The Scientific Basis of Child Custody Decisions

The Scientific Basis of Child Custody Decisions

edited by
Robert M. Galatzer-Levy
Louis Kraus

John Wiley & Sons, Inc.

New York • Chichester • Weinheim • Brisbane • Singapore • Toronto

This book is printed on acid-free paper.∞

Copyright © 1999 by John Wiley & Sons, Inc. All rights reserved.

Published simultaneously in Canada.

No part of this publication may be reproduced, stored in a retrieval system or transmitted in any form or by any means, electronic, mechanical, photocopying, recording, scanning or otherwise, except as permitted under Section 107 or 108 of the 1976 United States Copyright Act, without either the prior written permission of the Publisher, or authorization through payment of the appropriate per-copy fee to the Copyright Clearance Center, 222 Rosewood Drive, Danvers, MA 01923, (978) 750-8400, fax (978) 750-4744. Requests to the Publisher for permission should be addressed to the Permissions Department, John Wiley & Sons, Inc., 605 Third Avenue, New York, NY 10158-0012, (212) 850-6011, fax (212) 850-6008, E-Mail: PERMREQ@WILEY.COM.

This publication is designed to provide accurate and authoritative information in regard to the subject matter covered. It is sold with the understanding that the publisher is not engaged in rendering professional services. If legal, accounting, medical, psychological or any other ex-pert assistance is required, the services of a competent professional person should be sought.

Library of Congress Cataloging-in-Publication Data

The scientific basis of child custody decisions / edited by Robert
    Galatzer-Levy and Louis Kraus.
        p.   cm.
    Includes index.
    ISBN 0-471-17478-5 (CLOTH : acid-free paper)
    1. Custody of children—United States.   2. Forensic psychiatry—
United States.   3. Psychology, Forensic—United States.   4. Social
work with children.   5. Child psychiatry.   6. Child psychology.
    I. Galatzer-Levy, Robert M., 1944–   II. Kraus, Louis.
    KF547.A75S38   1999
    346.7301'73—dc21   98-55271

Printed in the United States of America.

10 9 8 7 6 5 4 3 2 1

Editors

Robert M. Galatzer-Levy, M.D.
The Institute for Psychoanalysis
University of Chicago
Chicago, Illinois

Louis Kraus, M.D.
Child and Adolescent Psychiatry
Evanston Hospital
Evanston, Illinois

Contributors

John Baker
Emmanuel Convalescent Foundation
Aurora, Ontario, Canada

Barry Bricklin, Ph.D.
Professional Academy of Custody
Evaluators
Wayne, Pennsylvania

Brenda Bursch, Ph.D.
UCLA Neuropsychiatric Institute
and Hospital
Los Angeles, California

Amity Pierce Buxton, Ph.D.
El Cerrito, California

Bertram J. Cohler, Ph.D.
University of Chicago
Chicago, Illinois

Shauna B. Corbin, Ph.D.
Emmanuel Convalescent Foundation
Aurora, Ontario, Canada

Robin Deutsch, Ph.D.
Massachusetts General Hospital
Boston, Massachusetts

David B. Doolittle, Psy.D.
Law and Psychiatry Services
Massachusetts General Hospital
Harvard Medical School
Boston, Massachusetts

Richard Erickson
Broening, Oberg, Wilson and Cass
Phoenix, Arizona

Frank D. Fincham
School of Psychology
Cardiff University
Cardiff, Great Britain

Susan M. Fisher, M.D.
Department of Psychiatry
University of Chicago
Chicago, Illinois

John H. Grych, Ph.D.
Department of Psychology
Marquette University
Milwaukee, Wisconsin

Michael J. Jenuwine, M.A.
University of Chicago
Chicago, Illinois

Joshua Kelman, M.D.
University of Chicago
Chicago, Illinois

Margaret Bull Kovera, Ph.D.
Assistant Professor of Psychology
Florida International University
North Miami, Florida

Jay Lebow, Ph.D.
The Family Institute
Northwestern University
Evanston, Illinois

Bennett Leventhal, M.D.
Department of Psychiatry
University of Chicago
Chicago, Illinois

Linda C. Mayes, M.D.
Child Study Center
Yale University School of Medicine
New Haven, Connecticut

Bradley D. McAuliff, M.S.
Department of Psychology
Florida International University
North Miami, Florida

Jade McGleughlin, L.I.C.S.W.
Children's Hospital
Boston, Massachusetts

Susanne Meyer
Children's Hospital
Boston, Massachusetts

Adriana Molitor-Siegl, Ph.D.
Yale University
New Haven, Connecticut

John E. B. Myers
University of the Pacific-McGeorge
School of Law
Sacramento, California

Eric Ostrov, Ph.D., J.D.
Forensic Psychology Association
Chicago, Illinois

Marsha Kline Pruett, Ph.D., M.S.L.
Department of Psychiatry
Child Study Center
Yale University School of Medicine
New Haven, Connecticut

Alan Ravitz, M.D.
Department of Psychiatry
University of Chicago
Chicago Lakeshore Hospital
Chicago, Illinois

John Rolland, M.D.
Department of Psychiatry
Center for Family Health
University of Chicago
Wilmette, Illinois

Christa Santangelo, Ph.D.
Department of Child and Adolescent
Psychiatry
University of California at San
Francisco
Langley Porter Psychiatric Institute
San Francisco, California

Lisa Vitti, M.A.
UCLA Neuropsychiatric Institute
and Hospital
Los Angeles, California

Judith S. Wallerstein, Ph.D.
Mill Valley, California

Froma Walsh, Ph.D.
School of Social Service
Administration and Department of
Psychiatry and Center Family Health
University of Chicago
Chicago, Illinois

Preface

THIS BOOK WAS born in a courtroom, but it is meant for a larger world. While listening to a particularly dreadful piece of expert testimony—that the "primary intrauterine bond of mother and infant" entailed that a 4-year-old should be returned to the care of her intermittently psychotic, substance-addicted, and abusive biological mother with whom she had almost no relationship—it occurred to one of us that none of the players in this drama, expert, lawyers, or judge, had a solid base from which to consider the testimony. Though examples are usually less glaring, as clinicians and expert witnesses, over the years, we have seen how difficult it is for both legal and mental health professionals to address the "best interest of the child." Lawyers and judges are often ignorant of basic psychological concepts, or worse, have latched onto a few ideas with which they were personally sympathetic. This creates situations in which the trial process functions poorly. Lawyers' lack of clarity about the testimony makes for muddled direct and cross examinations. Judges have difficulty understanding and evaluating the testimony. Divorcing families usually have limited resources, putting expert witnesses' and lawyers' time at a premium, so custody decisions are made without full benefit of the information available about children's best interests. Some judges and jurisdictions try to solve this problem by relying heavily on experts and agencies trusted by the court, including court-sponsored social service agencies. Difficulties arise in these situations because the opinions of mental health professionals in this position may be subject to little effective review and yet determine cases' outcome. Unfortunate situations can result when inadequately trained mental health professionals or individuals with idiosyncratic viewpoints essentially assume the judge's role in all but the most vigorously litigated cases.

Mental health professionals involved in custody determinations have often not thought through the difference between evaluations done in a forensic context and those appropriate for clinical work. Often mental health professionals are ill prepared to contribute to the legal process. Accustomed to treating mentally ill or distressed people, they commonly collect and formulate information in a way that is appropriate for that purpose, which is often quite different from what is required in forensic work. For example, although no rational person would try to mislead someone from whom he or she sought treatment, parties to a forensic evaluation can quite reasonably want to do so. The level of confidence with which a treater makes recommendations need only reach a conviction that the recommendation is the best choice available. Even then, the recommendation is subject to correction and reevaluation in the light of its effects. In contrast, expert opinions are expected to be highly reliable and defensible against close examination. They do not carry the expectation that they can be corrected as a result of subsequent experience with the client. The questions that treaters address are typically different from those raised in a forensic context. In most instances, the primary question for treating mental health professionals is what form of therapeutic intervention is most likely to aid the patient. This is a different type of question from those raised in custody evaluations, which concern the impact of various living arrangements on the child. Finally, the mental health professional who does not maintain a serious interest in these issues is unlikely to have kept up with the explosion in research concerning parenting, divorce, and children's developmental needs.

The end result of all these factors is that the vast information gathered through research in child development has less impact on custody and visitation decisions than it deserves. In that courtroom, several years ago it became clear that all those concerned, especially the child whose fate was being litigated, would benefit from a reliable reference that could clarify thinking about the psychological issues in the case. Such a book would have to be accessible, if at times with a little work, to both legal and mental health professionals. It would need not only to reflect the best current thinking available on topics affecting custody and visitation, but also provide information about the credibility of those current views. It would need to focus on the issues that courts address and although it could not possibly speak to every situation that might arise, it should at least discuss some of the common, particularly troublesome, situations confronted in custody decisions. Finally, it should be a book about what mental health professionals and knowledge of behavioral science can contribute to the decisions, with legal issues examined insofar as they impact those contributions.

We intend this book to be of use not only in situations involving litigation but also in the much more common situation where families are able to decide on custody and visitation arrangements for themselves. Families and their advisers should be guided by what is known about the impact of arrangements on children. The material presented here is applicable to any child involved in divorce.

As will quickly become apparent by perusing this volume, a surprisingly wide range of information is needed to address these questions. As editors, we tried to locate leading authorities. We soon discovered that some topics were far better investigated than others and that the extent to which topics were investigated did not necessarily relate to their significance to custody decisions. At this point, for example, a great deal is known about how parents facilitate growth of infants and young children but little is known directly about the details of effects of visitation schedules on children's psychological well-being in middle childhood. We have tried to ensure not only that this book includes the best available knowledge on a range of topics pertinent to custody decisions in divorce but that the reader is able to access how reliable that knowledge is. The chapters' authors have been generous in not only writing original drafts but in responding to our suggestions and queries designed to address these issues. For a variety of reasons, we were unable to address certain issues that commonly arise in custody disputes in the depth we would have liked. In some important areas, such as the impact of personality disorders (chronic maladaptive patterns of living) on child rearing, there was a surprising paucity of data. In some other areas, we simply could not locate an authority of adequate stature to address the issue. We hope to be able to rectify the latter limitation in later editions of this work.

ACKNOWLEDGMENTS

Completing a work such as this naturally reminds one of the many debts of gratitude owed not only to those who supported the effort directly but also to those who originally stimulated our interests and supported our efforts to think about these issues. Our teachers Bennett Leventhal, Alan Ravitz, and the late Ner Litner showed us that mental health professionals could benefit children outside the consulting room through informed participation in the legal process. Members of the Core Group of the Behavioral Science and Law Forum, including Leslie Star, Sandra Nye, Forrest Bayard, Randy Franklin, Frank Lani, Joy Feinberg, Richard Cozzola, Edward Wolpert, Jonathan Nye, Alan Ravitz, and Eric Ostrov have provided an exceptional forum to stimulate our thinking. Lawyers too numerous to mention have through their sometimes challenging questions brought many of the issues addressed in this book into sharp, even occasionally uncomfortably sharp, focus. Jeanne Galatzer-Levy has provided editorial support and more throughout this book's creation.

ROBERT M. GALATZER-LEVY, M.D.   LOUIS KRAUS, M.D.
Chicago, Illinois   *Evanston, Illinois*

Contents

CHAPTER 1

Introduction

ROBERT M. GALATZER-LEVY and LOUIS KRAUSS

IVORCE AFFECTS VAST numbers of American children, more than one million annually, an estimated 40% before the age of 18 (Glick, 1988, 1990). Although experts disagree about the effects of divorce on children, research supports the commonsense view that for many children their parents' divorce presents a serious challenge. Professionals agree that, within the limits imposed by the decision to divorce and the resources available to the family, arrangements should be based on the child's best interest.

The problem is to determine those best interests both generally and for particular children. Some of these decisions involve values—convictions about what constitutes a good life and the aims of child rearing. These questions can only be addressed through ethical analysis and public opinion, as reflected in legislation and judicial decisions. In many areas, it is easy to reach consensus on these matters. Few would argue that irrational anxiety or development in the direction of criminality are good for children. In other areas, consensus is less clear because of the diverse views in our society. Thus, some people believe it is of great importance to raise children with a strong religious sensibility, whereas others count this of little importance or even regard it as undesirable. Although many values about children's development are so widely shared that they do not need to be spelled out, discussions of children's interests are implicitly embedded in a context of values and some questions about children's best interests can only be addressed from within that context.

Other questions deal with matters of fact. They concern how particular arrangements are likely to affect children, for example, whether a child of a given age and background will be able to maintain a close relationship to a parent under a particular visitation schedule. These instrumental questions are subject to empirical investigation. Few researchers have explored the question directly, but often a body of empirical information is available about children's development that allows strong inferences about the likely impact of an arrangement on a child. For example, it might be proposed that a one-year-old child spend alternating weeks in the care of each parent. Although it is unlikely that anyone has performed an experiment with precisely these parameters, extensive research on children's capacities to maintain relationships with caregivers and the effects on development of failing to do so strongly suggest that this would be a very undesirable arrangement in terms of the child's psychological health. Our hope is that reliable information about children's needs and development can increasingly be brought to bear on decisions about living arrangements for children of divorce.

This book is intended to serve the needs of legal and mental health professionals involved in custody decisions about children of divorce. These decisions should be informed by the best available knowledge regarding their likely impact on children. Although several authors have addressed the performance of custody evaluations and the providing of expert testimony about them (Ackerman, 1995; Ackerman & Kane, 1998; Bricklin, Elliot, & Halbert, 1995; Gardner, 1989; Schutz, Dixon, & Lindenberger, 1989; Stahl, 1994) and there are many scholarly works about child development generally, we could not find a single ready source for authoritative statements about making custody decisions that included discussions of the reliability of those statements.

Whenever a couple separates or divorces, decisions must be made about their children's custody and visitation. Although society recognizes its interest in these arrangements, involving the family immediately with the legal system, the divorcing couple reaches most of these decisions with no input from any professionals. Other couples seek the counsel of mental health professionals, pediatricians, attorneys, and clergy to work out an agreeable arrangement. In approximately 10% of divorces involving children, parents initiate litigation because they are unable to agree about custody and visitation arrangements. The subsequent process of discovery, mandated mediation, and evaluation has been estimated to resolve approximately 90% of these disputes. Thus, overall, only about 1% of custody decisions are the result of trials (Melton, Petrila, Poythress, & Slobogin, 1997). However, this figure is misleading about the impact of the courts on custody arrangements. The pattern of actual decisions that the courts and legislatures reach on custody matters has a profound effect on the agreements that parents reach between themselves (Mnookin & Kornhauser, 1979). For many years, the "tender years doctrine" was widely applied by courts. It presumed that young children were best cared for by their mothers. As this doctrine lost sway, largely through legislation, fathers who previously had little hope of gaining custody of their children increasingly sought custody or a major role in young children's lives. Thus, in addition to affecting custody arrangements that actually go to trial, judicial decisions have a far-reaching impact on the lives of many children of divorce. The ever-present potential for litigation inevitably affects all actors in custody decisions so that the shadow of these cases is much longer than their numbers suggest.

The process for reaching custody decisions is unusual in that the individual most affected by the decision, the child, is rarely a party to the litigation. Additionally, custody-visitation arrangements are most often made as part of an overall divorce settlement so that, especially when the parties settle between themselves, considerations other than the child's best interests are likely to play an important role in the actual decision. For example, additional time with the child may be traded for increased financial support.

Mental health professionals who hope to contribute to custody arrangements must keep in mind both the intrinsic complexity of the issues involved and the context within which they will make their contribution. Because these decisions often require specific information about issues peculiar to divorce as well as the integration of multiple viewpoints, professionals need to do more than apply general child developmental and parenting principles. The divorcing family has distinct qualities, and its members are subject to forces that may not have been considered in investigations of broader developmental issues.

In addition to the particular problems associated with divorce, mental health professionals need to formulate and defend their views in a different fashion from that ordinarily used in their professional lives. The expert's job is to provide accurate information, and the function of the legal process is to assess the accuracy of that information. Recognition of these priorities affects every aspect of the mental health professional's work. Whereas in a therapeutic context, it is in the best interest of interviewees to provide information that is as accurate as possible, in a forensic context interviewees often have good reason to give inaccurate information. In a clinical setting, professionals properly provide information in a fashion that encourages the best clinical outcome; in a legal setting it is wrong to shape information to achieve a desirable goal. In a clinical setting, the credibility of a treatment provider's knowledge is rarely vigorously questioned, but mental health professionals engaged in forensic work should anticipate that their credibility will be carefully examined. Generally, mental health professionals need to be aware of the different world they enter when they become involved in forensic matters and to develop professional expertise in dealing with that world (Brodsky, 1991; Gutheil, 1998; Melton et al., 1997).

Mental health professionals commonly misunderstand the court's activities, believing that the judge's assignment is to do what is in a general sense best for the child. They often believe that the lawyers should also be working directly toward that end. Although judicial decisions hopefully correspond to doing what is best for the child, the judge's assignment remains, as it is in all matters, to apply the law to the particular case at hand. The attorney's responsibility is to vigorously represent the client's interest within the limits of the law. Through this adversarial process of litigation, the intention is to reach a decision based in law. Developed largely to resolve disputes about property and criminal behavior, even trials conducted with special rules based on the

difficulty of custody decisions often appear to be poor tools for society to ensure children's welfare. Indeed, an actual trial occurs only when other, less
rigid mechanisms for solving the problem have failed. When mental health professionals understand the legal process and appreciate the enormous difficulty
of the court's work, they can participate in it more effectively.

Within this context, the judge gathers information pertinent to the issues
before the court. It is here, as an expert witness, that the mental health professionals' input often enters into child custody decisions. Mental health professionals commonly misunderstand their own role and are tempted to exceed it.
Most mental health professionals, primarily trained to treat psychological illness and accustomed to having their opinions taken as authoritative, need to
"retool" to function well as experts for the courts. In particular, this means understanding that what they have to contribute is information about their particular expertise.* Mental health professionals need to understand what role is
being requested of them and then decide whether they can fill that role with
professional integrity. Similarly, lawyers and judges need to understand and
appreciate these limitations. Just as the appropriate role of legal professionals
may be difficult for nonlawyers to understand, legal professionals need to realize that for mental health professionals to function well, they must remain
within appropriate roles even when "common sense" might suggest that they
could extend their activities. All too often, mental health professionals are
pressed to opine on issues that they cannot adequately address.

Judges and lawyers frequently ask mental health professionals to predict the
consequences of a particular course of action. Will a visitation schedule provide sufficient contact to maintain a relationship with a noncustodial parent?
Will the child be better adjusted as a result of being in the custody of one parent rather than the other? If a parent assaulted a spouse, does that mean the
parent is likely to assault a child? In almost all instances, mental health professionals who base their opinions on reliable knowledge can only answer such
questions by describing the likelihood that some event will occur, and even
then the specification of that likelihood may be imprecise. Experts can provide
the court with the best information available but often information is limited.
The need to reach a decision can make it difficult for experts, lawyers, and
judges to exercise enough restraint to preserve the expert's useful function to
the court—the provision of accurate information.

---

*Mental health professionals are also called on by courts to serve many other roles in custody
matters. They may be asked to treat or educate the children, the parents, or the family. They
may serve as mediators. In some jurisdictions, they may even make decisions regarding custody and visitation under judicial supervision. Sometimes, the position of the court's supportive services is so significant that mental health professionals' opinions are almost always
adopted by the courts. The desire to have mental health professionals perform in these many
roles often leads to confusion on the part of both the court and the mental health professional.
We agree with Strasburger, Gutheil, and Brodsky's (1997) view that attempts to wear more than
one hat, for example to serve as both therapist and expert result only in an inadequate performance in both capacities.

The quality of information provided by experts in custody disputes has been particularly open to question. Melton and colleagues (1997), in their widely acclaimed text on psychological evaluations for the courts, refer to the validity of expert opinions in these matters: "There is probably no forensic question on which overreaching by mental health professionals has been so common and so egregious" (p. 484). Among other concerns, they and others observe that the scientific basis of many custody evaluations is questionable (see also Grisso, 1990; Heilbrun, 1995). This difficulty arises in part because both the training of custody evaluators and the methods they employ vary widely (Ackerman & Ackerman, 1997; Keilin & Bloom, 1986; LaFortune & Carpenter, 1998). An even more serious source of concern, however, is the weakness of the scientific database used to make many recommendations.

In many contexts, courts have increasingly demanded that expert testimony live up to some reasonable standards. Confronted with ever-increasing amounts of "junk science"—studies of dubious merit generated for the purpose of litigation (Huber, 1993)—courts have tried to better address issues of how to assess information provided by experts. In the *Daubert* decision (see Myers & Erickson, Chapter 2) the United States Supreme Court initiated a process designed to improve expert testimony. In particular, the court aimed to reserve the term "scientific" for information that would widely be regarded as meeting the high standards commonly associated with that term. The criteria suggested by the court will strike many trained in scientific methodology as somewhat problematic, but its spirit will be welcomed by those who hope that science can inform judicial process. Perhaps as important as the ruling's details is the indication that courts will increasingly try to assess the scientific merit of testimony presented. Experts of all types are expected to meet improved standards for the opinions they provide.

The core of a scientific attitude was first formulated by Francis Bacon in 1620 (Bacon, 1620). Science is characterized by its continuing and open assessment of the validity of its own facts and theories. Unlike arguments from authority, whose validity is claimed because of the status of the person putting forward a position, scientific arguments are assessed by the credibility of claimed observations and quality of the logic that connects observations and conclusions. Insofar as the theory of relativity is regarded as true by physicists, it is because observations and logical deductions based on it support the theory, not because it was created by the greatest physicist of the age. Thus the unique quality of scientific statements is that they are always accompanied by an explicit or implicit assessment of their own credibility. It is in this sense that we use the term scientific in this book. Thus, we include as scientific not only material that is accompanied by the apparatus of quantitative investigation but also research using other methods, provided the consequences and limitations of those methods are clear. We have tried not only to present the best current thinking from the behavioral sciences on issues involving custody in divorce but also to investigate the credibility of these statements: What evidence lies behind them? Such information can allow courts (and others) to weigh information from mental health experts with increased accuracy.

Frequently, evidence that lacks reasonable scientific backing is presented to the courts as though it had scientific merit. Although corrupt individuals occasionally may act as "hired guns," testifying in favor of those who retain them for a price, a much more common and pernicious problem is the uncorrupt but inaccurate expert who presents pet theories and personal prejudices as scientific fact. In the emotionally charged arena of child custody decisions, personal needs or inadequate training may lead some individuals with professional credentials to believe and testify in a manner that is inconsistent with reasonable standards for scientific information. We hope this book will assist both legal and mental health professionals in raising the quality of expert testimony and weeding out testimony that goes beyond the expert's credible knowledge.

Because custody decisions often involve the interface of two strong professions with distinctive outlooks that are difficult to integrate, clarifying the mental health professional's role in the legal process helps all involved to work more effectively toward good solutions for children. Chapter 2, by John E. B. Myers and Richard Erickson, provides an overview of the legal and ethical issues involving experts in custody litigation. Some of these issues, such as the courts' expectations regarding the scientific status of expert testimony and the protections afforded experts are rapidly evolving. Others may run contrary to the common assumptions of both mental health professionals and attorneys. In any case, a working knowledge of these issues helps all involved function more effectively.

We begin the book with a discussion of general issues important in custody evaluations. Chapter 3 addresses conceptualizing the scientifically based custody evaluation. In it, Robert Galatzer-Levy and Eric Ostrov describe how information from the behavioral sciences can be usefully brought to bear on custody issues by assessing its credibility and relevance to the case at hand. They point to the strengths and weaknesses of this kind of information and the tools available for accessing scientific information provided in custody decisions.

Discussions of custody arrangements usually involve theories about the relationship of children's well-being to their interactions with caretakers. These theories tend to either remain implicit or enter the discussions as authoritative, unquestioned statements. For these discussions to be rational, we need to be explicit about the theories and their credibility. Attachment theory, which originated in a combination of observational studies and psychoanalytic conceptualization, is emerging as among the most theoretically clear and empirically based means of thinking about the relationship of children and caretakers, as well as the impact of these relationships on development. In Chapter 4, Louis Krauss describes the major findings of attachment research and applies them to issues of custody and visitation.

Rational decisions about custody and visitation can only arise from an understanding of the impact of divorce, as discussed in Chapter 5. Based largely on an empirical longitudinal study of divorce, Judith S. Wallerstein and Shauna B. Corbin describe the impact of divorce on children and families. They show that regular patterns of adjustment emerge in divorcing families. Especially when examined in some depth, many children are significantly affected by divorce in predictable ways. In making custody decisions, these effects need to be carefully considered. Additionally, they show that families often go through regular stages in the process of divorce. When considering custody and visitation arrangements, professionals need to keep this process in mind because it is easy to mistake steps in the process for stable adjustments. In a later chapter (Chapter 6) addressing the impact of divorce, John Grych and Frank Fincham adopt a different emphasis, focusing more on the findings of quantitative research and its implication for assisting children of divorce. They describe how the findings of systematic empirical investigation point to the need to match intervention with the specific needs of children and what is known about the effectiveness of current intervention.

In making custody and visitation arrangements, decision makers work within a legal context and on multiple sources of information. One source of information is psychological testing, the subject of Chapter 7, by Barry Bricklin. Starting at the beginning of the 20th century, psychologists developed a vast collection of tools designed to systematically, reliably, and validly assess almost every aspect of psychological function (Groth-Marnat, 1997). Although many of these tests are fine tools for their intended purposes, extending their application beyond those purposes is often problematic. The relevance of their results to questions for which they were not designed is, at best, in need of clarification. At the same time, the complex issues relevant to custody and visitation could benefit greatly from reliable measures of significant qualities of the parent-child relationship. Bricklin outlines the fundamental ideas of psychological testing, the issues involved in using tests not originally designed for custody assessment in these evaluations, and the available tests specific to this purpose.

A very different source of information is the child's own statements, especially when the child is called on to testify. How reliable are the child's statements? How much are they influenced by the pressures the child is under? Are there means to facilitate the child's providing the most accurate information possible? In Chapter 8, on the child as witness, Margaret Bull Kovera and Bradley D. McAuliff explore these controversial issues with a particular eye to the question of helping the child give useful information.

We have devoted three chapters to an overview of child development as it relates to custody and visitation. For these chapters, the authors have not attempted exhaustive reviews of the literature on development, an undertaking that would require dozens of volumes the size of this one to encompass the massive findings of recent decades. Instead, we provide an overview, an entree into the literature, a discussion of how developmental concepts apply to custody and divorce, and an examination of particularly controversial issues during various developmental stages. At one time, infants were automatically assumed to need to reside with their mothers. Developmental theory went hand-in-hand in an increased societal appreciation that it is the functions the mother provides, not her person, that the child needs, so that issues of custody and visitation must be reframed in terms of the child's psychological needs. Linda C. Mayes and Adriana Molitor-Siegl (Chapter 9) describe contemporary developmental research about the manifestation of these needs in divorce situations and what is understood about the impact of various arrangements on the infant and young child.

Continuing in the same vein in Chapter 10, Bennett Levanthal, Joshua Kellman, Robert Galatzer-Levy, and Louis Kraus examine the development of young and school-age children emphasizing the several lines of development a child must traverse during this period. They emphasize how custody and visitation arrangements can facilitate or impede these developments.

Often adolescents are believed to be sufficiently mature to decide for themselves where they will live, and courts sometimes simply defer to their preferences. Yet, despite physical appearance and a wish to be mature enough to make such decisions, adolescents may lack the capacity to judge what is in their own best interest, especially in the emotionally charged context of divorce. In Chapter 11, which describes adolescent development, emphasizing some common myths about adolescents, Alan Ravitz describes the developmental needs of these young people, means for assessing their situation, and information about custody and visitation arrangements that facilitate their development.

Many custody arrangements must take into consideration special needs of particular children or potentially problematic aspects of parental function. The third section of this book is devoted to these issues. Very often, custody and visitation involves not only the parent but also the new family of which the parent has become a part through remarriage. In Chapter 12, Jay Lebow, Froma Walsh, and John Rolland describe the dynamics of the stepfamily and the child's relationship to it. Since custody arrangements should reflect the child's overall well-being, the child's engagement in the new family structure needs to be carefully considered. Another family configuration that changes the impact of divorce on children is adoption. Consideration of the adopted child's special vulnerability to loss and separation leads Susan Fisher (Chapter 13) to assert that, in making custody and visitation arrangements involving adopted children, special care should be taken to maintain the child's sense of security.

Another group of children for whom custody arrangements can be particularly difficult are youngsters with significant medical problems. A parent's realistic and imagined worries about the other parent's ability to care for the child, psychological needs of ill children, and rare but important problems of factitious illness all complicate custody decisions when children are medically ill. In Chapter 14, Brenda Bursch and Lisa Vitti explore these important problems.

In custody disputes, aspects of parental personality are commonly discussed, often without clearly identifying their significance relative to the parent's ability to rear a child. When the parent has qualities that may be problematic or simply socially frowned on, these qualities are often treated as though they were significant to custody decisions. Two groups who are often presumed to be inadequate parents are people suffering from severe psychiatric disturbances and homosexuals. The first step in addressing custody issues involving such parents is to focus on the impact of their conditions on parenting. Michael J. Jenuwine and Bertram J. Cohler show that the simple equation of severe psychiatric disorder with impaired parenting is wrong (Chapter 15). They demonstrate that different disorders affect parenting in different ways and that the presence of a severe psychiatric diagnosis, in itself, should not determine a child's custody. They also explore how parents whose illnesses do interfere with parenting may be involved with their children in a way that is most useful to the child. Homosexuality remains so controversial in our country that people with various attitudes toward it not uncommonly find different attitudes incomprehensible. It is precisely in such an emotionally charged context that empirical data may be most helpful in reaching rational decisions about the best interest of children of gay and lesbian parents. In Chapter 16, on gay and lesbian parents, Amity Pierce Buxton carefully reviews the available literature on the impact of parental sexual orientation on children to provide a clear picture of whether this factor should weigh in custody decisions.

When sexual abuse is alleged during custody disputes, the professionals involved are often confronted by an enormous problem. Failure to protect the child from abuse is unacceptable, but taking these steps when the allegations are false—especially when they are created for purposes of litigation—is likely to be seriously damaging to the child. Matters are even more troublesome because of the intense debate that accompanies a swinging pendulum of attitudes toward alleged sexual abuse of children. In Chapter 17, Jade McGleughlin, Susanne Meyer, and John Baker describe empirical research about these allegations and their assessment.

An ideal solution to the custody problem would be for children to continue to benefit fully from both parents and for parents to feel fairly treated in that they equally share their time and relationship with the child. The wide range of arrangements referred to as "joint custody" are intended to approximate this ideal. However, such arrangements are not a panacea. When parents cannot cooperate or, worse, enter into conflicts involving the child, joint custody can introduce great difficulties into the child's life. When attempts to be fair to the parents take precedence, the child, like the infant in the Solomon legend, may be sacrificed to achieve parental equity. For these reasons, it is important to differentiate those situations in which joint custody is likely to provide well for the child from those in which the child is likely to be hurt by it. In Chapter 18, Marsha Kline Pruett and Christa Santangelo draw on a wide range of studies to describe empirical research that has helped identify situations where joint custody works and where it fails.

High-conflict divorces can absorb the lives of parents and children for years with devastating consequences for all involved. Often, legal interventions designed to resolve the conflict seem only to intensify it. Effective means to end the Armageddon of these divorces require an understanding of their underlying dynamics. In Chapter 19, David Doolittle and Robin Deutsch describe the manifestations, psychological basis, and appropriate intervention in these most problematic of divorce cases.

Our book lacks some chapters we wish we could have included. Many observers believe that parents' chronic maladaptive psychological functions, often referred to as personality disorders, have particularly important effects on child development. We wanted to address this question but found that it has only been scantily studied using empirical methods. A much more extensive literature addresses the impact of parental substance abuse on children, but we failed to find an appropriate contributor to review this literature. Another area we would have liked to explore is the impact of the community in providing support for children's development (Bryant, 1985). We hope to remedy these limitations in a later edition.

This book is intended to help legal and mental health professionals come to the best possible decisions in assessing children's best interests. The ever growing empirical knowledge of child development and the impact of various arrangements on children can greatly improve these assessments. It is in the nature of scientific investigation that findings will change as more work is done and criticism will refine existing information. We hope that this book will move that process forward.

REFERENCES

Ackerman, M. (1995). *Clinician's guide to child custody evaluations.* New York: Wiley.

Ackerman, M., & Ackerman, M. (1997). Custody evaluations practices: A survey of experienced professionals (revisited). *Professional Psychology: Research and Practice, 28,* 137–145.

Ackerman, M., & Kane, A. (1998). *Psychological experts in divorce actions* (3rd ed.). New York: Aspen.

Bacon, F. (1620). Novum organum. In T. Fowler (Ed.), (2nd ed.). Oxford, England: Oxford University Press.

Bricklin, B., Elliot, G., & Halbert, M. (1995). *The custody evaluation handbook: Research based solutions and applications.* New York: Brunner/Mazel.

Brodsky, S. (1991). *Testifying in court: Guidelines and maxims for the expert witness.* Washington, DC: American Psychological Association.

Bryant, B. (1985). The neighborhood walk: Sources of support in middle childhood. *Monographs of the Society for Research in Child Development, 50*(3).

Gardner, R. (1989). *Family evaluation in child custody mediation, arbitration, and litigation* (Updated & Revised ed.). Cresskill: Creative Therapeutics.

Grisso, T. (1990). Evolving guidelines for divorce/custody evaluations. *Family and Counciliation Courts Review, 28,* 35–41.

Groth-Marnat, G. (1997). *Handbook of psychological assessment.* New York: Wiley.

Gutheil, T. (1998). *The psychiatrist as expert witness.* Washington, DC: American Psychiatric Press.

Heilbrun, K. (1995). Child custody evaluation: Critically assessing mental health experts and psychological tests. *Family Law Quarterly, 29,* 63–78.

Huber, P. (1993). *Galileo's revenge.* New York: Basic Books.

Keilin, W., & Bloom, L. (1986). Child custody evaluation practices: A survey of experienced professionals. *Professional Psychology: Research and Practice, 17,* 338–346.

LaFortune, K., & Carpenter, B. (1998). Custody evaluations: A survey of mental health professionals. *Behavioral Sciences and the Law, 16,* 207–224.

Melton, G., Petrila, J., Poythress, N., & Slobogin, C. (1997). *Psychological evaluations for the courts: A handbook for mental health professionals and lawyers.* New York: Guilford Press.

Mnookin, R., & Kornhauser, L. (1979). Bargaining in the shadow of the law: The case of divorce. *Yale Law Journal, 88,* 950.

Schutz, B., Dixon, E., & Lindenberger, J. (1989). *Solomon's sword: A practical guide to conducting child custody evaluations.* San Francisco: Jossey Bass.

Stahl, P. (1994). *Child custody evaluations: A comprehensive guide.* Thousand Oaks, CA: Sage.

Strasburger, L., Gutheil, T., & Brodsky, A. (1997). On wearing two hats: Role conflict in serving as both psychotherapist and expert witness. *American Journal of Psychiatry, 154*(4), 448–456.

CHAPTER 2

Legal and Ethical Issues in Child Custody Litigation

JOHN E. B. MYERS and RICHARD ERICKSON

AMILY COURT JUDGES make enormously important decisions affecting children and families. Yet, most judges have little training in psychology, child development, and family dynamics to equip them for this responsibility. Because judges lack essential expertise, they rely on expert testimony from mental health professionals. There are few other legal arenas in which mental health professionals make such an important contribution to judicial decisions. This chapter outlines legal and ethical principles governing expert testimony in child custody litigation.

CONTROLLING LEGAL AUTHORITY

The law governing the use and limits of expert testimony falls under the heading of evidence. Across the United States, similarities in rules of evidence far outnumber differences. In 1975, the *Federal Rules of Evidence* were enacted by Congress to govern trials in federal court. By 1998, forty states had adopted some version of the Federal Rules of Evidence. The ten states that do not have the Federal Rules nevertheless have rules on expert testimony closely paralleling the Federal Rules.

LAY TESTIMONY VERSUS EXPERT TESTIMONY

In court, there are two types of witnesses: lay witnesses and experts. A lay witness (also called a fact witness) is someone with personal knowledge of relevant facts. For example, a bystander who observes an auto accident testifies as a lay witness. The responsibility of the lay witness is to provide *factual* data about the accident to the jury or judge. The lay witness is not supposed to interpret the facts. Nor is the lay witness permitted to offer an opinion about what caused the accident or who was responsible. Again, the lay witness describes facts. The eyewitness to the auto accident describes *what* happened, not *why* it happened or *who was responsible.*

An expert witness helps the judge or jury understand technical, clinical, or scientific issues that the judge or jury is not fully equipped to comprehend. In the words of Rule 702 of the Federal Rules of Evidence:

> If scientific, technical, or other specialized knowledge will assist the [judge or jury] to understand the evidence or to determine a fact in issue, a witness qualified as an expert by knowledge, skill, experience, training, or education, may testify thereto in the form of an opinion or otherwise.

Unlike a lay witness, whose testimony is limited to factual data, and who is supposed to avoid opinion, expert witnesses routinely offer opinions. As provided in Rule 702, an expert "may testify in the form of an opinion." In an auto accident case, one party might offer expert testimony from an engineer specializing in accident reconstruction. The other party might offer expert testimony from the physician who treated the party. Both experts describe facts, and both offer their opinion.

In child custody cases, mental health professionals testify frequently. In some cases, the professional is a treatment provider. More often, however, the professional is a custody evaluator. If the professional is a therapist for the child or a parent, the professional's testimony may be limited to providing factual data about the client. Treating professionals typically avoid offering an opinion about custody. The generally accepted practice among treatment providers is to avoid the potentially conflicting roles of therapist and custody evaluator. The American Psychological Association *Guidelines for Child Custody Evaluations in Divorce Proceedings* (1994) state:

> Psychologists generally avoid conducting a child custody evaluation in a case in which the psychologist served in a therapeutic role for the child or his or her immediate family or has had other involvement that may compromise the psychologist's objectivity. This should not, however, preclude the psychologist from testifying in the case as a fact witness concerning treatment of the child. In addition, during the course of a child custody evaluation, a psychologist does not accept any of the involved participants in the evaluation as a therapy client. Therapeutic contact with the child or involved participants following a child custody evaluation is undertaken with caution.
>
> A psychologist asked to testify regarding a therapy client who is involved in a child custody case is aware of the limitations and possible biases inherent in such a role and the possible impact on the ongoing therapeutic relationship. Although the court may require the psychologist to testify as a fact witness regarding factual information he or she became aware of in a professional relationship

with a client, that psychologist should generally decline the role of an expert witness who gives a professional opinion regarding custody and visitation issues unless so ordered by the court. (Guideline II, paragraph 7)

THE REASONABLE CERTAINTY STANDARD FOR EXPERT TESTIMONY

When expert testimony is offered, experts must be reasonably confident of their conclusions and opinions. Judges and attorneys use the term "reasonable certainty" to describe the necessary degree of confidence. Thus, an attorney might ask a physician, "Do you have an opinion, based on a reasonable degree of medical certainty, whether the child's injuries were the result of an accident?" The question to a mental health professional might be, "Do you have an opinion, to a reasonable clinical certainty, whether the child's symptoms are consistent with clinical depression?"

A child custody evaluator may or may not be asked to state an opinion in the verbiage of the "reasonable certainty" standard. Regardless of the form of the attorney's question, however, the custody evaluator should possess the same level of certainty normally required for expert testimony.

Having advised custody evaluators to abide by the reasonable certainty standard, we have to admit that the reasonable certainty standard is not self-defining, and that the law does little to clarify the concept. It is clear that experts may not speculate or guess. It is equally clear that experts do not have to be completely certain. Thus, the degree of certainty required for expert testimony lies somewhere between the poles of guesswork and absolute certainty. Yet, placing reasonable certainty at some poorly defined location between these poles adds little to the concept. In the final analysis, the reasonable certainty standard fails to provide a meaningful tool to evaluate the value of expert testimony. A more productive approach to assessing expert testimony looks beyond the label of "reasonable certainty" and examines the following kinds of factors:

- In formulating an opinion, did the expert consider all relevant facts?
- How much confidence can be placed in the facts underlying the expert's opinion?
- Does the expert have an adequate understanding of pertinent clinical and scientific principles?
- To the extent the expert's opinion rests on scientific principles, have the principles been tested?
- Have the principles or theories relied on by the expert been published in peer-reviewed journals?
- Are the principles or theories relied on by the expert generally accepted as reliable by experts in the field?
- Did the expert employ appropriate methods of assessment?

- Are the inferences and conclusions drawn by the expert defensible?
- Is the expert reasonably objective?

The value of an expert's testimony depends on the answers to these and similar questions.

QUALIFICATION TO TESTIFY AS AN EXPERT WITNESS

Before a person may testify as an expert witness, the judge must be convinced that the person possesses sufficient "knowledge, skill, experience, training, or education" to qualify as an expert (Federal Rule of Evidence 702). The normal procedure is for the attorney offering the professional's testimony to ask about educational accomplishments, specialized training, and relevant experience. A professional does not have to be a well-known authority to testify as an expert. For example, publication of books or articles is normally not required. The important question is whether the professional can assist the judge or jury on technical or clinical matters.

The attorney opposed to proposed expert testimony may inquire into the professional's qualifications. Such questioning is called *voir dire.*

In many child custody cases, the opposing attorneys stipulate to the professional's qualifications, dispensing with formal qualification.

SOURCES OF INFORMATION ON WHICH EXPERTS MAY RELY FOR THEIR TESTIMONY

Professionals who provide expert testimony draw from many sources of information to formulate their conclusions. The law permits expert witnesses to base their in-court testimony on the same sources of information that they rely on in their day-to-day professional lives outside the courtroom. Thus, in a child custody case, an expert could rely on interviews of the child, parents, family members, teachers, and others. Additionally, the expert could rely on psychological tests and reports by other professionals. The expert may draw on the professional literature. Finally, the expert may fall back on his or her professional experience.

EXPERT TESTIMONY BASED ON NOVEL SCIENTIFIC PRINCIPLES

A special rule of evidence governs the admissibility of expert testimony based on scientific principles that are novel or of dubious reliability. The purpose of the special rule of evidence is to exclude unreliable expert testimony. The rule seldom applies to expert testimony in child custody cases because mental health professionals testifying in custody litigation rely on well-established (that is, non-novel) methods of assessment and on reliable psychological tests such as the MMPI. Despite the general inapplicability of the special rule of evidence in custody cases, mental health professionals have heard of the rule and may be curious to know something about it.

The special evidence rule for novel scientific evidence originated in a 1923 decision called *Frye v. United States*. In *Frye*, the court ruled that expert testimony based on a novel scientific principle becomes admissible in court only when the principle gains "general acceptance in the field in which it belongs" (p. 1014). An attorney offering expert testimony based on a novel scientific principle must convince the judge that the principle is generally accepted as reliable in the relevant professional community.

Until recently, the so-called *Frye* rule—also called the general acceptance rule—was the dominant rule in the United States for evaluating the admissibility of expert testimony based on novel scientific principles. An increasing number of courts have rejected the *Frye* rule, however, because *Frye* sometimes excludes scientific evidence that could assist the judge or jury. In 1993, the United States Supreme Court added momentum to the move away from *Frye* with its decision in *Daubert v. Merrell Dow Pharmaceuticals, Inc.* In *Daubert*, the Supreme Court rejected *Frye* for the federal courts in favor of a more flexible approach to novel scientific evidence. The more flexible approach is called the *Daubert* rule. Under *Daubert*, a judge faced with novel scientific evidence looks at more than general acceptance in the professional community. The judge conducts a searching inquiry into the reliability of the novel scientific principle. To assess reliability, the judge considers the following:

- Whether the principle has been tested to determine its reliability and validity.
- How often the principle yields accurate results.
- Existence of standards governing use of the principle to ensure accuracy.
- Publication in peer-reviewed journals.
- Whether the principle is generally accepted in the relevant scientific field (the *Frye* rule).

The Supreme Court's *Daubert* decision applies only to federal courts. State judges are free to accept *Daubert* or retain the venerable *Frye* rule. Although the trend in state courts is toward the *Daubert* approach, the supreme courts of California, Florida, Kansas, Mississippi, Nebraska, New York, Ohio, and Washington recently retained *Frye*.

THERE IS SOME DOUBT ABOUT THE APPLICATION OF *FRYE* AND *DAUBERT* TO EXPERT TESTIMONY FROM MENTAL HEALTH PROFESSIONALS

There is some uncertainty about when testimony from mental health professionals should be treated as scientific evidence subject to *Frye* or *Daubert* (Melton, Petrila, Poythress, & Slobogin, 1997; Rogers & Barrett, 1996). Faigman writes,

"*Daubert*'s application to social science is not obvious. The [*Daubert*] opinion itself is silent on the matter of social science. Moreover, much psychology-based expert testimony that today is routinely admitted bears little resemblance to 'science'" (1995, p. 961).

Despite uncertainty, courts apply *Frye* or *Daubert* to some mental health testimony. The California Supreme Court wrote "that given [*Frye*'s] prophylactic purpose, nothing precludes its application to 'a new scientific process operating on purely psychological evidence'" (*People v. Stoll*, 1989, p. 710). Courts have applied *Frye* or *Daubert* to rape trauma syndrome (*People v. Bledsoe*, 1984), some forms of expert testimony regarding child sexual abuse (*State v. Hadden*, 1997; *State v. Rimmasch*, 1989), and other types of psychological expertise.

CONTROLLING ETHICAL PRINCIPLES

Membership in a professional association brings with it the association's code of ethics. In addition to ethics codes promulgated by professional associations, state law imposes ethical responsibilities on professionals. In California, legislation provides that the State Board of Psychology "shall by rule or regulation, establish standards of ethical conduct relating to the practice of psychology" (Cal. Business and Professions Code § 2936, 1997).

Whether or not a mental health professional ever sets foot in a courtroom, the professional must adhere to ethical standards governing the profession. For professionals who testify, however, especially professionals who testify often, additional ethical requirements may attach. Professionals who provide more than occasional testimony, or who hold themselves out as forensic specialists, should comply not only with generally applicable ethical standards, but also with specialized ethical standards governing forensic practice.

It is not always easy to tell when a professional crosses the line into forensic practice. The American Psychological Association's *Specialty Guidelines for Forensic Psychologists* define forensic psychology as follows:

> "Forensic psychology" means all forms of professional psychological conduct when acting, with definable foreknowledge, as a psychological expert on explicitly psycholegal issues, in direct assistance to the courts, parties to legal proceedings, correctional and forensic mental health facilities, and administrative, judicial, and legislative agencies acting in an adjudicative capacity. (1991, p. 657)

The *Specialty Guidelines* state, "Individuals who provide only occasional service to the legal system and who do so without representing themselves as *forensic experts* may find these *Guidelines* helpful" (APA, 1991, p. 656).

The American Academy of Psychiatry and the Law defines forensic psychiatry as "a subspecialty of psychiatry in which scientific and clinical expertise is applied to legal issues in legal contexts embracing civil, criminal, correctional or legislative matters" (1995).

Mental health professionals who more than occasionally testify in child custody litigation should comply with ethical standards governing forensic practice. The same is true for professionals who regularly prepare custody evaluations for use in court, whether or not the professional testifies.

Failure to live up to applicable ethical standards can lead to disciplinary action by professional associations and licensing authorities. Additionally, serious ethical lapses can constitute malpractice (see Myers, 1998). Although witnesses generally enjoy immunity from civil liability for testimony in court, such immunity is not always impermeable. Immunity is discussed at the end of this chapter.

In this section, we draw on forensic ethics codes as well as general ethics codes to formulate recommendations for mental health professionals conducting custody evaluations and testifying in custody cases. Several ethics codes form the basis of our recommendations. Abbreviations used for text citations of these codes are indicated at the end of each entry in the following lists.

Generally Applicable Ethics Codes

- American Academy of Child and Adolescent Psychiatry. (1982). *Principles of Practice of Child and Adolescent Psychiatry.* 3615 Wisconsin Ave. NW, Washington, DC. (202) 966-7300. [cited as AACAP]
- American Association of Marriage and Family Therapy. (1991). *Code of Ethics.* 1100 17th St., NW, 10th Floor, Washington, DC 20036-4601. (202) 452–0109. [cited as AAMFT]
- American Medical Association. (1980). *Principles of Medical Ethics.* Chicago, IL: Author. [cited as AMA]
- American Medical Association. (1995). *Principles of Medical Ethics with Annotations Especially Applicable to Psychiatry.* Chicago, IL: Author. [cited as AMA- Psychiatry]
- American Professional Society on the Abuse of Children. (1997). *Code of Ethics.* 407 S. Dearborn, Suite 1300, Chicago, IL 60605. (312) 554-0166. [cited as APSAC]
- American Psychological Association. (1997). *Ethical Principles of Psychologists and Code of Conduct.* Washington, DC: Author. [cited as APA]
- National Association of Social Workers. (1997). *NASW Code of Ethics.* 750 First St., NE, Suite 700, Washington, DC 2002-4241. (202) 408-8600. [cited as NASW]

Forensic Ethics Codes

- American Academy of Psychiatry and the Law. (1987; Revised 1989, 1991, 1995). *Ethical Guidelines for the Practice of Forensic Psychiatry.* [cited as AAP&L]
- American Psychological Association. (1994). Guidelines for Child Custody Evaluations in Divorce Proceedings. *American Psychologist, 49,* 677–680. [cited as APA-Custody]

- American Psychological Association, Division 41 and the American Psychology Law Society. Committee on Ethical Guidelines for Forensic Psychologists. (1991). Specialty Guidelines for Forensic Psychologists. *Law and Human Behavior, 15,* 655–665. [cited as APA-Forensic]
- Association of Family and Conciliation Courts. (1994). *Model Standards of Practice.* 329 W. Wilson St., Madison, WI 53703. (608) 251–4001. [cited as AFCC]

Competence and Its Limits

Professionals must be competent (AAMFT, Standard 3; AMA-Psychiatry, Section 2. 3; APA, Principle A & Standard 1.04(a); APSAC, Standard III. A.; NASW, Ethical Principle & Standards 1.04(a) & 4.01(a)). When preparing an evaluation or testifying in court, professionals must not exceed the limits of their competence. Moreover, professionals should readily acknowledge the limits of their expertise. The American Psychological Association Forensic Guidelines provide:

> Forensic psychologists have an obligation to present to the court, regarding the specific matters to which they will testify, the boundaries of their competence, the factual bases (knowledge, skill, experience, training, and education) for their qualifications as an expert, and the relevance of those factual bases to their qualification as an expert on the specific matters at issue. (APA-Forensic, Guideline III. B)

The American Psychological Association's *Guidelines for Child Custody Evaluations in Divorce Proceedings* specifically recognize that "[i]n the course of conducting child custody evaluations, allegations of child abuse, neglect, family violence, or other issues may occur that are not necessarily within the scope of a particular evaluator's expertise" (APA-Custody, Guideline II. 5. C). The Association of Family and Conciliation Courts' *Model Standards for Practice* state, "In cases where issues arise that are beyond the scope of the evaluator's expertise, the evaluator shall seek consultation with a professional in the area of concern" (Principle VI. D). Most custody evaluators lack the expertise required to evaluate allegations of child abuse and should refer such matters to appropriate specialists (Myers, 1997).

Respect for Persons

Ethics codes reinforce the fundamental precept that professionals "respect the inherent dignity and worth of the person" (NASW, Ethical Principle). Moreover, professionals "respect the rights of individuals to privacy, confidentiality, self-determination, and autonomy" (APA, Principle D). Professionals avoid anything that could cause unnecessary harm to individuals (APA, Standard 1.14). With these principles in mind, custody evaluators should clarify the purpose of the evaluation, the use to which information will be put, and the degree of privacy that can be afforded to each participant.

BEST INTERESTS OF THE CHILD

The American Psychological Association's *Guidelines for Child Custody Evaluations in Divorce Proceedings* provide, "In a child custody evaluation, the child's interests and well being are paramount. Parents competing for custody, as well as others, may have legitimate concerns, but the child's best interests must prevail" (1994, Guideline I. 2).

TESTIMONY AND REPORTS MUST BE REASONABLY OBJECTIVE

The role of an expert witness is very different from that of an attorney. The attorney's responsibility is to be a zealous advocate for the client; to present the evidence that is most favorable to the client; and, hopefully, to win. The attorney is neither required nor expected to be objective. Expert witnesses, by contrast, are not, or at least should not, be partisan advocates. The expert's responsibility is not to win the case, but to help the judge make an informed custody decision. The *Standards of Practice* of the Association of Family and Conciliation Courts (1994) provide that custody "[e]valuators always serve impartially, never as an advocate for one parent or the other" (Preamble). The American Psychological Association's *Guidelines for Child Custody Evaluations in Divorce Proceedings* add, "The psychologist should be impartial regardless of whether he or she is retained by the court or by a party to the proceedings" (Guideline II. 4). This is not to say that expert witnesses must be entirely neutral regarding the outcome of a case. What is important is a degree of objectivity that is compatible with honest testimony. The American Academy of Psychiatry and Law provides, "Practicing forensic psychiatrists enhance the honesty and objectivity of their work by basing their forensic opinions, forensic reports and forensic testimony on all the data available to them" (Guideline IV). The American Psychological Association states, "In forensic testimony and reports, psychologists testify truthfully, honestly, and candidly" (APA, Standard 7.04(a)). The American Psychological Association's Forensic Guidelines state:

> When testifying, forensic psychologists have an obligation to all parties to a legal proceeding to present their findings, conclusions, evidence, or other professional products in a fair manner. This principle does not preclude forceful representation of the data and reasoning upon which a conclusion or professional product is based. It does, however, preclude an attempt, whether active or passive, to engage in partisan distortion or misrepresentation. Forensic psychologists do not, by either commission or omission, participate in a misrepresentation of their evidence, nor do they participate in partisan attempts to avoid, deny, or subvert the presentation of evidence contrary to their own position. (p. 664)

A professional who is appointed by a judge to evaluate a child and both parents may have an easier time maintaining neutrality than a professional retained by one parent. Nevertheless, the ethical principles previously cited make clear that a professional retained by one side of a custody dispute must refrain from stooping to the level of a "hired gun." Moreover, the best interest of the child is paramount.

CONFIDENTIALITY

Confidentiality is an overarching principle of mental health and medical practice (AAMFT, Standard 2; AACAP; AMA, Section 4; APSAC, Guideline III. B). For psychotherapy, "confidentiality is essential" (AMA-Psychiatric, Section 4. 1). In forensic settings, however, confidentiality is often limited. When a judge orders a custody evaluation, the expectation at the outset is that the evaluation will be submitted to the judge and attorneys, and that confidentiality will be limited or nonexistent.

It would be impossible in this short chapter to catalog the innumerable influences of law and ethics on confidentiality. Each case must be assessed on its own merits. It is important, however, to articulate the following principles: (1) Professionals have a duty to be aware of legal limits on confidentiality, (2) clients should be forewarned of the limits of confidentiality, (3) confidential information may be released only with client consent or as required by law, and (4) professionals should release only so much confidential information as is required by the situation.

Professionals Have a Duty to Be Aware of Legal Limits on Confidentiality

All professionals have an ethical responsibility to understand the limits of confidentiality (see AMA; APA; NASW). In particular, however, professionals who serve the courts must understand the legal limits of confidentiality. The American Psychological Association's *Guidelines for Forensic Psychologists* state, "Forensic psychologists have an obligation to be aware of the legal standards that may affect or limit the confidentiality or privilege that may attach to their services" (Guideline V. A).

Clients Should Be Forewarned of the Limits of Confidentiality

The requirement of informed consent is discussed later in this chapter. An important component of the consent process is informing clients of the limits of confidentiality (AFCC; APA-Custody; APA-Forensic, Guideline V. B; Deed, 1993). "Unless it is not feasible or is contraindicated, the discussion of confidentiality occurs at the outset of the relationship and thereafter as new circumstances may warrant" (APA, Standard 5.01(b)). Clients should be forewarned of "the nature of confidentiality and limitations of clients' right to confidentiality" (NASW, Standard 1.07(e)). "An evaluation for forensic purposes begins with notice to the evaluee of any limitations on confidentiality" (AAP&L, Guideline II).

In the forensic context, the professional "must fully describe the nature and purpose and lack of confidentiality of the examination to the examinee at the beginning of the examination" (AMA-Psychiatry, Section 4, paragraph 6).

It sometimes happens that a mental health professional conducting an evaluation wins the confidence of the client to such an extent that the original confidentiality forewarning is forgotten. The client may say, "Let me tell you something in confidence" or may start revealing information that the professional believes would be withheld if the forewarning were fresh in mind. In such cases, the professional should remind the person of the limits of confidentiality.

Confidential Information May Be Released Only with Client Consent or as Required by Law

Professionals release confidential information only with client consent or pursuant to law (AAMFT, Standard 2; AMA-Psychiatry, Section 4. paragraph 2.; APA, Standard 5.05(b); APA-Forensic, Guideline V. A. 2.; APSAC, Standard III. B). The American Psychological Association's *Ethical Principles of Psychologists and Code of Conduct* provides:

> Psychologists disclose confidential information without the consent of the individual only as mandated by law, or where permitted by law for a valid purpose, such as (1) to provide needed professional services to the patient or the individual or organizational client, (2) to obtain appropriate professional consultations, (3) to protect the patient or client or others from harm, or (4) to obtain payment for services, in which instance disclosure is limited to the minimum that is necessary to achieve the purpose (Standard 5.05(a)).

When confidentiality is circumscribed by the forensic nature of the evaluation, the client knows in advance because the professional forewarns the client. Moreover, the professional informs the client each time confidential information is released, to whom the information is released, the purpose of the disclosure, and the nature of the information disclosed. Limits on confidentiality include:

- *Child abuse reporting laws.* Laws in all states require professionals to report suspicion of child abuse to authorities (see Kalichman, 1993; Myers, 1998). The child abuse reporting laws override confidentiality.
- *Subpoenas.* A subpoena is issued by a court at the request of an attorney. A subpoena is a command from a court and cannot be ignored. There are two types of subpoena: (1) a subpoena that requires an individual to appear at a designated time and place to provide testimony, often called a subpoena *ad testificandum*, and (2) a subpoena that requires a person to produce documents, often called a subpoena *duces tecum*. Although professionals cannot ignore subpoenas, neither should they blindly obey them. Indeed, in the case of *Rost v. State Board of Psychology* (1995), a psychologist was reprimanded for *complying* with a subpoena! Before responding to a subpoena,

contact the client and consult an attorney. For guidance on responding to subpoenas see Committee on Legal Issues of the American Psychological Association (1996) and Myers (1998).

- *The dangerous client exception to confidentiality.* In most if not all states, when a mental health professional "determines, or pursuant to the standards of his profession should determine, that his patient presents a serious danger of violence to another, he incurs an obligation to use reasonable care to protect the intended victim against such danger" (*Tarasoff v. Regents of the University of California*, 1976, p. 334). The duty to warn potential victims of a dangerous patient overrides the ethical duty to protect the dangerous client's confidentiality. The American Medical Association's *Principles of Medical Ethics with Annotations Especially Applicable to Psychiatry* state, "When in the clinical judgment of the treating psychiatrist the risk of danger is deemed to be significant, the psychiatrist may reveal confidential information disclosed by the patient" (Section 4, paragraph 8).

- *Emergencies.* In emergencies, professionals may release confidential information without client consent. In some cases, there is no time to contact the client, or contacting the client may be contraindicated because the client is self-dangerous.

- *Limited confidentiality for psychotherapy records in child custody cases.* In some child custody cases, a parent's mental health is an issue. The judge may be called on to decide whether confidential mental health treatment records should be disclosed. On the one hand, the judge needs to know as much as possible about the parent, and treatment records may shed valuable light. On the other hand, stripping away confidentiality could undermine therapy. There is no easy answer to this dilemma, and judges reach different decisions depending on the facts of each case. The New Jersey Supreme Court observed:

[M]ost courts do not pierce the psychotherapist-patient privilege automatically in disputes over the best interests of the child, but may require disclosure only after careful balancing of the policies in favor of the privilege with the need for disclosure in the specific case before the court. (*Kinsella v. Kinsella*, 1997)

Professionals Should Release Only So Much Confidential Information as Is Required by the Situation

A client who consents to release of confidential information dictates the scope of release. When the law requires disclosure, the scope of disclosure is dictated by law. Whether disclosure follows the wishes of the client or the ditates of law, however, professionals should release only so much information as is necessitated by the situation (APA-Forensic, Guideline V. C). The American Psychological Association's *Ethical Principles of Psychologists and Code of Conduct* states, "In order to minimize intrusions on privacy, psychogists include in written and oral reports, consultations, and the like, only information germane to the purpose for which the communication is made" (Standard 5.03(a)). The

National Association of Social Workers' *Code of Ethics* provides, "In all instances, social workers should disclose the least amount of confidential information necessary to achieve the desired purpose; only information that is directly relevant to the purpose for which the disclosure is made should be revealed" (Standard 1.07(c)). Finally, the American Medical Association's *Principles of Medical Ethics with Annotations Especially Applicable to Psychiatry* provide, "In the event that the necessity for legal disclosure is demonstrated by the court, the psychiatrist may request the right to disclosure of only that information which is relevant to the legal question at hand" (Section 4, paragraph 9).

INFORMED CONSENT

Informed consent is a legal and ethical requirement for medical and mental health treatment (APA, Principle 4.02(a); NASW, Standard 1.03(a)). For purely forensic evaluations, when treatment is not provided, informed consent should nevertheless be obtained unless the evaluation is court-ordered and it is clear that consent is not required. The American Academy of Psychiatry and the Law's *Ethical Guidelines for the Practice of Forensic Psychiatry* provide, "The informed consent of the subject of a forensic evaluation is obtained when possible. Where consent is not required, notice is given to the evaluee of the nature of the evaluation. If the evaluee is not competent to give consent, substituted consent is obtained in accordance with the laws of the jurisdiction" (Guideline III). Along similar lines, the American Psychological Association's *Specialty Guidelines for Forensic Psychologists* provide:

> Forensic psychologists have an obligation to ensure that prospective clients are informed of their legal rights with respect to the anticipated forensic service, of the purposes of any evaluation, of the nature of procedures to be employed, of the intended uses of any product of their services, and of the party who has employed the forensic psychologist. Unless court ordered, forensic psychologists obtain the informed consent of the client or party, or their legal representative, before proceeding with such evaluations and procedures. (Guideline IV. E)

The American Psychological Association's *Guidelines for Child Custody Evaluations in Divorce Proceedings* specifically state, "The psychologist obtains informed consent from all adult participants and, as appropriate, informs child participants" (Guideline III, paragraph 8).

Consent should be obtained to videotape or audiotape an evaluation (APA, Standard 5.01(c); NASW, Standard 1.03(f)). The American Association for Marriage and Family Therapy's *Code of Ethics* provides, "Marriage and family therapists obtain written informed consent from clients before videotaping, audiorecording, or permitting third party observation" (1991, Standard 1.8).

Because children are legally incapable of consenting to most forms of medical and mental health treatment or evaluation, informed consent is obtained from parents or caretakers. Generally, if one parent has legal custody, it is the custodial parent who consents for the child. If there is any ambiguity about who is qualified to give consent for a youngster's participation in an evaluation, the professional should not proceed until the matter is resolved.

LIABILITY OF PROFESSIONALS

Liability is an increasing concern for mental health professionals. Twenty years ago, lawsuits against mental health professionals were rare. Today, the threat of litigation is real. Lawsuits and ethics complaints against mental health professionals have risen steadily in recent years. The remainder of this chapter briefly discusses professional liability in relation to custody evaluations.

MALPRACTICE BASED ON NEGLIGENCE

Malpractice is deficient practice that results in physical or mental injury to a patient (*Corpus Juris Secundum*, 1987, p. 455). Many malpractice cases are based on a claim of negligence (Myers, 1998; Smith, 1996). The person claiming negligent malpractice alleges that the professional fell below the standard of performance required of professionals. "Negligence on the part of a [professional] generally consists of the [professional] doing something a reasonable [professional] under the circumstances would not have done or omitting to do something a reasonable [professional] would have done" (Smith, 1986, pp. 5–6).

When a professional is sued for negligent malpractice, an ethics code may establish the standard of performance against which the professional's conduct is measured. Falling below the standard set by the ethics code can be evidence of negligence.

OTHER FORMS OF MALPRACTICE

Malpractice covers more than negligence. "Thus, malpractice consists of any professional misconduct, unreasonable lack of skill or fidelity in professional or fiduciary duties, evil practice, or illegal or immoral conduct" (Smith, 1986, p. 5). Failure to obtain informed consent can be malpractice, as can improper release of confidential information. Malpractice occurs when a professional negligently fails to refer a client to a specialist or a practitioner in a more appropriate discipline (Smith, 1996). For example, a custody evaluator could be liable for failing to refer allegations of child abuse to a specialist. Malpractice also includes criminal conduct by professionals, such as sexual assault of a client.

LIABILITY FOR COMMENTING ON THE FITNESS OF A PARENT THAT THE PROFESSIONAL DID NOT PERSONALLY EVALUATE

In some custody evaluations, the mental health professional evaluates both parents, and in such cases, it is proper to comment on each one's relative strengths and weaknesses. In other cases, however, the professional evaluates only one parent. In the latter case, should the professional comment on the comparative fitness of the parent who was *not* personally evaluated? Turning from the parents to the child, in most custody evaluations the child's relationship with each parent is important. Is it permissible for a professional to comment about a child whom the professional has not personally evaluated? Several ethics codes address these issues, and because the matter is highly significant to custody evaluators, relevant portions of ethics codes are quoted here.

The American Psychological Association's *Specialty Guidelines for Forensic Psychologists* provide:

> Forensic psychologists avoid giving written or oral evidence about the psychological characteristics of particular individuals when they have not had an opportunity to conduct an examination of the individual adequate to the scope of the statements, opinions, or conclusions to be issued. Forensic psychologists make every reasonable effort to conduct such examinations. When it is not possible or feasible to do so, they make clear the impact of such limitations on the reliability and validity of their professional products, evidence, or testimony. (Guideline VI. H)

The American Academy of Psychiatry and the Law's *Ethical Guidelines for the Practice of Forensic Psychiatry* state:

> Honesty, objectivity and the adequacy of the clinical evaluation may be called into question when an expert opinion is offered without a personal examination. While there are authorities who would bar an expert opinion in regard to an individual who has not been personally examined, it is the position of the Academy that if, after earnest effort, it is not possible to conduct a personal examination, an opinion may be rendered on the basis of other information. However, under such circumstances, it is the responsibility of forensic psychiatrists to assure that the statement of their opinion and any reports or testimony based on those opinions, clearly indicate that there was no personal examination and the opinion is thereby limited.
>
> In custody cases, honesty and objectivity require that all parties be interviewed, if possible, before an opinion is rendered. When this is not possible, or if for any reason not done, this fact should be clearly indicated in the forensic psychiatrist's report and testimony. Where one parent has not been interviewed, even after deliberate effort, it may be inappropriate to comment on that parent's fitness as a parent. Any comments on that parent's fitness should be qualified and the data for the opinion clearly indicated. (Guideline IV)

The American Psychological Association's *Ethical Principles of Psychologists and Code of Conduct* provides:

> [P]sychologists provide written or oral forensic reports or testimony of the psychological characteristics of an individual only after they have conducted an examination of the individual adequate to support their statements or conclusions. When, despite reasonable efforts, such an examination is not feasible, psychologists

clarify the impact of their limited information on the reliability and validity of their reports and testimony, and they appropriately limit the nature and extent of their conclusions or recommendations. (Standard 7.02(b), (c))

The American Psychological Association's *Guidelines for Child Custody Evaluations in Divorce Proceedings* add:

> Although comprehensive child custody evaluations generally require an evaluation of all parents or guardians and children, as well as observations of interactions between them, the scope of the assessment in a particular case may be limited to evaluating the parental capacity of one parent without attempting to compare the parents or to make recommendations. . . .
> The psychologist does not give any opinion regarding the psychological functioning of any individual who has not been personally evaluated. This guideline, however, does not preclude the psychologist from reporting what an evaluated individual (such as the parent or child) has stated or from addressing theoretical issues or hypothetical questions, so long as the limited basis of the information is noted. (Guideline III. paragraphs 8 and 13)

Finally, the Association of Family and Conciliation Courts' *Model Standards of Practice* state:

> Evaluators shall make every effort to include all parties involved in the custody dispute in the evaluation process itself. Evaluators shall not make statements of fact or inference about parties whom they have not seen. On occasion, evaluators will be unable to see all parties in a custody evaluation dispute, either because of refusal of one party to participate or because of logistical factors such as geography. In these cases the evaluator may perform a limited evaluation, but must limit his or her observations and conclusions. For example, if only one parent is seen, the evaluator must not make statements about the other parent and must not make a recommendation for custody because the other parent has not been seen. The evaluator may report on those individuals who have been seen and on their interactions with each other and may draw conclusions regarding the nature of those relationships, such as whether they should continue, not continue, or be modified in some way. The evaluator may also make comments or state opinions about the need for a more expanded evaluation. (Standard E)

PARENTS' CONSTITUTIONAL RIGHTS

When mental health professionals think of liability, they usually do not have the U.S. Constitution in mind. Yet, the Constitution plays an important role in some litigation against professionals. The Constitution protects parental rights. In *Prince v. Massachusetts*, the United States Supreme Court stated, "It is cardinal with us that the custody, care and nurture of the child reside first in the parents, whose primary function and freedom include preparation for obligations the state can neither supply nor hinder" (1944, p. 166). Professionals are occasionally sued by angry parents who claim that the professional interfered with their constitutionally protected parental rights.

Immunity from Liability

A mental health professional who is sued for malpractice or violation of constitutional rights may have qualified or absolute immunity. Before describing immunity, it is important to understand what immunity does *not* do: Immunity does *not* prevent a lawsuit from being filed. An angry parent may file suit against a professional even though a judge eventually determines that the professional has immunity. Although immunity does not prevent a lawsuit, it allows the professional to escape the lawsuit at an early stage, usually well before a trial. Moreover, if an angry parent is thinking about suing a professional, and the parent's attorney knows the professional will have immunity, the attorney may convince the parent not to sue in the first place.

A professional who lacks immunity—qualified or absolute—will not necessarily lose a lawsuit. After all, the professional may have done nothing wrong. If the professional lacks immunity, however, the professional's exposure to possible liability increases.

What is the difference between absolute and qualified immunity? With absolute immunity, the professional is nearly always entitled to early dismissal from a lawsuit. Moreover, "there can be no inquiry into the objective reasonableness of the absolutely immune [professional's] conduct" (Nahmod, 1991, p. 3). So long as the alleged wrongful conduct was within the scope of the immunity, there is no liability.

Qualified immunity provides less protection. A professional with qualified immunity is dismissed from a lawsuit only if the professional's conduct did not violate rights that a reasonable professional would know about. Still, qualified immunity is a powerful defense. Professionals "are not liable for bad guesses in gray areas; they are liable for transgressing bright lines" (*Maciariello v. Sumner*, 1992). Qualified immunity "provides ample protection to all but the plainly incompetent or those who knowingly violate the law" (*Malley v. Briggs*, 1986, p. 341).

Absolute Judicial Immunity and Its Application to Court-Appointed Custody Evaluators

Judges have absolute immunity for most judicial activities. A mental health professional who is appointed *by a judge* to conduct a custody evaluation *for the judge* is typically protected by absolute judicial immunity. In *Delcourt v. Silverman* (1996), for example, parents battled over custody of their young child. The judge appointed Dr. Silverman to evaluate the child and the parents. Eventually, the mother sued Dr. Silverman. In ruling that the doctor was absolutely immune from liability, the Texas Court of Appeals wrote:

> [A] party is entitled to absolute immunity when the party is acting as an integral part of the judicial system or an "arm of the court."
>
> [A] psychologist who is appointed by the court is entitled to absolute immunity if he or she is appointed to fulfill quasijudicial functions intimately related to the judicial process.

Numerous courts have extended absolute immunity to psychiatrists and other mental health experts assisting the court in criminal cases.

We believe this reasoning applies to mental health experts appointed to provide psychological expertise in child custody suits. Many courts recognize that psychiatrists and psychologists performing court-ordered custody evaluations perform a judicial function and enjoy absolute immunity. (pp. 782–783)

Thus, in custody litigation, a professional who is appointed by a judge to perform a custody evaluation is normally protected by absolute judicial immunity (*Lythgoe v. Guinn*, 1994). Immunity extends to the evaluation, the resulting report, and testimony in court. Generally speaking, however, a professional who is retained by one or both parents to conduct a custody evaluation does not enjoy absolute judicial immunity. Absolute immunity attaches only when a judge formally appoints the professional to conduct an evaluation for the court. Some professionals require one or both parents to agree that the professional will be court-appointed. The parents' agreement is put in writing and submitted to the judge. The judge signs the agreement, converting it into a court order appointing the professional. Absolute judicial immunity accompanies the appointment.

Absolute Witness Immunity

In most if not all states, witnesses, including experts, have absolute immunity from civil liability for their testimony in court. The California Court of Appeals wrote in *Gootee v. Lightner* (1990) that "freedom of access to the courts and encouragement of witnesses to testify truthfully will be harmed if neutral experts fear retaliatory lawsuits from litigants whose disagreement with an expert's opinions perforce convinces them the expert must have been negligent in forming such opinions" (p. 700).

Absolute witness immunity applies to testimony at a trial or hearing in court. Witness immunity also applies to testimony given at a deposition. Moreover, witness immunity extends to "preparatory activity leading to the witnesses' testimony" (*Gootee v. Lightner*, 1990, p. 701). Thus, a report prepared by an expert who is retained to testify in custody litigation is protected by absolute immunity so long as the report has some relation to the litigation. Even when litigation is not underway, absolute witness immunity may protect experts who are retained to evaluate potential litigation or to work on matters that may end up in court.

Gootee v. Lightner (1990) is a good example of absolute witness immunity in a child custody case. Irene and Michael Gootee were divorced and had three children. In 1985, Irene went to family court requesting a change in child custody. Irene and Michael retained Marshall Lightner to perform a custody evaluation of the family. Lightner prepared a report and testified in court, recommending that Irene have custody, with visitation for Michael. Upset with Lightner's report and testimony, Michael sued, alleging malpractice. The trial judge dismissed Michael's suit, ruling that Lightner's evaluation, report, and testimony were protected by absolute witness immunity. On appeal, the California Court of Appeals agreed with the trial judge, noting that "[i]t is undisputed that

[Lightner's] role was a limited one: to evaluate the partisans in the custody matter for purposes of testifying concerning the custody dispute. Because the gravamen of [Michael's] claim relies on negligent or intentional tortious conduct committed by [Lightner] in connection with the testimonial function, we conclude the absolute privilege bars civil lawsuits" (p. 699). The appellate court concluded that absolute witness immunity embraced not only testimony in court also any "prior preparatory activity leading to the witnesses' testimony" (p. 701).

In *Deatherage v. State Examining Board of Psychology* (1997), the Washington Supreme Court ruled that absolute witness immunity does not apply in disciplinary proceedings against professionals. Thus, in *Deatherage*, the state board of psychology could maintain a disciplinary action against a psychologist for work the psychologist performed in a child custody case.

CONCLUSION

Working with families embroiled in child custody litigation is difficult but important work. Not only must mental health professionals contend with daunting clinical issues, they also must come to grips with a plethora of legal and ethical questions. We hope this chapter helps these professionals more fully understand the complex legal and ethical aspects of custody practice. Professionals with a clear fix on their legal and ethical responsibilities have one less thing to worry about as they perform their vitally important function of helping the legal system restructure families and safeguard children's best interests.

REFERENCES

American Academy of Child and Adolescent Psychiatry. (1982). *Principles of practice of child and adolescent psychiatry.* Washington, DC: Author. [AACAP]

American Academy of Psychiatry and the Law. (1995). *Ethical guidelines for the practice of forensic psychiatry.* Bloomfield, CT: Author. [AAP&L]

American Association of Marriage and Family Therapy. (1991). *Code of ethics.* Washington, DC: Author. [AAMFT]

American Medical Association. (1980). *Principles of medical ethics.* Chicago: Author. [AMA]

American Medical Association. (1995). *Principles of medical ethics with annotations especially applicable to psychiatry.* Chicago: Author. [AMA-Psychiatry]

American Professional Society on the Abuse of Children. (1997). Code of ethics. *APSAC Advisor, 10,* 1–4. [APSAC]

American Psychological Association. (1997). *Ethical principles of psychologists and code of conduct.* Washington, DC: Author. [APA]

American Psychological Association. (1994). Guidelines for child custody evaluations in divorce proceedings. *American Psychologist, 49,* 677–680. [APA-Custody]

American Psychological Association, Division 41 and the American Psychology-Law Society. Committee on Ethical Guidelines for Forensic Psychologists. (1991). Specialty guidelines for forensic psychologists. *Law and Human Behavior, 15,* 655–665. [APA-Forensic]

Association of Family and Conciliation Courts. (1994). Model standards of practice. *Family and Conciliation Courts Review, 32,* 39–47. [AFCC]

California Business and Professions Code. (1997). St. Paul: West.

Committee on Legal Issues of the American Psychological Association. (1996). Strategies for private practitioners coping with subpoenas or compelled testimony for client records or test data. *Professional Psychology: Research and Practice, 27,* 245–251.

Corpus Juris Secundum. (1987). St. Paul: West.

Daubert v. Merrell Dow Pharmaceuticals, Inc., 509 U.S. 579 (1993).

Deatherage v. State Examining Board of Psychology, 948 P.2d 828 (Wash. 1997).

Deed, M. L. (1993). Mandated reporting revisited: *Roe v. Superior Court. Law and Policy, 14,* 219–239.

Delcourt v. Silverman, 919 S. W.2d 777 (Tex. Ct. App. 1996).

Faigman, D. L. (1995). The evidentiary status of social science under *Daubert:* Is it "scientific," "technical," or "other" knowledge? *Psychology, Public Policy, and Law, 1,* 960–979.

Federal Rules of Evidence. (1975). United States Code. Title 28.

Frye v. United States, 293 F. 1013 (D.C. Cir. 1923).

Gootee v. Lightner, 274 Cal. Rptr. 697 (Ct. App. 1990).

Kalichman, S. C. (1993). *Mandated reporting of suspected child abuse: Ethics, law & policy.* Washington, DC: American Psychological Association.

Kinsella v. Kinsella, 696 A.2d 556 (N.J. 1997).

Lythgoe v. Guinn, 884 P.2d 1085 (Alaska 1994).

Maciariello v. Sumner, 973 F.2d 295 (4th Cir. 1992).

Malley v. Briggs, 475 U.S. 335 (1986).

Melton, G. B., Petrila, J., Poythress, N. G., & Slobogin, C. (1997). *Psychological evaluations for the courts* (2nd ed.). New York: Guilford Press.

Myers, J. E. B. (1998). *Legal issues in child abuse and neglect practice* (2nd ed.). Newbury Park, CA: Sage.

Myers, J. E. B. (1997). *Evidence in child abuse and neglect cases* (3rd ed.). New York: Wiley.

Nahmod, S. H. (1991). *Civil rights and civil liberties litigation: The law of section 1983.* Colorado Springs: Shepards/McGraw Hill.

National Association of Social Workers. (1997). *NASW Code of Ethics.* Washington, DC: Author. [NASW]

People v. Bledsoe, 681 P.2d 291 (Cal. 1984).

People v. Stoll, 783 P.2d 698 (Cal. 1989).

Prince v. Massachusetts, 321 U.S. 158 (1944).

Rogers, F., & Barrett, D. (1996). *Daubert v. Merrell Dow* and expert testimony by clinical psychologists: Implications and recommendations for practice. *Professional Psychology: Research and Practice, 27,* 467–474.

Rost v. State Board of Psychology, 659 A.2d 626 (Pa. Commonwealth Ct. 1995).

Smith, J. T. (1986). *Medical malpractice: Psychiatric care.* New York: McGraw Hill.

Smith, S. R. (1996). Malpractice liability of mental health professionals and institutions. In B. D. Sales & D. W. Shuman (Eds.), *Law, mental health, and mental disorder.* Pacific Grove, CA: Brooks/Cole.

State v. Hadden, 690 So.2d 573 (Fla. 1997).

State v. Rimmasch, 775 P.2d 388 (Utah 1989).

Tarasoff v. Regents of the University of California, 551 P.2d 334 (Ca. 1976).

CHAPTER 3

From Empirical Findings to Custody Decisions

ROBERT M. GALATZER-LEVY and ERIC OSTROV

E VERYONE WORKING IN the area of child custody agrees that these decisions should be based credible information. In this chapter, we describe a framework for evaluating the significance of these findings.

Expert custody evaluators generally, though often informally, proceed through a three-stage process in forming opinions in custody matters:

1. Based on their knowledge of the kinds of facts that are likely to be relevant to the decision, they collect data about the particular situation.
2. Using previous knowledge and further research, they refer to studies that may be relevant to the facts they find, assess the pertinence of the studies to the situation, and apply their findings to the facts at hand.
3. Weighing the relative importance of these facts, they attempt to integrate the resulting conclusions into an overall scientifically reliable recommendation.

Often the evaluator will not carry out these steps in sequence or the process may loop back on itself. For example, on reviewing the pertinent scientific literature, the evaluator may see the need to gather additional facts before making a recommendation. In developing an opinion, evaluators commonly go through several iterations of this process. In practice, the care with which data about custody matters is gathered varies greatly. Many evaluators use their training and an unsystematic reading of the scientific literature as their sole source of information about the state of research in the matters about which they give opinions. Their process of reaching an opinion is incompletely thought through. Legal professionals are often uncertain about how to assess the statements of behavioral science experts in these matters. In this chapter, we describe several considerations that can lead to more credible opinions and more meaningful assessment of experts' statements.

Currently, the legal criteria for using scientific expert opinion are in flux (see Chapter 2). Roughly speaking, the courts appear to be moving from a sociologically based view of truth ("Truth is what experts in the field believe") toward a method-based view ("Truth is what is discovered through the appropriate application of scientific research methods"). This shift reflects an increasing unwillingness in our society to accept statements as true simply on the authority of credentialed experts. Most people familiar with the field would heartily endorse this move. Despite their limitation, scientifically based opinions are more likely to provide pertinent information to decision makers and information that is more easily evaluated than opinions with other bases, such a personal experience. Where possible, we want to use scientifically based opinions to inform decisions.

However, evaluating the merit of scientific evidence places tremendous demands on the courts. The boundaries of adequate scientific method generally, but especially in disciplines that study human behavior, are the subject of intense dispute among behavioral scientists and philosophers of science. Even when there is reasonable agreement about these boundaries, technically challenging questions arise in assessing research studies. These questions are often difficult for people with years of training in methodology to resolve. Attempts to resolve them in a legal context will demand much of the courts.

The main difference between scientific and other forms of knowledge is that scientific knowledge is always accompanied by an assessment of its own credibility. Each step in a scientifically conducted study is, at least potentially, subject to open scrutiny and evaluations. The question of the truth of the statement always remains open and subject to test. A typical scientific research report includes a section on "materials and methods" that describes how the reported data were collected and the means used for analysis. It does so in such a fashion that a reader could, at least potentially, replicate the research. The report also includes specific reasoning that shows how these data are related to any conclusion drawn and an indication of the extent to which alternative possibilities have been assessed and the likelihood of their being true. Thus, by their very nature, scientific opinions are never certain and their limitations and defects should be made particularly clear.

Although scientists have elaborate methods for assessing the credibility of scientifically based statements, no particular method is inherently necessary for an investigation to be scientific. In studying human behavior, many investigators find statistical methods extremely informative. However, when treated as a sort of magical ritual to make an investigation "scientific," statistics can provide a false impression of the status of the investigator's findings (Cohen, 1990; Salsburg, 1985). Nonquantitative studies have yielded some of the most useful information about human behavior and psychological function, whereas some studies, despite elaborate quantitative trappings are of little use. In the study of people, a trade-off commonly occurs between "extensive" and "intensive" study (Chassan, 1979). To reach statistically valid conclusions, many subjects are usually necessary. The richer the matters studied (in effect, the more variables studied) the more subjects are needed. However, studying many subjects in depth is difficult and time consuming. The following example displays this contrast:

> In studying the long-term effects of divorce Wallerstein (this volume) and McLanahan and Sandefur (1994) used distinctly different methods, which provide distinctly different results. Wallerstein studied a small number of subjects, in depth over an extended period of time using an open-ended interview technique. Her studies provide clear, rich pictures of some of the common psychological configurations seen in children of divorce, with particularly good insight into their subjective experience. They do not, however, tell us how common these configurations are, to what extent they result from interacting aspects of the subjects' lives, or the extent to which the subjects differed from other people like themselves. McLanahan and Sandefur base their studies on survey data collected by others. These surveys largely explored easily quantified aspects of the child's situation like family income and years of school completed. They involved very many subjects and systematically compared the subjects with individuals who had not been involved in divorce or who had lost parents in other ways. In return for a much less rich picture of the children's situation these authors provide reliable, quantitative information about the impact of divorce. Both researches are scientific in the sense that they are clear about the means by which their data was collected and the logic that ties their conclusions to those data. Each has advantages and disadvantages—the Wallerstein studies provide the kind of richness but not the level of certainty we would like; the McLanahan and Sandefur study is clear and convincing but does not reflect the psychological depth that most of us would want in reaching conclusions about children's well-being. In this instance, the studies complement one another in the sense of looking at matters from different views and coming to compatible conclusions.

In the following material, we will explore how custody evaluators collect information about specific cases, how they can assess literature on the subject and its applicability to the particular case, and a framework for thinking about the relative importance of the information obtained through these processes.

FACTS

In making custody assessments, mental health professionals make observations and collect reports from numerous sources. These provide a set of facts, which can be further processed. Decisions about what facts to collect and what credence to give them are of much importance.

The information an evaluator needs will depend on the questions to be answered. Too frequently, custody evaluators fail to focus on the specific issues pertinent to the situation and develop conclusions that go beyond or are irrelevant to the questions asked. They often collect both too much and too little information. Failure to gather pertinent information may leave the examiner ignorant of significant aspects of the situation. Irrelevant information can sway both the evaluator and the trier of fact in ways inconsistent with the goals of the evaluation. When working within a legal context, evaluators should develop a clear picture of the governing law in order to address the issues in the case. Many jurisdictions include specific issues that the court must consider in making decisions. For evaluators to be helpful in the decision process, they must collect information pertinent to these questions. Many states' statutes specify that the judge must consider the residential custodial parent's capacity to support a relationship with the noncustodial parent in deciding with whom the youngster should stay. Some experts in child custody do not agree that this should be a central consideration (Goldstein, Freud, & Solnit, 1975). However, whatever opinions examiners may have about the law, they impede the judicial process by failing to address the issues the court must address.

Most custody decisions do not depend per se on the general psychological health of the parents but do depend, in part, on the impact of the parents' psychological functioning on the child. Many mental health professionals, however, approach custody evaluations as they would the diagnostic assessment of a patient. The implications of the resulting diagnosis is often obscure in its meaning for the parent's interactions with the child. Nonetheless, the presence of a serious sounding diagnosis or test finding may sway the trier of fact or derail the focus of the evaluation. This is particularly problematic with regard to psychological test reports. Although the reports themselves are usually carefully worded to indicate that the subject shows a pattern of responses "consistent" with some condition or commonly observed among individuals with a particular condition, the inexperienced reader is likely to finish reading the report with a sense that the subject suffers from many and severe psychological disturbances.

The way in which "facts" are collected often profoundly affects their content and significance. The information collected in custody evaluations can be profoundly shaped by the collection process. For example, an interviewer who is perceived as sympathetic may be told many things that an apparently unfriendly interviewer is not told. Differentiating between the factors that substantially influence the data collection and those that do not can be difficult. This partly results because the subject's response to the interviewer may be so idiosyncratic that the interviewer is unaware of it (e.g., the interviewer may remind the subject of a pleasant or unpleasant person the subject has known). These problems are particularly marked in interviewing children, where such factors as the child's desire to please the interviewer or fears of parental disapproval may massively shift the information provided (Ceci & Bruck, 1995). The greatest danger occurs when the evaluator is unaware of the factors in the interview or testing situation that shape the information received. Although this hazard has been particularly well studied with regard to interviews about abuse allegations, interviewers are at constant risk of suggesting "correct" answers to the questions through responses such as approving remarks, gestures, and interested further questions when the interviewee responds in a certain fashion.

Because the respective attitudes of the interviewer and the intentions of the interviewee are so different during the performance of the roles of evaluator and therapist, these roles should not overlap (Greenberg & Daniel, 1997). In talking to a therapist, it is in the client's best interest to provide as full and accurate a picture as possible of the situation; in talking to an evaluator it is in the client's best interest to provide a picture that will lead the evaluator to concur with the client's opinions. The way in which an interviewer listens to the interviewee depends on an assessment of the interviewee's intentions. The intentions of subjects in forensic evaluations are generally different from those of clinical subjects. This distinction is important because most custody evaluators were primarily trained as clinicians. The clinical subject's own best interest is realistically served by providing the most accurate information possible to the evaluator because the more accurate the evaluator's assessment the better able the clinician is to assist the subject.

In a forensic situation, however, most subjects are highly motivated to have their point of view prevail. They are likely therefore to use whatever means they think will be effective to convince the evaluator of the merits of their own position. More or less subtle forms of dishonesty are common in custody evaluation. These range from overt lies, to significant omissions to enhance presentation of the subject's point of view. Attempts to form alliances with the subject in the interest of discovering what is best for the child sometimes help minimize the consequences of such tendencies. Nonetheless, evaluators should proceed on the basis that the information being provided is intended to influence them rather than to provide as accurate a picture as possible of the situation. When interviewers take on more than one role, they are likely to become confused about which role they occupy at a given time. The therapist's goal is often to communicate support and understanding to the client, which will aid the client in overcoming some difficulty. Evaluators have no such intention and are, in fact, appropriately skeptical that the information being given has any purpose other than persuasion. The vigorous questioning that may be appropriate in an evaluation and the use of collateral sources of information used by evaluators are rarely appropriate for the therapeutic situation. It is generally not possible to be both a good therapist and a good evaluator. For this reason, all guidelines for custody evaluators recommend avoiding a dual role (Ackerman, 1995).

As with other matters, a scientific attitude in collecting "facts" is not characterized by the search for absolute certainty but rather in careful attention to possible sources of error and their correction. To this end, evaluators note the apparent credibility of sources of information, including the motives an interviewee may have for distorting information, the manner in which the information is presented, knowledge of common forms of distortion including inaccuracies of memory, psychological test results that may pertain to credibility, and how consistent the information is both internally and with other sources of information. Some studies show that mental health clinicians are not particularly good judges of the veracity of the reports they receive (Ekman, 1992). Some of these studies are flawed in that they either placed the clinician in a "trick" position where he had little reason to anticipate that anyone would try to be less than honest or the clinician was given information of a type different from that ordinarily used by clinicians in making judgments of this kind. Methods are available to increase the clinician's detection of deceit (Ekman, 1992). Still, the clinical assessment of credibility remains significantly imperfect.

Human memory and perception are more fallible then most of us would like to think. In collecting information from many sources, it is essential to remember that distortions are common and not necessarily the result of intentional deception. Once people frame a view of a matter, they are likely to selectively perceive and recall events in a fashion that supports their preconceptions. For this reason, evaluators should, where practical, utilize collateral sources of information (Dietz, 1996) and weigh conflicting descriptions of events. Evaluators themselves may forget or misperceive aspects of a situation. The more carefully, systematically, and contemporaneously events are recorded, the less likely examiners are to introduce significant distortions into situations.[1] In addition to using ordinary thoroughness, many examiners follow comprehensive checklists when making observations during interviews and examinations to ensure the pertinent matters are recorded. These guides have the advantage that the examiner is likely to observe and record items on the checklist. They have the disadvantage that they may discourage pertinent open-ended exploration and the noting of observations that do not fit within the preassigned format.

---

[1] The pursuit of accurate and adequately recorded information is time consuming and expensive. It also often produces more complex findings than more superficial investigations. When the evaluation becomes part of a litigation process, this means that the scientific evaluator may appear to be at a disadvantage. Such an evaluator will be more explicit about the limitations of the evaluation, will acknowledge that certain investigations were not performed (or recorded). He or she will acknowledge lack of funds or time, will engage in more extensive and therefore more expensive evaluations whose cost may aid in suggesting that the expert is a hired gun, and at the end may come to conclusions that are less "black and white" than a less systematic investigator. Depending on the sophistication of the trier of fact, the scientifically oriented evaluator may thus appear at a distinct disadvantage as an expert witness than the less adequate examiner. As the courts move more in the direction of excluding "junk science" and develop increasingly sophisticated appreciation of the nature of scientific thinking, these apparent weakness are likely to turn into strengths. Scientifically oriented experts must be prepared to explain why their methods may appear less impressive than the false certainty of less careful evaluators.

When collecting information and making observations that are highly complex or available only once, recording the information may be useful. Many examiners have discovered the value of videotaping or audiotaping at least portions of the evaluation. Sometimes significant elements of interpersonal interactions between parent and child during an evaluation only become clear through the retrospective evaluation of recorded interactions.

> An experienced examiner observed the interaction between a mother and her 6-year-old child who had been removed from her care because of neglect associated with the mother's depression and substance abuse. Although the examiner felt ill at ease observing the interaction, the mother appeared animated, interactive, and concerned for the child's interests as manifested by her encouraging play with several toys that she knew he enjoyed. Reviewing a videotape of the session, the source of discomfort became clear. Over the 45-minute session, the mother never once responded to something the child initiated. In fact, when the child introduced a new topic, the mother continued speaking about the matter she had been focused on before the youngster "interrupted," giving no indication that she had heard what he had said. Even had the examiner been astute enough to pick up this pattern during the interview, without the videotape it would have been difficult to thoroughly and rigorously document it.

Studies of the suggestibility of children show that youngsters's reports may be profoundly influenced by subtle suggestion in previous and current interviews (Ceci & Bruck, 1995). Although this problem has been particularly noted in regard to sexual abuse allegations, it is important in any situation in which youngsters' historical reports become important. Simply having been asked about an event may constitute the basis for the later "recollection" of the occurrence. For this reason, it is extremely useful to retain videotapes of sessions in which children report historical events. Not only do such tapes make it more possible to assess the extent to which the examiner unwittingly employed various means that are known to produce distorted reports, they also make it possible to document situations in which the subject incorporated a question as a memory.

Selective recording may be challenged on cross-examination, however, where the question will naturally arise as to why the entire session was not recorded, or with implication of bias as to what was recorded. The evaluator should also expect that recordings will be subpoenaed, with the possibility of data being taken out of context for possible use in cross-examination.

THE EVALUATION OF STUDIES

The evaluator's opinions should be based in the knowledge accumulated in his field. In the behavioral sciences, as in any scientific discipline, the rate of growth of an evaluator's discipline is always too great for any one person to maintain a comprehensive knowledge of recent developments. Evaluators do have a responsibility, however, to remain aware of major recent trends in their field so that they can place specific knowledge in their discipline in context and reasonably evaluate whether older studies are consistent with current disciplinary thinking.

> Following World War II, researchers found substantial apparent evidence that certain styles of communication from parents to their children induced schizophrenia in the child (Lidz et al., 1958; Lidz, Fleck, & Cornelison, 1965). On the basis of these studies an examiner might reasonably conclude that a youngster with early signs of schizophrenia was the victim of a "schizophrenogenic" environment and would have appropriately considered this in making custody and visitation recommendation. More recent studies strongly suggest that the psychological environment in which the future schizophrenic grows up has a significantly smaller impact than biological factors in determining the course of the disease. Further exploration of the data on which the schizophrenogenic parent hypothesis was based demonstrated the flaws in the original studies (Lidz, 1984). (Rather than the child's schizophrenia being the result of abnormalities in parental behavior, the already disturbed child appears to produce the abnormalities.)

Scientific knowledge characteristically changes across time. New research changes the best information available on a topic. This is a strength, not a weakness, of scientific knowledge. As noted, an expert giving the best information available in the early 1960s would have stated that the parents of a schizophrenic youngster brought about or at least contributed significantly to their child's pathology through their disturbed form of communication. Today, this is not the view supported by available evidence and the expert would state that. Part of the expertise expected of evaluators is a sufficient knowledge of their discipline and a sufficient capacity for critical thought that they are able to assess the scientific status of published information they encounter.

In assessing particular studies, several factors are ordinarily considered including the source of the study, the status of the publication, the rigor of the reported study, and comparison of the study to related researches. Each of these factors will contribute to the evaluator's degree of confidence in a particular study.

Researchers' training should reflect the practical appreciation of sources of potential error, learning how to avoid elementary mistakes and becoming familiar with the range of problems that commonly beset a research effort. Various forms of direct and implicit certification identify the level of the researcher's training and experience. The researcher's highest academic degree and its source may indicate the extent of his or her research training. Many mental health professional degrees including the M.S.W., Psy.D., and M.D. include little or no formal training in research methods. A Ph.D. from a major university is very likely to have a strong background in research methodology. Similarly, the researcher's career as indicated by his academic rank, record of publication and the degree to which those publications are cited by other researchers suggests the level of regard with which the researcher is held within the professional community and the extent to which he has a track record of producing research that has been found to be of high quality by individuals qualified to review it.[2] A further indication that the work has been thoroughly reviewed is found in mention of sources of financial support. Major foundations and government agencies generally impose high standards of rigor for research proposals that they will fund, so that funding from such sources suggests the work is of high quality.

Scientific publications are of four types—publication in "refereed" or "peer reviewed" journals, journal publications in nonrefereed journals, chapters in edited volumes, and monographs. Publications may report new research findings or summarize and comment on older findings. Publication in a refereed journal indicates that two or more readers who are recognized authorities in the field concur that the article is of sufficient rigor and significance to merit publication. The quality of peer review itself varies substantially between journals, and failings of this system have been noted on numerous occasions (Burnham, 1990; Lock, 1990). Journals with many submissions are likely to impose higher standards on their authors than those that must work to fill their pages. Factors such as whether the peer-reviewer can identify the author (McNutt, Evans, Fletcher, & Fletcher, 1990) and peer-reviewer's conceptualization of his or her role (Horrobin, 1990) can strongly influence the peer review process. Nonetheless, it remains one of the more effective methods for ensuring the rigor of published materials.

The quality of non-peer-reviewed publication is more problematic. Sometimes these articles are of particularly high quality because they are written by leading researchers in the field, at an editor's invitation. The editorial review of chapters in edited books also varies markedly, resulting in uneven quality. In the "hard" sciences (chemistry, physics, etc.), researchers rarely publish significant new results in edited volumes or as monographs. The situation is different in the behavioral sciences, where significant research commonly appears in these formats. This means that in the behavioral sciences the consumer of research must often independently assess the quality of the research presented. An additional factor external to the study itself that should alert the reader's skepticism is the likelihood of the authors' financial gain from particular outcomes. For example, if a study demonstrates the validity of a commercially available test or the effectiveness of a drug in which the researcher has a financial interest, this should alert the reader to the greater likelihood of the report being shaped by those interests.

---

[2] Much research and scientific writing results from the collaboration of a seasoned researcher with a more junior colleague. The senior investigator, in essence, certifies the quality of the junior person's research and is regarded as responsible for the result.

Scientific literature suffers from a common problem with regard to negative results. A finding of the presence of some effect is more likely than the absence of an effect to stir interest both in those who decide whether an article should be published and those who write the article. As a result, negative findings tend to be underrepresented in the published literature (Dickersin, 1990). Negative results are of two kinds—those that show the absence of an effect and those that do not reproduce the findings of previous investigators. Though they are underrepresented in the literature of most sciences, in assessing the credibility of research findings, both of these results are of great importance. Despite researchers' best efforts, factors of which they are unaware may influence outcomes. The failure to reproduce a finding in another study is a strong indication of such factors.

ASSESSING THE CONTENT OF SCIENTIFIC PUBLICATIONS

The assessment of research on the basis of its content and process is a complex matter. We will simply outline here some major themes and particularly important areas. The reader should, however, refer to detailed treatises to learn about the means of assessing research findings (Campbell & Stanley, 1963).

Is It Science?

The Supreme Court's decision in *Daubert v. Merrell Dow Pharmaceutical, Inc.* (1993) attempted to address the question of what research and opinion should be characterized as "scientific." In doing so, the court attempted to answer a problem that has concerned those interested in the philosophy of science since at least the 16th century. Prior to this time, knowledge was regarded as embedded in authoritative texts from which correct information could be mined by those with the authority to do so. Starting with the work of Francis Bacon, a new way of knowing emerged, having as its chief reference observable facts about the external world. The interpretations of these facts was not a matter of authority but instead was based on the possibility that any adequately trained person could make the same observations and that the chain of reasoning from facts to interpretation could be made explicit. Over the past four centuries, but especially in this century, scientists and philosophers of science have refined and debated these core questions of what methods are "scientific" and when an investigation is properly labeled as such. The resulting ideas are both more technically[3] demanding and more controversial than the Supreme Court's decision suggests.

---

[3] Chief Justice Rehnquist in his partial dissent from the *Daubert* decision commented, "I defer to no one in my confidence in federal judges; but I am at a loss to know what is meant when it is said that the scientific status of a theory depends on its "falsifiability," and I suspect some of

The *Daubert* decision actually goes in the opposite direction from much of the most recent work in the philosophy of science. *Daubert* holds that science is characterized by its methods and that its claims to truth are based on those methods. This was the dominant view among methodologists until approximately 20 years ago. More recently, students of the history and sociology of science have argued that the actual way science is conducted is not related so much to method as to the social structure of scientific communities (Feyerabend, 1975; Kuhn, 1970; Latour & Woolgar, 1986). The newer picture of the nature of scientific knowledge is, in fact, more compatible with the *Frye* rule, which held that expert opinions must be compatible with widely accepted ideas within the expert's field.

However, if we accept the view that there are characteristic, if not utterly precise, methods of inquiry that set scientific knowledge apart from other kinds of knowledge, then the centerpiece of such knowledge is that ideas are tested against reliable observations about the world. If I say X is a scientific fact I must be able to demonstrate this through observations about the world. Moreover, terms must have commonly accepted, agreed-on definitions. Observations must be replicable both across raters and through time. The question of what data will determine whether X is a scientific fact is not simple. The things referred to in X must be clear enough so that researchers can agree whether what is observed is an example of this particular sort of thing. If someone says, "All hephalumps are green" there is no way in which this proposition can be scientifically tested until we know and agree what a hephalump is and how to define "green." This becomes a significant problem in many psychological researches because apparently meaningful terms may in fact have very unclear empirical referents. For example, mental health professionals are often asked to comment on the "dangerousness" of an individual. But until this term is defined in a way that refers to agreed-on specific empirically observable factors, the behavioral scientist has no way to collect data pertinent to the issue. In custody evaluation, phrases like "the best interest of the child" have little meaning in a scientific context until they are conceptualized in terms of reliable, observable phenomena.

Scientific statements are subject to test against observations. We will first look at this process conceptually. For many years, the proof of a hypothesis was regarded as the collection of observations that confirmed it. If a scientist claimed that all cells have nuclei, he could test and confirm this assertion by observing many cells under the microscope. This way of testing statements can prove faulty in two ways. First, it can involve a "sampling error"—the scientist

---

them will be, too." "Falsifiability" is one among many technical terms used in discussions of the philosophy of science and there is no reason that a federal court judge or any other layperson in this area would be expected to know its meaning. If principles derived from *Daubert* are to regulate the admissibility of evidence and opinions that claim to be scientific, the courts will require massive education about these matters.

may for some reason not look at those cells that lack nuclei. Second, although the statement appears to be about the external world, it may really be in a form in which no observation could show it to be wrong. For example, if a theory stated, "Every cell contains a nucleus but some of these nuclei are invisible," no microscope observation could prove the statement false, so any positive evidence about this matter would be essentially meaningless. Popper (1959) argued that only propositions for which one could imagine an experimental outcome contrary to the proposition should be regarded as scientific. This is the concept of "falsifiablity." For a hypothesis to be falsifiable, one must be able to design an experiment that would lead to the conclusion that the hypothesis was false. In the study of human behavior this can be a difficult requirement.

> Consider the psychoanalytic hypothesis that all young boys have anxiety-laden sexual desires for their mothers that they manage either by failing to become socialized to the taboo against incest or by forcing the idea from awareness, minimizing its emotional significance. Stated this way, no empirical data could possibly lead to the conclusion that the original statement was false because both the presence of erotic interest in the mother and *also* absence of such interest would be taken as confirming the hypothesis. Thus the proposition is not falsifiable.[4]

Not every investigation must involve a crucial experiment that tests a hypothesis. Most investigations simply provide additional reason to believe or disbelieve a statement. However, to be scientifically meaningful, a hypothesis must be capable of some form of critical test. As mentioned earlier, a major shift involved in scientific knowledge is that it rests on publicly available observation and reasoning. The argument that someone simply knows more or has more direct access to truth is unacceptable in scientific discourse. In some ways, this is a theoretical rather than a practical distinction. Most people cannot follow the reasoning involved in the theory of general relativity nor could they understand much less perform the experiments that confirm that theory. At no point, however, did Einstein say or imply, "I know more about the universe than you do and this theory is simply right." His reasoning was based on logical steps and empirical evidence (we are talking here about how the theory was substantiated, not how Einstein discovered it). When experts claim to be offering a scientific opinion about human psychological functioning, they must be held to this same standard. The empirical and logical steps leading to a statement must be capable of being laid out and not depend on authoritative

---

[4] This matter is introduced here as an example. Contemporary psychoanalysts would answer this criticism in two ways. Some would point out that the actual theory predicts the presence of certain observable residues of the oedipal situation so that the theory is actually falsifiable. Others would say that psychoanalysis is not a science in the same sense as the physical sciences and makes a different kind of claim to truth based on an enriched understanding of the psychological world rather than testable propositions about it.

assertion. This can be a real problem in behavioral science studies, in which a convincing rhetorical ability may be confused with scientific methodology (Spence, 1994). Vivid case histories are likely to impress readers and remain with them even when clear data contradict conclusions the researcher derives from them:

> In an experiment still often quoted in psychology textbooks, John B. Watson "demonstrated" his theory that phobias result from Pavlovian conditioned reflexes. In a conditioned reflex a stimulus that regularly elicits a response (the unconditioned stimulus) is paired with one that ordinarily does not elicit that response (conditioned stimulus). This often results in the conditioned stimulus eliciting the conditioned response—the most famous example being Pavlov's dogs who learned to salivate when a bell was rung after the bell and the presentation of food had been paired. Watson proposed that phobia resulted in a similar way when a noxious unconditioned stimulus was paired with an otherwise neutral situation. He vividly described an experiment in which "Little Albert" an 11-month-old child who had previously shown no fear of rats cried and avoided the rat after it was presented to him paired with a stimulus of a loud, clanging noise (Watson & Rayner, 1920). The experiment became the backbone of a theory of phobias which to this day has many adherents (Wolpe, 1990). Watson's original description still makes compelling reading. However, attempts to replicate Watson's experiment repeatedly failed (Seligman, 1971), a fact that received little notice as the rhetorical power of Watson's writing was so great.

It is worth keeping in mind that there are other kinds of valuable knowledge besides scientific knowledge. We only argue that if knowledge is presented as scientific it should be that. Because of the enormous prestige of science in our society, many people are tempted to describe their opinions and beliefs as scientific when they are not. Personal values and common sense may be presented as though they had scientific backing when they do not. This can be misleading when decision makers are relying on the information provided as having a scientific basis.[5]

---

[5] In child custody matters, experts often testify based on their "experience" or "clinical experience." It is important for all those concerned to treat these opinions for what they are worth. On one hand, they may be of considerable value, reflecting accumulated knowledge with real situations. However, they are subject to a variety of problems and rarely reflect the systematic collection of data characteristic of scientific investigation. That the expert does not recognize these limitations increases the problem. Some of the sources of error in "clinical experience" include (1) the experience reflects the expert's experience with a special subpopulation (e.g., a mental health professional who works with emotionally ill adults who were abused as children is likely to believe that abuse usually has devastating psychological effects because the abused individuals he sees are all psychologically disturbed). (2) Because information is not systematically collected or recorded, vivid experiences are likely to stand out. For several decades, tonsillectomy was a routine procedure in the United States because before the era of effective antibiotic therapy most physicians had the experience that some very ill children got dramatically better following the procedure; the children who were not affected did not stand out in the same way. Similarly, experiences that are congruent with the expert's views are likely to stand out. Every therapist of some experience has treated individuals who after an unrewarding experience with some other form of therapy did well in treatment with the therapist. Therapists are commonly convinced that

Do the Data Support the Conclusions?

In attempting to answer a question scientifically, data are collected that are believed to address the issue. In assessing whether data support a conclusion, it is important to ask how well this is accomplished. Doing research, especially research about people, is often extremely difficult and time consuming. At the same time, researchers want to produce meaningful findings. As a result, there is often some slippage between data and conclusions, usually in the direction of drawing stronger conclusions than the data warrant. Much of the methodology of scientific investigation is directed at attempting to get as much information from data as possible while avoiding reaching conclusions that are not supported by the data.

Many of the issues discussed earlier with regard to the information collected in assessments apply to data collected for research. Accurate descriptions of the setting in which the data are collected, attention to the accurate recording of that data, and the minimizing of reliance on memory and complex perception are even more important in the collection of research data. Most research publications carefully specify these matters. In assessing a research publication, the "methods" section should be reviewed with these considerations in mind. Surprisingly often, methods sections will indicate limitations in the work that otherwise would not be recognized. For example, in biomedical research it was for many years common to use only male subjects, at least ostensibly because the use of female subjects complicated the analysis of data. This information, which certainly opens the question of the applicability of these studies to women, is invariably present in the methods sections of the paper and can be used to correct the impression that the results are universally applicable. When a methods section is missing from a paper, this should raise a red flag about the soundness of the reported observations.

Much psychosocial research involves various instruments and test batteries designed to measure some aspect of psychological function. Several thousand such instruments are sufficiently well developed to have been described in multiple publications and reviews. Each claims to measure some aspect of human function. The validity of a measure is the extent to which it, in fact, measures what it claims. When the matter to be measured is clear and there is some sort of "gold standard" against which to compare the result, determining validity is relatively easy. Thus, if we wanted to decide whether a scale validly measures weight we would compare its results to widely accepted standards, much as are

---

such experiences indicate the general superiority of their own therapeutic approach, at least for this type of patient, and fail to appreciate that similar experience probably occur involving their own former patients and that other therapists probably enjoy success rates similar to their own. (3) Most clinical experience is time limited, usually to the period during which the subject is in treatment. This can easily lead to a misunderstanding of the long-term course of a situation. The mental health professional sees the "outcome" of a situation in terms of the situations when services were completed, which may not reflect more important issues of the course of the condition over years.

maintained by the National Bureau of Standards. But for many of the matters we try to address in studying people, no such simple absolute standards exist. We must first clarify what we mean by the terms we use and then see how well a measure reflects these concepts. For example, if we have a test that purports to measure whether a person is a "good parent," we would both need to clarify what was meant by this term and the extent to which the test measured the resulting qualities.[6]

The concept of validity always refers to a purpose for which the test is being used. A test may be valid for one purpose but not another (e.g., grades in college mathematics course may be valid predictors of grades in physical science courses but not grades in English courses). The concept of validity has been the subject of considerable refinement and clarification. *Face validity* refers to the observation that a test, on the face of it, is relevant to the quality measured. For example, performance on a test in which the subject is asked to do arithmetic problems on the face of it shows that subject's abilities to do that sort of problem. *Content validity* refers to a more thorough analysis in which we explore the extent to which a test measures matters pertinent to the question we are trying to answer. For example, a test of parenting ability might be shown to measure factors known or believed to contribute to parental function. However, useful measures need not have content validity. Certain important measures may accurately reflect an aspect of psychological function even though they do not necessarily directly address it. For example, although the presence of highly unusual experiences does not necessarily mean that an individual is delusional, reports of such experiences may be highly correlated with delusions.[7] Thus, *correlation validity* refers to the extent to which test results correlate with significant aspects of the person's current or future performance. The correlation need not reflect any other meaningful relationship between the item measured and its correlate. *Construct validity* refers to the extent to which a measure makes conceptual or scientific sense. In the absence of a gold standard, the validity of a measure is assessed by how well it fits within a network of measures

---

[6] Even when those who construct tests carefully describe what they do and do not measure, it remains easy to misconstrue their significance. Although "intelligence" tests were largely constructed to predict academic performance and although they have been shown to usefully measure a range of psychological functions, they are not adequate measures of overall psychological capacity or ability to function. Yet they are commonly treated as such not only by laypeople but also by professionals, often with negative consequences (see, e.g., Gould, 1981).

[7] The applications of psychological tests to individuals is discussed at greater length in Chapter 7. It is worth noting here that the application of psychological tests that lack content validity may lead to particular problems in assessing psychological function. One of the authors of this chapter recently had the experience, in two consecutive evaluations of MMPI-II test results suggesting that the subjects were psychotic and delusional. Their scores in these areas had been elevated because both answered affirmatively that their pictures had appeared on magazine covers. In fact, both individuals had been depicted on the covers of national magazines. A certain test-taking "set" or stance is more likely to distort results when subjects strive so hard to be "honest" that they overinterpret self-report test items, e.g., endorsing, "I have difficulty falling asleep" because they occasionally—not usually or often—have difficulty doing so.

that are used to study related concepts, the nomothetic net. In assessing the validity of a measure, researchers commonly combine several points of view about validity. It assessing the usefulness of a study, the various points of view regarding validity may serve as helpful guideposts in mapping the investigator's thinking. Looked at from a different angle, the reader of published studies should always be skeptical about the way in which the author uses terms. Simply because a test is said to measure a quality that goes by the same name as one with which the reader is familiar does not mean that the test measures that familiar quality. One must look at the way in which the test was put together and demonstrated to be related to the underlying construct to know whether, in fact, the test measures that construct well.

All the issues discussed in Chapter 7 apply to tests used in research studies. Especially in the case of projective tests and tests that have not been well studied, the reader should not assume they are as solidly based as one might hope. For many years, the standard text of psychological testing, which focused primarily on projective tests, was a volume by Rapaport, Gill, and Schafer (1945) based on the diagnostic test battery developed at the Menninger Clinic. This book formed the basis of many research and clinical studies. Though the studies on which the book was based included "normal controls," these turned out to be Kansas State Troopers. With no offense meant to these men, it is reasonable to doubt that they reflect the ordinary population of the community. Major criticism can be raised of the research supporting the validity of the most commonly used scoring system for the Rorschach, a widely used projective test (Groth-Marnat, 1997). Much of the supporting research is correlational with little information given about the actual false positive or false negative rates of inferences based on the use of this test.

An important aspect of validity is sensitivity. If the instruments used in a study cannot pick up significant differences between subjects, important aspects of the situation will not be adequately studied. The more sensitive a measure, the less reliable it is likely to be (i.e., the less likely it is that repeated measures of the same quantity or measures of the same quantity by different individuals will be the same). Obviously, for a measure to be meaningful it must also be reasonably reliable. Researchers must demonstrate or refer to demonstrations that the measures they use are both appropriately sensitive and reliable if their claims are to be credible.

In studying people, it is rare that research findings will show the clear delineation seen in the physical sciences. If we do a study of whether weights fall at the same rate when dropped in a vacuum, we expect that all the weights will so fall and would regard the experiment as incomplete if a small proportion of the weights fell at a different rate without explanation. In studies of people, things are rarely so straightforward; among the many factors that are likely to affect any significant aspect of human living, we rarely find one factor so powerful that it almost always causes a given effect. Because studies of people seldom have the sharp clarity of studies in the physical sciences, it became necessary to develop tools for assessing whether an observed relationship resulted from an actual re-lationship or occurred by chance. Over the past century and a half, scientists who have had to deal with the "messy" data typical of the study of people have developed a discipline that address this problem—statistics.

The massive discipline of statistics is devoted to the question of how to reli-ably extract information from observations and how to estimate the degree of certainty with which that information is asserted (Stigler, 1986). It is usually difficult to extract meaningful patterns from the welter of information with which an investigator is confronted. For example, we might observe declining school performance in youngsters following divorce. We would want to deter-mine the relationship of this finding to possible specific changes in the chil-dren's behavior (inattention in class, decreased attendance, indifference to good performance, unavailability of parental support in doing academic work) and the several changes in the children's environment (e.g., the fact of divorce, change of residence, parental reactions to divorce, community reaction to di-vorce). Finding a systematic approach to answering such questions is one job of statistics. A second job is estimating to what extent we should rely on the find-ings. In this example, if we study 10 youngsters involved in divorce and dis-cover that 8 of them are less attentive in class, 7 have parents who have become less engaged, and 6 of these cases overlap, are we justified in drawing any con-clusions about the relationship of these factors? To what extent is the overlap the result of chance? What is the likelihood that we would have a similar find-ing with another group of youngsters? How well do the 10 youngsters we have studied represent children with school difficulties following divorce? As any-one who has observed gambling or people estimating probabilities knows, human intuition about the likelihood of probabilistic events is poor. Statistics often provides quantitative estimates of how likely a finding is to result from chance and how likely it is to reflect a real difference; more generally it pro-duces estimates of how likely various experimental outcomes are given an un-derlying causal model. Even an outline of the statistical methods commonly used in studying the behavior science issues pertinent to divorce would re-quire far more space than we have available (see, e.g., Hopkins, Hopkins, & Glass, 1996, for a standard introduction to these issues; see Keren & Lewis, 1994, for a comprehensive review of them). However, we will briefly outline some common sources of confusion that arise from statistical studies in the be-havioral sciences and some common methodological problems of which read-ers should be aware in thinking about the usefulness of the study.

As discussed earlier, the mere presence of a statistical or quantitative treatment in a research paper may suggest a greater level of authority and credibility than the paper deserves. In assessing the quality of a study, re-member that statistics and quantity are only tools for finding information. If used wisely to gather important information, they can be exceedingly useful. However, because of their prestige, they can also hide substantial limitations in the study.

The concept of statistical significance is often misunderstood. Often given as a probability, statistical significance states the likelihood that a finding would arise by chance in a given situation. In the behavioral sciences, findings are generally regarded as significant if the likelihood of their being chance results is less than 1 in 20 ($p < .05$). Failure to demonstrate statistical significance in a study indicates nothing except that the study does not support a certain conclusion; it says nothing about the truth or falsity of propositions not being specifically studied. Providing a large enough sample to give statistical significance is difficult; the distinction between truth and statistical significance becomes particularly important. In long-term outcome studies it is far easier to collect information about such matters as economic well-being than it is about psychological states in depth. As a result, we do not have good statistical studies showing whether children's views of themselves are negatively altered by parental divorce. Some authors have concluded that the absence of such findings means that such effects do not occur or only occur as a result of other, incidental, factors. The data support no such conclusion. They instead point to the absence of adequate studies to address the question.

The presence of statistical significance may be equally confusing. If we look at enough relationships, a study may indicate a probability of less than 1 in 20 between two of the variables studied simply because we have studied so many variables. If we study 15 relationships, the probability that one of them will have a probability of less than 1 in 20 becomes substantial. Statistical significance does not necessarily point to meaningful relationship. In particular, such matters as causation cannot be properly inferred. A relationship between two variables may exist but this may result from a common cause. Statistical significance does not necessarily point to meaningful differences. It simply points to the extent of certainty with which one can say there is some difference. Some differences though definitely present are nonetheless practically meaningless. Statistical significance tells us little about the size of the effect being observed.

Although many journals now require that all articles involving statistical reasoning be reviewed by a competent statistician, publications that have not been subjected to such review surprisingly often have simple statistical mistakes. A common error is to use statistical tests that are not appropriate to the data. Many statistical tests assume that a variable is distributed in a certain way in a population (e.g., that a given variable, like height, is distributed in a bell-shaped curve). When this is not the case, the reasoning that supports the computation of various statistical measures may no longer apply and these measures may produce misleading results.

An important group of methods commonly used in statistics involve correlations and regressions. In almost all situations involving people, many things are happening at once and it is the job of the researcher to discover how these things are interrelated. A correlation study explores the extent to which two variables change together. Thus, the extent to which children's behavior becomes disruptive in the period immediately after a divorce varies with the age of the child.

The description of this relationship is a correlation. In many circumstances, correlations can be described as a single number, the correlation coefficient, which measures how much one variable changes with the other. In regression analysis, the situation is conceptualized somewhat differently. If many factors contribute to an observed change, one can think of that change as being the result of summing up those factors. Studying the change in many situations may allow the researcher to describe it as the sum of various factors each weighted by some constant. This is called a regression analysis. Both forms of analysis aim at showing the relationship between important variables. In the case of each analysis, we can discover how much of the change is *not* accounted for by the factors we have studied. Properly used correlation and regression analysis are powerful statistical tools for unraveling complex situations.

A common error, however, that particularly affects decision processes is equating correlation with causation. If two situations are causally linked it makes good sense to alter one to change the other. If the link is a mere correlation, however, such a change does not make sense. In the example discussed earlier concerning communications between parents and their schizophrenic children, we saw how correlation and causation can be confused. In the initial studies, a solid correlation was observed between the quality of parent-child interaction and the child's diagnosis. However, the researchers erroneously concluded that this correlation represented a causative relationship, in which the communication style caused the offspring's illness.

As mentioned earlier, statistical methods have obtained a status in the behavior science that sometimes goes beyond their actual usefulness. In particular, it is extremely difficult to study complex situations over time using the standard methods of sampling statistics. In the attempt to gather sufficient quantifiable data for statistical analysis, it often becomes necessary to simplify the situation to such an extent that factors that are commonly believed to be important cannot be addressed within a study. Additionally, for all their limitations, in-depth studies of individuals over time have contributed much of what we know about human psychological function in complex, emotion-laden situations, like the ones we are trying to address in custody evaluations. In recent years, many methodologists have recognized that the old, conceptually weak, case history method can be improved in several ways to produce very informative case studies (Yin, 1994). By paying close attention to the way in which conclusions are drawn and generalized, case studies have proved an increasingly effective means for studying complex psychological function. In addition to care in collecting and interpreting data, contemporary case study methodology often focuses on closely monitoring the time course of events (e.g., whether an improvement occurs in a subject at some regular interval following an intervention). When assessing reports of case studies or groups of case studies, readers should not follow the past style of simply discarding them as methodologically unsound but rather examine the extent to which they use contemporary methods to ensure their quality.

Is the Study Consistent with Other Research in the Subject?

Although a study may be carefully performed and its careful analysis may show no glaring failings, it is still appropriate to ask how well it coincides with related studies. In its most formal version, this process takes the form of replication, in which a study is repeated, usually in a different context. In studying behavioral and psychological issues, this is often particularly important because factors of which the investigator may be unaware can strikingly influence outcome. When a study appears significantly inconsistent with other research findings, a high level of skepticism about that study is appropriate and a search for the causes of the differences should be instituted. Because isolated studies are subject to substantial errors, behavior scientists only rely on them when they must.

Studies of the same subject matter are often difficult to compare. Differences in the population studied and the study procedure may make it unclear how much weight should be given to each study. In the past three decades, a means of comparing and consolidating groups of studies has emerged. Called meta-analysis, these methods are continuing to evolve and have at times been controversial (Garfield, 1991; Hunt, 1997). Yet they provide a systematic way in which to bring together, compare, and use comparable data on the same topic in a manner far superior to the traditional review article.

Findings that are inconsistent with other research are not necessarily in error. However, the differences in the findings must be explained for the work to be taken seriously. A particular group of problems arises with regard to studies of therapeutic and similar interventions. Initial evaluations are commonly performed by enthusiasts for the intervention, who in addition to other difficulties, are often naïve about methodology. The very enthusiasm of the investigators working on a new form of treatment may produce nonreplicable positive results unrelated to the purported mode of action of the treatment. Particularly when an intervention is reported as producing striking successes when other methods have not, the likelihood that the research can form a reliable basis for recommending that therapy is small. Custody decisions often require that a parent receive treatment for a condition that impacts the child negatively on the basis of the treatment's enthusiastic endorsement by a mental health professional. These recommendations may be contrary to broad consensus among students of the same conditions that these conditions are not significantly responsive to treatment.

APPLYING EMPIRICAL STUDIES TO PARTICULAR CASES

In the best of all possible worlds, experts would have a firm database of findings about the best interests of children in various circumstances, match the child's situation to the database and give a clear, empirically based opinion about how the particular youngster's best interests could be achieved.[8] Rarely is this possible. Several factors make the situation more complex and difficult. We have already discussed the challenges of both the assessment of the individual situation and reaching meaningful research conclusions. When we try to bring the two together additional questions arise. First, we need to ask whether the particular child's situation is actually an instance of the type studied in the research. Second, we need to ask how important the finding is to the child's situation. We also need to know whether the finding can be meaningfully translated into something that can actually be done in the real situation. Finally, we need to think through, given the imperfection of our knowledge, what standards should be applied to the quality of expert knowledge in custody decisions.

Does the Research Apply to This Child?

Research is always done on a sample drawn from a population. Thus, a researcher might study the impact of visits with a noncustodial parent taking his subjects from 8- to 10-year-old urban African American boys of low socioeconomic status whose parents have been divorced for at least two years. Assume that the study was of high quality and produced clear recommendations about the frequency of such visits that would most benefit the child. Is this study useful in making decisions about a middle-class white girl whose parents are in the midst of a divorce? Is it useful in making decisions about middle-class African American boys who are otherwise similar to the boys originally studied? Stated generally, if we find a situation where the subject of an evaluation belongs to the population from which the study sample is taken, we can apply the findings of the study directly. However, in other circumstances we need to ask how well or poorly the findings apply.

An approach to this problem begins with asking why we might expect the findings not to apply—in what way does the subject of evaluation differ from the research sample. In our example, many investigators might believe that low socioeconomic status African American boys tend to have limited relationships with paternal figures and would particularly benefit from those relationships compared with other youngsters. Insofar as this belief is correct, the importance of supportive contact with a noncustodial father is likely to be greater than for other populations of youngsters. Having identified likely perceived differences, one can than ask whether there are empirical studies that suggest these differences are meaningful. If (as is the case), most studies of the effects of father absence on the well-being of youngsters showed that there is little difference in its impact as a function of race (McLanahan & Sandefur, 1994) then the

---

[8] We use the "best interest" criterion here as an example both because it is widely accepted in the United States and because it points to the complexity of behavior science opinions. The same logic would apply to virtually any question that might be posed to the behavior scientist in this context, even though the issue at hand might not be the child's best interest.

evaluator may conclude the difference between a low social status, African American study population and the population from which the subject comes is unlikely to be significant for the purposes at hand. It is important to remember that scientific findings are characterized by the degree to which they are self-critical, not by their definitive nature. When applying studies to individual children, it is the evaluator's job to analyze the reasoning and findings that lead to his conclusions and the extent to which they are likely to be true—not to achieve absolute certainty.

How Important Is the Finding?

All real custody decisions involve factors that weigh on each side. One parent may be able to spend more time with the child, whereas the other may provide the child with access to superior schools. One parent may have a better sense of the child's emotional life while the other may provide a better model of socially acceptable behavior. In many instances, significant empirical evidence of the value or disadvantage of various parental qualities will be available from the research literature. However, the comparative importance of these various factors has rarely been systematically studied. Some methods of evaluating custody implicitly weight these factors in relation to one another (Bricklin, Elliot, & Halbert, 1995; this volume). Still, implicitly or explicitly in coming to a recommendation, the evaluator must weigh the relative importance of findings.

As discussed previously, studies should tell us not only that some factor makes a difference but also give some picture of the magnitude of that difference, the effect size. When comparing parents' abilities to care for the child, effect size from pertinent studies should be a central concern. Sometimes this is addressed in terms of common sense. If one parent engages in behavior that threatens the child's life while the other provides limited opportunity to play with peers, we do not need a systematic study to conclude that the latter parent should have custody. However, more subtle situations may require precisely such a comparative analysis; for example, with certain forms of parental psychiatric illness, empirical findings about the impact on children run contrary to most people's intuition (see Jenuwine & Cohler, this volume).

In many instances, the best evaluators can do is to make their analysis as explicit as possible. This will allow evaluators and others who use their findings to explore the extent to which implicit formulation, including the evaluator's personal values, have found their way into the recommendations.

Can the Recommendations Be Implemented?

In the course of custody studies, evaluators commonly observe situations that they believe could be improved if the parties acted in some particular fashion. The evaluator may conclude that a particular visitation schedule would be optimal for the child or that one or more of the parties would benefit from therapy;

the evaluator may conclude the peace could be maintained between the parents by the introduction of a third party who would supplement the custodial parent's caretaking function thereby making up for observed limitations in that parent. Whatever the intrinsic merits of these recommendations, they are of no value unless they can be implemented.

Parents may voluntarily adopt the recommendation for the child's benefit, although the process of convincing them to do so may involve the evaluator in problems of playing dual roles in the divorce process. It benefits the child little for parents to agree to terms in the midst of litigation unless the parents are likely to abide by those terms once the litigation is complete. Evaluators commonly confuse the court's role in custody matters with its role in child abuse and neglect cases. In the latter situation, the court or those acting with its implicit backing, freely exercise considerable power over parents, who have been shown to be inadequate in their parental functioning. The court can and does require parents to participate in arrangements for the child's benefit and through its agents often polices the parents' compliance. In contrast, in custody disputes in divorce there is no finding of parental incompetence and within very broad limits the court is likely to endorse a settlement reached by the parents whether or not it is optimal for the child (Weyrauch, Katz, & Olsen, 1994). Furthermore, whatever the court may order or whatever may be recommended to the parents, the court will not police compliance with its order unless the other parent actively complains of failure to comply. In making custody recommendations, evaluators should not accept parents' reports of their intention to behave differently than they currently are behaving because such promises are generally not enforceable. Although sometimes the outcome is positive, parents desiring custody often will describe plans that they are unlikely to carry out once an order is in place.

An arrangement workable for both parents is much more likely to be followed than a plan that is complex, crafted to absolutely optimize some aspect of the child's situation or is scrupulously "fair" to each parent. Part of the custody evaluator's work is to try to discover workable arrangements that minimize conflict between the parents and meet the child's needs.

THE GOALS AND STANDARDS OF EVALUATION

In their analysis of the best interest standard, Goldstein et al. (1975) observe that it is unrealistic to attempt to make recommendations that are optimal for the child and recommend instead that the evaluator attempt to find "the least detrimental alternative." Although some of the recommendations based on this formulation now appear mistaken and the concept has not found wide acceptance, a central problem to which they pointed remains of concern. It is generally not possible to frame a scientific opinion regarding a particular child in such a way that definitively solves all the problems associated with a custody decision. Almost always, any custody decision will have adverse as well as desirable affects.

Very often, the scientific evaluator will not be able to achieve the degree of certainty that all involved wish we had in making decisions that impact children as profoundly as custody decisions do.

Far from implying that the opinions of scientific custody evaluators are useless, this means that their opinions can be relied on to be accurate and sound insofar as they go. Courts and others who rely on these opinions may be less comfortable than they would be with more definitive statements but they will at least have the advantage of accurate information on which to reach conclusions. Although we know of no studies on the matter, it is our impression that custody evaluators are rarely hired guns in the sense of deliberately making recommendations favorable to the party that has retained them.[9] However, many experts believe it is useful to advocate for the opinion they have come to; sometimes they believe doing so is to advocate for the child. Such experts misunderstand their role in the legal process, that of providing the best information possible to those who must make custody decisions. The expert's job is to communicate accurately and informatively in a way that is useful to the court and other decision makers. To obtain reliable testimony, courts must tolerate the distress of decision making and the ambiguity that is part of the reality of complex human psychology. When courts displace their judicial responsibility for legal decision making onto enthusiastic experts, they create a situation in which the experts may fill this role at the expense of providing accurate information.

Increasingly in the behavioral sciences, researchers have recognized the value of framing findings in terms of specific risks and probabilities. In so-called second generation studies of the risk of violence, investigators have tried to make quantitative predictions of the likelihood of an individual being violent in various circumstances, rather than attempting the essentially impossible task of saying that the person will, in fact, be violent.

Following such a process, the expert's goal should be to reach the most reliable and valid opinion possible under the circumstances and to be able to describe how reliable and valid that opinion is. Rarely can the expert accurately forecast exactly what will or will not happen. (When an expert gives an opinion in this form, it almost always means that the opinion either is inaccurate or has been poorly expressed.) Experts should, however, be able to say whether the information changes the likelihood of some outcome and in some instances maybe able to quantify that conclusion. In all instances, experts should be prepared to describe the reliability and validity of their own opinions.

---

[9] The impression that hired guns are common arises from several sources. Most evaluators who do substantial work in this area develop reputations regarding the kind of opinions they are likely to render so that attorneys are likely to try to select evaluators who agree with their client's interests. When an evaluator comes to a conclusion contrary to the retaining attorney's position, the case often settles without trial or the expert is not called to testify so that at trial it usually appears that experts always agree with those who retain them. Finally, there are unethical individuals who, for a fee, will testify to almost anything. They stick out in memory because their behavior is often so egregious.

CONCLUSION

Custody evaluation can incorporate empirical information to reach credible conclusions. This involves three overlapping steps—the collection of information about the particular situation, the evaluation of pertinent published reports, and the informed use of published reports in reaching conclusions. The outcome, if the process is conducted properly may not be necessarily clear or definitive, but under the circumstances it is the best information to aid those making decisions.

REFERENCES

Ackerman, M. (1995). *Clinician's guide to child custody evaluations.* New York: Wiley.

Bricklin, B., Elliot, G., & Halbert, M. (1995). *The custody evaluation handbook: Research based solutions and applications.* New York: Brunner/Mazel.

Burnham, J. (1990). The evolution of editorial peer review. *Journal of the American Medical Association, 263*(10), 1323–1329.

Campbell, D., & Stanley, J. (1963). *Experiment in quasi-experimental designs for research.* Boston: Houghton Mifflin.

Ceci, S., & Bruck, M. (1995). *Jeopardy in the courtroom: A scientific analysis of children's testimony.* Washington, DC: American Psychological Association.

Chassan, J. (1979). *Research design in clinical psychology and psychiatry* (2nd ed.). New York: Irvington.

Cohen, J. (1990). Things I have learned (so far). *American Psychologist, 45,* 1304–1314.

Daubert v. Merrell Dow Pharmaceuticals, Inc., 509 U.S. 579 (1993).

Dickersin, K. (1990). The existence of publication bias and risk factors for its occurrence. *Journal of the American Medical Association, 263*(10), 1385–1389.

Dietz, P. (1996). The quest for excellence in forensic psychiatry. *Bulletin of the American Academy of Psychiatry & the Law, 24*(2), 153–163.

Ekman, P. (1992). *Telling lies.* New York: Norton.

Feyerabend, P. (1975). *Against method* (rev. ed.). New York: Verso.

Garfield, E. (1991). Current comments: Meta-analysis and the metamorphosis of the scientific literature review. *Current Contents,* (43), 5.

Goldstein, J., Freud, A., & Solnit, A. (1975). *Beyond the best interests of the child.* New York: Macmillan.

Gould, S. (1981). *The mismeasure of man.* New York: Norton.

Greenberg, S., & Daniel, W. (1997). Irreconcilable conflict between therapeutic and forensic roles. *Journal of Professional Psychology: Research and Practice, 28,* 50–57.

Groth-Marnat, G. (1997). *Handbook of psychological assessment* (3rd ed.). New York: Wiley.

Hopkins, K., Hopkins, R., & Glass, G. (1996). *Basic statistics for the behavioral sciences* (3rd ed.). Boston: Allyn & Bacon.

Horrobin, D. (1990). The philosophical basis of peer review and the suppression of innovation. *Journal of the American Medical Association, 263*(10), 1438–1441.

Hunt, M. (1997). *How science takes stock: The story of meta-analysis.* New York: Russell-Sage Foundation.

Keren, G., & Lewis, C. (Eds.) (1994). *A handbook for data analysis in the behavioral sciences: Statistical issues*. Hillsdale, NJ: Erlbaum.

Kuhn, T. (1970). *The structure of scientific revolutions* (2nd ed.). Chicago: University of Chicago Press.

Latour, B., & Woolgar, S. (1986). *Laboratory life: The construction of scientific facts* (2nd ed.). Princeton, NJ: Princeton University Press.

Lidz, T. (1984). A psychosocial orientation to schizophrenic disorders. *Yale Journal of Biology and Medicine, 58,* 209–217.

Lidz, T., Cornelison, A., & Fleck, S. (1958). The intrafamilial environment of the schizophrenic patient: VI. The transmission of irrationality. *AMA Archives of Neurology and Psychiatry, 79,* 305–316.

Lidz, T., Fleck, S., & Cornelison, A. (1965). *Schizophrenia and the family*. New York: International Universities Press.

Lock, J. (1990). Some aspects of medical hermeneutics: The role of dialectic and narrative. *Theoretical Medicine, 11*(1), 41–49.

McLanahan, S., & Sandefur, G. (1994). *Growing up with a single parent*. Cambridge, MA: Harvard University Press.

McNutt, R., Evans, A., Fletcher, R., & Fletcher, S. (1990). The effects of blinding on the quality of peer review. A randomized trial. *Journal of the American Medical Association, 263*(10), 1371–1376.

Popper, K. (1959). *The logic of scientific discovery*. London: Hutchinson.

Rapaport, D., Gill, M., & Schafer, R. (1945). *Diagnostic psychological testing*. New York: International Universities Press.

Salsburg, D. (1985). The religion of statistics as practiced in medical journals. *American Statistician, 39,* 220–223.

Seligman, M. (1971). Phobias and preparedness. *Behavior Therapy, 2*(3), 307–320.

Spence, D. (1994). *The rhetorical voice of psychoanalysis: Displacement of evidence by theory*. Cambridge, MA: Harvard University Press.

Stigler, S. (1986). *The history of statistics*. Cambridge, MA: Harvard University Press.

Watson, J., & Rayner, R. (1920). Conditioned emotional reactions. *Journal of Experimental Psychology, 3,* 1–14.

Weyrauch, W., Katz, S., & Olsen, F. (1994). *Cases and materials on family law: Legal concepts and changing human relationship*. St. Paul, MN: West.

Wolpe, J. (1990). *The practice of behavior therapy* (4th ed.). New York: Pergamon Press.

Yin, Y. (1994). *Case study research design and method* (2nd ed.). Newberry Park, CA: Sage.

CHAPTER 4

Understanding the Relationship between Children and Caregivers

LOUIS KRAUS

T HE SEARCH FOR the best interest of the child involves attempts to provide the best possible environment for the youngster's emotional growth. The idea that children need adequate opportunities for satisfactory relations with caretakers to develop well has gained wide endorsement among students of development. Attachment may be broadly defined as "an enduring emotional bond uniting one person with another . . . commonly manifest in efforts to seek proximity and contact to the attachment figure, especially when the individual is under stress" (Thompson, 1996, p. 127). Throughout this century researchers have worked to clarify the function and nature of attachment in developing children (Holmes, 1995). Starting in the 1970s, these ideas were applied to custody issues (Goldstein, Freud, & Solnit, 1979). While custody recommendations are based on a variety of issues beyond the attachment of children to their caregivers, the importance of the relationship between children and caregivers is universally recognized as an important component for deciding custody arrangements. However, detailed clarification of the significance of attachments, how they can be measured, and their relations to other factors that might be considered in custody evaluations remain active areas of investigation. This chapter describes the concept of attachment, its developmental significance, some of the means of measuring it, and its relevance to custody decisions. The chapter also examines the importance of the bond of the caregiver to the child.

HISTORICAL BACKGROUND

Sigmund Freud (1905) described the child's earliest attachment to the mother in terms of biological needs and sensual pleasures. Extending Freud's ideas, child psychoanalyst Melanie Klein posited that early psychological development involved making an image of the mother and the mother's functions part of the infant's psyche. Her focus emphasized the child's fantasies, as evidenced in the child's play, over the actual qualities of the mother in determining the child's experience of the caregiver. From these ideas, and the work of other psychoanalysts, there emerged a well-developed clinical theory, object relations theory, that attempts to describe how stable configurations of psychological functioning result from relations with other people (J. Greenberg & Mitchell, 1983). These theories evolved from the in-depth study of patients in psychoanalysis. The tragedies of World War II led to the direct observation of the impact of loss and separations from caretakers in young children.

The forced separation of London's young children and their families during the London Blitz led Anna Freud and Dorothy Burlingham to study the psychological impact of these separations (A. Freud, 1973). Anna Freud used direct infant observation to investigate the effects of loss on the development of infants and toddlers. She experimented with interventions designed to minimize the observed traumatic consequences and described the psychological solutions that the children found for themselves. One of her central findings was that children did better insofar as they were able to remain with their primary caregivers.

Also in consequence of World War II, many children in Europe were left without parents. Rene Spitz (1945, 1946) reported on approximately 100 infants, one year and younger. The study compared children of unwed incarcerated mothers reared by their mothers with infants raised in a highly sanitary environment in which they had little human contact. Despite the hygienic environment, the children in the nursery setting became ill and died at a far higher rate than infants who remained with their mothers, even though those caretakers were imprisoned young criminals. The orphanage-raised children who survived became unresponsive and immobile. Often they lay so still for so long that their bodies made indentations in their mattresses. Spitz termed the morbidity and mortality associated with early separation, *anaclitic depression* (Spitz, 1946).

A decade before Anna Freud's studies of separation, German ethologist, Konrad Lorenz, investigated mother-infant relationships in geese. Lorenz (1935) reported that goslings "imprint" on their mothers in a way that suggests a biological bonding mechanism wired into infant organisms. The concept that there could be a biological predisposition for human attachment and related behaviors challenged object relations and dynamic theories of development that characterized attachment as a consequence of other, more basic, biological needs.

In 1950, John Bowlby, an ethologist and psychoanalyst who had been exposed to Lorenz's work, was asked by the World Health Organization to advise on the mental health of homeless children (Bowlby, 1980). Bowlby explored childhood loss and its ramifications from multiple viewpoints. In particular, he integrated aspects of classical Freudian theory with evolution theory and attempted to remain close to empirical data. This led to a major synthesis published in 1969, *Attachment*, the first of three volumes devoted to attachment, separation and loss (Bowlby, 1969, 1973, 1980). Although Bowlby acknowledged the importance of Sigmund Freud's ideas that attachment grows from physiological need and sensual pleasure, and attempted to integrate his ideas with it, Bowlby faulted Freud's lack of direct infant observation. Looking at the same developmental lines as Freud but from a different perspective, Bowlby held, "Observation of how a very young child behaves toward his mother, both in her presence and especially her absence, can contribute greatly to our understanding of personality development." Empirical findings, such as Spitz's observation, strongly suggested that children require more than having their physiological needs met if they are to thrive. Combining these observations with the argument that proximity to caretakers greatly increases the chance of survival for mammalian young, Bowlby argued that mammals have a primary tendency to seek proximity to their caretakers, especially in times of danger. In humans, this tendency forms the basis of much psychological growth. Attachment is needed to help form the basic components of humanness. Bowlby found that responses to separation from the primary caretaker include love, hate, ambivalence, insecurity, anxiety, mourning, displacement (the attribution of negative aspects of the caretaker to other, less important persons), splitting (experiencing another as all good or bad), and repression (the barring of unacceptable ideas from awareness).

Bowlby's careful formulations gained considerable emotional force from a group of powerful films created by the Robertsons. These documentaries depicted children separated from their parents. In one film (Robertson & Robertson, 1969) we follow John, a likeable and loving child of 2½ years who is placed in residential care while his mother is hospitalized for nine days to deliver a baby. Over an amazingly brief period, John deteriorates from an active competent youngster, capable of being easily soothed and finding sources of pleasure and comfort, into a child who is chronically miserable, progressively less responsive to attempts to calm him physically and finally in a state of unresponsive depression. The pleasure and joy that characterized him seem to have disappeared. Most strikingly when he is finally reunited with his mother, with whom he had previously enjoyed an extremely positive relationship, he pulls away from her and refuses to look at her; when finally after much coaxing he does look, his expression is best characterized as hatred.

Bowlby's early work dealt with the separation of children from their primary attachment figures for periods up to several weeks. In 1969, Ainsworth developed a standardized laboratory procedure, the "strange situation" (described later in this chapter) for observing attachment behavior. Her studies looked at children 18 months of age and younger, and their primary attachment figures (Ainsworth, Blehar, Waters, & Wall, 1978). The strange situation allowed researchers to standardize and assess attachment in the laboratory using scientific method. Ainsworth's standardized measure has been modified and continues to be used as a framework to analyze parent-child interactions. Other systematic measures of attachment were developed and continue under development. These measures attempt to assess attachment during various developmental phases. A major problem facing researchers is to demonstrate that these measures tap a common, underlying psychological configuration, since the manifestations of attachment at different ages vary markedly.

Starting in 1950, a group of psychoanalysts, led by Saul Altshul and Joan Fleming, studied the impact of early parent loss on adult psychological function as it emerged in the treatment of psychoanalytic patients. They found, "The children continued to develop in an appropriate, but superficial, way. However, the traumatic scars would reveal themselves symptomatically during certain developmental periods throughout the life cycle." These adult survivors of childhood bereavement were described as exhibiting developmental arrests (i.e., failure to continue to develop in certain sectors of the personality), distortions of reality testing (the ability to differentiate fantasy from material reality), and chronic maladaptive patterns of behavior (Altshul, 1988). Children and adults are differently affected by loss. Even though a child may be able to have more than one attachment figure and to form new attachments, early parent loss, from whatever the cause, negatively affects children by increasing the insecurity in relationships and often leaving segments of development incomplete.

During the 1970s, Klaus and Kennell tried to apply Lorenz's theory of bonding to humans (Klaus & Kennell, 1982). They theorized that for "proper bonding" to occur, newborns needed to be placed immediately with their mothers. This led to a brief fad in which mothers, convinced by these publications, believed they needed immediate contact with their newborns to be "properly bonded" (Klaus & Kennell, 1982). Without this internal connection, mothers feared, and a few professionals suggested, their children were doomed to a life of psychopathology. This led to tragicomic events such as the young mother who ran down a hospital corridor, blood dripping from a ripped out IV cord, yelling, "I haven't yet bonded with my child." The concept of bonding, in the sense of some analogous process to Lorenz's observations is not, in fact, observed in human infants. The faddish popularity of bonding lingers in some court systems, particularly among certain well-meaning, but ill-informed, child welfare workers.

The term *bonding* has persisted in some legal contexts and has been used in a variety of ways. As defined by Lorenz, Klaus, and Kennell, it refers to a form of imprinting not observed in humans. Currently, it is often used vaguely to describe the parents' relationship to the child. The components of the parent-child relationship are profoundly important and critical to the best interest of the child. They include emotional availability, commitment, protection, provision of organized structure, responsiveness to the child's needs, teaching, appropriate play, and discipline (Sameroff & Emde, 1989); and it is in this sense that we use the term in this chapter. Attachment without bonding, though it occurs, leaves the child helpless in an unresponsive environment. Sometimes experts opine on the child's best interest based solely on the observation that a parent is the primary attachment figure without focusing on other important issues of parenting, including the parent's capacity to meet the child's needs or the complementary bond of parent to child.

THE NEED FOR ADEQUATE ATTACHMENTS

Children need consistent parenting to develop in an age-appropriate way. Attachment refers to the specific tie of an infant to the primary caregiver, which generally comes into focus after six months of age (see Mayes & Molitor-Siegl, this volume). As the development continues, the infant and young child begins to internalize this figure, in the sense of being able to evoke needed experience of the attachment figure in its physical absence. Premature or long separations from a primary attachment figure can be painful and the results can be devastating. The extreme disorganization and distress seen in many children reared in Romanian and Russian orphanages and their great difficulty in forming meaningful relationships with caretakers illustrate the profound effects of grossly inadequate attachment experiences. Early separation can lead to difficulties in forming new and trusting relationships. This is not to say, however, that new attachments cannot be formed. They can, but often the formation of these new attachments takes a long time and can only occur with difficulty in circumstances where skilled caretakers are willing to devote considerable effort to deal with children who are initially unrewarding.

Thompson (1996) describes guidelines for judicial decisions involving testimony on attachment, including (1) focusing on the psychological (as distinct from the biological) parent, (2) recognizing multiple attachments, (3) recognizing primary and secondary attachments, and (4) focusing on the child's need to maintain ties to noncustodial caregivers. For attachment theory to be used and to be helpful in a legal context, it must be used in conjunction with the complementary concept of bonding.

Characteristics of the infant contribute to parental bonding. From birth, many infants have a stable temperament, which continues to shape their personalities throughout life. Studying infant temperament and its interaction with parent-child relations, Chess and Thomas (1977) describe each influencing the other in an evolving process. They developed nine categories of childhood temperament, and three general descriptions of children, including the "easy child," "difficult child," and "slow to warm up" child. They relate development to these temperaments and to the "goodness of fit" between child and parent. By goodness of fit, they mean the extent to which the parents' personalities and preferences correspond to the needs of the child and vice versa. Thus an active demanding child may delight parents whose own personalities lead them to positively value these qualities but may prove undesirable to parents whose own energy level is such that the youngster seems too demanding to them. Similarly, unusually calm parents may do well with a child who is "difficult," while parents who tend to be reactive are likely to intensify the troublesomeness of the youngster. For this reason custody evaluators must always ask to what extent a parent fits with a particular child and to what extent the parent is bonded to the child, as well as the extent to which the child is attached to the parent.

Recent years have seen much discussion and debate over the relevance of "bonding" and some public confusion about Klaus and Kennell's version of bonding and attachment theory. Diane Eyer (1993) for example accurately criticizes the work of Klaus and Kennell, showing that there is no scientific basis for ideas of intrauterine or immediate postpartum imprinting of infants analogous to Lorenz's findings for birds. She then overgeneralizes her opinion, however, to include the work of Bowlby and other investigators, whose findings are more substantially based.

For those using ideas from attachment theory to form opinions about custody and visitation, an element of the history of attachment research is particularly problematic. Much more research and interest over the past 40 years has been devoted to mother-infant relationship than to the father-child relationship. When fathers and infants are studied, the subjects are often fathers who are unusually interested in attachment issues, raising the question of a significantly skewed sample (Ainsworth et al., 1978). The issue of father-infant attachment needs further study to ensure that scientifically informed recommendations are not biased by lack of information about attachments to fathers. In particular, the issue of the father as a secondary attachment figure and how potential disruption of this relationship may affect the child needs to be systematically explored.

An example of how further studies may give a richer picture of father's roles is provided by Marcus and Mirle's (1990) study of the attachment of 21 girls and 23 boys using a structured interview (The Parent Attachment Structured Interview). They described attachment of preschool and young school-age children from the perspective of the child's relationship with their primary caregiver. For boys, they a found a positive correlation between attachment to their father and future social competence. The boys with more positive attachments to their fathers exhibited less anxiety and depression than less attached boys. Maternal positive attachment for these boys was also positively related to social competence. Girls who had a greater positive attachment to their fathers also had less anxiety and depression. However, contrary to the expectations of the study, a greater maternal positive attachment for girls predicted less social competence. These researchers note that further study was necessary to better understand gender-related differences in attachment.

DISORDERS OF ATTACHMENT

The *Diagnostic and Statistical Manual of Mental Disorders* of the American Psychiatric Association (*DSM-IV;* 1994) describes *Reactive Attachment Disorder of Infancy or Early Childhood* as a markedly disturbed and developmentally inappropriate social relatedness in most contexts, beginning before age 5, as evidenced by a persistent failure to initiate or to respond in a developmentally appropriate fashion to most social interactions. This is seen in excessively inhibited, hypervigilant, or highly ambivalent and contradictory responses. The child, who is neither developmentally delayed nor suffering from a pervasive developmental disorder, may respond to caregivers with a mixture of approach, avoidance, and resistance to comforting, or may exhibit frozen watchfulness. The child may form diffuse attachments marked by indiscriminate sociability with marked inability to exhibit selectivity in choice of attachment figures (e.g., excessive familiarity with relative strangers). To be diagnosed with this disorder, the child must have been exposed to pathogenic care before developing symptoms as evidenced by at least one of the following:

Persistent disregard of the child's basic emotional needs for comfort, stimulation, and affection.

Persistent disregard of the child's basic physical needs.

Persistent changes of primary caregivers that prevent formation of stable attachments (e.g., frequent changes in foster care).

Reactive attachment disorders are divided into two types, inhibited or disinhibited, depending on whether the clinical picture is dominated by withdrawal from other people or inappropriate engagement with them (APA, 1994).

Sir Michael Rutter (1997) explores the psychopathology that can develop from disruptions of attachment. According to Rutter, these disorders are explained through attachment theory. He believes that *DSM-IV* oversimplifies and gives some erroneous information about attachment disorders. He underlines the importance of exploring the nature of the child's attachments as opposed to simply asking whether the child suffers from an attachment disorder as defined by *DSM-IV*. Difficult problematic attachments, worthy of careful scrutiny in making decisions about custody and visitation, are not necessarily associated with the child being diagnosable with a reactive attachment disorder. Nor are the manifestations of disturbed attachment sometimes seen in children of divorce necessarily the consequence of poor parenting by one of the parents alone. While children in divorce cases may exhibit any pattern of attachment, it is often the disruption of attachment in divorce that may devastate a child rather than difficulties with one parent or the other.

When considering whether a child has been the subject of pathogenic care, custody evaluators should carefully explore whether the child's emotional needs have been *persistently* disregarded. Rutter (1997) observes further that, in difficult divorce cases, the divorce per se is far less traumatic for the child than the extremely dysfunctional relationship that develops between the parents following the separation. In these pathological relationships, the parents often superficially define their focus as the best interest of their child, while they are actually primarily concerned to continue the pathological struggle between themselves (see Wallerstein & Corbin, this volume). In the process, although not intending to harm the youngster, they disregard the children's basic emotional needs. It is not surprising that in these situations children's behavioral problems, depression, anxiety symptoms, and school performance may worsen and social relationships deteriorate.

Disturbed attachment is associated with other forms of serious pathology as well as reactive attachment disorders. Benoit, Zeanah, and Barton (1989) describe attachment relationships in mothers of 25 children who were diagnosed with failure to thrive (a serious condition in which otherwise healthy infants fail to gain weight) and compared the attachment of 25 hospitalized mothers with normally growing infants. Their study matched the race, socioeconomic status, maternal education, and the infants' age and sex. They reported that 96% of the mothers with infants who were suffering from failure to thrive were classified as insecure with respect to attachment as assessed by the adult attachment interview.

ADOLESCENT ATTACHMENT

Psychoanalyst Peter Blos (1967) described adolescence as the second separation-individuation process, a period when youngsters normally decrease their engagement with primary caregivers and invest more fully in relationships outside the family. He suggested that much of the tension between adolescents and their parents reflects both parent and children's attempts to renegotiate this shifting investment. Though not normally so distressed a period as described in the older development literature (Offer & Sabshin, 1984), adolescence often includes increased affective turmoil and emotional lability. Consistent responsive parenting, even as children are attempting to create distance, remains important to normal development. Without this appropriate parenting, adolescent children often have difficulties, including depression, anxiety symptoms, substance abuse, and other behavioral problems that can develop into an adolescent-onset conduct disorder and continue into later life. During divorce, when parental capacities and empathy are commonly at their nadir, the adolescent's attempts to establish a more mature relationship with parents may go against the psychological needs of parents who turn to their children for support and solace. In evaluating custody when this occurs questions should be raised whether problematic situations reflect transient situations that are part of the first phase of divorce (see Wallerstein & Corbin, this volume) or whether they represent chronic problems in the parent's capacity to support the adolescent's growing independence. Disruptions of attachment in adolescence may be quite problematic. Precisely because the youngster and society are less willing to avow the importance of attachments to caregivers during this period, vitally important relationships to parents are less likely to be protected. In addition, youngsters vulnerable to disturbed attachments because of early problems in this area may be precipitated into considerable difficulty by threats to attachments in adolescence. It is not rare, for example, for an older adolescent or young adult child to be thrown into considerable distress by parental divorce even though that child had apparently moved far along the road to psychological independence from the parents.

LATER SEQUELAE OF EARLY ATTACHMENT PROBLEMS

Later effects of early attachment result because these early experiences become the basis for the person's conceptualization of what to expect in relations with other people throughout life. "Working models" or "states of mind" regarding what the self and others are like, whether relationships are likely to be secure or insecure, and the emotional tone of relationships shape psychological experience, often without the individual's conscious awareness (Bowlby, 1973; Bretherton, 1990; Main, 1991). These models, for better or worse, profoundly shape the individual's perception of self and other across a lifetime. Because they shape how parents deal with their children, the effects of attachment patterns pass from one generation to another by shaping the caregiver-infant relationship (Sroufe & Fleeson, 1986).

Though early attachment loss and disturbance may not produce immediate symptoms, pathology may express itself during later developmental periods. The disruption in attachment is particularly likely to resurface in adolescence when it can present as deficits in morality, empathy, caring, and commitment. Fonagy and his coworkers (1995) describe how impaired morality, disruptive behavior, and borderline personality disorder can emerge as sequelae of disturbed early attachment. Ordinarily as individuals mature, the functions performed for them by early attachment figures become part of the individual's own capacities. Having learned from caretakers how to evaluate one's own behavior, regulate impulses to action, and soothe oneself in distress, healthy individuals can largely perform these functions for themselves as adults. Failure of early attachment experiences interferes with learning these capacities and so puts the individual at risk of developing psychopathology rooted in the relative absence of these abilities. Individuals who have not learned to calm and soothe themselves in early attachment relationships are at increased risk of turning to maladaptive means of self-soothing such as drug and alcohol abuse, or promiscuous sexual activity.

THE ASSESSMENT OF ATTACHMENT

Having shown that attachment plays a central role in psychological development, we now turn to the question of how it is to be measured. In addition to its powerful conceptual framework, attachment theory became popular among behavioral scientists because, led by Mary Ainsworth, researchers worked to find systematic means to measure attachment. Ainsworth pioneered the study of the strange situation, a simple scripted procedure that explores young children's responses to brief separation. In the strange situation, mother and baby are introduced to a pleasant, toy-filled room and then left alone there for three minutes while the child explores the room. A stranger enters the room, speaks to the mother and tries to engage the child in play. The mother then leaves baby alone with the stranger, returning after three minutes, while the stranger leaves. After another three minutes the mother again leaves and the stranger returns. Finally the mother returns.

Researchers have found several patterns of response to this situation. The three most common responses are "secure," "insecure-avoidant" and "insecure-ambivalent/preoccupied." The securely attached baby is distressed by mother's absence but rapidly recovers and re-engages his interest in the world after his mother's return, which is greeted with pleasure. The "insecure-avoidant" youngster is less manifestly distressed by mother's departure. Mother's return evokes little or slightly negative responses from the baby. The "insecure-ambivalent/preoccupied" baby appears worried about the mother even when she is present, is greatly distressed by her departure and he continues to be distressed on her return, often appearing angry with the mother. Another important group of responses has been described as "insecure-disorganized/disoriented"—youngsters whose style is incoherent, confused, or inconsistent during reunions. Trained observers can make these classifications reliably. In recent years, further classification of responses to the strange situation have emerged (Main, 1995). The strange situation, properly conducted, gives a reliable classification of the child's attachment status. It also provides a framework for describing attachment responses.

Researchers are developing means to assess attachment beyond 2 years of age. The Attachment Q-sort (Waters & Deane, 1985) uses a sophisticated methodology to systematically describe attachment in young children. The relationship between this measure and the strange situation is not entirely clear, partly because of the different type of data that the Attachment-Q sort generates (Vaughn & Waters, 1990). Several research methods have been developed for exploring attachment in school-age children (M. Greenberg, Cicchetti, & Cummings, 1990). The Adult Attachment Interview (Kobak et al., 1993; Main, 1991) can also be employed with adolescents. It explores attachment by systematically examining adults' descriptions of their relationships to important figures. However, none of these measures has been standardized and studied to the extent that they can be used in ordinary clinical practice.

Most custody evaluators will assess attachment through a diagnostic interview of each parent, as well as interviewing the child/adolescent alone and with each parent. A thorough review of all available collateral information is recommended. Although there are a variety of interview schedules, at present they seem more relevant to research than the courts. The extent to which these scales measure attachment is still somewhat in doubt and few have been standardized. At present, clinical assessment gives more reliable information about attachment than any available test. As attachment research grows these tests, currently under development (Main, 1995), are likely to become more useful in assessing attachment. Some of the tests used specifically for custody evaluations incorporate aspects of attachment theory (see Bricklin, this volume).

STUDIES OF ATTACHMENT IN NONTRADITIONAL FAMILIES

In recent years, Israeli kibbutzim have been used for attachment studies and the evaluation of children following divorce. Sagi and coworkers (Sagi, van Ijzendoorn, Aviezer, Donnell, & Mayseless, 1994) investigated mother-infant attachments in two types of kibbutzim. In one, infants slept in a communal area without their mothers; in the other type infants slept at their mothers' residence. Where the children slept at home, the mother and infant shared attachment patterns in 76% of pairs as opposed to 40% in the communal sleeping kibbutzim. The researchers conclude that infants with less interaction with their mother/primary caregiver, in particular at nighttime, have less concordance of attachment pattern. In addition, there was a higher level of insecure attachment in the communal sleeping group. However, it is unclear whether attachment patterns in kibbutz-raised children are predictive of future psychopathology or relationship difficulties.

ATTACHMENT AND THE EVALUATION OF CUSTODY

Attachment theory has direct clinical application in custody evaluations in conjunction with other pertinent issues, including the child's needs and the parent's ability to meet those needs. Although living in a dysfunctional family can be traumatic to a child, research shows that children suffer from divorce (Wallerstein & Corbin, this volume). Unintentionally, children are often neglected and their needs are not met during the divorce process. Attachment theory suggests that the loss of one of the child's primary attachment figures complicates this trauma. Pagani Kurtz and Deverensky (1997) report that increased visitation minimizes the effects of divorce on school-age children. They evaluated elementary school-age children following divorce and found the children had lower levels of self-esteem, a poorer sense of efficacy, poorer social supports, and less effectual coping styles than children of nondivorced parents. These problems were somewhat improved with additional contact with the noncustodial parent.

CONCLUSION

When looking at the effects of divorce on a child, it can be difficult to pinpoint which variable has what effect. Such disparate effects as disruption in a primary attachment figure, perhaps an anxiety disorder, posttraumatic stress disorder, and changes in financial status with concomitant stress to the parent can all produce psychological distress in children and may, in actual situations, be difficult to differentiate from one another by their effect. There can be associated adjustment disorders, affective disorders, phobias, difficulty socializing and school disturbances. Do these disturbances result in disturbed attachments or do problems with attachment result in these disturbances? No simple cause-and-effect model explains the multifaceted psychological impact of divorce on children and rarely is only one factor at play. Nonetheless, problematic attachment is so detrimental to psychological well-being that attachment issues should be carefully addressed in any custody evaluation and attachment should be given a high priority in custody decisions. The usefulness of a careful and thoughtful review of collateral information, individual interviews, and interactional interviews can usually provide a reasonably clear picture of the child's attachment.

Implementing this necessary support for the child's attachments is often difficult. As discussed earlier, measurement of attachment has not achieved full precision. Evaluations are complicated because the child is likely to have more than one attachment figure. This can be a double-edged sword. The child will be able to remain with one attachment figure but may lose another significant attachment figure. The concept of "primary attachment figures" continues to be useful in infant and toddler evaluations. Most very young children have a single person to whom they are substantially more securely attached than to any other and maintaining this attachment is of primary psychological importance. After very early childhood, however, the psychological significance of other attachments increases so that the relative significance of figures to whom the youngster is attached becomes increasingly less clear.

Studies on attachment theory in children lead one to focus on the problems of loss and mourning. When visits with the noncustodial parent are sufficiently infrequent, from a psychological point of view, parent loss in divorce is in many ways equivalent to parent loss through death. Thus, our knowledge of mourning and loss is helpful in understanding some young children's response to divorce. Similarities in young children's responses to parental death and divorce include (1) aggressive behavior, (2) depressive symptoms, (3) anxiety symptoms, (4) socialization deficits, (5) school difficulties with associated behavioral difficulties. When children in the midst of divorce manifest symptoms, evaluators should first consider that these symptoms may result from the psychological impact of the divorce rather than immediately treating them as manifestations of a primary psychiatric disorder or mismanagement of the child by a custodial parent. Often these symptoms are usefully addressed in terms of disturbances in attachments that result from the divorce, and interventions based on the appreciation of this underlying problem may involve making custody and visitation arrangements that minimize the disruption of attachment or assisting the child in dealing with the distress that results from such disruptions.

Attachment theory is a valuable tool in custody evaluations and finding the best interest of the child. However, the assessment of attachment is only part of a custody evaluation. Though perhaps appropriately the single most important factor in many custody decisions, other factors also play an important role. The parent to whom the child is more securely attached may have significant deficiencies in parenting skills, which should outweigh attachment in deciding on custody. Children are not always wise in selecting figures to whom to become attached. They may, in fact, become intensely attached to overtly abusive and otherwise harmful parents. When Goldstein, Solnit, and Freud first introduced the concept of attachment by way of the "primary psychological parent" their correct emphasis on the importance of maintaining that relationship led them to minimize the importance of other aspects of the child's life, including other attachments. The maintenance of a firm relationship with a primary psychological parent does not preclude other attachment relationships. Instead of attempting to eliminate all possibility of other attachments, custody-visitation arrangements should ensure the maintenance of the primary attachment and attempt to address the child's other needs at the same time.

In considering statements about attachment and bonding, it is essential to keep in mind that there are many definitions of attachment theory and bonding and to clarify how the terms are being used in a given context. Given the varying use of these terms, custody evaluators should indicate how they are being used and triers of fact should insist on their clarification in reports and testimony.

The importance of providing the child with an opportunity for at least one stable, secure relationship is hard to overestimate. Yet the study of how to assess attachment, place it within the framework of an overall custody recommendation, and shape arrangements that best meet children's needs requires substantial additional investigation.

REFERENCES

Ainsworth, M., Blehar, M., Waters, E., & Wall, S. (1978). *Patterns of attachment*. Hillsdale, NJ: Erlbaum.

Ainsworth, M., Salter, M., & Witting, B. (1969). Attachment and exploratory behavior of one-year olds in a Strange Situation. In B. Foss (Ed.), *Determinants of infant behavior* (Vol. 4). London: Methuen.

Altshul, S. (1988). *Childhood bereavement and its aftermath*. Madison: International Universities Press.

American Psychiatric Association. (1994). *Diagnostic and statistical manual of mental disorders* (4th ed.). Washington, DC: American Psychiatric Press.

Baumrind, D. (1987). A developmental perspective on adolescent risk taking in contemporary America. *New Directions for Child Development, 37*, 93–125.

Belsky, J. (1984). The determinants of parenting. *Developmental Psychology, 55*, 83–96.

Benoit, D., Zeanah, C., & Barton, M. (1989). Maternal attachment disturbances in failure to thrive. *Infant Mental Health Journal, 10*, 185–202.

Blos, P. (1967). The second individuation process of adolescence. *Psychoanalytic Study of the Child, 22*, 162–86.

Bowlby, J. (1969). *Attachment & loss: Vol. I—Attachment*. New York: Basic Books.

Bowlby, J. (1973). *Attachment & loss: Vol. II—Separation.* New York: Basic Books.

Bowlby, J. (1980). *Attachment & loss: Vol. III—Loss.* New York: Basic Books.

Bretherton, I. (1990). Open communication and internal working models: Their role in the development of attachment relationships. In R. Thompson (Ed.), *Socioemotional development* (Nebraska Symposiums on Motivation, Vol. 36). Lincoln: University of Nebraska Press.

Burlingham, D., & Freud, A. (1942). *Young children in wartime England.* London: Allen & Unwin.

Burlingham, D., & Freud, A. (1973). *Infants without families. Reports on the Hampstead nurseries. The writings of Anna Freud* (Vol. III). New York: International Universities Press.

Chess, S., & Thomas, A. (1977). Temperament and the parent-child interaction. *Pediatric Annals, 6,* 26–45.

Easterbrooks, M., & Goldberg, W. (1984). Toddler development in the family: Impact of father involvement and parenting characteristics. *Child Development, 55,* 740–752.

Eyer, D. (1993). *Infant bonding: A scientific myth.* New Haven: Yale University Press

Fonagy, P., Steele, M., Steele, H., Leigh, T., Kennedy, R., Mattoon, G., & Target, M. (1995). Attachment, the reflective self, and borderline states: The predictive specificity of the adult attachment interview and pathological emotional development. In S. Goldberg, R. Muir, & J. Kerr (Eds.), *Attachment theory: Social developmental and clinical perspectives* (pp. 233–278). Hillsdale, NJ: Analytic Press.

Freud, A. (1973). *Infants without families: Reports on the Hampstead nurseries. The writings of Anna Freud* (Vol. III). New York: International Universities Press.

Freud, S. (1905). Three essays on the theory of sexuality. In J. Strachey (Ed. & Trans.), *The standard edition of the complete psychological works of Sigmund Freud* (Vol. 7, pp. 130–243). London: Hogarth Press.

Goldstein, J., Freud, A., & Solnit, A. (1979). *Before the best interests of the child.* New york: Free Press.

Greenberg, J., & Mitchell, S. (1983). *Object relations and psychoanalytic theory.* Cambridge, MA: Harvard University Press.

Greenberg, M., Cicchetti, D., & Cummings, M. (Eds.). (1990). *Attachment in the preschool years.* Chicago: University of Chicago Press.

Holmes, J. (1995). "Something there is that doesn't love a wall": John Bowlby, attachment theory, and psychoanalysis. In S. Goldberg, R. Muir, & J. Kerr (Eds.), *Attachment theory: Social development and clinical perspectives.* Hillsdale, NJ: Analytic Press.

Kaffman, M., (1993). Divorce in the kibbutz: Lessons to be drawn. *Family Process, 33,* 144–157.

Karen, R. (1994). *Becoming attached.* New York: Warner Books.

Klaus, M., & Kennell, J. (1982). *Parent–infant bonding* (2nd ed.). Saint Louis, MO: Mosby.

Kobak, R., Cole, H., & Frenz-Gillies, R. (1993). Attachment and emotion regulation during mother-teen problem solving: A control theory analysis. *Child Development, 64,* 231–245.

Lorenz, K. Z. (1957). Der Kumpan in Der Umuelt Des Vogels. F. Orn. Berl., 83. In C. Schiller (Ed. & Trans.), *Instinctive behavior.* New York: International Universities Press. (Original work published 1935)

Main, M. (1991). Metacognitive knowledge, metacognitive monitoring and singular (coherent) vs. multiple (incoherent) model of attachment: Findings and directions for further research. In C. Murray, J. Steveson-Hinde, & P. Marris (Eds.), *Attachment across the life cycle* (pp. 127–159). London: Routledge & Kegan Paul.

Main, M. (1995). Recent studies in attachment: Overview, with selected implications for clinical work. In S. Goldberg, R. Muir, & J. Kerr (Eds.), *Attachment theory: Social developmental and clinical prospectives.* Hillsdale, NJ: Analytic Press.

Marcus, R. & Mirle, V. (1990). Validity of a child interview measure of attachment as used in child custody evaluations. *Journal of Perceptual and Motor Skills, 70,* 1043–1054.

Offer, D., & Sabshin, M. (1984). Adolescence: Empirical perspectives. In D. Offer & M. Sabshin (Eds.), *Normality and the life cycle.* New York: Basic Books.

Pagani–Kurtz, L. & Deverensky, J. (1997). Access by noncustodial parents: Effects upon children's postdivorce resources. *Journal of Divorce and Remarriage, 27,* 43–55.

Robertson, J., & Robertson, J. (Producers). (1969). *Young children in brief separation: John, 17 months: For 9 days in a residential nursery* [Film]. London: Tavistock.

Rutter, M. (1997). Attachment and psychopathology. In L. Atkinson & K. Zucker (Eds.), *Clinical implications of attachment: Concepts retrospect and prospect* (p. 34). New York: Guilford.

Sagi, A., van IJzendoorn, M., Aviezer, O., Donnell, F., & Mayseless, O. (1994). Sleeping away from home in a kibbutz communal arrangement: It makes a difference for infant-mother attachment. *Child Development, 65,* 992–1004.

Sameroff, A., & Emde, R. (1989). *Relationship disturbances in early childhood.* New York: Basic Books.

Spitz, R. (1945). Hospitalism: An Inquiry into the genesis of psychiatric conditions in early childhood. *Psychoanalytic Study of the Child, 1,* 53–74.

Spitz, R. (1946). Anaclitic depression. *Psychoanalytic Study of the Child, 2,* 313–342.

Sroufe, L., & Fleeson, J. (1986). Attachment and construction of relationships. In W. Hartup & Z. Rubin (Eds.), *Relationships and development* (pp. 51–71). Hillsdale, NJ: Erlbaum.

Terr, L. (1991). Childhood traumas: An outline and overview. *American Journal of Psychiatry, 148,* 10–20.

Thompson, R. (1996). Attachment theory and research. In M. Lewis (Ed.), *Child and adolescent psychiatry: A comprehensive textbook* (pp. 126–134). Baltimore: Williams & Wilkins.

Vaughn, B., Lefever, B., Seifer, R., & Barglow, P. (1989). Attachment behavior, attachment security, and temperament during infancy. *Child Development, 60,* 728–737.

Vaughn, B., & Waters, E. (1990). Attachment behavior in home and in the laboratory: Z-sort observations and Strange Situations classifications of one-year-olds. *Child Development, 61,* 1965–1973.

Waters, E., & Deane, K. (1985). Defining and assessing individual differences in attachment relations: Q-methodology and the organization of behavior in infancy and early childhood. In I. Bretherton & E. Waters (Eds.), *Growing point in attachment theory and research* (pp. 41–65). Chicago: University of Chicago Press.

CHAPTER 5

The Child and the Vicissitudes of Divorce

JUDITH S. WALLERSTEIN and SHAUNA B. CORBIN

C HANGES WITHIN THE contemporary family are reshaping the experience of growing up in America. The steep rise in recent decades of the incidence of divorce is foremost among the changes that are profoundly influencing the lives of children and their parents. The number of children from divorced families more than doubled between 1960 and 1980 (Spanier & Glick, 1981). Demographers have estimated that 38% of all children born in the mid-1980s will experience the divorce of their parents (A.J. Norton, U.S. Bureau of Census, personal communication, April 1987). This phenomenon continues to newly affect no fewer than 1 million children each year.

Although many children weather the stress of marital discord and family rupture without psychopathological sequelae, a considerable number falter along the way. As a result, the high divorce rate has also had a notable effect on the makeup of clinical populations. Children of divorce are greatly overrepresented in the outpatient psychiatric, family agency, and private practice populations relative to their presence within the general population (Furstenberg et al., 1983; Gardner, 1976; Kalter, 1977). Parental divorce and parental loss significantly predict mental health referrals for school-age children (Felner, Stolberg, & Cowen, 1975). A national survey of adolescents whose parents had separated and divorced by the time the children were 7 years old found that 30% of these children had received psychotherapy before reaching adolescence, compared with 10% of adolescents in intact families (Zill, 1983); by young adulthood, 40% had received psychological help. The representation of children from divorced families is even higher among inpatient populations. Although national figures

are unavailable, many inpatient psychiatric facilities for adolescents report informally that 75% to 100% of their patients are from nonintact families. Overall, recent national data have shown that young people from single-parent or
stepfamilies have a 2 to 3 times greater likelihood of experiencing emotional or
behavioral problems, and a higher incidence of learning problems, than those
with both biological parents (Zill & Schoenborn, 1990).

The divorce literature, which scarcely existed prior to the 1970s, has prolifer-
ated as a growing number of investigators in psychiatry, psychology, and sociology have examined the processes of family separation and marital dissolution.
As a result, we have begun to acquire knowledge in many critical areas: the nature of the divorce process, the responses of children and adolescents by age
and gender, the impact of divorce and parental conflict on parent-child relationships, factors in good and poor outcome in the short- and long-term perspectives, patterns of custody and visitation, the role of the father, the roots and
dimensions of interparental conflict, and some of the issues that children and
adults confront in remarriage. More recently, as findings from longitudinal
studies have become available, we have been able to shed light on divorce-specific
anxieties that emerge belatedly in the lives of children of divorce, when they
enter young adulthood (Wallerstein & Blakeslee, 1989).

Much of the interest in exploring the theoretical issues inherent in the relatively new family forms that are being created (e.g., joint custody families; single-parent families in which one parent, usually the father, continues to visit;
remarried and/or redivorced families) has centered around reassessing the role
of the father in child development (Cath, Gurwitt, & Ross, 1982; Hanson &
Bozett, 1985). And although it is widely acknowledged that the psychological
theory that underlies established clinical interventions with children (whether
in psychoanalysis, family systems theory, or child development) was developed
within the paradigm of the intact two-parent family, there has been little theoretical exploration of how changes in family structure can or should modify the
goals or approach of the clinician, either in work with parents who find themselves cast in unfamiliar roles, or with the child, whose primary identification
figures are often shifting and unclear.

DIVORCE AS A PROCESS

Divorce is a process of social and psychological changes in the individual and in
family relationships that can extend over many years. It has no true counterpart
in other crises of adult life. Although it was initially considered analogous to
bereavement in the central significance of loss as the critical component of the
adult experience, we have come to recognize that, in divorce, grief is only one of
many powerful affects; rage, sexual jealously, and unrequited love share equal
power and significance (Wallerstein & Kelly, 1980). Divorce is not a time-limited
event for the adults or the children involved, in part because a complex undula-
tion of changes (many of them unanticipated and unforeseeable) leads to and,

in turn, is set into motion by the marital rupture. These changes often occupy a significant portion of the adult's postdivorce life. They typically occupy a significant portion of the youngster's childhood and adolescence and, as we are learning, of his or her own young adulthood.

Divorce can be broadly conceptualized as progressing through three successive phases (Wallerstein & Blakeslee, 1989). The ambience of the first, acute phase of dramatic and highly emotional responses is established by the fact that divorce in a family with children is rarely a mutual decision. Separation often occurs amid escalating spousal conflict that can include physical violence between the parents. During this acute phase, in extreme cases, one or both parents may experience depression with suicidal ideation and may regress considerably in behavior. Similarly, one or both parents may experience ego-syntonic rage, which can reach paranoid dimensions. In many of these people, there is a temporary weakening of ego control over aggressive and sexual impulses, accompanied by lapses in customary judgment. This acute phase may be relatively brief or may extend over several years. Sometimes, the divorcing couple remains fixated in this acute phase for years, reenacting the separation drama again and again, in the vain hope of modifying the events or the outcome, but never obtaining relief from the narcissistic injury that was initially sustained. These reenactments may take place in the courts or may be played out in the many other arenas available when there are children from the broken marriage. In most instances, the acute phase is followed by a transitional phase in which the parents begin to disengage from each other's lives and move into new relationships and new work and home settings. The physical, social, and emotional environments of the family during this time may be in continual flux. This intermediate period may be relatively brief or it, too, may last for several years. Finally, with the onset of the third phase, comes the establishment of the relatively stable postdivorce single- or remarried-parent household, each of which has its own associated strains and gratifications.

Ongoing stresses confront many postdivorce families. Some of these stresses are rooted in convergent economic and social issues that communities have been reluctant to address, particularly those that affect the serious economic disadvantaging of women and children following divorce (Weitzman, 1985). Other reports describe the many complex psychological issues that adults face in reconstructing their postdivorce lives and how their tasks are affected by the number of years invested in the marriage, the age of the adult at the divorce, and the discrepant opportunities that are available to divorced men and women in the sexual, social, and economic marketplaces (Wallerstein & Blakeslee, 1989). Moreover, recent observations on remarriage have called attention to the many psychological differences between first and subsequent marriages and the complex challenges that a second marriage, with children, poses to all the participants (Pasley & Ihinger-Tallman, 1987; Wallerstein & Blakeslee, 1989). These concerns have been reinforced by reports from demographers that the incidence of divorce in remarried families with children from a previous marriage is even higher than the divorce rate in first marriages (Pasley & Ihinger-Tallman, 1987).

EFFECTS OF DIVORCE ON THE PARENT-CHILD RELATIONSHIP—DIMINISHED PARENTING

Hess and Camara (1979) have pointed out that "for children, the threat of divorce lies in the disruption of relationships with the parents." This applies both to the availability of the parent and to the quality of the postdivorce relationship itself. Hetherington and her associates (Hetherington, Cox, & Cox, 1978, 1982) observed disorganization, deterioration of discipline, rising angers, and lowered expectations for appropriate social behavior by their children on the part of custodial mothers. Others (Santrock, Warshak, & Lindbergh, 1982) have noted the more conflicted postdivorce relationship of children with an opposite-sex custodial parent. The impairment of relationships between parent and child may appear early in the separation and divorce process or may remain latent, emerging only in young adulthood. Mother-child relationships that had previously weathered the storms of adolescence have been noted to deteriorate in young adulthood. This parallels Wallerstein's observed "sleeper effect" in young women from divorced families (Wallerstein, 1991).

Wallerstein (1985a) has suggested that a diminished capacity to parent is an expectable short-term consequence of divorce, which has the dangerous potential of becoming chronic when the custodial parent fails to reconstitute or becomes involved in new relationships that overshadow or replace the relationship with the child. This diminished capacity is most evident in the parent's decreased ability to separate the child's needs and reactions from those of the adult. She has proposed that the fantasy underlying the sometimes astonishing changes in the parent's relationship with the child is a conscious or unconscious wish to abandon the child coincident with the breakup of the marriage. As a fantasy, this impulse to leave the child behind may remain unacted upon, or it may unconsciously spur sudden flight or unexpected rejection by a parent of a child who had previously been well cared for. Whatever the conscious or unconscious roots of the disrupted parent-child relationship may be, the consequence is that the child's fears of abandonment at the time of the breakup are powerfully reinforced by a parent's changed attitudes or behavior. Often these fears lead to a hypervigilant tracking of the parent's responses and an intense anxiety that can dominate the child's inner life and intrude on his or her capacity to accomplish normative developmental tasks.

Wallerstein (1985a) has also proposed that a contrapuntal theme to the temporary rejection of the child at the time of the breakup in an intensified need of the parent for the child. This dependence on the child by one or both parents is often at the core of parental conflict and prolonged litigation over custody and visitation. In extreme cases, the dismantling of customary supports within the marriage, combined with the humiliation of the narcissistic injury inflicted by the divorce and the painful persistence of attachment to the divorcing partner, may result in severe ego regression in parents whose previous functioning, separately or together, may have been at least adequate. Feeling suddenly bereft and in need of help, such parents turn to their children for help in warding off the threatened depression.

In many divorcing families, the temporary dependence of the adult on the child is a transient phenomenon that has no lasting deleterious effects and may indeed be of benefit to a child suddenly elevated to unaccustomed importance. However, as Wallerstein (1985b) has pointed out, turning to a young son or daughter as a peer or, worse, as to a parent, may overwhelm the child with responsibility, placing the child at serious risk if the intense dependence continues. For these overburdened children—out of worry, guilt, compassion, or, indeed, out of their conviction that it is their assigned task to keep the parent alive—may devote themselves entirely to maintaining the psychic functioning and physical needs of the ailing parent and relinquish their responsiveness to their own needs over many years.

CHILDREN IN HIGH-CONFLICT DIVORCE

The struggle for and through the children embodies the intense conflicts that often accompany the failing marriage. Although competition for a child's affection may occur in an intact, even well-functioning family, disruption of the family system and its resulting angers bring the parents' competitiveness into sharpened focus. It is not uncommon for angry, sometimes distraught parents to cast their children in a great many roles during postmarital battles, ranging from that of audience, whose presence appears to be a necessary backdrop for the parental fighting, to that of fully positioned battle allies. The children often range in their participation from astonished, frightened observers to denunciatory Greek chorus, or in some instances, ardent champions of one parent against the other

Many of the anger-driven parent-child relationships that emerge at the time of the marital breakup are new alliances that diverge from the pattern that existed within the intact marriage. The child's conscious behavior may be powered by loyalty to the disrupted marriage or by the quixotic impulse to defend or rescue the parent who has been identified by the child (sometimes erroneously) as the victim. Not atypically, a child may take up the cause of the absent parent, representing his or her interests in the events of the custodial household. A child's active involvement in the marital battle is additionally fueled by the rise in physical violence between the parents that often erupts at the separation, even though it had never been a feature of the marriage (Wallerstein & Kelly, 1980).

Such alignments occur most often between a late latency or early adolescent child and the parent who has vehemently opposed the divorce. The adult's participation is almost always rooted in an entrenched sense of moral outrage at having been betrayed and cruelly exploited during the marriage. The avowed agenda of these alignments is likely to be the restoration of the failed marriage; the unspoken agenda is almost always revenge.

These anger-driven alliances serve a range of psychological purposes for both parent and child. The loneliness of the divorce period is reduced significantly by the new partnership. The child's own gnawing fear of being abandoned is alleviated by becoming the needy parent's trusted companion. Directing their anger outward against the absent parent serves as a powerful antidote to the intolerable pain of rejection and helplessness that the allied child and parent experience. Nor is it accidental that many children join cause with a parent with whom their relationship during the marriage had been tenuous or emotionally impoverished and take up an angry campaign against the parent they once had cherished. Additionally, for the child, the new alignment provides an opportunity to resolve any existing ambivalence of feeling toward the parents by creating a clear repository of virtue in one and villainy in the other.

There is evidence that such active alignments generally do not survive the adolescence of the young ally. Nevertheless, many young people come to adulthood complaining that their responses to the "villainous" parent had been governed by perceptions that they did not truly share. They regret deeply that they were not given the opportunity to form their own judgments, and their anger at having been cheated out of a true relationship with both parents is often intense. Some also express profound and pervasive guilt at having participated in lying or even more serious misbehavior directed at hurting their parent (Wallerstein & Blakeslee, 1989). These issues may underlie the negative shift seen in the maternal relationship once adolescence has been traversed (Zill, Morrison, & Coiro, 1993).

One of the most significant findings in family research concerns the serious hazard posed to the psychological health and development of children by continued exposure to high conflict between the parents whether in the context of an intact marriage or as part of ongoing postdivorce antagonism (Emery, 1982). In one recent California study of 1,124 divorcing families, one-quarter were characterized by high levels of conflict at an average of 3½ years postseparation (Maccoby & Mnookin, 1992). There is increasing interest in the plight and fate of children in such families and the impact of witnessing abuse and violence between the parents, especially if it is prolonged. The psychological effects and disturbances in parent-child attachments observed are not unlike those reported in families where the child has been the target of abuse directly. As yet, it is not clear whether this detrimental impact is mediated by the influence of the conflict on critical aspects of the parent-child relationship or whether it largely represents the intense reactions of the children who directly witness or overhear the fighting. Nor is it known whether children's reactions are primarily governed by the stimulation of seeing the parents fight, by the anxiety engendered from parents who appear to be out of control, by the fear that one or both parents—and perhaps the children as well—may be severely harmed by complex issues of identification, or by some combination of all these factors. The persistence of high conflict for many years, even after the parental divorce, may be particularly psychonoxious to children in that it appears to lack any remedy.

The link between parental conflict and the subsequent psychological adjustment of children represents one of the most fertile areas for increased theoretical understanding and new models of psychotherapeutic intervention. Johnston and Campbell (1988) have addressed the serious effect these lasting impasses create in some families after divorce, reporting severe reactions among the children, including impairment in reality testing. Adding to this concern is the report from a longitudinal study that at 10 and 15 years postdivorce, many young people remembered with great clarity incidents of physical conflict between their parents and described having been continually haunted by those memories during their waking and dream lives throughout the postdivorce decade and well into their young adulthood. A significant number of these children from homes where there was physical and verbal abuse between parents during the intact marriage became involved, as young adults, in abusive relationships of their own, although they had been separated by at least a decade from the trauma of witnessing their parents' quarrels (Wallerstein & Blakeslee, 1989).

At the cutting edge of research in this area is the work by Johnston and Roseby on the developmental impact of high-conflict divorce and separations in the context of violent relationships. Children caught in such circumstances show problems in psychological separation and individuation and disturbances of gender and sexual identity (Roseby, 1993; Roseby & Johnston, 1998; Roseby & Wallerstein, in press).

EFFECTS OF DIVORCE ON CHILDREN

INITIAL REACTIONS

Children and adolescents experience parental separation and its immediate aftermath as an immensely stressful period in their lives. Indeed, for middle-class children in America, their parents' divorce is likely to be the central stress of their growing-up years. The family rupture evokes an acute sense of shock, intense anxiety, and profound sorrow. Many children can feel relatively content and even well parented within families in which one or both parents are unhappy. A surprising number (one-third in one study) did not know that their parents' marriage was troubled (Wallerstein & Kelly, 1980). Few youngsters experience relief with the divorce decision; those who do are usually older and have witnessed open conflict between their parents. Children's initial responses are typically governed neither by an understanding of the issues leading to the divorce nor by the fact that divorce has a high incidence in their community. To children, their own parents' divorce signifies the collapse of the structure that was responsible for providing them basic nurturance and protection, even when the family was performing poorly in this role.

The initial pain experienced by children and adolescents in response to a marital separation is compounded by their fantasies of the catastrophes they fear the divorce will bring in its wake. Children suffer with a pervasive sense of vulnerability as they experience the family breaking apart. They grieve over the loss of the intact family, including the hopes and dreams attached to it, and over the absence of the noncustodial parent. Often they must also confront the additional losses of familiar friends, neighborhood, and school. Children worry about their distressed parents. They are concerned about who will take care of the parent who has left and whether the custodial parent will be able to manage alone. They experience intense anger toward one or both parents for disrupting the family. Some of their anger is reactive and defends them against their own feelings of powerlessness, their concern about being lost in the shuffle, and the fear that their needs will be disregarded as the parents give priority to their own wishes and needs. They often feel a painfully divided loyalty, as if they are being forced to choose between their parents, even when this question has not been put before them. They may suffer with imagined guilt over having caused the divorce. This is especially likely among young children, or where the parents have fought over child-related issues. Young children sometimes decide heroically that it is up to them to mend the broken marriage.

The responses of children, particularly their sense of loneliness and social isolation, are also strongly influenced by the social context of the divorce. Children all too often must face the tensions and sorrows of divorce with little outside help. Fewer than 10% of children in one widely reported study (Wallerstein & Kelly, 1980) had any support at the time of crisis from adults, other than relatives, who might have helped them, such as teachers, pediatricians, clergy, or family friends. Only 25% felt that grandparents came to their aid emotionally. Many children are poorly prepared by their parents for the impending upheaval, some not at all. Thus, it is a striking feature of divorce that when it occurs—unlike in bereavement or other stressful events that can occur in childhood—customary support systems, either through adult ignorance or diffidence, fall away.

DEVELOPMENTAL FACTORS

Developmental factors are critical in the responses of children and adolescents at the time of the marital rupture. Despite significant individual differences in children, in their families, and in parent-child relationships, it appears that children's dominant concern, their capacity to perceive and understand family events, their central psychological preoccupations and conflicts, their available repertoire of defenses and copies strategies, and the dominant patterning of their relationships and expectations, all primarily reflect their age and developmental stage at the time of the parental separation.

A major finding in divorce research has been these common patterns of response within age-related groups (Wallerstein & Kelly, 1980). The groups reported to share significant perceptions, responses, underlying fantasies, and behaviors are (a) preschool ages 3–5, (b) young school or early latency ages 6½–8, (c) later latency ages 8–12, and (d) adolescent ages 12–18. The responses of young adolescents have also been differentiated from those in mid- and late adolescence (Springer & Wallerstein, 1983). It may be that the similarities observed within the children's age groups represent their commonly shared responses to acute stress generally, not simply to marital rupture. Until recently there had been no systematic research addressing the short- or long-term effects of divorce on infants or toddlers under 3 years of age. The newest work in this area is a longitudinal study in progress by Solomon (1997), examining the effects of overnight visitation on the parent-child attachments of 100 children ages 12–18 months at the time of the family rupture. This is an important subgroup to understand as many divorces occur within the first 2 years of marriage.

Observations about preschool children derived from longitudinal studies in two widely divergent regions, northern California and Virginia, are remarkably similar (Hetherington et al., 1982; Wallerstein & Kelly, 1980). Preschool children are likely to regress following one parent's departure from home. The regression usually occurs in the most recent developmental achievement of the child. Intensified fears are frequent and are evoked by routine separations from the custodial parent during the day and at bedtime. Sleep disturbances are common. The preoccupying fantasy of many of these youngsters is fear of abandonment by both parents. Yearning for the departed parent is intense. Preschool children are likely to become irritable and demanding and to behave aggressively with parents, younger siblings, and peers.

Children ages 5–8 grieve openly for the departed parent. Many share the terrifying fantasy of replacement: "Will my daddy get a new dog, a new mommy, a new little boy?" Little girls weave elaborate Madame Butterfly fantasies, asserting that the departed father will someday return to them, that he loves them "the best." Many very young children cannot believe that the divorce is permanent. In their preoccupation with their fantasies, there is often a precipitous decline in their schoolwork (Wallerstein & Kelly, 1980).

For those 8½–12 years old, the central response often seems to be fierce anger at one or both parents. These children grieve over the loss of their intact world and suffer anxiety, loneliness, and a humiliating sense of their own powerlessness. They often see one parent as "good" and the other as "bad," and in this latency age period, they appear especially vulnerable to the blandishments of a parent to participate in the martial battles. They also have a high potential for assuming an empathetic and engrossing role in the care of a needy parent. School performance and peer relationships may consequently suffer (Wallerstein & Kelly, 1980).

Adolescents are also vulnerable to the impact of their parents' divorce. The incidence of acute depression, accompanied by suicidal preoccupation and acting out, is frequent enough to be alarming. Anger can be intense. Several instances have been reported of direct violent attacks on custodial parents by young adolescents who had not previously shown such behaviors (Springer & Wallerstein, 1983). Preoccupied with issues of morality, adolescents may sit in judgment on their parents' conduct around the divorce, and they may identify with one parent and do battle against the other. They are often anxious about their own future entry into adulthood, fearful that they may experience marital failure like their parents. Nevertheless, as researchers have pointed out, many adolescents show an impressive capacity to grow in maturity and independence as they respond to the family crisis and their parents' need for help (Weiss, 1979). The presence or absence of perceived fairness and integrity in their parents' postdivorce dealings with each other is not lost on them; yet, they are capable of considerable compassion for their parents' weaknesses and struggles, even as they continue to grapple with their own.

GENDER DIFFERENCES

Although it had been widely accepted by researchers that boys are more vulnerable than girls in both initial and long-term responses to divorce, this finding has been called into question by a critical analysis of the methodology employed in a range of studies (Zaslow, 1988, 1989). The picture is confusing, in part because the comparative developmental course of boys and girls in intact families, from infancy to young adulthood, is far from being clearly understood. The current state of our knowledge of divorce populations links gender differences to the different developmental stages. Thus, major differences between preschool boys and girls at approximately 4 years postseparation have been observed on a wide range of cognitive, social, and developmental measures (Hetherington et al., 1982). Although traditional sex-role typing in girls did not appear to be disrupted by divorce, boys scored lower on male preference and higher on female preference on the sex-role preference test at this same time. The boys were also spending more time playing with girls and with younger children. They showed affective narrowness and a constriction in fantasy and play and were more socially isolated than their female peers.

Gender differences were observed as well in the California Children of Divorce Study (Wallerstein & Kelly, 1980). Although boys and girls did not differ in their overall psychological adjustment at the time of the marital breakup, 18 months later the boys' psychological adjustment had deteriorated, whereas that of the girls had improved, making for a significant gap between the two groups (Wallerstein & Kelly, 1980). Guidubaldi and Perry (1985), in a national survey of elementary-school-age children at 6 years postdivorce, found that boys, but not girls, tested significantly below a matched control group from intact families in academic achievement and social relationships. Other evidence suggests that, in general, marital turmoil has a greater impact on boys than on girls, both in divorced families and in intact, discordant families (Block, Block,

& Morrison, 1981; Emery, 1982; Rutter, 1970). In fact, a report of two national, longitudinal studies of divorce effects on children in Great Britain and the United States suggests that, at least for boys, negative symptoms that are usually considered divorce sequelae are actually apparent before the marital split (Cherlin et al., 1991).

A critical question is how much of the reported differential response between the sexes, if it does exist, is mediated by mother custody. One small study from the late 1970s found that latency-age children in the custody of the same-sex parent showed greater sociability and independence than did those boys and girls in the custody of the opposite-sex parent (Santrock & Warshak, 1979).

Finally, there is increasing evidence that adolescent girls in divorced and remarried families confront particular difficulties. Kalter has described special problems that girls from divorced families face in their relationships with their mothers, especially the difficulties of separating at adolescence (Kalter, Reimer, & Brickman, 1985). Wallerstein's 10-year study (Wallerstein & Blakeslee, 1989) also reported that young women from divorced families often have a turbulent adolescence and a conflict-ridden entry into young adulthood. A significant number of young women at the 10-year mark were caught up in a web of short-lived sexual relationships, some with much older men. They described themselves as fearful of commitment, anticipating infidelity and betrayal. Many of the young women who encountered difficulties in late adolescence had done well during the early years after the divorce, when they were preschool and latency children. It may be that boys, especially oedipal and latency-age boys in mother-custody homes, have a more difficult time immediately following the divorce, whereas girls in mother custody find adolescence and entry into young adulthood particularly hazardous. Gender differences need to be explored further for the various age groups and within different family structures.

LONG-TERM OUTCOMES IN CHILDREN

There is mounting evidence that the effects of divorce in a general population extend well beyond the previous expectations of a several-year, but limited, aftermath to the marital rupture. Wallerstein's research over a 10- and 15-year period (Wallerstein & Blakeslee, 1989) represents the most extended longitudinal study of children and adults following divorce. Her findings show ongoing as well as delayed effects that come to the fore during the years from midadolescence to young adulthood, as relationships with the opposite sex move to center stage. The ongoing effects associated with good or poor adjustment are likely to reflect the quality of life and the parent-child relationships within the postdivorce and remarried family. The delayed (often long-delayed) effects are more likely to reflect concerns associated with the possibility of repeating the failure of relationship between a man and a woman that the child observed during the marriage, as well as with the parents' subsequent failures in coparenting or new love relationships that the child may have observed. Where the parents develop a more satisfactory postdivorce relationship, and where the parent individually is able to successfully reconstruct his or her life, the child's memories of the first poor parental relationship are less likely to be a disturbing influence.

Observations over the 10-year postdivorce period have led Wallerstein to propose that the inner developmental course of children of divorce is significantly altered by the parents' failed marriage and its frequently troubled, long-lasting aftermath (Wallerstein & Blakeslee, 1989; Wallerstein & Corbin, 1989). This is true whether or not the child falls into a more resilient group with better outcomes or into a more vulnerable group with poorer outcomes. The reports from the children over the many years of the follow-up suggest that the internal developmental tasks of establishing intimacy and trust in their own relationships with the opposite sex are felt to be persistently burdened to a greater or lesser degree by the template of a failed man-woman relationship that these children carry within them. Additionally, the fears of disappointment, betrayal, and abandonment that are legacies of the failed parental marriage are often reinforced by extended periods of diminished parenting during the postdivorce period. When many find as well that the bond with the father does not survive transplantation into the alien, rocky soil of arranged visitation, this too adds to their sense of the unreliability of relationships.

Other delayed effects of divorce may not emerge until many years later. There is evidence that at adolescence the need for the father increases in both boys and girls, and that feeling rejected by the father at this critical development time may pose special hazards. For the young adult, relationships with both parents appear burdened by divorce—specific issues surrounding the normative events of separation from home and family, which are emotionally much more complicated if the custodial parent will be left alone. Children of divorce face many tasks in addition to the usual ones of growing up. These tasks are formidable and may require more help than children in intact families in our society typically receive (Wallerstein, 1983). What seems very clear is that, over the years of their growing up, children of divorce find it necessary to work hard and consciously on the mastery of their experiences. It may be for this as well as other reasons that they continue to think of themselves as "children of divorce," as if that were their fixed identity (Wallerstein & Blakeslee, 1989).

FACTORS IN OUTCOME

The initial responses of children do not predict long-term consequences for psychosocial adjustment, either for those who did well at the time of the divorce or for those who fared poorly. Nor do preliminary findings at the 15-year mark of the California Children of Divorce Study indicate that even 10-year outcomes have remained stable (Wallerstein & Blakeslee, 1989). There appears to be considerable shifting in individual adjustment as the young people now in their third decade of life either seek psychotherapy for themselves after several relationship failures or succeed in building gratifying heterosexual relationships and marriages. No single theme appeared among the children in this study who were well functioning immediately following the separation and divorce, or over the years that followed. Nor was there a single thread associated with poor outcome. Many of the children who looked good at the 10-year mark were well parented or had had considerable help along the way from a parent or grandparent. Only a few were helped by both parents. Visiting frequency or patterns of visiting were unrelated to outcome, but whether or not the child felt rejected by the father remained a critical factor. Some were fortunate enough to find adult mentors and those who did showed particular promise in scholarship and athletics. Many had taken a great deal of responsibility for bringing themselves up.

Although in remarried families, the stepparent can, on occasion, play a critical role in the child's development, the extent to which this occurs is unclear. In the cited 10-year study, few stepparents took on a central role in the child's life. Also, in a significant number of remarried families, the children felt excluded from the orbit of the remarriage. The latest national figures provide no clear support for the protective or mitigating influence of remarriage for children of divorce, although when divorce had occurred early in the child's life, parental remarriage seemed to offer some benefit to the child (Zill et al., 1993).

In the Wallerstein study, the amount of stress noted in the postdivorce family was considerable. One of two children experienced a second parental divorce. One of two continued to live with intense anger between their parents that did not subside over the years. Three of five felt rejected by one or both parents. There were additional economic stresses, and a quarter of the youngsters experienced a significant drop in their standard of living, that they did not recoup during the postdivorce decade.

In effect, in investigating the long-term adjustment of the child of divorce, we have confronted a rich mix of individual issues in the resiliency and vulnerability of child and parent, the individual talents and staying power of the child, the nature of the relationship between the child and each parent (especially the custodial parent), the extent to which the postdivorce coparenting relationship is relatively free from continued conflict that involves the child, and the encouragement and support available to the child from whatever other sources are available within or outside the family.

DISPUTED CUSTODY AND VISITATION

The most tragic children of divorce are those aptly described as "the children of Armageddon" (Watson, 1969), who are caught in the entrenched legal battles of their parents. There are no national figures available on the numbers of families involved in full-scale legal battles over custody and visitation, but based on an early estimate, it is likely that 10% to 15% of families with children struggle in the courts over many years, and one-third of divorcing families return to court for modification of the initial orders (Freed & Foster, 1974). In the Maccoby and

Mnookin study, researchers estimated that 10% of families encountered "substantial" legal conflict (Maccoby & Mnookin, 1992). Thus, although most families make custody and visitation arrangements without recourse to the courts, many relying on the advice of their attorneys, even private arrangements are very much influenced by court decisions, which cast a long shadow over all postdivorce arrangements, including those that were never in dispute (Mnookin & Kornhauser, 1979).

The causes of continued legal contest between divorcing spouses are complex and multidetermined. Recent studies have begun to shed light on the interlocking issues that maintain the conflict at high intensity over many years. Johnston and Campbell (1988) have suggested a triad of factors that contribute to the impasse in the family: from the marital relationship and the changed interaction between the partners, and those factors in the social surround that support the continued litigation and contribute to the increasing stress of the parties involved. In the individual, a history of repeated unmourned losses is not uncommon and may go hand-in-hand with a pathological dependence on the constant presence of the child. The severe narcissistic injury of the divorce may trigger a rage against the divorcing spouse that continues to bind the partners to each other via conflict over the children. The same psychodynamics may underlie child stealing.

There is growing recognition among mental health professionals that the adversarial system of the courts is not only poorly suited to resolving family conflict but also may intensify it by further dividing the hapless parents and adding to the stress on the family. As Gardner (1982) has noted, "The adversarial system is ill suited to deal optimally with custody conflicts, is psychically detrimental to children, and is therefore antithetical to good psychiatric practice." The Group for the Advancement of Psychiatry (1980) has recognized the impact of the entire family's interrelationships during the postdivorce years and strongly advocates that all family members should be examined before a court decision on custody or visitation is made. Practitioners have increasingly refused to appear as an expert witness for one side in a custody or visitation dispute and have insisted on meeting with both parents before rendering a recommendation to the court.

Mediation

Mediation has attracted considerable interest in recent years as the intervention of choice for disputing families (Coogler, 1978; Haynes, 1981). Reports from a study of mediation in four court systems (Hartford, Denver, Minneapolis, and Los Angeles) indicate that families who agree to make use of the mediation services in the courts are generally pleased with the process and outcome. A significant number of families, however, reject mediation even when it is made available without charge. Many issues continue to hinder the full realization of mediation's early promise. Recent research shows that severely conflicted parents are unable to make use of the mediation process successfully (Kressal &

Pruitt, 1989). Still unresolved is the issue of whether mediation falls within the domain of the attorney or the mental health professional or whether they should work in concert with the disputing family. A critical issue is that the mediator's role may leave the child's interests without adequate protection, because mediators, by and large, lack training in child development or psychopathology and are unable, except from a commonsense vantage point, to assess how the mediated agreement will influence the child. Furthermore, the mediation process makes the assumption that the child's interests will be protected by the parents, an assumption often unwarranted at divorce, especially in the case of intensely conflicted parents. Finally, whereas the judge is charged with protecting the best interests of the child, the mediator in most settings does not share this responsibility.

In 1981, California enacted mandatory mediation for divorcing families who are disputing custody or visitation. Reports from different jurisdictions within that state show a high settlement rate, ranging from 55% to 85% of the disputing families in the different counties, who then refrain from taking their case to court. There is still much to be learned about the nature of these agreements and their impact on the psychological adjustment of the children or their parents. Overall, however, the courts have considered mediation services to be of great benefit, and the availability of mediation services has increased rapidly within courts throughout the country.

CUSTODY

The changing roles of men and women are mirrored in the courts and in legislation regarding custody and visitation. Early in the 1980s, the courts relied extensively on the concept of "the psychological parent," assuming that, except in unusual circumstances or for older children, the mother would fulfill this role. Our society has now moved away from the expectation that single-parent custody, combined with reasonable visitation with the noncustodial parent, is the legacy of divorce. Attention has increasingly focused on the contribution of the father as parent and as potential primary parent (Cath et al., 1982; Jacobs, 1982). Custodial arrangements have changed over the past 15 years (Maccoby & Mnookin, 1992). We still lack sufficient information about the extent of this change in the direction of joint custody. It is important, however, that during the 1980s over one-half of the states enacted legislation that permits joint custody. In several instances, the public policy has leaned toward a presumptive preference for joint custody. In California, in 1988, legislation went against the presumption of joint custody; while acknowledging the importance of both parents for the child, it emphasized the necessity of matching the custody arrangement to the needs of the individual family. Thus, community attitudes and social policy are in flux.

Joint custody remains a variously defined arrangement, differing not only among states but also even between local jurisdictions. Joint legal custody typically refers to an equally shared responsibility between parents for major decisions regarding their children's lives and well-being. Joint physical custody indicates that the child actually resides for substantial periods of time in each parent's home, although the proportion of time spent and the schedule of transitions between households may vary widely.

Joint physical custody can be properly regarded as a new family form. The motivation for its choice varies widely. Some parents select joint custody out of commitment to the child's continuing relationship with both parents; others, however, select this custody form out of the demands of the workplace; still others select joint custody because neither parent truly wishes to take responsibility for their child. Obviously, the experience of the child will vary with the parents' motivation and emotional investment.

Researchers have raised the question as to how important the custody arrangement itself is to the psychological adjustment of the child. Kline, in a sample of 93 white middle- and upper-class divorcing families, compared the psychological adjustment of those 38% of the children who were living in joint custody with that of the remaining group who were in sole custody (Kline et al., 1989). She and her colleagues found that neither the custody arrangement nor the frequency of access and visitation with the father influenced the child's psychological adjustment. The factors affecting the child's psychological and social adjustment, regardless of custody arrangement, were the prior psychological functioning of the parents and the degree of postdivorce hostility and conflict between the parents.

One study of intensely conflicted families, where the court had ordered joint custody over the considerable reluctance of one or even both parents, showed that children in involuntary custody situations looked seriously deteriorated in their psychological and social adjustment, school performance, and peer involvement, as observed over a several-year period. Both boys and girls seemed to suffer when frequent access to both parents was imposed on families locked in ongoing disputes (Johnston, Kline, & Tschann, 1989). This work addressed the very serious issue that has been raised in many jurisdictions as to whether the courts should award joint custody in the face of one parent's strong opposition. Findings from this study are very much in accord with the clinical opinions that practitioners have held over many years.

There is evidence from a number of studies that many children prefer joint custody to sole custody and that many children benefit from this arrangement (McKinnon & Wallerstein, 1986; Steinman, 1981). Our knowledge at present indicates that, when it is entered into voluntarily by both parents with dedication and conviction, joint physical custody can be regarded as a viable family form. Under appropriate circumstances, it serves well, especially in the transition from divorce to remarriage. Joint custody does demand special effort and commitment from the parents, the ability of the formerly married partners to remain in close touch with each other's lives, and considerable flexibility from both child and parents (Wallerstein & Blakeslee, 1989). There is an insufficiency of research in this entire domain, especially on the long-term effects of joint custody. We especially await findings from the study of infants and young children to shed light on how the frequency of going back and forth from one home to another affects bonding and development.

PUBLIC POLICY AND DIVORCE RESEARCH

Although policy makers, legislators, and judges have increasingly sought support from the findings of behavioral science and guidance from the mental health professions, the accumulation of psychological knowledge has not kept up with the rapid evolution of family law. Knowledge about children and parent-child relationships in the postdivorce family is still fragmentary and insufficient to support many of the legislative changes in family policy that have found powerful adherents. The subtleties of psychological thinking and shadings of individual difference that are so critical to the perspective of the behavioral scientist translate poorly into the arenas of court and legislature. The several years of follow-up required to assess the impact of changed circumstances on altered family structure are ill-suited to the pressured agendas of the political and judicial process. Despite the widespread acknowledgment given to the important interface between family law and mental health, the major task of building cooperation and mutual understanding on a firm basis of empirical knowledge and shared values still lies ahead.

INTERVENTIONS

Many families need professional advice and guidance in negotiating their way through the complex and tangled pathway of divorce and the postdivorce years. Moreover, it is important to provide these services to both adults and children when the need is greatest—at the marital rupture and at critical turning points along the arduous road ahead. Essentially, divorcing families confront two sets of divorce-related issues that fall within the domain of the clinician: those associated with rebuilding the family, and those related to subsequent families that will provide a "holding environment" for children and adults during the postdivorce years. These two sets of issues translate into a series of immediate and long-term psychological and social tasks for adults and children (Wallerstein, 1983; Wallerstein & Blakeslee, 1989). They translate as well into two separate preventive and clinical agendas: one addressed primarily to the amelioration of the psychological disequilibria of the separation crisis and its immediate aftermath and a second addressed to building or restoring family structure and parent-child relationships within the postdivorce or remarried family (Wallerstein, 1990a).

A third, clinical agenda is addressed to children who show relatively consolidated psychological disturbance. Although children in this group tend to present familiar clinical issues, the therapist's relationships with the parents and other significant adults will differ sharply from those with most intact families.

Thus, in the divorced family the issue of who bears primary financial responsibility for the child's therapy is often in dispute. The treatment, itself, whatever its course, has a high potential for being caught within the continuing angers between the parents, and the therapist is likely to be identified by one or both as allied with "the other side." Furthermore, there is the thorny issue, which needs to be resolved on a case-by-case basis, as to which adults should be included in the therapist's relationship with the family. When and under what circumstances should a biological father who has had little contact with the child be seen? When should a stepparent be dealt with as the primary parent? When and how should live-in lovers be included? The clinician needs to assess these multiple relationships not only for their bearing on the child but also because of their importance in constructing a network that will support the child's treatment (Wallerstein, 1990b).

Another critical issue that will influence treatment process and goals is that the development of a significant number of children is hindered by the continuing failure of their families to provide sufficient nurturance and protection to sustain the youngsters' developmental progress. As a consequence, in addition to addressing issues of neurotic conflict, the clinician may need to take a more supportive role. These supportive parameters, which so many of the children need, have implications not only for process but also for the duration of treatment.

TASKS OF DIVORCE

The reorganization and readjustments required of the child of divorce—the psychological tasks that need to be addressed—represent a major addition to the expectable tasks of childhood and adolescence in our society. In effect, the child of divorce faces a special set of challenges and carries an added burden that may indeed require professional help at different points along the developmental course. The individual child's resolution of these tasks is profoundly influenced by the family ambience and by the extent to which the parents have made progress in resolving the many issues to which divorce gives rise. Nevertheless, it is the child who must carry the burden of mastery and resolution on the way to successful adulthood; there is no necessarily determining relationship between the resolution and adjustment achieved by either of the parents and the outcome for any particular child in the family. There is in fact a widening difference in outcome among siblings as they approach young adulthood (Corbin, 1988).

These readjustments are likely to stretch over the growing-up years and through adolescence. They are the coping tasks that are shaped by psychological threats to the child's psychic integrity and development. These tasks have been conceptualized as a hierarchical series, which follows a particular time sequence beginning with the critical events of parental separation and culminating at late adolescence and young adulthood. They represent the agenda for the child as well as for the therapy.

The psychological tasks, as formulated by Wallerstein (1983), are six in number. They fall into an unfolding sequence and are accomplished in varying time spans. Task 1, *acknowledging the reality of the marital rupture*, and Task 2, *disengaging from parental conflict and distress and resuming customary pursuits*, need to be addressed immediately at the time of the decisive separation, and they are optimally resolved within the first year. The child's successful mastery of these two immediate tasks is tied to the maintenance of his or her appropriate academic pace and overall developmental agenda, after the initial dip at the time of crisis. But the child's unsuccessful mastery of divorce-engendered stress is only partially related to the early period following the marital rupture. Over many years, the child will work and rework Task 3, *the resolution of losses* (including the loss of the presence of one parent in the home); Task 4, *resolving anger and self-blame;* and Task 5, *accepting the permanence of the* divorce. These, along with the final Task 6, *achieving realistic hope regarding relationships,* will become salient at adolescence and entry into adulthood.

FUTURE DIRECTIONS IN INTERVENTIONS

There are indications of mounting community concern about the recent changes in the family in our society and their impact on children, particularly the initial and long-term effects of divorce. Whether this concern will translate into adequately funded preventive and clinical programs, we cannot predict. Thus far, mediation and court-based programs have traditionally excluded children, whereas school-based programs have typically excluded parents. Nevertheless, the possibility is greater that the decade of the future will see a proliferation of new and integrated educational and preventive programs that will address families at the time of the separation crisis. Such programs should ideally reach out to parents within a general divorcing population and provide guidance in making the many decisions that they face and offer specific advice about how to restore parenting and how to help their children during the crisis and its often extended aftermath.

One such demonstration project has been developed in northern California at the Center for the Family in Transition, funded by private foundations. The outreach includes a letter sent to every family within the county that files for divorce. Children and adolescents are assessed individually and receive intensive counseling over an initial 3-month period, returning for brief follow-ups at the 1- and 2-year marks (Wallerstein, 1990a). This model has been copied in several clinics within the United States and Canada. There has also been some recent interest in modifying the model to meet the demands of the private sector. The work of Johnston and her associates offers another important template for working with families in high-conflict situations.

Precisely because divorce impacts a large segment of the general population, it provides an unprecedented opportunity for developing and testing models of prevention in mental health. And because the subgroups at greater risk can often be identified at the time of the separation, among both parents and children, the clinician may be able to offer a range of intervention programs early on. One such subgroup that may well receive increased attention comprises high-conflict families who fall through the net of the mediation services provided by the court. It is possible that the courts will recognize the grave psychopathology among these children and their parents and develop referral networks within the private sector. The high incidence of allegations of physical and sexual abuse in divorcing families may also encourage the development of clinical services via a referral network attached to the courts.

Among the hopeful signs on this landscape is the new willingness of public, private, and parochial schools to recognize the link between the learning and behavioral problems of many children and the weakening in the family structure. School systems are increasingly willing to permit or even welcome groups for children within the school setting, especially in the elementary schools.

Finally, there is burgeoning recognition of the needs of children of divorce that emerge with new intensity at young adulthood. Group programs are being developed that primarily attract adults in their 20s and 30s who find their shared experience a useful supplement to individual therapy.

Overall, however, our society has been reluctant to undertake measures related to helping families deal with change. The mental health professions have not taken a leadership role, and children continue to lack a powerful voice raised on their behalf. Still critically needed are research that will address the large lacunae in our knowledge and programs in prevention and intensive clinical interventions that can push our knowledge far beyond its current compass. Both the research agenda and the intervention agenda appear to lengthen and to unfold before us as we come closer to understanding the psychodynamics of these new family forms.

REFERENCES

Block, J. H., Block, J., & Morrison, A. (1981). Parental agreement-disagreement on child rearing orientations and gender-related personality correlates in children. *Child Development, 52,* 965–974.

Cath, S. H., Gurwitt, A. R., & Ross, J. M. (1982). *Father and child: Developmental and clinical perspectives.* Boston: Little, Brown.

Cherlin, A. J., Furstenberg, F. F., Chase-Lansdale, P. L., Kiernan, K. E., Robbins, P. K., Morrison, D. R., & Teitler, J. O. (1991). Longitudinal studies of effects of divorce on children in Great Britain and the United States. *Science, 252,* 1386–1389.

Coogler, O. J. (1978). *Structural mediation in divorce settlement.* Lexington, MA: Lexington Books.

Corbin, S. B. (1988). *Factors affecting long-term similarities and differences among siblings following parental divorce.* Unpublished doctoral dissertation. Menlo Park, CA: Pacific Graduate School of Psychology.

Emery, R. E. (1982). Interparental conflict and the children of discord and divorce. *Psychological Bulletin, 92,* 310–330.

Felner, R. D., Stolberg, A. L., & Cowen, E. L. (1975). Crisis events and school mental health referral patterns of young children. *Journal of Consulting Clinical Psychology, 43,* 305–310.

Freed, D. J., & Foster, H. H. (1974). The shuffled child and divorce court. *Trial, 10,* 26–41.

Furstenberg, F. F., Nord, C. W., Peterson, J. L., & Zill, N. (1983). The life course of children of divorce: Marital disruption and parental contact. *American Sociological Review, 48,* 656–668.

Gardner, R. A. (1982). *Family evaluation in child custody litigation.* Cresskill, NJ: Creative Therapeutics.

Gardner, R. A. (1976). *Psychotherapy and children of divorce.* New York: Aronson.

Group for the Advancement of Psychiatry. (1980). *Divorce, child custody and the family.* New York: Mental Health Materials Center.

Guidubaldi, J., & Perry, J. D. (1985). Divorce and mental health sequelae for children: A two-year follow-up of a nationwide sample. *Journal of the American Academy of Child Psychiatry, 24,* 531–537.

Hanson, S. M. H., & Bozett F. W. (1985). *Dimensions of fatherhood.* Beverly Hills, CA: Sage.

Haynes, J. (1981). *Divorce mediation.* New York: Springer.

Hess, R. D., & Camara, K. A. (1979). Post-divorce family relationships as mediating factors in the consequences of divorce for children. *Journal of Social Issues, 35,* 79–96.

Hetherington, E. M., Cox, M., & Cox, R. (1978). The aftermath of divorce. In J. H. Stevens & M. Mathews (Eds.), *Mother/child, father/child relationships.* Washington, DC: National Association for the Education of Young Children.

Hetherington, E. M., Cox, M., & Cox, R. (1982). Effects of divorce on parents and children. In M. E. Lamb (Ed.), *Nontraditional families: Parenting and child development.* Hillsdale, NJ: Erlbaum.

Jacobs, J. (1982). The effect of divorce on fathers: An overview of the literature. *American Journal of Psychiatry, 139,* 62–66.

Johnston, J. R. (1994). High conflict divorce. *Future Child, 4.*

Johnston, J. R., & Campbell, L. E. G. (1988). *Impasses of divorce: The dynamics and resolution of family conflict.* New York: Free Press.

Johnston, J. R., Kline, M., & Tschann, J. M. (1989). Ongoing postdivorce conflict: Effects on children of joint custody and frequent access. *American Journal of Orthopsychiatry, 59,* 1–17.

Kalter, N. (1977). Children of divorce in an outpatient psychiatric population. *American Journal of Orthopsychiatry, 47,* 40–51.

Kalter, N., Reimer, B., & Brickman, A. (1985). Implications of divorce for female development. *Journal of the American Academy of Child Psychiatry, 24,* 538–544.

Kline, M., Tschann, J. M., Johnston, J. R., & Wallerstein, J. S. (1989). Children's adjustment in joint and sole physical custody families. *Developmental Psychology, 25,* 430–438.

Kressal, K., & Pruitt, D. G. (1989). *Mediation research: The process and effectiveness of third-party intervention.* San Francisco: Jossey-Bass.

Maccoby, E. E., & Mnookin, R. H. (1992). *Dividing the child: Social and legal dilemmas of custody.* Cambridge, MA: Harvard University Press.

McKinnon, R., & Wallerstein, J. S. (1986). Joint custody and the preschool child. *Behavior and Science Law, 4,* 169–183.

Mnookin, R. H., & Kornhauser, L. (1979). Bargaining in the shadow of the law: The case of divorce. *Yale Law Journal, 88,* 950–977.

Pasley, K., & Ihinger-Tallman, M. (1987). *Remarriage & stepparenting: Current research & theory.* New York: Guilford Press.

Roseby, V. (1993). *Conflicts in gender and sexual identity in children of high-conflict divorce.* Paper presented at The Vulnerable Child Discussion Group, Meeting of the American Psychoanalytic Association, San Francisco.

Roseby, V., & Johnston, J. R. (1995). Clinical interventions with children of high conflict and violence. *American Journal of Orthopsychiatry, 65,* 48–59.

Roseby, V., & Johnston, J. R. (1998). Children of Armaggedon: Common developmental threats in high-conflict divorcing families. In K. Pruitt & M. Klein-Pruitt (Eds.), Child & adolescent psychiatric clinics of North America [Special issue]. *Child Custody, 7,* 295–310.

Roseby, V., & Wallerstein, J. S. (in press). Impact of divorce on latency-age children: Assessment and intervention strategies. In J. Noshpitz (Ed.), *Handbook of child psychiatry* (Rev. ed.). New York: Basic Books.

Rutter, M. (1970). Sex differences in children's responses to family stress. In E. J. Anthony & C. Koupernik (Eds.), *The child in his family.* New York: Wiley.

Santrock, J. W., & Warshak, R. A. (1979). Father custody and social development in boys and girls. *Journal of Social Issues, 35,* 112–125.

Santrock, J. W., Warshak, R., & Lindbergh, C. (1982). Children's and parent's observed social behavior in step-father families. *Child Development, 53,* 472–480.

Solomon, J., & George, C. (1997, April). *Mother–child relationships in toddlerhood: Effects of early overnight visitation with father in divorced & separated families.* Paper presented at the meeting of the Society for Research in Child Development, Washington, DC.

Spanier, G. B., & Glick, P. C. (1981). Marital instability in the United States: Some correlates and recent changes. *Family Relations, 31,* 329–338.

Steinman, S. (1981). The experience of children in a joint custody arrangement: A report of a study. *American Journal of Orthopsychiatry, 51,* 403–414.

Wallerstein, J. S. (1983). Children of divorce: The psychological tasks of the child. *American Journal of Orthopsychiatry, 53,* 230–243.

Wallerstein, J. S. (1985a). Changes in parent-child relationships during and after divorce. In E. J. Anthony & G. H. Pollock (Eds.), *Parental influences in health and disease.* Boston: Little, Brown.

Wallerstein, J. S. (1985b). The overburdened child: Some long-term consequences of divorce. *Social Work, 30,* 116–123.

Wallerstein, J. S. (1990a). Preventive interventions with divorcing families: A reconceptualization. In S. E. Goldston, C. M. Heinicke, R. S. Pynoos, et al. (Eds.), *Preventing mental health disturbance in childhood* (pp. 167–185). Washington, DC: American Psychiatric Press.

Wallerstein, J. S. (1990b). Transferences and countertransferences in clinical interventions with divorcing families. *American Journal of Orthopsychiatry, 60,* 337–345.

Wallerstein, J. S. (1991). The long-term effects of divorce on children: A review. *Journal of the American Academy of Child Adolescent Psychiatry, 30,* 349–360.

Wallerstein, J. S., & Blakeslee, S. (1989). *Second chances: Men, women, and children a decade after divorce.* New York: Ticknor and Fields.

Wallerstein, J. S., & Corbin, S. B. (1989). Daughters of divorce: Report from a ten-year study. *American Journal of Orthopsychiatry, 59,* 593–604.

Wallerstein, J. S., & Kelly, J. B. (1980). *Surviving the breakup: How children and their parents cope with divorce.* New York: Basic Books.

Watson, A. (1969). The children of Armageddon: Problems of children following divorce. *Syracuse Law Review, 21,* 231–239.

Weiss, R. S. (1979). Growing up a little faster. *Journal of Social Issues, 35,* 97–111.

Weitzman, L. J. (1985). *The divorce revolution: The unexpected social and economic consequences for women and children in America.* New York: Free Press.

Zaslow, M. J. (1988). Sex differences in children's response to parental divorce: I. Research methodology and postdivorce family forms. *American Journal of Orthopsychiatry, 58,* 355–378.

Zaslow, M. J. (1989). Sex differences in children's response to parental divorce: II. Samples, variables, and sources. *American Journal of Orthopsychiatry, 59,* 118–141.

Zill, N. (1983). *Divorce, marital conflict, and children's mental health: Research findings and policy recommendations.* Testimony before the Subcommittee on Family and Human Services. U.S. Senate Committee on Labor and Human Resources, Senate Hearing 98-195, pp. 90–106. Washington, DC: U.S. Government Printing Office.

Zill, N., Morrison, D. R., & Coiro, M. J. (1993). Long-term effects of parental divorce on parent-child relationships, adjustment and achievement in young adulthood. *Journal of Family Psychology, 7*(1), 91–103.

Zill, N., & Schoenborn, C. A. (1990, November 16). *Developmental, learning and emotional problems: Health of our nation's children, United States, 1988* (Advance data, vital and health statistics of the national center for health statistics, no. 190). Washington, DC: National Center for Health Statistics.

CHAPTER 6

The Adjustment of Children from Divorced Families: Implications of Empirical Research for Clinical Intervention

JOHN H. GRYCH and FRANK D. FINCHAM

T HE IMPACT OF divorce on children has generated two contrasting viewpoints. One view is that so-called broken homes produce maladjusted children, whereas the other sees divorce as an experience that has benign or even beneficial effects on children. Debate on the impact of divorce on children has been fueled by values and attitudes regarding what kinds of families are healthy or unhealthy for children and continues despite convincing empirical evidence that neither of the preceding viewpoints is correct. Although early clinical reports and empirical research supported the idea that divorce led to behavior problems in children, more recent, methodologically sophisticated studies indicate that, on average, the difference in functioning between children from divorced and intact families is quite small (Amato & Keith, 1991; see also Grych & Fincham, 1990, 1997). Focusing only on averages can be misleading, however, because it neglects information about variability in children's functioning, and it is this variability that is the most salient feature of research on children's adjustment to parental divorce. Children from divorced families exhibit a range of adjustment outcomes: Many are as well-adjusted as their peers in intact families, but others exhibit significant and long-lasting problems.

From a clinical standpoint, the extent to which these children develop psychological problems serious enough to warrant therapeutic intervention is a primary consideration. Data on this issue come from two kinds of studies. First, a large nationwide survey found that approximately twice as many children from divorced families (13%) as intact families (6%) were evaluated or treated in mental health settings at some point following the divorce (Zill, 1978). Although factors other than their actual functioning influence whether a child will be referred for such services (e.g., parents' psychological adjustment), this estimate is supported by studies showing that at least twice as many children from divorced as intact families meet criteria for clinically significant levels of behavior problems on normed, well-validated measures of adjustment (Hetherington et al., 1992).

Taken together, these findings indicate that even though the percentage of children experiencing significant adjustment problems after divorce is relatively small, divorce is associated with increased risk for the development of psychopathology. Further, given the large number of divorces involving children each year, even a small percentage of children experiencing significant behavioral and emotional problems translates into a significant public health concern.

In response to the needs of this population, a number of approaches to intervening with children from divorced families have been developed. Some represent the application of traditional individual and family therapy techniques to the context of divorce (e.g., Gardner, 1991; Hodges, 1991), whereas others are self-contained programs specifically designed to help children cope with the challenges and difficulties posed by parental divorce. These approaches differ in the extent to which they are based on empirical data concerning the effects of divorce on children's functioning and in the degree to which they have documented their efficacy.

The purpose of the present chapter is to examine these interventions in the light of our knowledge of the processes that lead to maladjustment in children from divorced families. Toward this end, we first review empirical research on risk and protective factors associated with children's adaptation to divorce because this work can identify fruitful avenues for intervention. We then describe intervention programs designed to enhance the adjustment of children from divorced families and summarize evidence regarding their efficacy. Finally, we offer recommendations for better integrating basic and intervention research.

RISK AND PROTECTIVE FACTORS IN CHILDREN'S ADAPTATION TO DIVORCE

There now is widespread recognition that divorce is best understood as a process that begins prior to the physical separation of the parents and may continue long after. Although the separation may be the single most salient event in the divorce process, it represents just one of a long series of events that may challenge children's adaptation. Separation marks the end of months and often years of dissatisfaction and discord in the marriage, and the beginning of a new phase of family life in which new households are established and family relationships are reorganized. Children may be exposed to high levels of conflict as parents work out custody and visitation arrangements, their relationships with one or both parents may change considerably, they may be forced to move out of their home and neighborhood into unfamiliar surroundings, and they may suffer from economic deprivation. It is the nature of children's experiences and their ability to cope with stressful events that are primarily responsible for determining how they will adjust to divorce.

This is not to minimize the distress caused by the physical separation. Children rarely desire a divorce, and often display some kind of physical, emotional, or behavioral disturbance in the months following the separation, including sleep problems, sadness, anger, worry about themselves and their family, and aggressive behavior (Hetherington, 1989; Kelly, 1988; Wallerstein & Kelly, 1980). However, longitudinal investigations examining the course of children's adaptation to divorce indicate that these problems typically diminish over time (Allison & Furstenberg, 1989; Hetherington, Cox, & Cox, 1982; Kurdek, Blisk, & Siesky, 1981). In a sample of children who were 4 years old when their parents divorced, Hetherington and her colleagues found that both boys and girls demonstrated higher levels of problems 2 months and 1 year following divorce, but that by 2 years postdivorce, children's adjustment had improved significantly. These findings suggest that the first year or two following a divorce is a time of crisis for children and their families, but that most children adapt to this transition provided that they do not face new or continued stressors.

Unfortunately for many children, divorce often sets in motion a number of other changes that can adversely affect their functioning. In the next section, we summarize research on factors associated with children's adjustment following divorce. They can be categorized into processes occurring within the family, life stressors, and individual factors. Some increase the risk of developing adjustment problems whereas others may serve as protective factors that promote healthy adaptation.

FAMILY FACTORS

Given that divorce involves a fundamental rupture in family relationships, cooperative coparenting and the maintenance of good parent-child relationships provides a degree of stability and security in children's lives. In contrast, continued conflict between parents and strained or distant parent-child relations may create additional stress as children attempt to adjust to their new family situation. We consider the research on interparental conflict and parent-child relationships in turn.

Interparental Conflict

Children rate the conflict between their parents as one of the most stressful aspects of divorce (Wolchik, Sandler, Braver, & Fogas, 1989), and high levels of interparental conflict are consistently associated with child maladjustment in both intact and divorced families (Cummings & Davies, 1994; Grych & Fincham, 1990). In fact, children living in divorced families with low levels of conflict are better adjusted than those living in highly conflictual intact families (Hetherington et al., 1982), leading some to argue that the adverse effects attributed to divorce actually are due to the discord preceding and following the divorce (Hetherington et al., 1982; Shaw, Emery, & Tuer, 1993). After comparing evidence on several factors proposed to explain why children develop continuing problems after divorce, Amato (1993, 1994) concluded that conflict between parents was the single best predictor of maladjustment. In contrast, cooperation between ex-spouses is positively correlated with adjustment (Camara & Resnick, 1989; Hess & Camara, 1979).

Although levels of conflict between parents tend to diminish with time after the divorce (Maccoby, Buchanan, Mnookin, & Dornbusch, 1993), the process of determining child-related and financial issues may increase animosity between spouses, and postdivorce family life is rife with opportunities for disagreement as parents establish households with their own sets of rules and parenting styles. In addition, lingering resentment over problems in the marriage or the decision to divorce may fuel conflicts over unrelated issues after the separation. In the Stanford Custody Project, a longitudinal investigation of 1,124 divorcing couples, Maccoby, Depner, and Mnookin (1990) found that almost one third of the couples exhibited significant conflict 18 months after the separation and a smaller number remained locked in a conflictual relationship three years after separating. These couples tended to be those that previously had expressed higher levels of hostility, had more lengthy legal disputes, younger children, and concerns about the quality of parenting in the other's household (Maccoby et al., 1993).

The impact of conflict on children depends on how it is expressed, and the conflict associated with divorce is often expressed in a way that is likely to be particularly stressful for children. Conflict that is hostile and aggressive, poorly resolved, and child-related in content is more upsetting to children (Cummings & Davies, 1994; Grych & Fincham, 1993), and it is precisely these qualities that are likely to characterize interparental conflict occurring before and after divorce. Divorce often follows repeated unsuccessful attempts to resolve significant differences between spouses, and much of the conflict occurring after divorce involves child-related issues such as custody and visitation. Moreover, many ex-spouses have difficulty separating their marital and parental roles, and consequently feelings of anger toward a spouse may be expressed through the one tie that continues to bind them—their children (Emery, 1994).

The mechanisms by which parental conflict lead to maladjustment are not well understood, but one of the primary ways that postdivorce conflict can affect children is by creating situations in which they feel torn in their loyalty and affection for each parent (Buchanan, Maccoby, & Dornbusch, 1991). Although this might be as blatant as one parent disparaging their ex-spouse in front of the child, more often it is subtle, such as using a child to pass messages to the other spouse, questioning the child about the other parent's life, or making the child feel uncomfortable talking about one parent in the presence of the other. Buchanan and her colleagues (1991) found it was the perception of being caught between parents that accounted for associations between parental conflict and children's adjustment problems after divorce. Thus, an important factor in shaping children's adaptation to divorce appears to be parents' ability to keep their children out of the untenable position of feeling the need to choose between them. This is facilitated by resolving their differences without involving the children, but also suggests that parents' efforts to "win over" their child by undermining the other parent will have adverse effects. As Emery (1994) points out, some conflicts that appear to be struggles over power (e.g., making decisions about raising the child) actually reflect concerns about love (will the child continue to be close to the parent), which highlights the second important influence on children's postdivorce adaptation, the nature of parent-child relationships.

Parent-Child Relations

Divorce almost inevitably leads to changes in children's relationships with their parents, and two aspects of parent-child interaction have received the most attention in basic research: the support children receive from their parents, and the quality of discipline in both parents' households. Although almost all states allow or even encourage joint custody, most children still spend the majority of their time with one parent after divorce, usually their mother. Consequently, most children experience decreased contact with the nonresidential parent as well as changes in the relationship with the residential parent, who may take on additional responsibilities that make them less available to the children (e.g., increasing hours at work or beginning to work outside the home).

Many nonresidential fathers gradually become less involved in their children's lives, perhaps in response to the emotional difficulty of being only "part-time fathers" or because they remarry and focus their attention on their new family. The effect of this on children is not clear. Amato (1993) reviewed 32 studies on this topic and found that 16 supported the idea that frequency of contact with the nonresidential parent was associated with children's well-being and 16 did not. In fact, a few studies found that greater contact was associated with increased child problems. Although more research is needed on the relationship between children and nonresidential parents, it seems reasonable to conclude that fathers who see their children infrequently are unlikely to have much influence on them, but fathers who remain involved potentially play as important a role as fathers in intact families.

Disruptions in children's relationships with their parents can be quite distressing, especially during times of change and uncertainty. Children benefit from having stable, supportive relationships with their parents after divorce, particularly with the residential parent (Camara & Resnick, 1989; Hess & Camara, 1979; Hetherington et al., 1982; Peterson & Zill, 1986). However, it may be difficult for parents to be sensitive and responsive to their children in the wake of divorce because they too may be overwhelmed by the practical and emotional sequelae of separation. In addition, children at this time may be angry, clingy, or oppositional, and thus more difficult to parent. Parent-child relationships often are strained after divorce, especially between custodial mothers and sons, as parents attempt to maintain a household on their own.

In a richly detailed investigation of parent-child interaction, Hetherington and her colleagues (1982) found that residential mothers tended to become more controlling and/or inconsistent in their parenting style and communicated more poorly than mothers in intact families, and that their children responded with increasingly noncompliant and coercive behavior. In contrast, nonresidential fathers often become more permissive after the divorce, relaxing rules and consequences for children's behavior, perhaps in an attempt to maintain a good relationship with their children (Hetherington, 1993). These differences in expectations may be confusing to children and fuel discord between parents over how each is taking care of the children. Over time these differences tend to lessen, as both parents move toward more authoritative parenting styles (Hetherington, 1993). However, there is evidence that problems in parent-child relationships may reemerge in adolescence as children and parents deal with children's increasing autonomy (Hetherington, 1993).

Although divorce presents challenges for parent-child relationships, its impact is not necessarily negative; Hetherington and her colleagues found that 50% of divorced mothers and 25% of divorced fathers reported that their relationships with their children had improved over time (Hetherington et al., 1982). Residential mothers tend to develop particularly close relationships with their children, especially their daughters, that include a mixture of strong positive and negative experiences (Hetherington, 1993), and when freed from the tension and discord of the marriage, nonresidential parents may come to enjoy their children more.

LIFE STRESS

Another factor implicated in children's adaptation is the increase in stressful life events that often follows divorce. Although exposure to parental conflict and parent-child difficulties are stressful in their own right, children also may face a series of changes in daily routines as they shift from one household to another, or they may move to a different home, school, or neighborhood. Some changes involve the loss of friends, supportive adults, and familiar environs, and can include challenges that may tax the child's ability to adapt; however, divorce also may bring positive changes, such as a decrease in parental conflict, increased time spent with a parent, and the development of new competencies.

Empirical research provides consistent support for the hypothesis that experiencing a greater number of life changes is associated with poorer adjustment on a variety of indices, including academic functioning, behavioral problems, and self-esteem. Although some studies suggest that the number of life changes, positive or negative, predicts children's adjustment (e.g., Kurdek & Berg, 1983; Stolberg & Anker, 1983), others indicate that only negative life events correlate with adjustment (Sandler, Wolchik, & Braver, 1988; Walsh & Stolberg, 1989). Sandler, Wolchik, Braver, and Fogas (1991) provided the most detailed investigation of the kinds of life events associated with postdivorce adaptation. They examined both the quality (positive or negative) and stability (whether it represents a change or continuation of usual circumstances) of events encountered by 206 children aged 8 to 15 years from divorced families. They found that stable positive events were associated with lower levels of maladjustment and that increased negative change events were associated with higher maladjustment, though stable negative events were not. In this study, stable positive events primarily involved good interactions with their parents, which supports the role of parent-child relationships discussed earlier. Negative changes were viewed as particularly stressful because they contribute to a sense of unpredictability and uncertainty in children's lives that disrupt their functioning.

One of the most significant changes many children experience after divorce is a loss in family income. Residential mothers often experience a dramatic drop in income (Duncan & Hoffman, 1985), and economic deprivation is particularly likely to occur for African American women and White women whose income before the divorce was below the median. Child support and spousal maintenance payments, if they are made, generally are not sufficient to help these families maintain the standard of living they had before the divorce and for many women, this situation does not improve unless they remarry (Furstenberg, 1990). This loss of income means that children often must move to poorer quality housing and attend schools that do not provide the same educational opportunities and advantages that they previously had. It also may mean fewer opportunities to become involved in extracurricular activities that promote physical, social, and intellectual development.

Despite the potential importance of economic hardship following divorce, relatively few studies have directly investigated the link between changes in family income and child adjustment. Using a national sample of 699 first, third, and fifth graders, Guidubaldi, Perry, and Nastasi (1987) found that differences between children from intact and divorced families (an average of 4 years postdivorce) on several indices of adjustment were reduced when family income was controlled, and were reduced even further at a follow-up assessment 2 to 3 years later, especially for boys. However, some differences between the groups remained, indicating that income decline does not wholly account for the effects of divorce (Guidubaldi et al., 1987). Research examining the correlation between family income after divorce and child adjustment similarly presents moderate support for the role of income in children's adaptation to divorce, with about half of such studies documenting a significant association (see Amato, 1993).

INDIVIDUAL FACTORS

Stress and coping theorists have argued that the impact of a stressful event depends not just on the qualities of the event itself but on how an individual perceives and responds to it (Compas, 1987; Rutter, 1983). Research on divorce has examined several intraindividual characteristics in an effort to identify styles of thinking and responding that moderate the effect of the divorce process.

Children's beliefs about divorce, especially regarding their role in the divorce, have been a focus of researchers and clinicians. In particular, fear of abandonment, self-blame, and hope for reconciliation have been identified as common responses to divorce, especially by younger children (e.g., Wallerstein & Kelly, 1980), and are thought to be linked to increased anxiety and depression. However, quantitative empirical evidence for a relation between children's beliefs and their adjustment is mixed.

Kurdek and Berg (1983, 1987) found that "problematic" beliefs about divorce (which included the preceding three beliefs) were related to parent and teacher ratings of children's adjustment in one study (Kurdek & Berg, 1983) but only to child reports of adjustment in another (Kurdek & Berg, 1987). Other studies have examined these beliefs separately. Wolchik and her colleagues (1993) found that over half of fourth- to eighth-grade children from families separated an average of four years expressed the belief that their parents eventually would remarry and indicated that they feared being abandoned by both parents. However, only fear of abandonment was correlated with child and parent reports of adjustment. Although it might be expected that such beliefs would be more common among younger children, age was not correlated with either belief.

The idea that children tend to blame themselves for parental divorce also has received inconsistent support. Some studies indicate that young children in particular view themselves as being at least partly at fault for the divorce (Neal, 1983; Wallerstein & Kelly, 1980) whereas others have found that self-blame is uncommon in children of any age (Kurdek et al., 1981; Warshak & Santrock, 1983). These inconsistent findings may reflect changes in children's thinking over the course of adapting to the divorce. The studies reporting increased self-blame assessed children closer to the time of divorce than those that did not, suggesting that all children may try to understand why the divorce occurred and consider whether they had a role in it, but after a period of time come to understand that they are not responsible (Grych & Fincham, 1992b).

This possibility was supported by a longitudinal study assessing 6- to 12-year-old children within 8 months of parental separation and then one year later (Healy, Stewart, & Copeland, 1993). At the time of the initial assessment, 35% of the children believed that they may have been partially to blame for the divorce, but only 19% did so at follow-up. Self-blame was higher when children felt caught between their parents or were perceived as trying to play one parent off the other, providing further evidence of the adverse consequences of children becoming entangled in parental conflicts. However, it was not related to children's age or mothers' report that child raising disagreements or children's problems contributed to the divorce. Those children who did ascribe blame to themselves also reported lower perceived competence and greater psychological symptoms. Thus, although self-blame appears to become relatively rare as time passes after the divorce, it likely is more common in children who are referred for therapy, which may account for clinicians' overestimating its base rate in the population of children from divorced families.

Other types of beliefs also have been studied, including those that appear to serve a protective function. Whereas Mazur, Wolchik, and Sandler (1992) reported that "cognitive errors" (catastrophizing, overgeneralizing, personalizing) were related to higher levels of anxiety and behavior problems and lower self-esteem, what they termed "positive illusions" (high self-regard, personal control, optimism) correlated with lower levels of self-reported aggression. Moreover, these types of thoughts accounted for unique variance beyond that accounted for by the occurrence of negative divorce-related events. Similarly, having an internal locus of control has been associated with better adaptation to divorce. For example, Fogas and his coworkers (1992) reported that negative life events were less strongly related to maladjustment when children reported a more internal locus of control. How children think about events thus might be important for their efforts to cope with postdivorce stressors.

Because children often face a series of demanding and difficult life changes, their ability to marshal effective coping resources may be an important protective factor. The few studies conducted on children's coping with divorce-related events have measured coping strategies in different ways, making cross-study comparisons difficult. However, it appears that healthy adaptation is enhanced by active coping methods, which involve doing things or thinking of ways to directly address problems (Kliewer & Sandler, 1993; Krantz, Clark, Pruyn, & Usher, 1985; Sandler, Tein, & West, 1994), and by the use of distraction, which involves focusing one's attention on a pleasant activity rather than on the problem (Sandler et al., 1994). These approaches correspond to problem-focused and emotion-focused coping, respectively, which are adaptive in different types of situations (Lazarus & Folkman, 1984). Specifically, problem-focused coping is adaptive when the individual can do something to change the situation, whereas emotion-focused coping appears to be more effective when the person cannot directly affect the problem they are facing. In such circumstances it is likely to be more adaptive to regulate affect some other way. Age differences have been found in children's ability to use different types of coping methods, with emotion-focused coping developing later than problem-focused coping (Compas, Malcarne, & Fondacaro, 1988).

Children who try to cope with divorce-related stressors by simply trying not to think about them or engaging in wishful thinking show higher rates of maladjustment (Armistead et al., 1990; Kliewer & Sandler, 1993; Sandler et al., 1994).

This avoidance strategy has been distinguished from distraction; the former involves attempting to deny the reality of the situation whereas the latter involves recognizing the situation but focusing attention on something more positive (Sandler et al., 1994). Support-seeking also has been related to higher levels of adjustment problems, which may suggest that children who are more troubled perceived greater need for help from others, or perhaps reflects dissatisfaction with the support they are receiving from parents and others (Sandler et al., 1994).

Summary

Children's development after divorce is shaped by both risk and protective factors. Their adjustment is a product of the quality of relationships in the family, the kinds of life events they face, and their approach to thinking and responding to divorce-related events. Although the strongest evidence supports the role of parental conflict in mediating children's adaptation, all these factors may influence children's adaptation (Amato, 1993). Moreover, risk and protective factors are likely to be interrelated in complex ways. For example, children who are drawn into interparental hostilities are more likely to blame themselves for the divorce (Healy et al., 1993), but close relationships with one or both parents may reduce this tendency and thus buffer children from adverse effects of conflict. However, there have been few attempts to study the interaction of risk and protective factors, and so their combined effect on children is unknown. As more is learned about the influences on children's adaptation to divorce, empirical research can more fully inform interventions designed to reduce adjustment problems in these children. The development of intervention programs necessarily has had to proceed in the face of incomplete knowledge, and in the following section, we describe efforts to address the problems faced by children from divorced families.

INTERVENTIONS FOR CHILDREN FROM DIVORCED FAMILIES

Numerous books (e.g., Gardner, 1991; Hodges, 1991) and articles (e.g., Bird, 1992; Soldano, 1990) describe general principles and techniques for intervening with children and their families after divorce. Most of these are efforts to apply traditional individual or family therapy approaches to the context of divorce, but few present evidence, other than anecdotal reports, of their efficacy.

In a meta-analytic review of research studies on interventions for children and adults from divorced families, Lee, Picard, and Blain (1994) found that only 15 out of 100 published articles met minimal criteria for methodological rigor. Eight of these assessed group interventions for children and 7 assessed groups for adults. Although this represents a larger number of outcome studies than were available when Sprenkle and Storm (1983) reviewed this literature over 14 years ago, there remain relatively few interventions that provide empirical support of their efficacy. In part, this is due to the nature of most of the writing on clinical interventions with children from divorced families: they are not presented as structured interventions or interventions whose procedural details have been thoroughly described but as general frameworks for addressing maladjustment problems. Consequently, it is difficult to evaluate in any systematic way what does and does not work in these approaches.

On the other hand, several structured group interventions have been developed that present clearly specified goals and procedures, thus allowing for more rigorous evaluation of their efficacy. Most involve only children from divorced families, but one includes both parents and children, and another includes only parents. Several interventions also have been developed to address the needs of adults after divorce, but since our focus is on children's adjustment, we will discuss only those programs designed for either children or families.

INTERVENTIONS FOR CHILDREN

The groups designed for children of divorce share several common goals: to help children clarify misconceptions about divorce, understand and ameliorate troubling feelings, build coping skills, and enhance their perceptions of themselves and their families. Activities in the programs, which vary from 6 to 16 sessions, can include drawings, games, and audiovisual materials to facilitate discussion of thoughts and feelings about divorce. These programs also share the belief that involvement in a group of peers dealing with similar issues normalizes the experience of divorce and provides a support network for the children. Proponents argue that these group approaches, especially when conducted in schools, have distinct advantages over individual therapy. Groups can serve more children, which is important given the large number of children experiencing divorce, and can reach children who might not otherwise receive help, either because of a reluctance to seek therapy, difficulty affording therapy, or the perception that the child's problems are not severe enough. For children who are not experiencing significant problems, these groups may serve a preventive function by warding off difficulties before they get serious enough to warrant referral, or by stopping their development in the first place. In addition, conducting the groups in schools provides a natural support group because the other children in the group are classmates rather than strangers.

Of the children's groups that have been evaluated empirically, the Children of Divorce Intervention Project (CODIP) has shown the strongest evidence of its effectiveness (Alpert-Gillis, Pedro-Carroll, & Cowen, 1989; Pedro-Carroll, Alpert-Gillis, & Cowen, 1992; Pedro-Carroll & Cowen, 1985; Pedro-Carroll, Cowen, Hightower, & Guare, 1986). In addition to a focus on facilitating children's understanding of divorce-related thoughts and feelings, the CODIP group uses games to teach social problem-solving skills for dealing with divorce-related issues and interpersonal problem situations more generally, anger management, and how to distinguish solvable and unsolvable problems (Pedro-Carroll et al.,

1992). Pedro-Carroll and her colleagues have evaluated groups adapted for younger (2nd–3rd grade) and older (4th–6th grade) children from diverse ethnic and socioeconomic backgrounds, and reported positive effects in each.

The most consistent signs of efficacy have been found on children's reports of anxiety, teacher reports of competence (which includes frustration tolerance, assertiveness, social skills, shyness/anxiety, acting out), and parental reports of adjustment. Two of the studies showed improvement in children's attitudes and feelings about divorce, whereas two others failed to show such an effect. Finally, there was little evidence that the group had significant effects on children's or teachers' reports of adjustment problems. Children thus appear to feel more confident in their ability to cope with difficult circumstances and evidence positive changes in social interactions, both of which may be the result of learning social problem-solving skills. However, these changes do not translate consistently into lower levels of maladjustment. Why only two of the four studies demonstrated changes in divorce-related beliefs is not clear. The studies showing positive effects evaluated adaptations of the CODIP program for ethnically diverse, lower socioeconomic class children which placed greater emphasis on the extended family and acceptance of different family forms. It is possible that the changes made in the group strengthened the potency of this aspect of the intervention, or that differences in the samples included in the groups contributed to the disparate findings.

Another group intervention documenting positive effects was designed by Stolberg and his colleagues (Stolberg & Garrison, 1985; Stolberg & Mahler, 1994). Like the CODIP group, it teaches problem-solving and anger-management skills, but also involves parents in an effort to enhance the transfer of learning from the group to the home. To assess the program and its component parts, Stolberg and Mahler configured the groups three ways: one was devoted simply to enhancing support between members, one included support plus the skill-building sessions, and a third included support, skill-building, and parental involvement in homework from the group and participation in workshops. Children in the groups ranged in age from 8 to 12 years and on average had experienced parental divorce 3 years prior to the group. They found that participation in the skills plus support group resulted in the greatest immediate decreases in problems involving subjective distress and disturbed behavior, and that inclusion of parents in the "transfer" condition decreased children's reports of anxiety at the end of the group and parent reports of behavior problems at home one year later. Although the effects of the support only group were less apparent at the group's end, by the one year follow-up the adjustment patterns of children in all three groups were not significantly different. However, all three were better off than a comparison group of children from divorced families who did not participate in the intervention. The advantage of the skills training component thus appeared to be time limited.

Other evaluations of children's groups failed to document reliable effects on children's adjustment (Bornstein, Bornstein, & Walters, 1988; Kalter, Pickar, & Lesowitz, 1984; Kalter, Schaefer, Lesowitz, Alpern, & Pickar, 1988). Roseby and

Deutsch (1985) reported improvement in children's understanding of divorce after taking part in their group, but these improvements did not translate into more positive adjustment than a group of children who had participated in a placebo group involving discussion of thoughts and feelings about divorce. However, this control group experienced some elements of the intervention administered to the treatment group, and the children in it demonstrated improved adjustment that was not significantly different from those in the treatment group. The Bornstein group appeared to contain many of the same features as the other groups, but lasted only 6 sessions (as opposed to 14–16 for CODIP) and thus may not have been potent enough to have the desired impact (Bornstein et al., 1988).

These studies indicate that the programs most effective in improving children's adjustment to divorce teach constructive coping skills. Stolberg and Mahler (1994) reported short-term (but not long-term) advantages to the skill-building component of their intervention, and although Pedro-Carroll and colleagues did not do a component analysis of the CODIP program, their emphasis on enhancing coping skills distinguishes their group from others reporting less impressive results. Intervention research thus supports the findings from basic research in highlighting the role of coping as a mediator of children's postdivorce adaptation.

On the other hand, focusing on understanding divorce-related thoughts and feelings appears less effective in improving children's adjustment, which may be surprising given the emphasis placed on this component by all of the groups. This is most apparent in Roseby and Deutsch's (1985) group, which demonstrated the desired impact on children's understanding of the divorce, but failed to show that improvements in understanding enhanced their functioning. However, research described above (e.g., Healy et al., 1993) indicates that misconceptions about divorce tend to diminish over time, and most of the children participating in these groups experienced the divorce several years prior to participating in the intervention. Thus, it is likely that understanding feelings and clarifying misconceptions are no longer major issues for most of these children. They may still be very useful for children who have experienced divorce more recently and are still trying to understand it. This suggests that the content of the group may need to be adapted depending on how long ago children experienced divorce. Enhancing coping skills may also be important at that time; in fact, some of the skills taught in the groups may enhance the adjustment of all children, whether they are from divorced or intact families.

Finally, child-oriented interventions emphasize the role of peer support in the groups despite scant evidence that social support from friends is related to postdivorce adjustment, at least for preadolescents (Lustig, Wolchik, & Braver, 1992; Wolchik, Ruelhman, Braver, & Sandler, 1989; for contrasting results, see Cowen, Pedro-Carroll, & Alpert-Gillis, 1990). The finding that the group providing "only" support in Stolberg and Mahler's evaluation led to improved functioning one year after the intervention (compared with children not participating in the intervention) supports the value of the group setting. It may be that providing an opportunity to discuss thoughts and feelings about divorce with other children who have experienced it offers a more specific— and more powerful type of support to children than that provided by the presence of friends who are supportive in a general sense.

PARENT-ORIENTED INTERVENTIONS

Given the evidence for the importance of relations between parents and between parents and children in shaping children's adaptation to divorce, these relationships would seem to be an obvious target for intervention. However, there are only two published reports of interventions specifically targeting family processes (Stolberg & Garrison, 1985; Wolchik et al., 1993). Wolchik and her colleagues developed a group intervention for residential parents based on research regarding mediators of postdivorce adaptation. Their group is distinguished by its explicit specification of the processes hypothesized to mediate children's adjustment after divorce and its empirical evaluation of whether these factors in fact mediate effects of the group on children's functioning. The group was designed to improve children's relationship with their residential parent (in this case, all mothers), increase the amount of contact with nonresidential parent (fathers), decrease exposure to negative divorce events (including conflict between parents), enhance mothers' discipline strategies, and increase support from nonparental adults.

Their evaluation included 70 mothers of 8- to 15-year-old children, all divorced within the previous two years. The intervention emphasized teaching concrete skills to the parents. Sessions began with a short presentation in which particular skills were described and demonstrated, followed by time for group members to practice the skill. Homework was assigned to facilitate acquisition and application of the skills, and participants' experiences implementing the skills were discussed at the following session. Where possible, the techniques used in the group were based on prior evidence of their effectiveness. For example, the discipline strategies taught were based on research by Patterson (1975) and Forehand and McMahon (1981).

The largest changes seen in the intervention group compared with the waiting-list control group involved aspects of the mother-child relationship: constructive communication increased, mothers and their children engaged in more positive activities, and children reported greater maternal acceptance. Mothers also reported using effective discipline strategies more consistently (though children did not), lower levels of negative life events, and more positive attitudes toward their ex-husband's parenting ability. No differences between groups were found on children's exposure to conflict between parents or amount of contact with their father, and children reported less support from nonparental adults than the control group. Evidence for improved functioning in the intervention group was mixed: children reported lower aggression but did not differ from the control group on ratings of anxiety, depression, or conduct disorder, and maternal reports indicated that children exhibiting higher levels of adjustment problems prior to the group showed lower levels at the end. Moreover, as predicted, Wolchik and her colleagues found that changes in mother-child relationships partially mediated the impact of the group on child adjustment.

The failure of other group components to show positive effects may be due in part to the amount of time devoted to them during the sessions. The mother-child relationship was the focus of five sessions; whereas four were devoted to reducing negative divorce-related events, including attempts to reduce conflict between parents by teaching listening skills and anger management, two sessions addressed effective discipline, and single sessions were concerned with increasing contact with nonresidential parent and non-parental adults. The most potent effects thus were found on those issues that received the most extended treatment. They also were found on those factors over which mothers had the most control. Whereas mothers can directly affect their behavior toward their children, they cannot unilaterally decrease conflict with their ex-spouse or improve the child's relationship with the father, and perhaps it is unrealistic to expect that an intervention involving only mothers will significantly influence these factors. This evaluation is notable for documenting that positive outcomes are accounted for, at least in part, by a specified mechanism, here, parent-child relations. This study also is important for providing a quasi-experimental test of the role of parent-child relationship in postdivorce adjustment.

Stolberg and Garrison (1985) also evaluated a parent group conducted simultaneously with an earlier version of the child group described by Stolberg and Mahler (1994). The parents' group was designed to improve mothers' mental health and parenting skills. Two intervention conditions were evaluated; in one, parents participated in their group while their children participated in the child group, and in the other only parents were participants. Stolberg and Garrison reported that in the parent-only condition mothers reported more positive adjustment themselves, but there were no apparent effects on parenting skills, and the children of mothers taking part in the parent-only condition did not show signs of improvement. It may be that parent groups must focus more intensively on parenting issues, rather than the parents' own functioning, to have a significant impact on the parent-child relationship.

SUMMARY

Reviewing basic research on children's adaptation to divorce and evaluation research on interventions for children from divorced families reveals a gap between what is believed to cause or maintain child maladjustment and the programs designed to ameliorate it. Whereas basic research has underscored the significant role of family factors in shaping children's postdivorce adjustment, clinical inventions have focused primarily on the child as the locus for change.

This difference may be rooted in the historical interest of clinical psychology on internal causes of psychopathology and health, or to the practical issue that children are more accessible than families (e.g., through their schools) and therefore are easier to include in intervention efforts.

This is not to suggest that individually oriented interventions are without merit. On the contrary, there is evidence that beliefs and coping strategies mediate children's adaptation to divorce, and some individually oriented interventions have been shown to enhance children's functioning. However, it is unlikely that child-only interventions will be adequate for meeting the mental health needs of most children from divorced families. Interventions that target family processes, conflict between parents, and parent-child relationships are likely to be more effective in shaping the ecology of children's postdivorce life and promoting healthy adaptation. Such interventions will only be maximally effective if both parents are involved. As Wolchik and her colleagues' work showed, effects are strongest when participants can exercise direct control over the targeted interactions.

Although a gap remains between basic and applied research, there are signs that this gap is closing as these two types of research inform each other. The most recent interventions included parents, and basic research on intraindividual mediators of adjustment has increased in recent years. In the final section of the chapter, we offer suggestions for encouraging continued integration of basic and intervention outcome research.

TOWARD GREATER INTEGRATION OF BASIC AND APPLIED RESEARCH

MATCHING INTERVENTIONS TO CHILDREN'S NEEDS

To date, interventions have had a "one size fits all" quality that reflects the assumption that children from divorced families have similar needs and benefit from a similar approach. However, the evidence reviewed earlier suggests that this assumption is not true. All the group interventions attempt to reduce children's misconceptions about divorce, but there is little reason to believe that most children from divorced families hold such misconceptions. In the first year following divorce, a minority of children may believe that they had some responsibility for the divorce, but few continue to hold this belief after several years, when most interventions occur. Thus, self-blame may be important to discuss in a group of children whose parents recently separated, but it is not likely to be helpful to most children thereafter. To take another example, children whose parents remarry encounter a new set of challenges and demands that are different from those still living with a single parent. Adapting the structure of the group based on factors such as the length of time parents have been divorced or whether children live in stepfamilies will help ensure that group time is spent addressing issues of importance to the majority of children. The process of matching interventions to children's needs also will be facilitated by the use of screening measures to identify the kinds of problems children are experiencing (see Pillow, Sandler, Braver, Wolchik, & Gersten, 1991), and by postgroup analyses indicating whether certain children benefit more than others.

Customizing group interventions to fit the needs of participants depends on the generation of knowledge from basic research. There is a strong need to better understand the developmental course of divorce adjustment and the factors that shape it. Beyond Hetherington's longitudinal studies, the first of which is now almost 20 years old, there have been few attempts to chart the trajectory of parent and child adaptation over an extended period of time. Cultural attitudes and experiences with divorce have changed over that time, and it is not clear to what extent the conclusions from that work still apply.

ASSESSING THE PROCESS OF CHANGE

There is increasing recognition that intervention research is most useful when it specifies how the intervention affects children's adjustment. Knowing that a program has positive effects is limited if we do not know why it was effective. Therefore, it is important to articulate a theory of change that specifies the mediating processes leading to improved functioning, and then to assess whether these mediators are associated with changes in functioning. The intervention described by Wolchik and colleagues (1993) is a model for this approach. In addition to suggesting why or what aspect of an intervention was effective, attention to this issue can provide information on why an intervention did not work. This, in turn, offers clues about aspects of the intervention that need modification. In a similar vein, including integrity checks in the design of the study is important to ensure that the intervention was delivered as specified and facilitates understanding of the intervention process.

The choice of mediating processes to include in interventions can be informed by basic research, but mediational analyses in intervention research also can inform our general understanding of how children adapt to divorce. Assessing mediators in an intervention provides the opportunity to test conclusions drawn from basic research. Because experimental designs are not possible in this area of research, data from studies of divorce cannot be used to infer causal relationships between factors such as conflict between parents and child problems. However, intervention studies can be viewed as quasi-experimental designs in which changes in mediators can be linked to changes in adjustment. Although the factors that maintain disorder are not necessarily those that caused the disorder, showing that changes in a mediator lead to changes in adjustment can support causal hypotheses.

BROADENING THE SCOPE OF INTERVENTIONS

Because family processes play a major role in shaping children's adjustment to divorce, interventions that include at least one and preferably both parents are likely to have a broader impact than those involving only children. Involving both parents in interventions is more difficult to implement for practical reasons as there are no natural settings (parallel to schools for children) where ex-spouses can be found. In addition, it may be most effective to involve divorcing couples in interventions before children develop adjustment problems.

Perhaps the most effective way to prevent problems is to involve parents in an intervention focused on improving conflict resolution skills and cooperative parenting at the time they file for divorce. Such considerations are similar to those that have motivated the emergence of mediation programs in the context of divorce (see Emery, 1995). However, our suggestion is not limited to promoting communication and conflict management for the purpose of making mutually agreed arrangements regarding finances and/or child-related matters (as in mediation). Rather, the idea is to better equip parents for the task of being partners in the business of parenting (an implicit consideration in much of the mediation literature). Thus, we are suggesting that the role of the professional is closer to that of a therapist than of a mediator. Making participation in such a program court-mandated would provide access to all couples and ensure that couples at least have access to information that can help their children and the opportunity to gain guidance in the implementation of that knowledge. Programs that provide parents information (many are court-mandated) already exist (e.g., Kramer & Washoe, 1993), but they tend to be very brief (often 1–2 sessions) and do not speak adequately to parents' needs.

Because there is a widespread view that providing divorcing parents with information is beneficial for children, it is important to examine the assumptions on which such a belief is based. One assumption is that telling parents what is harmful for their children is equivalent to providing information about what is beneficial. This is a questionable assumption because parents may not be able to infer beneficial behavior from information about harmful behavior and the factors that promote children's adaptive functioning may not, in any event, simply be the inverse of those that cause harm. Second, it is assumed that parents can easily act on the information they acquire. But information by itself does not provide parents with the skills needed to change behavior or appropriately act on the information. Where there are long-standing patterns of ineffective conflict resolution, information provision by itself is obviously insufficient. If we want parents to successfully coparent after divorce, we need to make sure they have the relevant tools to do so. This requires more effort than providing brief programs that tell them what they should not do.

Enhancing Resiliency

One positive effect child-focused interventions have had on basic research is to highlight the role that intraindividual factors can play in adapting to divorce. However, there has been an overemphasis on identifying predictors of maladjustment and not enough study of the factors that promote positive adaptation.

As noted in the previous section, mental health is not necessarily the absence of maladaptive functioning and we clearly need more research on children who cope effectively with divorce. Some subset of these children may function well because they have not been exposed to risk factors such as conflict between parents or economic deprivation, but others may have faced challenging circumstances and thrived. Studying the children who do well will not only inform theory about adaptation to divorce but will provide important information for interventions. At present, most intervention efforts target factors that promote maladaptation and this may limit the effectiveness of interventions. Like the social skills training in the CODIP group, stronger effects may be found for processes that enhance children's ability to cope with adversity than for those that attempt to eliminate problems. Such approaches also may generalize to other situations not related to the divorce, contributing to a general sense of competence and resiliency.

CONCLUSION

In this chapter, we reviewed basic research on children's adaptation to divorce and interventions designed to promote children's adaptation to divorce. This helped to identify ways in which basic research and intervention research can inform each other, an issue discussed in the last section of the chapter. Although there is still much to be learned about how children adapt to divorce, empirical research has made great strides in the identification of risk and protective factors that shape their adjustment. Divorce does not typically lead to clinical problems in children and we have an increasingly solid understanding of the conditions under which it does. This knowledge has enhanced our capacity to intervene effectively with children who experience parental divorce. Although existing programs are promising, there remains a great deal of room for improving interventions by drawing on basic research findings and for improving basic research by drawing on ideas and findings in the intervention literature. This chapter has therefore attempted to integrate more fully basic and applied research to facilitate the development and evaluation of interventions that will be optimal for children from divorced families.

REFERENCES

Allison, P. D., & Furstenberg, F. F. (1989). How marital dissolution affects children: Variation by age and sex. *Developmental Psychology, 25,* 540–549.

Alpert-Gillis, L. J., Pedro-Carroll, J. L., & Cowen, E. L. (1989). The children of divorce intervention program: Development, implementation, and evaluation of a program for young urban children. *Journal of Consulting and Clinical Psychology, 57,* 583–589.

Amato, P. R. (1993). Children's adjustment to divorce: Theories, hypotheses, and empirical support. *Journal of Marriage and the Family, 55,* 23–38.

Amato, P. R. (1994). Life-span adjustment of children to their parent's divorce. *The Future of Children: Children and Divorce, 4,* 143–164.

Amato, P. R., & Keith, B. (1991). Consequences of parental divorce for the well-being of children: A meta-analysis. *Psychological Bulletin, 110*, 26–46.

Armistead, L., McCombs, A., Forehand, R., Wierson, M., Long, N., & Fauber, R. (1990). Coping with divorce: A study of young adolescents. *Journal of Clinical Child Psychology, 19*, 79–84.

Bird, H. R. (1992). Psychotherapy with children of divorce. In J. D. O'Brien, D. J. Pilowsky, & O. W. Lewis (Eds.), *Psychotherapies with children and adolescents* (pp. 255–268). Washington, DC: American Psychiatric Press.

Bornstein, M. T., Bornstein, P. H., & Walters, H. A. (1988). Children of divorce: Empirical evaluation of a group-treatment program. *Journal of Clinical Child Psychology, 17*, 248–254.

Buchanan, C. M., Maccoby, E. E., & Dornbusch, S. M. (1991). Caught between parents: Adolescents' experience in divorced homes. *Child Development, 62*, 1008–1029.

Camara, K. A., & Resnick, G. (1989). Styles of conflict, resolution and cooperation between preschoolers divorced parents: Effects on child behavior and adjustment. *American Journal of Orthopsychiatry, 59*, 560–575.

Compas, B. E. (1987). Coping with stress during childhood and adolescence. *Psychological Bulletin, 101*, 393–403.

Compas, B. E., Malcarne, V. L., & Fondacaro, K. M. (1988). Coping with stressful events in older children and adolescents. *Journal of Consulting and Clinical Psychology, 56*, 405–411.

Cowen, E. L., Pedro-Carroll, J. L., & Alpert-Gillis, L. J. (1990). Relationships between support and adjustment among children of divorce. *Journal of Child Psychology and Psychiatry and Allied Disciplines, 31*, 727–735.

Cummings, E. M., Ballard, M., El-Sheikh, M., & Lake, M. (1991). Resolution and children's responses to interadult anger. *Developmental Psychology, 27*, 462–470.

Cummings, E. M., & Davies, P. T. (1994). *Children and marital conflict.* New York: Guilford Press.

Cummings, E. M., Vogel, D., Cummings, J. S., & El-Sheikh, M. (1989). Children's responses to different forms of expression of anger between adults. *Child Development, 60*, 1392–1404.

Duncan, G. J., & Hoffman, S. D. (1985). Economic consequences of marital instability. In M. David & T. Smeeding (Eds.), *Horizontal equity, uncertainty, and economic well-being.* Chicago: University of Chicago Press.

Emery, R. E. (1994). *Renegotiating family relationships.* New York: Guilford Press.

Emery, R. E. (1995). Divorce mediation: Negotiating agreements and renegotiating relationships. *Family Relations, 44*, 377–383.

Fogas, B., Wolchik, S., Braver, S., Freedom, D. S., et al. (1992). Locus of control as a mediator of negative divorce-related events and adjustment problems in children. *American Journal of Orthopsychiatry, 62*, 589–598.

Forehand, R., & McMahon, R. J. (1981). *Helping the noncompliant child: A clinician's guide to parent teaching.* New York: Guilford Press.

Franklin, K. M., Janoff-Bulman, R., & Roberts, J. E. (1990). Long-term impact of parental divorce on optimism and trust: Changes in general assumptions or narrow beliefs? *Journal of Personality and Social Psychology, 59*, 743–755.

Furstenberg, F. F. (1990). Divorce and the American family. *Annual Review of Sociology, 16*, 379–403.

Gardner, R. (1991). *Psychotherapy with children of divorce.* Northvale, NJ: Aronson.

Grych, J. H., & Fincham, F. D. (1990). Marital conflict and children's adjustment: A cognitive-contextual framework. *Psychological Bulletin, 108,* 267–290.

Grych, J. H., & Fincham, F. D. (1992a). Interventions for children of divorce: Toward greater integration of research and action. *Psychological Bulletin, 110,* 434–454.

Grych, J. H., & Fincham, F. D. (1992b). Marital dissolution and family adjustment: An attributional analysis. In T. Orbuch (Ed.), *Close relationship loss: Theoretical perspectives.* New York: Springer-Verlag.

Grych, J. H., & Fincham, F. D. (1993). Children's appraisals of marital conflict: Initial investigations of the cognitive contextual framework. *Child Development, 64,* 215–230.

Grych, J. H., & Fincham, F. D. (1997). Children's adaptation to divorce: From description to explanation. In I. N. Sandler & S. A. Wolchik (Eds.), *Handbook of children's coping with common stressors: Linking theory and intervention* (pp. 159–194). New York: Plenum Press.

Guidubaldi, J., Perry, J. D., & Nastasi, B. K. (1987). Assessment and intervention for children of divorce: Implications of the NASP-KSU nationwide survey. In J. Vincent (Ed.), *Advances in family intervention, assessment, and theory* (Vol. 4, pp. 33–69). Greenwich, CT: JAI Press.

Healy, J. M., Stewart, A. J., & Copeland, A. P. (1993). The role of self-blame in children's adjustment to parental separation. *Personality and Social Psychology Bulletin, 19,* 279–289.

Hess, R. D., & Camara, K. A. (1979). Post-divorce relationships as mediating factors in the consequences of divorce for children. *Journal of Social Issues, 35,* 79–96.

Hetherington, E. M. (1989). Coping with family transitions: Winners, losers, and survivors. *Child Development, 60,* 1–14.

Hetherington, E. M. (1993). An overview of the Virginia longitudinal study of divorce and remarriage with a focus on early adolescence. *Journal of Family Psychology, 7,* 39–56.

Hetherington, E. M., Clingempeel, W. G., Anderson, E. R., Deal, J. E., Hagen, M. S., Holier, E. A., & Linder, M. S. (1992). Coping with marital transitions: A family systems perspective. *Monographs of the Society for Research in Child Development, 57.*

Hetherington, E. M., Cox, M., & Cox, R. (1982). Effects of divorce on parents and children. In M. Lamb (Ed.), *Nontraditional families* (pp. 233–288). Hillsdale, NJ: Erlbaum.

Hodges, W. F. (1991). *Interventions for children of divorce: Custody, access, and psychotherapy* (2nd ed.). New York: Wiley.

Kalter, N., Pickar, J., & Lesowitz, M. (1984). School-based developmental facilitation groups for children of divorce: A preventive intervention. *American Journal of Orthopsychiatry, 54,* 613–623.

Kalter, N., Schaefer, M., Lesowitz, M., Alpern, D., & Pickar, J. (1988). School-based support groups for children of divorce. In B. H. Gottlieb (Ed.), *Martialing social support: Formats, processes and effects* (pp. 165–185). Newbury Park, CA: Sage.

Kelly, J. B. (1988). Longer-term adjustment in children of divorce: Converging findings and implications for practice. *Journal of Family Psychology, 2,* 119–140.

Kinnaird, K. L., & Gerrard, M. (1986). Premarital sexual behavior and attitudes toward marriage and divorce among young women as a function of their mothers' marital status. *Journal of Marriage and the Family, 48,* 757–765.

Kliewer, W., & Sandler, I. N. (1993). Social competence and coping among children of divorce. *American Journal of Orthopsychiatry, 63,* 432–440.

Kramer, L., & Washoe, C. A. (1993). Evaluation of a court mandated prevention program for divorcing parents: The children first program. *Family Relations, 42,* 179–186.

Krantz, S. E., Clark, J., Pruyn, J. P., & Usher, M. (1985). Cognition and adjustment among children of separated or divorced parents. *Cognitive Therapy and Research, 9,* 61–77.

Kurdek, L. A., & Berg, B. (1983). Correlates of children's adjustment to their parent's divorces. In L. A. Kurdek (Ed.), *New directions in child development: Vol. 19. Children and divorce* (pp. 47–60). San Francisco: Jossey-Bass.

Kurdek, L. A., & Berg, B. (1987). Children's beliefs about parental divorce scale: Psychometric characteristics and concurrent validity. *Journal of Consulting and Clinical Psychology, 55,* 712–718.

Kurdek, L. A., Blisk, D., & Siesky, A. E. (1981). Correlates of children's long-term adjustment to their parent's divorce. *Developmental Psychology, 17,* 565–579.

Lazarus, R. S., & Folkman, S. (1984). *Stress, appraisal, and coping.* New York: Springer.

Lee, C. M., Picard, M., & Blain, M. D. (1994). Methodological and substantive review of intervention outcome studies for families undergoing divorce. *Journal of Family Psychology, 8,* 3–15.

Lustig, J. L., Wolchik, S. A., & Braver, S. L. (1992). Social support in chumships and adjustment in children of divorce. *American Journal of Community Psychology, 20,* 393–399.

Maccoby, E. E., Buchanan, C. M., Mnookin, R. H., & Dornbusch, S. M. (1993). Postdivorce roles of mothers and fathers in the lives of their children. *Journal of Family Psychology, 7,* 24–38.

Maccoby, E. E., Depner, C. E., & Mnookin, R. H. (1990). Coparenting in the second year after divorce. *Journal of Marriage and the Family, 52,* 141–155.

Mazur, E., Wolchik, S. A., & Sandler, I. N. (1992). Negative cognitive errors and positive illusions for negative divorce events: Predictors of children's psychological adjustment. *Journal of Abnormal Child Psychology, 20,* 523–542.

Neal, J. H. (1983). Children's understanding of their parents' divorce. In L. A. Kurdek (Ed.), *Children and divorce* (pp. 3–14). San Francisco: Jossey-Bass.

Patterson, G. R. (1975). *Families: Applications of social learning to family life.* Champaign, IL: Research Press.

Pedro-Carroll, J. L., Alpert-Gillis, L. J., & Cowen, E. L. (1992). An evaluation of the efficacy of a preventive intervention for 4th–6th grade urban children of divorce. *Journal of Primary Prevention, 13,* 115–130.

Pedro-Carroll, J. L., & Cowen, E. L. (1985). The children of divorce intervention program: An investigation of the efficacy of a school-based prevention program. *Journal of Consulting and Clinical Psychology, 53,* 603–611.

Pedro-Carroll, J. L., Cowen, E. L., Hightower, A. D., & Guare, J. C. (1986). Preventive intervention with latency-aged children of divorce: A replication study. *American Journal of Community Psychology, 14,* 277–289.

Peterson, J. L., & Zill, N. (1986). Marital disruption, parent-child relationships, and behavior problems in children. *Journal of Marriage and the Family, 48,* 295–307.

Pillow, D. R., Sandler, I. N., Braver, S. L., Wolchik, S. A., & Gersten, J. C. (1991). Theory-based screening for prevention: Focusing on mediating processes in children of divorce. *American Journal of Community Psychology, 9,* 809–836.

Roseby, V., & Deutsch, R. (1985). Children of separation and divorce: Effects of a social-role taking group intervention on fourth and fifth graders. *Journal of Clinical Child Psychology, 14,* 55–60.

Rutter, M. (1983). Stress, coping, and development: Some issues and some questions. In N. Garmezey & M. Rutter (Eds.), *Stress, coping, and development in children* (pp. 1–41). New York: McGraw-Hill.

Sandler, I. N., Tein, J., & West, S. G. (1994). Coping, stress and the psychological symptoms of children of divorce: A cross sectional and longitudinal study. *Child Development, 65,* 1744–1763.

Sandler, I. N., Wolchik, S. A., & Braver, S. L. (1988). The stressors of children's post-divorce environments. In S. A. Wolchik & P. Karoly (Eds.), *Children of divorce: Empirical perspectives on adjustment* (pp. 185–232). New York: Gardner Press.

Sandler, I. N., Wolchik, S. A., Braver, S. L., & Fogas, B. (1991). Stability and quality of life events and psychological symptomatology in children of divorce. *American Journal of Community Psychology, 19,* 501–520.

Shaw, D. S., Emery, R. E., & Tuer, M. D. (1993). Parental functioning and children's adjustment in families of divorce: A prospective study. *Journal of Abnormal Child Psychology, 21,* 119–134.

Soldano, K. (1990). Divorce: Clinical implications for the treatment of children. In B. D. Garfinkel, G. A. Carlson, & E. B. Weller (Eds.), *Psychiatric disorders in children and adolescents* (pp. 392–409). Philadelphia: Saunders.

Sprenkle, D. H., & Storm, C. L. (1983). Divorce therapy outcome research: A substantive and methodological review. *Journal of Marital and Family Therapy, 9,* 239–258.

Stolberg, A. L., & Anker, J. M. (1983). Cognitive and behavioral changes in children resulting from parental divorce and consequent environmental changes. *Journal of Divorce, 7,* 23–41.

Stolberg, A. L., & Garrison, K. M. (1985). Evaluating a primary prevention program for children of divorce: The divorce adjustment project. *American Journal of Community Psychology, 13,* 111–124.

Stolberg, A. L., & Mahler, J. (1994). Enhancing treatment gains in a school-based intervention for children of divorce through skill training, parental involvement, and transfer procedures. *Journal of Consulting and Clinical Psychology, 62,* 147–156.

Sweet, J. A., & Bumpass, L. L. (1992). Disruption of marital and cohabitation relationships: A social demographic perspective. In T. Orbuch (Ed.), *Close relationship loss: Theoretical perspectives* (pp. 67–89). New York: Springer-Verlag.

Wallerstein, J. S. (1991). The long-term effects of divorce on children: A review. *Journal of the Academy of Child and Adolescent Psychiatry, 30,* 349–360.

Wallerstein, J. S., & Kelly, J. B. (1980). *Surviving the breakup: How children actually cope with divorce.* New York: Basic Books.

Walsh, P. E., & Stolberg, A. L. (1989). Parental and environmental determinants of children's behavioral, affective, and cognitive adjustment to divorce. *Journal of Divorce, 12,* 265–282.

Warshak, R. A., & Santrock, J. W. (1983). The impact of divorce in father custody and mother-custody homes: The child's perspective. In L. A. Kurdek (Ed.), *Children and divorce* (pp. 29–46). San Francisco: Jossey-Bass.

Wolchik, S. A., Ruelhman, L. S., Braver, S. L., & Sandler, I. N. (1989). Social support of children of divorce: Direct and stress buffering effects. *American Journal of Community Psychology, 17,* 485–501.

Wolchik, S. A., Sandler, I. N., Braver, S. L., & Fogas, B. (1989). Events of parental divorce: Stressfulness ratings by children, parents, and clinicians. *American Journal of Community Psychology, 14,* 59–74.

Wolchik, S. A., West, S. G., Westover, S., Sandler, I. N., Martin, A., Lustig, J., Tein, J., & Fisher, J. (1993). The children of divorce parenting intervention: Outcome evaluation of an empirically-based program. *American Journal of Community Psychology, 21,* 293–331.

Zill, N. (1978). *Divorce, marital happiness, and the mental health of children: Findings from the FCD national survey of children.* Paper presented at the NIMH Workshop on Divorce and Children, Bethesda, MD.

CHAPTER 7

The Contribution of Psychological Tests to Custody-Relevant Evaluations

BARRY BRICKLIN

THE SCIENTIFIC BASES OF PSYCHOLOGICAL TESTS AND DECISION MAKING

S INCE FORMAL ASSESSMENT has been a core component in the psychologist's training, psychological tests have likely been used for comprehensive custody evaluations—rightly or wrongly as we will see—since the very first psychologists were asked to perform them. Over the years (from pre- to post-1986), there has been an increase in the number of psychologists who use tests in custody evaluations (from about 70% to 91%) and a shift in which tests are most frequently used, because in the mid-1980s, custody-specific tests appeared (Ackerman & Ackerman, 1997).

One thing should be made clear at the outset. Not even the most ardent test advocates believes tests should ever be used by themselves to make ultimate custody recommendations. (For an interesting point of view that there indeed may be circumstances in which one *would* rely on data from a single test, see Cizek, 1994.)

The author would like to express appreciation to the following individuals who assisted in the preparation of this chapter: Marc Ackerman, Ph.D.; Gail Elliot, Ph.D.; Michael Halbert; Paul W. Schenk, Ph.D.; Amy Altenhaus, Ph.D.

Those of us who have developed custody-specific-tests (Ackerman & Schoendorf, 1992; Bricklin, 1984, 1989, 1995) are sometimes challenged about our use of tests to address custody decisions. However, this is to confuse a *description* of how those tests are validated—by checking their accuracy in predicting which parent is the better candidate for primary custodial or residential parent compared with other ways of making such decisions—with a *pre*scription for how they should be used in the real psycholegal world. Neither Ackerman, Schoendorf, nor I advocate the use of any single instrument to make a custody decision.

Psychological tests *can assist* the custody decision maker in many ways. These include the elicitation of data relevant to (a) the degree of potential cooperativeness between the parents, to help decide such issues as the probability that mediation or joint parenting can be successful; (b) who should be designated the primary legal decision maker for the child (Both parents? One parent only? Neither?); (c) the creation of a time-sharing plan that optimizes the child's exposure to parental assets and minimizes exposure to parental liabilities.

A decision maker must think about the "scientific basis" of a psychological test within a broader general model of decision making. An often hidden but serious problem is not in deciding whether a test's data are scientific, but whether they are *relevant* for a particular decision. In this chapter, we show that the information needed to address this issue lies in the specific, often buried, details of how a test was validated, not in the usually quoted statistical indices of its scientific (i.e., psychometric) properties. Further, the total value to a decision maker of *any* source of information, including a test score, can never be known even if one is aware of its psychometric properties *and* has a solid grasp of its relevance for a specific decision. The full value can only be known if one knows how it compares with competing scores of available information. For example, in a custody case, the decision maker is often forced to wonder about how to compare the merits of a test score with modest accuracy against say, interview responses, which typically have poor and/or unknown credibility and accuracy (Ekman, 1992; Ekman & O'Sullivan, 1991; Grove & Meehl, 1996).

The scientific, or psychometric properties of a test refer to the degree to which: trained examiners can agree on how the test items are to be scored; obtained scores approximate (hypothetical) "true" scores (usually expressed by a score's stability over time); the scores can predict certain, specific outcomes; a person who takes the test matches the reference population used to generate the test scores. The last item refers to the confidence that a test measure can be used in regard to some particular person. Data from a psychological test can be valuable in ways unrelated to the test's psychometric properties. This happens when the evaluator is more interested in *how a respondent addresses and copes with the tasks of the test*, than in the numerical values attained. These, often highly idiosyncratic, coping styles may reveal themselves on the so-called projective tests (e.g., *Thematic Apperception Test* or *House-Tree-Person Test*) or on more formal and structured tests (e.g., intelligence tests). The practice of using information not referenced against a published database is called "idiographic" (pertaining to an individual in some unique way, or comparing a person's responses only with his or her own responses) rather than "nomothetic" (comparing a person's responses with those of a standard group). The latter is generally considered more scientific.

Keep in mind that when using a test to pinpoint how a respondent approaches a task rather than to discover some formal score, one is still dealing with a response pattern that is at least *potentially encodable*, and therefore subject to a nomothetic approach. Even a process that is truly idiographic (a person's performance is compared with other aspects of his or her own performance instead of with a reference group) can be encoded and tracked for accuracy-of-prediction. Suppose a person's past history suggests a high level of intelligence. Currently, the person shows inferior thinking skills. This could be very important information. Suppose further, however, that the current behavior which is "low" for this person is still quite "high" for others. If one only referenced this low-for-the-individual piece of behavior against a "normal" group (as may happen on a psychological test given a single time), this important change could go undetected.

Note that even complex scenarios like this can be potentially encoded and tracked for their predictive powers. Regardless of the source for any piece of information (nomothetic *or idiographic*), the critical aspect to a decision maker is understanding how the predictive value of the information is being established.

Decision makers should be aware that many tests can yield important information that is unrelated to their psychometric properties. However, decision makers must still question how the evaluator *can demonstrate* the predictive capabilities of the information. (For more on this often critically consequential issue—which often is the subject of furious arguments in courtrooms—see Nemeth, 1995.)

And because the value to a decision maker of a psychological test score has to do with much more than the degree to which the test and its scores were developed according to the tenets of good science, the focus here will be more on value-to-the-decision-maker than scientific requisites for their own sake. A test's scientific merits are only the beginning of a consideration of its usefulness.

PSYCHOLOGICAL TESTS AND CUSTODY ISSUES

The value of a psychological test score cannot be assessed unless the decision maker has a clear, explicit notion of what he or she wants to know. Before beginning to think about the value of a test score, the decision maker must define the outcome situations it would be useful to predict in a custody-relevant situation. The only value of a test score is to increase the confidence of a decision maker in predicting the differential likelihood of important future situations.

If the decision maker lacks a clear idea of what needs predicting, there is no way this value can be ascertained. For example, one of the most vexing problems facing legal decision makers is choosing a primary custodial parent. The "outcome situation" the decision maker must predict is the primary custodial parent whose care will provide for the child's "best interests." But what are the specific characteristics of a situation "in a child's best interests?" The child lives in nested and hierarchical family systems. It is often hard to discern what is "best" for a child in such systems. Older son A is a better match for Dad, while younger children B and C for Mom. But B and C are highly dependent on their older brother's presence. Who should sacrifice what for the sake of whom is often not clear.

Summarizing, the decision maker has two separate tasks. One is to consider the statistical properties of a test (described later). The other is to make sure a test is able to predict the outcome situations in which the decision maker is interested.

WHAT IS A PSYCHOLOGICAL TEST?

There are two broad categories of assessment procedures called "psychological tests." One includes precisely defined and highly systematized methods for making inferences that are based on the constructions of standard procedural models. A given model allows the accumulation of a database against which new information can be calibrated and understood. The other category includes less formal methods (e.g., judgment index numbers made from observation sessions). Most test developers aspire to create tools that fall in the former category.

A psychological test gathers information very differently than a clinical interview. It involves highly concrete and detailed procedures for collecting prespecified samples of information. The interpretation of the information is always with reference to a previously examined standardization group.

EVALUATING THE SCIENTIFIC BASIS AND VALUE OF PSYCHOLOGICAL TEST SCORES

Science can be described as a process which includes the creation and definition of a concept, the delineation of the empirical equivalents of that concept (i.e., what one looks for in the "real" sensory world that exemplifies the concept), the formation of principles (which describe or predict the relationships among the concepts) and validation of principles. The usefulness of formulated concepts along with hypothesized or discovered principles are validated when the correspondence between empirical referents in the real world match what is predicted by the principles (Piotrowski, 1957, pp. 12–23).

The development of a psychological test begins with the formulation and definition of a concept believed to be important. "Intelligence," "depression," and "good custody arrangements" are all examples of concepts. The developer then creates a pool or sample of items that are believed to measure the concept. Principles enter the picture when the developer more specifically formulates ideas as to what the test scores (which reflect the concept) could help to predict or understand. Validation studies seek to demonstrate that a specific test concept constitutes a useful way to describe and/or understand situations in the real world by sharpening the definition of the empirical equivalents of the concept, and/or proving that a particular test of that concept can result in useful predictions of other concepts.

For example, "intelligence" is believed to be a useful concept. Its empirical equivalents would be those behaviors in the real world that exemplify it. The latter would also guide the selection of test items. If, say, overall "school performance" is another concept, a principle (which defines relations among concepts) might predict that the higher the intelligence, the higher the school performance. Validation would involve proving that the empirical equivalents of intelligence, which might be exemplified by test behaviors, are associated with high levels of the empirical equivalents of school performance (scores on daily tests, grade-point average, etc.). Because all these conditions can be met to greater or lesser degrees, a test should not necessarily be described as "scientific" or "not scientific." Instead, we should ask the extent to which a test is scientific. Science seeks to create ways to look at and predict aspects of the world such that it is possible to at least roughly delineate the accuracy of specific predictions. A test is more scientific than a clinical interview because we can specify exactly how the procedure was developed, how it is to be administered, and the degree of trust that can be placed in its predictions.

Thus a test procedure can be very scientific, but not necessarily useful in a specific decision-required situation. The decision maker can best decide the value of test scores by understanding how tests are developed. Then the decision maker has a uniform way to compare competing sources of information. The psychometric numbers reported for a test are never enough to judge its value. The decision maker also needs to assess relevance and how the test information compares with competing sources of information (see Chapter 3).

TYPICAL TEST DEVELOPMENT

Tests are usually made up of *many* samples of the behaviors deemed to exemplify a useful concept. This is *one* of the reasons Cizek believes it is reasonable, in some instances, to rely on the results of a single test (Cizek, 1994). (We only need one accurate thermometer to measure a fever. But a dozen high-precision thermometers will not accurately measure blood pressure.)

The responses a test seeks of an individual can come in a huge number of informational forms (e.g., auditory, visual, kinesthetic, spoken words, tester observations, respondent body movements).

Test items believed to sample the involved concept are assembled, and they are administered in a standard way to a pool (or pools) of respondents. Various statistical procedures may be used to fine-tune the eventual lineup of items to be retained for a "final" (most tests are continually revised, so they are never really final) version of the test. The statistical procedures used to fine-tune the retained items may, depending on the concept the test developer wants to measure, aim at selecting "homogeneous" items (test items that share high correlations with a test's overall scores) or heterogeneous items (test items that share lower correlations with the test's overall scores).

After a final version of the test is assembled, it is typically administered to new groups of individuals. Measures of reliability and validity are determined (these terms are defined later in this section). Basically, they refer to the stability of the scores over time and between testers and how well the scores measure what they claim to measure. A test manual is printed. The manual should tell how the conceptual target of the test was defined, why it is assumed this conceptual target is useful, the principles that led to the choice of test items, the (standard) manner in which the test is to be administered, the categories into which responses are to be classified, and how to interpret information generated by the test. This last includes specifying the range of individuals to whom the test is appropriately administered, information on the stability of test scores over time, and the outcomes the test's scores might successfully predict.

Checklist of Ways to Consider the Value of a Psychological Test Score

1. The decision maker should understand the conceptual target that a test score aims to measure.
2. The decision maker should consider whether information about this conceptual target, even if highly accurate, would influence the decision. If the answer is it would not, there is no reason to analyze a score's value. If there *is* room for influence, the decision maker should consider how relevant and accurate the test scores need to be for a given score to have value in the overall decision scheme, and consider trade-offs between these two areas. For example, how is a very accurate intelligence test score showing one potential primary care parent is much brighter than the other to be weighed against a less accurate but more relevant test score showing that one parent has a better knowledge of the child's interests?
3. The decision maker should consider whether the person to whom the test was administered is sufficiently similar to the members of the standardization group(s). There is no easy formula here, since one could endlessly challenge the matchup between a respondent and the people in a normative group (e.g., "Yes, I know the respondent matches the group in age, gender, socioeconomic status and race, but this child is

extremely tall. Maybe tall children are psychologically different than other children, so these norms would not apply. How many children as tall as this child were in your sample?" The "robustness" of a test is the degree to which it is possible to depart from its assumptive structure and still obtain valid results. This is seldom known. If the family comes from a substantially different socioeconomic background than the standardization group, the decision maker should carefully think through how this is likely to affect test scores.

4. The decision maker should consider whether the test manual delineates an exact way the test is to be administered, and whether or not the person who administered the test followed its instructions. The decision maker should consider the precision of conclusions derived from the test score. If they are open to wide interpretation, the qualifications of the test interpreter become quite important.

5. The decision maker should consider whether the test results could be "faked" or manipulated. The critical question is not simply if this is so, but whether the examiner can spot such events, and reasonably compensate for them.

6. The decision maker should be familiar with a number of statistical devices that are commonly used to describe a test's performance in particular situations. Remember, it is not a test itself that is being described or evaluated, but its use in specific situations. The critical question is whether the validation and previous use of the test have generated a database by means of which a score can address a specific (predictive) issue. For shorthand, when we speak about the statistical characteristics of a test, we are referring to its use for specific purposes. The checklist items that follow define and describe the measures that will most commonly be encountered in reference to the performance of any given test.

   Since the two most important statistical things to know about the scores yielded by a test are their reliability and validity, it is helpful for the decision maker to understand what a correlation number is, since this is the statistical device most commonly used to express reliability and validity information. (Note: the legal system uses the term "reliability" very differently than mental health professionals.) For mental health professionals, reliability usually refers only to the stability of test scores over time, whereas in law, the term implies both stability *and* accuracy. Mental health professionals use the term "validity" to refer to agreement with a criterion (accuracy data).

7. A correlation number expresses the degree of association between two variables. It shows the intensity and direction of the relationship. The strength of a relationship is shown by the size of the correlation coefficient; the maximum value possible is 1.00, a perfect correlation. A positive or negative sign is used to indicate the direction of an association. When the sign is positive (+), or omitted, a high score on one measure is

associated with a high score on the other, while a negative sign (–) denotes an inverse relationship.

Whether reporting on reliability or validity, correlations of .80 and up indicate a strong association between the variables. The higher the correlation numbers, the more accurately scores on one variable can be predicted from information about the other variable.

8. Reliability figures address the internal consistency of the test items, whether the items might result in bias when used with special populations, the degree of agreement between raters, and the stability of test scores over time intervals. The latter is the most frequent concern. One way to think about this is in terms of the extent to which a person's test scores change over time when the "real" value of the measured variable (a statistical invention) is not changing.

   A problem with determining the reliability of psychological measures is that when scores change it is impossible to tell whether a test is yielding unreliable information, or there was a change in the underlying variable. If a test's scores seem to change without other relevant changes in a respondent's world that could explain the changes, the meaningfulness of the measure becomes more doubtful.

9. *Factor analysis*, another term the decision maker may encounter, is a mathematical procedure used to explore the underlying structure of data, including groups of tests. It assumes a set of underlying unobservable factors accounts for correlations among tests or variables. Factor analytic results are expressed as the amount (percentage) of total variance that can be attributed to a factor. Factor analysis is complex. The same data can produce different results depending on decisions made concerning the choice of factor analytic methods.

10. Validity, the most critical for a decision maker to understand, represents the degree to which a test is measuring what it aims to measure. A test with consistently good validity *must* have good reliability figures. The reverse is not true. Validity is typically given in a form, often a correlation coefficient, that tells the degree of association between the test scores and predicted standard outcome measures. A *test* is not valid or invalid. *Its scores can be assessed for validity only in regard to specific purposes and specific predictions.* The decision maker may encounter several forms of validity.

   - *Content validity*, based largely on experts' opinions, refers to the degree to which test items are seen as sampling the test's conceptual target. This term is frequently used interchangeably, but incorrectly, with *face validity*. The latter refers to what a test appears to measure. Face validity may be important in the sense that it inspires confidence in an individual taking the test. It is not a scientific necessity nor, for that matter, is content validity—so long as predictive validity holds up. The *Bricklin Perceptual Scales* (BPS) is made up of 64 items measuring a child's perception of each parent in 32 custody-relevant areas. Content validity is based on the fact that these items were selected on the basis of the judgments of psychological and legal experts in the areas (the items were derived from statutory guidelines, case law, family development experts, ect.).

- *Criterion-related validity* is the most important kind of validity information. It tells how well test scores predict something external to the test. Concurrent criterion-related validity describes the degree of association between the test scores and currently available external criteria; *predictive criterion validity* describes the test score's relation to future outcomes. The concurrent validity of the BPS is demonstrated by comparing the test's suggestions for primary custodial parents by those arrived at by mental health professionals based on two to seven years' worth of family therapy notes plus decisions of courtroom judges, and so on. To date, there are no custody test scores that have been compared with future outcomes. Reasons for this are given later in this chapter.

- *Construct validity* refers to how well a test measures a particular concept. It is empirically established over time based on experience with the test. "Good" construct validity means the test scores continuously achieve high positive correlations with other conceptual targets where the correlation should be positive, and negative correlations with targets where a negative relation would be expected. For example, if the BPS can suggest which parent is the better primary custodial parent, one would expect its scores to consistently achieve positive agreement rates with criteria of good child health when the child spends time with this parent. One would expect to find negative correlations between good BPS scores for a particular parent, and signs of *poor* health in that child when spending time with the parent.

Practical knowledge of how a test is validated is the most important information for a decision maker. Only with this information can the decision maker establish the relevance of a test score to what he or she wishes to predict or understand. (When the decision maker lacks the technical knowledge to assess this question, reliance on experts is essential. A competent expert is one who realizes that the most important facet of validity is in the relevance of the external criterion with which the test's predictions were compared.)

For example, if a test aims to predict or choose which of two parents would be the better match-up for a particular child as primary custodial parent, then the decision maker should inspect all the ways the test was validated to see if the external criteria studies used to demonstrate validity employed sensible methods (other than the test) to choose the better primary custodial parents. The decision maker might ask him- or herself: "If I didn't have the test scores, only the choices arrived at by the methods that were used in the external criteria study, would I feel comfortable that good choices were made?"

A test, no matter how prestigious, is only valuable to a decision maker insofar as it validly measures matters pertinent to the decision. Since this is such a critical issue, an example will be offered. When we developed our data-based tests, we used several different methods to show that the test scores were helpful in deciding which parent would be the better choice to be the primary custodial parent. The conceptual targets of the tests would have to make sense, the test would have to show appropriate reliability, and the test had to be capable of standard administration and scoring. Most important was that the criteria used in the validity studies be sensible. Here are some ways the test choices for primary custodial parent were validated: (a) agreement rates between test choices and those independently based on all clinical and life history data; (b) agreement rates for primary custodial parent choices between different but conceptually similar tests; (c) agreement rates between test choices and those of courtroom judges; (d) agreement rates between test choices and those made by several independent mental health professionals, based on their review of two to seven years of family therapy notes for given families, and consultation with the therapists.

Were I a legal decision maker, I would consider the last piece of information by far the most compelling. Ongoing and extensive family therapy sessions of *intact* families where no one has any reason to dissimulate on a regular basis, is perhaps the only forum in which parents and children will eventually act spontaneously, and reveal what actually happens in real life. Here, the therapy notes reflect actual interactions, from which the trained experts could glean data about which of the two parents the child viewed as being most helpful and supportive, who the child turned to for advice, and from whom the child sought solace when distressed. Such a setting is perhaps the closest we can come to recreating life-in-the-trenches, as it occurs on a day-to-day basis. (Although any individual therapist who recorded the interactions would not necessarily know which of them are most custody-relevant, the experts who reviewed the records would.)

In validity studies the devil is in the details. It is in these details that a decision maker can discover whether a test can predict the kinds of situations in which the decision maker is interested.

11. Finally, the value of a test score can only be fully known when the decision maker compares the quality (e.g., precision, etc., of the test information) with the quality of competing sources of available information, especially when there is disagreement in the recommendations flowing from the different sources. This forces a decision maker to think through

his opinion about information that has *known databases* with which to assess its usefulness, compared with information lacking such formal databases (e.g., interview data, observational data). The easiest scenario for the decision maker is when all or most of the information available leads to the same conclusions; the preceding issues become more critical when they do not. When this happens, the decision maker should explore the source of divergence. Were there special, unusual circumstances that were not addressed in the tests? Was the interview too narrowly focused? Were tests adequately performed? Were observation data gathered with a standardized protocol? The decision maker should have a clear picture of the sources of divergent opinion.

VALIDITY CHALLENGES IN CUSTODY MATTERS

Let us look at how validity issues apply to custody evaluations. There are conceptual/definitional complexities and measurement/methodological difficulties.

To show a test predicts which parent is better for a child, evaluators need to agree on *meanings* for quality of life and *indices* of quality of life. Is a nervously achieving child a better or worse outcome than a contented underachiever? Are many, but superficial, friends better or worse than a child's having one "best" friend? Is school attendance an appropriate measure of how well a child is doing? Or is it that some parents will not let a child stay home from school even if the child is ill, say because it is too much trouble for the parent to have a child at home during a school day? In almost any real-life situation, there is room for debate about how it reflects the child's overall well-being.

Furthermore, can we find forecasting predictors hardy enough to withstand the chaotic and unpredictable changes that follow divorce? Suppose a custody test shows mom is the better choice to be primary custodial parent for a given child. Four months later, she marries an angry and mean-spirited man. What was a good mother-child match may no longer be even a tolerable one. In the years following divorce, a child can find him- or herself with a new stepparent, new stepsiblings, a new school, a new neighborhood—each of which may be very supportive or toxic for the child. Especially during contested custody proceedings, parents are often at the nadir of their psychological and parental functioning, so evaluations of all kinds are even less likely to be good predictors of ongoing function than they usually are.

Some might claim it is perhaps too much to expect any test to have truly future-oriented predictive power, given the wildly swirling and often suddenly shifting conditions the postdivorce child faces. Perhaps *concurrent* criterion-related validity is all we can reasonably hope for in custody cases (correlating test predictions with currently available data). Even commonsense experience tells us that some parents who are placid and relaxed with young children may be nervous and irritable with older ones. Maybe this is why one of the best textbooks on custody evaluations (Schutz, Dixon, Lindenberger, & Ruther, 1989) describes its system as descriptive, not predictive. One might mistakenly conclude that in the chaos of the postdivorce world, it is not only in practical terms, *but theoretically impossible* to develop a predictive child custody test.

This gloomy state of affairs does not, however, seem to be the case. The *Bricklin Perceptual Scales* (Bricklin, 1984) for example, yields choices for primary custodial parent that manifest good predictive accuracy *and* reasonable stability. Reasonable stability means that if a score shows a marked change over time, there should be obvious reasons to explain the shift (e.g., a new stepparent, relocation, etc.). But two important points need to be made.

First, if a test targets the optimality of parent-child dyads, that target is much less stable than, say, intelligence.

Second, despite this, the measurement challenges are similar. Whether one deals with a conceptual target like "intelligence," which appears stable, or the "goodness" of a parent-child matchup, which conceptually is less stable, the evaluator must know under what conditions a score might change over time. Few things (e.g., brain trauma; greatly changed educational opportunities, etc.) shift IQ over time. Many things can change the optimality of parent-child congruence including continuing or heightened levels of parental conflict, a new live-in companion or stepparent, a new parent boy- or girlfriend, a changing child developmental level, a new home or new friends, a new school, a newly abusive sibling.

Typical measures of the stability of a test prediction over time—the reliability coefficient—do not address this area of concern. *Good evaluator judgment will remain critical.*

Returning to a consideration of conceptual and definitional challenges of validity studies, we must wonder: *What is the definition* of a custodial parent? One who spends 100%, 90%, 80% . . ?? of available time with the child? On this same topic, but from a methodological rather than conceptual perspective, how many parents actually follow with any precision a mandated or agreed-on custody plan to begin with? Not many.

The biggest problem of a validity study might be solvable in a "quantum world" where time flows in many directions and we can run the clock back and start over with a different custody arrangement.

A test is administered and the decision is made that the father is the better choice for primary custodial parent. The child lives predominantly with the father for one year. Let's pretend we have agreed on quality-of-life measures, and a team now comes in and evaluates the child. He is doing very well. Was the test prediction correct? Was it indeed the better choice for the child to spend most of his or her time with dad? The only way we could really know is if we could now roll the hands of time backward and have the child spend a year with the mother. In the absence of such data, we cannot really evaluate the prediction.

But since time cannot as yet be rolled backward, perhaps we can use a less strict definition of a "good prediction" at some follow-up interval (e.g., "The child shall at least be doing as well as he or she was doing when the prediction was made"). Would this be acceptable proof that the prediction was accurate? (It may be possible to find and test a sample wherein various judges assign children equally to test-predicted, and nonpredicted, parents. This is a tall order and involves complex ethical issues, but it probably can be done.) Not surprisingly then, in all the years that psychological tests have been used in custody cases, the only validity studies (Bricklin, 1984, 1989, plus all test manual supplements; Ackerman & Schoendorf, 1992) have used criterion-related concurrent, not predictive, validity information.

Another challenge manifests in equal measure conceptual *and* methodological problems. When a test developer introduces a new concept (see Bricklin, 1995, pp. 54–73), its validity cannot be proven by correlations with existing tests, since none exist that measure the concept. New and possibly innovative validational techniques are required.

Finally, some experts (Krauss & Sales, in press) argue that it is not only practically difficult but *theoretically impossible* to validate predictive child custody tests because there is no legally accepted definition of the "best interests of the child standard," and for practical and conceptual reasons, there may never be such a definition. Hence there is no way to define the outcome one is seeking to predict.

However, this argument places far too restrictive a noose around the notion of "validity." There is nothing in science that says a definition of a concept (e.g., "intelligence"; "cultural fairness") must be accepted by every segment of society before it can be useful. Whether predictions made on such bases would be accepted in court is *not a scientific issue*, and in any event, remains to be determined. Further, if one divides the custody evaluation task into two categories—choosing the legal custodian(s), devising a time-share plan—many of the difficulties vanish.

It may never be possible to validate all aspects of how a legal custodian is chosen, since there is no foreseeable way to judge the adequacy with which someone fulfills the role (apart from extremes in "goodness" or "badness"). There is simply no way to judge the merits of the huge array of *individual decisions* a legal custodian is entitled to make for a child (over the opposition of the other parent)—bedtime, naptime, whether a child can watch a PG-13 movie or go to bed "dirty," choice of friends, the exact amount of time to be spent on homework, and so on.

It is a vastly different story in the other category, the time-share plan. There exists a large body of research on attachment, resilience, ability to master developmental and real-life competency skills, and so on, such that it is possible to agree on desired outcomes, and to discover the antecedent conditions that lead to them. In this category, we seek to identify time-sustained behavioral patterns in parents and children with which to identify both the desired outcomes and the antecedent conditions. We do not need to judge the merits of an endless list of specific child-care decisions.

In our real-life courtroom experience, judges prefer to award joint legal custody whenever this is feasible, since it keeps both parents actively involved in a child's life without imposing any particular time-share plan on that child. However, when this is *not* feasible, either because of some glaring deficiency in one parent or because the parents can never agree on anything, the data used to address the time-share plan can legitimately be used to address the issue of recommending a legal custodian once it is seen that there is no obvious way to make such a recommendation from clinical and/or life-history data.

SPECIFIC PSYCHOLOGICAL TESTS AND SYSTEMS IN CUSTODY CASES

This chapter considers a group of tests and systems based on the usage patterns of American mental health professionals (Ackerman & Ackerman, 1997) and in model reports submitted to the *Professional Academy of Custody Evaluators* (PACE), a national organization made up of experienced evaluators. Greatest emphasis will be given to the two essentially data-based systems (both of which incorporate psychological tests) *that were expressly designed to assist in custody decision making.*

THE ACKERMAN-SCHOENDORF SCALES FOR PARENT EVALUATION OF CUSTODY (ASPECT)

The ASPECT (Ackerman & Schoendorf, 1992) was the first system to incorporate all the components of a custody evaluation. It provides a summary of appropriateness of parents for placement, by identifying the characteristics reported in the psychological literature demonstrative of fitness for custody.

Fifty-six variables were selected for use. The system incorporates several commonly used instruments in conjunction with clinical observations to quantify characteristics related to effective custodial parenting. It yields three standardized scales: The Observational Scale, The Social Scale, and the Cognitive-Emotional Scale. The Observational Scale assesses the quality of the parent's self-presentation during the evaluation. The Social Scale reflects interpersonal relationships as well as societal and intrafamilial concerns. The Cognitive-Emotional Scale measures the individual's affective and cognitive capabilities in relation to child rearing. The combination of the Observational and Social Scales is a measure of the outermost impressions conveyed by the individual of his or her parenting effectiveness. These two scales are therefore seen as an "overt" measure of fitness. On the other hand, the Cognitive-Emotional Scale is considered to be a measure of underlying cognitive and affective capabilities for parenting, and is therefore seen as a "covert" measure. The quantitative measure of these significant characteristics, relationships, and interactions is provided in the form of the Parental Custody Index (PCI), a score that may be regarded as an indicator of overall parenting effectiveness.

Each parent completes a Parent Questionnaire composed of questions regarding preferred custody arrangements, living and child-care arrangements, the children's development and education, and the relationship between the parents. It also includes questions about a parent's background, including past and present psychiatric treatment, past and current substance abuse, and legal history. The Cognitive-Emotional Scale utilizes information from the *MMPI/MMPI-2, Rorschach*, personality testing, and tests of cognitive functioning. It takes two to three hours to gather the test data in the latter category, and about 15 minutes to score all of the data in the ASPECT.

The ASPECT is intended for use with parents of children who are between 2 and 18 years of age. In cases where all the children are under 2, many items on the ASPECT will not be applicable. Furthermore, the ASPECT has not been standardized to determine stepparent, foster parent, or grandparent placement. The ASPECT scores are reported in raw scores, T-scores, and percentiles (T-scores tell the distance a given score is from the average (mean) score of a normative distribution of scores.)

The Parental Custody Index (PCI), an unweighted total of all three ASPECT subscales, is both an overall index of parenting effectiveness and a summary of all the system's components. The total PCI was constructed to assess the general appropriateness of the parent's self-presentation, the suitability of the social environment provided by the parent, and the extent of the parent's cognitive and emotional capacity to provide effective parenting. An interrater reliability study indicates that the ASPECT is relatively insensitive to the scoring idiosyncrasies of examiners. The PCIs of both parents are compared. Any T-score difference of 10 points or more is interpretable. In general, T-score differences of 10 to 15 points are significant, differences of 16 to 20 points are very significant, and differences of more than 20 points are marked. When both parents have high T-scores on the PCI (i.e., above 60), it is likely that either will be an effective parent, and even marked differences in their PCI scores would be less critical in making custody recommendations.

As is true with any test that is part of a complete psychological evaluation, the results of the ASPECT should not be the single criterion used to determine who should be the custodial parent. In certain situations, ASPECT scores would be irrelevant (e.g., if the father has been found guilty in court of sexually abusing his children, it is likely that the mother would be awarded custody regardless of the ASPECT scores).

Interpretation of the ASPECT, at this point, looks primarily at a comparison of the PCIs. With a standard deviation on the PCI of 10, a difference in scores of 10 points or more between the mother and the father is considered to be significant. When a significant difference occurs, the examiner can report: "Based on the results of the ASPECT, the mother/father would make a better custodial parent." Before reaching this conclusion, however, the examiner must evaluate the obtained significant difference based on cutoff score interpretations (scores above or below predetermined numbers). When no significant differences are reported on the PCI, the results of the ASPECT would suggest that neither parent would be a better custodial parent than the other.

There are situations in which the scores can be significantly different but of no particular value. For example, if both raw scores fall above 85, which is the 80th percentile, both parents would make appropriate custodial parents, even if their scores are more than 10 points apart. When both scores fall below a raw score of 65, which is the 12th percentile, it is likely that neither parent would make an appropriate custodial parent. As a result, interventions that include parenting classes, supervision, or even, in extreme cases, foster placement must be considered. When a significant difference occurs, it can be helpful to look at the actual items to determine which items are scored in the preferred direction for each individual.

Although they occur infrequently, there are situations in which significant differences could occur in the PCI that do not result in practical differences for purposes of interpretation. For example, one parent could be one or two points above the cutoff scores for various measures on the Cognitive-Emotional scale, while the other parent is one or two points below the cutoff scores. A three- or four-point difference in certain tests does not constitute a clinically interpretable difference. For example, one parent scoring 64 and the other 66 or 67 on a scale of the MMPI would result in the difference between a "yes" or "no" score on the ASPECT. However, this would not be a clinically interpretable difference. If the 10-point difference is the result of variables of lesser importance, less weight would be given to the significant difference in PCIs.

The ASPECT is considered to be content valid, because the questions were derived from the literature on custody issues. The ongoing research data (Ackerman & Schoendorf, 1992) show that the subscales do not correlate well with each other indicating they measure different variables, but do correlate well with the total score, which is desirable. Further, no bias in favor of mothers versus fathers is revealed. Taken together, these findings support construct validity. Predictive validity was measured in two separate ways. The first involved other psychologists who administer the ASPECT but do not tally the results until after they have already formulated custody recommendations. Their recommendations were compared with the ASPECT predictions, yielding a rate of 90% agreement.

A second predictive validity study involved comparing judges' custody decisions with the predictions made by the ASPECT. An outcome study of 56 cases compared the results of the ASPECT with the eventual outcome of the case, whether the outcome was the result of a stipulation or a judge's order. In 59% of the cases, the outcome was the result of a judge's order, and in 41% it was a result of a stipulation. Since the ASPECT does not predict who would make the best custodial parent if the difference is less than 10 points, the study compared results in cases where there was a 10-point or greater difference in ASPECT scores between the parents and cases where the difference was less. In 30 of the cases, there was a 10-point or greater difference. In 28 of those 30 cases, or 93.3% of the time, the ASPECT results agreed with the judge's final order. In those 26 cases where there was less than a 10-point difference in the ASPECT scores, the

ASPECT results agreed with the judge's decision 14 times and did not agree with the judge's decision 12 times. As a result, the 10-point difference cutoff was demonstrated as an accurate predictor of who would make the best custodial parent based on the judge's eventual recommendations after consideration of data from all relevant sources.

Furthermore, Ackerman and Schoendorf (1992) conclude that the result substantiates the conclusion that a difference of less than 10 points is not interpretable in making a recommendation because it represents close to an even split with the judges' ultimate decisions. The use of the decisions of judges as external validating criteria is complex. Some argue that if a judge is influenced to come to a particular decision on the basis of a test's score, then this particular judge's decision cannot be used to validate that test's scores, since validating criteria for test scores must arise from sources *independent* of that test's scores. However, others believe the fact that judges rely on massive amounts of information in reaching their conclusions, cancels out any test-favoring bias. Still another issue arises from those who claim judges lack the competency to make custody decisions in the first place, so it makes little sense to use their decisions as validators. The value to a decision maker of judges' decisions as adequate external validating criteria depends on which of these positions the decision maker believes is most sensible.

The research performed by Western Psychological Services indicated that overall interrater reliability on the PCI was .96, which is excellent.

A COMPREHENSIVE CUSTODY EVALUATION STANDARD SYSTEM (ACCESS)

ACCESS (Bricklin & Elliot, 1995) is an integrated system in which each tool is designed specifically to elicit custody-relevant information. It provides a *Model Contract* form that ensures the evaluation will cover the legally mandated guidelines of a specific jurisdiction, as well as pertinent ethical guidelines. Interview forms are provided for parents, children, stepparents, live-in companions, grandparents, pediatricians, psychotherapists, educators, and neighbors. Detailed observation formats ensure that the main focus used during observation sessions will be to discern not just what parents do, but the *impact* of parental behaviors on the children. (The importance of this will be explained later.)

The BPS and PORT (to be described), as well as the *Parent Awareness Skills Survey (PASS)*, which reflects a parent's awareness of optimum child care skills, the *Parent Perception of Child Profile (PPCP)*, which details a parent's range of knowledge about a child and the *Assessment of Parenting Skills: Infant and Preschooler (APSIP)*, a downward extension of the PPCP which also contains a special section for twins, constitute the core of the evaluation. Traditional tests (e.g., the *Rorschach*) are used on an as-needed basis, usually to rule out serious psychopathology.

The Bricklin-Elliot Home Visit Booklet guides extensive home studies, including the investigation of complex topics, like relocation.

A *Critical Targets* form informs and organizes the collection of information in about 40 essential custody-relevant areas such as each parent's ability to teach and model emotional support and behavioral self-sufficiency; avoid periods of irritability and distractibility; avoid episodes of neglect; demonstrate prior child-care skills; be aware of the child's routines, interpersonal relations, health needs, educational needs; be available time-wise. These assessment areas were formulated after a review of state statutory guidelines, case law, and the writings of experts in the field.

An Aggregation Booklet presents a formal model with which the evaluator can prioritize the gathered information in terms of what it all means to the involved children, and decide whether each piece of information truly discriminates between adequate and inadequate parenting. It is important to remember that the BPS and PORT are directly relevant to the issue of recommending a time-share plan only, while other parts of ACCESS address issues relevant to the choice of a legal custodian.

Briefly, highest importance is assigned to the data-based and observation-based information, each of which is cross-validated and fine-tuned by the other information. Hence, multiple sources are used to generate information and convergent lines of evidence sought.

Current visitation plans are modified to permit fair and balanced observations. It is recommended that the evaluation process unfold over a four- to six-week period, so that a dynamic, rather than freeze-frame picture is generated. In-person contact time for all participants collectively is usually 28 to 30 hours, and several more days are needed to review documents and prepare a report.

ACCESS comes from a different conceptual world than ASPECT and most other tests and methods that look at custody issues, in that it assumes "parental competence," as a concept, cannot be applied to any single individual (i.e., "parental competence" does not "reside" in a given parent). Just as in physics, where one cannot apply the concept "gravitational attraction" to a single body, *parental competence can only be understood as the property of a specific dyad.* For example, consider a father who gives long and detailed responses when a child asks a question. Such a response can be helpful and nurturant to a child who has good auditory-receptive abilities and assigns the following meaning to dad's response style: "Dad cares enough about me to take his time when he answers my questions." This *very same response pattern*, long detailed answers, *will be useless and toxic* to a child with poor auditory-receptive abilities, or assigns the following meaning to such a response: "Dad believes I can never figure anything out on my own." The data-based tests at the heart of the ACCESS model assume there is no such thing as "parental competence" outside of its impact on a particular child at a specific time in that child's development. This conceptual world allows the child to say to us: "Given my age, my developmental needs, the ways in which I process information and assign meaning to my world, in the life areas measured by ACCESS, Mom's/Dad's range of styles is a better match for me." Further, ACCESS tests seek ways to understand trade-offs that are useful for a given child; for example, a slightly learning-impaired child may require a parent who is highly organized even if that parent is on the cold side emotionally, while this trade-off, "greatly organized expressive style but cold emotionally," could be a disastrous trade-off for another child.

A brief example will illustrate how this concept goes beyond a traditional "interactional model," where it is presumed some relatively stable trait in one individual is interacting with a stable trait in another person.

Suppose, in the Bricklin tests, a 7-year-old boy experiences his father as "warm and supportive." Suppose also, say by means of an interview or a traditional test (e.g., the *Rorschach* test), an evaluator identifies the father as "emotionally cold."

What is happening here? Since personality is layered, is the lad seeing something others cannot see? Or is he seeing something that in fact does not exist? But what if there is something in the child's behavior that *elicits warmth from the father*, and what if no one else in the whole world can do this? Would it matter to the child? Probably not. A traditional approach that looks at custody evaluations as though they are a search for "parental traits" might well miss such findings. There would be no way to understand the totally unique qualities of any dyadic relation if all that was tested and observed was what parents know and do, and no way to measure what impact such behaviors were having on particular children. Hence, the ACCESS core tests, the *Bricklin Perceptual Scales* and the *Perception-of-Relationships Test* (PORT), are administered to the children and they yield these data. (Some may claim the preceding concept is less important when there is more than one child, since a decision maker will not separate siblings and therefore one parent must be chosen as "best." But this remains to be proven in individual cases. Futher, a visitation plan can vary widely on a child-by-child basis.)

Here is a brief illustration of the usefulness of these concepts in a case involving two parents, a 7-year-old son, and a 9-year-old daughter. On test, interview, and observation data, the father was seen as authoritarian and distractible. He fared more poorly than the mother in just about every assessment area.

However, the BPS and PORT revealed an interesting finding: although he was having an extremely negative effect on his son, he was having a (mildly) beneficial effect on his daughter.

We were able to obtain follow-up data 7 years after the evaluation. The mother, who was definitely no champion of the father, reported that her daughter *still* enjoyed seeing her father, and seemed to profit from interacting with him. The son disliked him at the time of the evaluation, and still did—despite repeated psychotherapeutic attempts to upgrade their relationship.

A standard approach that concentrated on discovering parental competencies rather than on the *idiosyncratic particularities of specific dyads*, would entirely miss seeing the nurturant qualities this father could offer his daughter.

The Perception-of-Relationships Test (PORT) and the *Bricklin Perceptual Scales (BPS)* are data-based tests that suggest a time-share plan. The original PORT research in 1961 ($n = 30$) used an exclusively Caucasian population, lower-middle or upper-middle class. The age range was 3 years to 14 years. The average age was 8 years. Since then, data have been collected on more than 1,600 cases, ranging in age from 2 years to 17 years. There is no real conceptual upper age limit, and the test can be used with older adolescents, although since children 14 years of age and up are usually considered competent to state a consciously held custody choice, very few older children are included in the test samples of either the PORT or BPS. Roughly 2% of the overall study population is non-Caucasian. BPS data include about 2,000 cases. The BPS, the most frequently used custody test for children (Ackerman & Ackerman, 1997) can be used with children 6 years of age through 14. The average age was 8 in the original samples ($n = 43$). In a new sample (1995 to 1997), in which 67 cases were given both the PORT and BPS, the age range was 5 to 13; the average was again 8 years. An equal number of boys and girls were included in both normative groups. Both the PORT and BPS are scored in terms of which parent is the parent-of-choice for a child on the greater number of test items. The conceptually important scores reflect the *magnitude of the difference between how each parent can serve the child in many critical life areas.*

Reliability data suggest that when BPS scores of a child's parental perceptions are close (a spread of only one or two points between the two caretakers), the reliability figures drop. In the Speth test-retest BPS data ($n = 20$) and in our own test-retest (over a 6-month interval, $n = 33$), there were six pre- to postchanges in parent of choice. In all instances, the mother/father "difference scores" were very close. In the PORT data ($n = 21$), there were two changes. When there is an item-difference score of one or two points on the BPS, or one on the PORT, there is a 10% chance the parent-of-choice could shift on retesting; when the difference is 3 or 4 points on the BPS or 2 points on the PORT there is a 2% chance of shift. Hence the decision maker must assume that when the mother/father scores are close, heightened attention must be given to the reliability data.

PORT choices for the primary custodial parents were compared with those arrived at independently in a number of different ways. External criterion-based (concurrent) validity studies used choices of primary custodial parents that represented the decisions of trained mental health professionals based on one-way mirror observations of children as they solved problems with the ability to ask either parent for help; courtroom judges; mental health professionals based on all available information (except the PORT); BPS scores; two mental health professionals based on an inspection of family therapy notes gathered over a 2- to 5-year period plus consultation with the relevant therapists.

The BPS studies used the decisions of the PORT; courtroom judges; parent and child questionnaires; mental health professionals based on all available clinical and life-history data (except the BPS); two mental health professionals with access to family therapy notes (and relevant therapists) gathered over a 2- to 7-year time span. The total validity populations include 1,600 cases for the PORT, and 2,000 for the BPS. The mean age of the samples was 7.8 for the PORT and 8.7 for the BPS. Two percent were non-Caucasians, and most were from the middle- to upper-middle socioeconomic class. Less than 1% were from very wealthy families. These data are considered quite generalizable for two reasons. As the sample sizes have increased, validity figures have remained stable. Second, the samples consist of children referred for custody evaluations, the same population on whom the test will mostly be used.

There are data ($n = 67$) where both the BPS and PORT were administered to each child. The tests will choose the same primary custodial parent about 80% to 87% of the time. Clinical data indicate that in the majority of instances (90%) where the tests disagree, the child is consciously manipulating his or her responses or has been the recipient of alienation ploys. When this happens, the less conscious responses are utilized to suggest a primary custodial parent; the validity figure ($n = 67$) based on the BPS and PORT used together and where each suggest the same parent of choice is 95% (test choices referenced against the choices of mental health professionals based on all available life-history and clinical data).

All validity figures for the BPS and PORT remain stable at approximately 90% throughout all studies. The only figure that departed from this was the original BPS-PORT comparison, which was 83%. The current PORT uses clearer scoring instructions (Bricklin, 1989).

Four important points can be made about such data. First, these validity figures (1,600 PORT cases and 2,000 BPS cases) continually achieve 90% validity. This tells us something about BPS and PORT score reliability. A test can be very reliable but lack validity. The converse is not true: reliability cannot be less than (large-scale) validity. There are three sources of change when a test score is unstable over time. Two involve errors of measurement, and the other actual changes in the measured variable. BPS and PORT scores are "wrong" 10% of the time. Hence, whatever part of this 10% is due to errors of measurement cannot be greater than 10%—and this 10% range also includes whatever changes would be due to actual changes in what is being measured.

Second, there is a difference between specifying the details of how a test has been validated, and specifying how a decision, legal or otherwise, should be made. The BPS and PORT were validated, in part, by comparing their predictions for primary custodial parents (time-share) with those arrived at in other ways. This is *not* the same as advocating that a decision to select a primary custodial parent in some given instance should be done solely with PORT and/or BPS scores. (ACCESS addresses 34 critical targets *in addition to* those assessed by the BPS and PORT.) This concern, how much and what kind of data does one need to feel justified in coming to a conclusion, overlaps with the "ultimate issue." An *ultimate issue* is basically the final decision needed in a given case. In custody situations, this might involve specifying who has the legal right to make decisions for and about a child, and some visitation plan. Among many others, we advocate that a mental health professional serving as an expert witness is wisest to refrain from addressing an ultimate issue, a point that would certainly preclude using a test score(s) to choose a primary custodial parent (Bricklin, 1995; Bricklin & Elliot, 1995). We follow the recommendations of Wagenaar (1988), that a judge can reason as follows: Given the evidence before me, what is the probability that some hypothesis (e.g., the mother is the better choice for primary custodial parent) is true? An expert witness should be directed only to the following kind of reasoning: If a hypothesis is true, what is the probability I would find some particular piece(s) of evidence? Some legal and mental health professionals advocate that evaluator's reports should more directly address ultimate issues. In practice, most evaluators would be wisest to seek clarification on this issue from a presiding judge.

Third, there is little merit in conducting an evaluation and having a ruling made about a parent-child living plan if the parents do not comprehend it. The various Bricklin measures use simple statistics (percentages of agreement) so they can be readily understood by all concerned (parents, attorneys, judges, etc.) even in tense and adversarial contexts. A parent's worst nightmare during an evaluation is that the mental health professional will be highly influenced by the interview-based lies and distortions of the "other side." The more parents can see that evaluator information offered to the courts is based on objective sources, the less this fear, and the greater the willingness to follow the plan (Bricklin, 1995, pp. 162–192).

The fourth point is a critical one for legal decision makers, and brings us back to validational complexities. We are going to refer to the validity information just presented, but the purpose is not to argue for these particular tests, but rather to make an important point about validity and the usefulness of a test to a decision maker. Many tests are validated by comparing their predictive assertions with information yielded by other tests (where it is unclear if the conceptual targets of the tests are similar), and/or by making use of the distribution of scores achieved in examining so-called known groups (e.g., groups of mental health patients; prison inmates; depressed people). Many of these studies use large samples. But the question remains as to what we can really learn when the members of such groups are identified by so few criteria of inclusion, especially when the aim is to predict something so complicated and individual as the parent who will be the "best" psychological matchup for a particular child, and when the "goodness of matchup" must predict how a parent will be able to guide a child through such a bewilderingly complex set of life circumstances— a postdivorce world of new relatives, possibly a new school and new friends, new eating, sleeping and homework patterns, and so on. Maybe we will eventually achieve agreement on what a "good" outcome would be in such circumstances, and maybe we will discover simple, "group statistics" forecasting markers powerful enough to predict such outcomes in the future. When the searched-for predictive signs are undecided or unclear, it is best to base validity criterion decisions on the richest amount of information available. And here we get to the heart of a main validity issue in using tests to help make custody decisions. A decision maker should ask him- or herself: "If I had to make the very best custody decision I could in choosing a primary custodial parent, would I rather have test results based on scores usually reported as differences in group averages obtained from very large samples of people about whom I know very little, or information from smaller samples of individuals I could meet with for several years on a weekly basis, and get to know as individuals?" The decision maker is essentially asking whether it would be preferable to validate a test on information collected, say, through observations made in a neutral and spontaneous setting over several years, or from average scores from a test of unknown custody-relevance (even if the tested group was a large one and the other group of modest size). The "richest amount of information" would be yielded by the repeated observation-scenario—the number and variety of details available through these sessions would be far more data-rich than those available via test scores of unclear custody-relevance. At this stage, the latter data-rich source would seem the better choice.

Hence, the value of a test to a decision maker has to do not only with appropriate reliability and validity figures, which are important, *but with the degree to which the criteria used in validating a test are those the decision maker would use if these criteria were the only information available to make the involved decision.*

Other Psychological Tests Used in Custody Evaluations

The Ackerman and Ackerman (1997) survey study strongly suggests that evaluators choose to use tests because they like and trust them, and not because there is any research available to support their direct relevance to custody decision making. Some examiners feel impelled to use tests because they anticipate their testimony will be impeached for failing to use them, despite the irrelevance of the tests to questions at hand. This is contrary to *Section 402* of the *Uniform Marriage and Divorce Act* (1979), which cautions that parental behaviors that have not been demonstrated to affect child-care responsibilities are irrelevant in a custody evaluation.

All the following tests (for either adults or children) were used by 20% or more of the evaluator-respondents to the aforementioned study, and yet there is no research to suggest the immediate relevance of any of them to custody decision making (with the possible exception of the MMPI-2, for which normative databases are being currently generated): various intelligence tests; the *Children's Apperception Test;* the *Thematic Apperception Test;* various sentence completion forms; various achievement tests; the *Rorschach* test; miscellaneous projective drawings; the MMPI-A (an MMPI-type test for adolescents); the *House-Tree-Person* test; and the *Millon Clinical Multiaxial Inventory* (the MCMI-II, MCMI-III).

Hence, the tests selected here for review are those for which there is either at least some research to support their use in the custody area (i.e., the

MMPI-2) or where the conceptual targets of the procedures are seen as directly relevant to custody issues (i.e., deal with parent or parent-child issues). However, many of the tests commonly used *could be* relevant to custody issues, in a second-level-inference manner: they deal with personality variables and it would be up to the evaluator to prove the relevance of such a variable to particular child-care issues.

The MMPI-2 (Butcher, Dahlstrom, Graham, Tellegen, & Kaemmer, 1989), the revision of the *Minnesota Multiphasic Personality Inventory* (Hathaway & McKinley, 1967), is widely used in custody evaluations. The basic concept behind the tests is the assumption that if a person endorses test items in much the same ways as do members of certain groups (e.g., people hospitalized for depression), they are likely to have personalities similar to these group members.

Pioneers who have attempted to adopt the test for use with custody issues include Ollendick (1984) and Ollendick and Otto (1984). Paul W. Schenk was among the first to publish normative data on the use of the MMPI-2 in contemporary custody cases (1996), as was Jeffrey C. Siegel (1996).

The test is made up of 567 true-false items. It provides objectively scored results on roughly 100 scales and subscales based on a large ($n = 2,600$) normative sample that was chosen to match the 1980 U.S. census on many dimensions. The test incorporates a variety of internal validity checks to assess whether the client was reasonably direct and forthright: efforts to look unrealistically good (e.g., job applicants) or unrealistically bad (e.g., malingerers) are typically detected by these scales. Custody litigants, for example, typically try to present themselves in the best possible light. Norms for a wide range of specific subpopulations have been developed over the years. Examples include patients in medical settings, prison inmates, psychiatric inpatients, airline pilots, and candidates for positions in law enforcement.

The norms are stable across such diverse factors as ethnicity, education, age, gender, and even nationality (i.e., the international norms look almost identical to the U.S. norms). The test can help identify areas of daily functioning that warrant further evaluation. Conversely, it can help support an impression that the individual is functioning well in day-to-day living. Since all scales use a standard deviation of 10 (mean = 50), it is easy to show graphically during testimony how a particular elevated score looks compared with a normative group.

The MMPI-2 can provide information about personality characteristics that could potentially impact parenting skills. Beyond screening for more serious psychopathology, such as a thought disorder or serious depression, it can provide insight into such factors as interpersonal relationships, capacity to give and receive love, maturity level, limit-setting, flexibility, judgment, impulse control, frustration tolerance, and possible substance abuse problems.

The MMPI-2 includes several validity scales that reduce the risk of a "fake good" profile. The common expectation is that parents will seek to minimize perceived shortcomings or personality flaws during an evaluation that is to be used in determining custody and visitation. On a test with obvious item content, safe interpretation of a "normal" profile is difficult because the test items make it easy to deny symptoms. Therefore, the inclusion of an instrument that is more difficult to fake becomes increasingly important when a "normal" profile has obvious benefits to the parent. However, almost all custody disputants want to make favorable impressions, and given what they are fighting about, this may be very reasonable. Further, no one knows if the desire to "look good" has a clear implication for assessing the value of a particular parent to a specific child.

A client's answers can be entered quickly into a computer by a secretary or the clinician (or the test can be administered directly on the computer). The answer sheet can be mailed to the test publisher for scoring. There is considerable disagreement among experts as to whether computer-written interpretations should ever be used as stand-alone items, or require further evaluator interpretation. There is also debate as to whether computer-written reports should be considered "raw psychological test data," which by ethical and contractual obligation should not be released to nonpsychologists, or revealed in a courtroom setting.

The *Uniform Marriage and Divorce Act, Section 402,* a model legal act widely followed by state statutes that deal with the criteria of child custody dispute resolution, expressly states that "the court shall not consider conduct of a proposed custodian that does not affect . . . (the custodian's) relationship to the child." Despite the MMPI-2's popularity, there is currently no research that directly addresses the relationship between what the test reveals and the direct impact on children of the traits revealed. One *can* find in the literature attempts to show how the MMPI-2 can be responsibly used to address issues of the nature and extent of a given parent's psychopathology (Otto & Collins, 1995), but dissenters to this focus would claim that no one has demonstrated that any particular kind of pathological behavior has some consistent (negative) impact on some specific child. Also, the pathology might be counterbalanced by some other asset that has great psychological value to the child. Also, at least some important MMPI authorities (e.g., Caldwell, 1997) believe that, in many instances, aspects of the MMPI-2 and the original MMPI should be used in combination. An up-to-date analysis of the current scientific status of the MMPI-2 has recently been published (Greene, Gwin, & Staal, 1997). The decision maker should also note that the very names of the scales (e.g., depression, psychopathic deviate, paranoia, schizophrenia) guarantee that interpretive statements based on the test will make people appear "sicker" than would be true were a different lens used to view them.

The *Rorschach* test, or the *Rorschach Inkblot Method* as some experts (e.g., Weiner, 1997) call it to stress that it can function both as a test *and* as a "method of generating structural, thematic and behavioral data . . ." (p. 219) that are useful in both quantitative *and qualitative* ways, was for many years the most widely used personality test in the country and now is second only to the MMPI/MMPI-2 in both usage and publication references (p. 14). It is typically welcome in court: a survey of 7,934 recent federal and state cases in which experts offered *Rorschach* testimony showed that *Rorschach* test information was seriously challenged only six times and deemed inadmissible only once (Weiner, Exner, & Sciara, 1996).

The basic task in using *Rorschach* data in a custody case is the same as that for the MMPI/MMPI-2. While both are reasonably good at red-flagging serious psychopathology and identifying personality attributes that are likely to remain stable over time, it is difficult to use either (except at scoring extremes) to make *first-level inferences* about the implications of their scores on a person's ability to be a good or adequate parent.

Even if one uses a very gross lens (i.e., identifying which parent is "sicker") in attempting to choose which of the two parents (or both, or neither) should be the legal decision maker and/or to fashion a visitation plan, serious challenges remain. Not only is it impossible at the present time to use either test to make first-level inferences about parenting skills, but the evaluator is often faced with two parents who are evenly matched in psychopathology. When I entered the custody field in the early 1960s and the only tests available were tests such as the *Rorschach* and MMPI, I often felt as if I were trading baseball cards: "I'll trade you two obsessive-compulsive conditions for one depressive condition" (are depressive symptoms twice as bad as obsessive-compulsive symptoms in their impact on parenting?). We did not know then, and still do not know now. We especially do not know, for a specific child, what a useful trade-off would be. Hoppe's data (1993) certainly suggest that custody litigants are not only fairly equal in psychopathology, but a diagnostically different-from-normals group to begin with, characterized by what he calls "relationship disorders." They show higher-then-expected amounts of self-centeredness, self-righteous indignation, rage, an inability to tolerate negative emotions, a tendency to project, and several more negative traits.

The *Rorschach* in the hands of competent users, achieves good scores in interrater scoring agreement (80% to 90% agreement), and good test-retest reliability (.70 to .80) over a 3-year time span (Weiner, 1997, pp. 6–7).

Validity studies in many areas show modest figures, about equal to those achieved by the MMPI (Parker, Hanson, & Hunsley, 1988). Ganellen (1996) found the *Rorschach* to be superior to both the MMPI and MCMI-II (see following section) in detecting serious psychopathology.

Certainly, all the tests reviewed here can at least be useful in helping an evaluator to generate hypotheses that account for what is revealed in observations, interviews, or data-based test results.

The Millon Multiaxial Clinical Inventory-III (MCMI-III)

The MCMI-III deals primarily with personality disorders (e.g., obsessive-compulsive). It has three modifying indexes (Scale X, Disclosure; Scale Y, Desirability; and Scale Z, Debasement) that address the client's approach to the testing and perhaps to the entire forensic evaluation.

The clinical scales of the MCMI-III have been developed with the notion of base rates for the specific disorders in the population. This is in contrast to MMPI T-scores, which do not take this into account. On the MCMI-III, a base rate of 60 is the median raw score. A base rate of 75 indicates the presence of what Millon labels a "trait" and a base rate of 85 indicates the presence of a "disorder" (Millon, 1997).

The issue of the use of the MCMI in custody evaluations has been questioned by some clinicians (Ackerman & Ackerman, 1997). Yet, the MCMI-III was recommended for individuals who were undergoing a "psychodiagnostic evaluation" or people with "interpersonal difficulties" (Millon, 1987). With the revisions of the MCMI-III, Millon included in his sample a modest number of persons undergoing forensic evaluations. Millon concludes that this makes his test useful in such evaluations. MCMI-III results can be reported in a probability format that addresses questions such as what is the probability of having a specific disorder if identified by the test as having the disorder on the test. The *Custody Newsletter* (edited by the author of this chapter) the official publication of the *Professional Academy of Custody Evaluators,* a national group of experienced custody evaluators, receives a good bit of mail concerning the appropriateness of the MCMI-III in such assessments. The positions are highly polarized. Detractors claim MCMI-III data are not appropriate in custody evaluations. Enthusiasts claim MCMI-III data achieve high correlations with information yielded by custody-specific tests such as the *Parent Awareness Skills Survey.*

The *Parenting Stress Index* (PSI) (Abidin, 1995) is intended for use with parents of children from 1 month to 12 years of age. It measures the "relative magnitude of stress in the parent-child system." Based on the Thomas and Chess "goodness-of-fit" model (Thomas, Chess, & Birch, 1968), it assesses interactions between a child's temperamental characteristics and situational (family context) variables that affect parenting ability—i.e., the child's behavior and its effect on the parent.

The Child Domain subscales assess the following child characteristics:

- Distractibility/hyperactivity: "My child is so active that it exhausts me."
- Adaptability to changes in the physical or social environment: "My child gets upset easily over the smallest thing."
- Ability to be a source of positive reinforcement to the parent: "My child smiles at me much less than I expected."
- Demandingness: "My child is always hanging on me."
- Unhappiness or depressed mood: "When playing, my child doesn't often giggle or laugh."
- Unacceptability to parents due to physical, emotional, or intellectual characteristics: "My child is not able to do as much as I expected."

The following are the parent characteristics and situational variables assessed by the Parent Domain subscales:

- Competence concerning parenting ability: "Being a parent is harder than I thought it would be."
- Social isolation: "I feel alone and without friends."
- Attachment to his/her child: "It takes a long time for parents to develop close, warm feelings for their children."
- Health: "Physically, I feel good most of the time."
- Depression: "There are quite a few things that bother me about my life."
- Degree to which the parenting role is seen as restrictive: "Most of my life is spent doing things for my child."

Extent of emotional and active support received from the spouse in the area of child care "Since having my child, I have not received as much help and support as I expected from my spouse [male/female friend]."

The Life Stress scale contains 19 optional items that assess current life stressors outside the parent-child relationship and often outside the parent's control. It is in Yes/No checklist form with possible stressors such as job loss or death in the family. The standardization sample included 2,633 mothers and 200 fathers of children in private pediatric practices, pediatric clinics, day-care centers, public schools, and a health maintenance program in Massachusetts, Virginia, New York, North Carolina, Georgia, and Wisconsin. Internal consistency reliability was established by using a standard method. The resulting correlations range from .70 to .83 for the Child Domain subscales, and were .90 or greater for each of the two domains and the Total Stress scale. These values indicate a range going from respectable to a high degree of internal consistency for these measures. Test-retest reliability was assessed in four different studies, with test-retest intervals of three weeks, one to three months, three months, and one year. Correlation coefficients ranged from .55 to .82 for the Child Domain, from .70 to .91 for the Parent Domain, and from .65 to .96 for the Total Stress score. These statistically significant correlations range from fairly weak to very good, indicating some stability for these scores over time. Validity has been established in the following way. Based on a literature review and clinical experience, the author identified characteristics believed to be determinants of parenting stress. Test items were then generated to assess these characteristics and were rated for relevancy of content and adequacy of construction by "six professionals in early parent-child relationships." Correlational studies led to further refinement of the instrument. Factorial (construct) validity was investigated by means of three factor analyses. The structure of the Child Domain was assessed by means of a factor analysis that resulted in a six-factor solution accounting for 41% of the variance. A seven-factor solution accounted for 44% of the variance on the Parent Domain data. Factor analysis of the data from the 13 subscales resulted in two factors that accounted for 58% of the variance. The results of these factor analyses suggest modest support for the notion that each domain is assessing the distinct characteristics or constructs that the test purports to measure, and that each of the two domains is measuring a different source of stress.

The author presents abstracts of many studies, which provide evidence for predictive and construct validity. These include studies in the areas of developmental issues, behavior problems, disabilities and illnesses, cross-cultural studies, at-risk families, parent characteristics, marital relations, and family transitions. There are abstracts of other studies in which the PSI was correlated with other measures. Very few statistics are presented in the abstracts. One study employed as subjects the children of separating parents. However, only one of the PSI subscales was used. Hence, one must exercise care in drawing conclusions about custody litigants from this measure, since there has been almost no research on this population.

The *Family Relations Test* (FRT; Bene & Anthony, 1985) evaluates the direction (positive or negative) and intensity of a child's feelings toward his or her family members and the child's perception of their feelings toward him or her—the child's experience of family relationships. The form for young children (no lower limit for age is given) contains items exploring positive and negative feelings coming from the child ("Who is nice?" "Who is nasty?") or perceived by the child as coming from other family members ("Who likes to kiss [child's name]?" "Who scolds [child's name]?") and feelings of dependency on others ("Who should help [child's name] get dressed in the morning?")

The form for older children (between 6 and 8 years of age, depending on the child's ability to handle the most complex questions) explores positive and negative attitudes emanating either from the child or another family member and varying in intensity from mild to strong:

- Mild positive coming from the child: "This person in the family is a good sport."
- Mild negative coming from the child: "This person in the family nags sometimes."
- Strong positive (sexualized) coming from the child: "I sometimes wish I could sleep in the same bed with this person in the family."
- Strong negative coming from the child: "This person in the family can make me feel very angry."
- Mild positive going toward the child: "This person in the family is kind to me."
- Strong positive (sexualized) going toward the child: "This person in the family likes to tickle me."

This scale also deals with parental overindulgence ("This is the person in the family mother spoils too much") and parental overprotection ("Mother worries that this person in the family might catch cold").

An Adult Version and a Married Couples Version are completed by adult family members. When used together, the three provide information about emotional interrelationships.

Test-retest reliability was not computed. The rationale provided was that with a short interval, memory influences performance and with a long interval, changes in the child are the expected effects of maturity and environmental influences, especially since the children and parents in the sample were receiving therapy. A modified version of split-half reliability was employed to determine internal consistency reliability. With this technique, the test is divided in half to create two alternate forms, and the correlation between the two forms is computed to determine the degree of consistency of measurement within the test. The correlations obtained from this procedure ranged from a modest .68 to a strong .90.

Validity studies employed two sets of outpatient children from a psychiatric hospital. They were referred for a variety of reasons "that are usual with child guidance cases." The children were 7 to 15 years of age. Case history material was compared with various aspects of the test results. Test responses concerning feelings coming from the father were predominantly negative for children whose fathers were identified by the mothers as hostile, cruel, punitive, and so on. Mothers identified by case records and interviews as either accepting of or rejecting of their child were also identified as such by their child's FRT results ($n = 16$, $p < .05$). There was 64% agreement (.05 level) between parents' reports of siblings feelings toward each other and those reported by the siblings. There was "full agreement" between parent reports of jealousy between siblings and test results regarding negative feelings for the sibling in conflict. Parent reports of a reciprocal dislike between siblings or a one-sided hostility toward a sibling was also reflected in the test results of the children in the study (64% agreement). In 34 cases, mothers' questionnaire responses about children's feelings toward fathers and siblings and the feelings of fathers and siblings toward the selected children were evaluated subjectively and compared with children's test results. There was partial or fair agreement in 38% of cases and good agreement in 47% of cases.

As with so many other tests reviewed here, it would be up to the evaluator to provide information on the credibility, accuracy, and relevance of data yielded by this test in relation to a specific decision-needed situation.

The *Parent-Child Relationship Inventory* (PCRI) (Gerard, 1994) assesses parents' attitudes toward their children and toward parenting. It yields a quantified description of the parent-child relationship and is intended for use in conjunction with other qualitative means of evaluating the parent-child relationship. It can be used to verify clinical hypotheses about family and individual disturbances. Other intended uses include evaluating the possibility that a parent is abusive and making custody recommendations (although it is cautioned that this should be done when the PCRI is used in conjunction with interviews and other means of clinical assessment.

A 78-item self-report questionnaire, the PCRI contains 7 scales in the following areas:

1. Level of social and emotional support the parent receives (SUP): "When it comes to raising my child, I feel alone most of the time."
2. Satisfaction with parenting (SAT): "I regret having children."
3. Parental interaction with and knowledge of a child (INV): "I spend very little time talking with my child."
4. Parental perception of effectiveness of communication with his/her child (COM): "If I have to say no to my child, I try to explain why."
5. Discipline style (LIM): "My child is out of control much of the time."
6. Parental ability to promote a child's independence (AUT): "I can't stand the thought of my child growing up."
7. Parental attitudes about gender roles in parenting (ROL): "Husbands should help with child care."

There are also two protocol validity indicators. One is the Social Desirability scale assessing the tendency to give socially desirable responses ("I never worry about my child"). The other assesses inconsistency between highly correlated responses, suggesting random responding or inattentiveness.

The standardization sample consisted of 1,100 mothers and fathers whose children attended day-care centers and schools in four different regions of the United States (Northeast, South, Midwest, and West). There are separate norms for mothers and fathers. Reliability was estimated from data gathered from the standardization sample. The internal consistency values for this sample were respectable, from .70 to .88. Test-retest reliability studies yielded correlations of weak to very solid (from .55 to .93).

Content validity was addressed in a number of ways. A review of parenting literature and factor analytic studies yielded dimensions of parenting attitudes on which the scale test items are based. Next, expert judges (item writing experts, school psychologists, clinicians, a minority psychologist, and a nationally known expert on child abuse) rated items for relevance, simplicity, and cultural fairness. Qualitative feedback from test-takers and mental health professionals, other empirical studies, and item analysis were also employed to generate scales representative of the assessment domains. Construct validity is demonstrated several ways. First, the measure of internal consistency (high reliability) reported here is presented as evidence of construct validity. Second, moderate intercorrelations among subscales (indicating relevance to the domain without redundancy) were reported. Most were significant at the .01 level, although none are above .64, a modest level. Evidence was also presented in the form of correlations demonstrating the relationships of individual items with their own scales. Additionally, factor analyses provided models that were applied to the normative data to demonstrate that the underlying factor structure is consistent with the patterns of intercorrelations yielded by the data. The resulting gamma values (a goodness-of-fit index expressed as confidence intervals), with one exception, all fall above .90, indicating good to excellent fit.

Predictive validity was demonstrated in three different ways. First, the PCRI and the *Personality Inventory for Children* (PIC) were administered to 35 couples involved in court-ordered custody mediation. The PIC assesses the child's cognitive ability, affect, and behavior and unlike the PCRI, its scores reflect the child's status rather than that of the parent-child relationship. Significant correlations among the two measures ranged from −.32 to −.71 (negative due to opposite scoring directions on the two scales). Second, there were significant relationships between parents' self-reports of their discipline practices (selected as a measure reflecting parent effectiveness) and their PCRI scores (.18 to .44). Finally, expected low PCRI scores (below the mean for the normative sample) were found in adolescent unmarried mothers, a group found to be at risk for experiencing difficulties in parenting. However, a study that compared PCRI data with custody-relevant data (from the ASPECT, Ackerman & Schoendorf, 1992) found no correlation at all between the two measures (Hubbard, 1997).

The *Parent Behavior Checklist* (Fox, 1994) defines parenting as ". . . a dynamic process that includes the unique behaviors of a parent that a child directly experiences and that significantly impact his or her development. Parenting also includes parental expectations that children indirectly experience through their parents' behaviors" (p. 3). The test yields scores in three areas: Expectations, Discipline, and Nurturing. It is designed to be given to child caretakers (parents) who have children between 1 and 4 years of age.

An example of expectations would be: "My child should use the toilet without help." An example of discipline would be: "I yell at my child for whining." An example of the nurturing subscale would be: "I read to my child at bedtime."

Normative data were gathered on 1,400 mothers from a large, urban area in the Midwest. Reliability figures are given for internal consistency, test-retest stability, and a domain comparison between mothers and fathers. All of the reliability scales are quite sound, ranging from .81 upward.

Although some data are given on validity studies, none have been carried out on custody populations. On a commonsense (face validity and content validity) basis, however, the areas the test measures are indeed relevant to custody concerns. Hence, it would be up to the evaluator to demonstrate the credibility, accuracy, and relevance of a test score to the demands of some particular decision. One drawback in custody cases may be that the possible examiner-interpretation of some test items would be quite manifest to the respondent (e.g., "I spank my child at least once a week"). Hence, it is likely that test-takers caught up in custody disputes would recognize some of the items of which to be wary.

The Family Apperception Test (FAT) (Sotile, Julian, Henry, & Sotile, 1991) consists of 21 stimulus cards that depict common family activities, constellations, and situations. They evoke wide-ranging projective associations about family processes and structures, as well as emotions that may affect specific family relationships. For example, Card 1, the so-called dinner card, pictures a man, a woman, and three children—two boys and a girl—seated around a dinner table. The adults are speaking as one child eats. It aims to elicit associations about family conflict, the quality of relationships, and frequently, marriage and divorce issues. Card 3, the "punishment" card, pictures a boy leaning over a broken vase with spilled water and flowers in the picture. An ambiguous human figure in the foreground faces the boy and holds a tubular object, semihidden. This card seeks information on discipline issues, a child's feelings about "justice" in the family, and the possibility of abuse. The FAT is specifically useful for children from ages 6 to 15. Essentially, the instructions to the participants go something like the following (paraphrased): I am going to show you several pictures about children and their families, one at a time. Please say what is happening in the picture, what led up to the situations, what the characters are saying and feeling, and how the story might end. Use your imagination and keep in mind that there are no right or wrong answers.

The scoring categories of the FAT are designed to illuminate areas of conflict (within the family, within the marriage, etc.), methods of resolving conflicts, methods of setting limits, the quality of relationships (in terms of whether significant figures are seen as allies or stressors), boundary factors (e.g., enmeshment), whether or not there are repeating dysfunctional patterns present, and also the possible appearance of the use of abusive remarks, unusual responses, refusal to deal with a certain thematic situation, and the emotional tones expressed.

The authors present data to show that interrater agreement in using the scoring categories is such that one can conclude the test can be reliably scored. Further reliability figures across various scoring categories are seen as "moderate to substantial." Most validity studies focused originally on distinguishing clinical from nonclinical groups in terms of a so-called conflict score, and then in terms of more of the scoring categories. The results range from quite modest to strong. This test could be highly relevant in certain situations, depending on whether the evaluator could point to an internal database gathered through experience and make a cogent presentation of the specific usefulness of this test in a given situation.

The Family Relationship Inventory (FRI) (the original authors are Michaelson and Bascom; the 1982 revision is authored by Nash, Morrison, & Taylor) can be used with children as young as 5 years. It basically consists of 50 items that can be used for a child to describe him- or herself or various family members. There are 25 positive items and 25 negative ones. Keep in mind that the child or respondent is answering in terms of some given individual. Some of the positives would read "loves me," "tries to act fair," "trusts me," "is strong and dependable." Some of the negatives involve "never believes me," "hates me," "is too noisy." After all 50 items have been administered, the tallies for each individual are collected. A score is derived for the self, and for all the other people that the respondent wants to include in his or her list. The person assigned the greatest number of positive responses is the family member whom the respondent views in the most positive terms and the converse is true with negatives. A so-called waste basket is used to shed additional light on the respondent's self-concept. "An analysis of the discarded items may reveal an absence of negative feelings, or unwillingness to assign either positive or negative statements to self or others" (p. 2).

The FRI helps the evaluator to understand the aspects of the family systems in which a child may be taking part, offering specific information on how a child perceives him- or herself, the parents, and other siblings and how he or she functions in relation to these people. Reliability (stability) coefficients are solid, ranging from .77 and up. While no validity figures are given for specific custody-relevant situations, it is clear that this test yields information that could be helpful in a comprehensive custody evaluation. Again, it would be up to the evaluator to prove credibility, accuracy, and relevance to the decision-required situation.

The Child Behavior Checklist (CBCL) (Achenbach, 1992) gives parents and teachers a standardized way to express their concerns about children. Parent-respondent forms apply to children from 2 years of age through 18 years, while the teacher form extends from 6 through 18 years. The test aims particularly at identifying children who may be withdrawn; have somatic complaints; seem anxious or depressed; manifest social problems; have thought or attention problems; show aggressive or delinquent behavior; manifest difficulties of a sexual nature. Reliability figures over various time spans range from .56 to .89 (the shorter the interval, the higher the reliability—which makes conceptual sense). Interparent agreement figures range from .65 to .76.

Since almost all state statutes relevant to custody evaluations and the UMDA direct evaluator attention to a child's overall status, including emotional condition, this test may be relevant in many cases. Validity figures are solid in the test's ability to differentiate clinical from nonclinical populations. The test is more useful in discriminating seriously disturbed from less disturbed children than it is in pointing to fine distinctions among children who do not manifest many problems.

The Personality Inventory for Children (PIC) (Wirt, Lachar, Klinedinst, & Seat, 1990), consists of 420 questions, which are asked of a parent about a child. It is designed to be useful with children from 3 to 16 years of age. The authors caution that anyone who would respond to such a form should have sufficient contact with a target-child such that it could reasonably be expected that answers could be given to such finely tuned inquiries. (This is an especially critical issue in cases where noncustodial parents are in disputes with custodial parents.)

In general, the test aims to offer information about a child's intellectual and psychological adjustment. Special scoring categories aim to demonstrate how a child may be doing: in his or her achievements, intellectually, developmentally, in "body feeling," in mood, with relationships within the family, in appropriateness of socialization, and in several other areas. Test-retest reliability is solid (most figures range from .82 to .97 over various time spans). Validity is somewhat less of an issue with this test (and others like it), which aim basically to describe a given child's current status (i.e., the "cost" of an error is not so compelling as would be the case in other areas of the decision maker's concerns). If a parent is a congruent match for a child (established via databased systems), then whether a child is correctly identified as a little more or a little less "disturbed" would not matter much, since the child will (hopefully) spend the majority of his or her time with the parent who can best address these needs. Of course, the cost of an incongruent parent-child match rises precipitously the more disturbed the child.

REFERENCES

Abidin, R. R. (1995). *Parenting stress index test manual* (3rd ed.). Odessa, FL: Psychological Assessment Resources, Inc.

Achenbach, T. M. (1992). *Child behavior checklist/2-3 and 1992 profile test manual*. Burlington: University of Vermont, Department of Psychiatry.

Ackerman, M. J., & Ackerman, M. C. (1997). Custody evaluation practices: A survey of experienced professionals (Revisited). *Professional psychology: Research and practice, 28*(2), 137–145.

Ackerman, M. J., & Schoendorf, K. (1992). *The Ackerman-Schoendorf parent evaluation of custody test*. Los Angeles: Western Psychological Services.

Bene, E., & Anthony, J. (1985). *Family relations test test manual* (Rev. ed.). Windsor, Great Britain: NFER-NELSON.

Bricklin, B. (1962, 1989). *The perception-of-relationships test*. Furlong, PA: Village.

Bricklin, B. (1984). *The Bricklin perceptual scales: Child-perception-of-parents series*. Furlong, PA: Village.

Bricklin, B. (1995). *The custody evaluation handbook: Research-based solutions and applications*. New York: Brunner/Mazel.

Bricklin, B. (1997). *Test manuals supplement update*. Furlong, PA: Village.

Bricklin, B., & Elliot, G. E. (1995). *ACCESS: A comprehensive custody evaluation standard system*. Furlong, PA: Village.

Bricklin, B., & Elliot, G. E. (1997). *Test manuals supplement for the BPS, PORT, PASS and PPCP*. Furlong, PA: Village.

Butcher, J. N., Dahlstrom, W. G., Graham, J. F., Tellegen, A. M., & Kaemmer, B. (1989). *MMPI-2: Manual for administration and scoring*. Minneapolis: University of Minnesota Press.

Caldwell, A. B. (1997). Whither goest our redoubtable mentor, the MMPI/MMPI-2? *Journal of Personality Assessment, 68*(1), 47–68.

Cizek, G. J. (1994). In defense of the test. *American Psychologist, 49*(6), 525–526.

Ekman, P. (1992), *Telling lies*. New York: Norton.

Ekman, P., & O'Sullivan, M. (1991). Who can catch a liar? *American Psychologist, 46*(9), 913–92.

Fox, R. A. (1994). *Parent behavior checklist test manual*. Brandon, VT: Clinical Psychology.

Ganellen, R. J. (1996). Comparing the efficiency of the MMPI, MCMI-II, and Rorschach: A review. *Journal of Personality Assessment, 67*(2), 219–243.

Gerard, A. B. (1994). *Parent-child relationship inventory test manual*. Los Angeles: Western Psychological Services.

Greene, R. L., Gwin, R., & Staal, M. (1997). Current status of MMPI-2 research: A methodologic overview. *Journal of Personality Assessment, 68*(1), 20–36.

Grove, W. M., & Meehl, P. E. (1996). Comparative efficiency of informal (subjective, impressionistic) and formal (mechanical, algorithmic) prediction procedures: The clinical-statistical controversy. *Psychology, Public Policy and Law, 2*(2), 293–323.

Hathaway, S. R., & McKinley, J. C. (1967). *The Minnesota multiphasic personality inventory* (Rev. ed.). New York: Psychological Corporation.

Hoppe, C. (1993, August). *A data-based description of relationship disorders*. Paper presented at the American Psychological Association, Toronto, Canada.

Hubbard, G. A. (1997). *Validity study of the parent-child relationship inventory for determining child custody*. Unpublished doctoral dissertation, Wisconsin School of Professional Psychology, Milwaukee, WI.

Krauss, D. A., & Sales, B. D. (in press). Legal standards, expertise, and experts in the resolution of contested child custody cases. *Psychology, Public Policy and Law*.

Millon, T. (1987). *Manual, MCMI-II* (2nd ed.). Minneapolis, MN: National Computer System.

Millon, T. (1997). *Manual, MCMI-III* (2nd ed.). Minneapolis, MN: National Computer System.

Nash, L., Morrison, W. L., & Taylor, R. M. (1982). *Family relationship inventory test manual*. Thousand Oaks, CA: Psychological.

Nemeth, A. J. (1995). Ambiguities caused by forensic psychologist's dual identity: How to deal with the prevailing quantitative bias and "scientific" posture. *American Journal of Forensic Psychology, 13*(4), 47–66.

Ollendick, D. G. (1984). Scores on three MMPI alcohol scales of parents who receive child custody. *Psychological Reports, 55*, 337–338.

Ollendick, D. G. & Otto, B. J. (1984). MMPI characteristics of parents referred for child-custody studies. *Journal of Psychology, 117*, 227–232.

Otto, R. K., & Collins, R. P. (1995). Use of the MMPI-2/MMPI-A in child custody evaluations. *Applied Psychology, 2*, 222–252.

Parker, K. C. H., Hanson, R. K., & Hunsley, J. (1988). MMPI, Rorschach and WAIS: A meta-analytic comparison of reliability, stability, and validity. *Psychological Bulletin, 103*, 367–373.

Piotrowski, Z. A. (1957). *Perceptanalysis*. New York: Macmillian.

Schenk, P. W. (1996). MMPI-2 norms for child custody litigants. *Georgia Psychological Association: The Georgia Psychologist, 50*(2), 51–54.

Schutz, B. M., Dixon, E. B., Lindenberger, J. C., & Ruther, N. J. (1989). *Solomon's sword: A practical guide to conducting child custody evaluations*. San Francisco: Jossey-Bass.

Siegel, J. C. (1996). Traditional MMPI-2 validity indicators and initial presentation in custody evaluations. *American Journal of Forensic Psychology, 14*(3), 55–63.

Sotile, W. M., Julian, A., III, Henry, S. E., & Sotile, M. O. (1991). *Family apperception test manual*. Los Angeles: Western Psychological Services.

Speth, E. (1992). *Test-retest reliability of the Bricklin perceptual scales*. Unpublished doctoral dissertation, Hahnemann University and Villanova School of Law.

Thomas, A., Chess, S., & Birch, H. G. (1968). *Temperament and behavior disorders in children*. New York: New York University Press.

Uniform Marriage and Divorce Act. (1979). *Uniform laws annotated*. (Previous versions: 1970, 1971 and 1973).

Wagenaar, W. A. (1988). The proper seat: A Bayesian discussion of the position of expert witnesses. *Law and Human Behavior, 12*(4), 499–510.

Weiner, I. B. (1997). Current status of the Rorschach inkblot method. *Journal of Personality Assessment, 68*(1), 5–19.

Weiner, I. B., Exner, J. E., & Sciara, A. (1996). Is the Rorschach welcome in the courtroom? *Journal of Personality Assessment, 67*(2), 422–424.

Wirt, R. D., Lachar, D., Klinedinst, J. K., & Seat, P. D. (1990). *Multidimensional description of child personality: A manual for the Personality Inventory for Children*. Los Angeles: Western Psychological Services.

CHAPTER 8

Child Witnesses in Custody Cases: The Effects of System and Estimator Variables on the Accuracy of Their Reports

MARGARET BULL KOVERA and BRADLEY D. McAULIFF

IN THIS CHAPTER, we discuss research on children's abilities to accurately report past events and the moderating factors that increase or decrease the accuracy of those reports. Many child witness researchers who focus on children's abilities to accurately recount traumatic experiences hope to generalize their findings to children who testify in sexual assault cases. Children sometimes are called to provide information about allegations of sexual abuse (Myers, 1993, 1995), but judges more frequently interview children about their preferences regarding their living arrangements (Jones, 1984; Lombard, 1984). Every state allows judges to consider children's wishes when making custody determinations (Crosby-Currie, 1996). Moreover, there is some evidence that judges consider these preferences to be very important to the decisions they make. In one survey, close to half of the surveyed judges viewed child preferences as one of the five most important criteria to use when making custody decisions (Felner, Terre, Farber, Primavera, & Bishop, 1985).

Crosby-Currie (1996) examined children's involvement in custody cases by surveying judges and family law attorneys. She found that many (53% in the survey) children participated in custody hearings, although the level of their participation varied. Practices varied widely among judges, even in the same jurisdiction. The children were less likely to give sworn testimony than to talk with the judge in chambers. Still, a significant number of children testify in custody cases. A third of the attorneys surveyed reported that they had asked a child to testify at some time in their career but almost all these attorneys indicated that their requests were influenced by a child's age. Although most of the empirical research on child witnesses has focused on situations in which children must remember and report their recollections of traumatic experiences (e.g., testifying about the abusive behavior of a parent), this body of research may also provide insight into the reliability of children's reports of their preferences and other factors influencing custody decisions.

Besides obtaining information about the children's preferences, judges may interview children to learn about parental behavior. In one sample of family court cases, sexual abuse allegations were made in 2% of contested custody cases (McIntosh & Prinz, 1993). In these cases, judges may interview children about the allegations to gather evidence about the charges. But this search for information about the family is not limited to cases in which abuse is alleged. Many judges responding to a survey conducted by Lombard (1984) reported that they interview a child involved in a custody dispute to gather information about the family. Indeed, 54% of the surveyed judges indicated that at times these interviews about children's preferences uncovered information about maltreatment of the child or parental drug/alcohol abuse. Other surveys revealed the use of judicial interviews with children to corroborate parental evidence or to elicit new information about parental behavior (Scott, Reppucci, & Aber, 1988). Many scholars question this practice on constitutional grounds (e.g., Crosby-Currie, 1996; Jones, 1984; Lombard, 1984). We raise a more fundamental question: Is the information gained in these interviews reliable? Can children provide accurate information about events they have experienced?

Moderating factors influence the accuracy of children's reports. Researchers on adult eyewitness capabilities have classified these moderating variables into one of two categories: estimator variables or system variables (Cutler, Penrod, & Martens, 1987; Narby, Cutler, & Penrod, 1996; Wells, 1978). Estimator variables are factors present in a witnessing condition that are not under the control of legal professionals (e.g., age of the child, coaching of testimony by a parent) but that, if known, can help the trier of fact predict the accuracy of the witness's report. System variables are factors influencing the accuracy of an eyewitness's report that are under the control of judges, attorneys, or other legal players (e.g., misleading questions, preparation of the child witness for the hearing). Thus, by attending to the potential impact of system variables on testimony and appropriately modifying their procedures, legal professionals can help make witness reports more accurate (Seelau & Wells, 1995). We first discuss the effects of two estimator variables on the accuracy of children's reports: the child's age and parental coaching of the child's testimony. Then we discuss the effects of system variables, including the child witness's preparation and type of questioning on the quality of information produced by children involved in legal proceedings.

ESTIMATOR VARIABLES

AGE OF THE CHILD

Survey research suggests that judges are wary about relying on information provided by young children. In one survey, for example, judges reported that, in custody decisions, they weigh the preferences of older children more heavily than those of younger children (Scott et al., 1988). These judges reported that they weighed information from children 14 years old and older most heavily, gave some weight to information from children between the ages of 10 and 14, and discounted information from children under the age of 10. Moreover, they stated they did not gather information from children under the age of 6 because such information would be unreliable. Newman and Collester (1980) also found that most courts presume that a child under the age of 10 is incapable of providing reliable information about their custodial preferences, although some judges argued that children as young as 6 should be interviewed to determine whether they have the ability to provide information about their preferences.

To what extent are judges' views consistent with psychological research examining the effects of age on the accuracy of children's reports? Research by Fivush and her colleagues suggests that judges may be underestimating children's abilities to remember autobiographical information (Fivush, 1993; Fivush & Shukat, 1995). Evidence that children can accurately recall autobiographical information is mounting. Gold and Neisser (1980) showed that children can accurately recall events from their kindergarten years even nine years later. Similarly, Hudson and Fivush (1987) examined children's memories of a kindergarten trip to a museum and found that children's recollections of the event remained accurate even six years later. Although both of these studies found that the amount of information children recalled was related to the amount of time that had passed since the event (i.e., children remembered more information when the event was more recent), this pattern of results is similar to the findings from studies of adult autobiographical memory (Linton, 1982; Wagenaar, 1986; Wagenaar & Groeneweg, 1990). Thus children's recollections may be as accurate as those of adults. In fact, research suggests that even preschoolers can remember unusual events (e.g., a trip to Disney World) that occurred 1 to 2 years previously (Fivush & Hamond, 1990; Hamond & Fivush, 1990). Children as young as 4 can retrieve accurate memories of everyday occurrences (e.g., what they did the previous summer) that occurred months earlier (Friedman, 1992).

School-age children appear capable of providing reports about personally experienced events that are consistent over time (Hudson & Fivush, 1987), although this ability is compromised if interviewers use suggestive or misleading questions to elicit information from the children (Poole & White, 1995). However, the consistency of a child's report may not always reflect its accuracy. Because at any one time very young children spontaneously recall few facts about events, over time preschoolers (e.g., 2½-year-olds) often provide inconsistent accounts of events even when nonleading questions are asked of them (Fivush & Hamond, 1990; Fivush, Hamond, Harsch, Singer, & Wolf, 1991; Fivush & Shukat, 1995). Yet when Fivush and her colleagues assessed the accuracy of these inconsistent reports with the children's parents, they found that over 90% of the children's statements were accurate (Fivush, Gray, & Fromhoff, 1987; Fivush & Hamond, 1990; Fivush et al., 1991).

There is some evidence that this inconsistency in preschoolers statements is caused by the questions adults ask. When adults ask children the same question over time, the children tend to produce consistent reports about personally experienced events (i.e., repeated reports agree with one another); when adults ask children different questions over time, the children tend to produce inconsistent reports (Fivush et al., 1991). Similar findings have been reported for adult witnesses. Although the consistency of witness reports is not strongly related to accuracy (i.e., the extent to which the report corresponds to actual events), consistency of reports over time is related to the consistency of interviewing procedures over time (Fisher & Cutler, 1996). Whatever the source of preschoolers' inconsistencies, judges should be careful not to rely on children's inconsistencies when judging the accuracy of their reports of family life, especially when the children are very young.

This research on autobiographical memory suggests that judges may want to revisit their assessments of children's capabilities. Surveys indicate that judges routinely devalue the reports of children younger than 10 (Newman & Collester, 1980; Scott et al., 1988). However, psychological research has repeatedly shown that even preschool children can give reliable information about their lives (Fivush et al., 1987, 1991; Fivush & Hamond, 1990). Therefore, young children may be able to provide important information about their current living situation and custodial preferences. Children's abilities to provide information about more stressful experiences may be less developed (Merritt, Ornstein, & Spicker, 1994; Peters, 1991), although other researchers find no discernible effects of stress on children's memory (Goodman, Hirschman, Hepps, & Rudy, 1991). Moreover, research examining 3-year-olds' memory for novel events (e.g., an unfamiliar adult reads them a new book) suggests that these preschool children have poorer memories for these events than do older children or adults (Ceci, Ross, & Toglia, 1987; Zaragoza, 1987, 1991). Thus, judges may wish to exercise caution when evaluating preschoolers' reports of unfamiliar or stressful experiences (e.g., sexual abuse).

PARENTAL COACHING OR REQUESTS FOR SECRECY

Although psychological research on autobiographical memory paints a promising picture of children's mnemonic capabilities, in certain circumstances children provide less accurate reports about experienced events because of social or motivational factors. One such situation arises when a parent coaches the child to provide or conceal particular information. To what extent do children conceal information if they are asked to keep it secret? How much are their reports of family life tainted by parental suggestion?

Pipe and Wilson (1994) showed that children may conceal from an authority figure information that they have been asked to keep secret by an adult. Children either assisted a magician with magic tricks or observed another child helping the magician. The child who assisted the magician was asked to wear white gloves, a cloak, and a hat. In the course of performing four tricks, the magician "accidentally" spilled ink on the child's white gloves, took the gloves from the child and hid them, and asked the child not to tell anyone about the accident. When children were asked to describe the event two weeks later, 75% of the 6-year-olds and 34% of the 10-year-olds failed to report the magician's transgression. Even when asked directly about the incident, 40% of the younger children and 16% of the older children denied any knowledge about the ink-stained gloves. Thus many, although not all, children will keep an adult's secret even in the face of direct questions about the secret event. Although another study of children's willingness to keep secrets to protect an unfamiliar adult suggests that children are unwilling to keep the adult's secret in the face of the experimenter's strong accusations that the adult has transgressed (Thompson, Clarke-Stewart, & Lepore, 1997), it is extremely unlikely that any judge would use this style of questioning to elicit information from a child during a custody matter.

What happens when children are asked by their parents to withhold information about certain events or experiences? For example, suppose a mother asks her children not to tell anyone that her new boyfriend spent the night in her bedroom, or a father asks his son not to tell the judge about the time that he kicked the family dog. Are children able to keep these secrets to protect their parents? Only one study has examined this issue. Bottoms, Goodman, Schwartz-Kenney, Sachsenmaier, and Thomas (1990) solicited mothers to assist in an investigation of children's ability to keep a secret. After arriving at the laboratory, mothers encouraged their children to play with toys that the experimenter had forbidden the children to touch. While the mother and child played with the forbidden toys, the mother accidentally broke one of the toys. Half of the mothers told the child that she would get in trouble if the experimenter discovered what happened, and asked the child not to tell the experimenter that they had played with the toys. These mothers told the child that they would be rewarded with a toy if they kept the secret. The remaining children were promised a toy after the experiment was over but were not asked to keep anything a secret.

Did children keep their mothers' secrets? Only one of the 49 children spontaneously reported the transgression to the experimenter. Thus it is unlikely that children will spontaneously report "secret" events to judges during a custodial interview. Children were more likely to divulge the secret in response to the experimenter's direct questions about the event. However, there were age differences in children's willingness to report the secret activity in response to direct questioning. Older children (5- and 6-year-olds) were more likely to keep the mothers' secrets under these conditions than were younger children (3- and 4-year-olds). Therefore, a judge may be able to elicit information from children—especially preschool children—about events that their parents have asked them to keep secret but it is unlikely that children will volunteer this information.

During custody disputes, one may also be concerned about parents who intentionally try to persuade their children that the other parent is unfit or otherwise unsuitable as a parent. Empirical evidence suggests that children incorporate parental suggestions into their memory for events (Poole & Lindsay, 1995). One could also be concerned about one parent coaching a child to lie about the actions of the other parent. Under some laboratory conditions, some children will deliberately tell a falsehood to an adult (i.e., that they had played with a toy that they had not actually touched) when asked to do so by another adult (Tate, Warren, & Hess, 1992). There were differences, however, in the reports provided by children who lied about playing with the toy and the reports provided by children who actually did play with the toy. Lying children provided shorter descriptions of their play activities and provided fewer details than did children who were telling the truth.

Also, parents may unintentionally use suggestive questioning that could alter their children's memories for interactions with the other parent. Suppose that a father suspects that his daughter is being maltreated by his ex-wife's new husband. Could this father's expectation influence the types of questions he asks his daughter about her interactions with her new stepfather and so influence the information that his daughter reports about these interactions? Research by Goodman, Sharma, Thomas, and Considine (1995) suggests that the answer to this question may be yes and no. In their study, children participated in a play session with an adult experimenter. The mothers of these children either received inaccurate information about the play session (biased mothers) or no information about the play session (unbiased mothers). Another group of women who were mothers but not the mothers of the child participants were given biasing information or no information about the play session. These women then interviewed a child to learn what that child remembered about the experimental session. Not surprisingly, biased interviewers asked more information about the misinformation they had received about the play session than did interviewers who had not been misled. More interestingly, children provided more incorrect information in response to questions from biased strangers than to questions from unbiased strangers; however, children provided equally accurate reports whether they were interviewed by a biased or unbiased mother. Thus, it appears that children may be more resistant to suggestions provided by their mothers than to suggestions made by strangers.

These studies may underestimate the influence of parental suggestion on children's event reports. Necessarily, the types of coercion that have been used in laboratory experiments are less threatening than those used in real custody situations. In addition, the transgressions that children have been asked to keep secret in these experiments are also not very serious. There is some evidence that children may be more likely to keep serious transgressions secret, perhaps because of the serious consequences that would result from their revelation (Bottoms et al., 1990).

Parental coaching or suggestion is not under the court's control. Thus, it may be impossible to eliminate parental influence on children's memory. Nor may it be possible to determine whether a child's statements have been influenced by their parent. Sometimes simply asking the child is sufficient to elicit descriptions of parental coaching. However, if there is collateral evidence that a parent has coaxed his or her child to make particular statements or to withhold certain information, this evidence should be considered when evaluating the accuracy of the child's statements about family life.

SYSTEM VARIABLES

PREPARATION OF THE CHILD WITNESS

If participation in a legal proceeding is often stressful for adults, it should be no surprise that testifying in court can be a frightening experience for a young child (Goodman et al., 1992). Even if a child is not called to testify in open court during a custody dispute, being interviewed by a judge in chambers is likely to be stressful, especially for young children who have only the vaguest understanding of the court process. Some children even fear that they are going to court because they are going to be put in jail (Dezwirek-Sas, 1992). Recognizing the difficulty that children may experience when participating in court proceedings, various courts and agencies have developed programs to prepare children for their day in court (Aldridge & Freshwater, 1993; Dezwirek-Sas, 1992; Keeney, Amacher, & Kastanakis, 1992; Melton et al., 1992).

Without preparation, child witnesses may not understand their role in court, may not know how courts generally work, and may misunderstand the judges' and attorneys' language. For example, a child understood the judge's decree that the "minor" would live with her grandmother to mean that the judge had sent a coal miner to live with her grandmother (Saywitz, Jaenicke, & Camparo, 1990). Saywitz and her colleagues found that children in elementary school had difficulty understanding many other legal terms (e.g., motion, petition, competence, and allegation). Children younger than 7 years generally do not understand what a lawyer is or does and very few understand why people go to court (Warren-Leubecker, Tate, Hinton, & Ozbek, 1989). Moreover, Warren-Leubecker and colleagues found that 82% of the 3-year-olds they questioned thought that court was a bad place. Although the numbers of children who indicated that court was a bad place decreased as the age of the children increased, fully a third of 7-year-olds still believed that court was "bad." In a study of children in Great Britain, Flin, Stevenson, and Davies (1989) also found that children view court as a negative place.

Because of children's misconceptions about the legal system and children's beliefs that court is something bad, various programs have been developed to educate children about the court proceedings and to reduce the stressfulness of the child's experience. One preparation program consists of teaching children about courtroom participants using dolls and books, allowing the children to practice speaking in court, touring an empty courtroom, and helping the child through stress reduction techniques such as relaxation (Dezwirek-Sas, 1992). Evaluation of this program suggested that the preparation program bettered the psychological adjustment of children who had appeared in court. In addition, attorneys who tried the cases for which the children had been prepared rated the prepared children as better witnesses than children whom they had previously encountered in court.

Preparation may not only benefit the psychological adjustment of the child—it may also help the child provide better information to the court. Because the Dezwirek-Sas (1992) study was conducted in the field (i.e., in the context of actual court cases), it is impossible to independently verify the accuracy of the children's statements to judge whether these prepared children truly were better witnesses than their unprepared counterparts. Only laboratory studies, in which the event to be remembered is known to the experimenter, allow for a clear picture of the impact of preparation on the accuracy of children's memory.

Several laboratory studies that examined the effect of child witness preparation on the quality of children's testimony have been conducted. In one of these studies, children witnessed a staged argument that occurred between two student teachers in the children's classroom (Saywitz & Snyder, 1996). Two weeks later, Saywitz and Snyder used memory training techniques to prepare some of these children for reporting the event they had witnessed. A subset of children were told that people can often provide more accurate accounts of events if they focus on describing different aspects of the event, such as the participants, the setting, actions, and what they heard. These children practiced this new memory technique by watching and recalling videotaped vignettes. The next day, all children were interviewed about the classroom altercation and their responses were compared with the videotape of the original event. Children who had been prepared for this memory task provided more correct information about the event than did children who were not prepared. Moreover, preparation did not increase the amount of incorrect information provided by the children.

Saywitz and Snyder (1993) described two additional laboratory studies of child witness preparation. In one study, researchers trained children to resist misleading questions by having them read a story about a child who acquiesced to misleading questions because the child did not want to hurt the feelings of the police officer asking the questions and was intimidated by the officer. Experimenters asked children to role-play the part of the child in the story so they could practice resisting misleading questions. The researchers praised the children when they resisted misleading questions, and when the children were misled reminded them of the dangers of acquiescing to misleading questions. Children with and without training watched a videotape and then were asked leading and nonleading questions about the events in the tape. Training improved children's accuracy when responding to misleading questions. In a second study, children received broader training about strategies to use when responding to questions. Prepared children were taught to recognize questions that were difficult to understand and to ask that they be rephrased. Compared with children who did not receive training, prepared children answered more questions correctly and made fewer errors.

A cautionary note about preparation programs is necessary. Attorneys report that court preparation results in children being more composed and confident in court (Kovera, Gresham, Borgida, Gray, & Regan, 1997). However, research by Kovera and coworkers suggests that fact finders may view composed and confident child witnesses negatively because they violate stereotypes about child witnesses (e.g., that child witnesses are often frightened and lack composure). Other studies suggest that children who are prepared for court testimony are more likely to respond "I don't know" in response to difficult or misleading questions (Saywitz & Snyder, 1993). Similarly, fact finders may view a prepared child who repeatedly answers, "I don't know" to be less accurate than an unprepared child who provides responses to questions, even though the prepared child is providing more correct information. Thus, the adoption of preparation programs should be tempered with the understanding that the programs may produce changes in child witness demeanor that make children look less credible even though they are providing accurate testimony.

These empirical studies of child witness preparation have some limitations. The well-controlled laboratory studies have not evaluated the types of preparation programs that are currently in existence (e.g., programs that familiarize children with the court and teach them to relax). Although providing useful information about how children might be prepared to provide better information in court, these studies tell us little about the effectiveness of preparation programs that are likely to be used with child witnesses. Moreover, researchers evaluating these preparation programs have focused on the preparation of children for open court testimony in criminal proceedings rather than for their likely role in family court proceedings. Nonetheless, this area of research provides important information about the needs of children to be prepared for their participation in custody proceedings. This research also highlights the benefits that court preparation may have for the accuracy of children's reports to a judge, whether they are asked to provide information about everyday occurrences in the home or testimony about sexual abuse allegations.

SOCIAL SUPPORT

Other system variables may relieve children from the stress attendant to their involvement in a custody proceeding. For example, children may benefit from receiving social support from a trusted adult, such as a *guardian ad litem*, during their *in camera* interview with the judge or during testimony in open court. In their study of the effects of social support on children's testimony, Goodman and colleagues (1992) conducted a 2-year field study in Denver, Colorado, in which they systematically observed children's emotional reactions to testifying in criminal court. They found that certain forms of social support were associated with positive outcomes. For example, children who had a loved one present in the courtroom during preliminary hearings were rated as being less frightened during testimony and were less likely to provide inconsistent testimony about details peripheral to the crime. Moreover, children testifying in the presence of a loved one were able to answer more of the prosecutors' questions. Though the generalizablity of these findings is limited because of the small number ($N = 17$) of children observed, the positive correlates of social support observed by Goodman and colleagues may hold for children testifying in custody proceedings.

Weighing the pros and cons associated with social support in this type of litigation is inherently arduous. On the one hand, research has demonstrated that various forms of social support, such as the presence of a support person, are associated with desirable outcomes, including increased accuracy and decreased levels of stress. On the other hand, children testifying in custody cases may find themselves stripped of their traditional social support systems or the source of support may be a litigant. Judges must decide who the appropriate support person should be and what that person's appropriate level of involvement should be. Neither parent should serve as a support person in a custody case in which he or she is a litigant. The value of children's reports, which often produce new insight into the family's life, could be limited by an involved parent's social support. For example, children are less likely to report the transgression of an adult when that adult is present than when the adult is absent (Dent, 1977; Peters, 1991).

QUESTIONING CHILDREN

Social scientists have carefully investigated the broad issue of interviewing children and the factors believed to influence the accuracy of children's reports. Our understanding of the cognitive, social, and emotional factors in the interview process has increased considerably over the past two decades. This literature can yield procedural recommendations that maximize the effectiveness with which children are interviewed in custody proceedings. Although the primary objectives of the judicial interview are to determine the child's custodial preference and, at times, to elicit a complete and accurate account of family life from the child, myriad factors in the interview process may cause even the most competent questioners of children to elicit inaccurate reports. Our goal in this section is to identify some of the pitfalls commonly encountered when questioning children. We will focus on three primary system variables relating to the questioning of children: (a) the creation and maintenance of a suitable interviewing atmosphere; (b) the use of age-appropriate vocabulary and sentence forms; and (c) the use of open- versus close-ended questions.

Atmosphere of the Interview

The ability to create and maintain an atmosphere conducive to questioning children is an often overlooked, yet essential, component of the interview process. An interviewer's ability to establish a positive atmosphere from the outset plays a paramount role in the ultimate success or failure of the interview. Optimal conditions for questioning witnesses rarely exist naturally, but require deliberate effort by the interviewer. Questioners of children, including judges, who do not take extra measures to ensure such an atmosphere may seriously compromise the consistency and accuracy of children's reports. Two strategies—restructuring children's everyday communication beliefs to better accommodate the interview task and using a supportive questioning style— foster an interview atmosphere that maximizes children's ability to provide useful information.

Children usually bring to court many preconceived notions about communicating with adults based on their experiences outside the legal domain. Though these implicit conversational rules may facilitate children's ordinary discourse, some are ill-suited for communicating in legal contexts. Research shows, for example, that younger children tend to assume that adults are honest and sincere, and that a speaker's comments are always congruent with his or her true beliefs and purpose (Demorest, Meyer, Phelps, Gardner, & Winner, 1984; Grice, 1975). Children also learn at a very young age (i.e., 2 to 3 years) that conversation is an interactive, cooperative exchange between people that involves a discernible pattern of one person asking a question, and the other providing an answer (Bloom, 1991). Children by the age of 2 years also believe that they should begin speaking immediately after their conversational partner has stopped doing so (Bloom, Rocissano, & Hood, 1976). Moreover, when an adult repeatedly questions a child about a specific topic or an event, the child may assume that the adult knows the correct answer to the question and may therefore employ a response "switching strategy" due to the demand characteristics inherent in the repeated questioning task (Siegal, Waters, & Dinwiddy, 1988); that is, the child will try to give the "right" answer.

These normative rules for communication may discourage children from scrutinizing information provided by adults and intimidate children from asking for clarification or further explanation when they fail to understand a question or idea. Even when provided ambiguous, uninformative messages from an adult speaker, younger children (i.e., 6-year-olds) may fail to report that an adult has communicated inadequately (Sonnenschein & Whitehurst, 1980). Markman (1977) investigated children's comprehension of an adult communicator's message and their tendency to ask clarifying questions by creating an experimental task in which children were asked to help evaluate the adequacy of instructions for a card game and a magic trick. For each of these tasks, crucial information was omitted from the instructions provided to the children. For example, the main objective of the card game was to determine who had the "special card"; however, the special card was never designated nor described in any way to the child. Results from this study revealed that first and second graders required a higher number of "probing" questions (i.e., questions such as "Do you have any questions?" or "Did I forget to tell you anything?" intended to help children realize and report their lack of understanding) than did third graders. Thus even in conditions where children are presented blatantly incomplete information and encouraged to evaluate the adequacy of the adult speaker's message, they may fail to voluntarily express the need for clarification or to request additional explanation from the interviewer.

Of perhaps even more concern are experimental findings that children may attempt to provide answers to unanswerable questions posed by adults (Hughes & Grieve, 1980) and may overestimate their ability to accurately communicate information to the message receiver (Asher, 1976). Hughes and Grieve asked 5- and 8-year-olds a series of "bizarre" questions (i.e., questions that did not permit direct answers, such as "Is milk bigger than water?" and "Is red heavier than yellow?") and discovered that children of both age groups frequently provided answers to such questions. Studies by Perry et al. (1995) and Carter, Bottoms, and Levine (1996) mirror the Hughes and Grieve study. Both groups of researchers have observed that children of various ages often attempt to answer questions that contain linguistically complex language features (e.g., double negatives, multiple parts, difficult vocabulary) that clearly exceed children's developmental capabilities.

What conclusions can we draw based on these studies? In general, it can be said that in certain situations, children overestimate the veridicality of adults' statements, may fail to communicate their lack of comprehension to an adult questioner, and may neglect to request additional clarifying information when they do not understand a message from an adult communicator. Moreover, children may attempt to answer extremely complex questions, even when a logical answer does not exist, and may overestimate their ability to accurately communicate information to the interviewer. Given these somewhat discouraging findings, what can interviewers do to circumvent the limitations associated with children's enigmatic assumptions about communicating with adults?

To better accommodate the interviewing task, interviewers can restructure children's preexisting notions about everyday communication. One of the most basic ways to achieve this goal is to begin the interview by explicitly stating what the interviewer expects of the child during the interview. In language a child can understand, interviewers should explain the purpose of the interview and stress that they are asking such questions because they do not know the answers. Interviewers should remind children that they are not being interviewed because they did something wrong or because they are in trouble, but instead because the judge needs the child's help and input to make an informed decision. Framing the task as a cooperative endeavor to discover the truth minimizes the confrontational nature of the interview, thus reducing children's worry about answering and expressing their lack of understanding or knowledge. Interviewers should make sure the child understands that there are no right or wrong answers, as long as the child is telling the truth. Children should be encouraged throughout the interview to ask for clarification when they do not understand a question or something the interviewer has said. An intentionally difficult practice question may be particularly effective in illustrating when and how the child should ask the judge to rephrase or restate a question or comment. Finally, interviewers should monitor children's comprehension of the questions and the specific answers provided by the child. To ensure that the child possesses an adequate understanding of the questions and responses, an interviewer can simply ask a child to rephrase the question in his or her own words (e.g., "Please tell me what I just asked you in your own words") or to explain the meaning of a statement in his or her own words (e.g., "You used the word X. What do you mean by the word X?").

Supportive Questioning Techniques

A second tool that can help to create and maintain an atmosphere suitable for the effective interviewing of children is the use of supportive questioning techniques. Interviewing children in a supportive, nonthreatening manner can lead to beneficial outcomes that are desirable to both fact finders and children (Carter et al., 1996; Goodman, Bottoms, Schwartz-Kenney, & Rudy, 1991; Marquis, Marshall, & Oskamp, 1972). One study explored how a reinforcing interviewer influenced the accuracy of children's memories for a stressful medical procedure. These researchers questioned 3- to 7-year-old children about a recent visit to a medical clinic during which they received an oral polio vaccine and inoculation (Goodman, Bottoms, et al., 1991). Interviewers in this study used a positively reinforcing interview style with half of the children, whereas the other half were questioned in a standard fashion. The reinforcing interview style consisted of the interviewer providing children with juice and cookies at the beginning of the interview session, as well as providing various verbal and nonverbal cues (e.g., smiling and praising the child) intended to put the child at ease during questioning. Results suggested that the reinforcing interview style could facilitate the accuracy of children's reports under some conditions. Specifically, children in the reinforcing interview condition made fewer inaccurate statements during free recall and made fewer commission errors (i.e., false statements) when presented with questions containing incorrect information four weeks after their visits to the medical clinic. Also, age-related differences in children's tendency to falsely report abuse in the standard interviewing condition disappeared for children interviewed in a reinforcing manner.

Subsequent research confirmed these findings in general and yielded a broader understanding of the positive effects associated with supportive questioning techniques (Carter et al., 1996). Interviewers in this study questioned 5- to 7-year-olds about an interactive play event using one of two questioning styles. In the supportive condition, interviewers used a number of techniques intended to put the child at ease during the interview, such as beginning the interview with a brief introduction and rapport-building session to reduce the perceived power differential between the interviewer and child; speaking in a warm, nonthreatening voice tone; displaying comforting nonverbal behaviors such as smiling and maintaining eye contact; and sitting in a relaxed body position during the interview. In the intimidating condition, interviewers used an interview style that lacked these features (e.g., the interviewer made no effort to establish rapport with the child, spoke in a monotonic voice, maintained minimal eye contact, smiled infrequently, and sat upright in a formal position). Children who were interviewed using supportive techniques gave more accurate responses to certain types of questions (i.e., those that were less personally relevant and those that were non-abuse-related).

Thus, it appears that under certain circumstances a supportive, positively-reinforcing interview style with children increases the accuracy of their reports. How else might this style of questioning increase the efficacy of interviews in custody cases? Marquis and colleagues (1972) found that the beneficial effects of supportive questioning techniques may do more than increase children's accuracy. In fact, they did not find positive effects of supportive interviewing on participants' responses to free recall and leading questions. However, adults interviewed in a supportive manner tended to like the interviewer more, evaluated the way in which the interview was conducted more favorably, and were slightly less likely to believe the interviewer wanted biased answers than adults questioned in a challenging manner. Though these outcomes may appear less advantageous and less forensically relevant than the improved memory performance observed by Goodman, Bottoms, et al. (1991) and Carter et al. (1996), children's (and parents') perceptions of procedural fairness are important—they may affect their reactions to a custody decision. Delays in children's improvement after legal proceedings, as reported by parents, are associated with perceptions that the legal system was unfair and unsatisfactory (Goodman et al., 1992). Moreover, perceptions of procedural fairness were found to be a powerful predictor of parents' overall satisfaction with court and the final decision reached in actual child custody cases studied by Kitzmann and Emery (1993). Finally, the extent to which individuals perceive legal procedures to be fair and just influences the perceived legitimacy of authorities in legal settings (Tyler, 1990) and the willingness to voluntarily accept a judge's decision (Lind & Tyler, 1988). Thus supportive questioning techniques that enhance children's and parents' perceptions of procedural fairness may lead to more positive responses to child custody litigation and decision making.

It is also noteworthy that Marquis and colleagues (1972) observed that witnesses in a challenging interview condition believed the interviewer held more negative evaluations of their performance and testimony than did witnesses in the supportive interview condition. Beliefs like these may inhibit a child's testimony and hinder a child's willingness to express confusion or to request additional needed information from the interviewer. If the supportive interviewing of children attenuates children's perceptions that the interviewer is distrusting and skeptical, as it did with adults in the Marquis experiment, this is yet another reason for interviewers to use these techniques. By doing so, judges may help children give more complete and accurate testimony as the children's feelings of intimidation and isolation during the interview are decreased.

Research on supportive questioning techniques in forensic settings is still in its infancy so additional research is needed before psychologists can provide informed, empirically sound recommendations to legal professionals about its use. The emerging picture appears promising in that a supportive or positively reinforcing questioning style has been shown to improve children's testimonial performance for certain questions in at least two recent experiments. None of the studies reviewed here documented negative or adverse effects of supportive questioning on children or their reports. Although these studies do not represent the final word on supportive questioning techniques, they can provide guidance for interviewing children in custody litigation. In addition to employing some of the supportive questioning techniques that yielded beneficial results in these studies, interviewers must carefully monitor their verbal and nonverbal behavior when questioning children. Interviewers should always strive to communicate consistent verbal and nonverbal messages to the child. For example, merely encouraging a child to speak up when he or she does not understand something the interviewer has said or asked may not be sufficient to create the positive interviewing atmosphere necessary to maximize children's testimonial capabilities. This especially may be the case if the interviewer's verbal message is not accompanied by complementary nonverbal behaviors that reinforce the idea that the child should be as relaxed and as comfortable as possible. Nonverbal behaviors such as smiling, nodding, maintaining eye contact, and sitting in a relaxed posture may serve this very purpose.

Future empirical studies should tease apart the effects of the various supportive interview components on children and their reports so the specific verbal and nonverbal acts that result in optimal outcomes can be identified and used. Social scientists should continue to investigate how children's reports are improved through supportive questioning. Remember, only one of the three studies we reviewed found beneficial effects of supportive questioning on children's free recall performance. Perhaps supportive interview techniques only increase the accuracy of children's responses to direct questions. Studies comparing the effects of supportive interviewing on different age groups are needed. Researchers also should examine children's reactions to an overly supportive interviewer. Is there a threshold for the positive effects of supportive interviewing? Can someone to be too supportive to the point of unknowingly encouraging partially or completely false reports from children?

Age-Appropriate Vocabulary and Language Structures

Two additional, closely related system variables are the vocabulary and linguistic complexity of the interview. A growing body of empirical research, from the laboratory and real world situations, shows that children often do not understand many of the words, phrases, and questions commonly used by professionals in legal settings (e.g., Brennan & Brennan, 1988; Carter et al., 1996; Perry et al., 1995). Not surprisingly, these studies also have revealed age-related differences in children's ability to understand legal terminology and question forms such that older children tend to understand more than do younger ones (Flin et al., 1989; Melton et al., 1992; Saywitz et al., 1990).

Walker (1993), for example, linguistically analyzed one child's trial testimony and found three sources of miscommunication: age-inappropriate vocabulary, complex syntax, and general ambiguity. Recall that Saywitz and colleagues (1990) examined elementary children's knowledge of terms commonly encountered in legal proceedings and found that many children were unable to provide basic definitions for words such as motion, petition, competence, and allegations. Many children mistook legal terms for a similar sounding word (e.g., "Jury is like the stuff ladies wear on their fingers and ears and around the neck") or attached a more familiar, nonlegal definition to the word (e.g., "A motion is like waving your arms"). In Great Britain, Flin and colleagues (1989) found that none of the 6-year-old children in their small sample understood the meaning of fundamental court-related terms such as evidence, lawyer, trial, witness, and going to court. Finally, evaluative research conducted in the United States and abroad confirms that legal professionals in actual cases use language beyond children's comprehension (Cashmore, 1992; Davies & Noon, 1991; Flin, Bull, Boon, & Knox, 1993; Murray, 1995; Tidwell et al., 1990). In some instances, attorneys interviewed posttrial have openly admitted their inadequacies in questioning children and have expressed a need for specialized training in this area (Cashmore, 1992; Murray, 1995).

How does children's well-documented inability to fully understand the language used in legal settings affect their testimony? How does the mismatch of legal professionals' and children's language influence the accuracy of children's accounts? Do children know when they do not understand? Social scientists have begun to uncover answers to many research questions such as these. Australian researchers Brennan and Brennan (1988) studied how the linguistic demands placed on children in various contexts affect their ability to process language. Drawing on questions used in actual trials involving children, Brennan and Brennan interviewed children in elementary and high school and asked them to repeat the three types of questions verbatim. Children performed most poorly on the questions taken from court transcripts, and the researchers concluded that as questions become increasingly courtroom specific and combative in nature, children's ability to respond in a truthful and meaningful way decreases dramatically.

Based on these findings, Perry and collaborators (1995) explored how accurately children respond to question forms frequently encountered in court. These researchers questioned children from four different age groups (kindergartners, fourth graders, ninth graders, and college students) about a previously viewed videotaped incident involving a brief interaction between a young girl and a man named Sam. These questions were phrased in either a normal, straightforward manner or contained linguistic and grammatical features common to the legal vernacular (e.g., negatives, multiple parts, difficult vocabulary, and complex syntax.) Two particularly relevant findings emerged from this study. First, as indicated by decreased levels of response accuracy, both children and young adults had more difficulty answering "lawyerese" questions compared with those phrased in standard English. Second, students of all ages demonstrated impaired metacognitive functioning in that they were often fooled into thinking they knew the answers to the lawyerese questions when in reality they did not. Thus, without respondents knowing it, certain linguistic and grammatical features common to questions posed by legal professionals can obfuscate communication and make inaccurate reports more likely.

Consistent with these findings, Carter and colleagues (1996) found that complex question forms reduce the accuracy of children's testimony about an experienced event. In this study, 5- and 7-year-old children interacted with an unfamiliar confederate in a play session and were later interviewed by researchers using questions of varying linguistic complexity. Children responding to complex, developmentally inappropriate questions were significantly less accurate than those answering simple questions. Moreover, similar to the findings of Perry and colleagues, the vast majority of children interviewed did not effectively communicate their inability to answer the complex questions to the interviewer. Among 30 children responding to over 900 total possible questions, only 5 children openly expressed a lack of understanding or asked for clarification. They raised these issues on a total of 9 questions.

Overall, those who question children can learn several important lessons from these empirical findings. First, interviewers must vigilantly monitor their vocabulary and the linguistic complexity of their interviews to ensure that they do not exceed the child's comprehension. Phrases and words such as "going to court," "motion," and "evidence" that are commonplace in the legal system are often problematic for children to understand, especially for those under 10 years of age. Certain question forms, such as those containing multiple parts that require mutually exclusive answers (e.g., "Did your mom leave you at home alone for a weekend and did she return with toys?") or those including negatives (e.g., "Is it not true that you've had problems getting along with your classmates at school?") may inadvertently thwart the truth-seeking function of the interview and, therefore, should be avoided. Complex sentences should be rephrased or broken down into shorter, simpler sentences to facilitate communication between parties. Taking these steps should increase the likelihood of gaining accurate information from child witnesses, thus making decision making in custody cases more effective.

Open- versus Close-Ended Questions

The use of open- versus close-ended questions poses perplexing dilemmas in a legal context. Open-ended questions are desirable because they give the child a chance to relate information from his or her point of view, using his or her own words, in a relatively uninterrupted manner. Although occasional prompts and cues may be necessary to guide the child, the nature and amount of information disclosed to the interviewer is largely determined by the child. On the other hand, close-ended questions are often useful and necessary to elicit more detailed and focused reports from children as well. Certainly, interviewers often have specific questions for which they need answers. For professionals who work with children, the challenge of questioning children becomes one of attempting to mutually satisfy these two competing goals. A delicate balance must be struck between allowing children to freely provide their own accounts and, at the same time, obtaining adequately specific, detailed information.

Empirical research has revealed a trade-off between the amount and the accuracy of information obtained via open- versus close-ended questions. Open-ended questions tend to yield highly accurate, although somewhat limited, accounts from children (Dent & Stephenson, 1979; Hutcheson, Baxter, Telfer, & Warden, 1995). Studies examining children's memories for a wide variety of events, ranging from fairly innocuous incidents such as playing games with an unfamiliar male confederate (Goodman & Reed, 1986) or performing and imagining various activities (Gordon, Jens, Shaddock, & Watson, 1991) to more serious events, such as participating in pediatric examinations (Baker-Ward, Gordon, Ornstein, Larus, & Clubb, 1993; Steward & Steward, 1996), visiting the dentist (Vandermaas, Hess, & Baker-Ward, 1993), or receiving venipuncture or inoculations (Goodman, Hirschman, et al., 1991) consistently have documented children's tendency to accurately, but incompletely, report events in response to open-ended and free recall questions. In contrast, studies of the effects of close-ended questions on children's reports show that this type of question typically elicits more complete and thorough, yet less accurate, accounts than open-ended questions do (Dent, 1992; King & Yuille, 1987). Thus, the additional information gained by using close-ended questions often comes at the cost of decreased accuracy.

How does the age of a witness affect the completeness and accuracy of his or responses to open- versus close-ended questions? Researchers employing a wide range of methodologies have studied witnesses of various ages and have found that as witness age increases, so does the completeness of their responses for both types of questions (Hutcheson et al., 1995; Laumann & Elliott, 1992). Similarly, as witness age increases, so do the levels of response accuracy for both open- and close-ended questions (Laumann & Elliott, 1992; Vandermaas et al., 1993). However, within each respective age group, the general trade-off between response completeness and accuracy for open- versus close-ended questions remains similar such that open-ended questions result in more accurate, yet incomplete reports, whereas close-ended questions result in more complete, yet less accurate, reports.

Based on the information gleaned from these experiments, professionals need to carefully contemplate the nature, quantity, and quality of the testimony they seek from children and adjust their style of questioning accordingly. Total reliance on one question type is often unfeasible, and sometimes detrimental. For example, Saywitz, Goodman, Nicholas, and Moan (1991) interviewed children about physical examinations involving anal and/or genital touch using a combined free recall (prompted by an open-ended question) and direct question procedure. Eighty-eight percent of the females who experienced vaginal touch and 89% who experienced anal touch failed to report these incidents during free recall alone. However, when asked directly about the occurrence of these activities, 86% correctly reported vaginal touch and 69% correctly disclosed anal touch. Thus, important information may go unreported when interviewers rely exclusively on open-ended questions.

Most researchers agree that interviewers should strive to maximize the use of open-ended questions when interviewing children. Others (e.g., Lamb, Sternberg, & Esplin, 1994; Steward & Steward, 1996) recommend that when more specific, directive questions are necessary, they should be followed by open-ended prompts to help shift the child back to the free recall response style (Lamb et al., 1996). Moreover, if a professional combines the open- and close-ended questioning strategies, every effort should be made to let the child relate the information in his or her own words before posing more specific, close-ended questions. This mixed strategy might best accommodate the needs and interests of decision makers in child custody cases, while minimizing the inaccuracy of reports.

Misleading Questions and Children's Suggestibility

To this point, we have discussed research on non-misleading close-ended questions. However, some forms of close-ended questions, specifically those that introduce misleading information to the child, have been shown to elicit less accurate information from children. Children's memories for an event can be influenced by exposure to misleading information. First, we explore a general description of the paradigm used by psychologists to study the suggestibility of children. Next, we describe research that has examined the relationship between exposure to misleading information and the accuracy of witness memory. Several variables that moderate the size and direction of the misinformation/accuracy relationship have been studied, and we discuss those that are of particular interest in custody cases. These moderating variables include the age of the witness, the level of witness participation in the event in question, and finally the prestige or perceived authority of the source providing the misleading information to the witness. Our discussion of these issues is not an exhaustive review of research on suggestibility. By providing an introduction to these concepts and findings, however, we hope to increase the reader's sensitivity to the problem and to reduce this type of questioning in court. For an authoritative review of children's suggestibility, see Ceci and Bruck (1993).

What do we mean when we say a witness is "suggestible" or "susceptible to misleading information?" What is the "misinformation effect" and why is it of relevance to judges and other professionals charged with questioning

witnesses? In general, psychologists have examined the influence of misleading information on witnesses' reports by exposing participants to some event
(or having them participate in some event) and later questioning them about
that event. Once participants have viewed the event, some or all of the participants are exposed to misleading information about that event. In some experiments, this misleading information is presented as a written summary of
the witnessed event; in others, the misleading information is presented in
questions asked of the witness by the experimenter. Researchers then compare the accuracy of participants who received misleading or incorrect information with those who received neutral or correct information. Alternatively,
researchers make comparisons within subjects, examining the accuracy of a
participant's responses to neutral or correct information versus responses to
misleading or incorrect information. A participant is said to be suggestible or
susceptible to misinformation to the extent that he or she incorporates the
suggested misinformation into his or her original memory for the event, as
evidenced by decreased accuracy on the final memory test. Psychologists
have termed this phenomenon the *misinformation effect*. This simply refers to
the tendency of witnesses to provide less accurate accounts of an event when
they have been misled to believe in some way that a certain aspect of the
event was different from what they originally observed.

In the laboratory, researchers can easily control children's exposure to misleading or incorrect information because researchers know whether questions
contain misleading or suggestive information. In the real world, however,
judges, attorneys, and criminal investigators seldom have such information.
Thus, an additional danger of using close-ended or specific questions is the risk
that these questions contain misleading information that can decrease the accuracy of a child's memory for the event. When asking children specific questions
about their homelife, for example, interviewers risk introducing incorrect information which, in turn, may alter or damage a child's original memory for a
given event. As a result, interviewers must be extremely careful to avoid the
questions containing misleading or suggestive information so as not to unintentionally contaminate children's memories.

Although our discussion of misinformation and suggestibility thus far may
suggest blatantly egregious errors or extremely suggestive questioning techniques, even subtle changes in the wording of a question have been shown to
result in dramatic differences in children's, as well as adults', overall accuracy
of memory for an event. For example, Elizabeth Loftus and her colleagues at
the University of Washington have conducted numerous studies demonstrating the powerful effects that the wording of a question can have on witness accuracy. In one such study, Dale, Loftus, and Rathbun (1978) interviewed
preschool children after they viewed a series of short films. In total, 16 different question forms were designed to test children's memories for entities that
either did or did not appear in the films. Within these different question forms
they manipulated whether each question contained affirmation or negation

(e.g., *"Did* you see . . . ?" versus *"Didn't* you see . . . ?") and an article or quantifier (e.g., *the* versus *a* for singular entities and *some* versus *any* for plural entities). Results showed that when children were asked questions about an entity that did not appear in the film, they were particularly likely to answer yes to the question forms "Did you see the . . . ," "Did you see any . . . ," and "Didn't you see some . . . ?" Thus, even minor changes in question composition can affect the accuracy of children's and adults' memories.

Of course, the extent to which a child is susceptible to suggestion is influenced by other variables. One of these variables is the child's age. With the increased reporting and prosecution of crimes committed against children, more and more child witnesses are appearing in court to provide testimony against alleged perpetrators. As a result, questions concerning the suggestibility of younger witnesses has come to the forefront of the child witness research agenda. Overall, this body of research has yielded mixed findings, some indicating that children tend to be more suggestible than adults (e.g., Ceci et al., 1987; Cohen & Harnick, 1980) and some indicating that children tend to be no more suggestible than adults (e.g., Flin, Boon, Knox, & Bull, 1992; Marin, Holmes, Guth, & Kovac, 1979). In their seminal analysis of this body of contradictory research findings, Ceci and Bruck (1993) concluded that there appear to be significant age differences in suggestibility, with preschool-age children being particularly susceptible to misleading information compared with older children and adults.

Research also suggests that the level of a child's participation in a witnessed event influences the magnitude of the suggestibility effect. Children recall activities that they have performed more easily than they recall activities that they observe other people perform (Baker-Ward, Hess, & Flanagan, 1990). Participation also helps make a child resistant to suggestion. Tobey and Goodman (1992) tested children's susceptibility to misleading questions while varying whether the child was a participant in or a mere witness to an event. Preschool children either interacted with a "babysitter" or watched another child play with the babysitter. These researchers found that children's free recall and their answers to misleading questions were more accurate when they actively participated in an event rather than passively observed an event. Similarly, Rudy and Goodman (1991) found that participation increased children's resistance to suggestion. Thus, children's reports about events in which they participated are likely to be more accurate than their reports about events they merely witnessed.

Finally, the characteristics of the source of the misleading information may also influence children's susceptibility to suggestion. Ceci and colleagues (1987) found that preschool children are more likely to incorporate inaccurate information about an event into their memory when the misleading information is provided by an adult source (high prestige) versus a same-age peer (low prestige). Credible adults are also more likely to mislead children than are adults who have been discredited. Lampinen and Smith (1995) found that when children were asked suggestive questions by an adult who was introduced as "a silly man" they were unlikely to be misled, whereas children were misled when asked suggestive questions by a credible adult.

The credibility of the source can also be manipulated by telling children whether the interviewer is knowledgeable about the event in question. For example, Toglia, Ross, Ceci, and Hembrooke (1992) found that children who were interviewed by an adult who claimed to know a lot about the witnessed event were more likely to be misled than were children who were interviewed by an adult who claimed to know little about the event. This research on the credibility of the interviewer suggests that children may be particularly likely to be misled by judges, whom children view as a highly authoritative source. However, research also suggests that children may be less likely to accept misleading information from a credible source if they are warned that the source may try to trick them by making incorrect statements (McDevitt & Carroll, 1988). Thus, when interviewing children, a judge may want to tell them that the children know more about the witnessed events than the judge does and that judges may accidentally say something that a child knows is untrue. This warning could help children resist the effects of any misleading information a judge may unwittingly introduce during the judicial interview.

One specific type of misleading question deserves special mention. In custody disputes involving allegations of child sexual abuse, decision makers should be particularly concerned about children's susceptibility to suggestions that they have been abused. Despite the overwhelming evidence that children, especially preschoolers, are often misled by suggestive questioning, evidence is mounting that children are particularly resistant to suggestions about abusive behaviors that did not occur. For example, children who are interviewed about a medical examination rarely provide false reports about genital touch even when they are directly asked about touching in this area (Saywitz et al., 1991).

Children also seem to resist false suggestions that they were abused during more commonplace interactions with adults. After children interacted with an adult male (a "babysitter") during a play session, Rudy and Goodman (1991) asked the children questions about events that had not occurred but that might be asked during a sexual abuse investigation (e.g., whether they had been kissed, how many times the man spanked them, and whether the man took off their clothes). Older children were more likely to resist these suggestions than were younger preschool children, but overall children were unlikely to accept these false suggestions. In a similar study, a police officer told some of the children that the babysitter might have done something wrong and that he was investigating the allegations; the remaining children were not given this information (Tobey & Goodman, 1992). Children were then asked abuse-related questions like the questions in the Rudy and Goodman study. Although one might anticipate that this forensic context would increase the number of false reports of abuse, children remained resistant to false suggestions of abuse.

The research evidence suggests that it is difficult to manipulate a child into producing a false report of abuse (Rudy & Goodman, 1991; Saywitz et al., 1991;

Tobey & Goodman, 1992). However, this resistance to being misled about abusive behaviors can be overcome if an interviewer uses an intimidating interview style with children (Goodman, Bottoms, et al., 1991). Although it is unlikely that children will be misled into falsely reporting sexual abuse during a judicial interview, we recommend that judges be careful and limit the extent to which they suggest information to children during their interviews.

Repeated Questioning

Some family court judges have advocated eliciting relevant information from a child when they are reluctant to express a clear custodial preference (Newman & Collester, 1980). When coaxing children to provide information about their family life, interviewers may ask repeated questions about the same topic to elicit more information from the child. This type of repeated questioning of a child on a particular topic could have one of two effects on children's memory. On the one hand, if a child is asked to repeatedly recall an event over time, it is possible that the repeated retrieval of the memory may reinforce or strengthen the representation of the event in memory, resulting in enhanced memory for the event (Fivush & Schwarzmueller, 1995). On the other hand, if children are repeatedly asked about the same events, it is possible that they may take the repetitive questioning as a sign that they provided the wrong answer to the question the first time it was asked (Siegal et al., 1988); otherwise, why would the adult repeat an answered question (Grice, 1975)?

Psychologists have begun to examine the impact of repeated questioning on the accuracy of children's event reports. Some studies find that repeated interviews (i.e., interviewing a child once, and then asking the same questions during a second interview) enhance the accuracy of children's memory for events (Baker-Ward et al., 1990; Flin et al., 1992; Goodman, Bottoms, et al., 1991; Memon, Wark, Bull, & Koehnken, 1997) or at least, do not decrease the accuracy of their reports (Baker-Ward et al., 1993; Tucker, Mertin, & Luszcz, 1990). Repeated questioning can take several forms, which may have a decidedly different impact on the accuracy of the memory reported by the child. Children may be subjected to multiple interviews with the interrogator asking the same questions in each interview or children may be asked repeated questions within the same interview.

Research suggests that when open-ended questions are repeated over time, appearing in different interviews between which a significant amount of time has elapsed, the repetition may have no effect on the accuracy of children's responses. In a study conducted by Poole and White (1991), children and adults witnessed an interaction between a male and a female experimenter. During the course of this exchange, the man and woman argued over a pen, the man grabbed the woman's arm to wrest the pen from her grasp, and the woman claimed to be hurt by this gesture. Participants were interviewed either once, a week after the event, or twice, a few minutes after the event and one week later. These interviews consisted of seven open-ended questions that were repeated three times during the course of each interview. The accuracy of children who were repeatedly questioned over different interview sessions did not differ from the accuracy of children who were questioned a single time. In a follow-up study, Poole and White (1993) interviewed a subset of the participants from their earlier study after a 2-year delay using the same procedure as was used in the previous interviews. There were still no differences in the accuracy of the memories reported by the children who had been questioned once or twice in the original study, even after this lengthy delay. Similarly, Cassidy and DeLoache (1995) found that children provided consistent responses to repeated questions for specific information (as opposed to open-ended questions) when the repeated questions appeared in five interviews that were several weeks apart.

How accurately do children respond to repeated questions contained within the same interview? Research by Memon and Vartoukian (1996) suggests that repetition of questions for a second time within the same interview will not affect the accuracy of children's responses to either open-ended or specific questions. Other evidence suggests that preschool children may be particularly likely to change their responses in the face of repeated questions within an interview (Poole & White, 1991; Siegal et al., 1988), especially if the repeated questions become increasingly suggestive over time (Cassel, Roebers, & Bjorklund, 1996). Children are particularly likely to change their responses to repeated questions if they make the attribution that the interviewer is repeating questions because they answered incorrectly the first time the question was asked or because the interviewer is looking for a different answer (Siegal et al., 1988). Thus, interviewers should avoid repeated questioning in an attempt to elicit additional information from very young children.

CONCLUSION

Because the research we have discussed has not been conducted to address questions that are specific to custody cases, there are limitations to our knowledge about the accuracy of children's reports in this context. Little research has been done on the accuracy of children's memory for family life (cf. Fivush & Shukat, 1995). Moreover, the stress levels that are present while the children are being interviewed in an experiment are necessarily lower—for ethical reasons—than the stress that children are likely to experience while being interviewed in judge's chambers or testifying in court. Despite these limitations, research on child witness memory has important implications for the treatment of children during custody cases and for judicial decision making in these cases.

Do judges have accurate beliefs about children's ability to remember? If judges, as suggested by survey data, routinely ignore statements of children under the age of 10 about the quality of their home life (Newman & Collester, 1980; Scott et al., 1988), they may be neglecting valuable information. Generally, judges seem to underestimate children's abilities by dismissing all information provided by young children. Research on the accuracy of children's autobiographical information demonstrates that even preschool children can provide accurate accounts of daily activities and special events (Fivush & Shukat, 1995). However, not all information provided by children is accurate; therefore, it is important to examine the factors associated with the accuracy of children's memory.

In our discussion of the variables that moderate the accuracy of children's reports, we have suggested that triers of fact pay attention to two classes of variables: estimator and system variables. Although little can be done to control the influence of estimator variables (e.g., parental coaching) on children's memory, judges need to be aware of the conditions under which children are providing information. Parental pressure to conceal information may or may not exist in any given case. If information about parental pressure is present, the trier of fact can then make a decision about the appropriate weight to be given to the child's testimony.

Much can be done, however, to increase the accuracy of children's reports if system variables are considered. Children should be adequately prepared for their experience in court if they are to give accurate testimony. Judges should work to maintain a supportive environment in the courtroom or in chambers so that the child is not intimidated by the questioning. Judges and attorneys must take care to use age-appropriate language and sentence structure. Although attorneys may be reluctant to ask open-ended questions because they would lose control of the evidence presentation, judges should be strongly encouraged to use open-ended questions when interviewing children. Not only do open-ended questions reduce the opportunity for the interviewer to introduce misleading or suggestive material into the questions being asked, children can accurately respond to open-ended questions even if they are repeated. If these recommendations are followed, it is more likely that children will provide the court with useful and accurate information about their living conditions.

REFERENCES

Aldridge, J., & Freshwater, K. (1993). The preparation of child witnesses. *Journal of Child Law, 5,* 25–27.

Asher, S. R. (1976). Children's ability to appraise their own and another person's communication performance. *Developmental Psychology, 12,* 24–32.

Baker-Ward, L., Gordon, B. N., Ornstein, P. A., Larus, D. M., & Clubb, P. A. (1993). Young children's long-term retention of a pediatric examination. *Child Development, 64,* 1519–1533.

Baker-Ward, L., Hess, T. M., & Flanagan, D. A. (1990). The effects of involvement on children's memory for events. *Cognitive Development, 5,* 55–69.

Bloom, L. (1991). *Language development from two to three.* New York: Cambridge University Press.

Bloom, L., Rocissano, L., & Hood, L. (1976). Adult-child discourse: Developmental interaction between information processing and linguistic knowledge. *Cognitive Psychology, 8,* 521–552.

Bottoms, B. L., Goodman, G. S., Schwartz-Kenney, B., Sachsenmaier, T., & Thomas, S. (1990, March). *Keeping secrets: Implications for children's testimony.* Paper presented at the biennial meeting of the American Psychology-Law Society, Williamsburg, VA.

Brennan, M., & Brennan, R. E. (1988). *Strange language: Child victims under cross-examination* (3rd ed.). Wagga Wagga, New South Wales: Charles Sturt University-Riverina.

Carter, C. A., Bottoms, B. L., & Levine, M. (1996). Linguistic and socioemotional influences on the accuracy of children's reports. *Law and Human Behavior, 20,* 335–358.

Cashmore, J. (1992). *The use of closed-circuit television for child witnesses in the ACT* (Children's Evidence Research Paper 1). Sydney, New South Wales: Australian Law Reform Commission.

Cassel, W. S., Roebers, C. E. M., & Bjorklund, D. F. (1996). Developmental patterns of eyewitness responses to repeated and increasingly suggestive questions. *Journal of Experimental Child Psychology, 61,* 116–133.

Cassidy, D. J., & DeLoache, J. S. (1995). The effect of questioning on young children's memory for an event. *Cognitive Development, 10,* 109–130.

Ceci, S. J., & Bruck, M. (1993). Suggestibility of the child witness: A historical review and synthesis. *Psychological Bulletin, 113,* 401–439.

Ceci, S. J., Ross, D. F., & Toglia, M. P. (1987). Suggestibility of children's memory: Psycholegal implications. *Journal of Experimental Psychology: General, 116,* 38–49.

Cohen, R. L., & Harnick, M. A. (1980). The susceptibility of child witnesses to suggestion: An empirical study. *Law and Human Behavior, 4,* 201–210.

Crosby-Currie, C. A. (1996). Children's involvement in contested custody cases: Practices and experiences of legal and mental health professionals. *Law and Human Behavior, 20,* 289–311.

Cutler, B. L., Penrod, S. D., & Martens, T. K. (1987). The reliability of eyewitness identification: The role of system and estimator variables. *Law and Human Behavior, 11,* 233–258.

Dale, P. S., Loftus, E. F., & Rathbun, L. (1978). The influence of the form of the question on the eyewitness testimony of preschool children. *Journal of Psycholinguistic Research, 7,* 269–277.

Davies, G., & Noon, E. (1991). *An evaluation of the live link for child witnesses* (Report commissioned by the Home Office). London, England: Home Office Library.

Demorest, A., Meyer, C., Phelps, E., Gardner, H., & Winner, E. (1984). Words speak louder than actions: Understanding deliberately false remarks. *Child Development, 55,* 1527–1534.

Dent, H. (1977). Stress as a factor influencing person recognition in identification parades. *Bulletin of the British Psychological Society, 27,* 13–17.

Dent, H. (1992). The effects of age and intelligence on eyewitnessing ability. In H. Dent & R. Flin (Eds.), *Children as witnesses* (pp. 1–13). Chichester, England: Wiley.

Dent, H. R., & Stephenson, G. M. (1979). An experimental study of the effectiveness of different techniques of questioning child witnesses. *British Journal of Social and Clinical Psychology, 18,* 41–51.

Dezwirek-Sas, L. (1992). Empowering child witnesses for sexual abuse prosecution. In H. Dent & R. Flin (Eds.), *Children as witnesses* (pp. 181–199). New York: Wiley.

Felner, R. D., Terre, L., Farber, S., Primavera, J., & Bishop, R. A. (1985). Child custody: Practices and perspectives of legal professionals. *Journal of Clinical Child Psychology, 14,* 27–34.

Fisher, R. P., & Cutler, B. L. (1996). The relation between consistency and accuracy of eyewitness testimony. In G. Davies, S. Lloyd-Bostock, M. McMurran, & C. Wilson (Eds.), *Psychology, law, and criminal justice: International developments in research and practice* (pp. 21–28). New York: Walter de Gruyter.

Fivush, R. (1993). Developmental perspectives on autobiographical recall. In G. S. Goodman & B. L. Bottoms (Eds.), *Child victims, child witnesses: Understanding and improving testimony* (pp. 1–24). New York: Guilford Press.

Fivush, R., Gray, J. T., & Fromhoff, F. A. (1987). Two year olds talk about the past. *Cognitive Development, 2,* 393–410.

Fivush, R., & Hamond, N. R. (1990). Autobiographical memory across the preschool years. In R. Fivush & J. A. Hudson (Eds.), *Knowing and remembering in young children* (pp. 223-248). New York: Cambridge University Press.

Fivush, R., Hamond, N. R., Harsch, N., Singer, N., & Wolf, A. (1991). Content and consistency in early autobiographical recall. *Discourse Processes, 14,* 373–388.

Fivush, R., & Schwarzmueller, A. (1995). Say it once again: Effects of repeated questions on children's event recall. *Journal of Traumatic Stress, 8,* 555–580.

Fivush, R., & Shukat, J. R. (1995). Content, consistency, and coherence of early autobiographical recall. In M. S. Zaragoza, J. R. Graham, G. C. N. Hall, R. Hirschman, & Y. S. Ben-Porath (Eds.), *Memory and testimony in the child witness* (pp. 5–23). Thousand Oaks, CA: Sage.

Flin, R., Boon, J., Knox, A., & Bull, R. (1992). The effect of a five-month delay on children's and adults' eyewitness testimony. *British Journal of Psychology, 83,* 323–336.

Flin, R., Bull, R., Boon, J., & Knox, A. (1993). Child witnesses in Scottish criminal trials. *International Review of Victimology, 2,* 309–329.

Flin, R. H., Stevenson, Y., & Davies, G. M. (1989). Children's knowledge of court proceedings. *British Journal of Psychology, 80,* 285–297.

Friedman, W. J. (1992). Children's time memory: The development of a differentiated past. *Cognitive Development, 7,* 171–187.

Gold, E., & Neisser, U. (1980). Recollections of kindergarten. *Quarterly Newsletter of the Laboratory of Comparative Human Cognition, 2,* 77–80.

Goodman, G. S., Bottoms, B. L., Schwartz-Kenney, B., & Rudy, L. (1991). Children's memory for a stressful event: Improving children's reports. *Journal of Narrative and Life History, 1,* 69–99.

Goodman, G. S., Hirschman, J., Hepps, D., & Rudy, L. (1991). Children's memory for stressful events. *Merrill-Palmer Quarterly, 37,* 109–158.

Goodman, G. S., & Reed, R. S. (1986). Age differences in eyewitness testimony. *Law and Human Behavior, 10,* 317–332.

Goodman, G. S., Sharma, A., Thomas, S. F., & Considine, M. G. (1995). Mother knows best: Effects of relationship status and interviewer bias on children's memory. *Journal of Experimental Child Psychology, 60,* 195–228.

Goodman, G. S., Taub, E. P., Jones, D. P. H., England, P., Port, L. K., Rudy, L., & Prado, L. (1992). Testifying in criminal court: Emotional effects on child sexual assault victims. *Monographs of the Society for Research in Child Development, 57*(5, Serial No. 229).

Gordon, B. N., Jens, K. G., Shaddock, A. J., & Watson, T. E. (1991). Children's ability to remember activities performed and imagined: Implications for testimony. *Child Psychiatry and Human Development, 21,* 301–314.

Grice, H. P. (1975). Logic and conversation. In P. Cole & J. L. Morgan (Eds.), *Syntax and semantics* (Vol. 3, pp. 41–58). New York: Academic Press.

Hamond, N. R., & Fivush, R. (1990). Memories of Mickey Mouse: Young children recount their trip to Disneyworld. *Cognitive Development, 6,* 433–448.

Hudson, J. A., & Fivush, R. (1987). *As time goes by: Sixth graders remember a kindergarten experience* (Emory Cognition Project Report #13). Atlanta: Emory University.

Hughes, M, & Grieve, R. (1980). On asking children bizarre questions. *First Language, 1,* 149–160.

Hutcheson, G. D., Baxter, J. S., Telfer, K., & Warden, D. (1995). Child witness statement quality: Question type and errors of omission. *Law and Human Behavior, 19,* 631–648.

Jones, C. (1984). Judicial questioning of children in custody and visitation proceedings. *Family Law Quarterly, 18,* 43–91.

Keeney, K. S., Amacher, E., & Kastanakis, J. A. (1992). The court prep group: A vital part of the court process. In H. Dent & R. Flin (Eds.), *Children as witnesses* (pp. 201–209). New York: Wiley.

King, M. A., & Yuille, J. C. (1987). Suggestibility and the child witness. In S. J. Ceci, D. F. Ross, & M. P. Toglia (Eds.), *Children's eyewitness memory* (pp. 24–35). New York: Springer-Verlag.

Kitzmann, K. M., & Emery, R. E. (1993). Procedural justice and parents' satisfaction in a field study of child custody dispute resolution. *Law and Human Behavior, 17,* 553–567.

Kovera, M. B., Gresham, A. W., Borgida, E., Gray, E., & Regan, P. C. (1997). Does expert testimony inform or influence juror decision-making? A social cognitive analysis. *Journal of Applied Psychology, 82.*

Lamb, M. E., Hershkowitz, I., Sternberg, K. J., Esplin, P. W., Hovav, M., Manor, T., & Yudilevitch, L. (1996). Effects of investigative utterance types on Israeli children's responses. *International Journal of Behavioral Development, 19,* 627–637.

Lamb, M. E., Sternberg, K. J., & Esplin, P. W. (1994). Factors influencing the reliability and validity of statements made by young victims of sexual maltreatment. *Journal of Applied Developmental Psychology, 15,* 255–280.

Lampinen, J. M., & Smith, V. L. (1995). The incredible (and sometimes incredulous) child witness: Child eyewitnesses' sensitivity to source credibility cues. *Journal of Applied Psychology, 80,* 621–627.

Laumann, L. A., & Elliott, R. (1992). Reporting what you have seen: Effects associated with age and mode of questioning on eyewitness reports. *Perceptual and Motor Skills, 75,* 799–818.

Lind, E. A., & Tyler, T. R. (1988). *The social psychology of procedural justice.* New York: Plenum Press.

Linton, M. (1982). Transformations of memory in everyday life. In U. Neisser (Ed.), *Memory observed* (pp. 77–92). San Francisco: Freeman.

Lombard, F. (1984). Judicial interviewing of children in custody cases: An empirical and analytical study. *University of California-Davis Law Review, 17,* 807–851.

Marin, B. V., Holmes, D. L., Guth, M., & Kovac, P. (1979). The potential of children as eyewitnesses: A comparison of children and adults on eyewitness tasks. *Law and Human Behavior, 3,* 295–306.

Markman, E. M. (1977). Realizing that you don't understand: A preliminary investigation. *Child Development, 48,* 986–992.

Marquis, K. H., Marshall, J., & Oskamp, S. (1972). Testimony validity as a function of question form, atmosphere, and item difficulty. *Journal of Applied Social Psychology, 2,* 167–186.

McDevitt, T. M., & Carroll, M. (1988). Are you trying to trick me? Some social influences on children's responses to problematic messages. *Merrill-Palmer Quarterly, 34,* 131–145.

McIntosh, J. A., & Prinz, R. J. (1993). The incidence of alleged sexual abuse in 603 family court cases. *Law and Human Behavior, 17,* 95–101.

Melton, G. B., Limber, S., Jacobs, J. E., Oberlander, L. B., Berliner, L., & Yamamoto, M. (1992). *Preparing sexually abused children for testimony: Children's perceptions of the legal process* (Final report to the National Center on Child Abuse and Neglect, Grant No. 90-CA-1274). Lincoln: University of Nebraska–Lincoln, Center on Children, Families, and the Law.

Memon, A., & Vartoukian, R. (1996). The effects of repeated questioning on young children's eyewitness testimony. *British Journal of Psychology, 87,* 403–415.

Memon, A., Wark, L., Bull, R., & Koehnken, G. (1997). Isolating the effects of the cognitive interview techniques. *British Journal of Psychology, 88,* 179–197.

Merritt, K., Ornstein, P. A., & Spicker, B. (1994). Children's memory for a salient medical procedure: Implications for testimony. *Pediatrics, 94,* 17–23.

Murray, K. (1995). *Live television link: An evaluation of its use by child witnesses in Scottish criminal trials* (Final Research Report). Edinburgh, Scotland: Central Research Unit.

Myers, J. E. B. (1993). Expert testimony regarding child sexual abuse. *Child Abuse & Neglect, 17,* 175–185.

Myers, J. E. B. (1995). New era of skepticism regarding children's credibility. *Psychology, Public Policy, and Law, 1,* 387–398.

Narby, D. J., Cutler, B. L., & Penrod, S. D. (1996). The effects of witness, target, and situational factors on eyewitness identifications. In S. L. Sporer, R. S. Malpass, & G. Koehnken (Eds.), *Psychological issues in eyewitness identification* (pp. 23–52). Mahwah, NJ: Erlbaum.

Newman, J. M., & Collester, D. G. (1980). Children should be seen and heard: Techniques for interviewing the child in contested custody proceedings. *Family Advocate, 8*–32.

Perry, N. W., McAuliff, B. D., Tam, P., Claycomb, L., Dostal, C., & Flanagan, C. (1995). When lawyers question children: Is justice served? *Law and Human Behavior, 19,* 609–629.

Peters, D. (1991). The influence of stress and arousal on the child witness. In J. Doris (Ed.), *The suggestibility of children's recollections: Implications for eyewitness testimony* (pp. 60–76). Washington, DC: American Psychological Association.

Pipe, M. E., & Wilson, J. C. (1994). Cues and secrets: Influences on children's event reports. *Developmental Psychology, 30,* 515–525.

Poole, D. A., & Lindsay, D. S. (1995). Interviewing preschoolers: Effects of nonsuggestive techniques, parental coaching, and leading questions on reports of nonexperienced events. *Journal of Experimental Child Psychology, 60,* 129–154.

Poole, D. A., & White, L. T. (1991). Effects of question repetition on the eyewitness testimony of children and adults. *Developmental Psychology, 27,* 975–986.

Poole, D. A., & White, L. T. (1993). Two years later: Effects of question repetition and retention interval on the eyewitness testimony of children and adults. *Developmental Psychology, 29*, 844–853.

Poole, D. A., & White, L. T. (1995). Tell me again and again: Stability and change in the repeated testimonies of children and adults. In M. S. Zaragoza, J. R. Graham, G. C. N. Hall, R. Hirschman, & Y. S. Ben-Porath (Eds.), *Memory and testimony in the child witness* (pp. 24–43). Thousand Oaks, CA: Sage.

Rudy, L., & Goodman, G. S. (1991). Effects of participation on children's reports: Implications for children's testimony. *Developmental Psychology, 27*, 527–538.

Saywitz, K. J. (1989). Children's conceptions of the legal system: "Court is a place to play basketball." In S. J. Ceci, D. F. Ross, & M. P. Toglia (Eds.), *Perspectives on children's testimony* (pp. 131–157). New York: Springer-Verlag.

Saywitz, K. J., Goodman, G. S., Nicholas, E., & Moan, S. F. (1991). Children's memories of a physical examination involving genital touch: Implications for reports of child sexual abuse. *Journal of Consulting and Clinical Psychology, 59*, 682–691.

Saywitz, K., Jaenicke, C., & Camparo, L. (1990). Children's knowledge of legal terminology. *Law and Human Behavior, 14*, 523–535.

Saywitz, K. J., & Snyder, L. (1993). Improving children's testimony with preparation. In B. L. Bottoms & G. S. Goodman (Eds.), *Child victims, child witnesses: Understanding and improving testimony* (pp. 117–146). New York: Guilford Press.

Saywitz, K. J., & Snyder, L. (1996). Narrative elaboration: Test of a new procedure for interviewing children. *Journal of Consulting and Clinical Psychology, 64*, 1347–1357.

Scott, E. S., Reppucci, N. D., & Aber, M. (1988). Children's preference in adjudicated custody decisions. *Georgia Law Review, 22*, 1035–1078.

Seelau, S. M., & Wells, G. L. (1995). Applied eyewitness research: The other mission. *Law and Human Behavior, 19*, 319–324.

Siegal, M., Waters, L. J., & Dinwiddy, L. S. (1988). Misleading children: Causal attributions for inconsistency under repeated questioning. *Journal of Experimental Child Psychology, 45*, 438–456.

Sonnenschein, S., & Whitehurst, G. J. (1980). The development of communication: When a bad model makes a good teacher. *Journal of Experimental Child Psychology, 3*, 371–390.

Steward, M. S., & Steward, D. S. (1996). Interviewing young children about bodily touch and handling. *Monographs of the Society for Research in Child Development, 61*(4, Serial No. 248).

Tate, C. S., Warren, A. R., & Hess., T. M. (1992). Adults' liability for children's "lie-ability": Can adults coach children to lie successfully? In S. J. Ceci, M. D. Leichtman, & M. E. Putnick (Eds.), *Cognitive and social factors in early deception* (pp. 69–87). Hillsdale, NJ: Erlbaum.

Thompson, W. C., Clarke-Stewart, A., & Lepore, S. J. (1997). What did the janitor do?: Suggestive interviewing and the accuracy of children's accounts. *Law and Human Behavior, 21*, 405–426.

Tidwell, R. P., Lipovsky, J. A., Crisp, J., Plum, H. J., Kilpatrick, D. G., Saunders, B. E., & Dawson, V. L. (1990). *Child victims and witnesses* (Final Report, Grant No. 88–11J-D-064). Washington, DC: Crime Victim Center.

Tobey, A. E., & Goodman, G. S. (1992). Children's eyewitness memory: Effects of participation and forensic context. *Child Abuse and Neglect, 16*, 779–296.

Toglia, M. P., Ross, D. F., Ceci, S. J., & Hembrooke, H. (1992). The suggestibility of children's memory: A social-psychological and cognitive interpretation. In M. L. Howe, C. J. Brainerd, & V. F. Reyna (Eds.), *Development of long-term retention* (pp. 217–241). New York: Springer-Verlag.

Tucker, A., Mertin, P., & Luszcz, M. (1990). The effect of a repeated interview on young children's eyewitness memory. *Australian and New Zealand Journal of Criminology, 23,* 117–124.

Tyler, T. R. (1990). *Why people obey the law.* New Haven, CT: Yale University Press.

Vandermaas, M. O., Hess, T. M., & Baker-Ward, L. (1993). Does anxiety affect children's reports of memory for a stressful event? *Applied Cognitive Psychology, 7,* 109–127.

Wagenaar, W. A. (1986). My memory: A study of autobiographic memory over six years. *Cognitive Psychology, 18,* 225–252.

Wagenaar, W. A., & Groeneweg, J. (1990). The memory of concentration camp survivors. *Applied Cognitive Psychology, 4,* 77–87.

Walker, A. G. (1993). Questioning young children in court: A linguistic case study. *Law and Human Behavior, 17,* 59–81.

Warren-Leubecker, A., Tate, C. S., Hinton, I. D., & Ozbek, I. N. (1989). What do children know about the legal system and when do they know it? First steps down a less traveled path in child witness research. In S. J. Ceci, D. F. Ross, & M. P. Toglia (Eds.), *Perspectives on children's testimony* (pp. 158–183). New York: Springer-Verlag.

Wells, G. L. (1978). Applied eyewitness-testimony research: System variables and estimator variables. *Journal of Personality and Social Psychology, 36,* 1546–1557.

Zaragoza, M. S. (1987). Memory, suggestibility, and eyewitness testimony in children and adults. In S. J. Ceci, M. P. Toglia, & D. F. Ross (Eds.), *Children's eyewitness memory* (pp. 53–78). New York: Springer-Verlag.

Zaragoza, M. S. (1991). Preschool children's susceptibility to memory impairment. In J. Doris (Ed.), *The suggestibility of children's recollections: Implications for eyewitness testimony* (pp. 27–39). Washington, DC: American Psychological Association.

CHAPTER 9

The Impact of Divorce on Infants
and Very Young Children

LINDA C. MAYES and ADRIANA MOLITOR-SIEGL

T HE QUESTION—WHAT contributes to the special tie between infants and their mothers and fathers—gains poignancy and urgency in the midst of parental divorce. Does a 3- or 6-month old infant experience the separation from a mother or father, and if so, how is separation experienced so early in psychological development? How does the nearly inevitable conflict between parents that accompanies divorce affect a preverbal child under age 2 years? What is the impact of parental loss or of shared custody? These questions are always an implicit and often an explicit part of divorces involving infants and very young children. Considerations of the effects of divorce on children are special instances of the more general problem of the effects of separations on infants and young children. The great dependency of very young children is widely recognized in the larger society, among mental health professionals and, to some extent, in law. For example, the now largely defunct "tender years" doctrine, that infants and young children should be in their mother's custody, reflected the traditional and enduring belief of some about a special primary relationship between a biological mother and her very young child.

Courts and mental health professionals are asked to make recommendations and decisions not only about the custody of infants but also about visitation and contact with the absent parent. These decisions emerge from a mixture of personal opinion, past experience, and prevailing cultural and legal standards of what is best for children. Less often, the opinions of experts, and most rarely data from case studies and theoretically driven empirical studies, affect these decisions. Personal opinion and past experience are strongly colored by the vagaries of individual differences among consulting experts, lawyers, judges, and other professionals involved with the family. Cultural views vary with time and place and are reflected indirectly in law and judicial opinion. Expert opinion and empirical data should go hand in hand, for the former should be at least partly grounded in the latter. In this review of the impact of divorce on preverbal children from birth through the first two years, we focus on expert opinion and the data on which those opinions are based.

Direct empirical data about the psychological impact of divorce on children under age 2 years are scant. To address the most relevant issues, we must turn to related investigations in which infants are exposed to nonfamilial caregivers and situations outside the traditional, albeit changing, two-parent family. First, however, it is useful to examine both the scope of the problem—how many children are affected—and the legal history and foundation surrounding the court's involvement.

DIVORCE, INFANTS, AND THE ROLE OF THE SOCIAL AND LEGAL COMMUNITY

Approximately three quarters of the estimated 1.1 million divorces per year in the United States involve children (Glick, 1988). As of 1992, approximately 48% of all couples in first marriages divorce (U.S. Bureau of the Census, 1992), and another 17% separate but do not divorce (Castro-Martin & Bumpass, 1989). It has been estimated that 40% to 50% of children in the United States will spend some time in a single-parent home (Glick & Lin, 1986), and many of these children will also experience life with a stepparent who may also have children from a previous marriage. How many children involved in divorce are under age 2 is usually unspecified in national averages and census data. However, while the incidence of divorce has risen across all age groups, the most dramatic rise has occurred among young adults (Norton, 1983). As a result, the children involved in the divorce more often include infants and preschool aged children (Wallerstein, 1985).

Court disputes over custody of an infant are historically less frequent because until recently the prevailing cultural and legal opinion was that the very young children belong in their mothers' care or the care of their closest female relatives. Among all divorces, 86% of mothers retain physical custody of their children (U.S. Bureau of the Census, 1992) and the proportion is surely higher when children under 2 years of age are involved. Traditionally, only in unusual situations, such as maternal unfitness, was consideration given to placing a young child with its father. However, in the past decade, the number of litigations involving infants and young children has increased as more fathers actively seek both custody and expanded visitation with their children. As cultural standards shift, fathers are beginning to expect and want to preserve contact and active involvement with their very young children.

At the same time that fathers have become more interested in preserving their relationships to their children despite divorce, increased national concern for the well-being of children generally has led to more sophisticated thinking about children's "best interests." Historically, the regulation of family life and of child custody rested with individual states in accordance with the Ninth and Tenth Amendments to the Constitution. In recent decades, however, the federal government has become far more active in regulating and defining family life, parenting, and child rights (for a review, see Horner & Guyer, 1993; Melton & Wilcox, 1989). Federal laws defining the enforcement of child support, the rights of adoptive parents in custody disputes, and the Parent Kidnapping Prevention Act are examples of the expanding role of the federal government in areas involving parent-child relations.

Judicial and legislative movements to protect children from neglect and abuse have brought more into focus the interface between basic developmental principles and legal issues involving children. For example, the 1974 Child Abuse Prevention and Treatment Act, providing federal support to states to develop programs for the prevention, identification, and treatment of child abuse and neglect, mandated reporting of suspected child maltreatment. The consequences included an enormously increased case load for child welfare agencies, a sharp increase in the number of abuse and neglect reports, and much increased public and governmental participation in matters previously regulated and known only within families. The government began to take on itself the guardianship of children's welfare. A second congressional act, the Adoption Assistance and Child Welfare Act, sought to regulate out-of-home placements for children and to establish a permanent home for displaced children. This legislation led to many efforts toward "family preservation" focused on improving family function to reunify children with their birth parents. Child welfare workers were obligated to evaluate the possibility of family preservation and to weigh the child's best interests. All of this federal legislation brought into focus the importance of defining the child's best interests, a doctrine that is also a critical part of considerations in parental divorce.

EXPERT OPINION AND AVAILABLE EMPIRICAL DATA

In 1973, Goldstein, Freud, and Solnit emphasized the essential role of clinical expertise and of expert opinion in serving the best interests of infants and children in custody disputes. Following this point of view, many courts increasingly relied on mental health and child development specialists in making custody decisions and determining parental fitness. Expert recommendations and judicial decisions show a high (85%) concordance (Ash & Guyer, 1986). Expert opinion and consultations often diminish conflicts in court, partly because the mental health consultants may formally or informally mediate between the parents. Mental health professionals have come to view themselves as uniquely qualified to evaluate, provide information, and make recommendations to the court regarding appropriate custody and parental visitation decisions (e.g., Black & Cantor, 1989). Professional guidelines for providing such consultations and opinions to the courts are beginning to appear (e.g., American Academy of Child and Adolescent Psychiatry, 1988).

Courts (and usually families) have as their goal maximizing the likelihood of the child's adequate development and minimizing negative outcomes. The notion of the "least detrimental alternative" (Goldstein, Freud, & Solnit, 1973, 1987) implies that with expert professional guidance, the courts may adequately weigh the developmental risks of several different alternatives for the child, recognizing that no alternative may be perfect or perhaps even good. Thus, opinions are almost always framed in terms of preventing or ameliorating certain adverse outcomes with the implied assumption that these outcomes can be reliably predicted from a given set of present circumstances—an assumption that can surely be questioned in several different contexts that involve predicting from early behaviors or abilities to later functioning.

The principle most often advanced in expert consultation by mental health professionals asked to advise the court regarding either custody or visitation is that there should be continuity of care and contact with the infant's "primary attachment figure" or "primary psychological parent." Although several conceptual conundrums are wrapped up in this principle, it underlies some of the more common court recommendations regarding custody (Horner & Guyer, 1993) including (1) an infant should be in the sole custody of one parent; (2) no overnight visitation with the noncustodial parent; and (3) no change in custody should be permitted once a permanent custodial arrangement is established for the infant (with the exception of obvious circumstances such as the incapacitation or death of the designated custodial parent). What is implied in and required by the principle of continuity of care?

First, insisting on continuity of care implies that infants can tolerate neither multiple persons in their world nor multiple transitions between or among different caring adults. Transitions among multiple caring persons and contexts are presumed uniformly stressful, if not traumatic, and not as opportunities for potentially developmentally promoting diversity and adaptation. The traumatic effects of multiple caregivers are not presumed to be evident immediately but to appear only much later as maladjustment, psychological distress, and crucial social deficits. There is little appreciation in the broadest interpretation of this assumption for individual differences among infants and the greater or lesser degree of adaptability imposed by maturation.

The second implicit assumption contained in the principle of continuity of care is that once infants have formed special, primary attachments to their parents, the infants then have specific physical and emotional requirements for how they are best handled, fed, and loved. Carried to its extreme, this second assumption implies that once intimately "in love" with their parents, infants have a far more restricted range of what they can tolerate from others and much more specified and delicate tastes in their physical and psychological needs. By this light, adequate parental care, at least temporarily, closes down rather than opens up an infant's capacities for adaptation and social engagement with others—a conclusion not supported by either clinical or empirical data. To the contrary, most clinical and empirical observations and prevailing developmental theories hold that in adequately nurturing and supportive care, infants are more free to explore others, feel comfortable with new persons made safe by their parents, and, within the range of their biologically given adaptive skills, adapt successfully to novel circumstances.

The third implicit assumption contained within the principle of continuity of care is that the "primary attachment figure" is usually singular and usually readily identified. All other persons, by implication, in the infant's life may leave without major impact. In our culture identifying who is most important psychologically to an infant is often a difficult, if not impossible, task. Moreover, as constructs, "continuity of care" and "primary attachment figure" do not allow for the multiplicity of services and persons involved in infants and young children's lives, including day-care teachers, at-home nannies, grandparents, aunts and uncles. Single parents, while apparently providing continuity in the legal sense, may be forced to have more persons involved in their infants' care as they adapt economically, socially, and psychologically to their changed circumstances. In 1972, 24% of mothers of infants under a year of age were employed; by 1987, over half (51%) were working outside the home and their infants were cared for by people other than their parents (Hayes, Palmer, & Zaslow, 1990).

The fourth assumption within the continuity-of-care principle is paradoxically a failure to acknowledge developmental differences even in the relatively narrow age range of birth to 2 years. Although very young children are certainly overall more vulnerable and more dependent than perhaps their 5- or 6-year-old counterpart, there is a vast difference in the elaboration of an 18-month-old's attachment to parents compared with a one-month-old. Eighteen-month-olds may be far less able to adapt to new custody arrangements or loss of a parent and may react more clearly to the separation inasmuch as they have a more secure attachment to both parents, or a more elaborated internalized object world—if all has gone well in the parenting relationship up to the time of the divorce. Mandates for continuity must be individualized by the child's level of maturation and history of parenting experiences.

What are the data regarding so-called continuity of care, or conversely, infants' abilities to tolerate and adapt to multiple persons and caregiving contexts and about the psychological definition of "primary attachment figure"? These data come from at least three sources—studies of day care and other group care programs in which infants are cared for by several nonfamilial adults, studies of differentiated attachment patterns between infants and their mothers or fathers, and infants' response to parental separation and loss. Following a discussion of these three areas, we review what is known specifically about the response of infants and toddlers to their parents' divorce.

OUT-OF-HOME CARE IN THE FIRST YEAR

Studies from infant day care yield a confusing array of data and interpretations. In terms of cognitive development, infant day care seems to have neither positive nor negative long-term effects on the cognitive development among middle-class children (Belsky, 1988; Clarke-Stewart, 1988, 1989). But children from economically impoverished homes appear to benefit from substitute, out-of-home care. There is an apparent prevention of declines in cognitive functioning in the early preschool years (Belsky, 1988). More relevant to concerns about parental divorce are those studies examining the influence of nonparental care on attachment to parents. Infants of working mothers are attached to their mothers and preferentially go to them over their day-to-day caregivers (Clark-Stewart, 1989).

There is more controversy about the quality or security of that attachment. Security of attachment at one year does predict later social adjustment and adaptation to school. Children who are securely attached at one year of age have been found to be more compliant and cooperative as preschoolers (Matas, Arend, & Sroufe, 1978; Sroufe, 1983) and more effective in problem-solving tasks (Matas et al., 1978). Out-of-home, substitute care for infants under one year of age appears to influence the quality of the relationship to mothers and fathers though the effects are not uniform and probably occur in response to extensive substitute care (e.g., more than 20 to 30 hours a week). The more very young infants are cared for by other persons, the more insecure the attachment between infant and parent (Clarke-Stewart, 1989; Lamb, Sternberg, & Prodromidis, 1992).

These findings using separation experiences and the Strange Situation (Ainsworth & Wittig, 1969; see Chapter 4) have been replicated and appear well founded. However, their implications for longer term development are less clear, and it is important to note that the majority of infants in out-of-home care are securely attached to their parents (Barton & Williams, 1993). As several researchers have pointed out, the Strange Situation paradigm is designed to elicit children's seeking their parents' comfort and safety under conditions of stress, that is, a separation in the presence of a stranger. However, children in out-of-home care experience separations routinely every morning and are likely far less stressed by a simulated separation (Barton & Williams, 1993). It may be that children in out-of-home care are less likely to seek out their mothers and remain playing comfortably with toys because the separation is not stressful (Doyle & Somers, 1978; Goosens, 1987; Hock, 1980).

On other measures of parent-child relationships, few differences have emerged between working and nonworking mothers on measures such as sensitivity to the infant, responsiveness, or amount of physical contact (Clarke-Stewart, 1989; Hock, 1980). Caruso (1990) reported that mothers of one-year-old infants with extensive day-care experience had higher quality interactions than did mothers of infants in exclusive home care. It maybe that the relationship among separation from mothers, out-of-home care, and altered attachment relations are profoundly influenced by maternal attitudes toward parenting and that the increase in insecure attachment patterns among day-care infants is not so much a factor of the separation for day care but of the relation with the mother before and after day care. Farber and Egeland (1982) reported that working mothers of insecurely attached infants reported less interest and desire prenatally for an infant and for motherhood. That is, maternal emotional and personality variables may be better predictors of infant attachment than arrangements for the child's physical care (Farber & Egeland, 1982), a point that is equally relevant to the infants of divorced parents.

The quality of the out-of-home care is also critical and another controversial area in considerations of the effects of nonmaternal care on infants. Even the definition of a quality variable for out-of-home care is complex and includes such factors as group size, staff training, and characteristics of the physical environment. Few published data include ratings of the quality of the nonmaternal care as a variable in the relationship between attachment and separation from parents. Howe and colleagues (Howes, Rodning, Galluzo, & Myers, 1988) reported that children are more likely to form secure attachments with their day-care teachers and caregivers in settings characterized by smaller child-to-adult ratios and more responsive care. Low child-to-staff ratios are also associated with more nurturant and nonrestrictive caregiver behavior (Howes, 1983) and increased talk and play behavior in toddlers (Howes & Rubenstein, 1985). Also, some data suggest that infants who are insecurely attached to their mothers were more likely to be placed in poor-quality care arrangements (Howes et al., 1988), a finding suggesting a complex interaction between family/parent characteristics and the selection of care settings (Barton & Williams, 1993). Families who are more stressed and more restrictive in their attitudes toward child rearing also tend to use low-quality child care (Howes & Stewart, 1987). Quality of care may have long-term effects on children's behavior that is, at least partly independent of the effects of parental separation. For example, Howes (1990) found that quality of care in infancy predicted social development in kindergarten. Children who had experienced low-quality out-of-home care were rated by their teachers as more hostile and less task-oriented than children who had experienced high-quality care. Children who had entered low-quality care in their first year of life were rated least positively by their kindergarten teachers on considerateness and distractibility.

As to long-term effects of out-of-home care, the findings are mixed. Several studies have reported enhanced social development among day-care children. Rubenstein and Howes (1979) compared the quality of social interaction and play among toddlers in day care and those in maternal care and noted more advanced play among day-care children as well as a greater range of affect and social behaviors. Advanced language has also been reported as a longer term effect of day care (McCartney, Scarr, Phillips, Grajeck, & Schwarz, 1982) and a tendency for children in day care to be more independent and socially confident (Andersson, 1989). On the other hand, early out-of-home care has also been associated with increased aggression and noncompliant behavior among preschoolers (Barton & Williams, 1993; McCartney et al., 1982) though these behaviors do not always reach maladaptive levels and in some circumstances may be more consistent with increased assertiveness and independence. It is also likely that increased aggression and similar behaviors reflect interactive relations with family circumstances and with the quality of the care arrangement.

Evidence suggests that multiple out-of-home caregivers for very young infants interacts complexly with such factors as parents' attitudes toward the child and parenting, infant temperament, quality of the out-of-home-care, and the amount of time in care. The majority of infants fare well with multiple caregivers; their attachments to their mothers (and fathers) are not disturbed. Infants who are less securely attached and more vulnerable bring familial and constitutional risks to the day-care situation. These findings imply that the notion that infants, whether from intact or divorced families, need one and one only caregiver is too simplistic.

GENDER DIFFERENCES IN PARENTAL CARE

In a two-parent family, mothers and fathers provide different styles of caring for their infant. Each style serves a crucial developmental function (Parke, 1995). In multiple studies and across cultures, researchers have observed differences between mothers and fathers in their interactions with infants. Mothers typically interact more verbally in displaying affection, hold, and engage in basic caregiving, whereas fathers are more physically stimulating, engaging in rough-and-tumble play (Lamb, 1977b; Power & Parke, 1982). Not only are fathers more stimulating; they stimulate in a qualitatively different way. The implications of these differences in style have not been fully explored. However, a few studies of fathers as the primary parent suggest that these sex-based differences in parenting style positively influence the behavior of infants and preschool children (Parke, 1995). A large literature has also emerged over the past three decades that shows relations between the quality of paternal involvement and children's social, emotional, and cognitive development (e.g., Biller, 1993; Lamb, Pleck, & Levine, 1985; Parke, 1981). At the same time, there is evidence for considerable overlap between mothers' and fathers' impact on infants and young children. Whether fathers make a unique contribution to infant development is less clear. Some data suggest that the more intense and active play that fathers provide their infants and toddlers uniquely and positively impacts social development and peer relations at ages 3 and 4 years (MacDonald & Parke, 1984). Thus, for decisions about infant custody in divorce, available evidence suggests both that fathers can parent their infants and toddlers as effectively and developmentally supportively as mothers and that the paternal parenting style may make unique and important contributions to an infant's early development.

SEPARATION AND LOSS IN THE FIRST YEAR

Many theoretical formulations of the impact of divorce on young children focus on the loss of a parent as the central psychological event. As several investigators have pointed out, however, the increased risk for short- and long-term psychological difficulties associated with divorce relates less to the loss of a parent and more to the amount of discord and stress between the parents before and after the divorce (Rutter, 1995a). Often divorce is a legal formality occurring after months or years of parental dissent and alienation (Lamb, 1977a) with attendant stressful and disruptive effects on infants and young children. In addition to its direct impact on the child or infant, parental separation and loss are stressful events for the remaining parent. This often affects the parenting capacity of the remaining parent.

Parental loss and separation are multidimensional events. The circumstances leading to either vary enormously, ranging from parental illness and depression to incarceration or abandonment. These varying circumstances affect the infant. In addition, from the infant's viewpoint, the loss is mediated by the caring adults who remain attentive and responsible for the baby. Since the circumstances of the loss are also likely to affect the remaining caretaker, the impact of these circumstances enter the child's life in yet another way. Further, separation and loss clouded in domestic violence and abuse have a different impact on the infant by virtue of the more stressful impact on all those caring for the baby. Thus, parental loss and separation is never simply the absence of a previously important person from the child's life—its impact is changed by the many additional factors besides the loss proper. Nonetheless, the complex literature on maternal deprivation is most germane to the issue of parental divorce in infancy. Much of the folklore and opinion surrounding parental separation with divorce and the emphasis on maternal care has its roots in notions of maternal deprivation from the 1950s. In his 1951 World Health Organization (WHO) monograph, Bowlby wrote, "The prolonged deprivation of the young child of maternal care may have grave and far-reaching effects on his character and so on the whole of his future life" (Bowlby, 1951, p. 46). Contained in this statement were several key elements others have summarized (e.g., Rutter, 1995b). Among those most important for parental divorce was that (1) "deprivation" involves the absence of nurturing, consistent *maternal* care; (2) the definition of deprivation included brief mother-child separations as well as long-term foster care; (3) the damaging psychological effects come from deprivation in infancy, not later, and these effects tend to be permanent and cannot be compensated for by better care later in life. Each of these claims has been singled out as flawed or controversial (see, e.g., Rutter, 1981). At the very least, the initial claims for the wide-reaching and serious effects of failures in maternal care have been tempered by recognition of the interaction among infant temperament, amount/intensity of environmental stress and discord, and the presence or absence of other adults in the child's world who are able to provide consistency and care. The postulate that infants and young children need loving, committed, and consistent parenting *is* substantially supported by studies from multiple perspectives (Rutter, 1995b). But that such care has to be with the mother has had to be qualified (e.g., Campos, Barrett, Lamb, Goldsmith, & Stenberg, 1983; Parke & Tinsley, 1987). Moreover, continuity and stability, while critical ingredients, are not the only aspects of parenting that have important effects on infants' development (Maccoby & Martin, 1983; Rutter, 1995b).

Although still not conclusively demonstrated, the idea that parenting disruptions in infancy have a unique effect on later outcomes has some support. Age-related differences in cognitive development suggest that environmental or experiential effects on later cognitive development may be relatively greater during the preschool years (2 to 3 years) after early infancy (e.g., Ramey, MacPhee, & Yeates, 1982; Yeates, MacPhee, Campbell, & Ramey, 1983). Conversely, for social development, rudimentary data on age-different effects raise the possibility that experiential effects are more pervasive in the first 2 years and are relatively persistent even when later family/parenting conditions are improved. In studies of institutional care, children admitted before age 2 years are more likely to show indiscriminate friendliness and no social inhibition (e.g., Wolkind, 1974). Again these data are sparse and institutional care or even foster care/adoption are not comparable to parental separation and divorce. Development must involve a mixture of continuities and discontinuities (e.g., Hinde, 1988) and an effect in infancy can begin a chain of events that influences later outcome. These chains of events include genetic mechanisms, constitutional or biological substrate, the shaping of the parenting environment by the baby's responses and behaviors, and the environment as shaped by the same factors in the parents. A negative or positive experience appears to make another of the same valence more likely (Rutter, 1989). In this way, the effects of parental divorce on infants may be indirect and transient rather than direct and enduring (see, e.g., Quinton & Rutter, 1988).

OUTCOME OF INFANTS AND TODDLERS FOLLOWING A DIVORCE

As already stated, the body of empirical literature specifically addressing the effects of parental divorce on infants and preverbal children is notably scant. And, as suggested in the previous section, even framing the question of whether divorce directly affects infant development in a persistent and enduring way may not be the theoretically soundest way to pose the issue. There is considerable controversy about the short- and long-term effects in many domains after divorce. It is probably true that any risks for adverse outcome in a child prior to a divorce (e.g., prematurity, developmental delay) are augmented by the divorce (Wallerstein, 1991). Much of the "clinical" if not statistical variance in children's outcome following a divorce is probably carried by the parental adjustment to the divorce (Kalter, 1990). The divorce itself is not so much the injurious event. Rather it serves as a marker for more or less severe disruptions in family functioning and by implication, possibly in parenting. Quality of parenting prior to the divorce mediates many of the potentially stressful effects of divorce (Hetherington, Law, & O'Connor, 1992).

Those effects of divorce on infants and toddlers that have been reported may be divided into the acute, short-term responses and the longer-term effects.

Data on long term effects are few—no published reports deal specifically with children under age two years of age. Data on short-term effects have appeared primarily in accumulated case reports. How infants and very young children react in the short term depends in part on their age and on the severity of the separation stress. Disruptions in usual sleeping or eating patterns, increased irritability or distress with usual separations, increased fear of strangers, more intense and frequent temper tantrums, or even temporary loss of recently acquired developmental skills such as first words or walking independently, may all emerge as short-term reaction to divorce and parental loss. In particular, preschool children show intensified fears during the day and at bedtime, worries about abandonment, yearning for the departed parents, and often increased aggressivity toward the parent most responsible for the child's day-to-day care (Wallerstein, 1985). Often, the baby's reactions are taken by one parent as indications of the other's deleterious effects on the infant. When the toddler cries and protests leaving one parent to go to another, not uncommonly the assumption is that the child does not want to go to the other parent rather than that the separation itself poses the upheaval and the stress. The pattern and severity of an infant's acute reaction to parental separation and divorce are influenced also by the temperamental characteristics of the infant. How a child reacts to change and transitions in general carries a great deal of explanatory clinical weight for how he or she may react to the upheaval of divorce.

REAL WORLD SITUATIONS AND DECISIONS OF SOLOMON

Despite their being more or less informed by available data, child mental health experts are rarely as impartial as they might wish or believe, and often custody cases involving very young children stir nearly as much controversy between the experts as between the parents (Horner & Guyer, 1993). There are many opportunities for expert consultants to inject personal belief and bias into their recommendations in these emotionally charged circumstances (Guyer & Horner, 1990; Melton & Wilcox, 1989). Indeed, when examined carefully, experts are as likely to disagree as to agree about findings and recommendations when they are presented with the same case material (Horner, Guyer, & Kalter, 1992). In part, this reflects the complexity of the few data from empirical studies just presented and the difficulty translating those data to individual experiences for children. Also, as already mentioned, there are particularly few data adequately addressing the central legal questions usually posed in an infant custody case.

The principle of continuity of care for an infant comes into practical application in two related ways around a parental divorce—decisions regarding custody and visitation or parent-child contact. The notion of custody is rooted historically in the practice of allocating children as property belonging to their parents and as such available for proprietary adjudication. Despite laws dictating arrangements based on the child's best interest, the proprietary notion persists often in the minds of parents and the legal system in arguments as to whom the child rightfully belongs "to" as much as "with" and concern that the custody arrangement be "fair" to the parents. The two custody alternatives, presuming that both parents are present and contending their wish to be involved in the child's life, are single-parent custody with visitation by the noncustodial parent and joint custody in which joint decision-making privileges and obligations of the separating parents are recognized by the court. By and large, for infants and preschool-age children, single-parent custody remains the most common decision. However, recently joint custody has been more often requested, if not granted, as more fathers act on their wish to remain intimately involved in the infants' lives and more mothers face the difficulties of raising a family as a single parent and working full time.

The data on joint custody and its effects on young children are slim and controversial. Some investigators suggest that joint custody poses unique challenges for the adjustment of young children to their parents' separation, and that some young children react adversely even when parents work cooperatively and attempt to meet the infant's needs (Gean, 1984; Steinman, 1981). However, there is no firm empirical basis for presuming that joint custody does or does not constitute a preferred alternative to single-parent custody (e.g., McKinnon & Wallerstein, 1986). Experiential case reports suggest that infants and very young children do better when parents minimize exposing the child to their discord and avoid using the child as a bargaining or negotiating point between them (McKinnon & Wallerstein, 1986; Wallerstein, 1991). Regardless of the impact of parental divorce or separation, infants and young children living in the midst of domestic violence and turmoil are more likely to evidence acute and chronic symptoms including failure to grow, developmental delays, and adjustment problems in day care and other settings outside the home. Single-parent custody does not necessarily eliminate the inherent conflicts between divorcing parents nor does joint custody automatically improve communication and parental attention to the infant's needs (Horner & Guyer, 1993).

In thinking about parent-child contact, that is, visitation with a noncustodial parent, it is important to remember that the needs of infants and toddlers do not change in the face of divorce. Many theorists have outlined the developmental tasks of infants and young children; in the concept of developmental lines (Freud, 1965), infants and very young children are described as facing the tasks of developing physical and emotional self-regulatory abilities, of moving from dependency to increasing separation and independence, of developing attachments and relationships with individuals other than their parents, and of elaborating an increasingly detailed and adaptive inner world of fantasy and imagination. The infant's place in these progressions influences how he or she responds to the presence or absence of a parent, including in divorce. Whatever parents do together to promote and support their infant's development is equally essential following parental separation. No systematic data are available comparing various models of visitation or parent-infant contact, but a few issues can be highlighted.

First, for infants, contact with the noncustodial parent is probably best regulated around the so-called homeostatic needs of the infant (Horner & Guyer, 1993), that is, around the infant's sleep-wake and feeding routines. Establishing regular rhythms of state regulation is a central and important task of infancy reflecting both central nervous system maturation and shaping by parental input. There are some data to suggest that failure to establish early, regular sleep-wake cycles (whether related to constitutional deficits in the infant or failure in the supporting environment) is associated with an increased incidence of developmental and behavioral problems in the later preschool years (Whitney & Thoman, 1993). Thus, it is probably better for the baby if visitation schedules minimally disrupt the infant's schedules. Such arrangements, however, may challenge fathers trying to maintain meaningful contact with their infant particularly when so much attention is paid to those basic rituals of physical care in which the noncustodial parent may be less involved.

Second, there are probably no consistently reliable signs that a given amount, time, or type of visitation is inappropriate. An individual infant is his or her best measure. Disruptions in feeding or sleeping that consistently follow a visit with the noncustodial parent suggest a need to change the timing or setting but do not indicate that visitation itself is harmful. Similarly, whereas it is true that most infants and young children do better with consistent and stable routines around feeding and bedtime, many infants tolerate multiple settings and routines (e.g., in day care or with in-home caregivers). Infants who are breast-feeding may need to sleep in one home as long as they continue to breast-feed but there are no consistent data suggesting that the traditional doctrine of one home for infants is absolutely essential or appropriate for all infants. Indeed, if it is possible for one parent to help out with arrangements such as child care while the other parent works and vice versa, it may be more developmentally adaptive for the infant to have two homes rather than extended time in out-of-home day care.

CONCLUSION

Data from several perspectives suggest a more complicated picture for the influences of divorce on infants than may be often tolerable in either the judicial system or social service agencies. The response of any given infant to parental divorce depends on the level of maturation in emotional regulation and parental attachment, the baby's physical health, conditions of vulnerability such as prematurity, physical handicaps, and the infant's prior parenting experiences. Into the variable mix must also go the presence of other caring adults, how the parents respond to their divorce (e.g., lability in parental mood, behavior, psychological and physical presence), and the degree of family cohesion or discord prior to the divorce. Data from related areas including studies of out-of-home day care, early separations, and gender differences among parenting behaviors provide useful perspectives for addressing the opinions most often used to speak for the interests of infants caught in divorce situations.

REFERENCES

Ainsworth, M. D., & Wittig, B. A. (1969). Attachment and exploratory behavior of one-year olds in a strange situation. In B. M. Foss (Ed.), *Determinants of infant behavior* (Vol. 4, pp. 113–136). London: Metheun.

American Academy of Child and Adolescent Psychiatry. (1988). Guidelines for the clinical evaluation of child and adolescent sexual abuse. *Journal of the American Academy of Child and Adolescent Psychiatry, 25,* 655–657.

Andersson, B. E. (1989). Effects of public day-care: A longitudinal study. *Child Development, 60,* 857–866.

Ash, P., & Guyer, M. J. (1986). Child custody and the law: The functions of psychiatric evaluation in contested child custody and visitation cases. *Journal of the American Academy of Child and Adolescent Psychiatry, 25,* 554–561.

Barton, M., & Williams, M. (1993). Infant day care. In C. H. Zeahnah (Ed.), *Handbook of infant mental health* (pp. 445–461). New York: Guilford Press.

Belsky, J. (1988). The effects' of infant daycare reconsidered. *Early Childhood Research Quarterly, 3,* 235–272.

Biller, H. B. (1971). *Fathers and families.* Westport, CT: Auburn House.

Biller, H. B. (1993). *Fathers and families: Paternal factors in child development.* Westport, CT: Auburn House.

Black, J. C., & Cantor, D. J. (1989). *Child custody.* New York: Columbia University Press.

Bowlby, J. (1951). *Maternal care and mental health* (WHO Monograph Series, No. 2). Geneva, Switzerland: World Health Organization.

Campos, J. J., Barrett, K., Lamb, M. E., Goldsmith, H. H., & Steinberg, C. (1983). Socioemotional development. In P. H. Mussen (Series Ed.) & M. M. Haith & J. J. Campos (Vol. Eds.), *Handbook of child psychology: Vol. 2. Infancy and developmental psychobiology* (4th ed., pp. 783–915). New York: Wiley.

Caruso, D. (1990). Infant day care and the concept of developmental risk. *Infant Mental Health Journal, 11,* 358–364.

Castro-Martin, T., & Bumpass, L. (1989). Recent trends and differentials in marital disruption. *Demography, 26,* 37–51.

Clarke-Stewart, K. A. (1988). The "effects" of infant day care reconsidered: Risks for parents, children, and researchers. *Early Childhood Research Quarterly, 3,* 293–318.

Clarke-Stewart, K. A. (1989). Infant day care: Maligned or malignant? *American Psychologist, 44,* 266–273.

Doyle, A., & Somers, K. (1978). The effects of group and family day care on infant attachment behaviours. *Canadian Journal of Infant Behavioural Science, 10,* 38–45.

Farber, E. A., & Egeland, B. (1982). Developmental consequences of out-of-home care for infants in a low-income population. In E. G. Zigler & E. W. Gordon (Eds.), *Day care: Scientific and social policy issues* (pp. 102–125). Boston: Auburn House.

Freud, A. (1965). *The writings of Anna Freud: Vol. 6. Normality and pathology in childhood.* New York: International Universities Press.

Gean, M. P. (1984). Psychiatric aspects of placement and visitation of children under three years. In J. D. Call, E. Galenson, & R. L. Tyson (Eds.), *Frontiers of infant psychiatry* (Vol. 2, pp. 495–501). New York: Basic Books.

Glick, P. C. (1988). The role of divorce in the changing family structure: Trends and variations. In S. A. Wolchik & P. Karoly (Eds.), *Children of divorce: Empirical perspectives on adjustment* (pp. 3–33). New York: Gardner Press.

Glick, P. C., & Lin, S. (1986). Recent changes in divorce and remarriage. *Journal of Marriage and the Family, 48*, 737–747.

Goldstein, J., Freud, A., & Solnit, A. J. (1973). *Beyond the best interests of the child.* New York: Free Press.

Goldstein, J., Freud, A., & Solnit, A. J. (1987). *Before the best interests of the child.* New York: Free Press.

Goosens, F. A. (1987). Maternal employment and day care: Effects on attachment. In L. W. C. Tavecchio & M. H. van Ijzendoorn (Eds.), *Attachment in social networks* (pp. 135–183). Amsterdam, The Netherlands: North Holland.

Guyer, M. J., & Horner, T. M. (1990). The activist expert in custody cases: A challenge to psychiatry. *Proceedings of the American Academy of Child and Adolescent Psychiatry, 6*, 22.

Hayes, C. D., Palmer, J. L., & Zaslow, M. I. (1990). *Who cares for America's children?* Washington, DC: National Academy Press.

Hetherington, E. M., Law, T. C., & O'Connor, T. G. (1992). Divorce: Challenges, changes, and new choices. In F. Walsh (Ed.), *Normal family processes* (pp. 208–234). New York: Guilford Press.

Hinde, R. A. (1988). Continuities and discontinuities: Conceptual issues and methodological considerations. In M. Rutter (Ed.), *Studies of psychosocial risk: The power of longitudinal data* (pp. 367–383). Cambridge, England: Cambridge University Press.

Hock, E. (1980). Working and non-working mothers and their infants: A comparative study of maternal caregiving characteristics and infants' social behavior. *Merrill-Palmer Quarterly, 46*, 79–101.

Horner, T. M., & Guyer, M. J. (1993). Infant placement and custody. In C. H. Zeahnah (Ed.), *Handbook of infant mental health* (pp. 462–479). New York: Guilford Press.

Horner, T. M., Guyer, M. J., & Kalter, N. M. (1992). Prediction, prevention, and clinical expertise in cases of child custody in which allegations of child sexual abuse have been made: III. Studies of expert opinion formation. *Family Law Quarterly, 26*, 141–170.

Howes, C. (1983). Caregiver behavior in center and family day care. *Journal of Applied Developmental Psychology, 4*(1), 99–107.

Howes, C. (1990). Can age of entry into child care predict adjustment in kindergarten? *Developmental Psychology, 26*, 292–303.

Howes, C., Rodning, C., Galluzo, D., & Myers, L. (1988). Attachment and child care: Relations with mother and caregiver. *Early Childhood Research Quarterly, 3*, 403–416.

Howes, C., & Rubenstein, J. (1985). Determinants of toddlers' experience in day care: Age of entry and quality of setting. *Child Care Quarterly, 14*, 140–151.

Howes, C., & Stewart, P. (1987). Child's play with adults, toys, and peers: An examination of family and child-care influences. *Developmental Psychology, 23*, 423–430.

Kalter, N. (1990). *Growing up with divorce.* New York: Free Press.

Lamb, M. E. (1977a). The effects of divorce on children's personality development. *Journal of Divorce, 2,* 163–174.

Lamb, M. E. (1977b). Father-infant and mother-infant interaction in the first year of life. *Child Development, 48,* 167–181.

Lamb, M. E., Pleck, J. H., & Levine, J. A. (1985). The role of the father in child development: The effects of increased paternal involvement. In B. Lahey & E. E. Kazdin (Eds.), *Advances in clinical child psychology* (Vol. 8). New York: Plenum Press.

Lamb, M. E., Sternberg, K. T., & Prodromidis, M. (1992). Non-maternal care and the security of infant-mother attachment: A reanalysis of the data. *Infant Behavior and Development, 15,* 71–83.

Maccoby, E. E., & Martin, J. A. M. (1983). Socialization in the context of the family: Parent-child interaction. In P. H. Mussen (Series Ed.) & E. M. Hetherington (Vol. Ed.), *Handbook of child psychology: Vol. 4. Socialization, personality, and social development* (4th ed., pp. 1–101). New York: Wiley.

MacDonald, K., & Parke, R. D. (1984). Bridging the gap: Parent-child play interaction and peer interactive competence. *Child Development, 55,* 1265–1277.

Matas, L., Arend, R. A., & Sroufe, L. A. (1978). Continuity of adaptation in the second year: The relationship between quality of attachment and later competence. *Child Development, 49,* 545–556.

McCartney, K., Scarr, S., Phillips, D. A., Grajeck, S., & Schwarz, J. C. (1982). Environmental differences among day care centers and their effects on children's development. In E. F. Zigler & E. W. Gordon (Eds.), *Day care: Scientific and social policy issues* (pp. 126–151). Boston: Auburn House.

McKinnon, R., & Wallerstein, J. S. (1986). Joint custody and the preschool child. *Behavioral Sciences and the Law, 4,* 169–183.

Melton, G. B., & Wilcox, B. L. (1989). Changes in family law and family life. *American Psychologist, 44,* 1213–1216.

Norton, A. J. (1983). Family life cycle: 1980. *Journal of Marriage and Family, 45,* 267–275.

Parke, R. D. (1981). *Fathers.* Cambridge, MA: Harvard University Press.

Parke, R. D. (1995). Fathers and families. In M. H. Bornstein (Ed.), *Handbook of Parenting* (Vol. 3, pp. 27–63). Mahwah, NJ: Erlbaum.

Parke, R. D., & Tinsley, B. J. (1987). Family interaction in infancy. In J. D. Osofsky (Ed.), *Handbook of infant development* (2nd ed., pp. 579–641). Chichester, England: Wiley.

Power, T. G., & Parke, R. D. (1982). Play as a context for early learning: Lab and home analyses. In I. E. Sigel & L. M. Laosa (Eds.), *The family as a learning environment* (pp. 147–178). New York: Plenum Press.

Quinton, D., & Rutter, M. (1988). *Parental breakdown: The making and breaking of intergenerational links.* Aldershot, England: Gower.

Ramey, C. T., MacPhee, D., & Yeates, K. (1982). Preventing developmental retardation: A general systems model. In L. Bond & J. Joffe (Eds.), *Facilitating infant and early childhood development* (pp. 343–401). Hanover, NH: University Press of New England.

Rubenstein, J. L., & Howes, C. (1979, January). Caregiving and infant behavior in day care and in homes. *Developmental Psychology, 15*(1), 1–24.

Rutter, M. (1981). *Maternal deprivation reassessed* (2nd ed.). Harmondsworth, Middlesex, England: Penguin.

Rutter, M. (1989). Pathways from childhood to adult life. *Journal of Child Psychology and Psychiatry, 30,* 499–513.

Rutter, M. (1995a). Clinical implications of attachment concepts: Retrospect and prospect. *Journal of Child Psychology and Psychiatry, 36,* 549–571.

Rutter, M. (1995b). Maternal deprivation. In M. H. Bornstein (Ed.), *Handbook of parenting* (Vol. 4, pp. 3–31). Mahwah, NJ: Erlbaum.

Sroufe, L. A. (1983). Infant caregiver attachment and patterns of adaptation in preschool: The rules of maladaptation and competence. In M. Perlmutter (Ed.), *Minnesota Symposium on Child Psychology: Development and policy concerning children with special needs* (Vol. 16, pp. 41–81). Hillsdale, NJ: Erlbaum.

Steinman, S. (1981). The experience of children in a joint custody arrangement: A report of a study. *American Journal of Orthopsychiatry, 51,* 403–414.

U.S. Bureau of the Census. (1992). Studies in marriage and the family: Married couple families with children. In *Current population reports* (Series P-23, No. 162). Washington, DC: US Government Printing Office.

Wallerstein, J. S. (1985). Children of divorce: Emerging trends. *Psychiatric Clinics of North America, 8,* 837–855.

Wallerstein, J. S. (1991). The long-term effects of divorce on children: A review. *Journal of the American Academy of Child and Adolescent Psychiatry, 30,* 349–360.

Whitney, M., & Thoman, E. (1993). Early sleep patterns of premature infants are differentially related to later developmental disabilities. *Journal of Developmental and Behavioral Pediatrics, 14,* 71–80.

Wolkind, S. (1974). The components of "affectionless psychopathy" in institutionalized children. *Journal of Child Psychology and Psychiatry, 15,* 215–220.

Yeates, K. O., MacPhee, D., Campbell, F. A., & Ramey, C. T. (1983). Maternal IQ and home environment as determinants of early childhood intellectual competence: A developmental analysis. *Developmental Psychology, 19,* 731–739.

CHAPTER 10

Divorce, Custody, and Visitation in Mid-Childhood

BENNETT LEVENTHAL, JOSHUA KELMAN,
ROBERT M. GALATZER-LEVY, and LOUIS KRAUS

C USTODY ARRANGEMENTS FOR children in early and middle childhood should reflect the developmental needs of the child. There is a vast literature, from many disciplines, describing normal and disturbed development during this period. Because children's welfare is a principal concern, much of this literature is closely tied to questions of how to facilitate optimal child development. Our goal in this chapter is to outline those developmental needs, particularly as they may be affected by custody and visitation arrangements.

As with other aspects of custody arrangements, these developmental needs can only be assessed for each particular child. Generalizations that describe a child's development in terms of the youngster's age or even as steps in a developmental sequence should be used only as tentative guidelines applied to that particular youngster after careful assessment. Although youngsters of a particular age may *on average* have certain capacities and needs, many youngsters will be significantly different from this average and wise decisions about custody and visitation will take these individual differences into account.

A word about terminology. We call the period from roughly age 3 years to 6 years the "preschool" period because, although formal education is initiated at ever earlier ages, this term captures the social status of most of these youngsters. Preschoolers are, at most, expected to learn in informal ways while opportunities for engaging in educational activities outside the family are present. This period is separated from the era we will call "mid-childhood" by a dramatic shift in cognitive and emotional functioning in which most children develop the abilities needed to read, to conceptualize the world from some other point of view than their own, and to commit to sustained efforts toward a goal (Shapiro & Perry, 1976). This shift appears to be largely independent of cultural factors. Sometime between ages 11 and 14, children enter adolescence. Adolescence refers to a psychosocial period whose initiation is usually proximate to the obvious biological changes of puberty. However, in addition to the physical maturation of puberty and the associated increase in sexual interest and reproductive capacity, adolescence includes a dramatic increase in the potential for abstract thought and a change in psychological focus toward the world beyond the nuclear family and immediate community. Because older psychological theories emphasized psychosexual development as at the core of the personality, the time we refer to as the preschool period is sometimes called the "oedipal period" and the era we call mid-childhood, "latency." The oedipal fantasy, typical of this period, is that the child will displace one of the parents in relationship to the other and fears retribution from the displaced parent. Latency refers to the greatly diminished interest in sensual pleasure thought to be typical of this period. The extent to which these are features of the respective periods is questionable and it is even more questionable whether they constitute their core psychological events. They are included here so that the reader may follow other psychological descriptions of this period.

DEVELOPMENT DURING THE PRESCHOOL AND MID-CHILDHOOD YEARS

Psychological development can be described along various lines. Although a description organized in this way is needed for clarity, the lines of development inevitably interact. With this in mind, we will examine fantasy, community influences, cognition, the concept of time, moral development, and religion in terms of children's development.

FANTASY

Personal fantasies, some of which are outside immediate awareness, are of varying degrees of importance throughout the life course. Childhood activities are commonly accompanied by fantasy: the boy stepping up to the plate imagines the cheering fans welcoming his major league hero or the girl putting on a dress pictures herself being transported to the royal ball. In contemporary America, fantasies may vary but their stirring impact remains important to children. The extent to which children are able to differentiate fantasy from actual occurrences is sometimes questioned. Recent studies suggest that children are usually well able to differentiate their fantasies from material reality. How robust this capacity is when dealing with highly emotionally charged matters is unclear. All indications suggest that children's descriptions of events should be taken at face value unless there is a specific reason to believe that fantasy and actuality have been confused.

However, the psychological importance of fantasy remains significant. The emotional impact of events is often contingent on the fantasies associated with it. Thus, the girl who imagines herself dressing for the royal ball will be affected more severely by a mishap to her dress than the youngster who sees it simply as a piece of clothing. Many of the events surrounding divorce are likely to stimulate intense fantasies.

As with people of any age, when material facts are unclear, fantasy is likely to gain in significance. Children are likely to fill the ambiguity of the divorce situation with fantasies, often very upsetting ones. Children who have no external reason to do so ordinarily do not question the stability of their personal situations. However, a dramatic change, such as divorce, puts all arrangements in doubt. Questions like "If Dad can leave the house, will he also abandon me?" are readily transformed into vivid fantasies of feared events. This is more true during the preschool years when the distinction between wishing for something and its occurrence is often weak. Thus, a 4-year-old enraged at a parent for leaving may, in anger, wish that parent dead and then be terrified that this wish will actually kill the parent or fearful that the parent is dead (Fraiberg, 1965). In addition to the direct distress they cause, frightening and painful fantasies naturally cause children to try to ward them off. Some of these attempts can themselves lead to problems, as they may consume considerable energy, lead the child to exclude other aspects of experience from awareness, or lead to other constrictions in the personality (A. Freud, 1966). For example, a boy of 5½, enraged at his mother, father, and stepfather during the year following his parents' divorce and his mother's immediate remarriage, was briefly plagued with vivid images of all three caretakers' bodies hacked with machetes. He discovered he could keep these painful images out of his mind if he focused on elaborate rituals of making his room immaculate. This, however, had many disadvantages—it kept him working hard much of the time; it eliminated not only the painful fantasies but the whole world of imagination from his life; and it prevented his thinking through and possibly resolving the underlying fantasy.

From the beginning of the preschool period until the end of middle childhood, fantasy remains an important part of the child's lived experience. However, its significance decreases across this time. The successful management of fantasy is generally a less urgent matter as the child becomes older. Certain fantasies are common in various age groups and may influence children's experience of divorce.

Oedipal Fantasies

Children between ages 3 and 6 years commonly imagine "marrying" one of their parents, having children with them, and generally taking the place of the other parent. Such fantasies are often accompanied by ideas of the displaced parent's retaliation. Fantasies may involve parents of either sex. Their specific content may vary from the vaguely romantic to the explicitly sensual. They may be a centerpiece of the child's psychology or of comparatively little significance (Abrams, 1984; Leavy, 1985). Classical psychoanalysts believe that the Oedipus complex is the centerpiece of child development and that its adequate resolution forms the basis for satisfactory love and rivalrous relations in later life and mature moral attitudes. However, there is no satisfactory empirical support for this proposition nor is it as widely accepted as it once was, even among psychoanalysts. Furthermore, the impact of particular family configurations on the Oedipus complex remains unclear (K. Pruett, 1985; Werman, 1980). That oedipal fantasies do not generally occupy the premier place suggested by classical analysts, however, does not mean that for some youngsters they are not of considerable importance or that the destabilization of the family inherent in divorce cannot serve as a strong problematic stimulus for these fantasies.

Fantasies of Heroes and Models

Another important group of fantasies concerns children's ideas of their own developmental needs and good parenting. Frequently, children imagine that a relationship to a powerful or admirable figure is essential to their own development (Kohut, 1971). Divorce may interrupt such fantasies because the child has less contact with the admired figure, or because that figure is seen as diminished by the failure of the marriage, or because the expectable adjustment to divorce leads parents to actually function less well than they ordinarily do (see Chapter 5, this volume).

Personal Grandeur

Another group of fantasies concerns personal grandeur and accomplishment. These fantasies may be a driving force toward accomplishment but also may be a source of painful shame. The capacity to maintain the sense of enthusiasm and pleasure in accomplishment while becoming increasingly realistic about one's actual abilities is among the major achievements of childhood. It is facilitated by parents who are able to help the child regulate the intensity of both positive and negative fantasies—to share the joy of being Superman saving the planet one minute and regulate the humiliation of being unable to tie one's shoe the next. Again, the interference with parental emotional availability associated with divorce poses a significant problem for the child.

Violence

A significant component of some fantasies concern violence. When physical or verbal violence is inadequately regulated, the youngster is likely to have particular difficulty separating fantasy from action (Campbell & Levandowski, 1997). Exposure to intense parental conflict, especially conflict that involves some form of violence, interferes with the child's clear differentiation of fantasy from actuality in this crucial area.

The importance of these and other fantasies in the child's psychological world implies that custody and visitation be arranged to promote optimal development in this area. Because continued ambiguity about the actual situation promotes difficulty in managing fantasy, custody and visitation arrangements should be made as promptly and unambiguously as possible. This also helps the divorcing couple get on with their lives and so makes each member of the couple more psychologically available to help the child work through fantasies. High levels of conflict between the parents, especially when they involve physical or verbal violence are particularly likely to stimulate unmanageable fantasies in children (Kilpatrick & Williams, 1997), and so stringent efforts should be made to minimize such interactions.

Childhood fantasies are a double-edged sword. On the one hand, they provide opportunities to work through matters of great psychological importance. They are much preferable to simply putting wishes and fears into action. On the other hand, fantasies may take on a frightening and destructive life of their own whose management interferes with the child's development. In assessing parental capacities, it is therefore important to explore how well parents assist children with fantasies. All cultures provide shared stories and images that engage the personally important material of children's fantasies. Many fairy tales and children's stories address youngsters' deep underlying concerns in symbolic and playful form (Bettelheim, 1976). On the other hand, children may be exposed to some materials that are too stimulating, so that rather than helping them work through problems, the material triggers intense anxiety and defenses that interfere with working through. Often children will signal that material is inappropriate by indicating that they do not enjoy it, or describing it as "icky" or "weird." Individual differences between children are quite marked in this area. Some youngsters enjoy depictions of graphic violence fully aware of its fantastic nature and use these depictions to playfully work through significant personal issues. Other children find similar depictions frightening and cannot process them well, as indicated by signs of anxiety such as nightmares. A few children mistake these depictions for social norms and emulate what they see. Parental capacity to help children in this area resides in sensitivity to the psychology of the particular child. The evaluator should ask not only whether the parent remains within wide social norms in the area of what is "age appropriate" to the child but also whether the parent has the capacity to note the child's needs and responses in this area.

The Place of the Community in the Child's Life

The focus of the child's interest changes dramatically between the 4th and 13th year of life. The 3-year-old's psychological life centers around the immediate family. At most, people outside the family constitute impingements into this close psychological world. Although the original family remains important in the years leading up to adolescence, a wide range of other people and institutions become important to children and provide opportunities for psychological development that could not be found within the family alone. Friends, teachers, neighbors, employers, group leaders, and coaches frequently become important figures for children as do institutions, including schools, churches, teams, after-school programs, and even the physical locale of the community (Bryant, 1985; Galatzer-Levy & Cohler, 1993). In addition to their intrinsic usefulness to the child, these resources commonly provide fail-safe mechanisms when the family becomes less able to support the child's development. These mechanisms can be particularly important for children of divorce who may find much of value to them in a trusted friend to whom they can confide, a teacher who can stand in for some of the functions of a largely absent parent, or a sense of security in the "old neighborhood" when the security of the family has been disrupted.

Because these resources are so valuable to youngsters, especially to children of divorce, custody and visitation arrangements should attempt to maintain these resources as intact as possible.

COGNITION

The ways children explain events to themselves change during childhood. The preschooler is likely to see all events as resulting from humanlike motives. By the time the children are eight or nine, they generally recognize that events can result from purely mechanical causes. Developmental psychologist, Jean Piaget (1929), who first systematically described these phenomena, gave the example of the child's conception of the appearance that the moon follows one as one walks. Children under age 6 generally and unromantically believed that the moon was trying to light their way. By age 8, most children explained the apparent motion in terms of an optical illusion. In similar fashion, children's theories about other people's mental states and the reasons for their actions evolve across this period. These shifts in cognition and social cognition are significantly dependent on an environment that supports such maturation. When a parent's cognition or social cognition is faulty, children are likely to have difficulty in fully developing in this area. For example, when parents, out of their own needs, are convinced that any action that causes them distress must arise from another's malice, it is hard for the child to learn that others may act in distressing ways for many other reasons including different views of the nature of a situation or different values.

During middle childhood, children are expected to master most of the fundamental intellectual skills needed to function effectively in our society. Although they may learn additional specific skills, many individuals reach their most mature fundamental level of thinking by the end of middle childhood. Children who fail to develop these basic competencies are in large measure doomed to economic disadvantage and marginal participation in many aspects of society. How much children learn in school, while significantly affected by their talent for learning and the quality of instruction, is profoundly affected by the child's home environment. Youngsters whose home situation is profoundly stressful or who have not learned ordered attention to a task at home cannot attend adequately to learn in the classroom. To varying extents educators rely on parental cooperation, from the mechanics of ensuring that children are present and timely at school, to providing an environment where children can do homework and education is valued, to active participation in the child's learning, for example assisting the child in preparing homework. Parents may actively decide on their children's schooling. Particularly if learning is problematic for a child (e.g., if the youngster suffers from a learning disability), the wise management of these decisions may be fateful for the child's overall well-being.

TIME

Most adults can easily recall that the experience of time is substantially different in childhood than it is in adult life. In particular, the passage of time during childhood seems far slower, so that a summer or an academic year seems to continue indefinitely and, when a child is distressed, even periods of an hour may seem interminable. Adult words for duration of time often have little meaning for children, who cannot translate terms like "a week" into a subjective experience of time. Meaningfully anticipating events is often not possible when the child cannot comprehend the time frame involved. Goldstein, Freud, and Solnit (1979) pointed out that the child's different experience of time should be a prime consideration in custody and visitation arrangements because it profoundly shapes the youngster's experience. A separation whose duration might seen tolerable from an adult perspective may make a child fearful that all relation to the absent parent is lost. Alternatively, the child may experience jarring discontinuities in relationships for this reason.

Although there is a clear trend across childhood to be able to tolerate longer separations without great distress, individual children's capacities in this regard are so variable that they should be assessed for each child. At the same time, trying to excessively fine-tune schedules according to children's needs may not be wise, first because precise assessment in this area is nearly impossible and second, because it invites changes of schedule rather than the stabilization of whatever arrangement has been put in place.

MORAL DEVELOPMENT

The lifelong process of the development of a moral capacity makes major strides during childhood. Although profoundly influenced by culture and gender, the sense of what it means to be "good" moves during this period from a desire to avoid punishment, loss of adult approval and affection or feelings of shame and imperfection to ideas that there are right actions and that failure to act right will result in painful feelings of guilt. In middle childhood, what is right is equated with what is conventionally accepted, not on the application of general principles to a particular situation. If the rules have been followed, right has prevailed (Kohlberg, 1984). Though less pronounced than it will become during adolescence, there is a difference in the way girls and boys think about right and wrong with girls generally more interested in maintaining relations between people while boys are more committed to the virtues of applying general rules to specific situations (Gilligan & Attanuicci, 1988). Although the rules are subject to revision and reconsideration with experience and maturity, there are enormous advantages in the capacity that develops during mid-childhood to more or less automatically follow the precepts of the society in which one lives. The youngster whose parent substantially deviates from society's norms is put in a difficult position. This child must either struggle with the ongoing belief that the parent is immoral or adopt the parent's attitudes, which then puts the child in conflict with society. In some instances, this tension may ultimately result in the child's developing a more mature, thought-through, moral stance. For example, when the parent takes a socially deviant but principled position, the child has an opportunity to engage questions of right and wrong from a position that transcends ordinary rule-following thinking. However, children are more frequently confronted with parental deviance resulting from failures in the parents' moral development or driven by parents' overriding emotional needs. Assessing the significance of mild to moderate delinquency in the parent for the child's moral development is complicated in our society by a lack of consensus about the moral significance of many delinquent actions. In this context, the evaluator or trier of fact is particularly at risk for introducing personal values into recommendations and decisions about custody and visitation. In the context of custody disputes, parents' moral failings often are brought forth in a fashion that suggests that the child will be profoundly corrupted by behaviors that in other contexts may be socially disapproved but are not treated with similar weight. In assessing such situations, the evaluator must get beyond the rhetoric and ask how the behavior is likely to impact the child. Does it materially endanger the youngster? Is it likely to shame the child? Is the child likely to learn that socially unacceptable conduct generally or the particular conduct should not be controlled? In the absence of these problematic effects on the child, is one parent's deviant behavior being used by the other parent as a means to interfere with the deviant parent's relationship with the child?

Religion

Disputes regarding children's religious upbringing may be explored from a psychological viewpoint. For many individuals, religious belief and practice provide profound emotional support across the course of a lifetime. Religious belief can provide moral guidance and meaning where it is otherwise missing. Religious practice can organize life activities and create powerful communal ties. Early psychoanalytic objections to religion (S. Freud, 1927), based on the idea that religion is unscientific and that religious precepts interfere with healthy erotic function, have largely given way to the recognition of the value of religion for many people's psychological adjustment. Although some people come to religion in later life and the nature of religious involvement normally changes as the individual matures, for most people the foundation of religious involvement is laid during mid-childhood (Rizzuto, 1979). The child is likely to make personal and therefore deeply emotionally meaningful the powerful concrete imagery of religious practice. From a psychological point of view, a child is most likely to effectively engage religion that is presented without contradiction and complication in its full emotional power. Insofar as the child's sustained investment in religion is desired, this is the preferred arrangement. Where parents disagree about religious upbringing, the importance of this factor must be weighed against the potential for the child to feel that one of the parents is in some way bad or lacking, the parent's sense of helplessness in seeing the child raised in a way the parent believes to be actively harmful, and the delicate problems associated with the legal system intervening the people's religious lives. As comforting as it may be to the adults involved and as soothing of conflict, it is a mistake to believe that a child's involvement in multiple religious viewpoints does not interfere with the youngster's long-term involvement with any one particular religious point of view.

THE CHILD CUSTODY EVALUATION IN EARLY AND MID-CHILDHOOD

A developmental understanding of early and mid-childhood has significant consequences for the evaluation of children during this period. Our understanding of normal development supports an evaluation of the child's current developmental status and factors that are likely to influence it. It also gives us a picture of the likely impact of elements of the evaluation process on the child and the findings that result from the evaluation.

THE EVALUATOR

Though the careful separation of the roles of treating and evaluating mental health professionals have been repeatedly emphasized and the interferences in performing either function well when one individual assumes both roles demonstrated (Strasburgel, Guttheil, Brodsky, 1997), when dealing with children it remains tempting to merge these roles. As a child's therapist, it may be tempting, feeling that one has the child's best interest in mind and that one knows the child well, to also assist in a custody decision about the child. This idea is supported by the common finding that custody evaluations are stressful for many children and that children, even more easily than adults, have trouble distinguishing evaluators from clinicians who provide treatment. However, precisely because children are likely to confuse these roles, it is essential that the adults keep them carefully separated. Therapists generally focus on the child's subjective and often irrational experience of parents, while evaluators will be interested to know how well these experiences correspond to external reality. Children can often make this distinction but will only do so when they understand the nature of the information the interviewer is seeking. Thus, a child's report, "My mother always yells at me." will be greeted by a therapist as a opportunity to explore the child's subjective experience of the mother with but slight focus on the extent to which the mother actually yells. In contrast, the custody evaluator will want to know how often and in what situations the yelling occurs. Children can cooperate in either exploration but only if they understand what kind of information the interviewer is seeking. It is generally accepted that attempting to fill the roles of custody evaluator and therapist at the same time is inappropriate and will likely have negative implications both to the ongoing therapy as well as the custody evaluation. As described by the custody practice parameter of the American Academy of Child and Adolescent Psychiatry:

> Treating clinicians are advocates or agents for children and ideally are partners with parents or guardians in the therapeutic alliance. In contrast, the forensic evaluator, while guided by the child's best interest, has no duty to the child or his parents. The forensic evaluator reports to the court or attorney involved rather than to the parties being evaluated. Thus, the aim of the forensic evaluation is not to relieve suffering or treat, but provide objective information and informed opinions to help the court render a custody decision. (American Academy of Child and Adolescent Psychiatry, pp. 4–5)

It is also recommended by the Academy that the evaluator should not refer any of the parties to themselves for treatment following the custody evaluation.

The Evaluation

Custody evaluations of children focus on the bond of each parent to the child and attachment to both parents, and the parenting capacities of each parent in regard to the particular child so as to attempt to determine the needs of the child and what will ultimately be in their best interest. Particular areas of importance include attachment issues, issues of parental alienation, special needs, education, gender issues, sibling relationships, and parents' physical and mental health. An area of particular concern is the child's preference for a particular parent. In many jurisdictions, judges are mandated by law to consider this preference in making custody decisions. Typically, courts give more weight to a child's preference the older the child. In assessing the child's preference, many factors must be kept in mind. Transient displeasure with a parent may lead to statements that do not accurately reflect the child's overall preference. Young children have limited capacities to recognize that their feelings of the moment may differ from their overall feelings about a situation. Another factor that may distort the children's reports regarding preference is a wish to please the interviewer. School-age children, consistent with their experience in school, may come to regard the "right answer" not as the one that is truthful but rather what the adult regards as correct. Thus, children are likely to be pulled in the direction of what they regard as the interviewer's preference, when asked to comment on their preference in custody arrangements. The child who understands the question of preference and the importance of the reply is often placed in a horrible bind realizing that any stated preference is likely to cause the other parent pain and risks damaging the relationship with the rejected parent. When children express a preference during an evaluation, the examiner should explore factors that point to the reliability of the statement.[1]

Sometimes children express very strong negative attitudes toward a parent. These may originate in conscious or unconscious efforts of the other parent. Gardner (1989) described what he regards as a "syndrome" of characteristic findings in children who have been actively turned against one parent by the other including unambivalent obsessive hatred often rationalized by apparently small failings on the part of the alienated parent. He asserts that children who fear loss of the alienating parent's love are particularly vulnerable. By analogy with radiological findings that are virtually only observed when the child has been physically abused, Gardner inferred that the presence of the symptoms of his syndrome showed that parents had actively alienated the child. Gardner's reasoning is mistaken. If A causes B, it is not correct to infer from the presence of B that A happened. (If the grass is always wet after it is watered, we cannot infer that every time we see wet grass someone has watered it.) Furthermore, empirical studies show that even when parents actively alienate children, the syndrome described by Gardner is not always found and that some children manifest symptoms like those he describes in the absence of active alienation by a parent (Dunne & Hedrick, 1994; Faller, 1998; Rand, 1997a, 1997b). All that can be concluded from the presence of these symptoms is that the child has a troubled relationship with at least one parent and that the examiner should attend to the possibility that the child is being actively alienated from the parent.

THE CHILD

During the custody dispute, children will often have special needs. These needs can be situational and related to the intense conflicts that both parents are undergoing as well as the children's relationship with each of their parents during this time. Researchers have in fact noted regular patterns of personal

---

[1] Because stating a preference directly is so problematic for children, many mental health professionals believe that children should not be asked their preferences directly and even discourage spontaneous statements by the child on this issue. In doing this, evaluators decrease the contribution they cam make to the custody decision when the court, as a matter of law, must consider the child's preference. Rather than avoiding the question, the evaluator may do better to address the issue with the child so that a statement is possible regarding the reliability of stated preferences. Additionally, by addressing the question directly, the evaluator may help the child understand that legitimate responses include not stating a preference or more complex responses that indicate factors favoring each parent.

distress associated with divorce (see Chapter 5,). Preschool-age children often exhibit regressive behavior, including difficulties separating from one or both parents, bedwetting, and increased dependency needs. It also is not uncommon to see anxiety or depressive symptoms. Regressive behaviors may occur in school-age children. Behavioral difficulties, anxiety symptoms, depressive symptoms, and worsening school performance are likely to predominate. These reactive states should be differentiated from more chronic and severe psychiatric symptoms, which may be pertinent to custody evaluations.

These responses to divorce should be differentiated, where possible, from pre-existing psychiatric disturbances in the child. Currently, children's psychiatric disturbances are recognized to have many, sometimes interacting causes (Lewis, 1996). These include biological predispositions, the impact of untoward experiences, the child's internal struggles between wishes and prohibitions against those wishes, and disturbances in caretaking. Factors that in isolation do not necessarily lead to psychopathology, may, through their interaction, result in psychological disturbance. For example, there is substantial evidence that children are born with characteristic temperaments (Chess & Thomas, 1984). Historically, ideas about the relationship of caretaking to children's psychiatric disturbances have shifted across the past half century. Misunderstandings of both psychoanalytic and behavioral concepts led many experts in child development and child psychiatry to endorse ideas that children's pathology resulted from failures in caretaking. For example, autism, a severe child psychiatric disturbance currently believed to result from disturbed brain function, was thought to be caused by "refrigerator mothers," women who were so emotionally cold that they blocked the emotional development of their children. Kanner (1973, p. 86), who was the first to systematically describe autism, observed that "the children haven't read those books" (i.e., observations of actual children did not support this and similar theories). Thus, confronted with a disturbed child during a custody evaluation, it is not appropriate to assume that the disturbance results from some failure of parenting. It is, however, appropriate to explore whether problematic parenting contributes to the child's illness. In the context of a custody evaluation, it is important to assess evidence for such contributions cautiously—hypotheses that may be useful for clinical exploration should not be confused with the reliable information on which courts can base decisions. In addition, even if a parent has contributed to a child's disturbance, the question remains of whether that contribution is ongoing and whether anything that the court can order is likely to have an impact on that contribution. When considering ordering treatment or other rehabilitation of a parent who contributes to a child's disturbance, it is important to carefully address the question of the likelihood of this order having the desired impact. It is important to have appropriate respect for the limitations of legal interventions to change well-established behavior patterns in individuals.

The willingness and ability of parents of psychiatrically ill children to support treatment and rehabilitation is easier to assess than their contribution to the illness. Considerations that apply to physically ill children also apply to children with psychiatric disturbances (see Chapter 14). Parental denial and concern about stigma are particularly likely to interfere with parents of psychiatrically ill children finding and supporting adequate care. Because there is significant controversy among professionals about the treatment of many child psychiatric disturbances, mental health professionals should be particularly cautious in assessing the significance of a parent's supporting an intervention the mental health professional does not endorse. Unless there is well-founded evidence of the superiority of the treatment that the mental health professional prefers, it is not appropriate to recommend it over other treatments in a legal context. Even when the treatment is superior to that which the child is receiving, it is inappropriate to take it as a measure of poor parental function that a parent has followed professional advice that a reasonable person would regard as authoritative.

Increasingly as children move through childhood, the world beyond the immediate family contributes to their psychological well-being. Especially when the family becomes disrupted, as in divorce, resources of school, neighborhood, friends, athletic activities, and religious institutions may become important sources of psychological support. Custody and visitation evaluations should explore the extent to which the child relies on these resources and how various custody and visitation arrangements are likely to affect the availability of these supports. Parents' attitudes and styles contribute to satisfaction with school. Reviewing research literature regarding the relationship of parenting to school performance, Collins, Harris, and Sussman (1995) note that a history of shared work and play between parent and child, as opposed to interactions between a controlling parent and resistant child, predict successful entry into school. They observe that children do better in school when the structure of authority at school and at home are similar and when that structure is authoritative (i.e., emphasizing encouragement, support for child-initiated efforts, clear communication, and a child-centered orientation). Also parental expectations are predictive of school function, as is parental involvement in school, especially homework. It should be kept in mind, however, in considering whether a child's school performance is being supported by a particular parenting style, that children observed during a divorce are likely, in any case, to do less well in school (see Chapter 5).

Parents' roles in the development of personal regulation and moral values have been extensively studied (Collins et al., 1995). The recurring finding from these studies is that the transformation of effective controls into internal values is the result of child-centered discipline. The intent of such discipline is the child's development, and the selection of techniques arises from observing the child's responses to discipline, and is communicated within a generally accepting attitude toward the child (Maccoby, 1984). In normal development, preschoolers tend to regard parents' authority as coming from power to reward or punish. In mid-childhood, children increasingly believe that the authority derives first from all the things parents do for children and then from the parents' great knowledge (Braine, Pomerantz, Lorber, & Krantz, 1991; Maccoby, 1984). Effective control in mid-childhood arises from the parents' monitoring of the child and fitting controls to what is observed, rather than generating attempts at control from the parents' own needs (Maccoby & Martin, 1983). Ineffective parental monitoring has been shown to be associated with antisocial behavior in mid-childhood and adolescence (Tolan & Loeber, 1993). Thus, in evaluating parental capacity, within a wide range, particular techniques of discipline are not so important as the extent to which the child's responses to discipline are monitored by the parent and the technique is consistently regulated by those responses and an effort to aid the child's development, as opposed to filling parental needs.

The impact of the gender of the custodial parent on children's well-being has been the subject of heated debate. This debate often becomes confluent with discussions of the impact of unfair assumptions about parenting as influencing mental health and judicial views on the appropriate placement of children. The polemical quality of much of the literature in the area makes it difficult to differentiate between scientifically reliable findings, informed theorizing, and personal political views. The demonstrable untoward impact of growing up in a single-parent household (McLanahan & Sandefur, 1994) is easily confused with the impact of being raised without a father, since the vast majority of single-parent households are headed by women. Thus the substantial literature showing the damaging impact of father absence on children (Popenoe, 1996) needs to be carefully assessed to determine what portion of the impact reflects gender-specific effects and what portion the effects of single parenthood itself. Both feminists and advocates of "fathers' rights" note that implicit assumptions about gender and parenting can inappropriately affect professionals' judgments in custody disputes. The widespread assumption that mothers are more appropriate custodial parents unless shown to be defective in some way places men who want to be involved with their children at substantial disadvantage in custody disputes (Leving & Dachman, 1997). The same set of assumptions may, however, be used against women who in some way do not fit gender-stereotyped visions of "good mothers"; likewise, a former husband's willingness to perform traditionally maternal activities might weigh heavily in the father's favor while similar activities by the mother are seen as merely fulfilling her appropriate role (Chesler, 1991). There is some indication that courts are moving in the direction of assessing parental competence and making fewer assumptions that qualities like interpersonal sensitivity and leadership are associated with one gender or the other (Brems, Carssow, Shook, Sturgill, & Cannava, 1995).

It is sometimes argued that during a period when children are learning gender roles and must become comfortable with seeing themselves as members of one gender or the other, it is particularly important that the child maintain close contact with the parent of the same sex in order to promote identification with that parent. Indeed, some boys deprived of a close relationship with a paternal figure exhibit intense longing for a close relationship with a man (Herzog, 1980,

1982). However, though less obvious than the opportunity for identification, the opposite-sex parent's role in promoting clear gender identity is also of great importance (Ross, 1979). Some empirical data is available to suggest that school-age boys do better in the custody of fathers (Clarke-Stewart & Hayward, 1996). These data do not support the idea that girls do better with their mothers. The data are also problematic in that fathers who have custody of their children are likely to differ in significant ways from those who do not and so the generalization that other boys would do better if in the fathers' custody is not warranted. For a particular child, the opportunity to have a closer relationship with a parent of a particular sex may prove important, but no generalization can be made about the impact of the gender of the custodial parent on the establishment of gender identity in the child.

Similarly, common expectations that mothers and fathers will differ in their commitment to certain aspects of development are not borne out by systematic research. Parents of both genders became increasingly and equally committed to homework and school achievement as their children grow older (Roberts, Block, & Block, 1984). Fathers and mothers have been found to be little different in their attitudes to competitiveness, autonomous achievement, cognitive competence, and play activities (Bronstein, 1984; Russell & Russell, 1987).

Particular qualities of the child are often relevant to the choice of custodial parent. Such issues as the child's temperament, talents, and interests, and their match to parents' capacities may make placement with a particular parent in the child's interest.

EVALUATION

In itself, the need for a formal custody evaluation indicates a breakdown in the parents' capacity to resolve differences for the benefit of the child. When custody evaluations are needed, the entire family and each of its members are likely to be under enormous stress and the evaluator should recognize this in conducting the evaluation. All family members are likely to be functioning less competently than usual and unconscious or conscious distortions are likely to become important as parents try to "win" custody battles. For this reason, attempts should be made to obtain all available collateral information from the parties involved, as well as from their attorneys. Although some custody evaluators attempt to meet with both parents together, it is generally recommended to meet with the parents separately. Unless a joint interview accomplishes a specific end, such as helping determine whether a couple can cooperate well enough that joint custody is an option, the stress of such meetings should be avoided.

The evaluator needs to acknowledge some level of anxiety that the parents will be under. The first meeting should allow the evaluator and the parent to become better acquainted. Often during this first meeting, parents describe how the separation and impending divorce came about and the current difficulties that brought them to the point of a custody evaluation. Providing the parent with sufficient time to explain the situation will provide a clearer picture than marching parents through a set of predetermined questions. At the same time, the evaluator should keep the range of information needed for the evaluation in mind and actively pursue those issues that the interviewee does not raise spontaneously. Often one will find inconsistencies between the statements of each parent. These inconsistencies should be further discussed with both parents to better clarify the statements. Where questions of the parents' cognitive capacities or issues of significant character pathology arise, psychological testing may be clarifying. It should not, however, be used unless it is likely to help answer specific questions pertinent to custody issues (see Chapter 7).

Following a fair understanding and interviewing of the parents, one should interview the children. Seeing each child with and without parents and siblings can provide valuable information not only about the child's psychology but also interpersonal relations with family members. Because attitudes may change depending on which parent has brought the child and parents may subtly or overtly encourage the child to give information that supports their positions, it is almost always best to interview the child at least twice with each parent bringing the child. Skillful interviews with children and observations of family interactions require a strong knowledge of child development, observation techniques, and interviewing skill. To conduct interviews as critical as these, the interviewer should be well trained and experienced in such matters. Among the numerous pitfalls in interviewing children, using language that is not shared with the child, failure to create an atmosphere in which the child can speak as freely as possible, mistaking ordinary responses to the stress of the interview for psychopathology, inadvertently leading the child to compliantly report what he or she believes the interviewer wants to hear, and failure to note important actions by the child because of ignorance of their significance are among the many errors into which insufficiently trained and experienced interviewers are likely to fall. For these reasons, if at all possible, the evaluator should be well trained and experienced in interviewing children and families.

While observing children interacting with their parents, it is important to allow them to interact as uninterrupted as possible. To assist with this interaction, appropriate toys, coloring materials, and so on should be in the office or one should request that the parent bring these into the office. There will be a relatively high level of anxiety when evaluating the parent-child interaction in the office situation, and this anxiety may account for some of any apparent dysfunction in the interaction between parent and child.

Interviewing techniques may vary depending on the verbal ability of the child and any potential anxiety or mental health issues present. In preschool children, often family drawings can be helpful in assessing the child's perspective of self as well as within the family. In addition, this is a way to assess fine motor skills and potential developmental delays. Experts vary in regard to what should be asked of the child during this interview process. On one extreme, some experts feel that children should not be asked anything about where they are currently living or thoughts of where they would want to live as this would add additional pressure. Many feel that an open-ended interview is appropriate for this situation and that the interview process should be modified with each child. It is important, both from the parent as well as from the child's perspective, to explore who has been the primary caregiver. Sattler described telling the parents to explain to the child that the evaluator is someone who will meet with each parent as well as with them to assist each in becoming a better parent (Sattler, 1997).

Through middle-school age, it is generally recommended to briefly explain aspects of the divorce to the child in somewhat greater detail. Each parent should express his or her care and love for the child in conjunction with explaining that mom and dad are unable to come to agreement in regard to the child and that the evaluator will assist with this process. It is important for the parents not to express their opinions and thoughts concerning the other parent, as this leads to much anxiety. However, whenever possible, the parents should allow a stage for their child to express any fears or thoughts concerning the divorce.

In making custody evaluations, the clinician often feels a tension between ensuring that pertinent issues are covered during the interview with the child and creating a situation in which children can tell about situations in their own way, which is often far more revealing than responses to preset questions. Semistructured interviews may be of value, especially as supplements to a more open-ended procedure (Sattler, 1997). Instruments that systematically explore the child's views and attitudes regarding parents' function may also be valuable (see Chapter 6).

VISITATION

Recommendations regarding visitation depend on the weight the evaluator gives to sometimes opposing factors. Because it is important that the child have at least one parent who provides a stable figure for attachment (see Chapter 4) and it is also in the child's interest that conflict between parents be minimized (see Chapters 6 and 19), visitation schedules should be designed with these factors in mind. When caretaking by the custodial parent is significantly disrupted by visitation, so that, for example, the child cannot develop an ordinary routine, the child ultimately suffers. In high-conflict divorce, the transfer of the child and conflict over many aspects of visitation become opportunities for ongoing warfare, which ultimately only harms the child. One study (Pagani-Kurtz & Derevensky, 1997) showed that longer visits promoted children's self-esteem and more frequent visits increased inter-parental conflict.

Too infrequent or too brief visits are likely to severely impair the child's relationship with the noncustodial parent. The child may lose valuable opportunities for development that can be provided by the noncustodial parent. Brief visits encourage the parent to disidentify with the parents' role and invite holidaylike visits in which the parent desperately tries to get all the "good things" into the brief time available. Especially when fathers are seen as visitors rather than as parents, their parental functioning is likely to deteriorate (M. Pruett & Pruett, 1998).

The child's experience of time and the capacity to maintain a relationship with an absent parent, either custodial or noncustodial, may be strained by visits that are spaced too far apart or that are too long in duration. Despite a trend toward being able to maintain a mental representation of the absent parent for increasing periods of time that occurs across childhood, each youngster's capacity in this regard must be individually assessed.

Experts are divided on the implications of these findings for visitation. Goldstein et al. (1979) in their groundbreaking work focused on the child's needs, rather than "fairness" to the parents, gave visitation a very secondary role compared with the maintenance of a strong bond with the custodial parent. In much the same spirit, Herman (1992) recommends that ultimately visitation planning will be left to the residential parent, so as to ensure that parent can exercise the full range of parental responsibility. Many evaluators assume it is important for the child to maintain as strong a relationship as possible with the noncustodial parent and have designed arrangements that promote such a relationship (Ackerman & Kane, 1998). To our knowledge, no systematic empirical investigations convincingly demonstrate the impact of various visitation schedules on the relationship of noncustodial parents to their children beyond the commonsense observation that too little visitation is likely to interfere with that relationship. In one of the few direct studies of these matters, Isaacs (1988) found that the regularity of visits rather than their frequency or duration was the most important factor for the child's adjustment.

In 80% to 90% of contested cases, child custody is awarded to the mother and visitation to the father. Nurcombe and Partlett (1994) reported that when both parents are equally fit, judges will often look at the parent who has been the primary caretaker for the child to determine best-interest issues. The primary caretaker can be determined by examining 10 specific areas: "(1) preparation and planning of meals, (2) bathing, grooming, and dressing the child, (3) buying, cleaning, and caring for the child's clothes, (4) providing medical care, (5) arranging for social activities, (6) arranging babysitting and/or day care, (7) putting the child to bed and waking him or her, (8) disciplining the child, (9) providing religious, cultural, and social education, and (10) teaching basic skills" all functions most likely to be performed by mothers in traditional family arrangements.[2] Thus, most of the discussion of visitation and almost all of the empirical data regarding it refer to situations in which the father is the visitor.

Hard data showing the advantages of visits are not very robust and indicate the major impact is in the area of academics (King, 1994). It was long thought that fathers' continued financial support of children was improved by visitation and that for this reason, if no other, it was to the child's advantage that such visits be promoted. Careful analysis of available data fail to support this idea (Veum, 1993).

Thus, the approach to visitation must involve the assessment of the individual child and noncustodial parent's capacities to maintain a parent-child relationship within a given schedule, and this factor must be weighed in relationship to issues such as the impact of visitation schedules on the parents' relationship and the relationship of the child to the custodial parent.

REFERENCES

Abrams, S. (1984). Fantasy and reality in the oedipal phase: A conceptual overview. *Psychoanalytic Study of the Child, 39,* 83–100.

Ackerman, M., & Kane, A. (1998). *Psychological experts in divorce actions* (3rd ed.). New York: Aspen.

American Academy of Child and Adolescent Psychiatry. (1997). *Practice Paramenters for Child Custody Evaluations.* Washington, DC.: Author.

Bettelheim, B. (1976). *The uses of enchantment.* New York: Knopf.

Braine, L., Pomerantz, E., Lorber, D., & Krantz, D. (1991). Conflicts with authority: Children's moral socialization. *Developmental Psychology, 27,* 829–840.

Brems, C., Carssow, K., Shook, C., Sturgill, S., & Cannava, P. (1995). Assessment of fairness in child custody decisions. *Child Abuse and Neglect, 19,* 345–353.

Bronstein, P. (1984). Differences in mothers' and fathers' behaviors toward children: A cross-cultural comparison. *Developmental Psychology, 20,* 995–1003.

Bryant, B. (1985). The neighborhood walk: Sources of support in middle childhood. *Monographs of the Society for Research in Child Development, 50*(3).

Campbell, J., & Levandowski, L. (1997). Mental and physical health effects of intimate violence on women and children. *Psychiatric Clinics of North America, 20,* 353–374.

Chesler, P. (1991). Mothers on trial: The custodial vulnerability of women. *Feminism and Psychology, 1,* 409–425.

Chess, S., & Thomas, A. (1984). *Origins and evolution of behavior disorders from infancy to early adult life.* New York: Brunner-Mazel.

Clarke-Stewart, K., & Hayward, C. (1996). Advantages of father custody and contact for the psychological well-being of school-age children. *Journal of Applied Developmental Psychology, 17,* 239–270.

Collins, W., Harris, M., & Sussman, A. (1995). Parenting during middle childhood. In M Bornstein (Ed.), *Handbook of parenting* (Vol. 1). Mahwah, NJ: Erlbaum.

---

[2] Available data suggest that this seemingly reasonable viewpoint may be mistaken since boys in the custody of the fathers appear to do better than boys in maternal custody (Clarke-Stewart & Hayward, 1996). This finding is difficult to interpret since, given the de facto presumption of custody for the mother, the fathers of these boys may be unusually dedicated.

Dunne, J., & Hedrick, M. (1994). The parental alienation syndrome: An analysis of six-teen selected cases. *Journal of Divorce and Remarriage, 21,* 21–38.

Faller, K. (1998). The parental alienation syndrome: What is it and what data support it? *Child Maltreatment, 3,* 100–115.

Fraiberg, S. (1965). *The magic years.* New York: Schribner.

Freud, A. (1966). *The ego and the mechanisms of defense* (rev. ed.). New York: International University Press.

Freud, S. (1961). *The future of an illusion.* In J. Strachey (Ed. & Trans.), *The standard edition of the complete psychological works of Sigmund Freud* (Vol. 21, pp. 1–56). London: Hogarth Press. (Original work published 1927)

Galatzer-Levy, R., & Cohler, B. (1993). *The essential other: A developmental psychology of the self.* New York: Basic Books.

Gardner, R. (1989). Family Evaluation in *Child custody mediation, arbitration, and litigation.* (2nd ed.) Cresskill: Creative Therapists.

Gilligan, C., & Attanuicci, J. (1988). Two moral orientations: Gender differences and similarities. *Merrill-Palmer Quarterly, 34,* 223–237.

Goldstein, J., Freud, A., & Solnit, A. (1979). *Before the best interest of the child.* New York: Free Press.

Herman, S. (1997). Practice parameters for child custody evaluation. *Journal of the American Academy of Child and Adolescent Psychiatry, 36*(10, Suppl.), 57S–68S.

Herman, S. (1992). Child custody evaluations. In D. Schetkey & E. Benedek (Eds.), *The clinical handbook of child psychiatry and the law* (pp. 91–103). Baltimore: Williams & Wilkins.

Herzog, J. (1982). On father hunger: The father's role in the modulation of aggressive drive and fantasy. In S. Cath (Ed.), *Father and child: Developmental and clinical perspectives.* Boston: Little, Brown.

Herzog, J. M. (1980). Sleep disturbance and father hunger in 18- to 28-month-old boys: The Erlkonig syndrome. *Psychoanalytic Study of the Child, 35,* 219–233.

Isaacs, M. (1988). The visitation schedule and child adjustment: A three-year study. *Family Process, 27,* 251–256.

Kanner, L. (1973). *Childhood psychosis.* Washington: Winston & Sons.

Kilpatrick, K., & Williams, L. (1997). Post-traumatic stress disorder in child witnesses to domestic violence. *American Journal of Orthopsychiatry, 67,* 639–644.

King, V. (1994). Nonresident father involvement and child well-being: Can dads make a difference? *Journal of Family Issues, 15,* 78–96.

Kohlberg, L. (1984). *The psychology of moral development.* San Francisco: Harper Rowe.

Kohut, H. (1971). *The analysis of the self.* New York: International Universities Press.

Leavy, S. (1985). Demythologizing oedipus. *Psychoanalytic Quarterly, 54,* 444–454.

Leving, J., & Dachman, K. (1997). *Fathers' rights.* New York: Basic Books.

Lewis, M. (Ed.). (1996). *Child and adolescent psychiatry: A comprehensive textbook* (2nd ed.). Baltimore: Williams & Wilkins.

Maccoby, E. (1984). Middle childhood in the context of the family. In W. Collins (Ed.), *Development during middle childhood: The years from six to twelve* (pp. 217–234). Washington, DC: National Academy of Sciences Press.

Maccoby, E., & Martin, J. (1983). Socialization in the context of the family: Parent-child interaction. In P. Mussen (Ed.), *Handbook of child psychology* (Vol. 4, pp. 1–101). New York: Wiley.

McLanahan, S., & Sandefur, G. (1994). *Growing up with a single parent.* Cambridge, MA: Harvard University Press.

Nurcombe, B., & Partlett, D. (1994). *Child mental health and the law.* New York: Free Press.

Pagani-Kurtz, L., & Derevensky, J. (1997). Access by noncustodial parents: Effects upon children's postdivorce coping resources. *Journal of Divorce & Remarriage, 27,* 43–55.

Piaget, J. (1929). *The child's conception of the world.* Patterson, NJ: Littlefield, Adams.

Popenoe, D. (1996). *Life without father.* New York: Free Press.

Pruett, K. (1985). Oedipal configurations in young father-raised children. *Psychoanalytic Study of the Child, 40,* 435–456.

Pruett, M., & Pruett, K. (1998). Fathers, divorce, and their children. *Child and Adolescent Psychiatric Clinics of North America, 7,* 389–407.

Rand, D. (1997a). The spectrum of parental alienation syndrome (Part I). *American Journal of Forensic Psychology, 15,* 23–52.

Rand, D. (1997b). The spectrum of parental alienation syndrome (Part II). *American Journal of Forensic Psychology , 15,* 39–92.

Rizzuto, A. (1979). *The birth of the living God: A psychoanalytic study.* Chicago: University of Chicago Press.

Roberts, G., Block, J., & Block, J. (1984). Continuity and change in parents' child-rearing. *Child Development, 55,* 586–597.

Ross, J. M. (1979). Fathering: A review of some psychoanalytic contributions on paternity. *International Journal of Psychoanalysis, 60,* 317–327.

Russell, G., & Russell, A. (1987). Mother-child and father-child relationships in middle childhood. *Child Development, 58,* 1573–1585.

Sameroff, A., & Emde, R. (1989). *Relationship disturbances in early childhood.* New York: Basic Books.

Sattler, J. (1997). *Clinical and forensic interviewing of children and families.* San Diego: Sattler.

Shapiro, T., & Perry, R. (1976). Latency revisited. The age 7 plus or minus 1. *Psychoanalytic Study of the Child, 31,* 79–105.

Strasburger, L., Gutheir, T., & Brodsky, A. (1997). On wearing two hats: Role conflict in serving as both psychotherapist and expert witness. *American Journal of Psychiatry, 154,* 448–456.

Tolan, P., & Loeber, R. (1993). Antisocial behavior. In P. Tolan & B. Cohler (Eds.), *Handbook of clinical research and practice with adolescents* (pp. 307–331). New York: Wiley.

Veum, J. (1993). The relationship between child support and visitation: Evidence from longitudinal data. *Social Science Research, 22,* 229–244.

Werman, D. (1980). Effects of family constellation and dynamics on the form of the Oedipus complex. *International Journal of Psychoanalysis, 61,* 505–512.

CHAPTER 11

Custody Evaluations of Adolescents

ALAN RAVITZ

T HE DEVELOPMENTAL CHANGES of adolescence are far more sweeping and dramatic than those of any other life period except infancy. Children enter puberty; they develop an interest in and the capacity for sexuality; their cognitive potential develops so that they are able to think in much more sophisticated ways; and concomitantly, they become increasingly aware of societal expectations for academic, social, and vocational functioning. By the end of this developmental period, successful adolescents will have established a relatively stable self-identity, some degree of physical and emotional autonomy from their parents, and the ability to form meaningful relationships with friends and romantic partners.

The goal of every custody evaluation, no matter what the age of the children, is to recommend a caretaking environment that has a reasonable chance of fostering healthy development. These recommendations should be based on a good understanding of developmental theory, but they should also recognize the specific developmental needs of the children involved in the case. A successful evaluation will take into consideration the complex fit between individual offspring and individual parents such that each child grows up with a realistic view of self and the world, the ability to tolerate strong feelings while remaining organized and adaptive, the capacity to initiate and maintain intimate relationships, and a tendency toward positive self-esteem so that he or she can sustain various developmental efforts in the face of life's inevitable obstacles.

The gathering and organization of clinical data should allow the mental health professional to address both general and specific questions. Each assessment requires slightly different information. Clinicians need to resist simplistic explanations. No single psychological theory will be universally relevant.

Rather, each family presents unique problems that require distinct solutions. A good custody evaluation will identify the specific problems that characterize the case and will make recommendations to address these issues.

Nevertheless, certain factors must be addressed in every evaluation. These include not only the biological/constitutional characteristics of the children and the caretaking capacities of the parents, but also the fit between the individual qualities of the child and the developmental expectations of each parent (Chess & Thomas, 1986). Furthermore, good custody evaluations should recognize that children and adolescents have an innate capacity to organize and attribute meaning to their experience, and that once these "working models" (Stern, 1985) are established, they are often very difficult to change. Therefore, another factor to be considered in every assessment is what meaning children will attribute to the custody and visitation recommendations given their past caretaking experience.

The course of life can be seen as a progression through a series of relatively age-specific psychosocial challenges (Erikson, 1963) with an implicit set of standards regarding performance and nonperformance at every age. Our society places sharp expectations on adolescents in terms of the relationship of age and performance. Adolescents enter high school at 14, drive when they are 16, vote when they are 18, and legally drink alcohol at 21. Chronological age, then, serves as one marker of developmental rank. Nevertheless, children achieve physical and psychological maturity at different rates. The new physical status of each child is also accompanied by a variety of social and psychological expectations. Thus, adolescence represents a developmental phase characterized by chronological age, physical maturation, psychological development, and social expectations, which can easily be out of synchrony. The transition to adulthood marks the end of adolescence, but again, adulthood is today a socially defined phase of life.

The onset of puberty, which usually occurs sometime between ages 10 and 14, represents a period of significant maturational change. The physical and cognitive development that occurs during this period is dramatic in both rate and magnitude. In fact, as noted, the degree of change is second only to that of infancy. Most pubertal development occurs over an average of four years. Girls usually begin and end puberty two years earlier than boys. Secondary sex characteristics (pubic and axillary hair, testicular enlargement and facial hair in boys, breast development and menstruation in girls) typically emerge with increases in body size (Petersen & Taylor, 1980). These physical changes are accompanied by cognitive developments, including an increased capacity for abstract thought (formal operational thinking). This leads adolescents to, on the one hand, be more interested in and aware of the feelings of others, and on the other, to be more egocentric and introspective, with a tendency to see themselves as the center of everyone's attention.

Brain growth is 90% complete by the age of 5 years, with the final 10% usually achieved by age 16. Thus, by mid-adolescence, brain anatomy, metabolism, and interactive dynamics are very well established (Rakic, 1996). This certainly leads to more adaptiveness and resiliency, but as a corollary, there is probably less inclination to modify underlying adaptive strategies. Thus, as children get older, they become more "set in their ways," and although they may have more capacity to adapt to change, they are often less willing to utilize these capacities.

The capacity for thinking undergoes major changes during adolescence. Teenagers develop new ways to manipulate ideas and assimilate more complex information. The body of knowledge that they possess increases as a result, as does their capacity for "metacognition." This ability to reflect on one's own thinking facilitates both understanding and empathy. Piaget characterized adolescent cognitive development as a transition from efficient but heavily subjective and relatively concrete memory and information processing into more objective and abstract concept manipulation (Gelman & Baillargeon, 1983). Throughout this developmental phase, children are capable of progressively higher levels of abstraction and conceptualization. They begin to understand and apply concepts in imaginative ways. They can test hypotheses and anticipate outcomes of actions without actually having to perform them. Adolescents can entertain ideas about possible alternatives that are not immediately in front of them. These new capacities are referred to as formal operational thinking. "Formal operational thinkers understand that logical arguments have a disembodied and passionless life of their own, at least in principle" (Showalter & Tobin, 1993). Many adolescents fail to establish a capacity for formal operational thinking.

Information processing theory posits an alternative explanation for the changes in cognitive capacity manifested by adolescents. It suggests that knowledge and experience influence both learning efficiency and techniques. "Development consists in part of going from the context-dependent state where resources are welded to the original learning situation to a *relatively* context independent state where the learner extends the ways in which initially highly constrained knowledge and procedures are used" (Brown, Bransford, & Ferrara, 1983). Data are scanned and processed more completely. There is an improved capacity to identify common elements and to utilize underlying concepts. As adolescents begin to regulate their cognitive activities, they have more capacity to exert executive control and self-reflection. "A deeper appreciation of the way others think and how their thinking influences their behavior reaches the grasp of the adolescent" (Showalter & Tobin, 1993).

To summarize, during adolescence, teenagers develop the capacity to step back from their experience, to identify common elements and conceptual underpinnings, and to think about their own and others' thoughts and feelings. Better skills at recognizing core elements shared by new and familiar experiences are critical in mastering developmental challenges. General adaptation is enhanced by more accurate perceptual skills, the flexible use of learning strategies, and the self-monitoring of information processing.

There has been massive research on the psychological and emotional changes that characterize adolescence (see, e.g., Tolan & Cohler, 1993; Offer, Schonert-Reciht, & Boxer, 1993, for overviews). Adolescence has long been a period that fascinates adults. From ever popular coming-of-age novels to psychological theories of adolescence, adults' fantasies of adolescent struggle and turmoil for many years dominated thinking about this developmental period (Galatzer-Levy & Cohler, 1993). In contrast to the way this developmental phase has been portrayed in literature, adolescence is probably not a period of tumultuous change. Psychologically healthy children become psychologically healthy adolescents. As long as biopsychosocial conditions remain the same, the course of adolescence can be reasonably well predicted by the course of earlier developmental phases. This is as true for children of divorce as it is for children from intact families. Thus, if early childhood has been characterized by intense familial conflict, it is likely that this will adversely effect adolescence.

Petersen (1988) noted that 11% of adolescents have serious chronic difficulties; 32% have more situational and intermittent difficulties; and 57% seem to manifest positive, healthy development. Offer and his group (Offer, Ostrov, & Howard, 1989) have also examined this phenomenon. They find that 21% of adolescents undergo "tumultuous growth," characterized by internal turmoil which manifests itself in behavioral problems in school and at home; 23% undergo "continuous growth," characterized by smoothness of purpose and psychological self-assurance; and 35% undergo "surgent growth," characterized by brief periods of turmoil in a context of generally adaptive functioning. Thus in evaluating adolescents and their families, the presence of notable strife and difficulty should not be attributed to ordinary adolescent development and other sources for it should be explored.

Cultural definitions of what is desirable and expectable play an important part in mediating the psychological experience of puberty, and children who are confronted with reasonable expectations will predictably do better than those who are not. In divorcing families, adolescents are often expected to serve as surrogate spouses, surrogate parents, or even parental caretakers (see Chapter 5, this volume). They are, in the overwhelming majority of cases, unprepared to take on these roles. It is therefore important to assess generational boundaries and roles in conducting custody evaluations involving adolescents.

As noted previously, turmoil and significant psychological disturbance does not characterize normal adolescence. Good coping and smooth transition into adulthood are more typical than not. Factors that complicate this process include less stable family backgrounds (including overt marital conflict and/or a history of parental mental illness), the timing of pubertal changes (early puberty for girls and late puberty for boys), and environmental instability (Petersen, 1988). Family and environmental instability often accompany the process of divorce, but more often than not, things stabilize within a couple of years. Therefore it is important to determine whether teenagers being assessed as part of a custody evaluation have long-standing problems, or whether the difficulties they may manifest are simply an accompaniment to the acute disruption the divorce is causing in their lives.

Adolescents have to confront various developmental challenges. Early during this phase, they must learn to cope with increased sexual and aggressive instincts as they struggle to accept their changing and growing bodies. Somewhat later, they have to begin to cope with the reality of their physical separation and psychological individuation from their parents. A good experience with this process leads to increased self-confidence and self-esteem. As adolescence comes to an end, teenagers redefine their peer relationships and crystallize their sexual orientations in the process of establishing a stable identity. By the end of this developmental phase, most adolescents have established themselves on a hierarchical scale of competence related to social, academic, and vocational functioning. The more realistic their self-assessments are, the better prepared they will be for independent functioning during adulthood.

How can parents best support adolescent development? First, they need to encourage independence while at the same time tolerating the child's continued need for their support. Parents must recognize that as much as their adolescent children assert their desire for independence, teenagers still need their parents to be available to them when challenges and crises occur. Second, parents need to have realistic expectations of their adolescents. As mentioned, relatively smooth development is the norm in adolescents. Psychopathological behavior must be recognized and treated early. Children who have problems during their teenage years have a very high probability of also having problems during adulthood unless something is done. Third, parents need to remember that no matter what their children say, core values of adolescents reflect the values held by their parents (Offer et al., 1989). Children learn by example. Parents need to establish firm and consistent behavioral expectations for both their children and themselves. Finally, parents of adolescents must learn to expect that their teenage children will be, to some degree, narcissistic and self-centered. Especially in the context of disputed custody, parents need to recognize that much of the frustration they encounter with their offspring is not engendered by the other parent, but rather is simply a normal by-product of the selfishness of adolescence.

Ultimately, adolescents have the same needs as other children. They need a secure relationship with a stable caretaker. Clear generational boundaries are especially important in this regard. Inverted attachment relationships are frequently problematic during separation and divorce because newly separated parents are often needy and require emotional support. Adolescents, given their newfound capacity for empathy and abstract thought, appear to be good sources of such emotional support, but in reality, adolescent children are still basically just children. They need their parents to sustain them rather than vice versa, even though they may present themselves as sources of emotional sustenance. Evaluators and parents need to distinguish between situations where the exercise of the child's new capacities augments development and those situations where parental need is so great that the limits of those capacities are ignored and the child is overburdened. It is also vitally important for parents to recognize that their children need a relationship with both parents, and that attempts to obtain psychological support may ultimately lead to alienation from the other parent.

Adolescents continue to require the same guidance and protection that younger children do. This is especially important considering the strength of their sexual and aggressive drives. Parents must be protective, but not overprotective. They should encourage independent decision making, but they cannot neglect their responsibility to ultimately control their children's behavior (Holmbeck, Paikoff, & Brooks-Gunn, 1995). Once again, the importance of clear generational roles and boundaries cannot be emphasized enough.

Like younger children, adolescents require their parents to provide them with physiological regulation and organized structure. Regular meals, regular bedtimes, and regular supervision are all necessary. Parents need to be responsive to the needs of their children. They must be able to step away from their own pain and focus on their children's needs instead of their own. This is often difficult in the context of a divorce or a custody battle (Hetherington & Clingempeel, 1992), but it is nevertheless necessary.

Helping children to recognize and regulate affect is an especially important parental function. Parents need to accurately identify their children's feelings and reflect this knowledge back so that they (a) have the experience of being emotionally recognized and responded to; and (b) begin to believe that sharing their feelings with others will lead to an alleviation of their distress. It is both painful and harmful to children when adults misread their emotional signals, yet divorcing parents are at great risk of doing this, given the intense psychological disruption they are experiencing. At the same time, parents must help their children to not let their emotions get out of control. They need to establish appropriate parameters of emotional expression, and to aid their children in avoiding emotional disorganization and/or trauma. Parents also must guard against using their children to act out their own feelings of hurt or anger.

Parents of teenagers, like those of children of other ages, need to encourage education and/or vocational training. They also, however, must appropriately and realistically assess the needs and capacities of their children. Parents also must recognize the importance of positive affect in development. They need to allow their children to step away from the divorce and have normal developmental experiences. Children need to play and have fun, and it is beneficial to them to share these positive experiences with their caretakers. This is best accomplished when parents genuinely know their children and share in activities with them.

Finally, adolescents require their parents to set firm and consistent limits (Lamborn, Mounts, Steinberg, & Dornbusch, 1991). It is vitally important to separate the meaning of an adolescent's behavior from that of his or her parents. Once again, it must be recognized that adolescents are often self-centered, and the motivation for their behavior frequently has little or nothing to do with the specific issues confronting a divorcing couple.

It is helpful to think of a divorcing family from a general systems point of view, which recognizes that the function of a family and its individual members can only be understood by exploring the interaction of the many elements in the family system. This orientation will lead one to carefully consider the biological, social, and (internalized) psychological aspects of each member of the family as an individual, and a consideration of how these individual variables interact with each other. The working models that children develop as a result of their experiences within the family serve as predictive templates that guide the way individuals perceive and interpret events, and the way in which they respond to them. As noted, people have an innate tendency to organize and attribute meaning to their experience. By the time children reach adolescence, they have developed relatively well elaborated explanatory systems. They are aware of how their parents have behaved in the past, and they, quite appropriately, expect that their parents will continue to behave this way in the future. It is difficult, although not impossible, for adolescents to alter these predictive templates. These belief systems play a large role in governing the response of children to custody and visitation recommendations.

Mrazek and colleagues (Mrazek, Mrazek, & Klinnert, 1995) identified five "key dimensions of parenting"—emotional availability (degree of warmth), control (degree of flexibility and permission), psychiatric disturbance, knowledge base (understanding of emotional and physical development and basic child care principles) and commitment. Each of these is important to consider in children of all ages, but special considerations apply to adolescents. Effective parents are emotionally warm and available. With adolescents, however, emotional availability becomes complicated. Teenage children are struggling with issues of autonomy and independence. Quite frequently, adolescents will oppose and/or reject the suggestions of their parents. It is important that divorcing parents not take this personally, that they not misidentify their children's strivings, and that they accept that it is in their children's best interest to at times make relatively bad decisions (although children should not be allowed to make terrible, self-destructive decisions). This may be extremely difficult to do during a period when parents are likely to feel deeply uncertain about many things including the wisdom of their perhaps most important life decision, whom to marry. In this frame of mind, parents often feel either desperately anxious to make sure that their children do not make mistakes and so become overly intrusive or, alternatively, they lack reasonable confidence in their own judgment. Effective parents set firm and consistent limits, but as children get older, they should more actively participate in these decision-making processes. Nevertheless, children need to be protected, and therefore if parents are too flexible or too permissive, this could be harmful to their children. This issue becomes especially relevant to the question of how large a role teenager's desires should play in determining custodial arrangements. In some jurisdictions, barring an egregious situation, adolescents' wishes are essentially determinative of custody arrangements. Besides putting a huge burden on the child in choosing between parents, this arrangement can easily repeat parental failures to recognize that despite physical appearance and protestations to the contrary, many adolescents are too immature to make such a decision.

The presence, type, and severity of psychological and/or psychiatric disturbance on the part of each parent is a major factor in determining the quality of parenting. Certainly, if parents are so disturbed that they cannot adequately function themselves, they should not be given responsibility for managing the development of their children. This is just as true of drug and alcohol abuse as it is of mental illness. On the other hand, the mere presence of a diagnosis does not rule out the capacity to make good child care decisions, especially when parents have adequately recognized and sought treatment for their problems (see Chapter 15, this volume). The more dangerous state of affairs, in fact, is the parent who does not have a diagnosis and does not recognize a problem, but who is in fact psychologically impaired. These are the parents who will not get help for themselves or for their children. Adolescents are especially adept at recognizing psychological impairment in their parents, and if impaired parents do not acknowledge their own problems, their children are likely to lose respect for them. Although there is good theoretical reason to believe that parent's personality disorders (chronic and fixed maladaptive ways of dealing with life situations) would strongly influence parenting, little empirical evidence directly addresses this issue (Rutter & Quinton, 1984; Weiss et al., 1996). Parents with antisocial personality disorders may encourage or provide ample opportunity for their adolescent children to become involved in antisocial behavior.

Effective parenting requires that parents have a basic understanding of the general principles of physical and emotional development, as well as a good knowledge base regarding basic child care principles such as those noted above. With adolescents especially, parents need to understand that dysfunction is the exception rather than the rule. They need to recognize the essential conflict between autonomy and independence with which every adolescent struggles, and additionally, parents need to understand that no matter how "rebellious" their adolescent child may be, in the end there is a very strong likelihood that the child's core values will reflect those of his or her primary caregivers.

Finally, parents must demonstrate an adequate commitment to their children. This means that good parents will place their children's welfare at the top of their list of priorities. And this means that they will be willing to not just support their children, but also to struggle with them if such a need arises. It is important to keep in mind that adolescents have well-elaborated, adaptive/defensive strategies, yet they are often quite intelligent and can intellectualize or rationalize even the most dysfunctional behaviors. Thus, managing them requires a great deal of time and energy. Custodial parents must be willing to devote to this task the considerable psychic resources that it requires. Past behavior in this regard is the best predictor of future behavior.

French (1979) identified four dimensions of family function as markers for the type of change that can be engendered in family therapy. These dimensions of family function are also relevant to making custody determinations. The first of them is the level of anxiety that each member of a family possesses.

Without anxiety, there is little motivation for change. Too much anxiety, however, is disorganizing and once again mitigates against change. Thus, custodial parents should realistically recognize the difficulties inherent in their situations. If they deny that there are problems, or if they are overwhelmed by their problems, they will not be effective. The second dimension of family function is the symptom-carrier role. In divorcing families, parents are often identified as victims or perpetrators, as morally good or bad, as strong or weak, and so on. Each family presents a slightly different constellation, and each situation attributes a different meaning to these roles. Simply being a victim does not necessarily imply parental fitness, just as being a perpetrator does not necessarily rule out effective parenting skills. The third dimension of family function is the capacity for change. In assessing the histories of the parents, one can estimate their capacity for genuine change. In looking at family background and early experience, one can make predictions about whether parents have relatively good or bad role models for parenting. This, in conjunction with their capacity for insight and their self-esteem, will go at least some of the way toward predicting their capacity for change. Finally, one has to assess power—which family members have power and which do not; which family members exert their power intelligently and benignly, and which do not. If a parent has no power, it is unlikely that he or she will be able to effectively manage an adolescent, no matter what the court mandates.

In the end, especially with adolescents, one has to deal with practicalities. One has to assess the capacity for change rather than what is morally right—evaluations that only take into consideration "what should be" are often profoundly unhelpful. The primary factor to consider is "what can be." This requires a thorough assessment of each parent and each child. One should make recommendations based on both what is good for the child and what is possible, with the recognition that adolescents, due to their sum of experience, often have relatively rigidly determined working models that limit the universe of effective caretaking arrangements. One has to make recommendations based on what set of circumstances will work best, given the current functional/adaptive predispositions of the adolescents, because it is unlikely that they will change in major ways. Although adolescents are somewhat more adaptive due to their more effective cognitive functioning, and they can cope relatively well with adversity in certain circumstances, it is nevertheless also true that their resiliency is to some extent contingent to their resistance to change.

Finally, in conducting custody evaluations, the number of variables often seems overwhelming. Maybe divorce itself is just one more factor that is variably important depending on the circumstances in which it occurs. Attempting to focus on the divorce as the only variable, or the most important variable, inevitably distorts the data gathering. Instead, evaluators should focus on identifying complex models of interrelationships, recognizing that past history is the best predictor of future behavior, and trying to identify those factors which govern the possibility of change.

REFERENCES

Brown, A. L., Bransford, J. D., & Ferrara, R. A. (1983). Learning, remembering, and understanding. In J. H. Flavell & E. M. Markman (Eds.), *Handbook of child psychology* (pp. 77–167). New York: Wiley.

Chess, S., & Thomas, A. (1986). *Temperament in clinical practice.* New York: Guilford Press.

Erikson, E. (1963). *Childhood and society* (2nd ed.). New York: Norton.

French, A. P. (1979). *Disturbed children and their families.* New York: Human Sciences Press.

Galatzer-Levy, R., & Cohler, B. (1993). *The essential other: A developmental psychology of the self.* New York: Basic Books.

Gelman, R., & Baillargeon, R. (1983). A review of Piagetian concepts. In J. H. Flavell & E. M. Markman (Eds.), *Handbook of child psychology* (pp. 167–230). Wiley: New York.

Hetherington, E., & Clingempeel, W. (1992). Coping with marital transitions. *Monographs of the Society for Research in Child Development, 57.*

Holmbeck, G., Paikoff, R., & Brooks-Gunn, J. (1995). Parenting adolescents. In M. Bornstein (Ed.), *Handbook of parenting: Children and parenting* (Vol. 1, pp. 91–118). Mahwah, NJ: Erlbaum.

Lamborn, S., Mounts, N., Steinberg, L., & Dornbusch, S. (1991). Patterns of competence and adjustment among adolescents from authoritative, authoritarian, indulgent and neglectful families. *Child Development, 62,* 1049–1065.

Mrazek, D., Mrazek, P., & Klinnert, M. (1995). Clinical assessment of parenting. *Journal of the American Academy of Child & Adolescent Psychiatry, 34*(3), 272–282.

Offer, D., Ostrov, E., & Howard, K. I. (1989). Adolescence: What is normal? *American Journal of Disabled Children, 143,* 731–736.

Offer, D., Schonert-Reciht, K., & Boxer, A. (1993). Normal adolescent development: Empirical research findings. In M. Lewis (Ed.), *Comprehensive textbook of child and adolescent psychiatry* (3rd ed., pp. 278–290). Baltimore: Williams & Wilkins.

Petersen, A. C. (1988). Adolescent development. *Annual Review of Psychology, 39,* 583–607.

Petersen, A., & Taylor, B. (1980). The biological approach to adolescence. In J. Adelson (Ed.), *Handbook of adolescent psychology.* New York: Wiley

Rakic, P. (1996). Development of the cerebral cortex in human and nonhuman primates. In M. Lewis (Ed.), *A comprehensive textbook of child and adolescent psychiatry* (pp. 9–29). Baltimore: Williams & Wilkins.

Rutter, M., & Quinton, D. (1984). Parental psychiatric disorder effects on children. *Psychological Medicine, 14,* 853–880.

Showalter, J., & Tobin, K. (1993). Adolescent development. In A. Tasman, J. Kay, & J. A. Lieberman (Eds.), *Psychiatry* (pp. 127–144). Philadelphia: Saunders.

Stern, D. (1985). *The interpersonal world of the infant: A view from psychoanalysis and developmental psychology.* New York: Basic Books.

Tolan, P., & Cohler, B. (1993). *Clinical research and practice with adolescents.* New York: Wiley.

Weiss, M., Zulkowitz, P., Feldman, R., Vogel, J., Heyman, M., & Paris, J. (1996). Psychopathology in offspring of mothers with Borderline Personality Disorder: A pilot study. *Canadian Journal of Psychiatry, 41,* 285–290.

CHAPTER 12

The Remarriage Family in Custody Evaluation

JAY LEBOW, FROMA WALSH, and JOHN ROLLAND

Vignette One

Susan and her two children, Brad 7 and Ted, 5, have been living with a great deal of stress over the past few years. Ever since Susan's divorce, money has been hard to come by. The family needed to relocate into a less desirable neighborhood than the one they had lived in earlier. The children also acutely felt the loss of their father, who like many fathers, had stopped visiting regularly. Susan's remarriage began to solve many of the family's problems. Combining Susan's income with her new husband, Joe's, allowed them to buy a new home in a better neighborhood. Together, Susan and Joe had more time for the children than Susan had alone. Now Susan could spend more time structuring the children's lives. Susan was much happier in her new life, and Joe felt he had gained an entire family he could love. Joe and the children bonded well, yet he remained respectful of the children's feelings about their biological father. Although the kinds of issues remarriage families face regularly emerged, life in this remarriage family was better for all family members.

Vignette Two

Natalie married George soon after her divorce from Rob. Todd and Tim, Natalie's children, immediately disliked George. George was different from their parents. He believed in "running a tight ship," unlike Natalie and Rob, who had been very laissez-faire. George saw himself as the new head of the household and demanded allegiance from all. He frequently had angry outbursts and shamed the children for their misbehavior. Rob heard of these outbursts from the children and complained to the child protective agency about George and filed suit to change custody. The conflict had an enormously destructive effect on the children, who began to act out in a variety of ways and threaten to move to live with their father. Natalie felt caught between her loyalty to George and to the children, leading to many difficult triangles, and much conflict in the remarriage family.

T HESE TWO EXAMPLES point to the powerful and varied effects of remarriage on the life of the postdivorce family. In most families, the predominant impact is positive, providing a foundation for enriching family life. For some, the impact of the stepfamily is primarily negative. For yet others, remarriage family life is simply a different form, neither better nor worse than life in the postdivorce family. The creation of a remarriage family is always a powerful transition that must be negotiated. How the family system reorganizes to meet the challenges of remarriage substantially impacts children, for better or worse.

Given the power of this influence, it is ironic that custody evaluators frequently ignore or minimally evaluate new partners/stepparents and their children from previous marriages. Rather than recognizing the children's place in complex postdivorce social systems, custody evaluations are often framed as a competition between mother and father over which individual is the superior parent, thus minimizing the importance of other relationships (Ackerman, 1995; Bricklin, 1995).

Parents do not function in isolation, nor do children in remarriage families relate to their parents without regard to others in the family. Stepparents and stepsiblings have many direct and indirect effects on children, who, in turn, have enormous impact on the relationships of adults in remarried families. This circular causal process is ongoing, with better interactions in each subsystem likely to foster greater satisfaction in other relationships. Parents' levels of satisfaction in their adult relationships facilitate better parenting, and children's satisfaction with life in the remarried family promotes better relationships between the remarried partners (Buchanan, Maccoby, & Dornbusch, 1996).

DIVORCE AND REMARRIAGE FAMILIES

Divorce and remarriage are not simply discrete events. They involve transactional processes that unfold over time, in the context of the evolving life cycle passage of all members in the multigenerational family system from the first consideration of separation, through tangled emotions and legal proceedings, to transitional upheavals in the immediate aftermath, and into varying postdivorce reconfigurations (Walsh, Jacob, & Simons, 1995; Whiteside, 1998). Thus, it is important in any custody evaluation to track the developmental passage of divorced and remarried families. We need to inquire about the history of previous marriages and family units, how they dissolved, and the future directions anticipated, to understand the current situation in developmental perspective and in the context of the entire relationship system.

Families undergo many challenges and transitions in the adaptation to divorce (see Chapter 5, this volume). The first phase, typically lasting 1 to 2 years postdivorce, is a period of high stress and turmoil. Since most families are more distressed after 1 year than immediately after the divorce, many families feel overwhelmed and discouraged at that time. However, longitudinal research (Hetherington, Cox, & Cox, 1982) has found a remarkable recovery for most families by the end of the 2nd year. Most families restabilize in 2 years and most parents and children are functioning well when followed up 6 years later. Still, many families undergo multiple transitions, as residences and custody arrangements change over time. When remarriage occurs, the complicated process of restructuring old relationships in concert with the new can require as long as 4 to 5 years for restabilization in many families, especially those with children in early adolescence.

It is important to understand that the initial postdivorce crisis period is transitional, and to identify its common issues. It is crucial not to pathologize distress. During the first phase of divorce, family members may appear disturbed to an extent that will not be borne out over time. Evaluators, legal professionals, treaters, and, if possible, families need to maintain a normative developmental perspective, distinguishing both immediate and long-term challenges and expectations. Clinical assessments often mistake divorced parents and children who are overwhelmed, undersupported, and depleted by the challenges inherent in their situation with individuals suffering from significant underlying psychopathology (Walsh, 1993). Although "failure" to stay married sometimes derives from individual character deficits, there usually are many other reasons for divorce. Children are not inevitably worse off with divorce. Where there has been chronic high conflict or abuse, children, in fact do better when parents separate than when families remain intact (Hetherington, 1993).

The high divorce rates do not mean that individuals have given up on marriage. On the contrary, nearly two-thirds of women and three-fourths of men remarry after divorce (Glick, 1989). Yet, the tremendous stresses inherent in the transitional processes of divorce and remarriage and the complexity of these relationship networks contribute to a divorce rate of nearly 60% among remarried couples, highest among those with children from former unions.

Added to the lack of behavioral guidelines and ambivalent feelings is the ambiguity of social norms about involvement between former spouses, between parents and children, and with new partners/stepparents (Ahrons & Rodgers, 1987). Role definitions become unclear. Divorce, like other major life transitions, disrupts a family's paradigm, the worldview, and basic premises that underlie the family identity and guide its actions. Parents' sense of mastery and competence are shaken. When individuals share unrealistic expectations that the post-divorce family should function like an intact two-parent family; failure to meet these fantasies results in a sense of disappointment and deficiency (Bray, 1988). Similarly, although most divorced adults do eventually remarry, it is crucial that clinicians view single-parent households not merely as waystations in transition to remarriage, but rather as potentially viable family structures in their own right (Herz, 1989). Whereas many men rush into remarriage to fill the gap, a third of custodial mothers never remarry.

Keys to Successful Remarriage

Remarriage most often occurs within 3 to 5 years of a divorce, with men tending to remarry sooner than women. Over half of remarrying adults have children from previous marriages, and they are twice as likely as those without children to divorce early in remarriage, principally due to child-related problems (White & Booth, 1985). Couples who can survive that transitional period, however, are no more likely to divorce than those in first marriages. It is vital for professionals evaluating custody arrangements to grasp the predictable emotional and organizational challenges in remarriage (Bernstein, 1990; Bray & Kelly, 1998; McGoldrick & Carter, 1989; Visher & Visher, 1988, 1993; Walsh, 1991).

When divorced individuals remarry, an open, flexible structure with permeable boundaries and clear roles and rules is optimal (Bernstein, 1990; Bray & Kelly, 1998). McGoldrick and Carter (1989) identify three key "enabling attitudes" that facilitate transition through the steps involved in the formation and stabilization process of remarriage. First is resolution of the emotional attachment to ex-spouses. Second is giving up the unrealistic and inappropriate ideal of emulating an intact, first-family structure and forming a new conceptual model of family. Third is accepting the time and space involved in stepfamily organization, as well as expectable ambivalences and difficulties.

The needs of newly constructed families are often hard to integrate. Permeable boundaries between households help children access both parents as agreed on in custody and visitation arrangements. Yet, new couples need to solidify the marital bond. In first marriages a "honeymoon period," during which the couple can focus exclusively on one another facilitates this process. The presence of children and relations with former spouses and their new families largely deprives the remarriage couple of such an opportunity. The range of empathy needs to enlarge. Each adult needs to understand the difficulties faced by others. Parents need to understand the difficult position of the stepparent, and stepparents need to accept and support the biological parent's attachments and responsibilities for children.

Couples also need to revise traditional gender roles that are dysfunctional in remarriage because attempts to fill these roles can easily lead to conflict.

Traditional gender role expectations pressure women to take responsibility for the emotional well-being of the family. A new wife trying to fill this role can easily be seen as competitive with her stepdaughters and the ex-wife/mother, so that an adversarial relationship develops. In other cases, a new stepfather who attempts to take charge as the new authority figure is likely to be met with defiance, especially by adolescents. Attempts to model the stepfamily along traditional lines commonly break down. Our clinical experience and the relevant research suggest that the new family works best when each parent takes primary responsibility for his or her own children and financial support is equitably shared.

Remarriage thrusts all participants into instant multiple roles and child-rearing responsibilities, without the stepwise progression of a first marriage (Bernstein, 1990). Confusion abounds concerning kinship labels, differing names, interactional rules, and guidelines for functioning. Members must navigate complex and ambiguous boundaries of the system involving such basic issues as membership (Who are considered family members?); space and time (Where do children really belong? How much time is spent where, when, with whom?); and authority (Who is in charge and whom should a child obey?). This cluster of issues must be renegotiated over time. Flexibility is required to enable the new family to expand and contract boundaries, to include visiting children and then let them go while also establishing a stable family unit.

Many problems stem from an attempt to replicate the intact family or its ideal image, with inappropriate roles and rules (McGoldrick & Carter, 1989). Rigid boundaries may shut out members and reminders of the former family unit. Because the strong parent-child bond predates the marital bond, competition for primacy with the spouse/parent may blur the distinction that the relationships are not on the same generational level.

Remarriage families must overcome the wish for instant unity and tendencies toward fusion and conflict avoidance stemming from their past pain, vulnerability, and fear of failing in the new marriage. It is important for them to take the process a step at a time and to realize that successful remarried family integration occurs gradually.

Every remarriage is grounded in loss. When the previous task of mourning the loss of a past marriage and family unit has not been dealt with, remarriage can reactivate painful issues. Unresolved issues from the past marriage, the process of divorce, and the period between marriages are all carried into remarriage. To the extent that each spouse can resolve emotional issues with significant people from the past, the new relationship can proceed on its own merits.

Remarried family integration can be more difficult following divorce than widowhood, given the emotional and practical complications. The remarriage of a former spouse is often accompanied by feelings of depression, helplessness, anger, and anxiety. Financial and custody battles frequently ensue at this time, mostly as noncustodial fathers seek changes in custodial arrangements.

It is crucial to explore the dynamics that drive the father's newly emerged wish for custody. These motives may include unresolved issues from the first marriage that are reactivated by the new marriage, such as jealousy of the ex-wife's remarriage, fears of being displaced in relations with the children by the new husband, or conviction that father's new wife can care for the children better than their biological mother, who is still seen in a negative light. Economics may play an important role as the financial demands of the new household may make payment of child support more difficult. Sometimes remarriage reflects significant personal growth, so that the father may have an increased capacity to commit to caring for the children. Careful assessment of these and other motives for attempting to change custody at the time of remarriage is an essential part of custody evaluation.

If ex-spouses are not speaking directly to each other or are in continual conflict, destructive bonds maintained by anger and communicated through children need to be altered so that they will not foster the children's distress or undermine remarried family formation. Loyalty conflicts for children are a common source of difficulty, in fears that becoming close to a stepparent will hurt or alienate the other parent. Divided loyalties, confusion, and mixed feelings about where a child "belongs" may be expressed in behavior problems or "triangulations," in which the child plays off one side against the other, especially at transition times between households.

Precisely when communication between biological parents is poor, they may fail to appreciate such triangulations. Custody evaluators need to be vigilant for such configurations because, as in the following example, they may lead to misunderstandings of the actualities of the homes involved, especially if the evaluator fails to explore the entire family system:

> The parents of a perceptive 10-year-old girl each tended to become overinvolved in new interests. The child, with good reason, feared that her mother's remarriage and father's ongoing relationship with another woman threatened each parent's commitment to her. She sought to ensure that her parents would remain involved with one another and disengage from their new relationships. Thus, she reported at length to mother how father's new girlfriend drank heavily and endangered the child by driving while drinking. She reported to the father, that her stepfather was a "gold digger" who used child support money to buy luxuries for himself. The resulting custody litigation was complicated because evaluators assumed that the child would have no motive to dissemble and took her statements as simply true, without carefully exploring the alleged behaviors. In this painful way, the youngster managed to interfere in both parents' new relationships and to retain their attention on her.

Difficulty in forming new attachments may arise from persisting conflict or cutoffs from one's ex-spouse, children, or other family members as a result of a bitter divorce. Men who have been disengaged from their own children may be unable to develop a relationship with stepchildren out of feelings of disloyalty, guilt, or fear that they will only lose them. Others may seek to compensate for a sense of failure in the first family by attempting to be a "perfect wife" or "superparent" in remarriage. With normal tensions of remarried family life and unresponsiveness of children, the sense of failure may fuel feelings of anger and futility. The best interest of children is not served when stepparents remain conflicted in relating to them or use the relationship in attempts to solve residual problems from their previous marriage. In evaluating custody and visitation, consideration should be given to the extent to which stepparents are likely to use the relationship to the child for such purposes and whether intervention is likely to help the stepparent engage the youngster in a more psychologically healthy way.

Remarriage shatters lingering reunion fantasies for the old family. Parents and stepparents may need help in encouraging and tolerating expression of the range of feelings children are likely to have and their need for ongoing involvement with the other parent. Reassuring children that the new stepparent relationship does not replace the bond with the biological parent reduces conflict for the child. Children should not be pressured to call a stepparent "mom" or "dad," but to develop steprelations on their own terms. Parents' capacities to support children in these areas can be important factors in custody recommendations, especially since some jurisdictions explicitly name the capacity to support relationship with the noncustodial parent as among the factors judges should consider in making custody decisions.

After divorce, a number of studies find that most parents and their former partners can, at a minimum, develop mutual tolerance and maintain sufficient communication to deal with the child-focused issues that need to be negotiated (Whiteside, 1998). A substantial minority achieve full cooperation. In remarriage family situations, respectful relationships between ex-spouses and new marital partners are generally easier on all involved (Pasley & McBride, 1999).

Terminology remains a problem in referring to the complex network of relationships in remarriage families. The most commonly used label, stepparent, has many negative connotations, such as not the "natural" or "real" parent. Another problem lies in that the terms "stepparent" and "remarriage" imply marriage, when current partners may not be married. It is also problematic that stepparents have no legal relationship to stepchildren. Divorce or death of a parent leaves the stepparent with no legal rights vis-à-vis stepchildren unless explicit steps have been taken to create such rights. We include long-standing live-in heterosexual relationships and gay or lesbian committed partnerships as falling under the heading "remarriage family" in this chapter because they function psychologically as such even though they are not legally recognized. Even if a parent has a significant relationship with a partner who does not reside in the home, this may have crucial importance for the children. We suggest including in evaluations any partner who has come to have major involvement in the lives of the children. However, as Buchanan et al. (1996) have suggested, remarriage and living together may take on very different meanings for children in divorce. These meanings should be explored in each case.

STEPFAMILIES IN CUSTODY ASSESSMENT

Evaluators in custody disputes typically are presented with unusual and contentious relationships between divorced partners. It is important to know that research finds that most divorced partners, although not the best of friends, are able to form a workable coparental alliance, permitting children access to both parents, minimizing conflict, and cooperating to the extent possible (Ahrons, 1994; Pasley & McBride, 1999; Whiteside, 1998). Those undergoing custody evaluations usually have passed through many stages at which resolution might occur, leaving 5% to 10% of former partners who are unable to decide on a life plan for the children on their own.

Litigants in custody disputes are frequently involved in an escalating process in which the behavior (or reaction) of one party becomes the impetus for more difficult behavior of the other. These parties frequently construct narratives in their own minds in which they rewrite and punctuate their experience to support their beliefs that the form of custody they seek is far better than other alternatives (Hooper, 1993). Although custody disputes occasionally arise as a negotiation tactic by one party toward some other end (e.g., financial relief), in most cases these conflicts occur in the context of deep-seated beliefs about what is best for the children. These beliefs make perfect sense to that parent. For example, a mother may view a father as too demanding of time with their child and then will restrict access to the child, leading to an escalation in his efforts to gain greater access, which, in turn, confirms her conviction. Behaviors that are typical in children's adjustment to divorce, such as separation anxiety, frequently come to be viewed as the product of the negative actions of the other parent. Disputing parents often use the power they each hold over the other: a custodial mother may withhold visitation to retaliate for a father's nonpayment of child support. Here again, a vicious cycle can ensue: Seeing less of his children and tired of hassles with his ex-wife, he further withdraws and withholds support. Interrupting this reactive cycle and encouraging a positive virtuous circle should be a priority in custody-visitation arrangements.

Given delays in the legal system, disputes frequently continue for years before a judgment is rendered. Lawyers and extended family may stoke conflict, polarizing positions into victim/villain and discouraging direct contact or open communication. Heightened conflict, painful feelings about the failed marriage, and the charged atmosphere of negotiations between attorneys and court appearances create an adversarial environment that only intensifies feelings of antipathy and the breakdown of communication.

A systemic understanding helps deconstruct such processes, placing behaviors in context, and can be utilized to help locate the solutions that work best for the family and, most especially, for the children involved. We stress a framework for using evaluations in a constructive way toward the creation of a resolution that can work best for the divorced family system over the long run. The central question is not who is the better parent, as in much custody evaluation, but what arrangements will work best for all concerned, most of all the children. Such a perspective helps mitigate the highly competitive winner-loser orientation in custody determinations, and the frequent tendency to describe all the participants in terms of personal psychopathology. It also helps the evaluator avoid the frequently encountered pitfall of the evaluation becoming part of the problem, in prolonging litigation and serving as a weapon in the conflict.

Following the thoughtful discussions about causality in abuse (Dell, 1986; Goldner, Penn, Sheinberg, & Walter, 1990), a systemic understanding in this context does not ignore individual responsibility and the powerful inevitable effects brought on by certain behaviors, but attempts to understand the complex determinants of the behavior occurring, and to utilize these understandings to arrive at the best arrangements possible. In a custody dispute, there may well be unacceptable, provocative, or even outrageous behavior by one party that rightly assumes central importance. Part of the responsibility of the evaluator lies in appropriately recognizing such behavior and making recommendations that offer protection when it is needed.

Remarriage families become involved in custody assessments in two major ways. The most typical presenting situation is when evaluations occur in the context of a post-decree request for change in custody, visitation, or financial support following remarriage. In these instances, families typically have many years to form remarriage family relationships. At times, the remarriage itself represents the change in circumstance that is offered as the reason for the need for change in custody. A noncustodial father may seek to reduce support payments when he assumes stepparent obligations in remarriage or goes on to have other children. A custodial mother may seek to relocate because of her new husband's job. Not uncommonly, the emotional pain of seeing a former spouse remarry (and have other children) leads to retaliation (e.g., challenging custody or support arrangements) in anger or fear that children will become more attached to the new stepparent. Some men reduce contact and support of their children; others fight to gain custody or greater visitations.

Surprisingly, the second major way "remarriage families" become involved occurs in the context of the divorce process of the earlier marriage. This may occur when the original marriage has ended because one of the parents has formed a new relationship that has developed to the point of anticipating marriage. In cases in which divorce has been delayed by lack of agreement about its terms, so much time may have passed that a new "marriage" is underway during the divorce process, merely waiting for the legalities of divorce and remarriage. Given the unusual delays that are so frequent in the legal process in these cases, often, such relationships evolve even when partners deliberately choose to take their time in finding a new partner. Serious involvements before the divorce is complete can prove controversial. Litigants may accuse their partners of engaging in immoral relationships, or of being insensitive to their children's emotional or moral development because the involvement began while the parents are still legally married. In such situations, evaluators should recognize the complexities of protracted divorce, and focus on how well the parent has attended to the children's needs in relation to the new relationship, how well the children have been prepared for the relationship, and how their feelings have been processed.

At times, the behavior of a stepparent or stepsibling is particularly at issue. In particular, allegations of abuse and neglect often focus on stepparent behavior. When this is the case, the stepparent may be the most important person to individually evaluate. For example, the S family presented for evaluation after an allegation by father that John, the stepfather, had beaten Tom, his stepson, on a number of occasions. In individual interviews, Tom told of the abuse and also was generally allied with his father. The evaluator's primary task centered on the degree of risk that John presented for the children in the family.

RELEVANT RESEARCH ABOUT CHILDREN'S ADAPTATION IN REMARRIED FAMILIES

We do not have research that speaks to every particular issue in custody evaluation. However, we can draw on a substantial body of research describing patterns and relationships in remarried families as an anchor in assessing individual families. Such research as the state-of-the-art longitudinal study of divorce and remarriage by Hetherington and colleagues (Hetherington, 1993) and the landmark study focused on adolescents in divorcing and remarriage families by Buchanan et al. (1996) describe typical developmental trajectories in these families.

DEMOGRAPHIC DATA

Remarriage most often occurs within 3 to 5 years of a divorce. Approximately one half of women and three quarters of men remarry within 5 years of divorce (Coleman & Ganong, 1990). Ahrons and Rodgers (1987) found 59% of women and 77% of men had new partners after 3 years, and that in half of the cases both partners had recoupled. Sixty-five percent of remarrying adults have children from previous marriages (Norton & Miller, 1993). In stepfamilies following divorce, 86% of children live with a stepfather and biological mother, while only 14% live with a stepmother and biological father (Bray & Hetherington, 1993).* Among preschool-age children whose parents remarry, 25% will gain a stepsibling in the first 18 months after remarriage (Coleman & Ganong, 1990; Norton & Miller, 1993). Remarried couples are twice as likely to redivorce in early remarriage, often due to child-related problems, so that half the children whose parents divorce and remarry will experience their parents divorcing

---

*For this reason, the data on remarriage in divorced families is much more extensive in describing situations in which children reside with mother rather than father. Consequently, much of the research refers to situations in which children reside with the mother.

again (Coleman & Ganong, 1990). Of remarriages that end in divorce, 40% will go on to remarry again. These transitions often occur with great speed (Norton & Miller, 1993). However, it is worth underscoring that couples who survive the transitional period of the first few years of remarriage are no more likely to divorce than those in first marriages.

ECONOMIC CONSEQUENCES

The economic consequences of remarriage are significant. Divorce often results in financial crisis for women and children. Inadequate divorce settlements and poor enforcement of support by fathers are serious, widespread problems. The shift in divorce laws toward no-fault divorce and "equal division" of property was intended to facilitate the divorce process and to compensate women who assumed the primary homemaking and child-rearing responsibilities. However, equal division of property proves neither equitable nor adequate for women who continue to bear most child-rearing obligations and who experience job discrimination (McGoldrick & Carter, 1989). With divorce reform laws in many states, alimony, now termed "rehabilitative maintenance," is awarded in only a small percentage of cases and for only a short time. The child support decreed by the court is often inadequate. Furthermore, many fathers, in any case, fail to comply with the order. Custodial mothers confront numerous conflicts in managing financial, homemaking, and child-care responsibilities. Low-paying, inflexible jobs as well as inadequate and unaffordable child care complicate their dilemma. Researchers underscore the importance of financial support by fathers for both the immediate and long-term adjustment of their children (Furstenberg & Cherlin, 1991).

Remarriage allows partners to combine their incomes and restore financial stability, a change of substantial importance in the life of most divorced families. However, newly remarried couples confront numerous decisions about the division of resources among family members in current households and those of ex-spouses. These decisions are frequently sources of conflict, jealousy, and resentment (Hetherington, 1993). Rivalries are common between current and former spouses, children and stepchildren, and among step- and half-siblings.

THE IMPACT ON CHILDREN

Remarriage also represents a further significant transition for children. As Hetherington has highlighted, children whose parents remarry have usually experienced life in their family of origin, the uprooting of the divorce, and a period of time in a single-parent household before the remarriage. The multiple transitions experienced appear to be cumulative in producing stress (Hetherington, 1993). When divorce is accompanied by too many other stressful transitions, particularly other losses and dislocations, there is heightened risk of negative impact (Hetherington, 1993).

The picture of children in remarriage that emerges from research is far more complex than suggested by the frequently encountered belief that divorce and remarriage always have negative consequences for children. Following remarriage, many children do evidence problem behaviors, marked by intensification of behaviors already present in boys and reemergence of problems in girls (Bray, 1988; Hetherington & Clingempeel, 1992). However, most children do well, and in younger children, the difficulties that do emerge are likely to emerge only for a short period (Pasley & McBride, 1999).

The developmental tasks facing adolescents make them especially vulnerable to this transition (Bray & Kelly, 1998; Hetherington, 1987; Hetherington & Clingempeel, 1988). The push of needs for separation and autonomy clash with the desire of a new remarriage family to pull together. Moreover, adolescents are likely to balk at attempts by stepparents to exert authority and control. However, Buchanan and coworkers (1996) found that the adolescents they studied generally adapt quite well to remarriage. In this study, early adolescents were also closer and more accepting of new parents than older adolescents, a finding in contrast to that of several other studies which found older adolescents adapt better than younger adolescents (Hetherington, 1987). Interestingly, this research also found many more negative effects on the adolescents and their family relationships when custodial parents cohabited or were seriously dating than when they remarried.

Studies have found girls to have more problems in adapting to remarriage of their residential custodial mothers (Brand, Clingempeel, & Bowen-Woodward, 1988; Buchanan et al., 1996). Sons who are often involved in conflictual relations with their custodial mothers frequently gain much by the introduction of a stepfather, whereas daughters who have developed close relationships with their mothers while living as a single-parent family unit more often find the new couple relationship disruptive of that special bond (Hetherington, 1987).

PARENTING IN REMARRIAGE

Data about parenting in remarriage strongly suggests the importance of understanding that remarriage is a transition to be negotiated (Bray & Kelly, 1998). In the early months of remarriage, custodial mothers typically report being less effective and more authoritarian in their child rearing than nondivorced mothers (Bray, 1988). Newly remarried mothers also report poorer family communication, less effective problem resolution, less consistency in setting rules, and less emotional responsiveness. Both remarried mothers and stepfathers report less family cohesion and more poorly defined family roles and relationships in the early months of remarriage. However, control and monitoring of children's behavior improves over time (Hetherington, 1987) for children who are not yet adolescents. Parental control and monitoring remain low with adolescents, and these low levels have been associated with the development of adolescent disorders (Hetherington & Clingempeel, 1992).

The emotional bonds between children and stepparents are generally less close than those with biological parents and cohesion tends to be lower than in families of first marriages (Pasley & McBride, 1999). However, the relationships in these families between children and parents are often very positive. This is especially the case when there is little contact with the noncustodial parent (Coleman & Ganong, 1990; Pasley & McBride, 1999). In general, research shows that being a stepparent is more difficult than parenting one's own biological children. Stepparents communicate more poorly with stepchildren, feel less warmth toward them, express fewer positive feelings to them, and provide less support and monitoring than do biological parents (Pasley & McBride, 1999). Specific difficulties for stepparents include lack of shared history, unrealistic expectations, lack of previous parenting experience, and the ambiguity associated with this role (Palsey & McBride, 1999). Age of children is a factor in stepparenting; relationships with younger children are more likely to resemble those of first marriages (Pasley & McBride, 1999). Stepfathers are experienced by children in a more positive role (Ambert, 1986; Hobart, 1987), perhaps because stepmothers are more involved in the children's lives and therefore more likely to be involved in limit setting (Ahrons & Wallisch, 1987). The quality of stepfamily bonds with children does not seem to be affected by the couple having further children in the remarriage (Ahrons & Wallisch, 1987; Ganong & Coleman, 1988). High levels of parent satisfaction in remarriage are directly related to better stepparent-child relationships (Coleman & Ganong, 1987).

Both stepmothers and stepfathers take a considerably less active role in parenting than do biological parents (Bray, 1988; Hetherington, 1987). Even after 2 years, the most common style of parenting by stepparents is laissez-faire (Hetherington, 1987). Stepfathers who initially spend time establishing relations with their stepchildren by being warm and involved, but do not assert parental authority, eventually are accepted by boys (Hetherington, 1987). Acceptance of the stepfather by daughters, however, is more difficult to obtain and complicated by emerging sexuality in preadolescence and adolescence (Hetherington, 1987).

There is evidence that residential stepmothers are more involved in discipline than stepfathers (Santrock & Sitterle, 1987). Families in which the custodial father remarries experience more resistance to the stepparent and tend to show poorer adjustment among the children than when a stepfather enters the family (Brand et al., 1988; Clingempeel, Brand, & Ievoli, 1984; Furstenberg, 1988; Pasley & McBride, 1999; Zaslow & Hayes, 1987). Families in which both parents bring children from previous relationships are associated with the highest levels of difficulty (Hobart, 1987; Santrock & Sitterle, 1987). Here, potentially competitive relationships between stepsiblings are added to the stresses of adapting to the remarriage family.

THE QUALITY OF THE REMARRIAGE RELATIONSHIP

Despite the high levels of risk for divorce in remarriage, remarriages of good quality show equally high levels of marital satisfaction compared with first marriages (Pasley & McBride, 1999). The quality of the marital relationship in the remarried family also has a clear association with the children's functioning. For boys, after the first 2 years of remarriage, positive marital adjustment is related to more positive functioning. In girls, however, the effect is paradoxical. Here, more satisfying marital relationships tend to be associated with negative child-parent interaction and poorer child adjustment (Brand et al., 1988; Hetherington, 1987). In Hetherington's (1993) longitudinal study of divorce, boys' behavior improved when stepfathers entered the system, whereas girls' behavior deteriorated. Similarly, Amato and Keith (1991) found better adjustment when boys gained stepfathers, whereas for girls the change had a neutral or negative effect.

In general, newly remarried parents report twice the stress of nondivorced parents (Bray, 1987, 1988). Much of this stress is concerned with parenting. Often, remarried parents' interactions around child-related issues are precipitants for divorce (Pasley & McBride, 1999). When couples achieve consensus about child rearing and the stepparents' involvement in parenting, there is far less difficulty in the remarriage.

EFFECTS ON COPARENTING BETWEEN BIOLOGICAL PARENTS

Remarriage also changes coparenting of biological parents. Maccoby and Mnookin's (1992) study of divorced parents of adolescents found that remarriage typically led to a more disengaged or conflictual coparenting style. Nonetheless, as Ahrons and others (1994) highlight, many families still are able to work out a collaborative team across households.

The introduction of a stepparent in a custodial home has not been found to be related to changes in involvement of the noncustodial parent, although remarriage of the noncustodial parent often does lead to such withdrawal (Furstenberg, 1988). There is a higher level of involvement of noncustodial mothers in families with stepmothers than of fathers in families with stepfathers (Brand et al., 1988; Furstenberg, 1988; Santrock & Sitterle, 1987). In general, after divorcing, noncustodial mothers remain more highly involved with their children than do most noncustodial fathers. Thus, this trend continues after remarriage.

Increased involvement of the noncustodial father has been associated with a positive or neutral role in the family for the stepfather, but increased involvement of noncustodial mothers frequently has been associated with increased levels of conflict in families with stepmothers, especially for girls (Brand et al., 1988). Buchanan and colleagues (1996) found maintaining a relationship with the nonresidential parent did not help or hinder adolescents' relationships with new residential partners. An exception to this finding was that girls who resided with their fathers were somewhat less accepting of a new stepmother when they were close to their own mothers. In families with low interparental conflict, the continued involvement of noncustodial fathers does not negatively impact close stepfamily relations. However, even in situations of low parental conflict, continued involvement of noncustodial mothers often is associated with loyalty conflicts and greater acrimony between children and stepmothers (Brand et al., 1988; Camara & Resnick, 1988). Thus, in father-custody families, children's conflicts with stepmothers, which are sometimes mistaken by evaluators as the result of alienation by the mother or difficulties in parenting by the stepmother, may only be a manifestation of expectable loyalty conflicts.

GUIDELINES FOR EVALUATING REMARRIAGE FAMILIES IN CHILD CUSTODY DISPUTES

The growing body of research and clinical experience with remarriage families can usefully inform assessment and interventions concerning custody issues.

1. First, always include all stepfamily members in evaluations, both in custodial and noncustodial households. Determine the time to spend with each member on the basis of the specific referral question. Beyond the separate interviews with biological parents and children, in most instances, an interview with each stepparent alone, one with each remarriage couple, and one with each stepfamily unit are valuable. These interviews should focus on learning about the stepparents as persons and parents, the relationships of the remarriage couple, the relationships between the children and the stepparent(s), and the relationships between the children and stepsiblings, as well as elucidating how they have dealt with remarriage family issues.

2. Carefully assess unresolved divorce issues that may surface at remarriage in challenges of custody arrangements. In separate interviews, hear each ex-spouse's story of the divorce and current feelings about it. For example, remarriage is predictably upsetting to an ex-spouse who was left for the new partner. Issues of abandonment, betrayal, and self-esteem may find expression in a challenge to custody, visitation, or support. When individuals feel powerless to challenge the ex-spouse's remarriage, they may resort to challenging custody arrangements in an effort to control or retaliate.

3. Consider the narratives family members bring about remarried life. What type of stories do the biological parents carry about each other and the new stepfamilies? How easily do normal stepfamily behaviors become the basis for questioning the behavior of a family member? Frequently, ordinary problems in adapting to the new member(s) of the remarriage family can be perceived by a former partner as reflecting severe difficulties, when they are, in fact, aspects of normal adaptation. Children may also express their loyalty to biological parents by complaining about the behavior of new family members. These complaints can readily fuel troubling beliefs in the other parent about life in the remarriage family.

4. Assess how the change consequent to remarriage(s) have affected the relative merits of life in each home and the various possible custodial and residential arrangements. Always consider the remarriage family as an essential factor. Parents do not parent in isolation, but in a specific context. In one case,

a parent who may have been completely available to a child may be far less available after a remarriage; in another, a parent may become much more available and more secure in parenting with remarriage. Consider, as well, the impact of the remarriage(s) on whatever specific ongoing arrangements have been in place. Some arrangements may become easier with remarriage, and others that worked well before may become more difficult. For example, cooperative coequal sharing of time between households may become more complicated and difficult to implement because of scheduling problems that may emerge with the increased commitments that often accompany the addition of new family members.

5. Pay particular attention to the relationships formed between the children and stepparents and stepsiblings. Does the level of bonding appear to be progressing at a pace that suggests successful adaptation? How actively do the biological parent and stepparent work to help the stepparent and/or stepsiblings build such bonds with the children? Beware of unrealistic expectations for immediate "blending"—remarriage family life tends to be complex and filled with the need for flexibility. Bear in mind that levels of cohesion are generally lower in remarriage families (Pasley & McBride, 1999). Further, the transition to remarriage family life almost always involves bumps in the road. Stepfamilies commonly take 4 to 5 years to master these challenges. Two years are typically required to get through the initial phase of the transition into stepfamily life. Thus, how long the new family has been together should be considered as a factor in assessing its functioning.

6. Evaluate risks when there are specific questions concerning the behavior of stepparent, stepsiblings, or the relationships with them. When there are suggestions or allegations of specific risk presented by a stepparent, take sufficient steps to make an adequate assessment. Are there histories of abuse or neglect or a negative attitude toward the children? Many evaluations are sought after complaints about the behavior of the new stepparent. Some of these complaints originate from typical difficulties in making the transition to remarried family. Others come when genuinely inappropriate behavior is occurring. It is crucial to evaluate whether accusations by the other biological parent are colored by anger at the remarriage or rivalry with the stepparent.

7. The evaluator may need to distinguish between true hostility and pseudo-hostility between children and stepparents, as well as between true closeness and pseudo-closeness, that is between real bonds and/or antipathy. Behavior of children in different contexts may be quite telling. For example, a child may complain about the behavior of a stepparent to father, but show obvious care and connection in the presence of that stepparent. Lack of congruence suggests conflicts over loyalty to a biological parent.

8. Consider the process by which the new partner has joined the family. How have the new partner and stepsiblings been introduced to the children and integrated into their lives? Has the process been primarily centered on the needs of adults or carried out in a way that promotes coping in children? Have

the adults introduced the new partner to the children in a timely way, neither prematurely labeling them as family before the relationship has solidified nor keeping the relationship secret after it is clear that an important new person will enter the children's lives? Has the new stepparent entered into parental authority in the kind of gradual way most amenable to successful adaptation or prematurely assumed power and control? There are many pathways to successful adaptation; rigid criteria about what should be done need to be avoided. Nonetheless, there generally are clear differences between families that engage in a stepwise process with appropriate rituals to help join new members into the family, and those who fail to attend to the psychological needs of children in this process.

9. Consider the parenting styles within the stepfamily. Do the new partners bring similar or different ways of parenting? How do remarriage couples negotiate these differences? Have they formed new ways of parenting different from the ways in the children's original home, or that have developed in the home of the other parent? If so, do they help the children deal with these differences? Are the differences explained and processed or is it left to the children to adapt? Children need help with understanding and respecting the differences between households.

10. Consider the complex relationships between biological parents, their partners, the children whose best interest is the focus of the evaluation, and their stepsiblings. How do the stepparent and stepsiblings interface with the other biological parent and any remarriage family that the other parent forms? How do the biological parents treat the new stepparents and siblings? Do they show them respect and accept the legitimacy of their roles or do they deny they have appropriate roles in the lives of the children? What kinds of overt and covert messages are given the children? Are stepparents scapegoated? Are the positive attributes of the stepparents used by their new spouses to diminish the children's view of the other biological parent? Do triangles form between biological parents and children against new parents and stepsiblings, or between new partners against the other biological parent? Supportive comments or respectful neutrality are vastly preferable to overt or covert undermining.

11. What kind of communication occurs between family members at transitions between homes and in other special situations that bring them together? Although closeness between new and old partners may be rare, levels of mutual respect and hostility vary enormously. Often, much of the success of coparenting depends on the willingness of new partners to be cooperative. It obviously is better for new partners to support positive transitions between homes than to work, overtly or covertly, at making such transitions more difficult.

12. What do the families call the new partners of the parents? Again, it is not so much that there are correct names to call stepparents and other new relatives; rather it is important for parents to remain empathic to the needs of children and the other biological parent in the matter of names, which convey so much intense feeling.

13. Consider the bond between the new marital partners. How stable does the relationship between the partners in the remarriage family appear to be? Would couple or family therapy promote stepfamily integration? More than 60% of second marriages end in divorce, and the last thing children need is a second divorce to negotiate.

14. Is the new relationship one in which there is a permanent commitment of partners or one not so solidified? Buchanan and coworkers (1996) found that, in general, adolescents function better in homes where there is such a permanent commitment. This is not to say that all live-in relationships do not work for children. Indeed, living together is most often the behavioral step that divorced parents engage in before they are married. Nonetheless, committed relationships are more beneficial for children, especially adolescents (see Chapter 16, for a discussion of gay and lesbian partnerships in this regard).

15. Consider the number of transitions the children have faced. In some instances, a remarriage involving a move to a new location may make for one transition too many for the children. In other instances, a relocation to the other biological parent's house may have the same negative effect.

16. When families present with overly idealized versions of remarriage family life, look beyond their presentation. It may be they have achieved the optimal solution, but we rarely encounter the Brady bunch, where there are no difficulties. (Remember, the Bradys had no ex-spouse in the wings!) If it looks too good, it may be they are presenting the image they believe they should be living up to rather than real family life.

17. In assessing stepfamily factors that argue for and against a particular recommendation about the question at hand, whether custody or visitation, consider the stepfamily through the lens of normative and viable stepfamily relationships. Understand typical paths of development in these families, as described earlier in this chapter. Do not undervalue normal distance or coping mechanisms. How has the family dealt with the special tasks imposed by remarriage? Have the stepparent and children worked out a viable relationship? Have the parents worked out a way of coparenting? Have they incorporated stepparents into the parenting team? Have good enough relationships been formed to promote growth and development? Forms and solutions vary, so focus on the family's ability to adapt and find solutions rather than a preset template.

18. Given the choice between life in a stepfamily and life in the home of the other unmarried parent, the literature suggests that neither type of family organization is innately superior. Each has its strengths and difficulties. Choices between family life in a comfortable home with one well-known parent, and another in a new and challenging environment with stepparents and stepsiblings are especially difficult. Assessment of the best interest of the children should be on the basis of strengths within each household and what works best for these children, not on the basis of there being a preferred mode of postdivorce life.

19. At times, a major part of the evaluator's tasks lies in predicting the course of life in new relationships. It is useful to ask future-oriented questions: about the family life they envision, about the challenges they face, what they have learned from their prior marriage and divorce experience, and how committed they are to work through expectable difficulties. When there is too much uncertainly for the evaluator to be confident about how family relationships are likely to develop, it is best to clearly say so in the report. It may be that if a stepfamily relationship is quite new that a reevaluation of the custody or visitation issues should be suggested after a 2-year period that would allow a better sense of life in the remarried family to emerge. The evaluator is assessing a developmental process and, at times, when the transition is particularly stressful, it may be better to frame the recommendations as an interim set of suggestions, with follow-up at a time that would allow for a better sense of what life will be like in the remarriage family to emerge. It is essential to identify the limits of the examiner's ability to predict future development.

REFERENCES

Ackerman, M. J. (1995). *Clinician's guide to child custody evaluation.* New York: Wiley.

Ahrons, C. (1994). *The good divorce.* New York: HarperCollins.

Ahrons, C., & Rodgers, R. (1987). *Divorced families: Meeting the challenge of divorce and remarriage.* New York: Norton.

Ahrons, C., & Wallisch, L. (1987). Parenting in the binuclear family: Relationships between biological and stepparents. In K. Pasley & M. Ihinger-Tallman (Eds.), *Remarriage and stepparenting: Current research and theory.* New York: Guilford Press.

Amato, P. R., & Keith, B. (1991). Parental divorce and the well being of children: A meta-analysis. *Psychological Bulletin, 110,* 26–46.

Ambert, A. M. (1986). Being a stepparent: Live-in and visiting stepchildren. *Journal of Marriage and the Family, 48,* 795–804.

Bernstein, A. (1990). *Yours, mine, and ours.* New York: Norton.

Brand, E., & Clingempeel, W. (1987). The interdependence of marital and stepparent-stepchild relationships and children's psychological adjustment: Research finding and clinical implications. *Family Relations, 36,* 140–145.

Brand, E., Clingempeel, W., & Bowen-Woodward, K. (1988). Family relationships and children's psychological adjustment in stepmother and stepfather families: Findings and conclusions from the Philadelphia stepfamily research project. In E. M. Hetherington & J. D. Arasteh (Eds.), *Impact of divorce, single-parenting, and stepparenting on children* (pp. 299–324). Hillsdale, NJ: Erlbaum.

Bray, J. H. (1988). Children's development during early remarriage. In E. M. Hetherington & J. Arasteh (Eds.), *Impact of divorce, single parenting and stepparenting on children* (pp. 279–298). Hillsdale, NJ: Erlbaum.

Bray, J., & Hetherington, E. M. (1993). Families in transition: Introduction and overview. *Journal of Family Psychology, 7,* 3–8.

Bray, J. H., & Kelly, J. (1998). *Stepfamilies: Love, marriage, and parenting in the first decade.* New York: Broadway Books.

Bricklin, B. (1995). *The custody evaluation handbook.* New York: Brunner-Mazel.

Buchanan, C. M., Maccoby, E. E., & Dornbusch, S. M. (1991). Caught between parents: Adolescents' experience in divorced homes. *Child Development, 62*, 1008–1029.

Buchanan, C. M., Maccoby, E. E., & Dornbusch, S. M. (1996). *Adolescents after divorce.* Cambridge, MA: Harvard University Press.

Camara, K. A., & Resnick, G. (1988). Interparental conflict and cooperation: Factors moderating children's post-divorce adjustment. In E. M. Hetherington & J. D. Arasteh (Eds.), *Impact of divorce, single parenting, and stepparenting on children* (pp. 169–195). Hillsdale, NJ: Erlbaum.

Clingempeel, W. G., Brand, E., & Ievoli, R. (1984). Stepparent-stepchild relationships in stepmother and stepfather families: A multimethod study. *Family Relations, 33*, 465–473.

Coleman, J., & Ganong, L. (1987). Marital conflict in stepfamilies: Effects on children. *Youth and Society, 19*, 151–172.

Coleman, M., & Ganong, L. H. (1990). Remarriage and stepfamily research in the 1980s: Increased interest in an old family form. *Journal of Marriage and the Family, 52*, 925–940.

Dell, P. (1986). In defense of lineal causality. *Family Process, 25*, 515–524.

Furstenberg, F. (1988). Child care after divorce and remarriage. In E. M. Hetherington & J. Arasteh (Eds.), *Impact of divorce, single-parenting, and stepparenting on children* (pp. 245–261). Hillsdale, NJ: Erlbaum.

Furstenberg, F. (1990). Divorce and the American family. *Annual Review of Sociology, 16*, 379–403.

Furstenberg, F., & Cherlin, A. (1991). *Divided families: What happens to children when parents part.* Cambridge, MA: Harvard University Press.

Ganong, L. H., & Coleman, M. (1988). Do mutual children cement bonds in stepfamilies? *Journal of Marriage and the Family, 50*, 687–698.

Glick, P. C. (1989). Remarried families, stepfamilies, and stepchildren: A brief demographic profile. *Family Relations, 38*, 24–27.

Goldner, V., Penn, P., Sheinberg, M., & Walter, G. (1990). Love and violence: Gender paradoxes in volatile attachments. *Family Process, 29*, 343–65.

Herz, F. (1989). The postdivorce family. In B. Carter & M. McGoldrick (Eds.), *The changing family life cycle.* Boston: Allyn & Bacon.

Hetherington, E. M. (1987). Family relations six years after divorce. In K. Pasley & M. Ihinger-Tallman (Eds.), *Remarriage and stepparenting: Current research and theory* (pp. 185–205). New York: Guilford Press.

Hetherington, E. M. (1993). An overview of the Virginia longitudinal study of divorce and remarriage with a focus on early adolescence. *Journal of Family Psychology, 7*(1), 39–58.

Hetherington, E. M., & Clingempeel, W. G. (1992). Coping with marital transitions: A family systems perspective. *Monographs of the Society for Research in Child Development*, (Serial No. 227, 57, Nos. 2–3).

Hetherington, E. M., Cox, M., & Cox, R. (1982). Effects of divorce on parents and children. In M. Lamb (Ed.), *Nontraditional families* (pp. 233–288). Hillsdale, NJ: Erlbaum.

Hetherington, E. M., Law, T. C., & O'Connor, T. G. (1993). Divorce: Challenges, changes, and new chances. In F. Walsh (Ed.), *Normal family processes* (2nd ed.). New York: Guilford Press.

Hetherington, E. M., & Tryon, A. S. (1989). His and her divorces. *Family Therapy Networker, 13,* 58–61.

Hobart, C. W. (1987). Parent-child relations in remarried families. *Journal of Family Issues, 8,* 259–277.

Hooper, J. (1993). The rhetoric of motives in divorce. *Journal of Marriage and the Family, 55,* 801–813.

Maccoby, E., & Mnookin, R. (1992). *Dividing the child: Social and legal dilemmas of custody.* Cambridge, MA: Harvard University Press.

McGoldrick, M., & Carter, B. (1989). Forming a remarried family. In B. Carter & M. McGoldrick (Eds.), *The changing family life cycle: Framework for family therapy.* Boston: Allyn & Bacon.

Norton, A., & Miller, L. (1993). *Marriage, divorce and remarriage in the 1990s* (Current Population Reports, Series P-23 #180). Washington, DC: Government Printing Office.

Pasley, K., & McBride, J. (1999). The new American step-family: Insights from a gestalt of research findings. *Journal of Marital and Family Therapy, 25.*

Santrock, J. W., & Sitterle, K. A. (1987). Parent-child relationships in stepmother families. In K. Pasley & M. Ihinger-Tallman (Eds.), *Remarriage and stepparenting: Current research and theory* (pp. 135–154). New York: Guilford Press.

Visher, E., & Visher, J. (1988). *Old loyalties, new ties: Therapeutic strategies with stepfamilies.* New York: Brunner/Mazel.

Visher, E., & Visher, J. (1993). Remarriage families and stepparenting. In F. Walsh (Ed.), *Normal family processes* (2nd ed.). New York: Guilford Press.

Walsh, F. (1991). Promoting healthy functioning in divorced and remarried families. In A. Gurman & D. Kniskern (Eds.), *Handbook of family therapy* (Vol. 2). New York: Brunner/Mazel.

Walsh, F. (1993). Conceptualization of normal family processes. In F. Walsh (Ed.), *Normal family processes* (2nd ed.). New York: Guilford Press.

Walsh, F. (1998). *Strengthening family resilience.* New York: Guilford Press.

Walsh, F., Jacob, L., & Simons, V. (1995). Facilitating healthy divorce processes: Therapy and mediation approaches. In N. Jacobson & A. Gurman (Eds.), *Clinical handbook of couple therapy.* New York: Guilford Press.

White, L. K., & Booth, A. (1985). The quality and stability of remarriages: The role of stepchildren. *American Sociological Review, 50,* 689–698.

Whiteside, M. (1982). Remarriage: A family developmental process. *Journal of Marital and Family Therapy, 8,* 59–68.

Whiteside, M. (1998). The parental alliance following divorce: Literature review and policy implications. *Journal of Marital and Family Therapy, 24,* 3–24.

Zaslow, M. J., & Hayes, C. D. (1987, September). *Sex difference in children's responses to psychosocial stress.* In W. Morrill (Chair) Symposium conducted at the meeting of the National Academy of Sciences Summer Study Center, Woods Hole, MA.

CHAPTER 13

Adopted Children and Custody Arrangements

SUSAN M. FISHER

W HAT IS VALID, wise, and true about custody arrangements for birth-children is equally valid, wise, and true for adopted children—only more so. Whether the "only more so" derives from a sense of loss re-sulting from knowledge of having been moved around, either at birth or later in development with actual memories of previous caretakers, or whether the "only more so" derives from necessary information wisely provided by adop-tive parents about the adoption so that adoptees are inevitably sensitized to loss and separation, adopted children's vulnerability to concerns about aban-donment are likely to be heightened (Watkins & Fisher, 1993).

Children, whether by birth or adoption, are always, at some level, disori-ented and disrupted by parental separation, even when the child knows it was for the best and actually desires and is, in fact, relieved, even affirmed and lib-erated, by the divorce (Chapter 5, this volume; Wallerstein & Blakeslee, 1989). Whatever an adopted child will feel during a divorce will be intensified by an extra measure of anxiety and sensitivity, derived either from his or her own life experience or from the way the larger culture responds to adopted chil-dren, looking for, even expecting, a vulnerability to loss (Bartholet, 1993; Kirk, 1964, 1984; Rothman, 1989; Wegar, 1997).

Here are two examples of sensitivity to loss and separation that arise in the lives of adopted children that are less likely to arise in the lives of children raised by their birthparents, assuming equivalent family situations. An adop-tive mother told me that she had to explain to her devoted parents that the kind of loving joking she grew up with about "being sent back to Woolworth's if she wasn't a good girl" was absolutely forbidden in regard to their adopted grandchildren—that there could be "no kidding around" about being "sent back." Another adoptive mother told me of a startling moment with her young teenage son, adopted at birth, comfortable with his adoption by every measure, and doing well in his life, by every measure. There was talk between them about exchanging the newest addition to his turtle collection, a very small turtle, for a larger one, the larger turtle having been unavailable the day before. When the mother suggested an exchange, to her utter astonishment, the boy began to sob and was unable to explain what was wrong. It took her a few seconds to "get it" and she then said to him, her hand on his shoulder, only this: "We'll keep them both. In our family, nobody gets sent back."

These two vignettes demonstrate appropriate parental sensitivity to a background of concern within the child about loss—loss of people, of pets, of objects to whom the child is attached. This heightened awareness of loss in the adopted child is neither pathological nor particularly problematic. It is usually not conscious and is often talked about comfortably within adoptive families. It can even heighten sensitivity to others in ways that enhance relationships. But there can be "no kidding around" about the inviolability of the adoptee's connection to the adoptive parents.

My premise is that attachments are primarily psychosocial phenomena (see Chapter 4, this volume). Whatever controversy exists around the nature of early attachment—is it biological, is it evolutionarily driven, are there prenatal connections (unlikely), does a response to the birthmother's smell or gaze mean that there is a primal bonding (very unlikely) or simply a response to the birthmother's smell or gaze with little psychological significance—there is no doubt in infant researchers' minds that infants form an attachment to the person who can be depended on to care for them. To quote Charles Zeanah, professor of psychiatry at Louisiana State University, a leading researcher in this area, "There is compelling evidence that it is not necessary to give birth to a child for the parent to become attached to the child and the child to the parent. There is not a shred of evidence that babies adopted soon after birth don't get attached to their caregivers" (Melina, 1997, p. 2).

Young children understand naturally that it is love that defines family relationships (Pederson & Gilby, 1986; Wegar, 1997). Zeanah and Alan Sroufe, professor of psychology at the University of Minnesota Institute of Child Development, agree that there is no evidence of a prenatal "bond" between the birth mother and infant that predisposes the infant to attach to her, or that gives the biological mother a head start in attachment. "Attachment has to do with relationship experiences," said Sroufe (Melina, 1997, p. 3), and there are no relationships in utero. There are certainly fantasies during the pregnancy as there are fantasies during the waiting period for an adopted baby. These fantasies prepare the mother for the child's arrival, whatever its source, from within her body, as in a pregnancy, or from elsewhere, as in an adoption. Every mother, birth or adoptive, has to be prepared to relinquish aspects of her fantasy when the real baby arrives, for the real baby can never exactly match any fantasy.

There has been a serious confusion between the development of emotional attachment over time between mother and infant and "bonding," a quasibiological event purported to happen shortly after birth. As noted by Kraus (Chapter 4, this volume), the term "bonding" has been used by some investigators to refer to the emotional investment of the caretaker in the child. We consider such emotional investment to be a measure of "attachment," a psychosocial process that deepens over time. Despite its discredited status among scientific researchers, bonding theory has remained persistently popular, and Eyer (1992) concludes that the concept of bonding was a magical one, invoked to distract childbirth reformers, necessitate medical interventions, and single out mothers for blame for the emotional problems of their children rather than place appropriate focus on the socioeconomic and cultural issues that militate against proper care and nurture of children. The myth of bonding as a magical rite that confers emotional protection on a child has haunted adoptive mothers, as well as the mothers of premature infants and others who were unable to connect at the appropriate time because they or the infants were ill. For such mothers, bonding is a maternal event that they have already failed to perform in the prescribed hours after birth. Without an understanding of the mythical nature of the bonding notion and its confusion with healthy attachment (which adoptive children do achieve in loving, caring settings), adoptive families, educators, and therapists can mistakenly blame any later difficulties of adoptees on either the failure of bonding or the separation of an infant even a few days old from the birth mother he has already "bonded to."

Infant research is notorious for the way in which bits and pieces of it have been used to bolster one side or the other in ideological debates. Findings on the resiliency of the infant, for example, have been used to argue for the positive side of adoption; work on the effects of the disruption of bonds has been cited to support negative prognostications about adoption. That the infant early on recognizes mother's smell, for example, is used to support the contention that the adoptee is wounded by the adoption process because the infant has switched from one smell to another by leaving the birthmother. A fact about olfactory perception is given a psychological significance one would be hard-pressed to prove.

So we have, on the one hand, a romanticization of the mother-infant relation, with an image of the baby as easily harmed by separation (Rutter, 1981). On the other hand, resiliency studies offer a quite different, hardier image of the infant. From our current cultural viewpoint, we have taken it for granted that the mother-child relationship in infancy and early childhood is all-important. Now studies question these commonplace assumptions, focusing on other highly significant variables such as sibling relations, that correlate with adult outcome. These studies suggest that early experience may not matter as much as we thought it did, that children can make up for lost time—at least cognitively (Anthony, 1987; Clarke & Clarke, 1976; Cohler, 1987, 1992; Kagan, 1980). Moreover, in most cultures infants and children have multiple caretakers and concern focuses on the quality of care rather than on the presence or loss of a particular caretaker (see Watkins & Fisher, 1993).

If a child has been adopted later in development and has had a disrupted early life and is thereby potentially even more insecure, it is particularly important to reinforce the reality and reliability of the legal ties to the adoptive parents in the face of divorce. Whatever the timing of the adoption, in the eyes of the law and in the hearts and minds of the adoptive family this child belongs with them in the same way that a birthchild belongs in his birthfamily. The fantasies and projections adoptive parents will have for the adopted child will be as variable and idiosyncratic as the fantasies and projections within a birthfamily for a birthchild. All children are vulnerable. Adopted children are potentially more vulnerable because their claims and attachments, being social in origin, can be more threatened by an insensitive and demeaning social milieu (see Wegar, 1997). It is therefore particularly crucial that these claims and attachments, their reality and their meanings, be respected, even sanctified, within the legal system. This is true for all children, only more so for adopted children.

There is a moving quote by a child in H. David Kirk's remarkable classic *Shared Fate* (1984, p. 160): "The child who is born into his family is like a board that's nailed down from the start. But the adopted child, him the parents have to nail down, otherwise he is like a loose board in mid-air." In this context, the Baby Richard case is a well-publicized example. This child had been adopted at birth. His birthmother had falsely stated that she did not know the whereabouts of the baby's father. Subsequently the father returned and challenged the adoption. The case became the object of intense public attention. Ultimately, the Illinois Supreme Court held for the birthparents finding a hearing regarding the child's best interest was not pertinent to the case. The child was abruptly transferred to his birthparents during his third year. These parents have not allowed contact between him and his adoptive parents or sibling. The case did lead to the passage of a law requiring a "best interest" hearing in similar situations but the impact of this law remains uncertain.

The Baby Richard case is a lightning rod for every fearful fantasy of every member of an adoptive family. In the stories collected for our book (Watkins & Fisher, 1993) in which parents describe their conversations with their adopted children, one of the common themes expressed by very young children was a fear that the birthparents would kidnap them. Though very much like children's fairy stories and images and fantasies of bogeymen and dragons that may represent desires masked as fears, or the reverse, the threat of an actual abandonment of the adopted child by the adoptive parents is captured by the Baby Richard case. Many adopted children talk about the fear that, since their birthparents gave them up, could not/would not their adoptive parents do the same? It is in the context of such an expressed fear that adoptive parents often clarify the context in which the original relinquishment occurred. The Baby Richard case is every adopted child's horror story. Many adoptive parents had to pull out legal records and go over them with their children, reassuring them many times over that their adoption was untouchable, unquestionable, and inviolable and explain the legal differences of the Baby Richard situation from their own in ways their children could understand. The notion of children as "left luggage" to be reclaimed as parental property does not sit well in the minds of the adopted children we studied.

There are now many complex studies, both retrospective and longitudinal, comparing three groups of children: children born into two-parent families who then raise them (the control group); children born to single mothers who keep them; and children born to single mothers of the same social class who are given up for adoption into a social class and environment similar to the biological children in the first group. The findings of large-scale studies from New Zealand (1,265 children), Sweden (624 children), and the United States are remarkably consistent (Bohman & Sigvardsson, 1978, 1980; Feigelman, 1997; Fergusson, Lynskey, & Horwood, 1995). Children kept by single mothers who had considered and then rejected adoption and children raised in foster families do not fare as well as the other two groupings in terms of family stability, social enrichment activities, response to stressful life events, and the quality of emotional responsiveness between mother and child.

A more enriched upbringing is no guarantee, however, of a well-balanced, self-regulating human being. What appears to be the case in all these studies is that adopted and birthchildren, at adulthood, are equivalent on all fronts except that, during adolescence, adoptees are at higher risk for externalizing behavior disorders that appear to straighten themselves out by maturity. Externalizing behaviors refer to conduct disorders, attention deficit hyperactivity disorders, acting-out behaviors and substance abuse disorders. There is no difference in any of these well-controlled large-scale studies between adoptees and birthchildren in areas of what are called internalizing symptoms: depression, social withdrawal, self-esteem, anxiety disorders, mood disorders (children of single mothers, however, in the New Zealand study had lower self-esteem).

During adolescence, adopted children had more problems in the area of externalizing behaviors than birthchildren raised in two-parent families but, once again, significantly fewer difficulties than children of single mothers. Since these adolescent acting-out behaviors tend to resolve by adulthood when the two groups of children raised in two-parent families look the same to trained observers, the present hypothesis is that these adolescent externalizing behaviors are not the manifestation of internal psychological difficulties related to the adoption because there are no signs of what are called the "internalizing behaviors," the signs of intrapsychic conflict, deficit, and despair that would manifest themselves in the expression of anxiety, depression, and suicidal ideation, none of which are present.

The New Zealand researchers put it best. They suggest what all the previous studies have implied—that the increased rate of externalizing behaviors in adolescence were due to "genetic or congenital factors that place adopted children at high risk for such disorders." Simply put, the adoptive pool consists of children whose prenatal experience is more likely to have included a higher incidence of exposure to the effects of substance abuse and poor nutrition, both factors that predispose not only to what is included under "externalizing behaviors" but to learning disabilities as well. When not managed carefully and successfully, these factors can lead to frustrations and tensions expressed in behavioral ways.

Absolutely no data suggest that an adopted child's genetic endowment alone predisposes to later externalizing behaviors. No one has yet designed a study in which it is possible to sort out genetic effects from the effects of less than optimal intrauterine environments. In the New Zealand study of 1,265 children "adoptive children had rates of (externalizing) disorder that were higher than would have been expected on the basis of the social characteristics of their adoptive mothers but lower than would have been expected on the basis of the social characteristics of their biological mothers. These results clearly suggest adoptive children may have been a biologically high-risk group for externalizing behaviors but that the generally advantaged childhood they received in the adoptive family may have mitigated this risk somewhat with the result that adoptive children had risks of adolescent externalizing behaviors that were between the elevated risks of children with a similar biological parental background and the lower risks of children with a similar social background to the adoptive family."

Impressively, and most significantly, the two groups, birth and adoptee, look the same in adulthood suggesting that the adequate self-concept and self-esteem of adoptees help get them through adolescence when they are well supported by an enriched and responsive environment. The birthchildren of the control group families are not at similar risk for adolescent externalizing behaviors.

A famous pair of French studies on intelligence were able to compare siblings, one adopted away and one remaining at home with the birthparents (Schiff et al., 1978) and then elaborately expand on their work by comparing four groups of adopted children (Capron & Duyme, 1989): (1) those born to high socioeconomic status (SES) parents and raised by high-SES adoptive parents; (2) high-SES babies adopted into low-SES families; (3) low-SES babies adopted into high-SES families; and (4) low-SES babies adopted into low-SES families. They found that children adopted by high-SES parents scored higher than children adopted by low-SES parents by 12 points on IQ tests. They also found, however, that children born to high-SES parents scored 15 points higher than children born to low-SES parents regardless of the SES of the adoptive parents. The children with the highest IQs were those of high-SES birthparents adopted into high-SES families; the lowest scores were achieved by children from low-SES birthfamilies adopted into low-SES families. The authors concluded:

> Although these findings clearly indicate that the biological parent's background contributes to observed differences in IQ between extreme groups, as does that of the adoptive parents, more detailed interpretation is difficult. The adoption method provides a means of dissociating the pooled effects of genetic and prenatal factors from factors related to the postnatal environment. But it is not

equipped to differentiate prenatal from genetic factors. This precludes interpreting the effects of the biological parents' background solely in genetic terms,
or concluding that observed effects could be prenatal or prenatal acting either in
additive or interactive manner with genotype. On the contrary, the effect attributed to the adoptive parents is clearly environmental. (p. 553)

What is the significance of these large-scale statistical studies of complex
populations of adopted, birth, single-parent, fostered children for the courtroom? What is the relevance of our understanding of the vulnerabilities of
adopted children? Once again, that the need for clarity, order, respect, reliability, humanity, and sanity in dealing with the needs of all developing children
will be intensified for the adopted child, particularly during adolescence. They
need the same qualities as any child during adolescence—only more so. All
children need sensitivity and care during divorce and adopted children are
particularly sensitive to issues of abandonment. If the adopted child of a divorcing family happens to be one of the children vulnerable to externalizing
behaviors because of constitutional or developmental predispositions, it will
be even more significant for the child's future development that there be clo-
sure and clarity about procedures and results as well as empathic, sensitive responsiveness to his or her particular needs.

For all adopted children, particularly those with any special needs, at any
age, all else being equal, the primary custodial parent should be the one with
the most committed attachment to the child and to whom the child is most attached. Once again, this is the case for all children. It is only that for adopted
children the palette is brighter, the shadows potentially darker. It is also of particular importance that the noncustodial parent be given visitation arrangements that will support his or her connection with the child. In the case of an
open adoption where contact with birthfamilies may have been maintained,
whatever arrangements had been meaningful to the child before the divorce
should be maintained afterward. Everything should be done to maintain the
network of attachments of the adopted child to the significant figures in his life,
just as it should be done for a birthchild.

Perhaps the theme of loss for the adoptee can sensitize and mobilize judicial
personnel to give to adopted children the quality of careful attention that will
be a model for all children under their protection.

REFERENCES

Anthony, E. J. (1987). Risk, vulnerability and resilience: An overview. In E. J. Anthony
& B. J. Cohler (Eds.), *The invulnerable child*. New York: Guilford Press.
Bartholet, E. (1993). *Family bonds: Adoption and the politics of parenting*. Boston:
Houghton Mifflin.
Bohman, M., & Sigvardsson, S. (1978). An 18-year prospective, longitudinal study of
adopted boys. In J. Anthony, C. Koupernik, & C. Chiland (Eds.), *The child in his fam-
ily: Vulnerable children*. London: Wiley.

Bohman, M., & Sigvardsson, S. (1980). A prospective, longitudinal study of children registered for adoption: A 15-year follow-up. *Acta Paediatrica Scandinavia, 61*, 339–355.

Capron, C., & Duyme, M. (1989). Assessment of effects of socio-economic status on IQ in a full cross-fostering study. *Nature, 340*, 552–554.

Clarke, A. M., & Clarke, A. D. B. (1976). *Early experience: Myth and evidence.* New York: Free Press.

Cohler, B. J. (1987). Adversity, resilience, and the study of lives. In E. J. Anthony & B. J. Cohler (Eds.), *The invulnerable child.* New York: Guilford Press.

Cohler, B. J. (1992). Culture, vulnerability, and resilience in the study of risk for major psychopathology. In D. Cicchetti & D. J. Cohen (Eds.), *Manual of developmental psychopathology.* New York: Wiley.

Eyer, D. (1992). *Mother-infant bonding: A scientific fiction.* New Haven, CT: Yale University Press.

Feigelman, W. (1997). Adopted adults: Comparisons with persons raised in conventional families. In H. E. Gross & M. B. Sussman (Eds.), *Families and adoption.* New York: Haworth Press.

Fergusson, D. M., Lynskey, M., & Horwood, L. J. (1995). The adolescent outcomes of adoption: A 16-year longitudinal study. *Journal of Child Psychology and Psychiatry, 36*(4), 597–615.

Kagan, J. (1980). Perspectives on continuity. In O. G. Brim, Jr. & J. Kagan (Eds.), *Continuity and change in human development* (pp. 26–74). Cambridge, MA: Harvard University Press.

Kirk, H. D. (1964). *Shared fate: A theory of adoption and mental health.* New York: Free Press.

Kirk, H. D. (1984). *Shared fate: A theory and method of adoptive relationships* (2nd ed.). Port Angeles, WA: Ben-Simon.

Melina, L. (1997). Recent studies examine adoption outcome, birth mothers' decision-making. *Adopted Child, 16*(1), 1–4.

Pederson, D. R., & Gilby, R. L. (1986). Children's concepts of the family. In R. D. Ashmore & D. M. Brodzinsky (Eds.), *Thinking about the family: Views of parents and children* (pp. 119–20). Hillsdale, NJ: Erlbaum.

Rothman, B. K. (1989). *Recreating motherhood: Ideology and technology in a patriarchal society.* New York: Norton.

Rutter, M. (1981). *Maternal deprivation reassessed* (2nd ed.). London: Penguin.

Schiff, M., Duyme, M., Dumaret, A., Stewart, J., Tomkiewicz, S., & Feingold, J. (1978). Intellectual status of working-class children adopted early into upper-middle-class families. *Science, 200*, 1503–1504.

Wallerstein, J. S., & Blakeslee, S. (1989). *Second chances: Men, women and children a decade after divorce.* New York: Ticknor & Fields.

Watkins, M., & Fisher, S. (1993). *Talking with young children about adoption.* New Haven & London: Yale University Press.

Wegar, K. (1997). *Adoption, identity, and kinship: The debate over sealed birth records.* New Haven & London: Yale University Press.

CHAPTER 14

Custody Evaluations for Medically Ill Children and Adolescents

BRENDA BURSCH and LISA VITTI

A LMOST ONE-THIRD OF all children in the United States under the age of 18 were classified as suffering from a chronic health condition in the 1988 National Health Interview Survey (Newacheck & Taylor, 1992). About one million children a year experience divorce, with 38,000 of those children having a disease or handicapping condition (Barbero, 1995). Surprisingly, no research has been specifically conducted on the outcome of custody decisions on chronically ill children, or on the optimal matching of children with chronic illnesses and caregivers. Although standard custody evaluations may be sufficient for many families with chronically ill children, knowledge of those factors that are relevant to families with medically ill children may assist an evaluator in making a decision in the best interest of the child. Recommendations made in this chapter are not intended to replace a standard custody evaluation, but to augment the evaluation when appropriate.

The first part of this chapter will review relevant research literature. The following factors have been studied and considered to be important predictors of health status: the nature of the illness, stress, and medical treatment. Relevant research findings pertaining to the child, the parents, and/or developmental issues will be presented when available. The second part will incorporate research findings into recommendations for professionals conducting custody evaluations involving an ill child or adolescent.

NATURE OF THE ILLNESS

The demands placed on the child and parents depend in part on the characteristics of the child's illness. When evaluating a family, it may be helpful to understand aspects of the child's illness such as the degree and type of incapacitation; the visibility of the condition; the prognosis or life expectancy; whether the course of the illness is constant, relapsing, or progressive; the amount of home and professional treatment and expertise required; and the amount of pain or other symptoms experienced. It is possible that within the same family one parent might be the optimal caregiver if the child suffered from chronic asthma and the other parent might be the optimal caregiver if the child had terminal cancer due to the differing demands and issues raised by these very different illnesses.

Overview of Chronically Ill Children

Comprising the one-third of children in the United States with chronic health conditions in 1988 were 20% with mild conditions, 9% with moderately severe conditions, and 2% with severe conditions (Newacheck & Taylor, 1992). Children in the mild group were most likely to suffer from respiratory allergies and chronic ear infections. Conditions that were identified as most common in the severe group included musculoskeletal impairments, cerebral palsy, diabetes, asthma, epilepsy, and arthritis. On average, children in the severe group had 2.6 medical conditions compared with 1.3 conditions in the mild group.

Of those children with one or more chronic conditions, 13% were limited in their usual activities, experiencing an average of about two days in bed and three days home from school in the previous year due to their chronic condition (not due to acute illnesses such as the flu, injuries, or colds). Eight percent of chronically ill children accounted for about three-fourths of all bed days, with this group spending an average of 7 or more days in bed due to their chronic conditions. Similarly, 12% accounted for about three-fourths of lost school days with an average of 7 or more school days missed during the year. Consideration of the number of expected lost school days and the ability of the parent to provide care for the child during those days without jeopardizing employment, and possibly health insurance coverage, is important to the long-term care of the child. Depending on the family, it may be helpful to inquire about the number of extended family members or friends who are available to assist with unexpected child care needs.

Among chronically ill children, approximately two-thirds were reported by their parents to have used medications recommended by a doctor, and 4% were reported to have been hospitalized to treat their chronic health problems during the year prior to the interview. The children averaged close to five physician visits each year for their chronic conditions alone. Again, a relatively small number of chronically ill children, mostly in the severely ill group, accounted for the vast majority of physician contacts and hospital days. Severely chronically ill children had an average of 16 physician visits annually and accounted for one-third of all hospital days due to chronic illness. Also, 85% of this group reportedly used physician-recommended medications. The need for the parent to regularly interact with health care personnel typically requires some form of health insurance or way to pay for service, transportation to an appropriate health care facility, and the ability to communicate with health care providers.

Community prevalence rates of childhood psychopathology are about 20% (Costello, 1989). It has been estimated that at least 12% of children and adolescents have serious mental disorders, and at least half of them are severely disordered or impaired by their condition (Institute of Medicine, 1989). The prevalence of psychopathology among chronically ill children is higher. The Ontario Child Health Study (Cadman, Boyle, Szatmari, & Offord, 1987) found that chronically ill children had twice as many psychological disorders as healthy children. Stocking, Rothney, Grosser, and Goodwin (1972) found that almost two-thirds of 80 pediatric hospital inpatients had significant psychopathology, with about half of the psychological disorders being unrelated to their medical illnesses. Kashani, Venzke, and Millar (1981) found that 7% of school-age children who were medical inpatients had a major depression, and that one-fourth of children admitted for orthopedic procedures showed evidence of depression. This research suggests that when evaluating the needs of a chronically ill child, it is important to consider potential comorbid emotional problems.

The course of a chronic illness can usually be categorized into one of three types: constant, relapsing, or progressive (Patterson & Garwick, 1994). Constant conditions, such as a spinal cord injury, often require a huge initial adjustment by the family at the onset and considerable perseverance over time. For families with a child with a constant condition, it may be helpful to consider caregiver respite opportunities as part of the custody plan. Relapsing conditions, such as epilepsy or recurrent cancer, usually require the flexibility to shift between a lower level of care to an acute model of care. Frequent shifts may take a toll on the family resources. Progressive conditions, such as cystic fibrosis, often require increasing caretaking demands over time and the need to address issues of dependency, loss, and death. Although not empirically studied, comparing the expected course of the child's illness with the abilities and coping styles of each parent may minimize the amount of burden experienced by the custodial parent and the amount of long-term stress experienced by the child.

BASIC DISEASE-SPECIFIC INFORMATION

Although space does not allow for a review of each of the many childhood illnesses, it is important for an evaluator to obtain basic information about the particular condition to determine the adequacy of the parents' knowledge, expectations and plans. For example, there are many issues specific to insulin-dependent diabetes mellitus (IDDM) that may be important for a custody evaluator to know. IDDM is used as an example to demonstrate the types of information that might be helpful for an evaluator to obtain regarding a specific condition.

IDDM is typically diagnosed in childhood and affects 1 out of every 600 children. It is characterized by failure of the pancreas and, consequently, requires daily insulin replacement by injection (usually one injection before breakfast and one before dinner). Because of the current use of exogenous insulin, IDDM is now considered a long-term chronic illness (constant) with a life expectancy of about 75% of normal. Typically after 15 to 20 years, common complications of IDDM start to occur, including blindness, renal failure, nerve damage, and heart disease. Maintaining a blood glucose level in the near-normal range has been found to prevent, delay, or minimize these complications (American Diabetes Association, 1993). To help maintain a relatively even blood glucose level, the patient is usually instructed to eat small amounts of food frequently throughout the day. Factors such as exercise, illness, stress, and emotional state also impact insulin action and, consequently, blood glucose level. Because the blood glucose level can vary over the course of a day due to these many factors, it is often necessary to closely monitor the child's blood glucose level by conducting blood tests at home or school. This requires a finger stick to produce a drop of blood that is analyzed by a sensitized strip or small computerized glucose meter. Death can result from either excessively high or low blood glucose levels. About 2–3% of children die of IDDM within the first 10 years after diagnosis, and 12–13% die within 20 years.

Even with this small amount of information on IDDM, a number of issues are relevant for a custody evaluation. For example, if the child is young, the custodial parent must be prepared and able to give insulin shots, monitor blood glucose, provide an appropriate diet, monitor exercise, and help manage stress for the child. If the child is a normal adolescent, a parent who is supportive of the adolescent's illness self-management behaviors and age-appropriate independence might be more effective than a parent who continues to want to personally manage the adolescent's diabetes care. The custodial parent, regardless of the child's age, must be able to identify the signs and symptoms of hypo- and hyperglycemia, potentially life-threatening events, and know how to respond.

CONCEPTUAL UNDERPINNINGS: STRESS, SELF-EFFICACY, AND COPING

Among children, stress has been found to be linked with headaches, asthma, cancer outcome, hemophilia bleeding episodes, chronic diarrhea, and diabetes control. It is expected that, as research in this area progresses, stress links with other illnesses will also be identified. It has been proposed that patient expectations and beliefs about their ability to care for themselves (self-efficacy) may play an important role directly on health outcome due to the activation of health-promoting behaviors and better adaptation to the stress associated with illness (Horwitz & Horwitz, 1993). The body of research that has examined these variables has provided a conceptual framework for understanding health behaviors and outcomes, and for predictions about the effects of various sources of stress and support on health status.

Patient expectancies and self-efficacy beliefs are two concepts derived from an extensively studied and widely accepted conceptual framework called Social Cognitive Theory. Social Cognitive Theory utilizes a biopsychosocial model of human behavior which specifies that human behavior is the result of the interactions of one's actions, thoughts, emotions, other personal factors, and environmental influences (Bandura, 1989). This framework includes the concept of efficacy expectations that has received much attention within the health behavior literature. From this model, the probability that a person will perform a behavior (such as seeking health care services or engaging in self-management of a problem) is related to the person's beliefs that he or she has the knowledge and ability to perform the behavior (self-efficacy) and that the behavior will result in beneficial outcomes (treatment efficacy). Efficacy expectations are influenced by several factors, including previous accomplishments and vicarious experiences. The development of self-efficacy requires experience mastering challenges with persevering effort. Research supports this model with efficacy expectations influencing health behaviors, including medical adherence, across a broad spectrum of illnesses.

Self-inefficacy beliefs are thought to play a role in the development of illness and increased use of health care services by negatively influencing one's stress level, functioning, and emotions, which can affect the person's appraisal of demanding situations. Thoughts that one is unable to manage potential threats are distressing and impair functioning (Bandura, 1988a, 1988b; Lazarus & Folkman, 1984; Meichenbaum, 1977; Sarason, 1975). Perceived coping self-inefficacy has been linked to high ratings of subjective distress, physiological arousal, and secretion of stress-related substances into the body (Bandura, Reese, & Adams, 1982; Bandura, Taylor, Williams, Mefford, & Barchas, 1985). Interestingly, it is not the number of negative thoughts, but the perceived self-inefficacy to turn them off, that leads to high levels of distress (Kent, 1987; Salkovskis & Harrison, 1984). This finding is consistent with other research which revealed that exposure to physical stressors with the ability to control them has no adverse physiological effects, but exposure to the same stressors without such personal control impairs cellular components of the immune system (Maier, Laudenslager, & Ryan, 1985). There is some evidence to suggest that stress that occurs while increasing one's coping efficacy actually enhances immune function (Wiedenfeld et al., 1990).

Self-inefficacy beliefs have also been linked to avoidant behavior and depression. Research on self-efficacy, anxiety, and avoidant behavior has revealed that avoidant behavior is not driven by anxiety, but rather by the belief that one is inefficacious to manage a situation (Williams, Dooseman, & Kleifield, 1984; Williams, Kinney, & Falbo, 1989; Williams, Turner, & Peer, 1985). Perceived self-inefficacy to achieve goals and attain life satisfaction has been linked to depression (Bandura, 1988c; Cutrona & Troutman, 1986; Holahan & Holahan,

1987a, 1987b; Kanfer & Zeiss, 1983). By impairing functioning, thoughts of self-inefficacy further diminish perceptions of self-efficacy (Kavanagh & Bower, 1985). Similar to findings regarding self-efficacy and anxiety, it is the perceived self-efficacy to turn off negative thoughts that is important to the occurrence, duration, and recurrence of depressive episodes (Kavanagh & Wilson, 1988). As people tend to avoid environments in which they perceive they are inefficacious and choose those in which they feel a higher degree of self-efficacy, decisions people make serve to reinforce their perceived competencies, values, and interests (Bandura, 1986; Betz & Hackett, 1986; Lent & Hackett, 1987; Snyder, 1986).

MEDICAL TREATMENT ADHERENCE

Adherence to medical treatment is of significant concern to health care providers and has been demonstrated to be a significant problem, sometimes fatal, for chronically ill children and adolescents. Overall pediatric adherence rates are estimated to average 50%, typically varying between 20% and 80% (Dunbar & Waszak, 1990). Many factors have been found to be related to adherence, often because they impact stress, self-efficacy, and/or coping. Custody evaluation in families with an ill child or adolescent should include the examination of relevant factors related to medical adherence, and strategies employed by the parents to optimize adherence as well as the appropriateness of medical adherence. The following factors will be reviewed as they are potentially relevant for child custody evaluations: family functioning, social support, psychological characteristics of the parent, and psychological characteristics of the child. Although many of the studies reviewed suffered from small sample sizes, the results across studies appear to be consistent in most cases. Differences will be discussed when they exist.

FAMILY FUNCTIONING AND SOCIAL SUPPORT

Several studies have found an inverse relationship between family conflict and treatment adherence among children (Christiaanse, Lavigne, & Lerner, 1989; Friedman et al., 1986; Hauser et al., 1990) and a number of studies suggest that medication adherence in particular is negatively impacted by family dysfunction. For example, nonadherence with immunosuppressive medications following renal transplant was found to be related to families that were fatherless, had lower income, and had more communication problems, and to the pediatric patients feeling they receive the most emotional support from someone outside the family (Korsch, Fine, & Negrete, 1978). Underscoring the importance of adherence to immunosuppresive medications in this population, 8 out of the 14 noncompliant patients experienced organ rejection and return to dialysis. In another study, Miller-Johnson et al. (1994) studied 88 children and adolescents with insulin-dependent diabetes from two clinics and found that ratings of parent-child discipline, warmth, and behavioral support were not significantly associated with diabetes outcome, but both parent and child ratings of parent-child conflict was a consistent correlate of medical adherence. Finally, nonadherence with seizure medication among children having epilepsy has been associated with families with less perceived harmony (Friedman et al., 1986).

Looking at it from the other side, children and adolescents who have parents who provide more social support for their diabetic care activities have been found to be more adherent (Hanson, Henggeler, & Burghen, 1987; LaGreca et al., 1995). Similarly, Shenkel, Rogers, Perfetto, and Levin (1985) reported that social support was important in moderating behavioral intentions, although not necessarily the resulting behaviors, of diabetic adolescents. Chaney and Peterson (1989) found that medication adherence among children with juvenile rheumatoid arthritis was related to higher levels of family cohesion and adaptability, lower degrees of stress from family life, mother's coping and father's family satisfaction. Finally, Hanson, DeGuire, Schinkel, Henggeler, and Burghen (1992) found better dietary adherence among adolescents with diabetes from families who were more flexible and less nonsupportive (nagging, criticizing).

One adherence study suggests that family functioning might interact with the type of disorder. Brown, Borden, and Clingerman (1985) found that hyperactive children were more likely to drop out of treatment if their family was intact, and the families of the medication-adherent children reported higher levels of family conflict.

Although family functioning appears to have a relationship with adherence, the direction of the relationship might depend on the disorder. The limited number of studies in this area do not allow making strong conclusions, but suggest that issues such as family cohesion, adaptability, conflict, communication, emotional support, and stress be evaluated considering the circumstances involved with the various custody options.

PSYCHOLOGICAL CHARACTERISTICS OF THE PARENT

Knowledge defined here refers to an understanding of the disease process, the tasks that are required for successful illness management, the ability to execute the tasks, and the ability to problem-solve. Knowledge requirements vary greatly by disease and individual child. Parental knowledge has been found to be an important factor related to adherence in many childhood illnesses, including asthma, cystic fibrosis, hemophilia, phenylketonuria, and diabetes (Alexander, 1983; Creer, 1993; Fehrenbach & Peterson, 1989; Johnson, 1995; Sergis-Deavenport & Varni, 1982, 1983). However, the degree of importance that needs to be attached to parental knowledge may vary by developmental level of the child. For example, maternal knowledge has been linked to treatment adherence among preadolescent children with diabetes, but not for adolescents. It is the knowledge level of the diabetic adolescents themselves that has been found to predict their adherence to treatment recommendations (LaGreca, Follansbee, & Skyler, 1990).

Health beliefs of mothers have been studied using adherence as an outcome measure in a number of studies. Mothers have been found to be more adherent with asthma medication for their children if they had a preventive orientation, believed in their personal capabilities, considered the medication efficacious, felt better when following physician advice, and believed their child would be more susceptible to an asthma attack if they were not compliant (Radius et al., 1978). The belief in their child's susceptibility to illness has also been found to be associated with treatment adherence among mothers of well children and of children with ear infections and obesity (Becker, Drachman, & Kirscht, 1974; Becker, Maiman, Kirscht, Haefner, & Drachman, 1977; Becker, Nathanson, Drachman & Kirscht, 1977). Severity of the risks believed to be associated with noncompliance has also been found to be an important factor among mothers (Becker et al., 1974; Becker, Maiman et al., 1977; Becker, Nathanson, et al., 1977).

Other adherence studies that have examined psychological characteristics of the parents have not been replicated, making it difficult to discern the importance of the findings. For example, as presented, Chaney and Peterson (1989) found that medication adherence among children with juvenile rheumatoid arthritis was related to mother's coping and father's family satisfaction. Another study focused on the psychological characteristics of mothers who refused cancer treatment for their children (Blotcky, Cohen, Conatser, & Klopovich, 1985). They were found to report greater religiousity and greater trait anxiety.

Research on the psychological characteristics of parents related to medical adherence suggest that it might be important to evaluate parental knowledge about their child's medical status and needs, and parental health beliefs. In particular, parental beliefs regarding their child's susceptibility to illness and severity of the risks appear to be related to adherence. The importance placed on this portion of the evaluation will likely vary depending on the developmental stage of the child. Other beliefs or psychopathology that might interfere with prudent health care decisions should also be evaluated as appropriate.

Relevant Psychological Characteristics of the Child

Although a number of psychological characteristics of the child have been studied using adherence as an outcome measure, only those characteristics that are most likely to be relevant during a custody evaluation will be reviewed here. They include independence and locus of control.

Several studies have examined independence and autonomy in relationship to adherence among adolescents. Increased independence has been found to be related to increased adherence with appointment keeping, antiseizure medication, and contraceptive use (Durant, Jay, Linder, Shoffitt, & Litt, 1984; Friedmen et al., 1986; Litt & Cuskey, 1984; Neel, Jay, & Litt, 1985). These findings suggest that, among families in which the ill child is an adolescent, it may be important to determine which parent is most supportive of the adolescent's independence and medical self-management.

A number of studies have measured locus of control and adherence with somewhat inconsistent results. Locus of control refers to the degree to which one has the general belief that one personally impacts life events (internal locus) or that external forces impact life events (external locus). Among adolescents with cancer, those with an external locus of control (believing external forces, rather than they, were in control) were more likely to be nonadherent with treatment and to refuse treatment than those with an internal locus of control (Blotcky et al., 1985; Jamison, Lewis, & Burish, 1986). In one study of pediatric patients with diabetes, internally oriented girls and externally oriented boys were more adherent (Hamburg & Inoff, 1982), and in another study of diabetic patients, locus of control was not found to be related to adherence (Gross, Delcher, Snitzer, Bianchi, & Epstein, 1984). The inconsistencies in the research regarding locus of control suggest that another factor may interact with locus of control to impact adherence. Inquiry regarding locus of control might not be fruitful unless it is clear that the focus of the child or adolescent is extreme in a way that would impede prudent health care decisions if not mediated by appropriate parental involvement.

STRATEGIES TO OPTIMIZE ADHERENCE

Strategies employed to optimize adherence should reflect those variables that are most likely to cause nonadherence for the particular child in question and may vary depending on which aspect of the treatment recommendations (medications, diet, exercise, etc.) is being targeted (Stark, Jelalian, & Miller, 1995). For example, one would expect that a controlling parent will be prone to exacerbate the nonadherence of an adolescent who is struggling to achieve independence. Few studies have specifically compared various parental strategies to optimize medical adherence in their children. However, some studies have identified or suggested successful parental strategies. Particularly where there is a history of medical nonadherence, it may be important to assess the types of strategies each parent uses to optimize adherence. If adherence has historically been optimized, it is important to understand what has worked in order to preserve the program to the extent possible.

Although most of the studies were conducted with small sizes, positive reinforcement has been used effectively to increase adherence across a number of childhood disease categories including diabetes, hemophilia, spina bifida, asthma, and renal failure (Carney, Schechter, & Davis, 1983; Epstein et al., 1981; Finney, Lemanek, Brophy, & Cataldo, 1990; Greenan-Fowler, Powell, & Varni, 1987; Killam, Apodaca, Manella, & Varni, 1983; Lowe & Lutzker, 1979; Magrab & Papadopoulou, 1977; Wysocki, Green, & Huxtable, 1989). The nature of the positive reinforcement should be evaluated in terms of the developmental functioning of the child and the type of illness. Younger or less motivated children may require more immediate and frequent reinforcement (Friedman & Litt, 1987). Adjunctive strategies and alterations in the reinforcement plan are likely to be important for chronic conditions as adherence often decreases over time or if the reinforcer is removed. Use of a token system (such as points that can be exchanged for various rewards) easily allows for changes in the reinforcer and has been found to be effective in improving adherence in children with rheumatoid arthritis (Rapoff, Lindsley, & Christophersen, 1984), with diabetes (Carney et al., 1983; Daneman et al., 1982), and on hemodialysis (Magrab & Papadopoulou, 1977).

Strategies used with adolescents will likely need to be different from those used with younger children. Adolescents have been found to be nonadherent to avoid appearing different from their peers (Dolgin, Katz, Doctors, & Siegel, 1986; Friedman & Litt, 1987; Korsch et al., 1978). Among organ transplant adolescents, who require medications that often cause physical disfigurement, dissatisfaction with body image is related to nonadherence to medications (Klein, Simmons, & Anderson, 1984). A parent who is able to model and provide support for coping assertively with peer pressure and social demands may be most useful for adolescents.

Parent involvement in efforts to improve family communication and reduce conflict may also improve adherence. Improvements in illness-related family communication skills, problem-solving strategies, and family support for adolescent self-care have been demonstrated in a randomized, controlled trial to improve diabetes adherence 6 months after intervention (Satin, LaGreca, Zigo, & Skylar, 1989). A program designed to train parents of children with diabetes to set clear expectations, avoid power struggles with the child, and effectively use reinforcement strategies, and motivation techniques resulted in improved adherence with diet, insulin administration, and glucose monitoring.

It is not clear whether direct parent supervision is consistently helpful or unhelpful for adherence. Among children with diabetes, increased parental supervision has been found to be positively correlated with improved exercise and insulin injection adherence, but negatively correlated with dietary behaviors and unrelated to glucose testing (Johnson, 1995).

Positive reinforcement, modeling of effective coping, and interventions geared toward improved family functioning have all been linked to medical adherence, whereas the efficacy of educational efforts alone, self-monitoring alone, graduated goal setting alone, reminders, contingency contracting alone, and increased parental supervision have not been consistently demonstrated to improve adherence (Dunbar & Waszak, 1990).

APPROPRIATENESS OF HEALTH SERVICE UTILIZATION AND MEDICAL ADHERENCE

The parent who appears to be more committed to the health care needs of the child is not always the best parent to have primary responsibility for the child. Variables other than the child's medical needs have been shown to be related to health care utilization. Such variables may complicate the difficult task of balancing the importance of illness self-management and appropriate health care.

Finally, there are instances when the acquisition of medical care may not be in the best interests of the child or may be harmful to the child. An evaluation of the *appropriateness* of parental concern, desire for medical intervention, and support for the sick role are important when considering custody options.

FAMILY VARIABLES AND HEALTH CARE UTILIZATION

Although the child's health status is consistently found to be the strongest statistical predictor of general pediatric service utilization, there is also clear indication that family variables are important to health care utilization (Alexander & Markowitz, 1986; Newacheck & Halfon, 1986; Tessler & Mechanic, 1978; Wolfe, 1980). For example, mothers who are experiencing significant stress are more likely to seek medical care for their children (Alexander & Markowitz, 1986; Gortmaker, Eckenrode, & Gore, 1982; Roghmann & Haggerty, 1973; Slessinger, Tessler, & Mechanic, 1976; Tessler & Mechanic, 1978). It is not clear from the published research if a mother's stress impacts her perceptions of her child's health status or if the mother's stress actually impacts her child's health. Also found to contribute to health care service use in general pediatrics are having a young child, urban area of residence, higher number of chronic medical problems in the child, families with a medical history of similar symptoms, more parental control, less expressiveness, more achievement orientation, fewer social activities, and higher level of maternal education (Alexander & Markowitz, 1986; Newacheck & Halfon, 1986; Slessinger et al., 1976; Weimer, Hatcher, & Gould, 1983).

EFFICACY OF ILLNESS SELF-MANAGEMENT VERSUS HEALTH CARE UTILIZATION

There are medical problems for which a careful balance of medical care and self-management are important to the health outcomes of children. Overreliance on health care systems might undermine illness self-management and consequently negatively impact the health status of the child. For example, research on pediatric pain syndromes suggest that children with severe and persistent pain often have inadequate coping responses and perceive themselves to have little control over their pain (Branson & Craig, 1988; Dunne-Geier, McGrath, Rouke, Latter, & D'Astous, 1986). The coping strategy used by a child has been shown to influence the impact of their pain with more active coping strategies increasing the child's sense of control and more passive strategies leading to withdrawal, inactivity, and increased pain (Flor, Birbaumer, & Rudy, 1990; Siegal & Smith, 1989). Because a child's ability to utilize adaptive coping skills is influenced by the family environment (Dolgin & Phipps, 1989; Dunne-Geier et al., 1986) via discriminate cues and selective reinforcement of pain behavior (Fordyce, 1976; Kerns et al., 1991; Turk, Flor, & Rudy, 1987), parental influence appears to be an important consideration in symptom development and maintenance. Specific parental behaviors that have been found

to reinforce pain behaviors include providing excessive sympathy and attention for symptoms, external help seeking, strong emotional responses, modeling of symptoms, and support for task avoidance (Fordyce, 1976; Payne &
Norfleet, 1986; Philips, 1987; Whitehead, Busch, Heller, & Costa, 1986). Overreliance on the medical system may, at times, hinder more effective coping and
the resolution of symptoms.

Quality of Life

There may be times when the costs of adhering to medical protocols are not in
the best interest of the child, even if it results in the deteriorating or subopti-
mal health of the child. Other factors that influence the child's quality of life
must be considered when evaluating the importance of adherence. Costs such
treatment side effects, financial burden, impact on functioning, and interference with daily activities may at times outweigh the benefits of treatment adherence and must be determined on a case-by-case basis. The weighing of such
costs and benefits may be most poignant in the case of a terminally ill child,
but may be of equal importance in cases of chronically ill children.

Munchausen by Proxy

The acquisition of medical care and administration of prescribed medications
for children who do not require it can take the form of child abuse such as in
Munchausen by proxy. In Munchausen by proxy, a caretaker fabricates or in-
duces illness in a child so that others view the child as ill. The child might
have a true illness which is manipulated or might be healthy. Most typically,
the child is frequently brought to medical professionals for evaluation and
treatment of the fabricated or induced signs and symptoms. The stress of a divorce can be sufficient to cause an onset or exacerbation of this form of abuse
in a parent who is vulnerable to this type of behavior. Also, the child's reported "special health care needs" might be used as an argument for custody.
Consideration of the health of the child when under the care of each parent
may be helpful in identifying Munchausen by proxy (MBP), and/or related
forms of child abuse, as victims usually improve or become symptom-free
when separated from the abuser.

When considering custody issues in a family where it is known that the child
has been a victim of MBP, it is important to keep in mind the seriousness of MBP
behavior. It is not unusual for a MBP parent to refrain from MBP behaviors while
under supervision. Frequently, however, the abuse begins again slowly and esca-
lates over time. Of six MBP children followed by McGuire and Feldman (1989),
five continued to be abused after referral to child protective services and all six
continued to be abused during and after the abuser had participated in psychotherapy. Parents who are truly interested primarily in their child's safety, are
usually open to monitoring and support. It is in the cases of extreme MBP that

complete denial, hostility, threats of lawsuits, and the garnering of outside support is most frequently observed (Kinscherff & Famularo, 1991). For most cases, considering the child's use of medical services before social services intervention compared with the child's use of services during separation from the abuser is a helpful indication of risk. For example, a child who had significant medical intervention or impairment before separation (doctor's office visits, use of medications, low functioning or hospitalizations) and little or no medical intervention or impairment during separation (fewer medications, higher functioning or fewer use of medical services) is at risk to return to his or her previous level of medical intervention or impairment over time if returned to the abuser. There is danger in relying on the child's medical status during unsupervised visitations or while the child is in the custody of a relative or family friend as a point of reference, however. Abuse often reoccurs over time and once external monitoring has ceased. Additionally, it sometimes continues with the conscious or unconscious collusion of other family members or family friends who have temporary custody.

When evaluating a previous or suspected MBP abuser for child custody, is important to consider the health care arrangements made for the children to minimize the danger of future abuse. It is often recommended that all pediatric medical care be coordinated by one or a team of two pediatricians (to cover each other) who have (1) the relevant medical history of the child, (2) a summary of the MBP evaluation, and (3) MBP experience or access to someone with MBP expertise. The pediatrician should (1) monitor the child's health and, if the child becomes ill, treat or refer the child for appropriate care, (2) assess the child's development, and (3) answer medical questions. If the child is in the custody of the abuser, arrangements can sometimes be made with insurance companies so any attempts at utilizing their insurance to seek care outside this arrangement can be reported. The diagnosing professionals should be included in the long-term evaluation of the family if possible. Likewise, mental health professionals who participated in the diagnosis can be helpful to reassess the progress made by the abuser(s) in psychotherapy.

When evaluating a previous abuser for suitability for custody, it is important to consider the quality of psychiatric treatment the person has received. Like other forms of child abuse, those abusers who admit MBP are generally considered to be more likely to benefit from psychotherapy. Following are recommendations for psychotherapy with the abuser and spouse:

- Mental health professionals evaluating or treating a suspected MBP family should have training and experience, or access to someone with training and experience, with MBP. This recommendation is consistent with legal and ethical mandates to practice within one's scope of expertise.
- Evaluating and treating mental health professionals should have access to all available records (sent directly from health care providers or organizations rather than provided by the family) and other professionals, and should utilize this information in their evaluation and treatments.

- Treating psychotherapists must provide service consistent with the determination of the court. If the court finds MBP, the therapist must provide services to treat MBP. If the therapist does not believe MBP occurred, is not convinced of MBP when provided with available records, or is unwilling to provide appropriate treatment, the therapist's view should be investigated for validity and/or a new therapist should be obtained. If the treating psychotherapist argues with the court that the parents are loving and concerned parents who have been wrongly accused, it is important to consider that the therapist may have been fooled by the parents, making the therapist ineffective. Again, a new therapist should be seriously considered.
- Similar to other forms of child abuse, some indicators of successful treatment include (1) the abuser(s) have admitted to the abuse and have been able to describe specifically how they abused the child, (2) the abuser(s) have experienced an appropriate emotional response to their behaviors and the harm they have caused their child, (3) they have developed strategies to better manage their needs and to avoid abusing their child in the future, and (4) they have demonstrated these skills, with monitoring, over a significant period. It is important that the partners of the suspected abusers also be included in therapy as they have either colluded with the abuser (consciously or unconsciously) or for other reasons have been unable to protect their child.

RECOMMENDATIONS

- Obtain a good understanding of the disease and determine the specific disease management requirements before conducting any other portion of the evaluation. Minimally, the following disease-related information should be obtained: the degree and type of incapacitation; the visibility of the condition; the prognosis or life expectancy; whether the course of the illness is constant, relapsing, or progressive; the expected amount of interface required with health care systems; the amount and types of home and professional treatment and expertise required; and the amount of pain or other symptoms typically experienced by those with the disease.
- Determine how illness management has previously worked in the family and evaluate the multiple perceptions of how effective the illness management has been (including the perspective of the child's physician(s)). Identifying what has worked well in addition to the specific areas of concern, from multiple perspectives, may help shape the direction of the evaluation. If custody is currently shared, determine (to the degree possible) whether the health of the child varies depending on whom the child is with.
- Evaluate the knowledge, specific skills, previous experience, and care philosophy of each parent, including parental beliefs regarding their child's susceptibility to illness and severity of the risks, strategies employed to

optimize medical adherence, and views regarding the appropriateness of medical care intervention. The importance placed on this portion of the evaluation will vary depending on the developmental stage (but not necessarily the age) of the child.

- Evaluate stress, social support, and possible barriers to meeting the child's needs. The specific concepts of family cohesion, adaptability, conflict, communication, emotional support, and perceived stress have been identified as important family variables. Additionally, parental and/or child psychopathology that might interfere with prudent health care decisions should also be evaluated as appropriate.

- Consider recommending parent training, if indicated, on the topics of understanding the illness, recognizing important medical signs and symptoms, and using appropriate disease management techniques. Most medical centers have parent training available for the parents of children with a common chronic illnesses.

- Consider parent and/or child psychotherapy if medical noncompliance or poor illness management appears to be partially due to family conflict, difficulties with parenting, and/or major psychopathology.

REFERENCES

Alexander, A. B. (1983). The nature of asthma. In P. J. McGrath & P. Firestone (Eds.), *Pediatric and adolescent behavioral medicine: Issues in treatment.* New York: Springer.

Alexander, C. S., & Markowitz, R. (1986). Maternal employment and use of pediatric clinic services. *Medical Care, 24,* 134–147.

American Diabetes Association. (1993). Position statement: Implications of the diabetes control and complications trial. *Diabetes Care, 16,* 1517–1520.

Bandura, A. (1986). *Social foundations of thought and action: A social cognitive theory.* Englewood Cliffs, NJ: Prentice-Hall.

Bandura, A. (1988a). Perceived self-efficacy: Exercise of control through self-belief. In J. P. Dauwalder, M. Perez, & R. Hobi (Eds.), *Annual series of European research in behavior therapy.* Lisse, The Netherlands: Swets & Zeitlinger.

Bandura, A. (1988b). Self-efficacy conception of anxiety. *Anxiety Research, 1,* 77–98.

Bandura, A. (1988c). Self-regulation of motivation and action through goal systems. In V. Hamilton, G. H. Bower, & N. H. Frijda (Eds.), *Cognitive perspectives on emotion and motivation* (pp. 37–61). Dordrecht, The Netherlands: Kluwer Academic.

Bandura, A. (1989). Human agency in social cognitive theory. *American Psychologist, 44,* 1175–1184.

Bandura, A., Reese, L., & Adams, N. E. (1982). Microanalysis of action and fear arousal as a function of differential levels of perceived self-efficacy. *Journal of Consulting and Clinical Psychology, 53,* 406–414.

Bandura, A., Taylor, C. B., Williams, S. L., Mefford, I. N., & Barchas, J. D. (1985). Catecholamine secretion as a function of perceived coping self-efficacy. *Journal of Consulting and Clinical Psychology, 53,* 406–414.

Barbero, G. J. (1995). Divorce and the child with cystic fibrosis: The therapeutic and legal implications. *Journal of Divorce & Remarriage, 22,* 13–23.

Becker, M. H., Drachman, R. H., & Kirscht, J. P. (1974). A new approach to explaining sick-role behavior in low-income populations. *American Journal of Public Health, 64,* 205–216.

Becker, M. H., Maiman, L. A., Kirscht, J. P., Haefner, D. P., & Drachman, R. H. (1977). The health belief model and prediction of dietary compliance: A field experiment. *Journal of Health and Social Behavior, 18,* 348–366.

Becker, M. H., Nathanson, C. A., Drachman, R. H., & Kirscht, J. P. (1977). Mother's health beliefs and children's clinic visits: A prospective study. *Journal of Community Health, 3,* 125–135.

Betz, N. E., & Hackett, G. (1986). Applications of self-efficacy theory to understanding career choice behavior. *Journal of Social and Clinical Psychology, 4,* 279–289.

Blotcky, A. D., Cohen, D. G., Conatser, C., & Klopovich, P. (1985). Psychosocial characteristics of adolescents who refuse cancer treatment. *Journal of Consulting and Clinical Psychology, 53,* 729–731.

Branson, S. M., & Craig, K. D. (1988). Children's spontaneous strategies for coping with pain: A review of the literature. *Canadian Journal of Behavioural Science, 20,* 402–412.

Brown, R. T., Borden, K. A., & Clingerman, S. R. (1985). Adherence to methylphenidate therapy in a pediatric population: A preliminary investigation. *Psychopharmacology Bulletin, 21*(1), 28–36.

Cadman, D., Boyle, M., Szatmari, P., & Offord, D. R. (1987). Chronic illness, disability, and mental and social well-being: Findings of the Ontario child health study. *Pediatrics, 79,* 805–813.

Carney, R. M., Schechter, K., & Davis, T. (1983). Improving adherence to blood glucose testing in insulin dependent diabetic children. *Behavior Therapy, 14,* 247–254.

Chaney, J. M., & Peterson, L. (1989). Family variables and disease management in juvenile rheumatoid arthritis. *Journal of Pediatric Psychology, 14,* 389–403.

Christiaanse, M. E., Lavigne, J. V., & Lerner, C. V. (1989). Psychosocial aspects of compliance in children and adolescents with asthma. *Journal of Developmental and Behavioral Pediatrics, 10,* 75–80.

Costello, E. (1989). Developments in child psychiatric epidemiology. *Journal of the American Academy of Child and Adolescent Psychiatry, 28*(6), 836–841.

Creer, T. L. (1993). Medication compliance and childhood asthma. In N. A. Krasnegor, L. Epstein, S. B. Johnson, & S. J. Yaffe (Eds.), *Developmental aspects of health compliance behavior* (pp. 303–333). Hillsdale, NJ: Erlbaum.

Cutrona, C. E., & Troutman, B. R. (1986). Social support, infant temperament, and parenting self-efficacy: A mediational model of post-partum depression. *Child Development, 57,* 1507–1518.

Daneman, D., Epstein, L. H., Siminerio, L., Beck, S., Farkas, G., Figueroa, J., Becker, D. J., & Drash, A. L. (1982). Effects of enhanced conventional therapy on metabolic control in children with insulin-dependent diabetes mellitus. *Diabetes Care, 5,* 472–478.

Dolgin, M. J., Katz, E. R., Doctors, S. R., & Siegel, S. E. (1986). Caregivers' perceptions of medical compliance in adolescents with cancer. *Journal of Adolescent Health, 7,* 22–27.

Dolgin, M. J., & Phipps, S. (1989). Pediatric pain: The parents' role. *Pediatrician, 16,* 103–109.

Dunbar, J., & Waszak, L. (1990). Patient compliance: Pediatric and adolescent populations. In A. M. Gross & R. S. Drabman (Eds.), *Handbook of clinical behavioral pediatrics.* New York: Plenum Press.

Dunne-Geier, B., McGrath, P. J., Rouke, B. P., Latter, J., & D'Astous, J. (1986). Adolescent chronic pain: The ability to cope. *Pain, 26,* 23–32.

Durant, R. H., Jay, M. S., Linder, C. W., Shoffitt, T., & Litt, I. (1984). Influence of psychosocial factors on adolescent compliance with oral contraceptives. *Journal of Adolescent Health Care, 5*(1), 1–6.

Epstein, L. H., Beck, S., Figueroa, I., Farkas, G., Daxdin, A. E., Daneman, D., & Becker, D. (1981). The effects of targeting improvements in urine glucose on metabolic control in children with insulin dependent diabetes. *Journal of Applied Behavior Analysis, 14,* 365–375.

Fehrenbach, A. M. B., & Peterson, L. (1989). Parental problem-solving skills, stress, and dietary compliance in phenykletonuria. *Journal of Consulting and Clinical Psychology, 57,* 237–241.

Finney, J. W., Lemanek, K. L., Brophy, C. J., & Cataldo, M. F. (1990). Pediatric appointment keeping: Improving adherence in a primary care allergy clinic. *Journal of Pediatric Psychology, 15,* 571–579.

Flor, H., Birbaumer, N., & Rudy, D. C. (1990). The psychobiology of chronic pain. *Advances in Behaviour Research and Therapy, 12,* 47–84.

Fordyce, W. E. (1976). *Behavioral methods for chronic pain and illness.* St. Louis, MO: Mosby.

Friedman, I. M., & Litt, I. F. (1987). Adolescents' compliance with therapeutic regimens: Psychological and social aspects and intervention. *Journal of Adolescent Health Care, 8,* 52–65.

Friedman, I. M., Litt, I. F., King, D. R., Henson, R., Holtzman, D., Halverson, D., & Kraemer, H. C. (1986). Compliance with anticonvulsant therapy by epileptic youth: Relationships to psychosocial aspects of adolescent development. *Journal of Adolescent Health Care, 7,* 12–17.

Gortmaker, S. L., Eckenrode, J., & Gore, S. (1982). Stress and the utilization of health services: A time series and cross-sectional analysis. *Journal of Health & Social Behavior, 23*(1), 25–38.

Greenan-Fowler, E., Powell, C., & Varni, J. W. (1987). Behavioral treatment of adherence to therapeutic exercise by children with hemophilia. *Archives of Physical Medicine and Rehabilitation, 68*(12), 846–849.

Gross, A. M., Delcher, H. K., Snitzer, J., Bianchi, B., & Epstein, S. (1984). Personality variables and metabolic control in children with diabetes. *Journal of Genetic Psychology, 146,* 19–26.

Hamburg, B. A., & Inoff, G. E. (1982). Relationships between behavioral factors and diabetic control in children and adolescents: A camp study. *Psychosomatic Medicine, 44,* 321–339.

Hanson, C. L., DeGuire, M. J., Schinkel, A. M., Henggeler, S. W., & Burghen, G. A. (1992). Comparing social learning and family systems correlates of adaptation in youths with IDDM. *Journal of Pediatric Psychology, 17*(5), 555–572.

Hanson, C. L., Henggeler, S. W., & Burghen, G. A. (1987). Social competence and parental support as mediators of the link between stress and metabolic control in adolescents with insulin-dependent diabetes mellitus. *Journal of Consulting and Clinical Psychology, 55*(4), 529–533.

Hauser, S. T., Jacobson, A. M., Savori, P., Wolfsdorf, F. I., Herskowitz, R. D., Milley, J. E., Bliss, R., Wertlieb, D., & Stein, F. (1990). Adherence among children and adolescents with insulin-dependent diabetes mellitus over a four-year longitudinal follow-up: II. Immediate and long-term likages with the family milieu. *Journal of Pediatric Psychology, 15,* 527–542.

Holahan, C. K., & Holahan, C. J. (1987a). Life stress, hassles, and self-efficacy in aging: A replication and extension. *Journal of Applied Social Psychology, 17,* 574–592.

Holahan, C. K., & Holahan, C. J. (1987b). Self-efficacy, social support, and depression in aging: A longitudinal analysis. *Journal of Gerontology, 42,* 65–68.

Horwitz, R. I., & Horwitz, S. M. (1993). Adherence to treatment and health outcomes. *Archives of Internal Medicine, 153,* 1863–1868.

Institute of Medicine. (1989). *Research on children and adolescents with mental, behavioral and developmental disorders.* Washington, DC: National Academy Press.

Jamison, R. N., Lewis, S., & Burish, T. G. (1986). Cooperation with treatment in adolescent cancer patients. *Journal of Adolescent Health Care, 7,* 162–167.

Johnson, S. B. (1995). Managing insulin dependent diabetes mellitus: A developmental perspective. In J. Wallander & L. Siegel (Eds.), *Adolescent health problems: Behavioral perspectives.* New York: Guilford Press.

Kanfer, R., & Zeiss, A. M. (1983). Depression, interpersonal standard-setting, and judgments of self-efficacy. *Journal of Abnormal Psychology, 92,* 319–329.

Kashani, J. H., Venzke, R., & Millar, E. A. (1981). Depression in hospitalized pediatric patients. *Journal of the American Academy of Child Psychiatry, 20,* 123–134.

Kavanagh, D. J., & Bower, G. H. (1985). Mood and self-efficacy: Impact of joy and sadness on perceived capabilities. *Cognitive Therapy and Research, 9,* 507–525.

Kavanagh, D. J., & Wilson, P. H. (1988). *Prediction of outcome with a group version of cognitive therapy for depression.* Unpublished manuscript, University of Sydney, Australia.

Kent, G. (1987). Self-efficacious control over reported physiological, cognitive and behavioural symptoms of dental anxiety. *Behaviour Research and Therapy, 25,* 341–347.

Kerns, R. D., Southwick, S., Giller, E. G., Haythornthwaite, J. A., Jacob, M. C., & Rosenberg, R. (1991). The relationship between reports of pain-related social interactions and expressions of pain and affective distress. *Behavior Therapy, 22,* 101–111.

Killam, P. E., Apodaca, L., Manella, K. J., & Varni, J. W. (1983). Behavioral pediatric weight rehabilitation for children with myelomeningocele. *American Journal of Maternal Child Nursing, 8,* 280–286.

Kinscherff, R., & Famularo, R. (1991). Extreme Munchausen syndrome by proxy: The case for termination of parental rights. *Juvenile & Family Court Journal, 40,* 41–53.

Klein, S. D., Simmons, R. G., & Anderson, C. R. (1984). Chronic kidney disease and transplantation in childhood and adolescence. In R. W. Blum (Ed.), *Chronic illness and disabilities in childhood and adolescence.* Orlando, FL: Grune and Stratton.

Korsch, B. M., Fine, R. N., & Negrete, V. F. (1978). Noncompliance in children with renal transplants. *Pediatrics, 61,* 872–876.

LaGreca, A. M., Auslander, W. F., Greco, P., Spetter, D., Fisher, E. B., Jr., & Santiago, J. V. (1995). I get by with a little help from my family and friends: Adolescents' support for diabetes care. *Journal of Pediatric Psychology, 20*(4), 449–476.

LaGreca, A. M., Follansbee, D., & Skyler, J. S. (1990). Developmental and behavioral aspects of diabetes management in youngsters. *Children's Health Care, 19,* 132–137.

Lazarus, R. S., & Folkman, S. (1984). *Stress, appraisal and coping.* New York: Springer.

Lent, R. W., & Hackett, G. (1987). Career self-efficacy: Empirical status and future directions. *Journal of Vocational Behavior, 30,* 347–382.

Litt, I. F., & Cuskey, W. R. (1984). Satisfaction with health care: A predictor of adolescents' appointment keeping. *Journal of Adolescent Health Care, 135,* 434–436.

Lowe, K., & Lutzker, J. R. (1979). Increasing compliance to a medical regimen with a juvenile diabetic. *Behavior Therapy, 10,* 57–64.

Magrab, P. R., & Papadopoulou, L. (1977). The effect of a token economy on dietary compliance for children on hemodialysis. *Journal of Applied Behavior Analysis, 10,* 573–578.

Maier, S. F., Laudenslager, M. L., & Ryan, S. M. (1985). Stressor controllability, immune function, and endogenous opiates. In F. R. Brush & J. B. Overmier (Eds.), *Affect, conditioning and cognition: Essays on the determinants of behavior* (pp. 183- 201). Hillsdale, NJ: Erlbaum.

McGuire, T. L., & Feldman, K. W. (1989). Psychologic morbidity of children subjected to Munchausen syndrome by proxy. *Pediatrics, 83*(2), 289–292.

Meichenbaum, D. H. (1977). *Cognitive-behavior modification: An integrative approach.* New York: Plenum Press.

Miller-Johnson, S., Emery, R. E., Marvin, R. S., Clarke, W., Lovinger, R., & Martin, M. (1994). Parent-child relationships and the management of insulin-dependent diabetes mellitus. *Journal of Consulting and Clinical Psychology, 62*(3), 603–610.

Neel, E. U., Jay, S., & Litt, I. F. (1985). The relationship of self-concept and autonomy to oral contraceptive compliance among adolescent females. *Journal of Adolescent Health Care, 6,* 445–447.

Newacheck, P. W., & Halfon, W. (1986). The association between mother's and children's use of physician services. *Medical Care, 24,* 30–38.

Newacheck, P. W., & Taylor, W. R. (1992). Childhood chronic illness: Prevalence, severity and impact. *American Journal of Public Health, 82,* 364–371.

Patterson, J. M., & Garwick, A. W. (1994). The impact of chronic illness on families: A family systems perspective. *Annals of Behavioral Medicine, 16,* 131–142.

Payne, B., & Norfleet, M. A. (1986). Chronic pain and the family. *Pain, 26,* 1–22.

Philips, H. C. (1987). Avoidance behavior and its role in sustaining chronic pain. *Behavior Research and Therapy, 25,* 273–279.

Radius, S. M., Becker, M. H., Rosenstock, I. M., Drachman, R. H., Schuberth, K. C., & Teets, K. C. (1978). Factors influencing mothers' compliance with a medication regimen for asthmatic children. *Journal of Asthma Research, 15,* 133–149.

Rapoff, M. A., Lindsley, C. B., & Christophersen, E. R. (1984). Improving compliance with medical regimens: Case study with juvenile rheumatoid arthritis. *Archives of Physical Medicine and Rehabilitation, 65,* 267–269.

Roghmann, K. J., & Haggerty, R. J. (1973). Daily stress, illness, and use of health service in young families. *Pediatric Research, 7*(5), 520–526.

Salkovskis, P. M., & Harrison, J. (1984). Abnormal and normal obsessions: A replication. *Behaviour Research and Therapy, 22,* 549–552.

Sarason, I. G. (1975). Anxiety and self-preoccupation. In I. G. Sarason & D. C. Spielberger (Eds.), *Stress and anxiety* (Vol. 2, pp. 27–44). Washington, DC: Hemisphere.

Satin, W., LaGreca, A. M., Zigo, M. A., & Skyler, J. S. (1989). Diabetes in adolescence: Effects of multifamily group intervention and parent simulation of diabetes. *Journal of Pediatric Psychology, 14*(2), 259–275.

Sergis-Deavenport, E., & Varni, J. (1982). Behavioral techniques in teaching hemophilia factor replacement procedures to families. *Pediatric Nursing, 8,* 416–419.

Sergis-Deavenport, E., & Varni, J. (1983). Behavioral assessment and management of adherence to factor replacement therapy in hemophilia. *Journal of Pediatric Psychology, 8,* 367–377.

Shenkel, R. J., Rogers, J. P., Perfetto, G., & Levin, R. A. (1985). Importance of "significant others" in predicting cooperation with diabetic regimen. *International Journal of Psychiatry in Medicine, 15*(2), 149–155.

Siegal, L. J., & Smith, K. E. (1989). Children's strategies for coping with pain. *Pediatrician, 16,* 110–118.

Slessinger, D. P., Tessler, R. C., & Mechanic, D. (1976). The effects of social characteristics on utilization of preventive medical services in contrasting health programs. *Medical Care, 24,* 392–404.

Snyder, M. (1986). *Public appearances, private realities: The psychology of self-monitoring.* New York: Freeman.

Stark, L. J., Jelalian, E., & Miller, D. L. (1995). Cystic fibrosis. In M. C. Roberts (Ed.), *Handbook of pediatric psychology* (2nd ed., pp. 241–262). New York: Guilford Press.

Stocking, M., Rothney, W., Grosser, G., & Goodwin, R. (1972). Psychopathology in the pediatric hospital: Implications for community health. *American Journal of Public Health, 62,* 551–556.

Tessler, R., & Mechanic, D. (1978). Factors affecting children's use of physician services in a prepaid group practice. *Medical Care, 16,* 33–46.

Turk, D. C., Flor, H., & Rudy, T. E. (1987). Pain and families: I. Etiology, maintenance, and psychosocial impact. *Pain, 30,* 3–27.

Weimer, S. R., Hatcher, C., & Gould, E. (1983). Family characteristics in high and low health care utilization. *General Hospital Psychiatry, 5*(1), 55–61.

Whitehead, W. E., Busch, C. M., Heller, B. R., & Costa, P. T. (1986). Social learning influences on menstrual symptoms and illness behavior. *Health Psychology, 5,* 13–23.

Wiedenfeld, S. A., O' Leary, A., Bandura, A., Brown, S., Levine, S., & Raska, K. (1990). Impact of perceived self-efficacy in coping with stressors on immune function. *Journal of Personality & Social Psychology, 59*(5), 1082–1094.

Williams, S. L., Dooseman, G., & Kleifield, E. (1984). Comparative power of guided mastery and exposure treatments for intractable phobias. *Journal of Consulting and Clinical Psychology, 52,* 505–518.

Williams, S. L., Kinney, P. J., & Falbo, J. (1989). Generalization of therapeutic changes in agoraphobia: The role of perceived self-efficacy. *Journal of Consulting and Clinical Psychology, 57,* 436–442.

Williams, S. L., Turner, S. M., & Peer, D. F. (1985). Guided mastery and performance desensitization treatments for severe acrophobia. *Journal of Consulting and Clinical Psychology, 53,* 237–247.

Wolfe, B. L. (1980). Children's utilization of medical care. *Medical Care, 18*(12), 1196–1207.

Wysocki, T., Green, L., & Huxtable, K. (1989). Blood glucose monitoring by diabetic adolescents: Compliance and metabolic control. *Health Psychology, 8,* 267–284.

CHAPTER 15

Major Parental Psychopathology and Child Custody

MICHAEL J. JENUWINE and BERTRAM J. COHLER

T HE PARENTAL ROLE is one which is inherently a source of strain in contemporary society. Cross-cultural studies show that parents in American society express levels of both anxiety and hostility regarding the parental role that are not found elsewhere. Not only is there little preparation for the reality of assuming total care of another, but shared expectations regarding the significance of care of the offspring's personality and adjustment pose unheralded demands from birth forward. Indeed, the phenomenon of post partum blues is a common response to becoming a parent. Survey findings (Campbell, Converse, & Rodgers, 1976; Thoits, 1986) show that the advent of parenthood leads to diminished morale among both mothers and fathers, but particularly among mothers, and that morale only rises to levels characteristic of the pre-parental years after all offspring are adults. These expectable problems posed by the advent of parenthood are only compounded by a major psychiatric illness that exists prior to becoming a parent or one that emerges over the years after assuming the parental role.

Child custody disputes often involve litigants asserting that the other party is mentally ill, hence less able to parent the couple's children than they are. The two parts of this assertion both require investigation: First, is the parent, in fact, mentally ill? And second, what effects will the illness have on that parent's ability to care for his or her children? This chapter will provide a context for understanding the effects of major psychiatric illness on child care, review what is known about the interplay of parenthood and major psychiatric illness, and examine the role of parental psychopathology in custody decisions.

Broad systematic information is available about the impact on parenting of only two groups of psychiatric disorders-schizophrenic and mood (or major affective) disorders. These major categories of mental illness will be the focus of this chapter. Mood disorders are characterized by pervasive, prolonged and disabling exaggerations of mood and affect with associated changes in other psychological and physical function. Broadly, these disorders can be categorized as unipolar or major depressive disorder which is characterized by periods of severe depression and bipolar disorder in which both depressive and manic episodes occur. Schizophrenic disorders are characterized by the presence of hallucinations, delusions, and/or disorganized thought and behavior lasting at least 6 months. Schizophrenia need not present as a florid disorder but may instead manifest itself as a kind of disengagement, symptoms of disordered thought and reality testing only showing themselves on close examination.

Most of the studies examined discuss the impact of psychiatric illness on mothering. Obviously, fathers can also be psychiatrically ill in ways that interfere with parenting. However, the reality of contemporary family life places much of the day-to-day responsibility for child care on mothers (Rodnick & Goldstein, 1974) so that the vast majority of research on the impact of parental psychopathology focuses on them. In many instances, we can appropriately extrapolate from research on mothers to caregivers generally, so that in custody evaluations similar pathology weighs equally for father and mother. However, where psychopathology has gender-specific aspects, such an extrapolation is not appropriate. Additionally, the absence of studies showing untoward effects of particular psychopathology on paternal function should certainly not be interpreted to mean that such effects are absent, but rather, like many aspects of fathering, they have been inadequately studied (Cath, Gurwitt, & Munder-Ross, 1982).

PARENTHOOD AND THE GENESIS
OF PSYCHOPATHOLOGY

Adequate social supports for the new role are often lacking during pregnancy (Dragonas & Christodoulou, 1998). Improved social support reduces the incidence of post-partum depressive symptoms (Brugha et al., 1998). These symptoms reach clinical levels in 5% to 8.8% of women who give birth (Richards, 1990). Mothers with postpartum depression are vulnerable to chronic or recurrent psychiatric problems (True-Soderstrom, Buckwalter, & Kerfoot, 1983).

Murray, Fiori-Cowley, Hooper, and Cooper (1996) report that the postpartum blues may affect the child during the first 2 years. At 18 months, children of mothers with postpartum depression were less able than similar children of nondepressed mothers to perform cognitive tasks. However, much of the effect reported in this study may have resulted from adversity in these mothers' lives, which contributed to the depression. Longer follow-up studies (Sinclair & Murray, 1998) show negative effects continuing at least through age 6 years. Meta-analysis of the small number of studies of long-term effects of postpartum depression reveals small but significant effects (Beck, 1998).

Some mothers develop postpartum psychosis. These psychoses often include delusional content related to childbirth, confusion, and mania (Beck, 1991). Although such psychoses occur infrequently (in 1 in every 500 to 1,000 births), they illustrate the extreme emotional burdens that can accompany childbirth (Bagedahl-Strindlund, 1986; Buist, Dennerstein, & Burrows, 1990; Thiels & Kumar, 1987). Apfel and Handel (1993) have discussed the complex issue of the more rarely occurring development of transitory psychotic episodes in men with the advent of fatherhood. Posttraumatic stress disorders are also observed, especially following difficult births (Reynolds, 1997).

Among women, who still generally accept rather than initiate marriage proposals, major psychopathology is less likely to preclude becoming a parent than it is for men because greater social competence is needed to find a marital partner than to respond to another's initiative (Zigler & Glick 1986; Zigler & Phillips, 1961, 1962). Since courtship and marriage involve some degree of social assertiveness, episodically or persistently psychiatrically ill men are unlikely to have the social skills needed to sustain a relationship leading to marriage and a family (Glick, 1997; Zigler & Glick, 1986; Zigler & Phillips, 1961, 1962). Similarly because severely psychiatrically ill men are less likely to become parents than women with similar levels of disturbance less is known about the impact of paternal psychiatric illness on the family and childcare than is known about the effects of similar maternal pathology. Studies of the impact of paternal major mental illness on offspring are largely anecdotal clinical reports (Apfel & Handel, 1993; Wainwright, 1966). Thus, women may marry and have children but succumb to a first episode of psychiatric illness during the expectably stressful first years of parenthood. The stress associated with various phases of parenting, such as dealing with difficult adolescents may precipitate psychiatric illness in some vulnerable individuals.

PARENTHOOD AND CONTEMPORARY SOCIETY

The Advent of Parenthood as a "Crisis"

Our culture is unique both in maintaining that the child's present and future adjustment are determined by parental personality and child care and in the worry and guilt that parents express about parenting (Fischer & Fischer, 1963; LeVine & White, 1987; Minturn & Lambert, 1964). These beliefs strain parents. Witness the huge number of books and intense media attention focused on parenting (Clarke-Stewart, 1978). In the past two decades, parents have been additionally strained by the intense reconsideration of gender roles and increasing demands that both parents join the workforce. Today a majority of mothers of preschool children have at least part-time work. Many parents, especially mothers, experience strain and overload as they attempt to care for children, create substantial incomes, and fill often unclear social roles with spouses.

Virtually all evidence to date shows marked gender differences in mood and adjustment in adult life. Women report lower mood than men, from adolescence through mid-life, but particularly during the years of family formation and active parenting of young children (Andrews & Withey, 1976; Campbell et al., 1976; McLanahan & Adams, 1987; Petersen, 1988; Petersen, Sarigiani, & Kennedy, 1991; Thoits, 1986). This gender difference is in large part accounted for by the position of women in contemporary society, juggling conflicting demands on their time and energy (Hagestad, 1974). Women's lives are more disrupted by marriage and parenthood than the lives of men (Hogan, 1980, 1984; Marini, 1978, 1984; Waite & Moore, 1978). Men enjoy relatively continuous careers, but women are forced to enter and leave the labor force by their husband's career and the demands of child care.

Gutmann (1975, 1987) suggests that regardless of careers before parenthood, parenthood creates a feeling of crisis that increases men's concern with the economic-instrumental role in the family, whereas women become more involved with child care, housework, and tending to emotional expressive needs in the family. When husbands have problems at work, they take their problems home to their wife. Although the wife's support and understanding soothes the husband, these problems are then assumed by the wife who then suffers from her husband's work problems (Brown & Harris, 1975; Siassi, Crocetti, & Spiro, 1974).

Chodorow (1978) described gender socialization in contemporary society as leading boys to be socialized to become men, whereas girls are socialized to become mothers. Chodorow believes that this pattern could be altered if men and women equally shared in child-care tasks. However, despite rhetoric to the contrary, there appears to have been little change in the distribution of tasks in the family during the past half century. Women continue as kin-keeper, responsible for managing relations within the family and across generations, while men view their role as that of provider (Bardwick & Douvan, 1971; Bart, 1971; Bernard, 1975; Chodorow, 1978; Firth, Hubert, & Forge, 1970). Only during midlife, with the end of active parenting, are women again able to return to school or work on a full-time basis and enjoy participating in the larger society in the same way as men. This description of "settled adulthood" helps explain difference in rates of depressive illness in men and women. Reviews of the literature on gender and mood in adult life, based on both biological and psychosocial evidence agree that the lowered morale reported among women results from the course of their adult lives and is not biologically inherent (Angold & Rutter, 1992; Goldman & David, 1980; Gove & Tudor, 1972; McGrath, Keita, Strickland, & Russo, 1990; Thoits, 1986; Weissman & Klerman, 1978). Further, the interdependence that characterizes the lives of women from adolescence through adulthood (Gilligan, 1983; Gilligan, Lyons, & Hanmer, 1990) is inconsistent with the self-reliant mode of success widely touted as the American ideal. Over time, many women in our society experience a sense of futility, akin to "learned helplessness" (Seligman, 1974, 1975) and so feel lowered morale and depressed mood.

Belsky and his students (Belsky, 1984; Belsky & Vondura, 1989) note the complex interplay of the social context of parenthood including the parents' portfolio of roles and the parents' life experiences in determining the response to caring for offspring generally and caring for a particular child from the moment of conception to the parents' relationship with their adult children. A child who is difficult to quiet poses different issues for parents than one who is easily calmed. So simple a matter as the child's sleep pattern can make huge differences in the level of parental stress, especially when parents must get up for a full day of work at a specified time. As the child moves through developmental phases, the parents' own conflicts and experiences from those periods are likely to be reawakened so that "ghosts (of the parents' own past) in the nursery" are likely to become important factors in parenting (Benedek, 1973; Fraiberg, Adelson, & Shapiro, 1975).

PARENTS WITH PSYCHIATRIC ILLNESS

Given strain associated with motherhood and the importance of motherhood to many women's identity (Belle, 1980), it is not surprising that issues of parenting are intertwined in the conflicts leading to episodes of major mental illness in women from adolescence to midlife (Gove, 1972; Gove & Tudor, 1972; Radloff, 1975; Thoits, 1986). Conversely, when men are hospitalized for episodes of major mental illness, these episodes are usually associated with work and marriage, and much less often with fatherhood and conflicts about child care. This difference reflects gender differences in the salience of adult roles and the less significant immersion of fathers in child care (Rodnick & Garmezy, 1975). Chesler's (1991) case examples suggest that courts dealing with child custody see maternal psychiatric illness as more likely to affect child care and view allegations of mental illness in women much more adversely than comparable allegations about men.

Mental illness complicates parenting, leads to a series of adverse changes for both the psychiatrically ill parent and other family members, and poses challenges for research, service, and social policy. Research suggests that the stresses of parenting may exacerbate mental illness and, so interfere with parenting (Zemencuk, 1995). However, merely relieving parents with psychiatric illness of their responsibility as parents does not solve the resulting problem. Rather, increased effort must be devoted to care and support for these parents, if only because women with psychiatric illness remain sexually active (Coverdale & Aruffo, 1989) and not only have normal fertility rates (Saugstad, 1989), but actually have more children than their psychologically well counterparts

(Rudolph, Larson, Sweeny, Hough, & Arorian, 1990). Pregnancies are unplanned for approximately half of chronically mentally ill mothers (Buist et al., 1990; Forcier, 1990; Zemencuk, 1995). The majority of mentally ill mothers lose custody of their children even though a great number of mentally ill mothers could be successful parents if adequate support programs were available (Bazar, 1990; Coverdale & Aruffo, 1989; Miller, 1990; Spielvogel & Wile, 1986). Maintaining the parent role can have positive effects on the functioning of a mentally ill mother though few programs exist to support mentally ill mothers in parenting. In fact, Oyserman, Mowbray, and Zemencuk (1994) observe that having contact with her children often serves as a positive motivator for the mentally ill mother, and can enhance parenting quality.

Their own lack of adequate parental role models during childhood contributes to problems parenting by mentally ill parents. Zemencuk's research group (1995) found that less than half of the mentally ill mothers they studied lived with both parents while growing up, and that nearly one third had been separated from their mothers before adolescence. Test and Berlin (1981) stress the importance of providing chronically mentally ill mothers with opportunities to learn specific child-management skills.

THE IMPACT OF PARENTAL MENTAL ILLNESS ON CHILDREN—GENERAL CONSIDERATIONS

Although the problem of psychiatric illness accompanying parturition was familiar to the physicians of the seventeenth century (Grunebaum, Weiss, Cohler, Hartman, & Gallant, 1975/1982), the impact of these disturbances on children has only been studied recently. Following World War II, numerous investigations documented the impact of child care on intellectual and emotional development. Systematic studies of infancy and early childhood focusing on such variations in early care as group homes as contrasted with family-reared children (Freud, 1973; Freud & Burlingham, 1944/1974; Spitz, 1945, 1946), experiences of new mothers with their infants (Levy, 1958), family-reared children confronted with the temporary absence of parents such as related to the birth of a sibling (Robertson & Robertson, 1969), early parental death (Garber, 1981; Wolfenstein, 1966), or even temporary parental preoccupation (Carr & Leared, 1973; Cohn & Campbell, 1992; Cohn & Tronick, 1983; Emde & Source, 1983; Stern, 1985, 1991; Tronick & Gianino, 1986) converged to confirm earlier anecdotal reports of the profound effect of parenting on children.

A major theme in child development research has been the recognition that the capacity to function reasonably comfortably without immediate support from others rests on the adequate availability of caregivers during infancy and early childhood (Ainsworth, Blehar, Waters, & Wall, 1978; Bowlby, 1983; Bretherton & Waters, 1985; Mahler, Pine, & Bergman, 1975). Therefore separations, such as those accompanying maternal physical or psychiatric illness, are likely to be of particular significance. Additionally, studies of mentally ill mothers have determined that these women experience other risk factors likely to compromise their parenting ability (Zemencuk, 1995). These include poor education, falling socioeconomic status, few social supports, having given birth at an early age, being unmarried, and a history of multiple hospitalizations. The picture is, however, not entirely negative. Zemencuk and colleagues (Zemencuk, Rogosch, & Mowbray, 1995) stress that the majority of severely psychiatrically ill mothers have adaptive ideas about parenting which can be supported and strengthened.

Generally, it is important for the child's development to live in a stable family and have continuity of care. When children's mothers are hospitalized for episodes of psychiatric illness, this disruption in continuity creates a crisis. Family life and caregiving are first disturbed by the appearance of symptoms and then by mother's disappearance into the hospital. Even a single such hospitalization creates problems for the family (Reiss, Steinglass, & Howe, 1993). If the hospitalization can achieve even limited therapeutic goals, such as preventing additional hospitalizations, cementing the parent's relationship with a therapist, and adjusting medication, then the benefits for patient and family might outweigh the costs in terms of family life disruption. However, changes in delivery of mental health services over the past two decades have led to a pattern of successive short-term, crisis-oriented, palliative hospitalizations that often only ensure subsequent hospitalization further disrupting family relations and child care. These repeated hospitalizations of psychiatrically ill mothers lead children to become preoccupied with concerns regarding both their mother's welfare and their own care (Strohm, 1993). For example, one sixth-grade girl reported that she worried every day whether her repeatedly rehospitalized mother would still be at home when she came home from school in the afternoon. Repeated hospitalizations can lead husbands to become disgusted and seek marital dissolution (Grunebaum, Gamer, & Cohler, 1983). These findings suggest the importance of planning programs of sustaining care that might provide enhanced support and assistance for parents formerly hospitalized for psychiatric illness (Grunebaum et al., 1982). Finally, recognizing the reality that psychiatric illness within one member of the family affects everyone (Bell, 1968; Cohler, 1983; Pruchno, Blow, & Smyer, 1984; Spiegel, 1971; Vogel & Bell, 1960), it is necessary to consider the larger family constellation in planning programs designed to maintain troubled parents and their families in the community.

How much parental psychopathology interferes in responding to children is still unclear. Earlier discussions of this issue, based on a "critical period" model (Freedman, 1974; Hess, 1959; Hinde, 1963, 1966; Lorenz, 1957), assumed that both adverse life changes, such as the mother's temporary absence due to psychiatric hospitalization, as well as subtle parental empathic failure accompanying exacerbation of symptoms, would have particularly significant negative impact on the emerging parent-child tie because there are periods of particular vulnerability or sensitivity for later personality development during early childhood. Although this view gained some support from animal and human studies (Bowlby, 1983) and still has a few adherents (Klaus & Kennell, 1976), longitudinal study (Clarke & Clarke, 1976; Kagan, 1980) strongly indicates that critical periods do not play a major role in human development. Rutter (1972), examining the literature on maternal deprivation, reports that the effects of such deprivation are not as devastating as first claimed, while Lennenberg (1967) showed that the critical period hypothesis applies to a limited range of cognitive developments. The critical period hypothesis appears to apply to only a narrow range of human behaviors (Colombo, 1982).

Another implicit theory that emphasizes the negative impact of parental psychopathology on children assumes an essentially "forward" transmission of influence from parent to child independent of the child's impact on parenting. This model probably overestimates parental contributions to the child's personality development and adjustment. More contemporary views emphasize that from earliest infancy children have qualities of their own which do not result from interactions with the parents and which, in many instances, may shape how parents deal with them (Chess & Thomas, 1987; Thomas & Chess, 1977).

Following the discovery of the profound impact of interrupted or disturbed relations with caretakers on child development, investigators assumed that symptoms of major mental illness, including thought disturbance and inappropriate expression of affect, together with the disruption inevitably following psychiatric hospitalization, was noxious for the child's development. Supporting evidence emerged in clinical studies of children whose mothers experienced a transitory hospitalization for physical illness or due to the birth of a younger brother or sister, and from early study of the infants of parents showing major psychopathology (focusing largely on parental inadequacy in providing care). Pao (1960) provided a clinical report on the development of the offspring of five persistently ill schizophrenic mothers. Sobel (1961) noted anecdotally that children of persistently troubled schizophrenic mothers appear to fare better in foster care than at home. He observed depressive symptoms and depressive equivalent symptoms such as sadness, hyperactivity, and irritability among those infants cared for at home by their own mothers. Grunebaum and coworkers (1975/1982), reviewing findings of clinical investigators, found reports of developmental delay and distress among children cared for at home by their psychiatrically ill parents. In particular, as Anthony (1968, 1969) and Garmezy (1971) reported, young children of psychotic mothers might be socialized into the misperception of reality, ultimately adopting their parents' psychotic adaptation as their own lived experience.

These clinical observations and inferences led to more systematic study of the children of severely psychiatrically disturbed parents. Findings from a complex Scandinavian study matching parental psychiatric hospitalizations and records of birth of offspring (B. Mednick, 1973; S. Mednick, Parnas, & Schulsinger, 1987; S. Mednick & Schulsinger, 1968) suggested that late adolescent and adult offspring with one schizophrenic parent showed psychopathology in larger numbers than their peers without this risk factor. These investigators assumed that genetic transmission and life circumstances combined to put the offspring of schizophrenic parents at greater risk for major psychopathology than their counterparts from families in which both parents were psychologically well.

For schizophrenia investigators, concerned to better understand the origin and course of schizophrenic illness, S. Mednick and Schulsinger's (1968) report suggested that it might be possible to prospectively study the origin and course of schizophrenia among the offspring of at least one schizophrenic parent more economically than by screening a large number of persons in the population for a syndrome that is found in about 1% of the population. Over the next decade, additional study of schizophrenic parents and their young offspring began in the United States and the United Kingdom (Watt, Anthony, Wynne, & Rolf, 1984). Reports from these studies were ambiguous. Depending on the age of the child, parental diagnosis, number of parental psychiatric hospitalizations, and outcome measures used, there was considerable variation in risk. Since genetic factors operate over a lifetime, it is not surprising that short-term longitudinal studies would not show much impact from these factors (Hanson, Gottesman, & Heston, 1976, 1990). They show that the young children of one parent occasionally hospitalized for a schizophrenic episode have few differences from children of well counterparts (Grunebaum et al., 1982). In fact, Kauffman, Grunebaum, Cohler, and Gamer (1979) reported that the most creative children were those of schizophrenic mothers, whereas the children of depressed parents showed the greatest developmental interference.

Where differences appear among children of schizophrenic mothers, as contrasted with psychologically well mothers, these differences may not be the direct result of the parent's illness. Instead there may be a consequence of living in socially disorganized families, repeated parental hospitalizations, unstable living arrangements, poverty, and parental substance abuse. When the neglect of these children is sufficiently severe, child welfare agencies may intervene removing them from the home. Even though it may be necessary, this event, inevitably disrupts the child's life and poses additional difficulties for children already at risk. These children often fit well in a category described by Fish and her colleagues (Fish, 1987) as "pandysmaturation"—children with enhanced genetic loading and constitutional vulnerability leading to limitations on coping ability, pre- and perinatal birth complications, a history of abuse and neglect within a socially disorganized family and neighborhood, wretched poverty, and repeated parental absence due to hospitalizations or prison terms. Fish's work suggests that the impact of genetically determined risk may be intensified by particularly adverse life circumstances. Thus, studies showing that being raised by a schizophrenic parent increases children's vulnerability to severe psychiatric illness and other conditions need to be examined to ensure that other, associated, factors are not the major determinants of disturbed development.

Children with greater family and neighborhood stability show less adverse response to parental psychopathology and occasional parental hospitalizations. These more resilient children are able to realize significant achievements (Anthony, 1971/1976, 1974; Anthony & Cohler, 1987; Cohler, 1987; Cohler, Stott, & Musick, 1995; Garmezy, 1981, 1987; Luthar & Zigler, 1991; Masten, 1985; Masten, Best, & Garmezy, 1990). Although sufficiently noxious influences can lead to more or less lasting disruptions in development, the impact of this adversity has not been found to be as severe, or as lasting, as expected (Clarke & Clarke, 1976; Emde, 1984; Garmezy, 1984; Kagan, 1980; Werner & Smith, 1982). Given adequate resources, children often find ways around parental psychopathology and may even be moved to unusual achievement in the process. Anthony (1971/1976) notes that Piaget's mother was episodically psychiatrically ill. He suggests that this disturbance strengthened Piaget's determination to remain passionately committed to reality and to the study of the attainment of adaptation to reality. On a more mundane level, some children whose parents are episodically psychiatrically ill live in communities where there are resources for children outside the home and are able to take advantage of scouting, after-school sports programs, or even part-time work and thus are able to avoid the home and also to enjoy an enhanced sense of personal competence.

RISK AND VULNERABILITY AMONG OFFSPRING OF PSYCHIATRICALLY ILL PARENTS

The impact of parental psychiatric hospitalization has been investigated from the point of view of how it affects children's socialization within the family. Early studies concerned the impact of parental rehospitalization on marriage, as well as the interactions between parent and child (Clausen & Yarrow, 1955). Assuming that all of the impact went from parents to children, these investigators found that the family turmoil due to eruptive symptoms characteristic of parental mental illness, the child's age, and the timing of separations were all factors contributing to negative impact on the child.

A powerful group of studies that led to particular concern that parental pathology might permanently harm children's psychological development came from studies of severely disturbed adults. They seemed to indicate that certain patterns of parental communication and psychopathology literally drove children crazy. Some studies of young adult schizophrenic patients showed that the child's psychiatric illness was associated with an extreme form of deviant patterns of communication within the family and concluded that the illness resulted from the deviant communication pattern (Wynne, Singer, Bartko, & Toohey, 1977). However, these studies did not directly address the direction of causation. Further study, in fact, suggests that the communication problems result because potentially or actually disturbed children teach their parents to think in a disordered mode (Cook & Cohler, 1986). Equally likely, problems in the child's adjustment lead to anxiety within the family which, in turn, reduces clarity of transactions between troubled children and their parents.

Little is known about the child's response to life changes during the period immediately prior to parental hospitalization, or of techniques used by children to cope with this adverse life event. Further, although toddlers would appear to be most adversely affected by separation due to maternal hospitalization (Robertson, 1962; Robertson & Robertson, 1969), there has been little systematic study of the association between the child's age or gender at the time of separation due to maternal psychiatric hospitalization and response to maternal hospitalization. Since adverse life events have an impact on the interdependent lives of family members (Cohler, 1983; Pruchno et al., 1984), parental hospitalization also affects the larger family unit. Little is known about how variations in substitute care provided by grandparents and others might mitigate the impact of such hospitalizations, or of the impact of demands for such help. Further, just as in the case of divorce, hospitalization of an offspring for psychiatric illness is inevitably associated with feelings of guilt and personal distress among grandparents.

Findings from the Rochester study suggest that the impact of parental psychopathology is difficult to detect in observed parent-child interaction. Klehr, Cohler, and Musick (1983), in a first report of the comparison of mother-child interaction among psychiatrically disturbed and well parents, also report little difference in the nature and rate of play across diagnostic groups. To date, there has been little evidence showing that the presence or nature of parental psychopathology leads to discernible differences in this area.

SCHIZOPHRENIC PARENTS AND THEIR OFFSPRING

Initial reports by Mednick and his colleagues suggested that as many as half of the offspring of schizophrenic parents showed personality disorders by adolescence, although relatively few showed evidence of schizophrenia. Based on brief sketches of these supposed disorders, it is not clear whether these adverse outcomes are substantially different from the problems seen in the population at large. Other investigators of children of schizophrenics have been more concerned with group differences in psychological functioning than with rates of psychiatric illness. Summarizing this literature, Lewine (1984) notes considerable variation across studies in rates of observed impairment in either cognitive or psychosocial functioning (11%–25%), showing the need for additional research.

Early studies of offspring of troubled parents showed not only that children of schizophrenic parents had more global psychopathology than children of psychologically well parents, but also that differences in such diverse areas as apparent neurological deficit, attention, and emotional capacity to resonate affectively with the mother appear very early in life (Fish, 1984; Sobel, 1961) although the findings about attention turn out to be questionable (Lewine, 1984). In fact, much of the research on offspring of schizophrenic parents has significant methodological problems. Virtually all research in this area shows some loss in the cognitive and psychosocial functioning of children of schizophrenic mothers, generally as contrasted with children whose mothers have never sought psychiatric treatment. However, when these offspring are contrasted with children whose parents have been diagnosed with some other form of major psychopathology, such as affective disorder, and hospitalized for periods of time, the increased psychopathology shown by these offspring of schizophrenic parents is less striking; and it becomes difficult to differentiate the impact of the parents' particular illness from the general effects of crisis and disruption. For example, problems in deploying and sustaining attention were once believed to be the cardinal characteristics of schizophrenia as a clinical entity and were found among the children of schizophrenic parents (Asarnow, Steffy, MacCrimmon, & Cleghorn, 1977; Nuechterlein, 1983; Steffy, Asarnow, Asarnow, MacCrimmon, & Cleghorn, 1984) but were subsequently also found among children of parents with unipolar and bipolar disorders (Cohler, Grunebaum, Weiss, Gamer, & Gallant, 1977; Lewine, 1984; Neale, Winters, & Weintraub, 1984).

With these qualifications, particularly as contrasted with children of psychologically well parents, children of schizophrenics show some increased sensitivity to be distracted, show increased sensitivity and overresponding in tasks involving stimulus selection in attentional tasks or autonomic conditioning, and decrement in intelligence. In early infancy, children of schizophrenic mothers show problems in forming a close tie, but again, this may as much reflect disruption of caretaking (Grunebaum et al., 1975/1982) as early evidence of impairment in the capacity for relationships. Problems in cognitive development may also be reactive to disruptions in caretaking engendered by parental psychosis rather than evidence of the transmission of a particular form of irrationality and nonattentiveness to the environment characteristic of schizophrenia (Lidz, Fleck, & Cornelison, 1965; Wynne et al., 1977).

Considering the school-age children of schizophrenic parents, much of the work to date has concerned adjustment in the classroom and acceptance by peers, with most studies showing little difference between children of schizophrenic and well parents.

Consistent with previous findings on the childhood of later schizophrenics (Watt, Stolorow, Lubensky, & McClelland, 1970), the vulnerability of children of schizophrenic parents is more marked in terms of aggressive behavior rather than of social withdrawal (Rolf, Crowther, Teri, & Bond, 1984; Rolf & Hasazi,

1977; Watt, Grubb, & Erlenmeyer-Kimling, 1982). Where this aggressive behavior is seen, particularly among boys, who appear more vulnerable than girls to the effects of discontinuity in child care (Elder, 1979), this increased aggression is associated with an increased sense of social isolation from peers. However, these findings on adjustment problems among offspring of schizophrenic parents may also be accounted for by differences in parental social class and in problems in the use of intellectual abilities, reactive to long-standing parental psychopathology and accompanying social disorganization within the family, regardless of type of parental psychopathology.

To date, with the exception of Mednick's pioneering Scandinavian studies, there has been little opportunity to follow children of schizophrenic parents forward into adulthood. Although expectations of major psychopathology among children of schizophrenic parents range to as high as 50%, Bleuler's own (1978, 1984) reports suggest that only about 10% of these offspring become schizophrenic, about what would be expected on the basis of genetic loading alone. Overall, as both Lewine (1984) and Watt et al. (1984) conclude on the basis of the review of findings across a number of studies, there is little evidence to point to specific effects on the child development resulting from living in families with a schizophrenic parent.

PARENTS WITH BIPOLAR AND UNIPOLAR DEPRESSION: PARENTAL PREOCCUPATION AND CHILD DEVELOPMENT

Although not as thoroughly studied as children of schizophrenics, children of parents with major affective disorders show cognitive dysfunction and lowered mood (Beardslee, Bemporad, Keller, & Klerman, 1983; Keller et al., 1986; Reid & Morrison, 1983). Recently, the study of children of parents with mood disorder has shifted in the direction of more detailed focus on mechanism of transmission of mood from parent to offspring in relation to attunement and attachment (Cicchetti, Rogosch, & Toth, 1997; Field, 1984, 1992; Tronick & Gianino, 1986). Questions, such as whether being raised by a parent with an affective disorder raises the likelihood of suffering from such a disorder, have been less thoroughly explored although researchers have studied the epidemiology of the relationship of parental and offspring mood disorder, focusing on signs of lowered mood, or a depressive equivalent such as delinquency, substance abuse and other forms of sensation seeking, in determining the impact of parental disturbance on offspring adjustment (Weissman et al., 1984).

Studies of children through early adolescence show at least three important factors increase the impact of parental depression on the child's adjustment. Parental mood disorder is much more difficult for children to recognize and understand than the more bizarre and deviant symptoms of schizophrenia. In addition, children of depressed parents often feel responsible for their parents' mood disorder. Further, the often less dramatic quality of affective symptoms, compared with schizophrenic symptoms, joined with the tendency of depressed individuals to withdraw from social contacts makes it even more difficult for children of depressed parents to differentiate parental illness from their own failings.

Parental mood disorder has been shown to have both immediate and long-term adverse consequences for the child's development, even in the absence of other adversity. A large number of studies, reviewed by Beardslee et al. (1983) and Keller et al. (1986), show the high rate of concordance between parental and offspring diagnosis of unipolar depression, while a large number of studies have shown the dramatic impact of maternal depression on the development and present adjustment of offspring (Alpern & Lyons-Ruth, 1993; Bettes, 1988; Breznitz & Sherman, 1987; Cohler, Gallant, Grunebaum, & Kaufman, 1983; Conners, Himmelhock, Goyette, Ulrich, & Neil, 1979; Cytryn, McKnew, Bartko, Lamour, & Hamovitt, 1982; Ghodsian, Zajicek, & Wolkind, 1984; McKnew, Cytryn, Efron, Gershon, & Bunney, 1979; Weissman et al., 1987).

To the extent that the mother, usually the principal caregiver, is depressed, preoccupied, and withdrawn across the first years of the child's life, the child may experience this maternal unavailability as a failing of him- or herself, leading to the lifelong experience of deficit in capacity to soothe tensions and manage transactions with the world (Carr & Leared, 1973; Cohler, 1980; Galatzer-Levy & Cohler, 1993; Kohut, 1971, 1977; Kohut & Wolf, 1978; Winnicott, 1960). This deficit, initially inspired by lack of maternal availability, later leads to a sense of depletion and despondency that may be responded to by sensation seeking and other activities designed to create even the momentary sense of stimulation and aliveness.

Burdened by conflicting demands for housework, child care, and even part-time work, many mothers of young children in contemporary society express feelings of futility and dismay with their present life circumstances similar to those seen in mood disorders (Andrews & Withey, 1976; Cohler, 1984; Gove, 1972; Gove & Geerken, 1977; Weissman & Klerman, 1978). The emergence of unipolar depressive disorders appears, unlike schizophrenia and bipolar disorder, to be largely a consequence of adverse life circumstances. Weissman and her colleagues (Weissman & Myers, 1979; Weissman, Myers, & Hardin, 1978) found that over a third of women in an urban community experience mood disorders. At home alone with their young children, these depressed mothers are unavailable to their children, who thus become at risk for the development of disorders of self (Kohut & Wolfe, 1978). These depressive disorders often go unrecognized.

The impact of maternal depression on offspring adjustment was dramatically demonstrated in a study by Cohn and Tronick (1983) in which mothers of toddlers were asked to feign depression when with their children. Even feigned depression, characterized by withdrawal and disengagement from the child in the playroom, retreating into reading a newspaper and indifference to the child's distress, had an immediate, disorganizing impact on the child's play and on the child's own mood. Replication of this study with preschool-age children showed that even transitory, feigned emotional unavailability led to increased negativism in the children and to more unfocused and withdrawn action differing only from that of the younger group in that these children persisted somewhat longer in bids for their mother's attention (Seiner & Gelfand, 1995).

Depressive disorders increase self-preoccupation and lead to withdrawal from relationships and community involvement, so it is difficult for troubled parents to reach out to potentially helpful resources in the community. Programs like Family Focus, that provide drop-in centers where mothers and young children gather together and can gain social support, require that women be able to reach out to the community. Further, since one symptom of a depressive disorder is intensified anger, children of depressed parents are at increased risk for physical and emotional abuse.

The toll of parental depression is not limited to young children. Adolescent psychopathology and substance abuse may appear reciprocally to the onset of parental depression and to the adolescent's self-blame as the source of parental psychological distress (Weissman, Paykel, & Klerman, 1972).

Children of very depressed parents are likely to experience inadequate caretaking and to become involved in accidents around the house not only because they are inadequately supervised but also because they may identify with what they perceive as their parent's view that they are not worth being cared for. In contrast to children's parents who are clearly psychotic, not only do depressed parents' disturbances persist for longer periods before being diagnosed, but the nature of the disturbance tends to shut off the parent from the community and interfere with the child's contact with community institutions that might assist the child. Finally, since depressive symptoms such as lethargy, withdrawal, and sadness are less socially disruptive than schizophrenic symptoms, it may be more difficult for the child of the depressed parent than for the child of the schizophrenic parent to recognize that the parent's present state is abnormal. These impediments to the child's receiving assistance when a parent is depressed are particularly sad since interventions that resolve maternal depression also relieve the children's mood disorder (Field, 1992).

The most significant impact of any parental psychiatric disorder not involving direct attacks on the child derives from the loss of parental attention. Findings reported by Field (1992) suggest that the prolonged emotional unavailability of maternal depression is particularly problematic for children. Children of depressed parents may grow up with limited abilities to soothe and comfort themselves. This may lead them to withdraw from ordinary stimuli for fear of being overwhelmed or to seek stimulation in an effort to overcome feelings of depletion (Field, 1992).

The impact of maternal depression may have a cumulative effect on development of children across middle childhood; depressive episodes, hospitalizations, paternal discouragement leading to separation and divorce, and subsequent family instability create multiple risk factors that, together, interfere with satisfactory adjustment (Cohler et al., 1983; Goodman, Brogan, Lynch, & Fielding, 1993). This is consistent with the finding reported by Murray et al. (1996) that at least part of the impact of maternal depression on child development and adjustment may be attributed to the many sources of adversity in the lives of these mothers which led them to become depressed in the first place.

Children whose mothers have been separated from them by illness, or whose mothers have suffered emotional strain such as loss of their own parents during the preceding year react less well to a test of separation and reunion (the Strange Situation, see Chapter 4). Some of these children ignore their mother on her return, shutting her out of the activity, or both seek and avoid contact during reunion. Some children show increased disorganization on mother's departure and are not soothed by mother's reappearance. Evidence suggests that these disturbed reactions have long-term consequences (see Chapter 4).

Mothers' emotional unavailability has profound consequences for the child's ability to experience a secure base from which to continue mastery of the larger world. Living with a depressed mother over time interferes with the emergence of a sense of personal competence and worth. With little encouragement to explore the larger world, and little appreciation for their enthusiasm for the world, children of depressed mothers may withdraw from such exploration as demonstrated in a series of studies reported by Radke-Yarrow, Zahn-Waxler, and their colleagues at the National Institute of Mental Health (Radke-Yarrow, 1991; Radke-Yarrow, Cummings, Kuczynski, & Chapman, 1985; Zahn-Waxler, Chapman, & Cummings, 1984; Zahn-Waxler et al., 1988). Studying a group of nearly one hundred 2- and 3-year-old children of mothers with a bipolar disorder, another group of nearly 50 children whose mothers had a major unipolar affective disorder, 12 children of mothers with a minor mood disturbance, and about 30 children of mothers with no history of affective disorder, these workers found insecure attachment following reunion was most common among children of mothers with either a major unipolar or bipolar affective disorder, but was infrequently observed among women either without a disorder or with a mild disorder. A later study (Radke-Yarrow, 1991) with a larger group of mothers and children reports that 75% of families in the well comparison group had children rated as securely attached, as contrasted with 47% of children of mothers with a major affective disorder. In this larger group, the risk for disturbance in attachment among children is particularly significant for mothers with bipolar disorders. Indeed, it is difficult to distinguish statistically children of mothers with a unipolar illness from well counterparts. Children showing disturbance of attachment in both the unipolar and psychologically well groups had mothers who were less able to express affect and to signal to the infant their mood state.

FROM FOCUS ON RISK TO RESILIENCE AMONG OFFSPRING OF TROUBLED PARENTS

Although it is important to recognize that affective disorders increase the risk of psychological problems in children, it is also important to ask why 88% of these children remain relatively resilient to the impact of parental disability and whether custody-visitation arrangements can help support such resilience. Social competence, or the capacity to engage others in support of one's own continued psychological development, and to effectively use this support, affirmation, and admiration for enhancing feelings of personal integrity and vitality, appears to be central to the study of resilience.

Follow-back studies of students with varying mental health outcomes (Watt et al., 1970), follow-through studies of the children of psychiatrically ill parents, and studies of children raised in circumstances of poverty, violence, and family disorganization consistently show that the child with the engaging smile, who is energetic and able to reach out to others, as well as to support and comfort, gets more attention from adults and peers alike. More socially competent children are better able than their less socially competent counterparts to withstand family affliction and disruption. They seem to grow in psychological strength through overcoming difficulties. Beardslee and Podorefsky (1988) report that the capacity to differentiate between themselves and their troubled parents and to understand themselves are important factors in the resilience of adolescent children of mothers with unipolar depression.

Currently, many states have laws that allow a child to be taken from a parent for no reason other than parental mental illness (*Mental and Physical Disability Law Reports*, 1985, 1986a, 1986b). The litigant in custody-visitation disputes who suffers from a diagnosed psychiatric disorder is always at a marked disadvantage. This is despite evidence that women with mental illness report that having children serves as an organizing function, focusing their lives and providing a further impetus to avoid drugs, alcohol, and other maladaptive behaviors (Mowbray, Oyserman, Zemencuk, & Ross, 1995). Furthermore, researchers suggest that the emotional pain of mentally ill parents is exacerbated by the tendencies of the legal, welfare, and mental health systems to treat adults with mental illness as if they were children (Schwab, Clark, & Drake, 1991). These researchers contend that for some, parenthood, however brief, is the only time many mentally ill women have ever felt like an adult. This complicates treatment of mentally ill women who are involved in custody cases. These parents typically report that "the system" is controlling their lives, and view any professional behavior that does not immediately facilitate increased access to their children as part of the same frustrating, bureaucratic pattern (Schwab et al., 1991). Since it is always to children's advantage for parents, whether custodial or noncustodial, or even having minimal contact with their child, to be functioning at the highest possible level, consideration of arrangements for the child's best interest properly includes means to maintain parents at their highest level of function.

Courts' attempts to contribute to the mental health of parents by mandating treatment as a condition of custody or visitation may have complex, undesired results. Psychiatrically ill parents may perceive such treatment as a further extension of the oppressive system in which they feel trapped. When mandated treatment is reported to the court, as is necessary for the court to enforce its mandate, mentally ill parents are likely to view therapeutic interventions with skepticism, reasonably worrying that their therapists may provide negative information about them to the court. Clinicians often feel caught between the role of advocating for their client and taking responsibility for the welfare of the children (Schwab et al., 1991). Careful analysis of these situations shows that treating and forensically evaluating the same individual are fundamentally incompatible roles (Strasburger, Gutheil, & Brodsky, 1997) and that every effort should be made to separate them. The tempting argument that treaters know their patients best and hence their input would be of great value to legal decisions does not stand up to examination because the way in which treaters gather information and the nature of that information differ fundamentally from the information gathering found most useful in legal contexts. Additionally, courts must assess whether mandated treatments are likely to achieve their desired ends. Too often, judges make some kind of treatment a condition of custody or visitation without adequately enquiring into the likelihood of its actually achieving the changes needed to make the custody-visitation order in the child's best interest.

Fears arising from highly publicized cases may weigh heavily in judicial and legislative decisions affecting contact between psychiatrically ill parents and their children. In the Joey Wallace case, a 27-year-old mother with an extensive history of psychiatric hospitalizations including violent behaviors, regained custody of her two children after they were removed from her home following physical abuse. Shortly after the children were returned home, against the recommendations of a psychiatrist and the Public Guardian's office, 3-year-old Joey angered his mother, who tied an electrical cord around his neck and hung him from a door transom in their apartment (Gottesman & McWhirter, 1993). The resulting outcry by the media and elected officials led to administrative reorganization, the demotion and transfer of several judges, and the termination of case workers. The case was a catalyst that prompted the "best interests" doctrine to be prioritized above the interests of family reunification in Illinois. Those working in the juvenile courts agree that this case caused the pendulum to swing from one extreme, of family reunification at any cost, to the other end of the scale, which seems neglectful of the rights of mentally ill parents and the resulting impact of decreased parental involvement on children.

CONCLUSION

Major psychopathology presents problems not only for those afflicted, but also for the entire family (Cohler, 1983; Pruchno et al., 1984). This is nowhere more evident than in families where parents, predominately mothers, of young children succumb to an episode of psychiatric illness. Maternal psychiatric disturbance evokes a caregiving crisis in the extended family; the husband and father is most often working and not available to provide care. Other relatives, most often women, are expected to "fill in" and provide continuity of care during times when the mother is too impaired to provide care or is in the hospital. Repeated episodes of maternal psychiatric illness often lead the father and husband to seek divorce, further adding to the burden of caring for children and maintaining family continuity (Cohler et al., 1983). This further complicates the situation, adding issues of custody to an already difficult situation. As a matter of public policy, more would be gained by investing adequate resources in the mental health needs of mothers than in attempting to find the best arrangements for the family after catastrophic disruptions have already occurred. Still families, courts, and mental health professionals must do their best to address these situations as they occur.

Divorce increases the problems in providing care for the wife and mother and children. Except when the wife and mother is grossly neglecting and abusive, psychiatrically ill mothers are likely to maintain custody. The problem for many of these families is not the contest between parents for custody but various degrees of abandonment of the family by the father. When the mother cannot adequately care for the children, foster care is often associated with further exacerbation of the children's problems. The present crisis of inadequate care for the mentally ill thus puts their children at profound risk. Efforts must be made to maintain troubled parents in the community using effective after-care interventions following hospitalization and continuing assistance to the mother struggling to maintain tenuous adjustment while beset with such adversity as poverty and lack of help in caring for young children.

For those children fortunate enough to have two parents who desire custody or extensive visits, considerations based on parental mental illness are more complex than they may first appear. Even severe psychiatric illness in a parent may have less impact than might be anticipated. The significance of parental psychiatric illness for custody decisions can only be evaluated by examining the impact of the illness on the child. If the parent's illness puts the child at direct risk of abuse or neglect, arrangements must be made to protect the child. Findings that children are damaged by having psychiatrically ill parents need to be carefully reviewed since much of the negative impact of parental psychiatric illness results from its consequences, such as family disruption, and can be mitigated by managing these secondary consequences. Severe psychiatric illnesses have different effects on children. Parental mood disorders despite their less flamboyant manifestation appear to have significantly more untoward impact on children than schizophrenia. In fact, there is little evidence that parental schizophrenia in itself is harmful to children except through the disruption it may cause. Many children are successfully raised by psychiatrically ill parents and some even benefit from the experience of dealing with unusual problems. In assessing the child's best interest, it is important to note that the opportunity to care for a child may contribute to the mental health of severely mentally ill people and that the resulting improved function may benefit the child who now has the advantage of another involved parent and the peace of having to be less worried about that parent. Custody decisions involving psychiatrically ill parents thus need to go beyond a knee-jerk assumption that involvement with these parents is likely to harm a child to a careful assessment of the impact of the relationship and the careful design of arrangements that optimize factors contributing to the child's well-being.

APPENDIX: PSYCHIATRIC DIAGNOSIS

Custody evaluations commonly include psychiatric diagnoses, which are intended to aid in custody decisions. A clear understanding of the meaning of these statements will help in assessing the role they should play in custody decisions. In this appendix, we provide a view of the conceptual basis of the psychiatric diagnostic commonly used in the United States. Mental health professionals have attempted to develop psychiatric diagnoses that function in the same way as medical diagnoses do in understanding and managing nonpsychiatric illness. Medical diagnoses carry much information summarized in a few words. When a physician diagnoses streptococcal pharyngitis (strep throat), she immediately has a vast amount of information about the illness. She knows that the patient is likely to have a specific group of symptoms (subjective experiences) such as sore throat and difficulty swallowing. She also knows that a certain collection of signs (objective physical findings) such as swollen lymph nodes in the neck, fever, and an inflamed throat are likely to be manifest and the probabilities that they will be manifest. She knows that were she to examine certain of the patient's tissues under the microscope they would show a known pattern of change and that if she performs certain laboratory tests, such as a throat culture, these tests will yield characteristic results. She knows a great deal about the mechanism by which the disease operates (its pathophysiology). She can predict the likely course of the disease if it is untreated and provide probabilistic estimates for the various things that may happen to the patient. This is called the natural history of the disease. Finally, she can describe the likelihood that various interventions will change that natural history and lead to cure or amelioration of the condition. This is called the prognosis. Thus, for an ideal medical illness, diagnosis carries with it a clinical picture, pathological findings, pathophysiology, natural history, and prognosis.

Even in physical medicine, there are many conditions for which the full set of information described is unavailable. Some medical conditions simply have not been systematically studied to provide reasonably complete pictures of their clinical presentation. Others, especially chronic illnesses whose long-time course challenges researchers, do not have well understood natural histories. The understanding of the mechanism of medical diseases is the major fruit of the massive biomedical research efforts of the past century. Yet for many conditions, this picture remains, in varying degrees, incomplete. Especially for chronic illnesses, researchers often have surprising difficulty in describing the impact of treatment. Difficult problems include designing ethical studies that show convincing and meaningful differences in outcome as a result of treatment and properly extending research findings to the situation of ordinary patients. All of these problems are intensified when we work with psychiatric disturbances.

The 19th century saw a clear differentiation between organic psychiatric disorders, those conditions like tertiary syphilis, that were related to physical damage to the brain, and "functional" psychiatric disorders in which no gross brain pathology could be found. By the end of the nineteenth century, psychiatrists had begun to sort out the diagnosis of functional psychiatric disorders along lines consistent with the medical description of disease. They discovered symptom complexes that were characterized by collections of co-occurring findings in similar natural histories. The most successful of these findings was Kraeplin's (1899) recognition of the difference between two major groups of functional psychotic illnesses. One group of patients observed by Kraeplin commonly suffered from chronic hallucinations, highly unusual thought processes, and a flattening of emotional life. These patients, who today would be classified as falling into the schizophrenic spectrum, followed an essentially chronic, downhill course, usually beginning in mid-adolescence to young adulthood. A contrasting group of patients suffered primarily from intensely disordered moods, characterized either by profound depression and/or periods of euphoric excitement. The natural history of these disorders, currently called mood disorders, is strikingly different from that of schizophrenia. These conditions commonly first appeared later in life. Their course is intermittent: following an episode of disturbed mood that usually lasts several months, the patient spontaneously recovers to, or nearly to, the level of functioning he or she had prior to the episode. Inspired by these findings, descriptive psychiatrists studied an array of disorders. In addition to schizophrenia and mood disorders, they found that anxiety states, obsessive-compulsive conditions and hysteria (the presence of otherwise unexplained paralyses and seizurelike conditions, which are inconsistent with known neurological lesions), and certain disorders of sexual interest and function, were regularly associated with complexes of related symptoms, and to varying extents, had specific temporal patterns. However, the remarkable success that Kraeplin achieved with the functional psychoses was not to be had with the wider range of psychiatric disorders; many psychiatrically ill individuals failed to fall within its categories.

As therapy for psychiatric disorders became available, treatments were found to be differentially effective depending of patients' diagnoses. Psychoanalysis, for example, was found to be useful in the treatment of neurotic states, including anxiety disorder, obsessive-compulsive states, and hysteria. However, it was found to be ineffective, and even to be detrimental to a patient's functional psychoses. With the introduction of effective pharmacological means for treating several psychiatric disorders, differential diagnosis became even more important. However, even prior to having therapeutic implications, differential diagnosis in psychiatry was important because it helped physicians assist patients and families in predicting the course of illness, and so planning better for patients' lives has also aided in clarifying the situations in which organic illness was present. For example, prior to the development of the electrocardiogram, physicians had difficulty telling the difference between myocardial infarctions and anxiety attacks. Systematic study of the presenting symptoms of the patients with "heart problems" allowed researchers to separate them into two groups, one of which was likely to develop severe and obvious organic heart disease, the other of which, despite great distress, rarely progressed to clear organic illness.

The development of psychiatry along this medical model is referred to as descriptive (and sometimes "biological") psychiatry. Descriptive psychiatry remained the dominant point of view in Europe, and especially Great Britain throughout most of this century. In the United States, psychodynamic psychiatry ascended following World War II, but was largely eclipsed in the 1980s by a resurgent interest in bringing psychiatry closer to general medicine. The strength of descriptive psychiatry lies in its ability to translate readily and consentually observed aspects of disordered psychological function into meaningful diagnoses from which strong inferences can be drawn about the subject situation. Its weakness lies in the too wide-ranging application of this idea so that conditions for which information are unavailable are treated as if they were well understood and from its oversimplification of the complexity of human psychological life.

The most important embodiment of the descriptive point of view is the *Diagnostic and Statistical Manual of Mental Disorders,* Fourth Edition, of the American Psychiatric Association (1994; *DSM-IV*). This volume describes psychiatric disturbances along five axes—major psychiatric disorder, personality disorder (chronic maladaptive means of dealing with the world), physical illness, current stressors, and overall psychiatric severity. The various conditions listed in *DSM-IV* and their definitions reflect a consensus of members of committees of experts brought together by the American Psychiatric Association. Some of these opinions are based on careful systematic empirical studies, some have little basis beyond the clinical opinion of the authors. Patients are generally given a diagnosis when they meet a set of criteria listed in the volume. These criteria are often of the form that a certain number of signs and/or symptoms from a list are present. In addition, the clinician's judgment is explicitly given substantial weight.

The significance of *DSM-IV* diagnoses varies substantially. Some diagnoses represent devastating conditions, that can be reliably diagnosed and whose properties are well researched and understood. For other diagnoses, there is little evidence that clinicians would agree on their presence or that they represent stable entities. In its attempt to avoid controversy about the origin of psychiatric disturbance, the *DSM-IV* avoids etiologic statements except in a few instances. Thus, in using the *DSM-IV*, careful attention must be given to the meaning of a particular diagnosis, the reliability with which it is made and the extent to which the diagnosis has implications for the particular situation. This last is particular important in forensic contexts. The *DSM-IV* is designed to aid psychiatric clinicians in their work. The clinician's concerns are often markedly different from the court's and care must to taken to respect these differences. As discussed at length, for example, the mere presence of a psychiatric disorder, even a severe psychiatric disorder, may have little relevance to the individual's ability to parent a child. For certain tasks, other diagnostic classification may prove more useful in making decisions involving psychiatrically disturbed individuals. It is not rare in the courtroom to hear *DSM-IV* described as the "bible of psychiatry." Insofar as psychiatry is scientifically based, the idea that a particular text is absolutely authoritative is clearly mistaken (especially since that text is significantly revised approximately every 8 years). The *DSM-IV* is a compendium of professional opinion designed for a specific purpose, it is inappropriate to give it undue authority especially when it is being used for purposes different from those for which it was intended.

REFERENCES

Ainsworth, M. D. S., Blehar, M. C., Waters, E., & Wall, S. (1978). *Patterns of attachment: A psychological study of the strange situation.* Hillsdale, NJ: Erlbaum

Alpern, L., & Lyons-Ruth, K. (1993). Preschool children at social risk: Chronicity and timing of maternal depressive symptoms and child behavior problems at school and at home. *Development and Psychopathology, 5,* 371–387.

Andrews, F., & Withey, S. (1976). *Social indicators of well being: Americans' perception of life quality.* New York: Plenum Press.

Angold, A., & Rutter, M. (1992). Effects of age and pubertal status on depression in a large clinical sample. *Development and Psychopathology, 4,* 5–28.

Anthony, E. J. (1968). Research as an academic function of child psychiatry. *Archives of General Psychiatry, 21,* 385–391.

Anthony, E. J. (1969). A clinical evaluation of children with psychotic parents. *American Journal of Psychiatry, 126,* 177–184.

Anthony, E. J. (1974). The syndrome of the psychologically invulnerable child. In E. J. Anthony & C. Koupernik (Eds.), *The child in his family: Children at psychiatric risk* (pp. 529–544). New York: Wiley.

Anthony, E. J. (1976). How children cope in families with a psychotic parent. In E. Rexford, L. Sander, & T. Shapiro (Eds.), *Infant psychiatry: A new synthesis* (pp. 239–250). New Haven, CT: Yale University Press.

Anthony, E. J., & Cohler, B. (Eds.). (1987). *The invulnerable child.* New York: Guilford Press.

Apfel, R., & Handel, M. (1993). *Madness and the loss of motherhood.* Washington, DC: American Psychiatric Press.

Asarnow, R. F., Steffy, R. A., MacCrimmon, D., & Cleghorn, J. (1977). An attentional assessment of foster children at risk for schizophrenia. *Journal of Abnormal Psychology, 86,* 267–275.

Bagedahl-Strindlund, M. (1986). Mentally ill mothers and their children. *Acta Psychiatrica Scandinavica, 74,* 32–40.

Bardwick, J., & Douvan, E. (1971). Ambivalence: The socialization of women. In V. Gornick & B. Moran (Eds.), *Women in a sexist society* (pp. 147–159). New York, Basic Books.

Bart, P. (1971). Depression in middle-aged women. In V. Gornick & B. K. Moran (Eds.), *Women in sexist society* (pp. 183–186). New York: Basic Books.

Bazar, J. (1990, December). Mentally ill moms aided in keeping their children. *APA Monitor, 32.*

Beardslee, W., Bemporad, J., Keller, M., & Klerman, G. (1983). Children of parents with major affective disorder: A review. *American Journal of Psychiatry, 140,* 825–832.

Beardslee, W., & Podorefsky, D. (1988). Resilient adolescents whose parents have serious affective and other psychiatric disorders. *American Journal of Psychiatry, 145,* 63–69.

Beck, C. T. (1991). Maternity blues research: A critical review. *Issues in Mental Health Nursing, 12,* 291–300.

Beck, C. T. (1998). The effects of postpartum depression on child development: A meta-analysis. *Archives of Psychiatric Nursing, 12,* 12–20.

Bell, R. (1968). A reinterpretation of the direction of effects in studies of socialization. *Psychological Review, 75,* 81–95.

Bell, R., & Harper, L. (1977). *Child effects on adults.* Hillsdale, NJ: Erlbaum.

Belle, D. (1980). Mothers and their children: A study of low-income families. In C. Heckerman (Ed.), *The evolving female: Women in a psychosocial context.* New York: Human Sciences Press, 74–91.

Belsky, J. (1984). The determinants of parenting: A process model. *Child Development, 55,* 83–96.

Belsky, J., & Vondura, J. (1989). Lessons from child abuse: The determinants of parenting. In D. Cicchetti & V. Carlson (Eds.), *Child maltreatment: Theory and research on the causes and consequences of child abuse and neglect* (pp. 153–202). New York: Cambridge University Press.

Benedek, T. (1973). Parenthood as a developmental phase of the libido (with discussion). In T. Benedek (Ed.), *Psychoanalytic investigations: Selected papers* (pp. 378–407). Chicago: Quadrangle Press. (Original work published 1959)

Bernard, J. (1975). *Women, wives and mothers: Values and options.* Chicago: Aldine.

Bettes, B. (1988). Maternal depression and motherese: Temporal and intonational features. *Child Development, 59,* 1089–1096.

Bleuler, M. (1978). *The schizophrenic disorders: Long-term patient and family studies* (S. Clems, Trans.). New Haven, CT: Yale University Press.

Bleuler, M. (1984). Different forms of childhood stress and patterns of adult psychiatric outcome. In N. Watt, E. J. Anthony, L. Wynne, & J. Rolf (Eds.), *Children at risk for schizophrenia: A longitudinal perspective* (pp. 537–542). New York: Cambridge University Press.

Bowlby, J. (1983). Attachment and loss: Retrospect and prospect. *American Journal of Orthopsychiatry, 52,* 664–678.

Boyle, M. (1990). Is schizophrenia what it was? A re-analysis of Kraepelin's and Bleuler's population. *Journal of the History of the Behavioral Sciences, 26,* 323–333.

Bretherton, I., & Waters, E. (1985). Growing points of attachment theory and research. *Monographs of the Society for Research in Child Development, 50*(Serial No. 209).

Breznitz, Z., & Sherman, T. (1987). Speech patterning of natural discourse of well and depressed mothers and their young offspring. *Child Development, 58,* 395–400.

Brown, G., & Harris, T. (1975). *Social origins of depression: A study of psychiatric disorder in women.* New York: Free Press-Macmillan.

Brugha, T., Sharp, H., Cooper, S., Weisender, C., Britto, D., Shinkwin, R., Sherif, T., & Kinwan, P. (1998). The Leicester 500 project. Social support and the development of postnatal depressive symptoms: A prospective cohort survey. *Psychological Medicine, 28,* 63–79.

Buist, A. E., Dennerstein, L., & Burrows, G. D. (1990). Review of a mother-baby unit in a psychiatric hospital. *Australian and New Zealand Journal of Psychiatry, 24,* 103–108.

Campbell, A., Converse, P., & Rodgers, W. (1976). *The quality of American life: Perceptions, evaluations, and satisfactions.* New York: Russell-Sage Foundation.

Carr, H., & Leared, J. (1973). The effect on a child of a mother who though physically present was emotionally unavailable. In R. Gosling (Ed.), *Support, innovation and autonomy: Tavistock clinic golden jubilee papers* (pp. 83–111). London: Tavistock Press.

Cath, S., Gurwitt, A., & Munder-Ross, J. (1982). *Father and child developments in clinical perspectives.* Boston: Little, Brown.

Chesler, P. (1991). Mothers on trial: The custodial vulnerability of women. *Feminism & Psychology, 1,* 409–425.

Chess, S., & Thomas, A. (1987). *Origins and evolution of behavior disorders: From infancy to early adult life.* Cambridge, MA: Harvard University Press.

Chodorow, N. (1978). *The reproduction of mothering.* Berkeley: University of California Press.

Cicchetti, D., Rogosch, F., & Toth, S. (1997). Ontogenesis, depressotypic organization, and the depressive syndrome. In S. Luthar, J. Burack, D. Cicchetti, & J. Weisz (Eds.), *Developmental psychopathology: Perspectives on adjustment, risk and disorder* (pp. 273–316). New York: Cambridge University Press.

Clarke, A., & Clarke, A. D. B. (Eds.). (1976). *Early experience: Myth and evidence.* New York: Free Press.

Clarke-Stewart, A. (1978). Popular primers for parents. *American Psychologist, 33,* 359–369.

Clausen, J., & Yarrow, M. (1955). The impact of mental illness on the family. *Journal of Social Issues, 11*(Whole Issue No. 4).

Cohler, B. (1980). Developmental perspectives on the psychology of the self. In A. Goldberg (Ed.), *Advances in self psychology.* New York: International Universities Press.

Cohler, B. (1983). Autonomy and interdependence in the family of adulthood. *The Gerontologist, 23,* 33–39.

Cohler, B. (1984). Parenthood, psychopathology, and child-care. In R. Cohen, B. Cohler, & S. Weissman (Eds.), *Parenthood: A psychodynamic approach* (pp. 119–147). New York: Guilford Press.

Cohler, B. (1987). Resilience and the study of lives. In E. J. Anthony & B. J. Cohler (Eds.), *The invulnerable child* (pp. 363–424). New York: Guilford Press.

Cohler, B., Gallant, D., Grunebaum, H., & Kaufman, C. (1983). Social adjustment among schizophrenic, depressed, and well mothers and their school aged children. In H. Morrison (Ed.), *Children of depressed parents: Risk, identification and intervention* (pp. 65–98). New York: Grune & Stratton.

Cohler, B., & Grunebaum, H. (With D. Gallant & C. Hartman). (1982). Afterword: Beyond the hospital—Aftercare intervention programs and the study of vulnerable children. In H. Grunebaum, J. Weiss, B. Cohler, C. Hartman, & D. Gallant (Eds.), *Mentally ill mothers and their children* (2nd ed., pp. 341–385). Chicago: University of Chicago Press.

Cohler, B., Grunebaum H., Weiss, J., Gamer, E., & Gallant, D. (1977). Disturbance of attention among schizophrenic, depressed, and well mothers and their young children. *Journal of Child Psychology and Psychiatry, 18,* 115–135.

Cohler, B., Grunebaum, H., Weiss, J., Hartman, C., & Gallant, D. (1975). Perceived life-stress and psychopathology among mothers of young children. *American Journal of Orthopsychiatry, 46,* 123–134.

Cohler, B., Stott, F., & Musick, J. (1995). Vulnerability, resilience and response to personal adversity: Cultural and developmental perspectives. In D. Cicchetti & D. Cohen (Eds.), *Developmental psychopathology* (pp. 753–800). New York: Wiley.

Cohler, B., Stott, F., & Musick, J. (1996). Distressed parents and their young children: Interventions for families at risk. In M. Göpfert, J. Webster, & M. Seeman (Eds.), *Parental psychiatric disorder: Distressed parents and their families* (pp. 107–134). New York: Cambridge University Press.

Cohn, J., & Campbell, S. (1992). Influence of maternal depression on infant affect regulation. In D. Cicchetti & S. Toth (Eds.), *Developmental perspectives on depression* (pp. 103–130). Rochester, NY: University of Rochester Press.

Cohn, J., & Tronick, E. (1983). Three-month-old infants' reaction to simulated maternal depression. *Child Development, 54,* 185–193.

Colombo, J. (1982). The critical period concept: Research, methodology, and theoretical issues. *Psychological Bulletin, 91,* 260–275.

Conners, C. K., Himmelhock, J., Goyette, C., Ulrich, R., & Neil, J. (1979). Children of parents with affective illness. *Journal of the American Academy of Child Psychiatry, 18,* 600–607.

Cook, J., & Cohler, B. (1986). Reciprocal socialization and the care of offspring with cancer and with schizophrenia. In N. Datan, H. Reese, & A. Greene (Eds.), *Intergenerational networks: Families in context* (pp. 223–224). Hillsdale, NJ: Erlbaum.

Coverdale, J. H., & Aruffo, J. A. (1989). Family planning needs of female chronic psychiatric outpatients. *American Journal of Psychiatry, 146,* 1489–1491.

Cowan, C., & Cowan, P. (1992). *When partners become parents: The big life-change for couples.* New York: Basic Books.

Cytryn, L., McKnew, D., Bartko, J., Lamour, M., & Hamovitt, J. (1982). Offspring of patients with affective disorders: II. *Journal of the American Academy of Child Psychiatry, 21,* 389–391.

Daniels, P., & Weingarten, K. (1982). *Sooner or later: The timing of parenthood in adult lives*. New York: Norton.

Dragonas, T., & Christodoulou, G. (1998). Prenatal care. *Clinical Psychology Review, 18*, 127–142.

Elder, G. (1979). Historical change in life patterns and personality. In P. Baltes & O. G. Brim, Jr. (Eds.), *Life span development and behavior* (pp. 117–159). New York: Academic Press.

Emde, R. (1984). The affective self: Continuities and transformations from infancy. In J. Call, E. Galenson, & R. Tyson (Eds.), *Frontiers in infant psychiatry* (Vol. 2, pp. 38–54). New York: Basic Books.

Emde, R., & Source, J. (1983). The rewards of infancy: Emotional availability and maternal referencing. In J. Call, E. Galenson, & R. Tyson (Eds.), *Frontiers of infant psychiatry* (Vol. 1, pp. 38–54). New York: Basic Books.

Entwisle, D., & Doering, S. (1981). *The first birth: A family turning point*. Baltimore: Johns Hopkins University Press.

Feldman, S., & Nash, S. (1984). The transition from expectancy to parenthood: Impact of the firstborn child on men and women. *Sex Roles, 11*, 61–78.

Field, T. (1984). Early interactions between infants and their post-partum depressed mothers. *Infant Behavior and Development, 7*, 527–532.

Field, T. (1992). Infants of depressed mothers. *Development and Psychopathology, 4*, 49–66.

Firth, R., Hubert, J., & Forge, A. (1970). *Families and their relatives: Kinship in a middle class section of London*. London: Humanities Press.

Fischer, J., & Fischer, A. (1963). The New Englanders of Orchard Town. In B. Whiting (Ed.), *Six cultures: Studies of childrearing* (pp. 869–1010). New York: Wiley.

Fish, B. (1984). Characteristics and sequelae of the neurointegrative disorder in infants at risk for schizophrenia 1952–1982. In N. Watt, E. J. Anthony, & L. C. Wynne (Eds.), *Children at risk for schizophrenia: A longitudinal perspective* (pp. 423–439). New York: Cambridge University Press.

Fish, B. (1987). Infant predictors of the longitudinal course of schizophrenic development. *Schizophrenia Bulletin, 13*, 395–410.

Forcier, K. I. (1990). Management and care of pregnant psychiatric patients. *Journal of Psychosocial Nursing, 28*, 11–16.

Fraiberg, S., Adelson, E., & Shapiro, V. (1975). Ghosts in the nursery. *Journal of the American Academy of Child Psychiatry, 14*, 387–421.

Freedman, D. G. (1974). *Human infancy: An evolutionary approach*. New York: Erlbaum/Halsted/Wiley.

Freud, A. (1973). Infants without families: Reports on the Hampstead nurseries, 1939–1945. In A. Freud (Ed.), *The writings of Anna Freud*. New York: International Universities Press,

Freud, A., & Burlingham, D. (1974). Infants without families: The case for and against residential nurseries. In A. Freud (Ed.), *The writings of Anna Freud* (Vol. 3, pp. 543–669). New York: International Universities Press. (Original work published 1944)

Galatzer-Levy, R., & Cohler, B. (1993). *The essential other: The developmental psychology of the self*. New York: Basic Books.

Garber, B. (1981). Mourning in children: Toward a theoretical synthesis. *Annual for Psychoanalysis, 9*, 9–19.

Garmezy, N. (1971). Vulnerability research and the issue of primary prevention. *American Journal of Orthopsychiatry, 41*, 101–116.

Garmezy, N. (1981). Children under stress: Perspectives on antecedents and corre-lates of vulnerability and resistance to psychopathology. In A. Rabin, J. Aronoff, A. Barclay, & R. Zucker (Eds.), *Further explorations in personality* (pp. 196–269). New York: Wiley.

Garmezy, N. (1984). Children vulnerable to major mental disorders: Risk and protec-tive factors. In L. Grinspoon (Ed.), *Psychiatry update* (Vol. 3, pp. 91–103). Washing-ton, DC: The American Psychiatric Association.

Garmezy, N. (1987). Stress, competence, and development: Continuities in the study of schizophrenic adults, children vulnerable to psychopathology, and the search for stress-resistant children. *American Journal of Orthopsychiatry, 57,* 159–174.

Ghodsian, M., Zajicek, E., & Wolkind, S. (1984). A longitudinal study of maternal de-pression and child behavior problems. *Journal of Child Psychology and Psychiatry, 25,* 91–109.

Gilligan, C. (1983). *In a different voice.* Cambridge, MA: Harvard University Press.

Gilligan, C., Lyons, N., & Hanmer, T. (Eds.). (1990). *Making connections: The relational worlds of adolescent girls at Emma Willard School.* Cambridge, MA: Harvard University Press.

Glick, M. (1997). The developmental approach to adult psychopathology. In S. Luthar, J. Burak, D. Cicchetti, & J. Weisz (Eds.), *Developmental psychopathology: Perspectives on adjustment, risk and disorder* (pp. 227–247). New York: Cambridge University Press.

Goldberg, W., & Michaels, G. (1988). Conclusion. The transition to parenthood: Syn-thesis and future directions. In G. Michaels & W. Goldberg (Eds.), *The transition to parenthood: Current theory and research* (pp. 342–360). New York: Cambridge Univer-sity Press.

Goldman, N., & David, R. (1980). Community surveys: Sex differences in mental ill-ness. In M. Guttentag, S. Salasin, & D. Belle (Eds.), *The mental health of women.* New York: Academic Press.

Goodman, S., Brogan, D., Lynch, M. E., & Fielding, B. (1993). Social and emotional competence in children of depressed mothers. *Child Development, 64,* 516–521.

Gottesman, A., & McWhirter, C. (1993, April 20). In the end, everyone failed Joseph. *The Chicago Tribune.*

Gove, W. (1972). The relationship between sex roles, marital status, and mental illness. *Social Forces, 51,* 34–44.

Gove, W., & Geerken, M. (1977). The effect of children and employment on the mental health of married men and women. *Social Forces, 56,* 66–76.

Gove, W., & Tudor, J. (1972). Adult sex roles and mental illness. *American Journal of So-ciology, 78,* 812–835.

Grossman, F., Eichler, L., & Winickoff, S. (1980). *Pregnancy, birth and parenthood.* San Francisco: Jossey-Bass.

Grunebaum, H., Gamer, E., & Cohler, B. (1983). The spouse in depressed families. In H. Morrison (Ed.), *Children of depressed parents: Risk, identification, and intervention* (pp. 139–158). New York: Grune & Stratton.

Grunebaum H., Weiss, J., Cohler, B., Hartman, C., & Gallant, D. (1982). *Mentally ill mothers and their children* (2nd ed.). Chicago: University of Chicago Press.

Gutmann, D. (1975). Parenthood: Key to the comparative study of the life-cycle. In N. Datan & L. Ginsberg (Eds.), *Life-span developmental psychology: Normative life-crises* (pp. 167–184). New York: Academic Press.

Gutmann, D. (1987). *Reclaimed powers: Toward a psychology of men and women in later life.* New York: Basic Books.

Hagestad, G. (1974). *Middle-aged women and their children: Exploring changes in a role relationship.* Unpublished doctoral dissertation, University of Minnesota.

Hanson, D., Gottesman, I., & Heston, L. (1976). Some possible childhood indicators of adult schizophrenia inferred from children of schizophrenics. *British Journal of Psychiatry, 129,* 142–154.

Hanson, D., Gottesman, I., & Heston, L. (1990). Long-range schizophrenia forecasting: Many a slip twixt cup and lip. In J. Rolf, A. Masten, D. Cicchetti, K. Nuechterlein, & S. Weintraub (Eds.), *Risk and protective factor in the development of psychopathology* (pp. 424–444). New York: Cambridge University Press.

Hess, E. (1959). Imprinting. *Science, 130,* 133–144.

Hinde, R. (1963). The nature of imprinting. In B. Foss (Ed.), *The determinants of infant behavior* (Vol. 2, 227–234). New York: Wiley.

Hinde, R. (1966). *Animal behavior: A synthesis of ethology and comparative psychology.* New York: McGraw Hill.

Hobbs, D. (1965). Parenthood as crisis: A third study. *Marriage and Family Living, 27,* 367–372.

Hobbs, D. (1968). Transition to parenthood: A replication and extension. *Journal of Marriage and the Family, 30,* 413–417.

Hobbs, D., & Cole, S. P. (1976). Transition to parenthood: A decade of replication. *Journal of Marriage and the Family, 38,* 723–731.

Hogan, D. (1980). The transition to adulthood as a career contingency. *American Sociological Review, 45,* 216–276.

Hogan, D. (1984). The demography of life-course transitions: Temporal and gender considerations. In A. Rossi (Ed.), *Gender and the life-course* (pp. 65–78). New York: Aldine/Atherton.

Jacoby, A. (1969). Transition to parenthood: A reassessment. *Journal of Marriage and the Family, 31,* 720–727.

Kagan, J. (1980). Perspectives on continuity. In O. G. Brim, Jr. & J. Kagan (Eds.), *Constance and change in human development* (pp. 26–74). Cambridge, MA: Harvard University Press.

Kauffman, C., Grunebaum, H., Cohler, B., & Gamer, E. (1979). Superkids: Competent children of psychotic mothers. *American Journal of Psychiatry, 136,* 1398–1402.

Keller, M., Beardslee, W., Dorer, D., Lavori, P., Samuelson, H., & Klerman, G. (1986). Impact of severity and chronicity of parental affective illness on adaptive functioning and psychopathology in children. *Archives of General Psychiatry, 43,* 930–937.

Klaus, M., & Kennell, J. (1976). *Maternal-infant bonding.* St. Louis: Mosby.

Klehr, K., Cohler, B., & Musick, J. (1983). Character and behavior in the mentally ill and well mother. In J. Musick & B. Cohler (Eds.), *Parental psychopathology and infant development* (Infant Mental Health Journal Vol. 4, No. 3, pp. 250–271). New York: Behavioral Sciences Press.

Kohut, H. (1971). *The analysis of the self.* New York: International Universities Press.

Kohut, H. (1977). *The restoration of the self.* New York: International Universities Press.

Kohut, H., & Wolfe, E. (1978). The disorders of the self and their treatment: An outline. *International Journal of Psychoanalysis, 59,* 413–425.

Leifer, M. (1980). *Psychological effects of motherhood: A study of first pregnancy.* New York: Praeger.

LeMasters, E. E. (1957). Parenthood as crisis. *Marriage and Family Living, 19,* 352–355.

LeMasters, E. E. (1970). *Parents in modern America.* Homewood, IL: Dorsey Press.

Lennenberg, E. (1967). *Biological foundations of language.* New York: Wiley.

LeVine, R., & White, M. (1987). Parenthood in social transformation. In J. Lancaster, J. Altmann, A. Rossi, & L. Sherrod (Eds.), *Parenting across the life span: Biological dimensions* (pp. 271–294). New York: Aldine de Gruyter.

Levy, D. (1958). *Behavioral analysis.* Springfield, IL: Thomas.

Lewine, R. (1984). Stalking the schizophrenia marker: Evidence for a general vulnerability model of psychopathology. In N. Watt, E. J. Anthony, L. Wynne, & J. Rolf (Eds.), *Children at risk for schizophrenia: A longitudinal perspective* (pp. 545–564). New York: Cambridge University Press.

Lidz, T., Fleck, S., & Cornelison, A. (1965). *Schizophrenia and the family.* New York: International Universities Press.

Lorenz, K. (1957). The nature of instinct. In C. Schiller (Ed.), *Instinctive behavior* (pp. 129–175). New York: International Universities Press. (Original work published 1937)

Luthar, S., & Zigler, E. (1991). Vulnerability and competence: A review of research on resilience in childhood. *American Journal of Orthopsychiatry, 61,* 6–22.

Mahler, M., Pine, F., & Bergman, A. (1975). *The psychological birth of a human infant.* New York: Basic Books.

Marini, M. (1978). The transition to adulthood: Sex difference in educational attainment and age at marriage. *American Sociological Review, 43,* 483–507.

Marini, M. (1984). Age and sequencing norms in the transition to adulthood. *Social Forces, 63,* 229–244.

Masten, A. (1985). Risk, vulnerability and protective factors in development. In B. Lahey & A. Kazdin (Eds.), *Advances in clinical child psychology* (Vol. 8, pp. 1–52). New York: Plenum Press.

Masten, A., Best, K., & Garmezy, N. (1990). Resilience and development: Contributions from the study of children who overcame adversity. *Development and Psychopathology, 2,* 425–444.

McGrath, E., Keita, G., Strickland, B., & Russo, N. (1990). *Women and depression: Risk factors and treatment issues.* Washington, DC: American Psychological Association.

McKnew, D., Cytryn, L., Efron, A., Gershon, E., & Bunney, W. (1979). Offspring of parents with affective disorders. *British Journal of Psychiatry, 134,* 148–15.

McLanahan, S., & Adams, J. (1987). Parenthood and psychological well-being. *Annual Review of Sociology, 5,* 237–257.

Mednick, B. (1973). Breakdown in high-risk subjects: Familial and early environment factors. *Journal of Abnormal Psychology, 82,* 469–475.

Mednick, S., Parnas, J., & Schulsinger, F. (1987). The Copenhagen high-risk project, 1962–1986. *Schizophrenia Bulletin, 13,* 485–496.

Mednick, S., & Schulsinger, F. (1968). Some premorbid characteristics related to breakdown in children with schizophrenic mothers. *Journal of Psychiatric Research, 6*(Supp. 1), 354–362.

Mental and Physical Disability Law Reports. (1985). 9, 187–189.

Mental and Physical Disability Law Reports. (1986b). 10, 182–183.

Mental and Physical Disability Law Reports. (1986a). 10, 104–106.

Miller, L. J. (1990). Psychotic denial of pregnancy: Phenomenology and clinical management. *Hospital and Community Psychiatry, 41,* 1233–1237.

Minturn, L., & Lambert, W. (1964). *Mothers of six cultures: Antecedents of childrearing.* New York: Wiley.

Mowbray, C. T., Oyserman, D., Zemencuk, J., & Ross, S. (1995). Motherhood for women with serious mental illness: Pregnancy, childbirth, and the postpartum period. *American Journal of Orthopsychiatry, 65,* 21–38.

Murray, L., Fiori-Cowley, A., Hooper, R., & Cooper, P. (1996). The impact of postnatal depression and associated adversity on early mother-infant interactions and later infant outcome. *Child Development, 67,* 2512–2526.

Neale, J., Winters, K., & Weintraub, S. (1984). Information processing deficits in children at high risk for schizophrenia. In N. Watt, E. J. Anthony, L. C. Wynne, & J. Rolf (Eds.), *Children at risk for schizophrenia: A longitudinal perspective* (pp. 264–285). New York: Cambridge University Press.

Neuchterlein, K. (1983). Signal detection in vigilance tasks and behavioral attributes among offspring of schizophrenic mothers and among hyperactive children. *Journal of Abnormal Psychology, 92,* 4–28.

Nydegger, C. (1980). Role and age transitions: A potpourri of issues. In C. Fry & J. Keith (Eds.), *New methods of old age research: Anthropological alternatives* (pp. 127–145). Chicago: Loyola University of Chicago, Center for Urban Studies.

Oyserman, D., Mowbray, C. T., & Zemencuk, J. K. (1994). Resources and supports for mothers with severe mental illness. *Health and Social Work, 19,* 132–142.

Petersen, A. (1988). Adolescent development. *Annual Review of Psychology, 39,* 583–607.

Petersen, A., Sarigiani, P., & Kennedy, R. (1991). Adolescent depression: Why more girls? *Journal of Youth and Adolescence, 20,* 247–271.

Pruchno, R., Blow, F., & Smyer, M. (1984). Life events and interdependent lives: Implications for research and intervention. *Human Development, 27,* 31–41.

Radke-Yarrow, M. (1991). Attachment patterns in children of depressed mothers. In C. M. Parkes, J. Stevenson-Hinde, & P. Marris (Eds.), *Attachment across the life-cycle* (pp. 115–126). New York: Routledge.

Radke-Yarrow, M., Chapman, M., & Cummings, E. M. (1984). Cognitive and social development in infants and toddlers with a bipolar parent. *Child Psychiatry and Human Development, 15,* 75–85.

Radke-Yarrow, M., Cummings, E. M., Kuczynski, L., & Chapman, M. (1985). Patterns of attachment in two- and three-year-olds in normal families and families with parental depression. *Child Development, 56,* 884–893.

Radke-Yarrow, M., Zahn-Waxler, C., Richardson, D., Susman, A., & Martinez, P. (1994). Caring behavior in children of clinically depressed and well mothers. *Child Development, 65,* 1405–1414.

Radloff, L. (1975). Sex differences in depression: The effects of occupation and marital status. *Sex Roles, 1,* 249–265.

Reid, W., & Morrison, H. (1983). Risk factors in children of depressed parents. In H. Morrison (Ed.), *Children of depressed parents: Risk, identification, and intervention* (pp. 33–46). New York: Grune & Stratton.

Reiss, D., Steinglass, P., & Howe, G. (1993). The family's organization around the illness. In R. E. Cole & D. Reiss (Eds.), *How do families cope with chronic illness* (pp. 173–214). Hillsdale, NJ: Erlbaum.

Reynolds, C. (1997). Treatment of major depression in later life: A life cycle perspective. *Psychiatric Quarterly, 68,* 221–246.

Richards, J. P. (1990). Postnatal depression: A review of recent literature. *British Journal of General Practice, 40,* 472–476.

Robertson, J. (1962). Mothering as an influence on early development. *Psychoanalytic Study of the Child, 17,* 245–264.

Robertson, J., & Robertson, J. (1969). *Young children in brief separation: Film no. 3: John, 17 months, for 9 days in a residential nursery.* London: Tavistock.

Rodnick, E., & Garmezy, N. (1957). An experimental approach to the study of motivation in schizophrenia. In R. M. Jones (Ed.), *Nebraska Symposium on Motivation* (pp. 109–184). Lincoln: University of Nebraska Press.

Rodnick, E., & Goldstein, M. (1974). Premorbid adjustment and the recovery of mothering function in acute schizophrenic women. *Journal of Abnormal Psychology, 83,* 623–628.

Rolf, J., Crowther, J., Teri, L., & Bond, L. (1984). Contrasting developmental risks in preschool children of psychiatrically hospitalized parents. In N. Watt, E. J. Anthony, L. Wynne, & J. Rolf (Eds.), *Children at risk for schizophrenia: A longitudinal perspective* (pp. 526–534). New York: Cambridge University Press.

Rolf, J., & Hasazi, J. (1977). Identification of preschool children at risk and some guidelines for primary intervention. In G. Albee & J. Joffe (Eds.), *Primary prevention for psychopathology* (Vol. 1, pp. 121–152). Hanover, NH: University Press of New England.

Rudolph, B., Larson, G. L., Sweeny, S., Hough, E. E., & Arorian, K. (1990). Hospitalized pregnant psychotic women: Characteristics and treatment issues. *Hospital and Community Psychiatry, 41,* 159–163.

Rutter, M. (1972). Relationships between child and adult psychiatric disorders: Some research considerations. *Acta Psychiatrica Scandinavica, 48,* 3–21.

Saugstad, L. (1989). Social class, marriage, and fertility in schizophrenia. *Schizophrenia Bulletin, 15,* 9–43.

Schwab, B., Clark, N. E., & Drake, R. E. (1991). An ethnographic note on clients as parents. *Psychosocial Rehabilitation Journal, 15,* 95–99.

Seiner, S., & Gelfand, D. (1995). Effects of mothers' simulated withdrawal and depressed affect on mother-toddler interactions. *Child Development, 66,* 1519–1528.

Seligman, M. (1974). Depression and learned helplessness. In R. Friedman & M. Katz (Eds.), *The psychology of depression: Contemporary theory and research.* Washington, DC: Winston.

Seligman, M. (1975). *Helplessness: On depression, development and death.* San Francisco: Freeman.

Shereshefsky, P., & Yarrow, L. (Eds.). (1973). *Psychological aspects of a first pregnancy and early postnatal adaptation.* New York: Raven Press.

Siassi, G., Crocetti, G., & Spiro, H. (1974). Loneliness and dissatisfaction in a blue collar population. *Archives of General Psychiatry, 30,* 261–265.

Sinclair, D., & Murray, L. (1998). Effects of postnatal depression on children's adjustment to school. Teacher's reports. *British Journal of Psychiatry, 172,* 58–3.

Sobel, D. (1961). Children of schizophrenic patients: preliminary observations on early development. *American Journal of Psychiatry, 118,* 512–517.

Spiegel, J. (1971). *Transactions: The interplay between individual, family, and society.* New York: Science House/Aronson.

Spielvogel, A., & Wile, J. (1986). Treatment of the psychotic pregnant patient. *Psychosomatics, 27,* 487–492.

Spitz, R. (1945). Hospitalism: An inquiry into the genesis of psychiatric conditions in early childhood. *Psychoanalytic Study of the Child, 1,* 53–72.

Spitz, R. (1946). Anaclitic depression. *Psychoanalytic Study of the Child, 2,* 313–342.

Steffy, R., Asarnow, R., Asarnow, J., MacCrimmon, D., & Cleghorn, J. (1984). The McMaster-Waterloo high-risk project: Multifaceted strategy for high risk research. In N. Watt, E. J. Anthony, L. C. Wynne, & J. Rolf (Eds.), *Children at risk for schizophrenia: A longitudinal perspective* (pp. 401–413). New York: Cambridge University Press.

Stern, D. (1985). *The interpersonal world of the infant.* New York: Basic Books.

Stern, D. (1991). Maternal representations: A clinical and subjective phenomenological view. *Infant Mental Health Journal, 12,* 174–186.

Stratsburger, L., Gutheil, T., & Brodsky, A. (1997). On wearing two hats: Role conflict in serving as both psychotherapist and expert witness. *American Journal of Psychiatry, 154,* 448–456.

Strohm, A. (1993). Coping and development in children of psychiatrically ill mothers: A longitudinal follow-up. *Dissertation Abstracts International, 54,* 2774.

Test, M. A., & Berlin, S. B. (1981). Issues of special concern to chronically mentally ill women. *Professional Psychology, 12,* 136–145.

Thiels, C., & Kumar, R. (1987). Severe puerperal mental illness and disturbances of maternal behavior. *Journal of Psychosomatic Obstetrics and Gynecology, 7,* 27–38.

Thoits, P. (1986). Multiple identities: Examining gender and marital status differences in distress. *American Sociological Review, 51,* 259–272.

Thomas, A., & Chess, S. (1977). *Temperament and development.* New York: Brunner/ Mazel.

Tronick, E., & Gianino, A. (1986). Interactive mismatch and repair: Challenges to the coping infant. *Zero to Three: Bulletin of the National Center for Clinical Infant Programs, 6,* 1–5.

True-Soderstrom, B. A., Buckwalter, K. C., & Kerfoot, K. M. (1983). Postpartum depression. *Maternal Child Nursing Journal, 12,* 109–118.

Vogel, E., & Bell, N. (1960). The emotionally disturbed child as the family scapegoat. In N. Bell & E. Vogel (Eds.), *A modern introduction to the family* (pp. 382–397). New York: Free Press.

Wainwright, W. (1966). Fatherhood as a precipitant of mental illness. *American Journal of Psychiatry, 123,* 40–44.

Waite, L., & Moore, K. (1978). The impact of an early first birth on young women's educational attainment. *Social Forces, 56,* 845–865.

Watt, N., Anthony, E. J., Wynne, L., & Rolf, J. (Eds.). (1984). *Children at risk for schizophrenia: A longitudinal perspective.* New York: Cambridge University Press.

Watt, N., Grubb, T., & Erlenmeyer-Kimling, L. (1982). Social, emotional and intellectual behavior at school among children at high risk for schizophrenia. *Journal of Consulting and Clinical Psychology, 50,* 171–181.

Watt, N., Stolorow, R., Lubensky, A., & McClelland, D. (1970). School adjustment and behavior of children hospitalized for schizophrenia as adults. *American Journal of Orthopsychiatry, 40,* 637–657.

Weissman, M., Gammon, G. D., John, K., Merikangas, K., Warner, V., Prusoff, B., & Sholomskas, D. (1987). Children of depressed parents. *Archives of General Psychiatry, 44,* 847–853.

Weissman, M., & Klerman, G. (1978). Epidemiology of mental disorders: Emerging trends in the United States. *Archives of General Psychiatry, 35*, 705–71.

Weissman, M., & Myers, J. (1979). The New Haven community survey, 1967–75: Depressive symptoms and diagnosis. In S. B. Sells, R. Crandall, & M. Roff (Eds.), *Human functioning in longitudinal perspective: Studies of normal and psychopathological functioning* (pp. 74–88). Baltimore: Williams & Wilkins.

Weissman, M., Myers, J., & Hardin, P. (1978). Psychiatric disorders in a U.S. urban community. *American Journal of Psychiatry, 135*, 459–462.

Weissman, M., Myers, J., & Thompson, D. (1981). Depression and its treatment in a U.S. urban community 1975–1976. *Archives of General Psychiatry, 38*, 417–421.

Weissman, M., Paykel, E., & Klerman, G. (1972). The depressed woman as mother. *Social Psychiatry, 7*, 98–108.

Weissman, M., Prusoff, B., Gammon, C. D., Merikangas, K., Leckman, J., & Kidd, K. K. (1984). Psychopathology in the children (ages 6–18) of depressed and normal parents. *Journal of the American Academy of Child Psychiatry, 23*, 78–84.

Werner, E., & Smith, R. (1982). *Vulnerable but invincible: A study of resilient youth.* New York: McGraw-Hill.

Winnicott, D. W. (1960). The theory of the parent-infant relationship. *International Journal of Psychoanalysis, 41*, 585–595.

Wolfenstein, M. (1966). How is mourning possible? *Psychoanalytic Study of the Child, 21*, 93.

Wynne, L., Singer, M., Bartko, J., & Toohey, M. (1977). Schizophrenics and their families: Recent research on parental communication. In J. Tanner (Eds.), *Developments in psychiatric research* (pp. 254–286). London: Hodder and Stoughton.

Zahn-Waxler, C., Chapman, M., & Cummings, E. M. (1984). Cognitive and social development in infants and toddlers with a bipolar parent. *Child Psychiatry and Human Development, 15*, 75–85.

Zahn-Waxler, C., Mayfield, A., Radke-Yarrow, M., McKnew, D., Cytryn, L., & Davenport, Y. (1988). A follow-up investigation of offspring of parents with bipolar disorder. *American Journal of Psychiatry, 145*, 506–509.

Zemencuk, J., Rogosch, F. A., & Mowbray, C. T. (1995). The seriously mentally ill woman in the role of parent: Characteristics, parenting, sensitivity, and needs. *Psychosocial Rehabilitation Journal, 15*, 95–99.

Zigler, E., & Glick, M. (1986). *A developmental approach to adult psychopathology.* New York: Wiley.

Zigler, E., & Phillips, L. (1961). Social competence and outcome in psychiatric disorder. *Journal of Abnormal and Social Psychology, 63*, 264–271.

Zigler, E., & Phillips, L. (1962). Social competence and the process-reactive distinction in psychopathology. *Journal of Abnormal and Social Psychology, 65*, 215–222.

CHAPTER 16

The Best Interest of Children of Gay and Lesbian Parents

AMITY PIERCE BUXTON

C ONTROVERSIES OVER CUSTODY and visitation often heighten when one of the parents is gay or lesbian. Arguments on either side become fraught with political, social, psychological, and moral assumptions about sexual orientation and child development. Such assumptions are hard to amend without empirical evidence about what actually happens when children live with or visit their homosexual parents. This chapter reviews the research about gay and lesbian parents, their home environments, and their children.

Deliberations about gay and lesbian parenting are affected by accelerating change in attitudes about families and sexuality in general and gay and lesbian people in particular. These issues provoke polarized views, the influence of which is difficult to avoid. When discussing political or social issues involving gay or lesbian persons, it is sometimes easier to endorse or to condemn homosexuality than to seek empirical facts and to reason with logic. This chapter on gay and lesbian parents focuses on the common concern: the welfare of their children. The task is to present research evidence on the growing-up experiences of children of divorced parents, one or both of whom has disclosed homosexuality.

WHAT RESEARCH SAYS AND DOES NOT SAY

Research on gay and lesbian parents and/or their children is barely 25 years old; systematic empirical research, just 20. Reviewed as a whole, the findings indicate that, all other variables being equal, divorced gay and lesbian parents can be good parents and their sexual orientation per se does not have a detrimental effect on their children. However, problems of methodology and sampling make it impossible to generalize with certainty to all parents and children in this situation. The consistency and breadth of findings outweigh their limitations to some degree. Given mutually reinforcing, complementary data from quantitative and qualitative studies, there appears to be little reason to doubt the overall picture the research presents.

Several caveats: First, no one theory explains with any certainty two focal issues of our question: sexual orientation and child development. Recent scientific discoveries challenge traditional theories of human and sexual development. Sexual orientation and child development processes involve such complex interactions of the individual and his and her environment that it is hard to identify, isolate, and measure all relevant variables. Second, most empirical studies of gay and lesbian parents or their children involve small homogeneous samples. Control groups, when used, are not always comparable. Qualitative studies often include only self-reports without independent validation. Since it is hard to find study participants, due to fear of stigmatization, most groups studied are convenience samples, predominantly well-educated, middle and upper class, and Caucasian, located through gay, lesbian, feminist or gay-related organizations; friendship pyramiding; snowballing; parent groups; university connections; heterosexual spouse support groups; or counseling populations. Also, most subjects live in large metropolitan areas where the highest concentrations of gay and lesbian citizens are found. Thus, there is no large random probability sample from which to generalize with certainty.

For these theoretical, societal, and methodological reasons, there is not yet and may never be a complete bank of knowledge validated with certainty about all children and their gay and lesbian parents. However, the existing studies, representative of diverse pockets of gay and lesbian parents and their children, yield enough significant and suggestive findings from which to make reasonable judgments in evaluating individual parents and homes for custody and visitation decisions.

At a conservative estimate, there are approximately 1,000,000 married or once married gay men and lesbians in the United States, a figure considerably lower than previous estimates including my own (1994). The lower figure comes from more reliable percentages of the incidence and prevalence of homosexuality, 1% to 2% (based on several measures) calculated in the most comprehensive probability study to date (Laumann, Gagnon, Michael, & Michaels, 1994). This study revealed extreme variations of percentages depending on the place of residence, with higher concentrations of gay men and lesbians in urban compared with suburban and rural areas. Based on census figures on adults, 18 years or older, and generally accepted though uncertain estimates of percentages of gay men and lesbians who marry and have children (Bell & Weinberg, 1978; Moser & Auerback, 1987; Saghir & Robins, 1973), such marriages have produced 1,750,000 to 2,000,000 children, including those who are now adults.

Research about lesbian parenting began in the 1970s as more lesbian mothers came out following the start of the Gay Liberation movement in 1969. Studies on gay fathers followed, totalling fewer in number, only 16, as of 1990, based on eight samples (Barret & Robinson, 1990) plus one in 1992. Following the first systematic empirical research in 1978, investigators gradually looked at a wider range of variables of parenting and child development. Recent studies examine lesbian couples who raise children from conception.

Studies include quantitative and qualitative research. The empirical studies, all relatively small, often include comparison groups, standardized assessment tools or coded protocols, and statistical analyses to test hypotheses. The qualitative studies, based on clinical case studies, interviews, participant observation, or surveys, generally provide information from the perspective of parents and children. Two investigations are longitudinal. The most recent is the British Longitudinal Study. Using questionnaires and interviews, the researchers compared 27 divorced lesbian mothers and their 39 children with 27 divorced heterosexual mothers and their 39 children in 1976; and, 20 years later, compared 25 of the original 39 children of lesbian mothers with 21 of the original 39 children of heterosexual mothers through statistical analysis of outcome variables (Tasker & Golombok, 1997). The other is a naturalistic 8-year examination of self-reports of 1,000 spouses (heterosexual, gay, lesbian, and bisexual) and 35 children of mixed-orientation couples across the United States regarding the impact of a spouse's disclosure of homosexuality over time, using a phenomenological perspective (Buxton, 1994). Together, the quantitative and qualitative studies represent diverse disciplines, from psychiatry to sociology. What the data lack in depth or statistical certainty is made up for in the recurrence of many findings across several disciplines. The following review of the research presents first what is known about mixed-orientation couples and their children at the time of divorce, followed by research findings on divorced gay and lesbian parents, their home environment, and their children's development.

GAY-RELATED FACTORS THAT IMPACT A DIVORCING MIXED-ORIENTATION COUPLE AND THEIR CHILDREN

For mixed-orientation couples who divorce after one of the spouses discloses he or she is gay or lesbian, the disclosed homosexuality intensifies typical divorce conflicts and adds more conflictual factors. Because gay-related factors so easily become intertwined with other divorce and custody problems, it is critical to isolate them for accurate evaluation. This section examines homosexuality issues that typically impact a divorcing mixed-orientation couple and their children. The description is drawn from self-reports gathered in my study over the past 12 years from some 2,000 heterosexual, gay, and lesbian spouses and 50 children across the United States and several foreign countries. It is the only study to date that looks at experiences of both spouses and children.

In most cases, the homosexual orientation of the gay or lesbian spouse is not known or disclosed at the time of marriage. When he or she "comes out," the disclosure devastates the heterosexual spouse, confuses the children, and in most cases breaks up the family. The disclosed gayness exacerbates problems common to any disuniting couple (see Chapter 5). Homosexuality may not be the decisive cause of the divorce for some couples, but the last straw that reveals flaws in the marriage. In most cases, the sexual mismatch and the gay or lesbian spouse's desire to live as an openly gay man or lesbian are the major reasons for divorce. If the couple have children, the gay factor rarely becomes a tool to allege that the homosexual parent is less fit than the heterosexual parent or that living in his or her home will harm the children.

The impact on the family of the spouse's disclosure occurs in waves. First, the gay or lesbian spouse comes out after a long struggle; then the heterosexual spouse has to deal with the new information; and finally the children are told that their parent is gay or lesbian. Having to cope with the parent's sexual orientation adds another major challenge to their growing up. "Growing up is hard enough," commented a teenage son of a lesbian, "without having to deal with a parent's homosexuality."

The revealed gayness affects everyone in the family in six areas of concern: sexuality, marriage and family, parent role, identity, integrity, and belief system. As parents and children try to come to terms with those issues, each is at a different stage, proceeding at a different rate, and viewing them from his or her perspective: homosexual or heterosexual, adult or child, male or female.

Problems of sexuality and personal integrity present unique challenges. While the gay or lesbian spouse can now satisfy repressed same-sex desires, the heterosexual spouse typically feels rejected as a man or woman and may feel sexually inadequate. The wife of a gay man fears exposure to AIDS. The sense of wholeness felt by the gay or lesbian partner because of honest disclosure contrasts with the heterosexual spouse's feelings of deception and of distrust in his or her own judgment of what is true or real.

Emotions of both spouses are the most volatile during the first 2 years or so after disclosure. The gay or lesbian mate often enters into what many call their "teenage period." Coiffure, clothes, and mannerisms may change so much that he or she seems like a stranger to the family. The heterosexual spouse, meanwhile, remains in a state of disbelief, accomplishing household and job tasks in a survival mode and often behaving in atypical ways. Within a repeating cycle of hope and disappointment, anger or distrust can explode unexpectedly. If the couple separate in this period, soon after disclosure, neither home may reflect their typical home setting. Developmental needs of the children are often forgotten.

While the gay or lesbian spouse generally finds a social support system within their new community, the straight wife or husband has few persons who understand the unique issues involved and typically retreats into isolation to cope alone. Since lesbian wives tend to leave soon after disclosing, the straight husband faces disclosure, divorce, and custody issues simultaneously. By the time a couple is considering divorce and custody arrangements, the gay or lesbian spouse has largely resolved disclosure issues, whereas the heterosexual spouse has yet to rebuild her or his self-concept and integrity.

Meanwhile, the children, sensitive to their parents' tension (or upset by the disclosure if they have been told) may act out in home or school. Reactions of children to the parent's disclosure reflect their age and development stage. Preschool youngsters usually take the announcement as a matter of fact. School-age children tend to feel embarrassed but not seriously upset by changes in their gay or lesbian parent's appearance or behavior that match stereotypes of gay men and lesbians. They feel conflicted when hearing outsiders' antigay remarks that reflect on their gay parent and indirectly on themselves. Adolescents, facing puberty issues of sexuality and identity and feeling increased sensitivity to peer attitudes against homosexuality, sometimes feel confused about their own sexual identity and often keep their parent's gayness secret so they are not seen as different. Older teenagers, having worked out their own identity and sexuality issues and formed a personal value system, are typically less disturbed but may judge the parent's homosexuality in its moral, political, or social dimensions. In retrospect, however, the majority of children say that finding out that Dad is gay or Mom is lesbian is not the major crisis. The divorce crisis is worse.

In view of the postdisclosure volatility, allegations made in divorce negotiations and conditions demanded for custody are sometimes couched as gay-related concerns. Deliberations by the straight spouse may be colored by anger about unfulfilled sexuality and distrust about deception issues. These emotions are sometimes countered by the gay or lesbian spouse's expressed guilt or defensiveness, fueled by fear that contact with the children might be curtailed because of their sexual orientation. In some cases, accusations of homophobia or heterosexism cover up psychological problems or family dysfunction. In other cases, genuine respect and affection between the spouses lie beneath their gay versus straight arguments.

During custody negotiations, it is easy to forget that the impact of homosexuality on the spousal relationship is significantly different from its effects on the parent-child relationship. While the spousal relationship is unalterably changed, the parents and children retain their distinctive roles and bond, which operate independently of the sexual orientation of either parent. In addition, research on postdivorce parenting by gay and lesbian parents demonstrates that their sexual orientation does not appear to have a serious or long-term detrimental effect on their parenting, the homes they establish, or their children's development.

GAY AND LESBIAN PARENTS

Concerns raised about gay and lesbian parents typically revolve around possible differences between them and heterosexual parents that might make them less fit parents. Questions arise about their mental health, attitudes toward marriage and children, attitudes toward gender, parenting behaviors, and sexual orientation as a potential for child molestation or encouragement for the child to become homosexual. Research studies related to these concerns demonstrate more similarities than differences between homosexual and heterosexual parents, and the differences are neither serious nor highly significant. Further, the sexuality of gay and lesbian parents has not been shown to be an operative factor in parent effectiveness or ineffectiveness.

In this and subsequent sections, quantitative research is presented first followed by data from qualitative research studies that carry weight by virtue of consistency, numbers, or breadth of representation. At the end of the chapter, further research is suggested to close significant gaps in our knowledge about these families.

MENTAL HEALTH

Questions continue to arise about the psychological health of gay and lesbian parents (Cameron & Cameron, 1997) despite the removal of homosexuality from the *Diagnostic and Statistical Manual of Mental Disorders* by the American Psychiatric Association in 1973. Research since then indicates that gay and lesbian persons fall on the normal curve of mental health and that sexual orientation *per se* does not account for unusual scores that may appear in psychological assessments (Green, 1986; Whitlin, 1983).

No study has shown a disproportionate degree of mental health problems among the lesbian or gay parent groups examined. Rather, studies demonstrate a high correlation between the mental health of homosexual parents and their acceptance and disclosure of their sexual orientation (Falk, 1994).

One study of 25 lesbian mothers, selected by friendship pyramiding in a Midwestern community and examined by responses to the California Psychological Inventory on self-acceptance and achievement and the sense of well-being, demonstrated that the lesbian mothers were as psychologically healthy as the large standardization sample (Rand, Graham, & Rawlings, 1982). The mean score for self-acceptance and achievement was one standard deviation above the norm. On well-being, the mean score was about a half of one standard deviation below. Of note, statistical analysis revealed a significant correlation between the lesbian mothers' increased sense of well-being and their openly discussing their lesbianism with their employer, ex-husband, and children; and their self-acceptance was significantly and positively correlated with feminist activism.

Studies related to the mental health of gay fathers focus on how they resolve the dissonance they initially feel when facing the two identities: father and gay man. Based on societal attitudes that are internalized, these two identities conflict, the one seen as desirable, the other less so, even though it is an enduring element of their psyche (Bozett, 1980, 1981; Cramer, 1986; Humphrey &

Humphrey, 1988). The more a socially negative image is part of one's self-image, as in the case of gay fathers, the more difficult it is to achieve psychological health (Green, cited in Bozett, 1981). Interview studies of 40 gay fathers going through the stages of "stigmatized careers" (Miller, 1979a; Miller, cited in Bozett, 1981) indicate a sense of well-being when the two identities are integrated. Openly gay fathers who divorce achieve a better mental state than those who remain closeted and married (Bozett, 1981; Miller, cited in Bozett, 1981). The integrative process takes considerable time (Green & Bozett, 1991).

ATTITUDES TOWARD MARRIAGE AND THE FAMILY

Marriage and family are values shared by divorced lesbian and gay parents and their heterosexual counterparts. Kirkpatrick (1987) reviewing studies on divorced lesbians and a comparable group of divorced heterosexual women and adding clinical examples, found no difference between the number of women in each group who mentioned love of their husbands and desire for marriage as motives for marrying. The only difference was the lesbians' major reason given for divorce: absence of psychological intimacy, not sexual dissatisfaction, in contrast to heterosexual wives' top mention: lack of intimacy and their husbands' negative or abusive behaviors (Kirkpatrick, Smith, & Roy, 1981).

Most gay men who marry do not view their homosexual activity before marriage as significant enough not to marry (Miller, cited in Bozett, 1981). Studies show that, like the lesbian wives, the gay men married for traditional reasons: desire of a stable family, love of future husband or wife, and desire for children (Golombok et al., 1983; Hoeffer, 1981; Kirkpatrick et al., 1981; Strommen, 1989). Different from lesbians, however, the men more often include desire for children among their top reasons for marrying (M. Ross, 1983; Strommen, 1989).

ATTITUDES TOWARD GENDER AND THE OPPOSITE SEX

Concerns raised about attitudes that gay and lesbian parents hold toward gender arise from two assumptions: lesbians hold negative attitudes about men and homosexual persons' attitudes about gender roles or sex-role typing differ from social norms. The latter assumption underlies fears that lesbian or gay parents might influence the children's concepts of gender role and thereby encourage homosexuality (Kweskin & Cook, 1992). Both assumptions are disproved by research studies. None of the studies, small in size but subjected to thorough statistical analysis, demonstrate any significant differences between homosexual and heterosexual parents in their attitudes toward the opposite sex. Despite sampling limitations, consistency among the findings lends them weight.

All studies to date indicate that lesbian mothers and gay fathers make an effort to provide opposite-gender adults in family activities more or less as often as do divorced heterosexual parents (Ostrow, 1977). Only one small questionnaire study of 10 gay and 2 nongay fathers and 13 lesbians (four never married) and 14 heterosexual mothers drawn from a university community, found that the nongay parents made more effort to have opposite gender adults in their children's lives than did gay parents (Harris & Turner, 1985/1986).

Although one often hears anti-male attitudes expressed by some feminist lesbian groups, no study of lesbian mothers has found any sizable difference of attitude toward men compared with attitudes expressed by heterosexual mothers, even study samples that included women active in feminist groups (Harris & Turner, 1985/1986; Hoeffer, 1981; Kirkpatrick et al., 1981; Kweskin & Cook, 1992; Turner et al., 1985). A theme found in recent interview studies is that lesbian mothers are more interested in rectifying gender disparities and developing nonsexist attitudes in their children than in instilling an antimen stance (Casper et al., 1992; Rohrbaugh, 1992).

Kirkpatrick's review (1987) and Golombok and Tasker's study (1994) suggest that lesbian mothers involve men in their children's lives more than their nongay counterparts. Kirkpatrick noted also that lesbians, in comparison to heterosexual mother samples, reported more congenial relationships with their ex-husbands and more contact between their children and their fathers, contrary to an earlier finding (Kirkpatrick et al., 1981). As for gay fathers, the 18 fathers interviewed by Bozett (1981) commonly expressed concern about the absence of the feminine influence in their homes.

Findings differ as to the degree to which lesbian and gay parents involve opposite-gender adult models. Harris and Turner (1985/1986), comparing structured interview responses of just the 11 lesbian and 10 gay parents, found that over half of the gay fathers provided an opposite gender role model for the children compared with less than half of the lesbian mothers. The majority of 30 lesbian mothers of young children in an exploratory study (Casper et al., 1992) wanted their children to be exposed to as many men and women as possible and to realize that there are many ways of being male or female. Gender was of less interest to the mothers than the individual child.

SEX-TYPED BEHAVIORS AND TOY SELECTION

Several studies examine the encouragement of sex-typed behaviors and sex-typed toys, that is, toys typically used primarily by boys and girls. Compared with heterosexual parents no group of gay or lesbian parents showed any significant differences in these areas. In 1982, Kweskin and Cook (1992) investigated 20 lesbian mothers (10 with partners) and 22 heterosexual mothers (2 with partners) as well as their children, 11 daughters and 11 sons in each mother group (Kweskin & Cook, 1982). Based on a self-description, the Bem Sex Role Inventory, and a social desirability scale, no significant difference was found regarding sex role behavior or the ideal gender behavior that the two groups of mothers espoused for their children. Of note was the significant correlation of the mothers' self-descriptions and their attitudes toward the ideal behavior they wanted for their children, regardless of the sexual orientation of the mothers.

When mothers' attitudes about sex-typed toys were examined by Hoeffer (1981) in a study of 40 children, aged 6 to 9 years, of 20 lesbian and 20 heterosexual mothers, the mothers' attitudes were more similar than different. The lesbian mothers, however, indicated more tolerance of their children's playing with opposite-sex-typed toys and more support for their daughters' developing autonomy and their sons, nurturant interests. The tendency for lesbian mothers here and in other studies not to encourage sex-typed toys appears to be directed at equalizing gender disparity, not at changing gender roles. Regarding gay fathers, Robinson and Skeen (1982) used the Bem Sex Role Inventory to study 285 members of Dignity, a national Catholic organization. More of the 30 gay fathers in the sample, compared with their heterosexual counterparts fell into the androgynous category, and they were more equally spread across the other categories (masculinity, femininity, and nondifferentiated).

Harris and Turner's (1985/1986) study of 10 gay, 13 lesbian, and 14 nongay single fathers and 14 single mothers, found the gay fathers tended to encourage the children to play with sex-typed toys more than did the nongay fathers. B. Miller (1979a) in his interviews of 40 gay fathers found that openly gay fathers were less sexist in reporting child-parent interactions than were closeted fathers.

VALUE OF CHILDREN

The extent to which gay and lesbian parents value children has been measured directly and can also be inferred from attitudes expressed in interview and questionnaire surveys. Quantitative and qualitative measures of diverse variables suggest that children are the major focus of their lives.

The fear of losing custody is a major stressor for gay and lesbian parents, especially lesbian mothers (Kirkpatrick, 1987; Lewis, 1980; Lott-Whitehead & Tully, 1992; Polikoff, 1986; Rohrbaugh, 1992). Some gay fathers fear disclosure will lead to being rejected by and losing contact with their children and therefore stay married while wanting to be free (Bozett, 1981, 1990; Dunne, 1987; M. Ross, 1983; Saghir & Robins, 1973; Wyers, 1987).

Concern about children's development, based on a review of research and clinical experience, was concluded as being no different among divorced lesbian mothers than among divorced heterosexual mothers (Kirkpatrick, 1987). Examining lesbian mothers of 20 children, aged 5 to 12, and a comparable group of heterosexual mothers and children, Kirkpatrick and her coworkers found no differences in concern for child care. Both groups expressed similar concerns and equally sought professional help for the children when problems arose.

In one of the largest studies of gay fathers, Bigner and Jacobsen (1989b) found similarities and some differences between views about children held by gay and nongay fathers, as expressed in responses given to a Value of Children questionnaire. Theirs was a cross-national study of 33 gay fathers (out of 68 support group members sent the questionnaire) and a matched sample of 33 divorced, presumably heterosexual fathers, selected from 1,700 men from various parenting meetings. The two groups of men cited similar reasons for having children, except for social status and tradition-continuity-security factors. Both groups were similar in believing that producing children enhances masculinity and provides an entrance into the adult and heterosexual communities. They also shared negative views toward child-rearing. Significantly fewer gay fathers, however, checked social status and more indicated motivation toward marriage and family as reflecting a traditional attitude and providing security from societal rejection. Also, the gay fathers believed less than the nongay fathers that having children enhanced the morality of their behavior.

Positive attitudes held by gay fathers about child rearing can also be inferred from qualitative studies. Children's needs were cited as top concerns by a majority of 18 gay fathers interviewed by Bozett (1981). In Miller's in-depth interview, of 40 gay fathers, most indicated that an explicit commitment to their children came with custody. Any potential gay relationship had to accept that commitment as primary.

The value gay and lesbian parents place on their children and their efforts to maintain quality parenting is noteworthy since neither the lesbian nor gay community is organized around children (Bigner & Jacobsen, 1989b; Bozett, 1981; B. Miller, 1979a; Rohrbaugh, 1992).

PARENTAL ATTITUDES AND ROLE

Most research into the parenting of lesbian and gay parents suggests that their maternal and paternal attitudes and roles are similar to those of their heterosexual counterparts and that the role of being a father or mother is a more important factor in their lives than their sexual orientation.

Parental Attitudes

Maternal attitudes examined by Kirkpatrick et al. (1981) as part of their larger study found no differences between the lesbian and heterosexual mothers involved. Three studies on parental attitudes and roles used the Adult Response to Child Behavior instrument, a presentation of 15 slides of child behaviors each with a narrative scenario. Accompanying each slide and scenario is a three-option question asking what the parent would do if his or her child did that behavior. The response options are designed to distinguish among three types of parent response: adult-oriented (assertion of adult power or control), child-oriented (concern for the child's development), and task-oriented (impact of an adult response on the child's learning or task).

Using the slides with 34 lesbian (74% partnered) and 47 heterosexual mothers, Mucklow and Phelan (1979) in their pilot study, found similar maternal attitudes among the two sets of mothers, confirmed by a self-rating instrument that showed comparable maternal attitudes and self-concept of confidence, dominance, and nurturance.

J. Miller, Jacobsen, and Bigner (1981) used the slides on 34 divorced lesbian mothers (74% of whom had partners) drawn from a feminist center and 47 married heterosexual mothers drawn from the local PTA in a large western mountain city. The modal responses given by the two groups of mothers to all the slides suggested that the lesbians were more child-oriented. However, there were no significant differences between responses to 13 of the slides. The significantly different responses were to two slides: disruption of furniture and bedtime stalling. Significantly more lesbian mothers (88%) gave a child-oriented response to the furniture disruption than heterosexual mothers (59.6%). To the bedtime stalling side, the largest percentage of lesbians gave an adult-oriented response, in contrast to task-oriented responses of the highest percentage of heterosexual mothers.

Bigner and Jacobsen (1992) also used the slide study with a convenience sample of 23 gay and 29 presumably nongay fathers from parent groups in a large western mountain city. Responses to the slides demonstrated a high degree of similarity of paternal attitudes between the two groups.

The small size of these convenience samples and different family configurations of the parent groups involve too many uncontrolled variables to generalize from the findings with any degree of certainty. The similarities found, however, are consistent enough to suggest some commonalities of parental attitudes between gay and lesbian parents and heterosexual parents. The nonsignificant differences need to be studied further. Arguments can also be raised as to which ultimately is the "best" response to give to an individual child's behavior.

In addition to the slide study, Bigner and Jacobsen (1992) gave the father groups a nonstandardized, self-administered questionnaire on attitudes toward fathering. For 36 items, five response options were designed to distinguish between having a traditional approach to children (authoritative; lesser degree of involvement in developing the child's personality; little affection or expressed concern for social, emotional, or mental development) and having a developmental approach (democratic behavior; training for self-reliance; help to grow socially, emotionally, and mentally; frequent demonstration of affection; and expression of concern for the child's happiness, well-being, and self-worth). Except for two items, both father groups, gay and straight, gave responses indicative of a developmental view toward their children. Since the questionnaire was not standardized and the convenience sample was small, the findings are but suggestive.

Based on a similar assumption that parents who are authoritative (control with warmth and acceptance) will more likely have well-adjusted children than authoritarian parents (control and little warmth) or permissive parents (either indulgent or neglectful), Miller (cited in Green & Bozett, 1991) used an authoritative versus authoritarian scale with two groups of gay fathers: married and closeted versus openly gay and divorced. The divorced, openly gay fathers were more authoritative, less physical in punishment, expressed a stronger desire to rear children with nonsexist, egalitarian parent-child interaction than were married dads still in the closet. This study suggests, consistent with studies cited earlier, that gay fathers' accepting their gay identity has integrative effects on their behavior.

Reinforcing the picture of a nonauthoritarian mode of gay fathering are data from a later study in which 20 gay fathers demonstrated more paternal nurturance and less traditional paternal attitudes in comparison with 20 nongay fathers (Scallen, 1981).

Parental Role

The several studies of parental role show few differences between maternal roles shown by lesbian mothers and paternal roles demonstrated by gay fathers in comparison with their heterosexual counterparts (Green & Bozett, 1991). Kirkpatrick (1987), surveying studies of lesbian mothers through 1987 and her own clinical work, generalizes that motherhood is their salient identity. Similarly, Lewin and Lyons (1982), in their semistructured interviews, found that, for 43 lesbian and 37 heterosexual divorced mothers in the San Francisco Bay area, all activities, preoccupations, social systems, and friendships revolved around the mother role. Lott-Whitehead and Tully (1992), in their questionnaire study of 46 lesbian mothers in Georgia, found the mothers had no problem reconciling being a lesbian and a mother. For the lesbian mothers and heterosexual mothers in the Kweskin and Cook (1992) study, the mother role, rather than sexual orientation, was the more important indicator of what they wanted for their children. The lesbian mothers felt that obligations toward their children superseded expressions of homosexuality.

Looking at gay fathers compared with nongay fathers, Scallen (1981) found both similarities and differences in certain aspects of the parent role based on responses to the Eversoll Father Role questionnaire. Compared with 20 heterosexual men, fewer of the gay fathers endorsed the concept of being an economic provider and more endorsed paternal nurturance and assessed their overall paternal role more positively. However, they resembled nongay fathers in paternal problem-solving, providing recreation, encouraging autonomy in their children and in taking an active role in caregiving. These findings contradict negative attitudes toward child rearing expressed in the Bigner study cited earlier, highlighting the effort gay fathers make to care for the children in real life.

Demands of the father's role conflict with participation in the gay community: being single, free, or uncommitted. In contrast to lesbians, many of whom willingly share a lesbian mother's child rearing tasks, many gay men do not want to be "stepparents" (Miller, cited in Bozett, 1981). Interview studies, however, report that isolation and negativity from the community do not weaken their identity as fathers. Being a father is more important than having a new superficial relationship. One study reported that the gay fathers more easily reconciled their parent role with their homosexuality than did the lesbian mothers (Turner, Scadden, & Harris, 1990).

The parenting attitudes and roles of gay fathers and lesbian mothers who have been studied fall within the normal range as measured against comparable groups of heterosexual parents and in some cases standardized measures. No significant correlation with or any direct effect of sexual orientation per se has been demonstrated to date.

SEXUAL ORIENTATION

Concerns raised about gay and lesbian parents' sexuality typically focus on issues of sexual molestation or causation of a homosexual orientation in the children. The sexual orientation of gay and lesbian parents, while a defining factor in their own self-identity, has not been shown to lead to molestation or to link to any significant degree to their children's turning out to be gay or lesbian if they live with or visit them.

Disagreements about the impact of a parent's homosexuality on children's sexuality stem from a lack of certainty about what factors "cause" homosexuality. Considerable confusion arises from the interchangeability of terms that describe distinctly different dimensions of sexuality: *sexual orientation* refers to a predominant cluster of emotions, desires, and attractions toward someone of the same or opposite gender or toward both genders; *sexual identity* is the way one sees and labels himself or herself as homosexual, heterosexual, or bisexual; and *sexual behavior* denotes conduct that covers a broad spectrum of sexual activities.

Sexual orientation, identity, and behavior are so intermingled that authors of the recent and most comprehensive study of sexuality and sexual practices in the United States refused to pin down an exact percentage for the prevalence of homosexual persons (Laumann et al., 1994). To present a more accurate picture, they conducted a statistical analysis of overlapping relationships among same-sex desire, behavior, and identity. Of the three dimensions, sexual behavior provokes the most controversies in custody disputes.

Child Molestation

No sexual molestation by gay or lesbian parents has been reported in research literature or in judicial records (Hall, as cited by Falk, 1989). Various reports indicate that molesters are more commonly older heterosexual men with young girls as their victims (Finkelhor, cited by Rivera, 1987; Groth & Birnbaum, 1978). No sexual molestation by gay or lesbian parents has been reported in research literature or in judicial records (Hall, as cited by Falk, 1989). Isolated incidents appear to be anomalies. In a recent reanalysis of 5,182 responses to a 6-city mail-back questionnaire study conducted in 1985 (Cameron & Cameron, 1997), only 2 men in the Dallas sample said they had had sex in their teens with their reportedly gay fathers. Surveys and reports of homosexual prostitution and man-boy love (Cameron & Coburn, 1986) describe subgroups of the gay community whose conduct, attitudes, and motives clearly differ from those of gay and lesbian parents.

Recruitment or Encouragement

No study to date indicates that gay and lesbian parents encourage their children to be gay or lesbian. Interviews and surveys indicate that they have no preference about their children's orientation, although some say they do not like the idea that their children's being gay would subject them to societal negativity. Most lesbian mothers studied want their children to be true to whatever their child's own orientation turns out to be (Green, 1982; Kirkpatrick, 1987). They want their youngsters to develop into mentally, physically, and socially adjusted persons more than that they have a particular sexual orientation. In the Tasker and Golombok follow-up study (1997), however, the two daughters of lesbian mothers who turned out to be lesbians as young adults thought their mothers preferred it but did not feel forced to be lesbian or influenced by their mothers' lesbianism.

Predictions that children are likely to become gay or lesbian if they live with or have contact with their homosexual parents (or their partners) are questionable, since no single route to homosexuality has yet been established with any certainty. Neither nature nor nurture has been proven to be "the" cause, nor has any particular combination of biological and environmental factors. Current thinking on the genesis of homosexuality highlights the absence of convincing data about causation (see Cohler & Galatzer-Levy, in press).

Most researchers believe that homosexuality results from some degree of interplay among biological components and factors in an individual's environment (Laumann et al., 1994). Essentialists emphasize the individual; social constructionists the society (Parker & Gagnon, 1995). The question then is what proportions of nature and nurture and what stages of a person's development make the difference. No empirical study provides an answer. Competing theories provide partial views. Traditional psychoanalytic theory posits that homosexuality indicates an unresolved oedipal conflict of a person with his or her father and/or mother, a dysfunction that operates differently for boys and girls (Freud, 1905/1953; Socarides, 1990). Similar theories state that homosexuality is a transitional stage toward heterosexuality, an outcome of emotional wounds (Moberly, 1983) or, for gay men, a reparable dysfunctional way of relating to other men (Nicolosi, 1991). Recent biological studies have shifted the focus back toward the nature side, pointing to possible genetic or hormonal factors. Investigations on homosexual twins (50% concordance) suggest a genetic component (Bailey & Pillard, 1991; Bailey et al., 1993). Other research has identified prenatal hormones of the mother as acting on neural substates of the brain of the fetus (Money et al.; Dittman et al., cited by Tasker & Golombok, 1997). The finding of a different-sized hypothalmus in a sample of deceased homosexual and presumably heterosexual men (LeVay, 1991) raises further questions about what biological and experiential factors might explain the structural difference. Though suggestive, none of these studies has sufficient empirical support to raise them above informed speculation.

More recent theories look at sexuality as a total phenomenon and focus on the interaction of the social environment and the individual in the formation of sexual orientation toward the same or the opposite sex. Social learning and cognitive development theories emphasize the social environment and observed sex-role behavior. Children learn gender behaviors through reinforcement by and modeling of behaviors of their parents and all females and males in their world: real life, fiction, or the media. From these examples, they abstract concepts of gender-appropriate behavior and imitate those "gender stereotypes" (Tasker & Golombok, 1997). Children become aware of those stereotypes as early as age 2 (Stern & Karraker; Martin; Singorella et al.; all cited by Tasker & Golombok, 1997). According to cognitive developmentalists, too, children develop this pre-operational, internal capacity to distinguish between the sexes by 2 years of age (Beall & Sternberg, 1993). Children establish abstract concepts of sex roles by age 11, when formal cognitive operations enable them to link sex roles with social systems, work, and family roles (Agbayewa, 1984).

Symbolic interactionist and social constructionist theories state that children are neither born with particular sexual feelings nor shown how to be sexual through interactions. Rather, they form their sexual identity or behavior from sexual scenarios or concepts found in their culture and through social interactions and then create their own meanings about sexuality and sexual behavior (Simon & Gagnon, 1987). Sexual identity, according to this theory, is continually constructed throughout life. Modifying the theory, symbolic interactionists stress the individual's identification with significant "others" in the social construction process. From the feminist perspective, lesbian relationships reflect a personal preference and represent a response to a patriarchal society (Tasker & Golombok, 1997).

All data considered, sexual orientation develops through the interaction of biological givens and environmental variables, that is, the child and his or her whole world of inputs. If overall psychological development toward maturity is the basis on which custody decisions are made and parent-child bonding is the most critical element in that process, then asking about possible effects from a parent's homosexual orientation is perhaps the wrong question. A more useful question is whether or not parents can provide the optimum conditions for the child to develop his or her given nature fully in all dimensions. The following section describes what research discloses about homes established by gay and lesbian parents and effects of such home environments on the children's development.

HOME ENVIRONMENT

The most salient factors in a home environment are the parent-child interactions. How the parent and child share feelings and ideas, solve problems, accomplish tasks, and learn to live together are more significant factors than the family structure or physical details of the home. These interactions are affected also by relationships with other family members in the home and the heterosexual parent and persons outside the family circle as well as by the societal context in which the child grows up. Most of the findings on home environment come from qualitative studies.

HOUSEHOLD SETTING

The predominant lifestyle of gay and lesbian parents is that of working parents who organize their lives around going to work, putting food on the table, keeping the house clean and safe, and providing recreation, medical resources, and support for the children's school and social activities (Buxton, 1994; Rohrbaugh, 1992). Kirkpatrick (1987), comparing how divorced lesbian mothers and heterosexual mothers shared household and child-care tasks, found only similarities.

Lesbian couples tend to share household tasks (Blumstein & Schwartz, 1983). Lesbian mothers who are partnered share child-care tasks, too (J. Miller et al., 1981). Patterson's (1995a) empirical investigation of ways by which lesbian couples organize household and child care for children raised from conception revealed a significant correlation of the degree of the children's sense of well-being and adjustment with the shared child rearing of the partners.

Regarding other sources for help with child care, Lewin and Lyons (1982) found no difference between the 43 lesbian and 37 heterosexual mothers in their use of social support systems (partners, relatives, and friends). One of the few studies on gay fathers that directly addresses shared child-rearing activities, found that, compared with 11 heterosexual fathers, 10 gay fathers indicated they had fewer disagreements with their partners over discipline (Harris & Turner, 1985/1986).

ECONOMICS, WORK, AND MOBILITY

Income level affects the quality of the physical home environment, and divorce creates a strain on any family, homosexual or heterosexual. In Kirkpatrick's (1987) study of single divorced heterosexual and divorced lesbian mothers, both groups experienced a decrease in income. The gay fathers in Miller's study (cited in Bozett, 1981) suffered downward mobility due to financial pressures to support two households.

Pagelow (1980), using interviews and participant observation of a number of urban women's groups and interviews, reported that the stress lesbian mothers felt from a lack of money, isolation, and the difficulty of finding suitable housing was no less than that experienced by divorced heterosexual mothers. However, the lesbian mothers reported greater problems in finding appropriate child care because of antigay attitudes in the community. Both groups felt oppressed as single mothers, but the degree of perceived oppression was greater for the lesbian mothers because of their sexual orientation. The number of moves made between homes and schools reported in studies of gay and lesbian parents and their heterosexual counterparts suggests a greater degree of mobility for lesbian parents (Huggins, 1989; Kirkpatrick et al., 1981).

FAMILY CONFIGURATION

The composition of postdivorce families headed by gay or lesbian parents varies widely (Martin, 1993). In most studies on divorced mothers, more of the divorced lesbian mothers have partners than their heterosexual counterparts. The samples of gay fathers are so diverse that no pattern emerges. One study (Turner et al., 1990) found less than half of the fathers had partners, compared with half of the lesbian mothers, while a survey of 32 gay fathers and 32 lesbian mother by Wyers (1987) discovered half of each group was partnered. Blended or stepfamilies seem to be common but not universal. Blended families described often include more variations of adults, such as adult friends of the same or opposite sex, than found in homes of divorced heterosexual parents (Hotvedt & Mandel, 1982; Pennington, 1987). Aside from extra adults and the presence of same-sex partners, the home settings of lesbian and gay parents appear to be more or less like most postdivorce heterosexual households.

FAMILY INTERRELATIONSHIPS

Within the diversity of family structure and household organization, family interactions in both the child's primary and secondary homes are the more significant factors in a child's development. Family relationships in each home, gay or lesbian and heterosexual, include those of the children with the parent, with the parent's partner (if any), and with his or her siblings and possibly stepsiblings. Research to date indicates no serious or long-term detrimental consequences of children's living in or visiting their gay or lesbian parent's home. Empirical studies and interviews, case studies, and surveys indicate problems and successes found in most families. Problems reported stem primarily from dysfunctional parent behaviors or an unstable home life related to factors other than the parent's sexual orientation (Buxton, 1994; O'Connell, 1990; Osman, 1972; Rafkin, 1990; J. Ross, 1988; Weekes, Derdeyn, & Langman, 1975). Specific issues related to the parent's homosexuality are mainly children's difficulties in trying to come to terms with having a parent who does not fit the heterosexual norm and coping with antigay community attitudes.

Gay or Lesbian Parent and Child

The gay or lesbian parent's having full responsibility for the child during their time together often increases parent-child time (West & Turner, 1995). On a questionnaire survey of 400 gay and lesbian parents across the country, out of 1,000 questionnaires sent, some divorced parents reported that they were spending more time with the children than they had during the marriage and that the time was of better quality because it was more "conscious" (Schulenberg, 1985). Research indicates normal, supportive child-parent interactions. In one study, lesbian mothers with partners, compared with mothers in two-parent heterosexual families, showed greater warmth and interaction and reported less frequent disputes with daughters (Golombok, Tasker, & Murray, cited in Tasker & Golombok, 1997).

Parent-child interrelationships between gay fathers and their children have been examined more often than have interactions between lesbian mothers and their children. Structured interviews with 10 single gay fathers and 11 single lesbian mothers revealed that both gay and lesbian parents reported they had a good relationship with their children and few problems related to their homosexuality (Turner et al., 1990). In another study comparing gay divorced fathers and married heterosexual men, gay fathers with partners rated as "good" on a 5-point scale their relationship with their children in cooperation, discipline, togetherness, mutual enjoyment, and communication (B. Miller, 1979a).

Several studies on gay fathers examine child-rearing approaches. Based primarily on questionnaires, interviews, and case studies, similarities were found between convenience samples of gay and heterosexual fathers in the areas of problem solving, provision of recreation activities, encouragement of autonomy, handling child-rearing problems, and promoting positive relationships (Bigner & Jacobsen, 1989; Harris & Turner, 1985/1986; B. Miller, 1979a; Riddle, 1978; Robinson & Skeen, 1982). Differences between gay and heterosexual fathers were revealed in some areas. Harris and Turner (1985/1986) found in their study comparing 10 gay and 10 nongay fathers, that the gay fathers were more child-centered, more consistent in discipline, went to greater lengths to promote cognitive skills and verbal communication, and perceived and responded more to the needs of children. Bigner and Jacobsen's (1989b) study of 33 gay and 33 nongay fathers showed the former group to be more responsive, more concerned about socialization, more promoting of cognitive skills, and stricter in enforcing limits.

Communication.   The practice of open communication between gay and lesbian parents and their children is revealed in many qualitative studies, which describe ways it strengthens the parent-child relationship and enables children to share concerns about the parent's homosexuality (Buxton, 1994; Pennington, 1987; Tasker & Golombok, 1997; West & Turner, 1995). Lesbian mothers are shown in most studies to be exceptionally open to having the children express intimate concerns, such as sexuality (Rafkin, 1990; Tasker & Golombok, 1997; West & Turner, 1995). In another study of gay fathers and lesbian mothers, more of the fathers were involved in parent-child communication (Clay, cited in Humphrey & Humphrey, 1988).

Disclosure and Monitoring Gay-Related Factors.   Disclosure of homosexuality to the child is one of the most difficult and significant events that a gay or lesbian parent experiences. Data accumulated from a variety of qualitative studies suggest that the longer parents wait to disclose their sexual orientation to children, the harder it is for the children and the more likely they may lose trust in the parent (Buxton, 1994; Lynch, 1993; Pennington, 1987). Telling them at the time of divorce seems to be a more traumatic event for children, introducing two drastic changes at once, I have found in my more recent study. Based on data from case studies and interviews with children, the coming-out event evokes a range of reactions, few of them explicitly positive (Buxton, 1994; Lewis, 1980; Lott-Whitehead & Tulley, 1992; O'Connell, 1990; Pennington, 1987; Tasker & Golombok, 1997). Viewed along with parent reports, initial reactions include disbelief, confusion, anger, surprise, shock, and confirmation (Bozett, 1981; Buxton, 1994; Harris & Turner, 1986; B. Miller, 1979a). Parents tend to add more positive inferences such as "supportive," "proud," "close," or "understanding" (Bozett, 1981; B. Miller, 1979a; Strommen, 1989; Turner et al., 1990; Wyers, 1987). Contrary to the parent's fear of rejection, most children accept the information when it is first communicated. Yet the first impression of the children's reaction does not always match their inner feelings, then or in the following months. Each child reacts differently according to personality, age, stage of development, and gender, as described earlier. In B. Miller's (1979a) study, for example, sons did not like seeing their fathers as sexual beings, while daughters saw their fathers' homosexuality in romantic terms. Other specific reactions are examined in the later section on children.

As children work through the jumble of feelings to put together the two seemingly contradictory identities of their parent, parents help or hinder their children's coping to the degree that they encourage the sharing of feelings and show sensitivity to the possibility that the children may be upset by visual evidence of their parent's homosexuality. Studies suggest that some gay fathers and lesbian mothers monitor gay-related books, pictures, magazines, or organizational literature on gay-related topics so their children are not embarrassed (Bozett, 1981, 1987a; Tasker & Golombok, 1997). Other parents do not. Some make a point of referring to the partners as "uncle" or "aunt" or "housemate" and try to be discreet about the degree of overt affection shown their partners in front of their children and particularly their friends (Bozett, 1981; Kirkpatrick et al., 1981; Tasker & Golombok, 1997). Although a small number include their children in social gatherings of gay friends (Buxton, 1994), some gay fathers emphasize a traditional male image (Bozett, 1981).

Child and Parent's Partner

A unique aspect of a gay or lesbian parent's home is the possible presence of a same-gender partner. Because a gay or lesbian couple currently has no legal recognition, the partner's role differs from that of a heterosexual stepparent (Baptiste, 1987b). Though not legally a stepparent or seen as one; the partner nevertheless serves as a resource for the children's care (B. Miller, 1979a) or sometimes a target for a child's displaced anger at the parent (Lewin & Lyons, 1982). Not having a typical stepparent role makes it difficult for the partner and children to know what rules govern their relationship. In addition, fear of community negativity often influences a gay or lesbian family to keep a low public profile (Baptiste, 1987a; Pennington, 1987). This closeting does not reinforce a "family" image. At the same time, feelings about the partner who is not of the same gender as the heterosexual parent, do not feed into the conflict of loyalties typically felt by children in traditional stepfamilies. Referred to as "aunt" or "friend," the partner is not seen as a pretend or replacement parent (Kirkpatrick, 1987; Pennington, 1987). Many children develop a close bond with the partner, and some children create a label and role with names like "my mentor" or "my two fathers" (Buxton, 1994). In Tasker and Golombok's (1997) follow-up study, the adult children of lesbian mothers who had partners, compared with children of divorced heterosexual mothers with male partners, recalled significantly better relationships with their mothers as adolescents and as young adults. When lesbian partner relationships dissolve, as a number do, the children feel the loss as a second divorce (Buxton, 1994). Some lesbian ex-partners stay connected with the parent and the children (Kirkpatrick, 1987), enabling the children to keep the same adults in their lives (Rohrbaugh, 1992).

Child and Siblings and Stepsiblings

Not much research has been done on sibling relationships, biological or "step." Some siblings support each other by sharing concerns about having a gay or lesbian parent (Buxton, 1994). Many do not (Lewis, 1980). As they relate to children of the parent's partner as stepsiblings, they, too, sometimes suffer from the ambiguity of not having a legal status (Baptiste, 1987a).

Heterosexual Parent and Child

Continued interaction with both mother and father parents ranks at the top of children's concerns, regardless of family problems or sexual orientation (Buxton, 1994; Rafkin, 1990). Since mothers more often have custody, studies have focused on contacts with fathers, gay and heterosexual.

Studies differ in reported percentages of fathers who stay involved in the lives of children of lesbian or heterosexual mothers. Several studies found that more ex-husbands of lesbians maintained a positive relationship or involved themselves more frequently in their children's lives than did ex-husbands of heterosexual mothers or that these groups did not differ (Golombok & Tasker, 1994; Kirkpatrick et al., 1981; Lewin & Lyons, 1982). B. Miller (1979a), for example, found that gay and heterosexual fathers are similarly reliable for staying in their children's lives.

Continued contact with the father is important for children of divorced lesbians no less than for children of divorced heterosexual mothers (Lewis, 1980). The Tasker and Golombok follow-up study (1997) found a significant correlation between the degree of contact the children had with their fathers in early postdivorce years and with both parents in later years, regardless of the sexual orientation of the mother with whom they lived. The less contact with the father, the poorer relationships with both parents. One study of children, aged 6 to 12, of divorced lesbian and heterosexual mothers examined how the two groups viewed their fathers in scenes they drew of their families (Puryear, 1983). All children included Dad in their pictures, but more children of heterosexual mothers drew him engaged in family activities. Possible negative effects of an apparent or real psychological or physical distancing of fathers is further suggested by a study of troubled youngsters which revealed that the loss of their father from the household or the children's lives was their greatest stressor, irrespective of the father's sexual orientation (O'Connell, 1990).

How the heterosexual father or mother views the gay or lesbian ex-spouse plays a significant role in how the children relate to their gay or lesbian parent. In accepting or respecting the homosexuality of the co-parent, heterosexual parents model positive acceptance. Most do so, although some, especially in the first few years after disclosure, find it hard to suppress hurt and anger, according to spouses' self-reports in my 12-year study. Parent and children's interviews indicate how a heterosexual parent's negativity can taint children's perception of the other parent, intensify the division of loyalties, and often lead to curtailing the noncustodial parent, usually the gay father (Buxton, 1994). Huggin's (1989) study of 18 adolescent children of lesbian mothers suggests that a father's attitude toward his lesbian ex-wife was the critical factor in the child's high or low self-esteem. In addition, if their parent has remarried, antigay attitudes of the stepparent affect negatively the frequency and quality of contact with the gay or lesbian parent (Buxton, 1994).

RELATIONSHIPS BEYOND THE FAMILY CIRCLE

Relationships outside the family present a mixture of supportive and negative reactions regarding the gay or lesbian parent. Generally, most responses are supportive or at least neutral. Yet, some are extremely negative (Buxton, 1994). Encountering responses that are explicitly or implicitly against homosexuality is a hurtful experience for children of gay and lesbian parents. According to every study that reports stigmatizing events, stressors range from isolated episodes focused on the children to outsiders' statements that express points of view that are explicitly antihomosexual or assume an exclusively heterosexual society (Bozett, 1987a; Falk, 1989; Lott-Whitehead & Tully, 1992; O'Connell, 1990; Suseoff, 1985). Antigay remarks or traditional attitudes that exclude homosexual options are expressed by some relatives, neighbors, friends, and people in church or temple, schools, and community organizations (Buxton, 1994; Casper et al., 1992; West & Turner, 1995; Wyers, 1987). Riddle and Arguelels found 63% of the families of 60 lesbian mothers and 22 gay fathers reported some negative input, most from the children's peers (cited in Falk, 1989).

Generally, direct harassment of children occurs as an individual episode of name-calling or teasing and appears not to be damaging in the long term (Green, 1978; Riddle, 1978). Teasing and stigmatization have never been a cause for removing a child from a home in custody cases (Rivera, 1991). Most studies find that children's stress stems primarily from hearing negative remarks of friends and schoolmates, such as "fag" and "dyke" jokes that are common in school chatter but that reflect on their parents and in turn on them. Also, neighbors who disapprove of homosexuality sometimes prohibit their children from playing in the gay or lesbian family's home. Publicly expressed antigay attitudes or reported events as well as fears of discrimination against their parent also trouble children (Bozett, 1980; Buxton, 1994; Hall, 1978; Suseoff, 1985; Tasker & Golombok, 1997; Wyers, 1987). To minimize the effects of such stressors, gay fathers report that they use discretion in selecting whom they tell about their homosexuality (B. Miller, 1979a). Both parents, homosexual and heterosexual, say they provide support, information, and counsel in handling hurtful events (Buxton, 1994; Lott-Whitehead & Tully, 1992).

Gay-related problems for children arise more from anticipated or actual negativity outside the home than from factors inside. Ineffective parenting and family interactions pose more significant problems for a child. Stress from overt evidence of homosexuality and external stigmatization can be ameliorated by parent discretion, communication, and guidance.

CHILDREN OF GAY AND LESBIAN PARENTS

Empirical studies of psychosexual and psychosocial factors reveal no significant differences between children growing up in homosexual homes and those living in heterosexual homes (Falk, 1994; Patterson, 1992). Reported psychological problems relate primarily to faulty family interactions, the parent's poor judgment or psychological problems, the divorce, the disclosure of homosexuality, or societal negativity toward homosexuality. Only the disclosure and stigmatization relate, albeit indirectly, to the parent's sexuality, and the negative impact of these experiences appears to be short-lived.

PSYCHOLOGICAL ADJUSTMENT

No study has shown children of gay or lesbian parents to be psychologically less well adjusted than other youngsters. Kirkpatrick and coworkers (1981) investigated the emotional pathology of 40 children aged 5 to 12, ten boys and ten girls living full time with a lesbian or heterosexual mother. Using the Holzman inkblot test, a human figure drawing, semistructured playroom interview, and blind evaluations on a Rutter Scale by a child psychiatrist and a psychologist, the only significant finding was that over half of each group were moderately to severely disturbed, possibly attributable to the fact that the authors offered free psychological evaluations in return for participation. Among the severely disturbed, marital discord in the family background, in some cases long and violent, had a higher correlation with the children's problem than their mothers' sexual orientation. Reinforcing evidence of psychological normalcy, children aged 3 to 9 who were conceived and raised by 15 lesbian mothers, demonstrated average or above average and normal cognitive functioning and behavioral adjustment compared with a matched sample of heterosexual mothers and their children, as measured by intelligence tests, a behavioral checklist, and teacher ratings (Flaks, Ficher, Masterpasqua, & Joseph, 1995). In a longitudinal study of 37 British children, aged 5 to 17, of 27 divorced lesbian mothers compared with a comparable group of 38 children of 27 heterosexual mothers, Golombok and her team (1983) found no emotional disadvantage in either group. Their follow-up study of over half the children as adults (Tasker & Golombok, 1997) also found no negative impact of the mothers' lesbianism on their psychological adjustment. No significantly different levels of anxiety or depression appeared between them and the group of adult children who had grown up with their heterosexual mothers. The only significant correlation was between mental health problems of the adult children and predivorce mental health problems of their mothers, irrespective of sexual orientation. The one other varible significantly linked to the adult children's mental health problems was the poor relationship that some children of heterosexual mothers had with their stepfathers.

Related to psychological factors, the maturity of moral judgment among adolescent children of heterosexual and lesbian mothers showed no differences in Rees' (1979) study. Similarly, assessment of intelligence of teenage children of lesbian and heterosexual single mothers as measured by standardized individual intelligence tests by Green and his colleagues (1986) revealed that both sets of children scored within the normal range.

SEPARATION-INDIVIDUATION

The process of separation and individuation into one's "self" is normally achieved by 3 years of age according to Mahler's (Mahler et al., 1975) developmental theories. Concerns are sometimes expressed that individuation might be hard for children raised by lesbian mothers. Steckel (1987) studied theseparation-individuation process of 11 children aged 3 to 4 of lesbian couples who were never married compared with children of heterosexual mothers. Parent interviews, parent and teacher Q-sorts, and structured doll play children interviews revealed no significant differences. However, qualities of self-image differed. Children of lesbians saw themselves as more lovable, and those of heterosexual mothers saw themselves as more aggressive and were seen by parents and teachers as more bossy, assertive, or negative. Though the statistical analysis is thorough, the small size and nondivorced nature of the lesbian sample make the results only suggestive.

Looking at separation anxiety, a related dimension, Golombok and colleagues found that children of lesbians compared with those of heterosexual couples demonstrated greater security of attachment as assessed by the Separation Anxiety test (Klagsbrun & Bowlby, cited in Tasker & Golombok, 1997).

Patterson (1994) examined the self-view as well as behavioral adjustment of 37 children, aged 4 to 9, born to or adopted by lesbian couples. In their responses to two standardized instruments, the Achenback and Edelbrock Child Behavior Checklist and five scales from the Eder Children's Self-View Questionnaire (Aggression, Social Closeness, Social Potency, and Well-Being, and Stress Reaction), the children scored in the normal range. They showed a greater sense of well-being and stronger reactions to stress. Since children raised from birth in lesbian-headed homes differ from those of once-married mothers, their "normalcy" is of interest. Puryear (1983) found no difference in self-concept or locus of control (of events in their lives) between two groups of children, aged 6 to 12, of lesbian and heterosexual parents. However, self-concepts revealed in their drawings differed. More children of the heterosexual mothers drew themselves in cooperative behavior with others, compared with the children of the lesbian mothers, a contradiction of Steckel's (1987) finding discussed earlier.

GENDER IDENTITY AND ROLE

Questions of gender development are often raised because of a possible linkage of nontypical gender-related behavior as a child and becoming gay or lesbian as an adult. Gender development includes gender identity (traits and behaviors considered to be typically masculine or feminine); gender role (sex-typed behaviors and attitudes appropriate for males and females in a culture); and sexual orientation (sexual attraction to the same or opposite gender). By age 5, children usually have a strong gender identity. Unclear and atypical gender identity is associated with gender deviance and disorder.

Some studies suggest that a nonconventional gender role or sex-typed behavior in childhood may be a precursor of adult homosexuality (Bell, Weinberg, & Hammersmith, 1981; Safer & Reiss, cited in Tasker & Golombok, 1997; Saghir & Robins, 1973). In these studies, adult gay men and lesbians recalled childhood activities typically associated with the opposite gender (boys playing with dolls and girls acting like a tomboy or wanting to be a boy). Similarly, prospective studies that followed children who expressed a strong desire to be the opposite sex and characteristically engaged in cross-gender behavior found that many became homosexual as adults (Green, 1985; Zuger, 1989). However, no certain linkage is determined since nearly a third of the Green study sample did not become gay or lesbian; and in the retrospective studies, some gay and lesbian adults did not recall cross-gender behaviors (Tasker & Golombok, 1997).

At least 14 studies of children of gay and lesbian parents, starting with Weekes et al. (1975) through Green (1986), examined gender role development or sex-role identity of children of lesbian mothers, usually in comparison with children of heterosexual mothers. None of the significant differences found related to the sexual orientation of the mothers (Hoeffer 1981; Hotvedt & Mandel, 1982; Robinson & Skeen, 1982; Turner et al., 1990). The most relevant investigations are discussed here.

Green (1978) investigated several variables of gender role identity, including peer group popularity, in a controlled study of 58 children, aged 3 to 11, of 50 divorced lesbian mothers and 43 same-aged children of 34 divorced heterosexual mothers, all single parents with no adult male in the home for at least 2 years. Based on children's responses to an intelligence test, Draw-A-Person test (Koppitz, 1968), the It Scale for Children (Brown, 1956), mothers' questionnaire responses, and interviews with the mothers and children, no significant differences were revealed in masculinity or femininity, sexual identity conflict, or peer group popularity. Only one child indicated some atypical choices.

Part of a study cited earlier, Kirkpatrick and colleagues (1981) examined the gender development of 20 children ages 5 to 12, living full time with their lesbian mothers, and a comparable group, living full time with their heterosexual mothers, by means of mothers, interviews, and, for the children, a psychological evaluation using an intelligence test, a projective ink blot test, Human Figure Drawing test (Koppitz, 1968) and a playroom interview by a psychiatrist. Of the sons of lesbians, 90% were within the norms, compared with 70% of the sons of the heterosexual mothers. The daughters' scores were reversed. Sons and daughters in each group who scored outside normal gender development had in common some physical difficulty early in life.

Hoeffer (1981) compared 20 boys and 20 girls, aged 6 to 9, of lesbian and of heterosexual mothers in the San Francisco Bay Area, using Block's Toy Preference Test, parental interview, and the Toy Selection Interview. The boys and girls did not differ in their selection of same-gender-typed toys. The mothers' sexual orientation did affect their preferences for their children's choice, but their toy preferences did not correlate positively with the children's selection. Influence of peers, the father, and television figures had affected the children's choices, according to all mothers. Sons of lesbian mothers rated themselves more gentle and aware of others' feelings, while daughters of lesbians rated themselves higher in leadership and more adventuresome than did the children of the heterosexual mothers.

Using the Bem Sex Role Inventory, Rees (1979) examined femininity, masculinity, and androgyny between groups of twelve children aged 10 to 20 of lesbian and of heterosexual mothers. No differences between the groups were found on the masculinity or androgyny scales, while the children of the lesbian mothers had higher though nonsignificant scores of psychological femininity than those of heterosexual mothers.

One investigation utilized one of the least constricted samples of all studies, drawing from urban and rural areas in five states located in three regions. Green and his team (1986) examined the psychosexual and psychosocial development of 56 children of 50 homosexual mothers compared with 48 children of 40 heterosexual mothers in ten states in the same region. None had an adult male in the household for at least 2 years. Based on questionnaires, audiotaped interviews, and standardized tests, no differences in intelligence, self-concept, or social adjustment and no evidence of gender identity conflict were found among the children of the lesbian mothers or any psychopathology related to the mothers' lesbianism. The only significant difference between the groups was between future job preferences expressed by the lesbians' daughters, more of whom cited traditionally masculine jobs (including lawyers and doctors) than did daughters of the heterosexual mothers. They were also less feminine in dress and activities at home and school, though a difference within the normal range. No differences were found between the two groups of sons. In view of the large sample and range of respondents, the findings strongly suggest that gender role development is not much different for children living with a lesbian mother than for those living with a heterosexual mother, except for sex-typed job preferences of daughters of lesbians—responses that may reflect the current times more than their mothers' sexual orientation. Boys in this and all other studies did not differ in their choice of masculine-typed activities or toys regardless of which activities their mothers preferred. This persistence in masculinity suggests the power of social stereotypes and the role of peers and other adults in children's lives.

Impact of Having a Gay or Lesbian Parent

Discovering they now have a gay or lesbian parent affects all children, regardless of gender. It is not the disclosed homosexuality per se that is troublesome as much as the changed picture of the parent imbedded in their sense of the child-parent bond. "I wanted so much to have a normal family," the 20-year-old daughter of a gay man exclaimed in a recent interview about her childhood. Many months, sometimes years, are needed for children to resolve discomfort about having a gay parent, confusion about their own and their parent's sexuality and stress from antigay attitudes in the community. Most come to terms with such concerns as they resolve their own identity issues in late adolescence. (Buxton, 1994)

Children who are told their parent is gay or lesbian after the divorce find the experience more stressful and manifest more difficulties than those told earlier (Pennington, 1987; Turner et al., 1990), except those told at the time of divorce. Teenagers have the most difficult time dealing with their parent's sexuality and often show acute symptoms of stress (Buxton, 1994; Deevey, 1989). Even if told when young, adolescents have to reprocess the information as they begin to understand sexuality, adult gender roles, intimate relationships, and life choices.

Negative concerns come to the fore for school-age children, as discomfort with the new identity of their parents becomes enmeshed with embarrassment about the parent's nontraditional orientation or stereotypical behavior; confusion about their own sexuality; conflicting loyalties to their two parents; fears about telling others lest they be rejected or hurt; and for children of gay fathers, anxiety they may lose their father to AIDS (Buxton, 1994; Gantz, 1982; Lynch, 1993; Paul, 1986).

Another common concern, discomfort about their gay parents' overt affection with partners, is no different from that felt by children of heterosexual parents (Tasker & Golombok, 1997). Lewis (1980) interviewed 21 children, aged 9 to 26, in the Greater Boston area. Those in the 9 to 13 age range feared the parent's sexuality might influence their own. Older children, 14 to 25, wondered about their own sexual preference even though they did not think that there was a genetic basis. Older children worry also about their own femininity and masculinity (Moses & Hawkins, 1982). The most thorough analysis of children's reactions is Paul's (1986) retrospective study of 34 children, aged 18 to 28, in the San Francisco Bay area. Of the variables with which they reported coping, one of the most difficult was the prejudice that some of them held and then had to unlearn in order to accept their gay parents.

Children's worries and hurt are often hidden by silence, masked by indifference, or expressed in tandem with pride in the bravery of their parents to have come out (Bozett, 1989; Buxton, 1994; Lewis, 1980; Lynch, 1993; O'Connell, 1990; Pennington, 1987). Difficulties communicating with their parents add to their stress about keeping the gayness and stigmatization secret. A number fear expressing negative feelings to their parent lest they be abandoned.

Targets of children's negativity include either parent, his or her partner, or the children themselves if they feel they cannot control their anger or the situation. In an 8-year study that included 57 children of 28 parents and an additional 22 children, self-destructive threats or actual incidents were reported for or by four sons, aged 9 to 11, and four daughters, aged 14 to16. All had gay fathers but were living with their heterosexual mothers or, in one case, the heterosexual mother and closeted father. Reported causes included fear or anger over feared or actual divorce, confusion about unspoken family concerns about the postdisclosure situation, and lack of control. All but one child regained mental health through therapy; one daughter is still angry over her father's detachment from her birth (Buxton, 1994).

Over time, negative feelings are generally replaced by positive attitudes (Buxton, 1994; Wyers, 1987). Young adults in the Tasker and Golombok (1997) follow-up study were more likely to accept their lesbian "family identity" if their mothers had a stable long-term relationship and welcomed their friends at home when they were adolescent. The only significant variables related to not feeling good about their lesbian family as adolescents were mothers' short-term relationships or being openly gay in front of the child's friends.

In most cases, concerns about having a gay or lesbian parent are resolved by the time children achieve autonomy as young adults and can identify unashamedly as children of gay and lesbian parents. Some children continue not to accept the parent's homosexuality on the basis of moral values but continue to love the parent (Buxton, 1994). Since most of the children interviewed were located through homosexual and heterosexual parents in support networks or through snowballing, we do not know if they speak for children in the broader society or those who declined to talk.

IMPACT OF ANTIGAY COMMUNITY ATTITUDES

Harmful effects of stigmatization by the community is a common issue brought into custody deliberations. Studies reveal that despite teasing or other hurtful acts, there are no significantly negative effects on peer relationships or self-esteem from teasing, harassment, rejection, or labeling (Suseoff, 1985). Given evidence that harassment occurs as isolated incidents, the major negative impact comes from fears that such events might occur and the secrecy or isolation many children impose upon themselves to avoid them (Buxton, 1994; Lewis, 1980; Lynch, 1993; O'Connell, 1990; Pennington, 1987; Rafkin, 1990). Children experience hurtful events no matter in which parent's home they reside, according to reports in my on-going study.

According to most interview studies, children fear rejection and ridicule of themselves and harm to their parents because of discrimination. This anxiety peaks in their teenage years, when they tend to keep the gayness secret or lie (Lewis, 1980). The problem then is self-imposed isolation to maintain peer approval. Boys do not want to mar peer approval of their fathers as well (Buxton, 1994). For girls, who ordinarily share and discuss a wide range of personal information with peers, it is particularly hard not to share information about parents' sexual orientation (Buxton, 1994). Keeping secrets makes it hard to develop intimacy skills. Deciding to tell someone becomes a major event, and reactions are sometimes hurtful.

All studies on stigmatization show that the children are resilient and create adaptive coping skills (Buxton, 1994; Green, 1978; Rafkin, 1990). Some decide that antigay negativity stems from the other person's ignorance. Others say discrimination is society's fault (Lynch, 1993; Schulenberg, 1985). Lynch (1993) writing as the child of a gay and a lesbian parent, notes that children's anxiety changes over time until criticism of the parents ceases being taken as criticism of the children themselves.

Children, aged 14 to 35, of gay fathers recount social control strategies they devised so others would see them as they wanted to be perceived (Bozett, 1980). Through such coping with painful discrimination, children learn social sensitivity and ways to detect trustworthiness (Baptiste, 1987b; Bozett, 1980; Buxton, 1994; Lynch, 1993; O'Connell, 1990; Paul, 1986; Pennington, 1987). Many become protective of their homosexual parent and some become active in gay rights causes.

In retrospective interviews, a number of children report more benefits than problems from dealing with societal negativity (Buxton, 1994; Lynch, 1993; O'Connell, 1990). Although they would "not wish the difficulties of the experience on anyone," they have a greater understanding of prejudice, feel free to change and have choices, and are more tolerant of differences and intolerant of discrimination (Buxton, 1994; Falk, 1994; Lynch, 1993; Paul, 1986). However, as mentioned, most of these studies involve convenience samples of children who might be expected to express more positive attitudes than would a random sample of all children of gay and lesbian parents. At the same time, we can never find out how they would have developed had their parents' sexual orientations been different.

PEER RELATIONSHIPS

One test of the impact of stigmatization is the quality of the children's peer relationships. No study has shown a deleterious effect on their ability to form relationships with peers. Wyers' (1987) survey of parents in the United States and Canada, found 21% of gay fathers reported some problems their children had in relationships with other people as did 58% of lesbian mothers. The major factors cited by mothers were indirect: fear of censure or concern about how to discuss homosexuality. Despite peer name-calling or rejections, no difference has been demonstrated between the popularity and friendship patterns of children of lesbian mothers compared with children of heterosexual mothers (Buxton, 1994; Hotvedt & Mandel, 1982; Rees, 1979). In the Golombok and Tasker data-based study (1994), two of the 39 children of the lesbian and heterosexual mothers alike exhibited distress, social impairment, or restricted activities; a third of each group showed minor difficulties related to peer relationships.

SELF-ESTEEM

The self-esteem of youngsters studied, interviewed, or observed does not appear to be damaged because of the parent's homosexuality. One empirical study of sex-typed toys and behaviors (reviewed earlier), showed a positive correlation between a child's self-concept and self-esteem and the mother's self-esteem, independent of sexual orientation (Kirkpatrick et al., 1981). Huggins (1989) studied the self-esteem of 36 teenagers, 9 sons and 9 daughters of both lesbian and heterosexual mothers in Los Angeles. Based on interviews with the mothers and children, questionnaire items on self-concept and peer relationships, and a scaled measure about home, school, and academics, no significant differences of self-esteem appeared in relation to either the mother's sexual orientation or the children's gender. Of note, those with higher self-esteem had mothers with partners, either lesbian or heterosexual male, and contact with their fathers.

Despite the isolation that comes with social stigmatization, the strain of not feeling "normal" does not appear to last (Baptiste, 1987b; Buxton, 1994). By the time children end their teen years, knowing their own identities and values, separated psychologically from their parents, and possibly out of the house, they feel free to tell others they have a gay or lesbian parent without regard to social reactions (Buxton, 1994; Lynch, 1993; Pennington, 1987).

SEXUAL ORIENTATION

The final and most sensitive issue is what the chances are of a child's becoming gay or lesbian by living full time or part time with the gay or lesbian parent. Research figures are unreliable because most studies are small, homogeneous convenience samples. The number of postpubertal children examined is even smaller. Furthermore, because of the difficulty of calculating the prevalence of homosexuality, no reliable norm exists.

Percentages of children who might be or did turn out to be gay or lesbian vary from study to study. All adolescent children in Rees's (1979) study were heterosexual, while Paul's (1986) sample of 34 adult children included two bisexual and two gay sons, three lesbian daughters, and one daughter who was "unsure." Green's study (1978) of 21 children of lesbian and heterosexual mothers identified one child who demonstrated a degree of deviant psychosexual development. In Huggins's study (1989) of 36 adolescent children, one child of a heterosexual mother identified as homosexual. The Gottman (1989) study found 16% of 35 adolescent daughters in her convenience sample self-identified as lesbian.

Golombok and her team (1983) found that one of nine postpubertal children showed signs of a homosexual orientation. In the follow-up study of 46 of the original 75 children, only children of the lesbian mothers had thought about or pursued same-sex relationships but only 2 of the 17 daughters of lesbian mothers self-identified as lesbian, had lesbian relationships, and expressed a commitment toward future lesbian relationships (Tasker & Golombok, 1997). However, the study found no difference in same-sex attraction (such as "crushes") reported by the children of either lesbian or heterosexual mothers. These findings suggest that same-sex attraction does not necessarily lead to sexual relationships or identity and that relationships do not automatically lead to homosexual orientation. These figures are viewed with caution, however, since the sample is small (the lesbian mother sample had 17 young adult daughters compared with 9 in the heterosexual mother group), and the young adult respondents do not represent those who did not participate.

Regarding children of gay fathers, Bailey and coworkers (Bailey, Bobrow, Wolfe, & Mikach, 1995) conducted the only study of adult sons and found that out of 43 adult sons, self-selected out of a possible 82, of 55 gay or bisexual fathers, 6 rated themselves as nonheterosexual and 4 were rated as such by their fathers. In B. Miller's study (1979) of 27 daughters and 21 sons of gay fathers, one son and three daughters were reported to be gay. Among 25 children of 18 fathers studied by Bozett (1981), no postpubertal child was homosexual. Among 19 children in another study, two sons reported being gay and one daughter bisexual (Bozett, 1987a). Two of the 26 divorced wives of gay men in Hays' (1989) study reported having a gay son and one had a lesbian daughter.

My own longitudinal study suggests that diverse variables are linked to a child's coming out and that where a child lives is not a key factor. Of four daughters whose fathers were gay and who self-identified as lesbian or bisexual as adults, the bisexual daughter had lived with her heterosexual mother until moving to her father's home at sixteen and, of the three lesbians, one lived with her mother (who later came out as lesbian) until a young adult, and the other two lived with married parents (mother and bisexual father and mother and closeted gay father).

The figures considered together, prove little about how living with a gay or lesbian parent affects a child's sexual orientation, except that the vast majority of such youngsters turned out to be heterosexual. All the children were biologically related to their parents, and only one interview study of lesbian mothers reports lesbian siblings (Rafkin, 1987). The more important concern of most parents interviewed, heterosexual and homosexual, is that the children develop into mature, responsible adults and, if they turn out to be homosexual, they need not repress or hide their sexual orientation.

CONCLUSION

The research, despite limitations of methodology, sampling, uncontrolled variables, lack of control groups or replication, provides a fairly consistent picture of gay and lesbian families. Taken as a whole, the findings, both empirical and qualitative, do not demonstrate any significantly damaging outcome on children's development from living with or visiting their gay or lesbian parent.

More significant are positive outcomes from interactions between gay and lesbian parents and their children. Parent behaviors and family interactions that create the home environment seem little different from those of nongay families undergoing postdivorce readjustment. Most children appear confident, sensitive, and resilient as they deal with the unique problems and challenges of having a homosexual parent. Negative community attitudes toward the homosexuality of their parents that reflect on them, while hurtful in the short run, appear not to create long-term damage to children's self-esteem or relationships, but rather to provoke the development of constructive coping and sensitive social skills. Moreover, concerns about having a gay or lesbian parent and upsets from antigay community attitudes impact them regardless of the parent with whom they reside.

However exploratory and limited, the findings describe the experience of real-life children and their parents. Since many samples are drawn from areas with large concentrations of gay and lesbian individuals, the data yield at least a descriptive picture of possibly the greatest proportion of parents. The picture is incomplete and the findings tentative, but, given the cross-referencing of the data, it might be well not to reject the findings totally out of hand.

Much more research is needed. The studies do not reveal any adverse effects of gay and lesbian parenting, yet they do not prove that there are none. We do not know much about parents who are not members of committed gay father or lesbian mother groups or about those who live outside major metropolitan areas and who are members of different ethnic, socioeconomic, or educational populations. We do not know about other children whose feelings and stresses have not been heard. We may never know all the relevant variables, since research in child development and sexuality continue to be in such flux and it is difficult if not impossible to gather a representative or random sample of all gay and lesbian parents. What is possible and needed is a longitudinal study, conducted by a team of researchers from several disciplines, and a research design that combines both quantitative and qualitative methods to examine the actual lives of a large, more diverse sample of divorced gay and lesbian parents and their children, including all significant variables of parent-child interactions.

In the meantime, there is enough evidence of expected normalcy in key developmental dimensions for children living and interacting with their gay or lesbian parents in postdivorce homes that custody deliberations can, with some degree of confidence, focus on questions of parent fitness and the best interests of the children, irrespective of the sexual orientation of either parent.

REFERENCES

Agbayewa, M. (1984). Fathers in the newer family forms: Male or female? *Canadian Journal of Psychiatry, 29*(5), 402–406.

Ainsworth, M. D. S. (1982). Attachment: Retrospect and prospect. In C. M. Parkes & J. Steenson-Hinde (Eds.), *The place of attachment in human behavior* (pp. 3–30). New York: Basic Books.

American Psychiatric Association. (1994). *Diagnostic and statistical manual of mental disorders* (4th ed.). Washington, DC: Author.

Baggett, C. R. (1992). Sexual orientation: Should it affect child custody rulings? *Law & Psychology Review, 16,* 189–200.

Bailey, J. M., Bobrow, D., Wolfe, M., & Mikach, S. (1995). Sexual orientation of adult sons of gay fathers. *Developmental Psychology, 31,* 12–129.

Bailey, J. M., & Pillard, R. C. (1991). A genetic study of male sexual orientation. *Archives of General Psychiatry, 48,* 1089–1096.

Bailey, J. M., Pillard, R. C., Neal, M. C., & Azyer, Y. (1993). Herritable factors influence sexual orientation in women. *Archives of General Psychiatry, 50,* 217–223.

Bailey, J. M., & Zucker, K. J. (1994). Childhood sex-typed behavior and sexual orientation: A conceptual analysis and quantitative review. *Developmental Psychology, 31,* 43–55.

Bandura, A. (1969). Social learning theory of identification processes. In D. Goslin (Ed.), *Handbook of socialization theory and research.* Chicago: Rand McNally.

Baptiste, D. A. (1987a). The gay and lesbian stepparent family. In F. Bozett (Ed.), *Gay and lesbian parents* (pp. 112–137). New York: Praeger.

Baptiste, D. A. (1987b). Psychotherapy with gay/lesbian couples and their children in "stepfamilies": Challenge for marriage and family therapists. *Journal of Homosexuality, 14*(1/2), 223–238.

Barret, R. L., & Robinson, B. E. (1990). *Gay fathers.* Lexington, MA: Lexington Books.

Barret, R. L., & Robinson, B. E. (1994). Gay dads. In A. E. Gottfried & A. W. Gottfried (Eds.), *Redefining families: Implications for children's development* (pp. 157–170). New York: Plenum Press.

Beall, A. E., & Sternberg, R. E. (Eds.). (1993). *The psychology of gender.* New York: Guilford Press.

Belcastro, P. A., Gramlich, T., Nicholson, T., Price, J., & Wilson, R. (1993). A review of data-based studies addressing the effects of homosexual parenting on children's sexual and social functioning. *Journal of Divorce and Remarriage, 20*(1/2), 105–122.

Bell, A. P., & Weinberg, M. S. (1978). *Homosexualities: A study of diversity among men and women.* New York: Simon & Schuster.

Bell, A. P., Weinberg, M. S., & Hammersmith, S. K. (1981). *Sexual preference: Its development in men and women.* Bloomington: Indiana University Press.

Benkov, L. (1994). *Reinventing the family: The emerging story of lesbian and gay parents.* New York: Crown.

Bieber, I. (1988). Introduction. In I. Bieber (Ed.), *Homosexuality: A psychoanalytic theory.* Northvale, NJ: Aronson.

Bigner, J. J., & Bozett, F. W. (1990). Parenting by gay fathers. *Marriage and Family Review, 14*(3/4), 155–175.

Bigner, J. J., & Jacobsen, R. B. (1989a). Parenting behaviors of homosexual and heterosexual fathers. *Journal of Homosexuality, 18*(1/2) 173–186.

Bigner, J. J., & Jacobsen, R. B. (1989b). The value of children to gay and heterosexual fathers. *Journal of Homosexuality, 18*(1/2), 163–173.

Bigner, J. J., & Jacobsen, R. B. (1992). Adult responses to children's behavior and attitudes toward fathering: Gay and nongay fathers. *Journal of Homosexuality, 23*(3), 99–112.

Blumstein, P., & Schwartz, P. (1983). *American couples: Money, work, and sex.* New York: Morrow.

Bozett, F. W. (1980). Gay fathers: How and why they disclose their homosexuality to their children. *Family Relations, 29*(2), 173–179.

Bozett, F. W. (1981). Gay fathers: Evolution of the gay-father identity. *American Journal of Orthopsychiatry, 51*(3), 552–559.

Bozett, F. W. (1987a). Children of gay fathers. In F. W. Bozett (Ed.), *Gay and lesbian parents* (pp. 39–57). New York: Praeger.

Bozett, F. W. (Ed.). (1987b). *Gay and lesbian parents.* New York: Praeger.

Bozett, F. W. (1987c). Gay and lesbian parents: Future perspectives. In F. W. Bozett (Ed.), *Gay and lesbian parents* (pp. 231–236). New York: Praeger.

Bozett, F. W. (1988). Gay fatherhood. In P. Brownstein & C. P. Cowan (Eds.), *Fatherhood today: Men's changing role in the family* (pp. 214–235). New York: Wiley.

Bozett, F. W. (1989). Gay fathers: A review of literature. *Journal of Homosexuality, 18*(1/2), 137–162.

Bozett, F. W., & Sussman, M. B. (1990). Homosexuality and family relations: Views and research issues. *Marriage & Family Review, 14*(3/4), 1–8.

Brown, D. G. (1956). Sex-role preference in young children. *Psychological Monographs, 70*(14, Whole No. 421).

Buxton, A. P. (1994). *The other side of the closet: The coming-out crisis for straight spouses and families, revised and expanded.* New York: Wiley.

Cameron, P., & Cameron, K. (1997). Homosexual parents. *Adolesence, 31,* 727–776.

Cameron, P., & Coburn, W. (1986). Child molestation and homosexuality. *Psychological Reports, 58,* 327–337.

Casper, V., Schultz, S., & Wickens, E. (1992). Breaking the silences: Lesbian and gay parents and the schools. *Teachers College Record, 94*(1), 109–137.

Cohler, B., & Galatzer-Levy, R. M. (in press). *Gay and lesbian lives.* Chicago: University of Chicago Press.

Cramer, D. (1986). Gay parents and their children: A review of research and practical implications. *Journal of Counseling & Development, 64*(8), 504–507.

D'Augelli, A. R., & Patterson, C. J. (Eds.). (1995). *Lesbian, gay, and bisexual identities over the lifespan: Psychological perspectives.* New York: Oxford University Press.

Deevey, S. (1989). When Mom or Dad comes out: Helping adolescents cope with homophobia. *Journal of Psychosocial Nursing, 27*(10) 33–36.

Dunne, E. J. (1987). Helping gay fathers come out to their children. *Journal of Homosexuality, 14*(1/2) 213–222.

Erikson, E. (1950). *Childhood and society* (pp. 247–274). New York: Norton.

Falk, P. J. (1989). Lesbian mothers—Psychosocial assumptions in family law. *American Psychologist, 44*(6), 941–947.

Falk, P. J. (1994). The gap between psychosocial assumptions and empirical research in lesbian-mother child custody cases. In A. E. Gottfried & A. W. Gottfried (Eds.), *Redefining families: Implications for children's development* (pp. 131–156). New York: Plenum Press.

Flaks, D. E., Ficher, I., Masterpasqua, F., & Joseph, G. (1995). Lesbians choosing motherhood: A comparative study of lesbian and heterosexual parents and their children: Sexual orientation and human development [Special issue]. *Developmental Psychology, 31*(1), 105–114.

Fowler, J. G. (1995). Homosexual parents: Implications for custody cases. *Family & Conciliation Courts Review, 33*(3), 361–376.

Freud, S. (1953). Three essays on the theory of sexuality. In J. Strachey (Ed. & Trans.), *The standard edition of the complete psychological works of Sigmund Freud* (Vol. 7, pp. 125–263). London: Hogarth. (Original work published 1905)

Gantz, J. (1982). *Whose child cries: Children of gay parents talk about their lives.* Rolling Hills Estates, CA: Jalmar Press.

Gibbs, E. D. (1988). Psychosocial development of children raised by lesbian mothers: A review of research. *Women and Therapy, 8,* 65–75.

Golombok, S., Spencer, A., & Rutter, M. (1983). Children in lesbian and single-parent households: Psychosexual and psychiatric appraisal. *Journal of Child Psychology and Psychiatry & Allied Disciplines, 24*(4), 551–572.

Golombok, S., & Tasker, F. (1994). Children in lesbian and gay families: Theories and evidence. *Annual Review of Sex Research, 5,* 73–100.

Gonsiorek, J. C., & Weinrich, J. D. (1991). The definition and scope of sexual orientation. In J. C. Gonsiorek & J. D. Weinrich (Eds.), *Homosexuality: Research implications for public policy* (pp. 1–12). Newbury Park, CA: Sage.

Goodman, B. (1973). The lesbian mother. *American Journal of Orthopsychiatry, 43,* 283–284.

Gottman, J. S. (1989). Children of gay and lesbian parents. *Marriage & Family Review, 14*(3/4), 177–196.

Gottsfield, R. L. (1985). Child custody and sexual lifestyle. *Conciliation Courts Review, 23*(1), 43–46.

Green, G. D., & Bozett, F. W. (1991). Lesbian mothers and gay fathers. In J. C. Gonsiorek & J. D. Weinrich (Eds.) *Homosexuality: Research implications for public policy* (pp. 97–121). Newbury Park, CA.

Green, R. (1975). *Sexual identity conflict in children and adults.* Baltimore: Penguin.

Green, R. (1978). Sexual identity of 37 children raised by homosexual or transsexual parents. *American Journal of Psychiatry, 135*(6), 692–697.

Green, R. (1982). The best interests of the child with a lesbian mother. *Bulletin of the American Academy of Psychiatry and the Law, 10*(1), 7–15.

Green, R. (1985). Gender identity in childhood and later sexual orientation: Follow up of 70 males. *American Journal of Psychiatry, 42,* 339–341.

Green, R. (1986). Lesbian mothers and their children: A comparison with solo parent heterosexual mothers and their children. *Archives of Sexual Behavior, 15*(2), 167–184.

Green, R., Mandel, J. B., Hotvedt, M. E., Gray, J., & Smith, L. (1986). Lesbian mothers and their children: A comparison with solo parent heterosexual mothers and their children. *Archives of Sexual Behavior, 15*, 167–184.

Groth, A. N., & Birnbaum, J. (1978). Adult sexual orientation and attraction to under-age persons. *Archives of Sexual Behavior, 7*, 175–181.

Hall, M. (1978). Lesbian families: Cultural and clinical issues. *Social Work, 23*, 380–385.

Harris, M. B., & Turner, P. H. (1986). Gay and lesbian parents. *Journal of Homosexuality, 12*, 101–113.

Hays, D., & Samuels, A. (1989). Heterosexual women's perceptions of their marriages to bisexual or homosexual men. *Journal of Homosexuality, 18*, 81–101.

Hoeffer, B. (1981). Children's acquisition of sex-role behavior in lesbian-mother families. *American Journal of Orthopsychiatry, 51*, 536–544.

Hotvedt, M. E., & Mandel, J. B. (1982). Children of lesbian mothers. In W. Paul, J. D. Weinrich, J. C. Gonsiorek, & M. Hotvedt (Eds.), *Homosexuality: Social, psychological, and biological issues* (pp. 275–285). Beverly Hills, CA: Sage.

Huggins, S. L. (1989). A comparative study of self-esteem of adolescent children of divorced lesbian mothers and divorced heterosexual mothers. *Journal of Homosexuality, 18*(1/2), 123–135.

Humphrey, M., & Humphrey, H. (1988). *Families with a difference: Varieties of surrogate parenthood.* London, England: Routledge & Kegan Paul.

Javaid, G. A. (1983). The sexual development of the adolescent daughter of a homosexual mother. *Journal of the American Academy of Child Psychiatry, 22*, 196–201.

Kinsey, A. C., Pomeroy, W. B., & Martin, E. (1948). *Sexual behavior in the human male.* Philadelphia: Saunders.

Kinsey, A. C., Pomeroy, W. B., & Martin, E. (1953). *Sexual behavior in the human female.* Philadelphia: Saunders.

Kirkpatrick, M. (1987). Clinical implications of lesbian mother studies. *Journal of Homosexuality, 14*(1/2), 201–211.

Kirkpatrick, M., Smith, C., & Roy, R. (1981). Lesbian mothers and their children: A comparative survey. *American Journal of Orthopsychiatry, 51*(3), 545–551.

Kleber, D. J., Howell, R. J., & Tibbits-Keber, A. L. (1986). The impact of parental homosexuality in child custody cases: A review of literature. *Bulletin of the American Academy of Psychiatry and the Law, 14*, 81–87.

Koppitz, E. M. (1968). *Psychological evaluation of children's human figure drawings.* New York: Grune & Stratton.

Kweskin & Cook (1992). Data generated by research. In W. Dynes & S. Donaldson (Eds.), Homosexuality: Discrimination, criminology, and the law. *Studies in Homosexuality, 6*, 323–329. (Reprinted from Kweskin & Cook, 1982)

Lamb, M. E. (1988). The father's role in the infant's social world: Mother/child: Father/child relationships. In J. A. Stevens & M. Matthews (Eds.), *National association of young children* (pp. 87–108). Washington, DC: National Association of Young Children.

Laumann, E. O., Gagnon, J. H., Michael, R. T., & Michaels, S. (1994). *The social organization of sexuality: Sexual practices in the United States* (pp. 283–320). Chicago: University of Chicago Press.

LeVay, S. (1991). A difference in hypothalamic structure between heterosexual and homosexual men. *Science, 258*, 1034–1037.

Lewin, E. (1984). Lesbianism and motherhood: Implications for child custody. In T. Darty & S. Potter (Eds.), *Women-identified women* (pp. 163–183). Palo Alto, CA: Mayfield.

Lewin, E., & Lyons, T. A. (1982). Everything in its place: The coexistence of lesbianism and motherhood. In W. Paul, J. D. Weinrich, J. C. Gonsiorek, & M. E. Hotvedt (Eds.), *Homosexuality: Social, psychological, and biological issues* (pp. 249–273). Beverly Hills, CA: Sage.

Lewis, K. G. (1980). Children of lesbians: Their point of view. *Social Work, 25,* 198–203.

Lott-Whitehead, L., & Tully, C. T. (1992). The family lives of lesbian mothers. *Smith College Studies in Social Work, 63,* 265–280.

Louis, A. J. (1986). Homosexual parent families: Gay parents, partners, and their children. *Dissertation Abstracts International, 46*(9-A), 27–29.

Lynch, S. (1993). *Fags, dykes, and kids: A guidebook for daughters and sons of lesbians and gay men.* Unpublished senior thesis, Simon's Rock College of Bard, Great Barrington, MA.

Lyons, T. A. (1983). Lesbian mothers' custody fear. Women changing therapy: New assessments, value and strategies in feminist therapy [Special issue]. *Women and Therapy, 2*(2/3), 231–240.

Mahler, M., Pine, F., & Bergman, A. (1975). *The psychological birth of a human infant: Symbiosis and individuation.* New York: Basic Books.

Martin, A. (1993). *The gay and lesbian parenting handbook.* New York: HarperCollins.

Mayadas, N. S., & Duehn, W. (1976). Children in gay families: An investigation of services. *Homosexual Counseling Journal, 3,* 70–83.

McCandlish, M. (1987). Against all odds: Lesbian family dynamics. In F. W. Bozett (Ed.), *Gay and lesbian parents* (pp. 23–26). New York: Praeger.

Miller, B. (1979a). Gay fathers and their children. *The Family Coordinator, 28,* 544–552.

Miller, B. (1979b). Unpromised paternity: Lifestyles of gay fathers. In M. Levine (Ed.), *Gay men: The sociology of male homosexuality* (pp. 239–252). New York: Harper & Row.

Miller, J. A., Jacobsen, R. B., & Bigner, J. J. (1981). The child's home environment for lesbian vs. heterosexual mothers: A neglected area of research. *Journal of Homosexuality, 7,* 49–56.

Moberly, E. R. (1983). *Psychogenesis: Early development of gender identity.* London: Routledge & Kegan Paul.

Money, J. (1988). *Gay, straight, or in-between: The sexology of erotic orientation.* New York: Oxford University Press.

Money, J., & Ehrhard, A. A. (1972). *Man and woman, boy and girl: The differentiation and dimorphism of gender identity from conception to maturity.* Baltimore: Johns Hopkins University Press.

Moser, C., & Auerback, S. (1987, July–August). Groups for the wives of gay and bisexual men. *Social Work,* 321–325.

Moses, A. E., & Hawkins, R. O. (1982). *Counseling lesbian women and gay men: A life issue approach.* St. Louis: Mosby.

Mucklow, B. M., & Phelan, G. K. (1979). Lesbian and traditional mothers' responses to adult response to child behavior and self-concept. *Psychological Reports, 44,* 880–882.

Nicolosi, J. (1991). *Reparative therapy of male homosexuality: A new clinical approach.* Northvale, NJ: Aronson.

Nungesser, L. G. (1980). Theoretical basis for research on the acquisition of social sex roles by children of lesbian mothers. *Journal of Homosexuality, 5*(3), 177–187.

O'Connell, A. (1990). Voices from the heart: The developmental impact of a mothers' lesbianism on her adolescent children. *Smith College Studies in Social Work, 63,* 281–299.

Osman, S. (1972). My stepfather is a she. *Family Process, 11,* 209–218.

Ostrow, E. (1977). *Gay and straight parents: What about the children?* Unpublished bachelors's thesis, Hampshire College, Amherst, MA.

Pagelow, M. D. (1980). Heterosexual and lesbian single mothers: A comparison of problems, coping, and solutions. *Journal of Homosexuality, 5,* 198–204.

Parker, R. G., & Gagnon, J. H. (Eds.). (1995). *Conceiving sexuality: Approaches to sex research in a postmodern world.* New York: Routledge & Kegan Paul.

Patterson, C. J. (1992). Children of lesbian and gay parents. *Child Development, 63,* 1025–1042.

Patterson, C. J. (1994). Children of the lesbian baby-boom: Behavioral adjustment, self-concepts, and sex-role identity. In B. Greene & G. Herek (Eds.), *Lesbian and gay psychology: Theory, research, and clinical applications* (pp. 156–175). Beverly Hills, CA: Sage.

Patterson, C. J. (1995a). Families of the lesbian baby boom: Parents' division of labor and children's adjustment. *Developmental Psychology, 31*(1), 115–123.

Patterson, C. J. (1995b). Lesbian mothers, gay fathers, and their children. In A. R. D'Augelli & C. J. Patterson (Eds.), *Lesbian, gay, and bisexual identities over the lifespan: Psychological perspectives* (pp. 262–290). New York: Oxford University Press.

Paul, J. (1986). *Growing up with a gay, lesbian or bisexual parent: An exploratory study of experiences and perceptions.* Unpublished dissertation, University of California, Berkeley.

Pennington, S. B. (1987). Children of lesbian mothers. In F. W. Bozett (Ed.), *Gay and lesbian parents* (pp. 58–74). New York: Praeger.

Polikoff, N. (1986). Lesbian mothers, lesbian families: Legal obstacles, legal challenges. *Review of Law and Social Change, 14*(4), 907–914.

Puryear, D. (1983). *A comparison between the children of lesbian mothers and the children of heterosexual mothers.* Unpublished doctoral dissertation, California School of Professional Psychology, Berkeley.

Rafkin, L. (1987). *Different daughters: A book by mothers of lesbians.* San Francisco: Cleis Press.

Rafkin, L. (Ed.). (1990). *Different mothers: Sons and daughters of lesbians talk about their lives.* San Francisco: Cleis Press.

Rand, C., Graham, D. L., & Rawlings, E. I. (1982). Psychological health and factors the court seeks to control in lesbian mother custody trials. *Journal of Homosexuality, 8*(1), 27–39.

Rees, R. L. (1979). A comparison of children of lesbian and single heterosexual mothers on three measures of socialization. *Dissertation Abstracts International,* (Section B:3418).

Riddle, D., & Arguelles, M. (1981). Children of gay parents: Homophobia's victims. In *Children of separation and divorce* (pp. 174–197). New York: Van Nostrand-Reinhold.

Riddle, D. I. (1978). Relating to children: Gays as role models. *Journal of Social Issues, 34,* 38–58.

Rivera, R. R. (1991). Legal issues in gay and lesbian parenting. In F. W. Bozett (Ed.), *Gay and lesbian parents* (pp. 199–227). New York: Praeger.

Robinson, B., & Skeen, P. (1982). Sex-role orientation of gay fathers versus gay nonfathers. *Perceptual and Motor Skills, 55,* 1055–1059.

Rohrbaugh, J. B. (1992). Lesbian families: Clinical issues and theoretical implications. *Professional Psychology–Research & Practice, 23*(6) 467–473.

Ross, J. L. (1988). Challenging boundaries: An adolescent in a homosexual family. *Journal of Family Psychology, 2*(2), 227–240.

Ross, M. (1983). *The married homosexual male.* Boston: Routledge & Kegan Paul.

Roy, S., & Cook, A. S. (1982). Heterosexual and homosexual mothers' self-described sex-role behavior and ideal sex-role behavior in children. *Sex Roles, 8,* 967–974.

Saghir, M. T., & Robins, E. (1973). *Male and female homosexuality: A comprehensive investigation.* Baltimore: Williams and Wilkins.

Scallen, R. M. (1981). An investigation of paternal attitudes and behavior in homosexual and heterosexual fathers. *Dissertations Abstract International, 41,* 3809B.

Schulenberg, J. (1985). *Gay parenting: A complete guide for gay men and lesbians with children.* New York: Anchor.

Sigelman, C. K., Howell, J. L., Cornell, D. P., Cutright, J. D., & Dewey, J. C. (1991). Courtesy stigma: The social implications of associating with a gay person. *Journal of Social Psychology, 131,* 45–56.

Simon, W., & Gagnon, J. H. (1987). A sexual scripts approach. In J. H. Geer & W. T. O'Donoghue (Eds.), *Theories of sexuality* (pp. 363–383). London: Plenum Press.

Socarides, C. W. (1990). Homosexuality: A psychoanalytic clarification. In C. Socarides & V. Volken (Eds.), *Homosexuality: Reality, fantasy and the arts.* Madison, CT: International University Press.

Steckel, A. (1987). Psychosocial development of children of lesbian mothers. In F. W. Bozett (Ed.), *Gay and lesbian parents* (pp. 75–85). New York: Praeger.

Steinhorn, A. (1982). Lesbian mothers—the invisible minority: Role of the mental health worker. *Women and Therapy, 1*(4), 35–48.

Strommen, E. F. (1989). "You're a what?": Family member reactions to the disclosure of homosexuality. *Journal of homosexuality, 18,* 37–58.

Suseoff, S. (1985). Assessing children's best interests: When child of gay or lesbian: Toward a rational custody standard. *UCLA Law Review, 852,* 882.

Tasker, F., & Golombok, S. (1997). *Growing up in a lesbian family: Effects on child development.* New York: Guilford.

Turner, P. H., Scadden, L., & Harris, M. B. (1990). Parenting in gay and lesbian families. *Journal of Gay and Lesbian Psychotherapy, 1*(3), 55–66.

United States Bureau of the Census. (1995). *Statistical abstracts of the United States* (117th ed., p. 15). Washington, DC: US Government Printing Office.

Weekes, R. B., Derdeyn, A. P., & Langman, M. (1975). Two cases of children of homosexuals. *Child Psychiatry and Human Development, 6,* 26–32.

West, R., & Turner, L. H. (1995). Communication in lesbian and gay families: Building a descriptive base. In T. J. Socha & G. H. Stamp (Eds.), *Parents, children and communication: Frontiers of theory and research* (pp. 147–169). Mahwah, NJ: Erlbaum.

Whitlin, W. (1983). Homosexuality and child custody: A psychiatric viewpoint. *Conciliation Courts Reviews, 21*(1), 77–79.

Whitman, F. (1977). Childhood indicators of male homosexuality. *Archives of Sexual Behavior, 6,* 2.

Wyers, N. (1987, March/April). Homosexuality in the family: Lesbian and gay spouses. *Social Work,* 143–148.

Zuger, B. (1989). Homosexuality in families of boys with early effeminate behavior: An epidemiological study. *Archives of Sexual Behavior, 18*(2), 155–166.

CHAPTER 17

Assessing Sexual Abuse Allegations in Divorce, Custody, and Visitation Disputes

JADE McGLEUGHLIN, SUSANNE MEYER, and JOHN BAKER

I NCREASING PUBLIC AWARENESS of allegations of sexual abuse emerging in disputes over divorce custody and visitation has ignited an impassioned debate about the veracity of sexual abuse allegations in those contexts. This debate is lodged in a larger discourse about the prevalence of child sexual abuse in our society, whether interviewers contaminate children's accounts and/or elicit false disclosures through leading and suggestive interviewing techniques, whether parents frequently make false allegations to alienate the other parent from the children, and whether memories of abuse are repressed and later recovered. While the public debate rages, little empirical data support either side of this increasingly polarized dispute.

This chapter reviews what is known about the prevalence and validity of sexual abuse allegations in the context of divorce/custody/visitation disputes. Key issues are raised that must be considered when assessing these allegations and illustrate the dilemmas faced by professionals attempting to determine the desirability of contact between a child and the allegedly abusive parent following a sexual abuse allegation. Using the existing research and clinical literature on divorce and sexual abuse, we examine whether sexual abuse allegations are rampant in divorce cases, and whether evaluators can accurately assess the credibility of such allegations. We then describe guidelines for judging the adequacy of an evaluation and criteria that must be considered to differentiate between the effects of sexual abuse and the impact of high-conflict divorce.

In American law, custody decisions in divorce are primarily guided by criteria known as "the best interest of the child." Children's rights take precedence over those of their parents. When the veracity of allegations is unclear, judges face a critical dilemma choosing between returning a child to a possibly abusive parent or rupturing a parent-child relationship. The judicial process often grinds to a halt while the judge seeks the consultation of a guardian ad litem, expert evaluator, or mental health professional. Since the stakes are so high, the authors agree with Bresee and coworkers (Bresee, Stearns, Bess, & Packer, 1986) that "an allegation of child abuse is clear evidence that the child is at risk, whether or not the allegation can be proved." While a valid allegation has obvious implications for the future of the child's relationship with the abusive parent, a false allegation needs to be understood in the context of what it signifies about the conflict between the parents. Assessment of an allegation can be long and arduous, and yield inconclusive findings with grave implications for children.

Mental health professionals are increasingly called on to make recommendations regarding visitation and custody of children in cases involving sexual abuse allegations because there is no coherent body of empirically based data on which evaluators can base their decision making. Instead, they are forced to integrate research data from other domains. For example, as discussed elsewhere in this volume, there is a body of research which examines the psychological impact of divorce on children at various ages and stages of development and the effects of high-conflict divorce on children. Similarly there is research on the psychological impact of sexual abuse on children. Studies by Briere (1988) and Browne and Finkelhor (1986) show the immediate and long-term sequella of child sexual abuse in repeated well-designed studies characterized by large sample sizes and longitudinal data.

However, research examining allegations of sexual abuse within a divorce/ custody context is just beginning to emerge. Although there is some research on the incidence of true and false allegations in divorce cases, empirical research examining "false allegations" has been characterized by small and biased samples. Moreover, there are major flaws in the grouping of cases—unsubstantiated cases are all lumped together whether they include a parent's honest suspicion, which is unfounded; a child's inability to make a clear disclosure; or a deliberately "false" or fictitious allegation. This lack of differentiation erroneously inflates the prevalence of false allegations, and little is known about the actual breakdown of cases among these three categories.

When there is no finding of sexual abuse, a child's relationship with the accused parent may nonetheless have been compromised. There are no empirical data on children who lose a parent through unfounded allegations of sexual abuse. In those few cases where false allegations were deliberate and malicious, not based on well-intended misinterpretations of the child's behavior or statements, the child is placed at risk by the allegations themselves.

In the following sections, research on the frequency with which sexual abuse allegations arise in custody/visitation disputes is reviewed. Subsequent sections review research on the accuracy of findings in sexual abuse evaluations and on differentiating the effects of sexual abuse from the impact of divorce on children. Finally, we suggest guidelines for evaluating children and families in these situations, and issues to be considered when planning visitation with parents accused of having sexually abused a child.

HOW COMMON ARE SEXUAL ABUSE ALLEGATIONS IN THE CONTEXT OF DIVORCE/CUSTODY/VISITATION DISPUTES?

The media focus on a few high-profile cases in which one spouse vindictively accused the other of child sexual abuse to affect custody and visitation arrangements has led to a common perception that such situations are common. There is little empirical support for such beliefs. Several early studies demonstrated relatively high rates of "false allegations" in divorce/custody disputes. However, the data were based on small and selective samples generally drawn from the authors' clinical practice. Later samples based on larger, more representative samples revealed that the prevalence of sexual abuse allegations in divorce/custody disputes was actually quite low. Those studies will be reviewed later in this section. The prevalence of *false* allegations among these cases remains unclear.

In an early study of their own client population, Benedek and Schetky (1985) found that among 18 cases, 10 involved false allegations. Similarly, Green (1986) reported that 4 of 11 cases, were false allegations. In addition to sampling problems, these investigators failed to identify the criteria for "true" versus "false" allegations, nor did they differentiate unsubstantiated cases where concerns were warranted, but unsupported (e.g., a child makes a genuine statement about being touched in a questionable manner), from cases of deliberately false and vindictive allegations. They did note, however, that among those cases defined as false, allegations were usually made by a parent without any disclosure by the child. Despite the methodological shortcomings of these studies, the authors concluded that although false allegations are generally rare, they are more likely to occur in the context of disputes over custody and visitation.

In a more comprehensive report on a sample of cases involving sexual abuse allegations in divorce that had been referred to a large, regional child abuse evaluation center, Jones and Selig (1988) found that 14 of 20 cases were "valid" allegations of sexual abuse. One case was "uncertain" (inconclusive), another was an unsubstantiated suspicion, and four were "fictitious." Their procedures included a series of separate interviews with the child and with each parent. The authors give a detailed description of the characteristics of "valid" cases as opposed to "fictitious" ones. In those cases determined to be fictitious, the details of the child's disclosure were inconsistent, sparse, or implausible. In three of the four fictitious cases, they report that the parent making the allegation appeared prematurely convinced of the abuse and unable to entertain alternative explanations for the child's statements or presentation. In the fourth case, the allegation was made by an 11-year-old boy with a prior history of sexual abuse by a friend of his father, although he was now accusing a different adult. It is noteworthy that the authors found that the children's psychological state appeared equally compromised whether or not the allegation was valid, suggesting that the trauma of divorce conflict may be as emotionally damaging as that of sexual abuse.

Faller (1991) examined a much larger sample of 136 cases referred to a child abuse center by child protective agencies, courts, community agencies, and parents. Of the 120 cases she included in her analysis, 75% ($n = 89$) were "confirmed" cases of sexual abuse. Faller divided these cases into three categories: (1) sexual abuse precipitating the divorce; (2) abuse revealed during the divorce process; (3) abuse precipitated by divorce (e.g., occurring after the marital separation). The third category comprised the largest group, with 58% of confirmed cases falling into this category. Faller defined the remaining cases (25%, $n = 31$) either inconclusive ($n = 12$) or false ($n = 19$). Among the "false" cases, some seemed based on distorted perceptions on the part of the accusing parent, while others were based on observed behaviors of the child that might be suggestive of sexual abuse, but might also be attributed to other sources. In three of the "false" cases, sexual abuse was found to have occurred, however the perpetrator was found to be someone other than the ex-spouse. Only 3 of the 19 "false" cases were thought to be deliberate fabrications on the part of the accusing parent.

Only two studies (McIntosh & Prinz, 1993; Thoennes & Tjaden, 1990) have examined the prevalence and patterns of sexual abuse allegations in the context of divorce among unselected, unbiased, representative samples. Thoennes and Tjaden collected data from court evaluators and child protective workers in 12 cities across the United States. Participants were asked to document demographic and allegation-specific information for *all* cases of sexual abuse allegations within the sample. Of the 9,000 cases across all courts where custody was in dispute, slightly less than 2% ($n = 165$) involved allegations of sexual abuse. This percentage varied across sites. It ranged from less than 1% in one area to 8% in another. Results indicated that allegations were initiated by mothers in 67% of the cases and by fathers in 22%. Approximately half of the children in those cases involving allegations were 6 years or younger, and 65% were female. Overall, with respect to the total number of divorce-related actions in these courts, sexual abuse allegations occurred in only a very small percentage of cases.

Among cases where allegations of sexual abuse were made, evaluators were able to judge the veracity of these allegations in 129 cases. Fifty percent of these cases were believed to involve sexual abuse, and 33% were believed to be "unlikely cases" of sexual abuse. Seventeen percent were cases in which sufficient information was available, but no determination could be made as to whether abuse had occurred. The authors compared these figures with rates of validation found in general (nondivorce) samples involving sexual abuse allegations (Jones & McGraw, 1987 [53%]; Solomon, 1986 [50%]) and found that sexual abuse allegations in divorce/custody disputes are just as likely to be confirmed as sexual abuse allegations arising in other circumstances. They conclude, therefore, that a very small percentage of custody and visitation disputes involve allegations of sexual abuse, and that allegations arising in that context are as likely to be confirmed as allegations of sexual abuse arising within other contexts.

In addition to reporting on the prevalence of sexual abuse allegations, Thoennes and Tjaden (1990) found that a number of factors were related to the validation of allegations in their sample. Reports were more likely to be confirmed if the child was older, if the abuse had gone on for a longer period, if there had been a previous report of abuse, and if the allegation emerged long after the initial divorce filing. Allegations that coincided with the filing for divorce were less likely to be validated than allegations made a few years postdivorce when custody was no longer the major issue before the court. Thoennes and Tjaden did not comment on the basis for their "unlikely" cases, nor did they comment on the motives for the allegations.

Results from a study by McIntosh and Prinz (1993) of 603 cases involving custody and access in a single county in South Carolina revealed a remarkably similar prevalence of allegations of sexual abuse. During a one-year period, they found that 85 of 603 divorce cases involved disputes over custody and access. Only 3 (3%) of these contested cases involved allegations of sexual abuse. They found two additional cases of allegations of sexual abuse in noncontested cases. McIntosh and Prinz did not report on the prevalence of confirmed versus unconfirmed or indeterminate cases so their study cannot be compared with that of Thoennes and Tjaden on these variables. Their findings confirm that allegations of sexual abuse arise in a small percentage of contested divorce cases.

Thus, despite the prevailing public opinion, available research indicates a low prevalence of such allegations. Whether these allegations can be confirmed at the same rate as similar allegations arising in other contexts as Thoennes and Tjaden's (1990) study bears out, has not yet been conclusively determined. Studies to date do not tell us how often false allegations are part of a strategy of intentional efforts to gain custody or punish a spouse. These rates are difficult to determine for several reasons. First, methodological differences and poorly defined guidelines for assessing valid versus false accusations across studies make it difficult to compare prevalence rates. Second, because agencies lump together all unsubstantiated cases in assembling data, it is impossible to distinguish between qualitatively different types of false allegations. It is crucial to differentiate among (1) valid, but unfounded allegations (a child's statements or behaviors are consistent with sexual abuse, but are found to be attributable to other causes); (2) inconclusive allegations, with insufficient data to make a determination; (3) credible allegations, but with a perpetrator who is other than the accused parent; (4) false allegations (deliberate fabrications). Development and implementation of such a classification system and the systematic collection of data across large and representative samples are essential if we are to understand the relationship of sexual abuse allegations to divorce and custody cases.

HOW WELL CAN WE ASSESS SEXUAL ABUSE ALLEGATIONS?

In addition to the myths and problematic data regarding the prevalence of sexual abuse allegations in divorce cases, little is known about the accuracy of sexual abuse evaluations. Although there is common sentiment that professionals can validate sexual abuse in an accurate and reliable manner, few studies have examined these questions, and the existing data are equivocal.

Evaluating children experiencing the emotional stress of parental separation and divorce is, by itself, difficult and complicated. Combining allegations of sexual abuse with such circumstances vastly increases this complexity. Evaluation of sexual abuse allegations in the midst of parental separation and divorce is an exceedingly serious clinical challenge for mental health professionals.

To our knowledge, the evaluation of sexual abuse specifically within the context of divorce/custody disputes has not been examined empirically. The following section, therefore, will review the current literature on the accuracy of sexual abuse assessments in general. These studies may be divided into those examining the relationship between the occurrence of sexual abuse and certain child symptoms and behaviors, those examining the accuracy of child interview data to assess the presence of sexual abuse, and those that examine consensus among professionals in diagnosing the presence of sexual abuse.

SYMPTOMS AND BEHAVIORS

One method of diagnosis is to identify those symptoms and behaviors that are characteristic of sexually abused children. If sexually abused children are found to have a distinctive behavioral profile, this profile might aid in identifying those children who have been sexually abused.

In an effort to determine which emotional and behavioral problems were correlated with substantiated cases of sexual abuse, Conte, Sorenson, Fogarty, and Dalla Rosa (1991) surveyed 212 mental health professionals with expertise in child sexual abuse. Respondents identified a wide variety of behaviors. However, four indicators were most commonly identified across at least 90% of the sample. These behaviors included sexualized play, precocious or seductive behavior, excessive masturbation, and a consistent account by the child over time of alleged abuse that included pressure or coercion. Other indicators of sexual abuse identified by at least 90% of the sample included physical findings, and inappropriate sexual knowledge.

A number of research studies have been conducted to compare the behavioral characteristics of sexually abused children with those of nonabused children (Wells, McCann, Adams, Voris, & Ensign, 1995) or emotionally disturbed controls (Kolko, Moser, & Weldy, 1988). In a comprehensive review of studies examining the effects of sexual abuse on children, Kendall-Tackett, Williams, and Finkelhor (1993) reported consistent differences between sexually abused children and control groups of "normal" (nonclinical) children who had not been abused. The abused children were more likely to present with fears, nightmares, a diagnosis of posttraumatic stress disorder (PTSD), withdrawn behavior, neurotic symptoms, cruelty, delinquency, sexually inappropriate behavior, regressive behavior (including enuresis), running away, and self-injurious behavior. Abused children also scored higher on overall indexes of internalizing behavior (e.g., anxiety and depression) and externalizing behavior (e.g., aggressive and disruptive behavior).

Kendall-Tackett et al. (1993) note that although these behaviors are more characteristic of sexually abused children than of "normal" controls, they may also be more prevalent among nonabused children with emotional problems, or those exposed to other environmental stressors or traumas. In comparisons of sexually abused children and nonsexually abused, but emotionally disturbed children, Kendall-Tackett et al. found that fewer symptoms distinguished sexually abused children. However, sexually abused children were still more likely to exhibit inappropriate sexual behavior, and to qualify for a diagnosis of posttraumatic stress disorder. Among adolescents, promiscuity was also a common behavior. Although certain symptoms were more prevalent among sexually abused children, none of the symptoms were found in a majority of children, and most were exhibited by far less than half the children studied. They estimated that approximately 20% to 30% of sexually abused children are asymptomatic; they do not show any unusual pattern of symptoms or behaviors and cannot be distinguished from normal, nonabused children.

The current research on symptoms and behavior associated with sexual abuse indicates: (1) *No symptom profile is found consistently across the majority of sexually abused children;* (2) *symptoms or behavior associated with sexual abuse is found in all or most sexually abused children.* Thus, a behavioral or symptom profile of sexually abused children *cannot be delineated* for diagnosis of sexual abuse, and the presence of particular symptoms *does not provide conclusive evidence* that a child has been sexually abused. Conversely, however, the *absence of symptoms is not indicative of the absence of abuse* because at least 20% of abused children may be asymptomatic at the time of assessment. Thus, certain symptoms are associated with sexual abuse, and may indicate that abuse has occurred, however, they are not, in and of themselves, sufficient to confirm that abuse has occurred.

INTERVIEW DATA

Historically, an interview with the child has been the most commonly relied on clinical method for identifying sexual abuse in children. Clinical evaluators have shown a high degree of consensus about the characteristics of a child interview that indicate sexual abuse (Kuehnle, 1996). However, definitive assessments of the accuracy of a sexual abuse assessment following explicit disclosure are rarely possible because most acts of sexual abuse leave no physical evidence, are unobserved by witnesses, and are not revealed through confession of the offender. An interview-based assessment of sexual abuse may result in four possible outcomes:

1. An assessment may accurately determine that sexual abuse occurred (true positive).
2. It may accurately determine that no abuse occurred (true negative).
3. It may confirm sexual abuse inaccurately (false positive).
4. It may deny abuse inaccurately (false negative).

A few recent studies have attempted to examine the ability of a clinical interviewer to accurately detect the presence of sexual abuse. For example, Esplin, Houed, and Raskin (1988) developed a coding system to evaluate the accuracy of clinical interviewing in assessing abuse in cases where the alleged offender had confessed. The coding system, "Content-Based Criteria Analysis" (CBCA) used 19 criteria by which to measure the logical structure of the child's statement, including whether the statement was made spontaneously, whether it had specific as well as idiosyncratic details, and whether it indicated some degree of self-doubt, which would be natural in a child. The authors compared those abuse cases where the offender had confessed, with those considered "doubtful" because of a lack of physical evidence and/or judicial findings. (Note that this is an ambiguous category, because it most likely includes some cases of actual abuse, though there was lack of sufficient evidence to meet the legal standard.) The authors found that the confirmed cases averaged significantly higher on the CBCA system (24.8 vs. 3.6), indicating that children known to be abused exhibit the characteristics assessed by the CBCA during clinical interviewing. In a more recent study, Anson and Gully (1989) applied the CBCA to another sample of offender-confessed abuse cases. They found a much lower average score (10.4) among their sample, indicating that the CBCA may not be as useful in diagnosing sexual abuse as had been hoped. The authors noted however, that methodological differences between studies may account for the discrepancy in findings (see Faller & Corwin, 1995 for a full description of these studies).

Faller (1988) described a second coding system in her examination of 103 sexual abuse cases confirmed by an offender confession. Her coding system divided interview characteristics into three categories:

1. A description of the context in which the abuse occurred, including details about the setting of the abuse and whether the offender said anything to gain the child's cooperation.

2. An explicit description of the abuse as well as knowledge of sexual behavior beyond the child's developmental level.
3. An emotional reaction during the account that was consistent with its
   content, such as the child avoiding a discussion of the abuse or showing
   emotions such as anxiety, depression, or embarrassment.

She found that the majority (68%) of her cases contained items in all three coding categories. Her coding system accurately identified the majority of the
abused children. Still 32% of the abused children did not meet the criteria in
all three categories. The author concludes, therefore, that regardless of an interviewer's skill, some children may be unable to disclose much about their
abuse and therefore it is impossible to make accurate determinations based
solely on a child's account.

In addition to studies of interview data, analogue studies have been conducted to assess the reliability of clinical assessments of sexual abuse. These
studies differ from interview research in that they do not represent actual clinical practice, but ask study participants to make clinical assessments based on
case-study data presented by another clinician. Horner, Guyer, and Kalter (1993)
presented a detailed case description to a group of 48 professionals attending a
conference on sexual abuse in preschool children. The professionals heard an extensive case presentation by the individual who had evaluated a 3-year-old girl.
The presentation included the professional's own observations as well as police
and child protective reports, medical examinations, polygraph tests, and a second opinion sexual abuse evaluation secured by the mother. After the presentation, participants estimated the likelihood that sexual abuse had occurred, and
made recommendations for visitation/contact with the parent alleged to have
abused the child. Estimations of the likelihood of abuse were made again following a group discussion period. The authors found a great deal of variability in
the initial estimates, ranging from a low of 1% to a high of 100% probability that
abuse occurred. Among mental health professionals, the range was only slightly
smaller, from 5% to 90%. The average estimation across all participants was
approximately 50%, but was somewhat lower (43%) in the group of clinical
psychologists ($n = 11$), and somewhat higher (63%) among clinical social workers
($n = 11$). The group consensus increased considerably after the group discussion
period, and the estimation of the likelihood of an occurrence of sexual abuse decreased to about 29%. Recommendations about contact also varied, with most
recommending that contact with the accused parent be supervised pending further evaluation of allegations.

The authors concluded, "In cases of alleged sexual abuse, clinical experts
have yet to demonstrate that they possess any unique ability to find the truth,
to determine the credibility of persons giving testimony, or to divine either
the past or future from immediate clinical observations and facts" (p. 930).
They therefore recommended that courts be cautious in relying on the findings of clinical experts regarding sexual abuse allegations in the context of

custody disputes. A number of limitations to the study however, including over-generalizing, make such strong conclusions highly problematic. For example, this was not a sample of sexual abuse experts or mental health professionals (less that half the sample qualified for this designation). Many participants were probably attending the conference to *learn* about sexual abuse and fewer still would meet the criteria for expert testimony. In addition, only one, highly ambiguous case study was presented, which included inconsistent "disclosures" by the child, a situation that would tend to lower agreement in any event. Thus, the results of this study are important in that they indicate that the ability of professionals to assess sexual abuse is limited in some cases and should not be presumed, but neither should it be discounted entirely as recommended by the authors. Assessment of sexual abuse is a specialty area requiring advanced levels of training.

Research and clinical experience demonstrate that assessment of sexual abuse and the standardization of evaluation techniques is complicated by the impact of developmental processes. Symptoms and behaviors consistent with sexual abuse, and the ability to identify and collect reliable interview data are influenced by the age and developmental status of the child (Kendall-Tackett et al., 1993). Thus, different assessment measures and interview formats are appropriate for different children, and these variables need to be incorporated into the research as data become available.

Currently validated, standardized, assessment protocols are not available for any age group. Researchers have begun to investigate techniques such as the cognitive interview (Geiselman et al., 1991) and narrative elaboration (Saywitz & Snyder, 1993) to enhance the completeness of children's narrative accounts. A cognitive interview protocol, a structured technique that uses memory strategies to enhance children's accounts of their experiences, is in development. Preliminary data suggest that this format increases by 20% the number of correct facts recalled, without increasing the reporting of incorrect information (Geiselman & Padilla, 1988; Geiselman, Saywitz, & Bernstein, 1991). Fisher and McCauley (1995) note that this new technique enhances children's narratives, but is less effective with younger children.

Finally any evaluation of the assessment of sexual abuse in children must address the complex controversial issue of children's suggestibility. The research to date is compelling, but equivocal. Ceci and Bruck (1993) describe pervasive methodological differences between studies, including differences in children's ages, sample size, number of misleading questions, and variable linguistic complexity, which make it difficult to draw valid conclusions about the nature and impact of children's suggestibility on evaluation of sexual abuse.

Current research on the accuracy of evaluation of child sexual abuse is promising but inconclusive. Studies show that sexual abuse can be accurately assessed by clinical interview by trained mental health professionals in a majority of cases, and that certain symptoms and behaviors are associated with experiences of abuse in children. In addition, interview research shows that certain content areas are related to accurate assessment and should therefore be used in the development of interview protocols, and integrated into clinical decision making about sexual abuse determinations. Despite these findings, however, accuracy continues to be imperfect, and cases are incorrectly identified both positively and negatively. In addition, the reliance in empirical studies on cases confirmed by offender confession or physical evidence, is problematic in that these cases represent the minority of confirmed sexual abuse cases, and may therefore be atypical among all cases of sexual abuse. Finally, the effect of developmental level on the accuracy of assessment techniques has not been sufficiently examined. Thus, improved methods and continued research on the assessment of sexual abuse allegations are needed.

CAN EVALUATORS DIFFERENTIATE BETWEEN THE EFFECTS OF SEXUAL ABUSE AND THE EFFECTS OF DIVORCE?

After discussing the difficulties in formulating a diagnosis of child sexual abuse, it is important to consider a related diagnostic question. How well can clinical evaluators distinguish between the effects of sexual abuse and the impact of a conflictual divorce on children? Considerable anxiety and tension are inherent in cases of high-conflict divorce. This section will address whether these conflicts could account for sexual abuse allegations and examines the research data on the psychological characteristics exhibited by children whose parents remain in highly conflicted postdivorce relationships.

Studies of abused children tend to use measures of specific symptoms, or they measure the frequency with which abused children received different psychiatric diagnoses. Studies of children whose parents are divorced use fewer measures and tend to rely on more broad-spectrum measures of adjustment (see Chapter 5). Comparing the numerous studies in this area is difficult because of the differences in methodology. There are no studies that directly compare sexually abused children with children of divorce.

Studies on the psychological functioning of children from divorced families show some variation in the degree of the disturbance found in the children when they are compared with children in intact families. In a longitudinal study lasting from childhood into adolescence, Hetherington, (1993) found that children from divorced and blended families showed a higher overall degree of disturbance than children from intact families. In this study, 16% to 36% of teenage children of divorce manifest psychological symptoms, depending on whether the father or mother was rating their behavior. The children showed greater disturbance in all areas measured: externalizing behaviors, internalizing behaviors, and socially competent behaviors. Amato and Keith's (1991) meta-analysis of a large number of studies of children from divorced families compared with nondivorced families found that most studies revealed differences between children from divorced families, but that the differences were small. The strongest difference was in the presence of conduct problems and academic difficulties in children from divorced families, and there were significant, but smaller differences in emotional adjustment, self-concept, and social adjustment. Studies of children from more conflicted postdivorce families reveal a much greater degree of emotional distress and behavioral disturbance than found in Amato and Keith's review. Johnston, Gonzalez, and Campbell (1987) found differences on a measure of childhood behavior problems (The Child Behavioral Checklist, total behavioral problems scale) where at least 21% of the children of high-conflict divorce had scores in the clinical range and up to 43% fell in this range if either parent's rating was accepted. This rate is 2 to 4 times that seen in a normal group of children. In addition, they found that children from more aggressive families that were also more involved in the parental conflict, had higher scores on depression, withdrawal/uncommunicative, somatic symptoms, and aggression as well as on total behavioral problems.

In a subsequent study, Johnston, Kline, and Tschann (1989) studied the effects of frequent access to the noncustodial parent and visitation on children in high-conflict divorces. The findings indicated that greater access to both parents, which required more frequent transitions, led to psychological symptoms including depression, withdrawal, and somatic symptoms as well as total behavioral problems.

These data are difficult to compare with studies of symptoms in sexually abused children, which were reviewed earlier. While similar symptoms may be observed in both sexually abused children and children of divorce, the measures are different and not comparable.

Restricting ourselves to studies that have used one particular measure (CBCL) a parental report of behavioral symptoms, both sexually abused children and children of divorce are more likely to score in the higher, "clinical" range similar to children referred for psychiatric treatment. For sexually abused children, Kendall-Tackett et al. (1993) reported that in four studies reviewed, approximately 30% of the children scored in the clinically elevated range on measures of internalizing symptoms, and 23% showed elevations on externalizing symptoms. In comparison, Hetherington (1993) found that in their sample of children of divorce, approximately 30% in divorced families showed clinically elevated scores on the overall behavior problems scale, and 29% in remarried families. These figures are strikingly similar.

Another way to compare the groups is to look at the size of the differences between these two groups and a normal control group ("effect size"). This method looks not at the percentage of children that receive elevated scores, but on the size of the differences, if they are found, between the target group (abuse or divorce) and the normal group. On this comparison, it appears that abused children show greater effects on their adjustment due to their history of abuse. The effect sizes quoted by Kendall-Tackett et al. (1993) were .38 for internalizing behavior and .32 for externalizing behavior. The equivalent effect sizes quoted by Amato and Keith (1991) were .23 for conduct problems (i.e., externalizing behavior) and .08 for psychological adjustment (similar to internalizing behavior). This comparison suggests that, although both adversely affect children, the effects of sexual abuse are stronger than the effects of divorce. Since these studies used somewhat different methods to measure effect size, these findings must be viewed with caution.

On the other hand, sexually abused children do not appear to exhibit more overall symptoms than children from high-conflict divorces. Children from high-conflict divorces, who as a group are more symptomatic than children of divorce generally, often show a great deal of anxiety, withdrawal, and depression. The increased incidence of behavioral problems would make it more difficult to distinguish them from sexually abused children on the basis of behavioral indicators alone.

Both sexually abused children and children of divorce show greater disturbance than normal controls. There is a suggestion that sexually abused children exhibit more internalizing symptoms such as anxiety and depression than children of divorce in general. This difference disappears when they are compared with children from high-conflict divorce who also show many signs of anxiety, fearfulness, and depression. In addition, there are large areas of overlap of the types of symptoms observed in sexually abused children and children of divorce: aggressive and conduct problems, depression, withdrawn behavior, and somatic symptoms. Clinically, anxious and avoidant behavior, as well as separation anxiety, are frequently seen in children from high-conflict divorce further increasing the overlap between the clinical appearance of these two groups of children.

The most distinctive symptoms between the two groups may also show overlap. Higher levels of sexualized behavior are the most distinctive characteristic of sexually abused children (Kendall-Tackett et al., 1993). However, some children who exhibit highly sexualized behavior have not been abused. Yates (1991) described four types of so-called "eroticized" behavior: (1) behavior caused by nonabusive sexual overstimulation; (2) compulsive sexual behavior; (3) behavior due to posttraumatic stress disorder; (4) learned behavior due to abusive contact. Sexualized symptoms may result from sexual abuse or other kinds of overstimulation or understimulation.

These data have significant implications for the clinical evaluation of children who are suspected of having been sexually abused while a custody dispute is ongoing. The presence of anxiety, avoidance, separation anxiety, nightmares, aggressive behavior, and somatic symptoms, either before or after a visit with the noncustodial parent, should not be assumed to be indicative of sexual abuse unless there is clear and compelling data from the child or other sources that abuse is occurring. These same symptoms could indicate, instead, the presence of severe emotional stress before or after the visits based on a fear of the eruption of parental conflict, or a fear of losing one parent or the other.

RECOMMENDED CLINICAL GUIDELINES
FOR EVALUATIONS

Many dilemmas face clinicians attempting to evaluate allegations of sexual abuse that arise in disputes over custody and visitation. These cases precipitate strong emotional reactions and may bias the evaluator. Child protective workers, mental health professionals, attorneys and judges as well, are particularly susceptible to bias when sexual abuse is alleged. Some are biased toward making false negative errors (finding no abuse when abuse did, in fact, occur) and others to making false positive errors (finding abuse when none, in fact, occurred.) Often professionals line up on one side of a case and extreme polarizations occur not only between the parties, but among the professionals. Such polarized positions make it difficult for an evaluator to remain neutral and child focused.

VULNERABILITY TO FALSE NEGATIVE ERRORS

In addition to the problems of personal bias, there is the vulnerability to procedural bias (Klawsnik, 1994) that is inherent in the expectation that children should be able to share the details of the alleged sexual abuse whenever they are interviewed. In the absence of a clear personalized statement with adequate detail, the child protective and/or legal system runs the risk of dismissing a credible allegation. Moreover, the prevailing presumption that sexually abused children are always capable of making a coherent and detailed verbal disclosure of sexual abuse is not supported by empirical data. Children cannot always make clear disclosures even when sexual abuse has occurred.

PROCESS OF DISCLOSURE

The process of disclosure often mitigates against a clear verbal statement. For some time, there has been consensus validity regarding the "Yes-No-Maybe" syndrome (MacFarlane & Krebs, 1986) previously described by Summit (1983) whereby sexually abused children characteristically vacillate between acknowledging and denying credible allegations of sexual abuse. Clinicians have historically accepted that denial (Courtois, 1988) and retraction (Faller, 1988) are part of the normal disclosure process when children become frightened or are threatened. Sorenson and Snow (1991) gathered empirical data that supports consensus validity on the process of children's disclosure. From their sample of 630 children, they culled 116 cases in which sexual abuse was confirmed as defined by either perpetrator confession (80%), criminal conviction (14%), or a diagnosis of a sexually transmitted disease (6%). Retrospective analysis of the children's accounts revealed that almost 72% of the children initially denied having been sexually abused. Only 7% of these denying children moved directly to the phase of active disclosure, which was defined as the ability to provide a detailed coherent first-person account of their experience. Seventy-eight percent of the children moved to a phase of tentative disclosure in which they appeared confused, inaccurate, uncertain, and vacillated from acknowledgment to denial. Ninety-six percent of the children went on to reconfirm their original disclosures; and 22% of children recanted valid allegations. Sorenson and Snow's findings support the notion that disclosure of sexual abuse is a dynamic process, not a one-time event and highlight the problem that virtually all investigative protocols are only effective when children are in the active phase of disclosure. A child's initial failure to provide adequate detail or a recantation may result in the dismissal of a valid disclosure.

The fact that the pattern of children's disclosures is not always congruent with the procedures relied on by investigators in the child protective and legal systems is further supported by the work of Lawson and Chaffin (1992) who examined 28 children with sexually transmitted diseases who had never disclosed sexual abuse. Fifty-seven percent of these children denied being abused during an interview with a well-trained clinician.

As Sorenson and Snow (1991) point out, issues of suggestibility, contamination, and fear of false allegations have increasingly restricted the kind of support that the clinical, protective, and investigative systems have made available to support children during the disclosure process. Klawsnik (1994) has noted that children with supportive caretakers are more likely to disclose. This is supported by Lawson and Chaffin (1992) who found that nondisclosing children were more likely to have nonbelieving mothers. Elliott and Briere (1994) in their study of 399 children noted that 50% of nondisclosing children whose abuse was confirmed via external sources had nonbelieving mothers. Despite these findings, supportive caretakers may well be viewed by the child protective system as vindictive spouses. Thus the manner in which children disclose can lead to false negative errors. The support they require to disclose sexual abuse may be viewed as biased by forensic standards.

VULNERABILITY TO FALSE POSITIVE ERRORS

There are serious limitations in the scope of many sexual abuse evaluations conducted when the allegations have emerged in divorce/custody conflicts. Evaluators often fail to consider the effects of protracted parental conflict on children when assessing allegations of sexual abuse. Furthermore, limited or brief evaluations may be leading or suggestive and may preclude the evaluator from gathering information to facilitate his or her understanding of the family dynamics and context in which a false or erroneous allegation can emerge. Finally, little consideration has been given to the uniquely polarizing effect that sexual abuse allegations have on professionals working with parties engaged in contested custody or visitation disputes.

In determining the adequacy of an evaluation and its potential usefulness, the following factors should be considered.

Qualifications of the Evaluator

Cases involving allegations of sexual abuse in the context of divorce require a level of assessment that can only be undertaken by experienced evaluators with advanced degrees in a recognized mental health discipline. Such evaluators should possess special expertise in the area of child sexual abuse including knowledge of the current literature, child development, family dynamics, cultural competency, the psychological impact of divorce and separation on children and parents, as well as knowledge and experience regarding the judicial system and forensic issues. Although the American Professional Society on the Abuse of Children (1990), the American Academy of Child and Adolescent Psychiatry (1990), and the American Academy of Pediatrics (1991) have all put forth guidelines regarding who should perform sexual abuse assessments in general, these guidelines fall short when it comes to cases of high-conflict divorce.

Role of Evaluator

The evaluator should be a fair and impartial mental health professional whose role is clear to all parties involved. Kuehnle (1996) points out that some of the most legitimate criticisms of evaluations conducted by mental health professionals have focused on individuals assuming multiple professional roles leading to conflicts of interest. To avoid role confusion, it is essential that the evaluator specifically delineate his or her role as a neutral forensic evaluator whose primary goal is to obtain uncontaminated information, who entertains multiple hypotheses for the child's presentation, and whose primary client is the judicial system. This markedly differs from the position of a clinical evaluator whose goal is most often that of assessing the child's psychological state, whose role may be that of an advocate, and whose primary client is the child and parent(s). It is impossible for a clinician to perform multiple roles simultaneously and maintain credibility. Any attempt to do so will undoubtedly compromise the outcome of the evaluation (Guidelines from the American Academy of Child and Adolescent Psychiatry [1990] and American Psychological Association's *Ethical Principles* [1992] and American Psychological Association's *Guidelines for Child Custody Evaluations in Divorce Proceedings* [1994]).

Structure of Evaluation

Sexual abuse evaluations in the context of divorce are complicated by the extreme polarization of the involved parties, which makes it difficult for an evaluator to remain neutral. Professional consensus is emerging whereby it is recommended that evaluators first establish themselves as neutral by requesting that the evaluation be court ordered. This may prevent the child from being referred for multiple interviews if one of the parties disagrees with the findings. Careful arrangements should be made to ensure that the evaluator is operating so as to avoid legal and ethical entanglements that are both distressing to the evaluator and jeopardize the outcome. Protections such as court orders for the evaluation, clear and specific guidelines about the nature and scope of the work shared in advance with all parties, and clarity about legal procedures all help ensure that the evaluator's work can be completed and avoid ensnarement into tangled unproductive situations. It is often helpful to have a guardian ad litem assigned to the case. In most states, the guardian ad litem is required to be an attorney whose task is to complete fact findings relevant to court proceedings. Attorneys functioning as guardians ad litem must work closely with a mental health professional who can collect and weigh the data as well as develop clinical impressions based on diagnostic interviewing in order to interpret the data to the court.

Models of Evaluation

Historically, there have been four models for conducting sexual abuse evaluations: (1) the child interview model; (2) parent/child observation model; (3) child observation model; (4) the comprehensive model (Everson, 1993).

Based on the assumption that false allegations were rare, most practitioners conducting sexual abuse evaluations between 1960 and 1980 utilized the child interview model whereby statements made by children were presumed reliable and therefore the child's statements were given undue weight (Kuehnle, 1996). This model, while acceptable under some conditions, does not have consensus validity when allegations of sexual abuse emerge in the context of disputes over divorce, custody, and visitation. Given the greater likelihood that children have been exposed to discussions or prevention programs about sexual abuse, children's accounts are no longer thought of as "pure" or uncontaminated and can no longer be relied on as the sole basis for determining sexual abuse.

The parent-child observation model presumes that observations of a child interacting with an allegedly abusive parent is an important source of data. However, the parent-child observation model when used in isolation has been strongly criticized. It erroneously assumes that observing the interaction between an allegedly abusive parent and a child is the most reliable source of data. While research indicates that the use of the parent-child observation model provides useful data in cases involving physically abusive parents (Ainsworth & Bell, 1970; Egeland & Farber, 1984), there is no empirical support for the assumption that observing a child and the allegedly offending parent will guarantee that the evaluator can accurately differentiate between a sexually abused and nonsexually abused child. One assessment format has been proposed (Haynes-Seman & Baumgarten, 1994), but there is no empirical support for its validity.

Very few professionals support the use of a model of interviewing children about abuse in the presence of the alleged abuser since it potentially places a child at psychological risk (Conte, Sorenson, Fogarty, & Dalla Rosa, 1991). In Conte's study using a sample of 212 experts in the field, 96% refrained from doing so (Kuehnle, 1996). Even when used as part of the comprehensive model, there is debate about the advisability of observing a parent and child during the evaluation process. Faller, Fronig, and Lipovsky (1991) question the use of this model while the APSAC Guidelines suggest it may be helpful in obtaining information about the overall quality of the parent-child relationship, but not helpful in determining whether sexual abuse occurred.

The child observation model presumes that direct interviewing of the child is less useful than long-term observation of a child's play and assumes that play will allow for the most natural expression of thoughts and feelings. However analysis of the play of both nonsexually and sexually abused children has not revealed any useful or statistically reliable data differentiating between these children. Everson and Boat (1994) suggested that observation of children's doll play is useful but cannot be the basis for any conclusion regarding sexual abuse. The child observation model is useful in evaluating sexual abuse allegations in the context of divorce custody disputes as part of the comprehensive model.

State-of-the-art sexual abuse evaluations in divorce-custody disputes require a comprehensive model whereby the evaluator assumes that multiple sources of information are essential for conducting an adequate evaluation including data obtained from collateral contacts (e.g., extended family members, friends, teachers). Subsumed under this model are all the other models (the child interview model, the child observation model, and the child-parent observation model). This model appears to have consensus validity. However, no research studies have been conducted to directly test this widely held opinion.

We propose a team model whereby one evaluator interviews the parents and another interviews the child. This speeds up the process and reduces personal bias since the model requires evaluators to integrate their data. The evaluation comprises three to four individual diagnostic interviews with the child and each parent, as well as interviews with collateral contacts who would have knowledge relevant to the question of sexual abuse. On completion of the individual interviews, if not clinically contraindicated, a conjoint session is conducted with the child and each parent. The goal of the latter is not to determine whether sexual abuse occurred, but rather to ascertain level of attachment, parenting style, a parent's strengths and weaknesses, and so on. If on completion of the process, the data supports the credibility of the allegation, the alleged abuser is referred for an evaluation by a professional with expertise in evaluating persons who have had sexual allegations made against them (if the parent interviewer does not possess this expertise).

Assessing the Timing and Function of an Allegation

Divorce can precipitate a disclosure, create the preconditions for sexual abuse to occur, or create a climate that is rife for misinterpretation or false allegations. Each of these possibilities warrants careful exploration with particular attention to the timing and potential function of an allegation. Thorough evaluations include a psychological assessment of each involved person. Assessments should include all the elements of an ordinary sexual abuse evaluation—

a review of prenatal and developmental history; history of medical problems, particularly any intrusive genitourinary procedures; caregiving history; school progress, significant parent-child separations, significant behavioral or emotional problems, and a child's past and present living circumstances. Additionally, a psychosocial history of the family unit should be taken including the family's daily routines; family mores relative to privacy and nudity; approach to sexuality and sex education; history of the child's exposure to sexually explicit materials and/or adult sexual intimacy; and the child's sexual development as well as detailed sexual histories of both parents. A review of the child's symptoms should include the history and current status of trauma-specific symptoms (sexualized behaviors and/or statements; precocious sexual knowledge); history of abuse-reactive or perpetrating behavior; and any history of prior sexual or physical abuse of child and/or parents. These evaluations should explore the level and pattern of family conflict, history of the child's relationship with each parent including the child's attachment to each parent; the child's level of compliance with parents; the child's degree of alienation from either parent; the presence or absence of a united front concerning an allegation or denial of abuse and the chronology of events that raised a parent's concerns about possible sexual abuse.

When Marital Separation Precipitates Disclosure. There is significant data regarding barriers to disclosure of sexual abuse when children remain in an abusive situation. Because of these barriers, children are more likely to disclose following a marital separation when they are no longer living in an abusive situation (Faller, 1991). Furthermore, parents are more likely to recognize longstanding abuse of their children when they are no longer intimately involved with an abusive spouse. For these reasons, marital separation may actually precipitate disclosures of long-standing abuse. Therefore an evaluator should consider the following: Did the marital separation precipitate a disclosure either because a child felt safe enough to report long-standing abuse once the perpetrator left the home or because a parent was more likely to recognize possible signs of sexual abuse?

When Marital Separation Increases Vulnerability to Abuse. Despite the widespread assumption that allegations in divorce-custody conflicts are usually suspect, one of the factors that puts children most at risk for abuse is divorce. Inherent in the divorce context are circumstances that may increase a child's vulnerability to possible sexual abuse due to the complementary needs of child and parent. The impact of divorce on parents may include feelings of abandonment, loneliness, depression, and sadness for which they compensate by increased emotional investment in children. Other risk factors noted by Finkelhor (1984) include maternal emotional unavailability, a father deprived of physical affection, the presence of a stepfather, and low income.

Eastman and Moran (1991) identified additional factors associated with divorce that may increase a child's vulnerability to sexual abuse. One example would be the blurring of boundaries whereby children become involved in meeting the needs of adults (e.g., a depressed parent who is looking for nurturance and support coupled with a child who is trying to nurture the abandoned parent and has a fantasy of reuniting the parents). Children of divorce almost always wish for their parents to be reunited. Other factors include the increased opportunity for boundary violations by virtue of unsupervised contact between child and parent. Additionally, parents of preschoolers may have to perform intimate caregiving for the first time. Other factors include the potential for regression precipitated by the loss of a sexual relationship coupled with anger at a partner who may have a new sexual relationship. Since marital separation can increase a child's vulnerability to sexual abuse, evaluators should consider this possibility.

When Marital Separation Creates a False Allegation

Although marital separation can precipitate a disclosure of long-standing abuse, or create the preconditions for abuse to occur, it can also foster a climate where anger, hostility, and the wish to "be rid of" the other spouse results in fictitious allegations. The timing of the allegation becomes a critical piece of data when entertaining the possibility of fictitiously generated allegations. Did the allegation emerge at the time of filing for divorce or did it emerge sometime later? Did it emerge at the time of some other legal motion? As noted earlier, there is considerable debate, but no empirical data, to support the idea that a greater number of unfounded allegations occur in divorce cases (Berliner, 1990; Jones & Selig, 1988; Thoennes & Tjaden, 1990). Although certain professionals (Gardner, 1994) assert that sexual abuse allegations which emerge after the onset of disputes are most likely false, this opinion is unsubstantiated by empirical data. Still, the possibility of a fictitiously generated allegation must be considered. What is the function of the allegation in the family system? Is there a history of escalating allegations? Can the parent(s) entertain alternative explanations for the child's presentation?

Regardless of the timing of the allegation, it is important to note the initial response of the person hearing the alleged disclosure and his or her response at the time of interview because parental responses to allegations often shift. Parents who were originally disbelieving of an allegation often come to believe it during the process of evaluation when they may receive feedback from professionals that their child might have been abused. As the process unfolds and affects people's willingness to entertain multiple possibilities, it is particularly useful to be able to gather historical information on a parent's initial response since one or more sexual abuse assessments may have taken place prior to the current evaluation. A parent's current conviction may arise from professional input rather than a too ready propensity to endorse allegations against a former spouse.

When Marital Separation Precipitates Symptoms That Mimic Sexual Abuse. There are a significant number of cases in which sexual abuse is ruled out after careful evaluation although the initial concerns seemed warranted. This most often involves misinterpretation of caregiving functions. When children comment on touch to their genitals and they are symptomatic from trauma associated with the marital separation, allegations of sexual abuse often arise. This is particularly relevant in cases involving preschoolers where the potential for confusing divorce-related trauma with sexual abuse is high.

Given the strong possibility for misinterpretations, it is important to note the context of the original disclosure. If a parent heard the initial disclosure statement(s) what was the context in which the disclosure was made? Research indicates that preschool children disclose most often in situations that trigger association, such as diaper changing or bathing (Campis, Hebden-Curtis, & DeMaso, 1993). Was the disclosure accidental or purposeful? Sorenson and Snow (1991) note that disclosures of preschool children tend to be accidental and disclosures by latency age and adolescent children tend to be purposeful. Therefore the context in which the disclosure emerged becomes significant.

Children's responses to divorce differ depending on their stage of development (Chapter 5) and it is incumbent on the evaluator to be well versed in this area. Preschoolers tend to respond to divorce with overwhelming fears of abandonment. They understand divorce from an egocentric perspective that precludes their taking another's point of view, so the potential for feeling that they caused the divorce is high. Since preschoolers see the world in cause-and-effect terms, they often blame themselves for their perceived abandonment. They often develop symptoms such as anxiety, sleep disturbance, and separation difficulties, especially when asked to separate from a primary caretaker to visit a noncustodial parent (see section "Visitation," later in this chapter). These symptoms can be mistakenly interpreted as indicative of sexual abuse, particularly if they occur in conjunction with a statement about genital touching. The response of latency-age children and adolescents are not here because their symptom presentation is less likely to be confused with sexual abuse symptoms.

Children may exhibit sexualized behaviors during any developmental stage. Some children are highly anxious and display sexualized behavior as a means of soothing themselves; others feel depressed and neglected and soothe themselves by masturbating. These children may be mistaken for abuse victims when other emotional stresses are causing the sexualized behavior. Additionally, other forms of sexual overstimulation may occur as a result of being exposed to a separated or divorced parent engaging in a sexual relationship with a new partner. The knowledge and awareness of a parent's sexual relationship can also be highly stimulating to vulnerable children following a separation or divorce. Thus, it should be emphasized that sexualized behavior per se should not be used as a definitive indicator of sexual abuse. It can result from the child's reaction to the divorce itself.

Emotionally stressed or angry parents may be more likely to jump to unfounded conclusions when their child is symptomatic and talking about genital touch.

The effects of divorce on a child's development are unique for each child and include temperamental differences, experience of control over the situation, social environment, informal and formal supports, extent of exposure to ongoing conflict, violence, and substance abuse. How contentious is the divorce? Does the family retain any cohesiveness? Can the child maintain predictable routines and structures? Has the child witnessed violence, observed emotional or physical abuse, experienced both or witnessed sexual abuse of others?

Assessing the Credibility of a Child's Statement

As discussed earlier, empirical data are limited with respect to criteria that reliably differentiate sexually abused children from their nonsexually abused counterparts. Still, there appears to be widespread acceptance of certain criteria relied on by experienced clinicians to assess the credibility of children's statements. In Kuehnle's comprehensive review of existing empirical research (1996) she drew on Faller et al.'s review of the literature (1993) which put forth eight criteria most often considered when assessing the veracity of a child's statement regarding sexual abuse. Although only Raskin and Esplin (1991) and Faller (1984) have attempted to establish empirical validity, these criteria are widely accepted and thought to have consensus validity.

In assessing the credibility of an allegation, these eight elements should be considered when interpreting data:

1. What is the timing of the disclosure and the circumstances surrounding it, as reviewed in the previous section? When did the allegations emerge and what might be their function in the family system or divorce process?
2. Is the language of the disclosure congruent with the child's developmental level? Is the vocabulary and sentence structure age-appropriate or reminiscent of adult language construction?
3. What is the quantity and quality of detail? Is the child able to supply sufficient detail to contextualize the data he or she presents? For example, a description of a genital touch is not useful unless the context of that touch is clearly understood. Sparse detail can indicate the need for more focused questions to facilitate the child's ability to provide additional details or it can be indicative that the alleged event did not occur.
4. Is the child's sexual knowledge developmentally appropriate? Does the child's sexual knowledge exceed what is expected for a child of that age? Are there alternative explanations for a child's advanced knowledge?
5. Does the disclosure reflect both internal and external consistency? External consistency refers to a child's ability to remember and repeat salient features of the description across interviews. Internal consistency refers to the details within the account. While a child might lose sight of the color or placement of an object, he or she can usually recall the essential or core details of the event. External consistency as a category is being reconsidered, however, as researchers learn more about how children remember. It appears that children store and retrieve memory in fragments rather than in narrative forms and may report different fragments at different times to different interviewers (Loftus & Ketcham, 1991).

6. Can a child describe the offender's behavior beyond the specific touch? The evaluator should listen for statements reportedly made by the offender including threats, bribes, or the need for secrecy regarding the sexual interaction.
7. Is the alleged abuse plausible? Is the narrative possible in terms of other data known about the event or circumstances surrounding the event?
8. What is the child's emotional reaction during the interview? Is the child able to comment on his or her affective state at the time of the abuse?

This framework for assessing disclosure statements must be utilized within an overall developmental framework considering age, temperament of the child, relationship with the allegedly abusive parent, and the unique meaning the child has made of his or her experience.

Evaluation Report

There are important considerations to be kept in mind when preparing the evaluation report. Failure to include the following may leave evaluators open to criticism and potentially nullify their conclusions. The evaluation report should include a definition of the evaluation question; comment on the format and scope of the evaluation; comment on the multiple hypotheses entertained and why alternatives were ruled in/out; comment on data obtained from collateral sources and weight given to that data; comment on both sides of the question (include data both consistent with/not consistent with sexual abuse); comment on the limitations of the evaluation; comment on the decision-making criteria for the conclusions reached (to document that interpretations did not extend beyond the bounds of the data); and some comment regarding how the recommendations are related to the evaluation findings.

Finally, it is incumbent on the evaluator to adequately document how he or she went about interpreting and weighting data obtained during the child interviews in the larger context of the data obtained from other sources, and formulate an opinion regarding whether or not the child was sexually abused. The report is critical, and an exemplary evaluation is all for naught if it is not adequately documented and written in a manner that is useful to the trier of fact.

VISITATION

Currently, there is scant clinical data, little research, and few legal precedents on which to draw when attempting to address the issue of contact between a child and an allegedly abusive parent. The dilemmas of how to preserve the attachment between child and parent while simultaneously ensuring a child's safety give rise to a series of questions: Should a child visit with the alleged abuser? If so, on what basis? Who should supervise the visit? Should the visit be supervised by a mental health professional? How should the professional be selected? How long should the professional remain involved? What should the professional's role be during the visits? Who is financially responsible for the cost of supervision? What happens when the allegations are unclear? What if the child does not want to visit with the alleged abuser? What happens when the custodial parent cannot support the visitation plan? What factors influence the abusing parent's support of the visitation plan?

DEFINITION OF VISITATION

Any contact between a child and his or her parent ranging from a birthday card to telephone calls to personal contact may be considered visitation. From his review of the literature, Barnum (1987) notes that there are both positive and negative outcomes associated with visitation between a child and a non-custodial parent. Positive visitation experiences have been associated with enhancing a child's self-esteem, since contact promotes feelings of being cared about; facilitating the child's identification with the absent parent so that the parent is retained as an important part of the child's external and internal world; facilitating an attachment that is realistic rather than fantasied as the child can make his or her own appraisal of the parent's strengths and limitations. In the absence of ongoing contact a child is obliged to rely on wishes or fears to keep the image of the absent parent alive, a situation with great potential for distortion.

Barnum notes that negative visitation experiences have been associated with fueling parental conflict, which is detrimental since research supports that children's exposure to toxic parental relationships is a major contributor to child psychopathology; perpetuating loyalty conflicts when parents make conflicting demands; disrupting a child's development when mandated visitation requires the child to separate and connect at points that conflict with normal developmental needs; undermining the custodial parent's sense of autonomy; producing confusion about discipline; and disrupting family routines.

Research findings of Johnston et al. (1989) challenge long-held beliefs on which visitation has been historically based. They point out that beliefs about joint custody were based on families who wanted to share custody of their children and were therefore not in "high conflict" over the divorce or custody. In cases of high-conflict divorce, custody and visitation are highly contested. Their findings indicate that children in such families with frequent access to both parents were more emotionally troubled and behaviorally disturbed. Children with more extensive visitation and those making more frequent transitions between parent's homes were more likely to be emotionally disturbed regardless of the level of conflict between the parents. When high conflict was also present, children's mental health was even more seriously compromised. These findings indicate the need for considerable caution when implementing any visitation plan.

IMPLEMENTATION OF VISITATION

One of the more challenging decisions facing a judge is whether to allow or suspend the visitation rights of an accused parent. Denying a parent's right of access because of a vague accusation may appear fundamentally unfair to the parent. Rupturing a parent-child relationship may be traumatizing to a child, while permitting continued contact with an alleged perpetrator risks physical and/or emotional harm to the child. Judges often solicit recommendations regarding parent-child contact from mental health professionals in the form of evaluations. To make those determinations, evaluators seek to answer a number of questions.

TEMPORARY SUSPENSION OF CONTACT

While essential information is gathered, we recommend the development of a standard which, on a case-by-case basis, allows temporary suspension of contact between a child and an alleged perpetrator. This is essential for the following reasons:

- Suspending contact with the alleged abuser may facilitate a disclosure if an allegation is valid. Previous research data support the position that it is much more difficult for children to disclose when the alleged perpetrator has continued access to them (Faller, 1991).
- Standardization of temporary suspension of visitation during the portion of the evaluation that involves child interviews allows evaluators to retain their position as neutral if they are not called on to make recommendations regarding visitation *before* the evaluation.
- Parent-child contact can be restored, if not contraindicated, as part of that evaluation in the form of a conjoint session which can potentially yield important information about attachment and parenting style.

Because of the stress placed on all parties by the interruption of visits, everything possible should be done to complete the evaluation promptly.

SUPERVISED VISITATION

Supervised visitation is a model of contact that is frequently recommended to provide for the parent's contact with the child while ensuring the child's safety. It helps preserve parent-child attachment, protects parents' and children's rights, and provides an opportunity to observe the quality of a parent-child relationship (Barnum, 1987). The purposes of supervised visitation vary from case to case. Frequently, supervised visitation has been defined as a mechanism for guaranteeing a child's physical and psychological safety, a means of psychologically supporting the child, and an opportunity to educate the parent (Barnum, 1987).

CLINICAL CONSIDERATIONS REGARDING SUPERVISED VISITATION

Recommendations for supervised visits should be based on assessments of the credibility of the child's disclosure, and the child's wishes.

The following clinical considerations may be included:

- The nature of the prior relationship between child and alleged perpetrator including consideration of whether the parent was involved in early caretaking or whether his or her interest in visitation developed after separation or divorce.
- Whether the motivation for the visits is the wish for motherly or fatherly contact with child, a means to pressure the child to recant, a desire to gain access to the child's mother or father, or a wish for preservation of mutually positive contact.
- The willingness of the alleged abuser to seek treatment. If not, can he or she attend to the child's needs? Can the alleged abuser allow the child to maintain his or her reality as he or she maintains innocence? To what extent will the child's reality be undermined by the visit?
- The custodial parent's ability to value preservation of the relationship between noncustodial parent and child. If not, why not? Has the marital relationship been characterized by battering or intimidation? Will visitation result in physical danger (e.g., by revealing the whereabouts of the custodial parent and child)? How will the custodial parent cope when the child is forced to visit against his or her and/or the child's will?

Temporary suspension of supervised visitation may be necessary when an allegation includes coercion or threats; when fear and intimidation are communicated as part of the child's experience; when the child's mental status is a matter of concern; or when the child is unwilling to visit.

STRUCTURE OF SUPERVISED VISITATION

Orders for "supervised visitation" often fail to specify crucial aspects of the situation such as the management of risk of abuse. It is important to consider who determines the structure of visitation including how changes in the visitation order and in the structure of visits are implemented and by whom? How will the alleged abuser's risk be assessed, how will allegations raised during visits be managed? When will supervision of visits no longer be necessary? Supervisors must have information about the victim's experience of the alleged abuse. Issues such as under what circumstances the visit should be interrupted need to be considered in advance. In highly contested custody matters with allegations of sexual abuse, the supervised visit can become extremely complicated. We have found these issues are best addressed by mental health practitioners who collaborate with legal counsel on a regular basis to continually monitor the situation from the perspective of all parties.

ROLE OF VISITATION SUPERVISOR

If visitation is recommended, the supervisor's role must be clearly defined. Possible roles include (1) fact recorder, whose observations are recorded without interpretation; (2) evaluator, whose clinical impressions are recorded; (3) role model or facilitator.

We recommend that the visits not be used to reevaluate of the parent-child relationship since the data obtained is biased. Supervision does not guarantee access to the child's internal experience or to input from the noncustodial parent and is seldom of a type that supports an overall evaluation.

PARENTAL DYNAMICS OF SUPERVISED VISITATION

It is important to consider the dynamics of the supervised visitation model for both the custodial parent and the allegedly abusive parent. For the custodial parent, usually the mother, the supervisor's role may supersede that of the primary caretaker's role as protector and so symbolically replicates the mother's perceived failure as a parent. This problem is compounded when the mother's attempts to protect postdisclosure are perceived as controlling or vindictive. The visitation situation may also replicate the original trauma whereby the mother is excluded from the secrets between the father and daughter because the supervisors develop relationships with fathers as a result of the time spent together, in contrast with mothers with whom they interact briefly when they pick up and drop off the child. For the allegedly abusive father having his parenting skills and interactions with his child scrutinized by a stranger can lead to profound feelings of embarrassment and shame. He often views the supervisor as a judge and therefore tries to prove his innocence which may at some point be used against him.

ROLE OF CUSTODIAL OR NONOFFENDING PARENT

Despite the research findings of Thoennes indicating that sexual abuse allegations emerge in only 2% of contested divorce cases, the credibility of the custodial parent, usually the mother, is immediately suspect. Mothers are often wary of a system that they perceive as failing to protect their child. Anxiety-generated questions by mothers are often interpreted as attempts to wrest control. It is important to determine whether the questions are motivated by knowledge she has that the professionals do not have (e.g., battering relationship) or stem from her own anger and hatred toward the noncustodial parent.

ASSESSING THE IMPACT OF VISITATION

Assessing the impact of visitation is a complicated process because of the many confounding variables. As noted, frequent transitions between parents and children are stressful and themselves promote a range of symptoms and problematic behaviors. Barnum (1987) provides a useful frame for assessing the impact of visitation on children that includes three contexts:

1. *Intrapsychic Context.* Are the child's symptoms a manifestation of something intrinsic to the child? Does the very act of confronting the person who hurt him or her result in the child becoming flooded or overwhelmed with anxiety?
2. *Visitation Context.* Are the child's symptoms a manifestation of the visitation context itself? Something is actually going wrong in the visit such as a conflict between the supervisor and the parent.
3. *Custodial Parent Context.* Do the child's symptoms have to do with the conflict between the parents or the custodial parent's conflict over the visitation arrangement?

Often custodial parents are frustrated by having to adhere to someone else's schedule. Additionally, they may become acutely distressed because of fears that harm may result from visitation. If a parent is anxious, fearful, sad, or feeling coerced, these messages get transmitted to children and affect the child's response to the visitation experience. While the custodial parent context is the one most frequently pointed to for the source of visitation conflicts, all three need to be closely examined. Certainly, the child's experience of visits must be assessed periodically.

CONCLUSION

The public perception is that sexual abuse allegations are rampant in cases involving high-conflict divorce and are used in retaliation by a vindictive spouse to exclude the other spouse from the lives of the children. In actuality, only a small percentage of contested cases involve allegations of sexual abuse and the rate at which allegations of sexually abuse are validated in the few studies available appears to be about equal to rates of general (nondivorce) samples. However, when such allegations arise in the context of disputes over custody and visitation, they pose particular challenges because the trauma of divorce often results in a symptom presentation that is remarkably similar to symptom presentations observed in sexually abused children. The authors have put forth a comprehensive model for conducting these complicated evaluations.

Judges face a critical dilemma when they have to choose between allowing a child to remain in contact with a possibly abusive parent or conversely rupturing a parent-child relationship. Additionally, the judge is faced with how best to preserve an accused parent's relationship with the child during the evaluation, which may be a long and arduous process. If the findings of the evaluation are inconclusive, the judge is left with the same dilemma. The authors have raised a number of issues to be considered before implementing any kind of contact between the child and allegedly abusive parent.

REFERENCES

Ainsworth, M. D., & Bell, S. M. (1970). Attachment, exploration, and separation: Illustrated by the behavior of one-year-olds in a strange situation. *Child Development, 41,* 49–67.

Amato, P. R., & Keith, B. (1991). Parental divorce and the well-being of children: A meta-analysis. *Psychological Bulletin, 110,* 26–46.

American Academy of Child and Adolescent Psychiatry. (1990). *Guidelines for clinical evaluation of child sexual abuse.* Washington, DC: Author.

American Academy of Child and Adolescent Psychiatry. (1997). Practice parameters for the forensic evaluation of children and adolescents who may have been sexually abused. *Journal of the American Academy of Child and Adolescent Psychiatry, 36*(3), 423–442.

American Academy of Pediatrics. (1991). Guidelines for the evaluation of sexual abuse of children. *Pediatrics, 87*(2), 254–260.

American Professional Society on the Abuse of Children. (1990). *Guidelines for psychosocial evaluation of suspected sexual abuse in young children.* Chicago: Author. (Available from: APSAC 332 South Michigan Av. Suite 1600, Chicago, IL 60064.)

American Psychological Association. (1992). Ethical principles of psychologists and code of conduct. *American Psychologist, 47*(12), 1597–1611.

American Psychological Association. (1994). Guidelines for child custody evaluations in divorce proceedings. *American Psychologist, 49*(7), 677–680.

Anson, D. A., & Gully, K. J. (1989). *Valid child sexual abuse cases: The relationship of child and interview characteristics with the child's allegation.* Paper presented at the eighth national conference on Child Abuse and Neglect, Salt Lake City, UT.

Barnum, R. (1987). Understanding controversies in visitation. *Journal of the American Academy of Child and Adolescent Psychiatry, 26*(5), 788–792.

Benedek, E., & Schetky, D. (1985). Allegations of sexual abuse in child custody cases. In E. Schetky & E. Benedeck (Eds.), *Emerging issues in child psychiatry and the law* (pp. 145–156). New York: Brunner/Mazel.

Berliner, L. (1990). Protecting or harming? Parents who flee with their children. *Journal of Interpersonal Violence, 5*(1), 119–120.

Bresee, P., Stearns, G. B., Bess, B. H., & Packer, L. S. (1986). Allegations of child sexual abuse in child custody disputes: A therapeutic assessment model. *American Journal of Orthopsychiatry, 56*(4), 560–569.

Briere, J. (1988). The long-term clinical correlates of childhood sexual victimization. In R. A. Prentley & V. L. Quinsey (Eds.), Human sexual aggression: Current perspectives. *Annal of the New York Academy of Sciences, 528,* 327–334.

Browne, A., & Finkelhor, D. (1986). Impact of child sexual abuse: A review of the research. *Psychological Bulletin, 99,* 66–77.

Campis, L. B., Hebden-Curtis, J., & DeMaso, D. R. (1993). Developmental differences in detection and disclosure of sexual abuse. *Journal of the American Academy of Child and Adolescent Psychiatry, 32*(5), 920–924.

Conte, J. R., Sorenson, E., Fogarty, L., & Dalla Rosa, J. (1991). Evaluating children's reports of sexual abuse: Results from a survey of professionals. *American Journal of Orthopsychiatry, 61*, 428–437.

Courtois, C. (1988). *Healing the incest wound.* New York: Norton.

Eastman, A. M., & Moran, T. J. (1991). Multiple perspectives: Factors related to differential diagnosis of sex abuse and divorce trauma in children under six. *Child and Youth Services, 15*(2), 159–175.

Egeland, B., & Farber, E. A. (1984). Infant-mother attachment: Factors related to its development and changes over time. *Child Development, 55*(3), 753–771.

Elliott, D. M., & Briere, J. (1994). Forensic sexual abuse evaluations of older children: Disclosures and symptomatology. *Behavioral Sciences and the Law, 12*(3), 261–277.

Esplin, P. W., Houed, T. D., & Raskin, D. C. (1988). *Applications of statement validity assessment.* Paper presented at NATO Advance Study Institute on Credibility Assessment, Maratea, Italy.

Everson, M. D. (1993). *Evaluating young children for suspected sexual abuse.* Paper presented at the San Diego Conference on Responding to Child Maltreatment, San Diego, CA.

Everson, M. D., & Boat, B. W. (1994). Putting the anatomical doll controversy in perspective: An explanation of the major uses and criticisms of the dolls in child sexual abuse evaluations. *Child Abuse and Neglect, 18*(2), 113–129.

Faller, K. C. (1984). Is the child victim of sexual abuse telling the truth? *Child Abuse and Neglect, 8,* 473–481.

Faller, K. C. (1988). Criteria for judging the credibility of children's statements about their sexual abuse. *Child Welfare, 67,* 389–401.

Faller K. C. (1991). Possible explanations for child sexual abuse allegations in divorce. *American Journal of Orthopsychiatry, 61*(1), 86–91.

Faller, K. C. (1993, January). *Evaluating young children for possible sexual abuse.* Paper presented at the San Diego Conference on Responding to Child Maltreatment.

Faller, K. C., & Corwin, D. (1995). Children's interview statements and behaviors: Role in identifying sexually abused children. *Child Abuse and Neglect, 19,* 71–82.

Faller, K. C., Corwin, D. L., & Olafson, E. (1993). Research on false allegations of sexual abuse in divorce. *APSAC Advisor, 6*(3), 6–10.

Faller, K., Fronig, M., & Lipovsky, J. (1991). The parent-child interview: Use in evaluating allegations of sexual abuse by parents. *American Journal of Orthopsychiatry, 61*(4), 552–557.

Finkelhor, D. (1984). *Child sexual abuse: New theory and research.* New York: Free Press.

Fisher, R. P., & McCauley, M. R. (1995). Improving eyewitness testimony with the cognitive interview. In M. Zaragoza, J. Graham, G. Hall, R. Heschman, & Y. Ben-Proth (Eds.), *Memory and testimony in the child witness* (pp. 141–159). Thousand Oaks, CA: Sage.

Gardner, R. A. (1994). Differentiating between true and false sex-abuse accusations in child-custody disputes. *Journal of Divorce and Remarriage, 21,* 1–20.

Geiselman, R. E., & Padilla, J. (1988). Interviewing child witnesses with the cognitive interview. *Journal of Police Science and Administration, 16,* 236–242.

Geiselman, R. E., Saywitz, K., & Bornstein, G. K. (1991). *Effects of cognitive interviewing, practice, and interview style on children's recall performance.* Washington, DC: National Institute of Justice.

Goldstein, S., Freud, A., & Solnit, A. J. (1979). *Before the best interests of the child.* New York: Free Press.

Green, A. (1986). True and false allegations of sexual abuse in child custody disputes. *Journal of the American Academy of Child and Adolescent Psychiatry, 25,* 449–455.

Haynes-Seman, C., & Baumgarten, D. (1994). *Children speak for themselves.* New York: Brunner/Mazel.

Hetherington, E. M. (1993). An overview of the Virginia longitudinal study of divorce and remarriage with a focus on early adolescence. *Journal of Family Psychology, 7,* 39–56.

Horner, T. M., Guyer, M. J., & Kalter, N. M. (1993). Clinical expertise and the assessment of child sexual abuse. *Journal of the American Academy of Child and Adolescent Psychiatry, 32,* 925–931.

Johnston, J. R., Gonzalez, R., & Campbell, L. E. G. (1987). Ongoing postdivorce conflict and child disturbance. *Journal of Abnormal Child Psychology, 15,* 493–509.

Johnston, J. R., Kline, M., & Tschann, J. M. (1989). Ongoing postdivorce conflict: Effects on children of joint custody and frequent access. *American Journal of Orthopsychiatry, 59,* 576–592.

Jones, D. P., & McGraw, J. M. (1987). Reliable and fictitious accounts of sexual abuse to children. *Journal of Interpersonal Violence, 2*(1), 27–45.

Jones, D. P. H., & Selig, A. (1988). Child sexual abuse allegations in custody of visitation disputes: A report of 20 cases. In J. Nicholson & J. Bulkley (Eds.), *Sexual abuse allegations in custody and visitation cases.* Washington, DC: American Bar Association.

Kendall-Tackett, K. A., Williams, L. M., & Finkelhor, D. (1993). Impact of sexual abuse on children: A review and synthesis of recent empirical studies. *Psychological Bulletin, 113,* 164–180.

Klawsnik, C. (1994, November 5). *Sexual abuse allegations: Myths and biases.* Presented at MAGAL Conference Dilemmas in Child Custody and Visitation Decisions.

Kolko, D. J., Moser, J. T., & Weldy, S. R. (1988). Behavioral/emotional indicators of sexual abuse in child psychiatric inpatients: A controlled comparison with physical abuse. *Child Abuse and Neglect, 12,* 529–541.

Kuehnle, K. (1996). *Assessing allegations of child sexual abuse.* Sarasota, FL: Professional Resource Press.

Lawson, L., & Chaffin, M. (1992). False negatives in sexual abuse disclosure interviews. *Journal of Interpersonal Violence, 7*(4), 532–542.

Loftus, E. F., & Ketcham, K. (1991). *Witness for the defense.* New York: St. Martin's Press.

MacFarlane, K., & Krebs, S. (1986). Techniques for interviewing and evidence gathering. In K. MacFarlane & J. Waterman (Eds.), *Sexual abuse of young children* (pp. 67–100). New York: Guilford Press.

McIntosh, J. A., & Prinz, R. J. (1993). The incidence of alleged sexual abuse in 603 family court cases. *Law and Human Behavior, 17,* 95–101.

Raskin, D. C., & Esplin, P. W. (1991). Assessment of children's statements of sexual abuse. In J. Doris (Ed.), *The suggestibility of children's recollections* (pp. 153–164). Washington, DC: American Psychological Association.

Saywitz, K. J., & Snyder, L. (1993). Improving children's testimony with preparation. In G. S. Goodman & D. L. Bottoms (Eds.), *Child victims, child witnesses: Understanding and improving testimony* (pp. 117–146). New York: Guilford Press.

Solomon, P. (1986). *Tracing of sexual abuse cases reported to the Cuyahoga County Department of Social Services, January 1983 through November 1984.* Cleveland OH: Federation for Community Planning.

Sorenson, T., & Snow, B. (1991). How children tell: The process of disclosure in child sexual abuse. *Child Welfare, 70,* 3–15.

Summit, R. C. (1983). Child abuse accommodation syndrome. *Child Abuse and Neglect, 7,* 177–193.

Thoennes, N., & Tjaden, P. G. (1990). The extent, nature, and validity of sexual abuse allegations in custody/visitation disputes. *Child Abuse and Neglect, 14,* 151–163.

Wakefield, H., & Underwager, R. (1988). *Accusations of child sexual abuse.* Springfield, IL: Thomas.

Wallerstein, J., & Kelly, J. (1980). *Surviving the breakup: How children and parents cope with divorce.* New York: Basic Books.

Wells, R. D., McCann, J., Adams, J., Voris, J., & Ensign, J. (1995). Emotional, behavioral, and physical symptoms reported by parents of sexually abused, nonabused, and allegedly abused prepubescent females. *Child Abuse and Neglect, 19,* 155–163.

Yates, A. (1991). Differentiating hyperotic states in the evaluation of sexual abuse. *Journal of the American Academy of Child and Adolescent Psychiatry, 30,* 791–795.

CHAPTER 18

Joint Custody and Empirical Knowledge: The Estranged Bedfellows of Divorce

MARSHA KLINE PRUETT and CHRISTA SANTANGELO

T HE EMERGENCE OF joint custody as an option in divorce settlements has far outdistanced the empirical knowledge that supposedly informs it. The relationship between joint custody and research began with impassioned intensity, suggesting that they were well positioned as both psychologically and politically suitable partners. Divorce research in the 1970s and early 1980s indicated that children fared better when they had ongoing, quality relationships with both parents. A growing men's movement called attention to fathers' determination to maintain relationships with their children after divorce. The women's movement made it equally clear that men would be welcomed as more involved partners in child-rearing and home responsibilities. Consistent research evidence about the negative impact of marital and postdivorce conflict on child adjustment further welcomed joint custody into legal arenas as a viable alternative to the more traditional "custody with visitation." Finally, concerns about the ways in which the legal system could exacerbate hostility and conflict between ex-spouses suggested that joint custody might offer divorcing parents a respectful alternative to the adversarial process. Despite these auspicious beginnings, rigorous research into the potentials and pitfalls of joint custody developed little beyond initial inquiries. This estrangement of joint custody from research left decision makers out on a limb, without a sufficient knowledge base, just as they were being faced with increasingly complex choices.

This chapter examines what is known about the legal status, living arrangements, outcomes, and legal contexts of joint custody and reflects on what is not known. The first two sections (1) lay the foundation for subsequent analysis of empirical knowledge, providing a brief overview of the historical circumstances that generated joint custody as a legal option, and (2) clarify definitions of legal and physical forms of custody. The latter section also highlights the diversity of custody arrangements families choose, elucidating the discrepancy between how custody is *defined* and how it is *lived*. The third section presents the salient dimensions examined in the joint custody literature. Next, we review legal contexts that influence the potential impact of joint custody on children and families, and conclude with a summary and directions for future research.

HISTORICAL BACKGROUND

Although the country's first joint custody statute was established in North Carolina in 1957, the majority of joint custody laws have been enacted only in the past decade (Folberg, 1991). Prevailing tradition for the greater part of Western history, in accordance with common law, gave fathers custody of their children as part of their property rights. In fact, men's authority over their families changed little through the Middle Ages (Derdeyn, 1976). By the nineteenth century, fathers maintained their primary right to custody, but a movement toward custodial preference from fathers to mothers occurred with the *tender years presumption.* Mothers, according to this doctrine, were considered superior caretakers of children in their "tender years," a supposition that some historians trace to the specialization in men's and women's roles initiated by the industrial revolution (Grossberg, 1985). By the 1960s, maternal preference, limited only by a showing of unfitness or fault for divorce, had entirely replaced the presumption of father custody based on men's authority over the family. The enactment of no-fault divorce laws in the 1960s and 1970s, alongside challenges to traditional ideas about men's and women's family roles in the 1970s and 1980s, eroded the former tender years presumption until it was eliminated from statutory law (Emery, 1994).

The *best interests of the child* standard which replaced the tender years presumption, dictates that custody decisions be based on the child's present and future best interests (Mnookin, 1975). However, the best interest standard offers little direction for judicial discretion, especially when two competent parents desire custody of their children. Consequently, two standards, the *primary caretaker parent* and *joint custody,* have emerged (Emery, 1994). The former grants custody to the parent who was the primary caretaker of the child during the marriage; the latter attempts to foster a shared caretaking arrangement between parents. Over the past 20 years, although mothers continue to be recognized as the primary caretaker in a large majority of cases, states have increasingly recognized joint custody as a feasible arrangement for the children of divorcing families.

These two standards are often expressed as opposing custody decision possibilities. Advantages of joint custody touted by supporters include the preservation of continuity of care and affection that children need from both parents (Roman & Haddad, 1978), the expansion of children's support network (Stack, 1976), and the elimination of single-parenting burdens and child behavioral disorders linked with father absence (Hetherington, Cox, & Cox, 1985; Jacobson, 1978; Kelly, 1988). Potential dangers of joint custody include the engendering of loyalty conflicts and instability that sole custody mitigates against by preserving continuity of caretaking and support for the autonomy of one primary parent, without interruption (Goldstein, Solnit, Goldstein, & Freud, 1996). Others also highlight potential difficulties associated with joint custody arrangements. Kuehl (1989) describes joint custody as harmful because it robs children of security and predictability. Weiss (1979) focuses on the problems created by contact that may result in the intensification of attachment bonds between divorcing parents which, he believes, renders emotional divorce difficult. These ideas are useful in identifying central questions in the joint custody debate, and are instrumental in suggesting what is possible in postdivorce parenting.

While joint custody becomes more visible as an option for postdivorce parenting, states continue to implement their support of it to varying degrees. As of 1990, 18 states have passed a statutory presumption for joint custody, with eleven of those specifying that the presumption holds only when parents agree. An additional three states specify a preference for joint custody, and 19 states consider it an option. Ten states have not addressed it statutorily, but many of these recognize it as an option through case law (Emery, 1994). Support for joint custody ranges in these states from viewing it as an option on request to acceptable only under exceptional circumstances.

DEFINITIONS AND APPLICATIONS

The statutory laws regarding joint custody are usually focused on legal custody status as decreed at the time of divorce. Joint legal custody (JLC) grants rights and responsibilities for major decisions affecting the child (e.g., health, education, welfare) to both parents, but does not assume residential arrangements of any particular type. In joint physical custody (JPC), not only are legal responsibilities shared, but children also spend large portions of their time with each parent. Often, the term is used to connote near equal time sharing. Shared parenting or shared residences, as described in this chapter, refer to JPC arrangements.

Distributions Associated with Custody Status

Families may adopt at least three different constellations of custody: (1) joint legal and joint physical custody, (2) joint legal custody and sole physical custody and noncustodial parent visitation, or (3) sole legal and physical custody, with or without visitation.

JLC with JPC is a relatively rare event. Even in states at the forefront of the joint custody movement, such as Washington, Colorado or California, only 15%–20% of the children sampled lived in dual residences (Ellis, 1990; Maccoby & Mnookin, 1992; Pearson & Thoennes, 1990), with only 10% of the adolescents in the California study living with both parents (Maccoby, Buchanan, Mnookin, & Dornbusch, 1993). In California, arguably the vanguard of the JPC movement, maternal custody remains the usual arrangement from initial separation through at least the early postdivorce period (Maccoby & Mnookin, 1992). By contrast, the same researchers found that joint physical custodial arrangements were the least consistent over time. Although the percentage of adolescent children in dual households remained constant over a 3½-year period, there was a great deal of movement across residential groups. Significantly, only about half of the families awarded JPC retained dual residential arrangements (Maccoby & Mnookin, 1992). A smaller study located in California produced a higher percentage of JPC (38%) among 93 families sampled over a 2-year period (Kline, Tschann, Johnston, & Wallerstein, 1989). Again, the arrangements in this group were less stable than the arrangements in mother custody families. Data from the studies cited above represent only the northern part of the state of California, so the percentages are not necessarily generalizable to other areas. Given California's role in the joint custody movement, rates of JPC around the country are likely to be lower. In a study from Massachusetts, analysis of 500 court records revealed that only 11 cases designated both parents as having physical custody (Phear, Beck, Hauser, Clark, & Whitney, 1984), with a small percentage (6%) also reported in an Arizona study (see Pearson & Thoennes, 1990).

Compared with the relatively rare status of JPC, the majority of states specify joint legal custody as an option or a preference, as described earlier, making it more common across many jurisdictions (Maccoby & Mnookin, 1992; Phear et al., 1984; Racusin, Albertini, Wishik, Schnurr, & Mayberry, 1989). Just how normative it is varies significantly across the country. Since 80% of all states have passed statutes either explicitly allowing or encouraging joint custody (Folberg, 1991), the incidence is likely to increase as the concept gains in familiarity.

APPLICATIONS: FROM LEGAL STATUS TO LIVING ARRANGEMENTS

Despite the clear definitions of JLC and JPC, the realities of these arrangements are not so clear. It is possible for JPC arrangements to look more like parallel parenting than highly communicative shared decision making. Conversely, parents may implement JLC in a variety of idiosyncratic schedules, such that JLC with frequent visitation is nearly indistinguishable from JPC. The amount of time a parent and child spend together is also qualitatively different from the type of time they spend together in terms of the impact it is likely to have on the child's development. If the child spends the bulk of his or her time with dad on weekends, there will be a considerable difference in their relationship than if dad is responsible for getting the child to bed on time with homework completed. Changing distributions of living arrangements over time further confound data emerging from studies that are not specific in describing original custody situations. It is with this cautionary note that we proceed to establish a context for the assessment of joint custody research which is available to inform decision making.

THE DIMENSIONS OF JOINT CUSTODY

Efforts to understand joint custody have relied on the broader divorce literature, which consistently identifies certain variables as critical to child and family adjustment. Dimensions of the pre- and postdivorce family that are most commonly addressed are family characteristics (e.g., socioeconomic status), child attributes (gender, age, temperament), parent functioning, father involvement and loss of contact, the parental relationship, and parent-child relationships (e.g., Amato & Keith, 1991; Tschann, Johnston, Kline, & Wallerstein, 1990). Results across multiple studies and populations concur that children of divorce show more behavioral and emotional problems than do children in never-divorced families (Camara & Resnick, 1988; Emery, 1988; Guidubaldi, Perry, & Cleminshaw, 1984; Hetherington, Cox, & Cox, 1982; Wallerstein & Kelly, 1980; Zill, 1983).

Findings are most consistent about child and parental reactions to divorce in the first 3 years following the separation; for some portion of the children, symptoms persist into young adulthood (Chase-Lansdale, Cherlin, & Kiernan, 1995; Hetherington et al., 1985; Kelly, 1990; Wallerstein & Blakeslee, 1989). Problems are exacerbated by father loss (see Healy, Malley, & Stewart, 1990; Hetherington, 1972; Santrock & Warshak, 1979), marital and postdivorce parental conflict (Camara & Resnick, 1988; Davies & Cummings, 1994; Emery, 1982; Johnston & Campbell, 1988), parent adjustment problems (Kalter, Kloner, Schreier, & Okla, 1989; Wallerstein & Kelly, 1980), and diminished parental authority and closeness to the child (Hess & Camara, 1979; Hetherington et al., 1982; Wallerstein & Kelly, 1980). Boys appear more reactive than girls (Guidubaldi & Perry, 1985; Tschann et al., 1990), and symptoms vary in accordance with developmental stage. Difficulties attributed to divorce may be ameliorated by high quality parent-child relationships (Clingempeel & Reppucci, 1982; Hetherington, 1989; Kline, Johnston, & Tschann, 1991; Tschann, Johnston, Kline, & Wallerstein, 1989); while father contact and involvement have proven to be less clearly related to child adjustment except through their association to quality parent-child connections (King, 1994; Thomas & Forehand, 1993). The question that remains is how joint custody, in its various manifestations, adds to our understanding of family adaptation.

OVERVIEW OF SELECTED RESEARCH

Table 18.1 provides a summary of the seminal studies in the joint custody literature discussed in this chapter. Not all studies that merited citation are included in the table. The included studies were focused specifically on joint custody. The researchers used reasonable sample sizes, published in peer-reviewed journals, and in most cases included comparison groups. A few exceptions were made for studies that did not include a comparison group but that do make a unique contribution to clinical understanding.

The *Legal Custody* studies almost all include a comparison of legal and joint custody families. In almost all cases, father custody participants were dropped from analyses because they were so few in number; however, four studies included reports only from fathers. About half of the studies restrict analysis to descriptive statistics, and the other half utilize quantitative analyses that require more rigorous accounting for the data observed. Child adjustment is examined in only four studies, and most of the studies examining the parents do not report the age of their children. Some investigations, as noted, do not maintain independent samples by including couples data, or by mixing couple and individual data and reporting them all as individuals. The joint custody samples are often much smaller than the sole custody groups studied. It is unclear the extent to which the size difference between the groups is controlled for statistically, suggesting that it was not.

The *Physical Custody* studies were conducted predominantly by two research groups from northern California: the Maccoby group (includes Depner, Mnookin, Buchanan, and Albiston) and the Johnston group (includes Kline, Tschann, Wallerstein, Coysh, and Nelson). Johnston's other colleagues and the Steinman papers also collected data from the same area of the country. These groups rely on quantitative methods described in appropriate detail, and draw from multiple data sources (combining self-report with clinical data or self-report from several family members). Children are differentiated by gender and developmental status. The major drawback of these studies is that they represent a narrow geographic area and, despite efforts to include both parents, data is more often obtained from mothers.

A small group of legal studies that provide descriptive information about legal processes or court recorded data will be referred to separately in Table 18.1.

Enough research has included legal and physical custody as a central focus to elucidate patterns of parental and child adjustment. However, California is overrepresented across studies, particularly among descriptive and physical custody categories. Moreover, the effects of joint custody on child adjustment are the focus of relatively few studies. We know most about the benefits and drawbacks of joint custody, from parents' perspectives. Also, the JLC literature is more extensive and representative than JPC research. Therefore, throughout this chapter, joint custody will refer to JLC unless specified otherwise.

Table 18.1

Summary of Selected Custody Studies

Author(s), Date of Publication	Sample Size (% J. C.)	Participants	LEGAL CUSTODY STUDIES						Ages of Children	State
			Descriptive Only	Sole Custody Comparison Group	Parental Self-Report	Parent Assesses Child	Child Assessed by Self or Non-Parent			
Albiston et al., 1990	449 (73%)	Mothers Fathers			✓	✓		NA*	CA
Arditti, 1992	212 (19%)	Fathers	✓	✓	✓				VA
Bautz & Hill, 1991	216 (37%)	Mothers Fathers		✓	✓			< 19	National
Bowman & Adams, 1985	82 (34%)	Fathers		✓	✓				WI
Donnelly & Finkelhor, 1993[1]	320 (13%)	Mothers Fathers		✓	✓				National
Greif, 1979	40 (20%)	Fathers		✓	✓				NY
Ilfeld et al., 1982	414 (33%)	Court Data	✓	✓					CA
Irving et al., 1984	201 (50%)	Mothers Fathers	✓	✓					Canada
Luepnitz, 1986	43 (26%)	Mothers/Fathers Children		✓	✓		✓	NA*	PA
Patrician, 1984	90 (33%)	Fathers	✓	✓	✓				CA
Phear et al., 1984	500 (22%)	Public Divorce Records	✓	✓					MA
Shiller, 1986	40 (50%)	Parents Teachers				✓	✓	Boys 6–11	CT
Shrier et al., 1991	112 (31%)	Mothers Fathers	✓						NJ
Wolchik et al., 1985	133 (30%)	Mothers/Fathers Children		✓	✓	✓	✓	8–15	AZ

* NA = Not Available

[1] Legal/physical not differentiated; data more suggestive of legal.

(continued)

395

Table 18.1 (Continued)

PHYSICAL CUSTODY STUDIES

Author(s), Date of Publication	Sample Size (% J.C.)	Participants	Descriptive Only	Sole Custody Comparison Group	Parental Self-Report	Parent Assesses Child	Child Assessed by Self or Non-Parent	Ages of Children	State
Benjamin & Irving, 1990	395 (51%)	Mothers Fathers		✓	✓				Canada
Buchanan et al., 1991	522 (10%)	Adolescents		✓	✓		✓	< 16	CA
Buchanan et al., 1996	664 (26%)	Mothers/Fathers Adolescents		✓	✓		✓	< 16	CA
Coysh et al., 1989	184 (34%)	Mothers Fathers		✓	✓				CA
Ehrenberg et al., 1996	32 (100%)	Mothers Fathers	✓		✓				CA
Johnston, Campbell & Edmund, 1987	126 (28%)	Mothers Fathers Children			✓	✓	✓	1–15	CA
Johnston, Gonzales & Campbell, 1987	56 (33%)	Children				✓	✓	4–12	CA
Johnston, Kline & Tschann, 1988	52 (23%)	Mothers Fathers Children		✓	✓	✓	✓	1–12	CA
Kline et al., 1989	93 (38%)	Mothers/Fathers Children		✓	✓	✓	✓	3–14	CA
Maccoby et al., 1990	664 (26%)	Mothers Fathers		✓	✓			< 16	CA
Maccoby & Mnookin, 1992; Maccoby et al., 1993	917+ (10%)	Mothers Fathers Adolescents		✓	✓		✓	< 16	CA
McKinnon & Wallerstein, 1986	25 (100%)	Mothers Fathers Children	✓			✓		< 5	CA

Author(s), Date of Publication	Sample Size (% J.C.)	Participants	Descriptive Only	Sole Custody Comparison Group	Parental Self-Report	Parent Assesses Child	Child Assessed by Self or Non-Parent	Ages of Children	State
Nelson, 1989	121 (28%)	Mothers Fathers		✓	✓				CA
Pearson & Theonnes, 1990	686 (9%)	Mothers Fathers		✓	✓	✓		NA*	CO CA
Radovanic et al., 1994	49 (61%)	Mothers Fathers	✓		✓	✓		7–18	Canada
Rothberg, 1991	30 (100%)	Mothers Fathers	✓		✓			<8 at Time 1	NY
Steinman, 1981 Steinman et al., 1986	48 (100%)	Mothers Fathers Children		✓	✓		✓	1–15	CA

* NA = Not Available

JOINT CUSTODY INCLUDED BUT SECONDARY

Author(s), Date of Publication	Sample Size (% J.C.)	Participants	Descriptive Only	Sole Custody Comparison Group	Parental Self-Report	Parent Assesses Child	Child Assessed by Self or Non-Parent	Ages of Children	State
Bautz & Hill, 1991	216 (37%)			✓	✓			< 19	National
Buchanan et al., 1991; 1996	522+ (10%)			✓	✓		✓	< 16	CA
Buchanan et al., 1996	664 (26%)	Mothers/Fathers Adolescents	✓	✓	✓		✓	< 16	CA
Maccoby et al., 1990; 1993	697+ (26%)	Mothers/Fathers Adolescents	✓	✓			✓	< 16	CA

STUDIES WITH LEGAL SYSTEM FOCUS

Author(s), Date of Publication	Sample Size (% J.C.)	Participants	Descriptive Only	Sole Custody Comparison Group	Parental Self-Report	Parent Assesses Child	Child Assessed by Self or Non-Parent	Ages of Children	State
Bahr et al., 1994 (legal custody)	1087 (21%)	Court Records	✓	✓					UT
Felner et al., 1985	117 % not relevant	Judges Attorneys	✓						Northeast
Sorensen et al., 1995	60 % not relevant	Court Records	✓	✓					FL

DIRECT IMPACT OF CUSTODY TYPE ON CHILD ADJUSTMENT

A substantial research effort in the past two decades has focused on child adjustment postdivorce, with custody being one variable of interest. Actual studies examining adjustment in joint versus sole custody arrangements indicate that custody status *in and of itself* does not significantly predict child postdivorce adjustment (Kline et al., 1989; Luepnitz, 1982, 1986; Warshak & Santrock, 1983). As with the divorce research preceding it, the role of family process emerges as more determinative than custody structures (Folberg, 1991; Shiller, 1986; Wolchik, Braver, & Sandler, 1985). Each type of family structure sets the stage for different patterns of parent-child interactions. Descriptive studies have reported increased self-esteem and competence, and a diminished sense of loss among joint custody children, but also noted that a substantial proportion of children were visibly distressed and confused (McKinnon & Wallerstein, 1986; Steinman, 1981; Steinman, Zemmelman, & Knoblauch, 1986).

However, some evidence supports that boys, in particular, benefit from joint custody. There was less emotional loss experienced by school-age boys in shared physical custody (Luepnitz, 1982; Shiller, 1986), and fewer joint custody boys had emotional and behavioral problems than did maternal custody boys (Shiller, 1986). JLC boys also reported fewer negative experiences over a 3-month period (Wolchik et al., 1985). In this latter study, boys and girls reported higher self-esteem than children living in sole legal custody arrangements. Joint custody may also buffer boys from being coopted in their parents' conflict, since they are more likely than girls to be used between warring parents (Johnston, Gonzales, & Campbell, 1987).

MODERATING VARIABLES FROM THE DIVORCE LITERATURE

The primary determinants of family adjustment postdivorce that have been addressed in the joint custody literature are parental characteristics and adjustment, child characteristics and adjustment, parent-child relationships, and parental cooperation and conflict.

PARENTAL CHARACTERISTICS AND ADJUSTMENT

Socioeconomic Status

Families who choose joint custody voluntarily appear to have higher economic standards of living than their sole custody comparison groups. In a national survey, joint custody families lived predominantly in large cities, and parents had higher education and income levels than families who did not have joint custody (Donnelly & Finkelhor, 1993). Other evidence supports the assumption that joint custody parents tend to be older, wealthier, and better educated than sole custody parents (Luepnitz, 1982; Pearson & Thoennes, 1990; Racusin et al., 1989).

Satisfactions and Challenges

Although there is some evidence showing that fathers with joint custody have lower levels of depression than sole custody fathers (Greif, 1979), most research about parental adjustment emphasizes parental satisfactions and challenges. Whereas mental health professionals have written from clinical impressions about the satisfactions and challenges inherent in joint custody, few have empirically explored family members' reactions. Children have been assessed to a lesser extent than their parents. Overall, children have reported greater satisfaction living in JPC than in sole physical custody arrangements, citing their interest in remaining close to both parents as the primary reason for this preference (Steinman et al., 1986). These studies drew from samples of highly motivated participants. Since JPC is relatively rare, it is likely that the select population who choose and sustain shared residences are more likely to have family dynamics that support positive experiences of shared living.

Similarly, studies report higher parental satisfaction with joint custody than sole custody (Ahrons, 1979, 1981; Greif, 1979; Luepnitz, 1982; Nehls & Morgenbesser, 1980). Even when parents are not initially desirous of joint custody, some are satisfied with it 6 months to a year later (Benjamin & Irving, 1990). Both fathers and mothers tout their satisfaction with shared parenting. Fathers with joint physical custody generally report more satisfaction than fathers with visiting status (Ahrons, 1983; Irving, Benjamin, & Trocme, 1984; Kelly, 1990; Steinman, 1981). Maccoby et al. (1990) identified mothers with dual-residence arrangements as more satisfied than mothers with primary physical custody whose children saw their fathers.

Benjamin and Irving (1990) interviewed 395 ex-spouses to compare the experiences of shared parenting for satisfied versus dissatisfied parents. Most of their sample ($n = 350$) described themselves as satisfied; the dissatisfied partners ($n = 68$) may be underrepresented in the results as no statistical accommodations for the largely discrepant sample sizes were reported. The satisfied subgroup were more likely to have mild or moderate interparental conflict, to have selected shared parenting mutually, and to describe their ex-spouse as participatory and available when needed.

An alternative view is suggested by Rothberg (1983) who assessed a group of 30 JLC parents with children in private school about their satisfaction with joint custody. About two-thirds of the sample reported having generally good feelings about it, 13% reported negative feelings, and 20% reported feeling largely ambivalent. The majority of the Satisfied Parents group would recommend joint custody to other families (80%), but stipulated that it is not for everyone once the compromises and sacrifices involved in maintaining close contact with a former spouse are taken into account. These results must be viewed with caution since the sample obviously limits generalizability and responses were purely descriptive with no formal methodology articulated.

Characteristics of Parents Most Likely to Create a Positive Joint Custody Environment for Their Child

Only a few studies move beyond clinical impressions to investigate which parental characteristics are associated with the ability to sustain shared parenting. Steinman et al. (1986) describe the qualities of parents who most easily master the tasks required for cooperative parenting. Empathy, ability to maintain appropriate boundaries between the parental and parent-child dyads, the capacity to separate personal needs from the child's perspective, the ability to shift emotional expectations from those consistent with a spousal role to a co-parental one, and flexibility were key qualities. Parents who were least successful utilized coping strategies that included blaming and projecting feelings of hurt and anger onto the ex-spouse's parenting behaviors. More recent clinical research has further elucidated qualities of the parents that facilitate or hinder successful shared parenting (Ehrenberg, Hunter, & Elterman, 1996). These authors found that parents who were able to agree on a coparenting arrangement proved to be less narcissistic, more empathic, less self-oriented, and more child-oriented in their parenting attitudes. The majority of couples (75%) could be correctly classified by whether they agreed or not on a coparenting arrangement on the basis of these qualities. This research, in addition to employing a rigorous methodology, provides provocative information that begins to address for whom joint custody is appropriate. One interesting pathway shows that for some self-oriented partners this stance may be situationally determined, arising from coping mechanisms that soften the psychological injury of the divorce. These persons overlap but are not the same group as the narcissistic individuals, whose self-orientation is personality based. This points to a group for whom shared parenting may be successfully agreed on and maintained if services and supports are in place to cope with the vulnerabilities produced by the divorce.

CHILD CHARACTERISTICS AND SATISFACTIONS

Gender

Empirical knowledge offers few differences between boys' and girls' reactions and adjustment to joint custody. There are not enough studies in which other variables, such as age and time of assessment, are held constant so that the relative contributions of gender can be determined. Several studies suggest that boys benefit from shared parenting arrangements through fewer behavioral and emotional problems and self-defined negative experiences compared with sole custody children (Shiller, 1986; Wolchik et al., 1985). Among high-conflict families, girls are at particular risk for developing symptoms, although boys are more vulnerable to being triangulated in parental conflict (e.g., Johnston et al., 1987; Johnston, Kline, & Tschann, 1989). Since the general divorce literature indicates that boys are more likely to exhibit negative reactions, joint custody may ameliorate some of the negative impact of divorce for boys. The larger question of how joint custody lends support to healthy male development in divorced families longitudinally remains an open empirical question.

Developmental Level

Two age groups of special concern when divorce occurs are young children and adolescents. Developmentally, these groups require large doses of parental coordination and sensitivity to help them master the autonomy and relational issues that become magnified in these stages of development.

Children under Six. The tender years doctrine that formed child custody law arose from the awareness that the youngest children have great needs but are least able to express them directly or to act on their own behalf. Furthermore, parents and their young children confront a number of risk factors that are exacerbated by divorce. The group comprising children under the age of 6 years is the fastest growing segment exposed to the effects of parental separation and divorce, comprising 60% to 66% of large-scale study samples (Maccoby & Mnookin, 1992; Weitzman, 1985). These families are more likely to present disagreements over parenting arrangements than are parents of older children (Maccoby & Mnookin, 1992). Married couples with young children have had less time to become adjusted to partnerhood or parenthood, and are more likely to be younger, less educated, and to have fewer economic resources than older couples (Weitzman, 1985; Whiteside, 1995). Many postdivorce issues are related to socioeconomic status, including the decision to participate in joint custody.

In a comprehensive summary and meta-analysis of divorce literature pertaining to the youngest children of divorce, Whiteside (1995) found that the data for these children closely parallels the general divorce literature, with a few developmental caveats. More frequent father-child contact and father's preseparation level of involvement were related to a positive father-child relationship. One factor that may be of particular importance to the development of father-child relationships is having overnight time together. The loss of father contact among infants and toddlers occurred primarily in families where the children did not spend overnights with their father (Maccoby & Mnookin, 1992). Time spent together without adequate opportunity for fathers to assume direct responsibility for the child's care may not provide a sufficient foundation to establish a primary relationship. The infant needs enough time with each parent to establish an intimate relationship. For this to occur, it is crucial in the early stages of the marital separation to achieve a balance of child-care responsibilities that reinforces the competence of both parents. For the majority of families, this will mean reorganizing family labor division after divorce, since in most married families with infants and toddlers, women are the primary parents.

Whiteside (1995) concluded from the meta-analysis that no information available from research suggests how long a young child can go without contact with one of his or her parents, the number of transitions/week a baby can handle, or how long the child should stay in each household. To fill this gap, Whiteside conducted semistructured interviews with 11 experienced legal and mental health professionals working in the California court system. These practitioners identified factors that must be attended to in custody decisions with young children, including the length of time the child goes without seeing a parent, number of overnights in each house, and number of transitions between parents and with day-care providers. Although even the youngest children were assumed to be capable of handling overnights, the practitioners concurred that the schedule should protect the child's relationship with a primary caretaker. Frequent, shorter periods of contact were recommended for youngest children, with longer visits spaced further apart as the children grow beyond infancy and toddlerhood. However, more questions were raised than answered in Whiteside's report, since empirical validation from shared parenting studies has not yet been derived.

Relying on studies that differentiated results for youngest children from children in other developmental stages (Johnston & Campbell, 1988; McKinnon & Wallerstein, 1986; Steinman et al., 1986), results about cooperation and conflict within these families are as applicable for young children as for older ones. In short, high contact and high conflict provide a harmful environment. Infants and toddlers whose parents are in frequent contact and who are supportive of one another appear to be well-adjusted, even when they spend overnights in different households (also see Solomon & George, 1996). An absence of contact between spouses does not show a consistent relationship with adjustment; other factors become more important moderators. Three clinical studies of paternal access and young children (Brotsky, Steinman, & Zemmelman, 1988; Johnston & Campbell, 1988; McKinnon & Wallerstein, 1986) found that parents' commitment to the child and the quality of the interparental relationship were more closely linked to child adjustment than the schedule of contact in and of itself. Regardless of the amount of time children spent in two homes, high conflict, low cooperation, and disorganized care of the child resulted in aggression and regression. The conflict level was important, but so was the parents' ability to protect the child from exposure or cooption. Brotsky et al. (1988) reported that the children's adjustment was negatively impacted by the conflict and the parents' distress associated with it. The children's difficulties fed back to the parents, increasing their conflict in a negative feedback loop.

The data debunk certain myths associated with young children and joint custody. These children can do well behaviorally when separated from their mothers for days or even overnights. Overnights are not inherently harmful. However, young children require a higher level of commitment to cooperation than is needed for older children.

Adolescents.   In the largest study of adolescents to date, Buchanan, Maccoby, and Dornbusch (1996) examined children 10 to 18 years of age from 1,100 families from diverse socioeconomic groups in Northern California. Fewer adolescents lived in shared parenting arrangements over a 3-year period than in mother or father custody arrangements. Boys selected JPC more often than did girls. The teenagers selected JPC when they wished to have more contact with both parents; they moved out of the arrangements when one parent moved away or when they had conflict with their primary custodial parent.

With regard to adjustment, adolescents living in shared arrangements did not differ significantly from those in sole custody situations on behavioral or emotional outcomes. No gender differences emerged. However, minor differences were found that favored shared custody arrangements. Dual-residence teens were less depressed, had better grades, and described their "worst problems" in less severe terms than their sole custody counterparts. Some differences also were found between groups on a number of variables pertaining to parent-child relationships on dimensions of closeness and control; all of the significant findings favored JPC families. The most important predictors of adjustment for all groups of teenagers were fewer numbers of life stressors, residential stability, parent-child closeness, and the degree of household management, especially monitoring. This suggests that older children can do well in any kind of custody arrangement so long as they have ongoing support and firm guidance from their parents, and that this may be facilitated by shared parenting arrangements.

PARENT-CHILD CONTACT AND RELATIONSHIP

Research regarding joint custody has devoted the lion's share of its energies to examining the father-child relationship. The usual focus of these inquiries is the extent of joint custody fathers' involvement with their children over time. Children in JPC families do see their less-seen parent (usually their father) more frequently than those in sole custody arrangements (Coysh, Johnston, Tschann, Wallerstein, & Kline, 1989; Greif, 1979; Johnston et al., 1989; Kline et al., 1989; Luepnitz, 1986). In Kline et al., fathers with JPC had more access to their children, their children made more transitions between homes, and the men were more likely to maintain contact with their children over a 2-year period. Children living in mother physical custody situations saw their fathers an average of only 4 days per month, compared with 20 days for children living in JPC. A high-conflict sample produced an average of 4 days compared with 12 days for sole versus joint physical custody families, respectively (Johnston et al., 1989).

As with JPC families, JLC families show increased father contact and involvement in child care for joint compared with sole custody families (Albiston, Maccoby, & Mnookin, 1990; Arditti, 1992; Bowman & Ahrons, 1985; Wolchik et al., 1985). In the latter study (Wolchik et al., 1985), children in joint custody homes spent an average of 7 hours more per week with their fathers than did children living in sole custody homes.

It is possible that the more frequent paternal contact associated with JLC may be attributable to the higher economic status of those families. Although

Albiston et al. (1990) found a link between paternal contact and joint custody after the separation, the link was not significant when income and education variables were controlled in subsequent analyses. The link *did* remain after controlling for SES in Kline et al. (1989) and Johnston et al. (1989), who assessed JPC families. Thus, the link between JLC and paternal contact may not be sufficiently independent of SES to show a correlation once the powerful effects of SES are introduced. However, JPC and paternal contact by definition are more highly related.

The fact that joint custody fathers stay involved in their children's lives raises a question about what difference that makes to children's adaptation to divorce and overall development. This question is not easily determinable because custody, amount of access, schedules, transitions between homes, parental responsibilities, and child developmental needs have not been adequately disentangled in joint custody research. To examine this question, we turn to the general divorce literature. Earlier studies of family adaptation to divorce have indicated that children desire and benefit from nurturing relationships with both of their parents (e.g., Hetherington, Cox, & Cox, 1979; Wallerstein & Kelly, 1980; Warshak & Santrock, 1983). However, the amount of time children spend with their parents is not the most salient dimension of adjustment. Although there have been some mixed results, consensus from the more rigorous research designs indicates that there is no direct relationship between time spent with the less-seen parent and child adjustment postdivorce (e.g., see discussions in King, 1994; Maccoby et al., 1993; Thomas & Forehand, 1993). This finding was echoed in the joint custody research (e.g., Kline et al., 1989).

In the general literature, studies have consistently found a link between father contact and child adjustment when the quality of the relationship, not the quantity of time, is employed as the independent variable (Healy et al., 1990; Hodges, 1991; see generally, Thomas & Forehand, 1993). One exception to this generalization from JPC research is that increased father-child contact was associated directly with child emotional and behavioral symptoms among high-conflict families (Johnston et al., 1987), discussed in more detail in a subsequent section.

One way joint custody fosters a positive father-child relationship is predicated on the connection between fathers' feeling like a parent and acting like one. The more fathers visited their children and stayed close to their activities, the more they assumed parental responsibility and felt they had an influence on the emotional life of their child (Greif, 1979). The kind of control the author describes occurs in the contexts of having the right to make important decisions on a child's behalf. One interesting link has been made between father involvement and the mother-child relationship among adolescents (Buchanan, Maccoby, & Dornbusch, 1991). Adolescents who felt closest to noncustodial fathers also felt closer to their custodial mothers. They tended to feel closer to both parents, rather than to one or the other. Adolescents living in dual residences were more likely than their sole physical custody counterparts to report close relationships with both parents. Teens in JPC situations appear to benefit from a structure and process that encourages active participation by both parents.

These studies lend credence to the probability that, taken together with evidence of parents' satisfaction with joint custody arrangements, parents who are sharing responsibility enjoy having a legal status that depicts their shared authority and involvement. Fathers with joint custody stay more involved with their children one year after the divorce than do fathers without custody (Bowman & Ahrons, 1985; Luepnitz, 1986), whereas father dropout is more likely among sole custody fathers (Kline et al., 1989). After controlling for potential mediating variables, legal custody status explained a significant but small portion (9%) of the variance in father-child contact as reported by 80 men (Bowman & Ahrons, 1985). However, research has not sufficiently determined whether the adoption of joint custody agreements fosters an increased sense of shared parental responsibility.

Some parents who did not prefer joint custody initially reported higher satisfaction with it at a follow-up (Benjamin & Irving, 1990). Therefore, some reluctant parents may find that adopting a coparenting agreement increases their satisfaction with parenting, and perhaps their involvement. The arrangements would need to provide parents with opportunities for increased responsibility and sense of influence in their child's life, as well as increased time together. Regularity, duration, and inclusion of overnights are important elements in fostering a warm, enduring bond between parents and young children (Whiteside, 1995). With teens, even a brief amount of time may be sufficient to produce a close relationship (Maccoby et al., 1993). We know little about how much time children need with their fathers, at various developmental stages, in married or divorced homes, to foster long-term positive outcomes (Maccoby, 1995). Without this information, we can conclude only that joint custody provides reinforcement to those parents who are motivated to stay involved with their children.

CHILD SUPPORT

Financial support is one aspect of father involvement that clearly impacts family adjustment. Monetary issues are central to familial adaptation after divorce, influencing the degree and nature of parental conflict, resources and physical environments available to a child and his or her residential parent(s), older children's opportunities for higher education, and all the health and mental health factors correlated with socioeconomic status.

Courts have tended to make fewer awards among parents sharing custody, raising concerns that joint custodial mothers will receive less child support than their sole custody counterparts. In Maccoby et al.'s (1993) study, child support was ordered in over 90% of the families in which the children lived primarily with their mothers and in two thirds of the families with joint custody. The authors did not report employment data after divorce, yet it is possible that some of the discrepancy can be attributed to the fact that joint custody parents are able to work more hours, earning more, than their sole custody counterparts. Joint custody mothers may also be in a higher socioeconomic bracket independently, since families who choose joint custody tend to be better educated and have a higher SES than other divorcing families (Luepnitz, 1982; Racusin et al., 1989).

One difficulty is that joint physical custody *may* denote equal sharing of time spent with a child and associated expenses. However, time sharing may vary from near equal time to an arrangement that approximates regular visitation, equivalent to approximately 20% of a regular calendar year (Garfinkel, Melli, & Robertson, 1994). A question that arises in joint custody situations is the amount by which child support is to be reduced, known as the threshold. Most states do not reduce child support until the time spent with the less-seen parent is 30% to 35% above standard visitation amounts (Garfinkel et al., 1994). According to Garfinkel et al.'s analysis of child support orders, the most commonly used approach to reduce child support is based on parents' incomes and time spent with the child. Although this formula appears to be fair, it is often implemented unfairly. In some states, for example, no reduction is made at 30% time, but at 35% time, a 35% reduction is introduced. The 35% economic support loss for the 5% time reduction obviously results in a hardship to the primary custodian, most often the mother. An alternative method the authors favor is to reduce support only for the amount of shared time beyond the threshold. Research has not yet examined these different methods and their relationship to the success of joint custody and family adjustment.

Researchers have also looked at the relationship between joint custody and compliance with child support. There is limited evidence that fathers participating in joint custody families stay current in their payment compared with fathers without custody (Arditti, 1992; Luepnitz, 1986; Pearson & Thoennes, 1986). In Pearson and Thoennes' research, fathers in joint custody arrangements had the best record of compliance (85%–95%), compared with fathers whose children lived in the sole custody of their mothers, who complied 65% of the time. Parents with joint custody also reported doing more financial extras for their children beyond the court-ordered agreement (Chambers, 1979). At worst, no differences have been found between joint and sole custody family situations (Shrier, Simring, Shapiro, Greif, & Lindenthal, 1991). These inconsistencies may be a function of the dynamic that parental cooperation and a positive relationship may have a decreasing, but significant impact on fathers' compliance with child support payments (Ahrons & Miller, 1993).

COOPERATION AND CONFLICT

As data emerges identifying the many variables that interact in joint custody arrangements, and it becomes clearer that the construct of joint custody itself is heterogeneous, scientific inquiries are guided by questions concerning the conditions under which these shared parenting arrangements will work best for certain types of family systems. A central concern about joint custody is that it increases the frequency of interactions between ex-spouses, thereby increasing demands for cooperative communication and the potential for ongoing conflict and hostility. This section will examine knowledge about cooperation and conflict in normative custody situations in which anger and hostility are present in low to moderate levels. It also will address issues of the high conflict and violent custody situations.

Three cumulative findings have emerged from research. First, the decision and implementation of joint custody is part of the ongoing family processes prior to the marital separation. A detailed assessment of a small sample of joint physical custody families indicated that those who are most successful at establishing and maintaining coparenting relationships are those who were less angry about the divorce from the beginning (Steinman et al., 1986). A much larger study of 678 persons concurred that the emotional state of the parents immediately following the separation had a significant impact on the coparenting relationship one year later (Maccoby, Depner, & Mnookin, 1990). Second, cooperative and conflictual parents are found in a range of custody and access configurations (Bowman & Ahrons, 1985; Kline et al., 1989; Maccoby et al., 1990; Pearson & Thoennes, 1990; Wolchik et al., 1985). This variability might explain conflicting findings about whether and how conflict impacts child adjustment across studies. Third, for cooperation and conflict to be useful predictors, they must be more discretely defined. They are affected by distal factors such as the amount of time passed since separation and child age, as well as proximal factors such as the content of discussion or conflict, its frequency, context, and the child's role in the conflict (e.g., Maccoby et al., 1990). These factors also affect whether the cooperation or conflict has a direct impact on child adjustment or an indirect impact through its effect on important moderators such as the frequency and quality of the noncustodial parent and child relationship (Kelly, 1993). Given these complexities, few generalizations can be made about the connection between custody and coparental communication. It is not prudent to make decisions about custody based solely, or even primarily, on the interparental relationship.

Cooperation between Joint Custody Parents

A central belief held about joint custody parents is that they will cooperate more than sole custody parents around child rearing. Empirical support for this assumption is limited, and therefore is an area that is frequently overinterpreted. Nelson (1989) reported that JPC parents did discuss their children more often than a sole custody control group. Similarly, JLC status predicted higher levels of parental interaction and its quality (Bowman & Ahrons, 1985). In an 18-month follow-up report from the Stanford group, Maccoby et al. (1990) also found that parents in dual-residence families cooperated to a higher degree. In a separate study from the same project, Albiston et al. (1990) reported that having joint legal custody did not predict higher levels of cooperation. The children's residence made little difference in the pattern of coparenting the parents adopted

(Maccoby et al., 1993). Across custody groups, one-fourth of their 664 family sample could be characterized as cooperative. Based on their previous reports, the percentage would be higher among the dual-residence group. However, the overall picture suggests that higher cooperation may be present among joint custody families, but it is not a characteristic that strongly differentiates the families from those in sole custody arrangements. A subsample from the project that focused on adolescents made the distinction that young people living in dual-residence situations benefited from cooperation more than their sole custody counterparts, such that the benefits of having cooperative parents are magnified under shared parenting conditions (Buchanan et al., 1991).

Viability of Joint Custody without Cooperation

The extent and nature of cooperation, like child adjustment outcomes, is not correlated directly with custody type or arrangement (Kline et al., 1989; Pearson & Thoennes, 1990; Wolchik et al., 1985). Parents may be able to sidestep cooperative parenting and still promote healthy adjustment if they stay attuned to their child's needs (Tschann et al., 1989). Also, Steinman et al.'s (1986) descriptive study of a 3-year longitudinal investigation identified qualities such as appreciation for the bond between the child and former spouse, maintenance of objectivity through the divorce process, and ability to empathize with the child and other parent as qualities of parents who successfully navigated joint custody. When one parent accepted or appreciated the other parent's needs with regard to their child, cooperation was not as important.

The age of the child may also determine the viability of joint custody without parental cooperation. Reports from the Stanford study indicate that parents tend to become more disengaged from each other over time, with the parents who engaged in discussions about their children declining from 67% to 40% over the 3 years of the study (Maccoby et al., 1993). Despite this occurrence, adolescents in shared custody situations fared at least as well as those in sole custody arrangements with less frequent visitation. By contrast, a meta-analysis of divorce studies pertinent to custody of younger children, though not specific to joint custody, indicated that a cooperative style and coparenting support are related to child and parent adjustment (Whiteside, 1995). This pattern makes intuitive sense based on younger children's developmental needs and the increased coordination and sharing of information required by parents of younger children. As children become more self-sufficient and independent, they can manage more of their own affairs in concert with their divorced parents even if they are moving between homes.

Viability under High-Conflict Situations

The deleterious effects of parental conflict on child development, in married and divorced families, is one of the consistent findings in family interaction research.

The evidence strongly suggests that the nature, severity, and management of conflict between parents is a feature of the quality of divorcing life that deserves primary consideration from legal decision makers. Although the area of conflict and cooperation has been extensively explored among the general divorce population, research has often meshed considerations of coparenting with greater access. Although increased access and visitation are obviously linked to the notion of joint custody, how much and where contact overlaps with shared residential arrangements and legal agreements is still vaguely understood.

The available knowledge about joint custody with regard to conflict indicates that conflict is not merely the mirror image of cooperation. Dual-residence parents may have engaged in higher levels of communication with their ex-spouses, but their levels of conflict did not differ from those of primary residential parents (Maccoby et al., 1990). Similarly, custody and conflict were not related between sole maternal custody and joint physical custody groups (Johnston et al., 1987; Kline et al., 1989), or when examined within joint physical custody groups defined by their success and satisfaction with their arrangements (Steinman et al., 1986). Levels of hostility and conflict did not differentiate those who had "successful, stressed, or failed" joint custody arrangements, nor did it differentiate those who maintained their arrangements from those who did not. By contrast, joint physical custody was associated with lower conflict among parents in one other study that employed a sole custody control group (Luepnitz, 1986), although only 11 persons were included in the sample.

Overall, it would seem that joint custody can be conducted in the midst of low to moderate levels of conflict. There is no evidence that, in itself, shared parenting will reduce conflict. In fact, it seems quite unrelated to conflict. Researchers have not yet determined whether conflict between parents in shared parenting arrangements will cause greater or fewer problems among children than would similar levels of conflict occurring in sole custody situations. It can be argued that the greater exposure to the conflict would increase children's vulnerability. It is equally likely that the cooperation among joint custody parents will mitigate some of the deleterious effects of conflict on the children's development.

The strongest empirical evidence that interparental conflict in shared parenting situations can adversely affect child adjustment emerges from two studies drawing from three distinct samples (Johnston et al., 1987, 1989). These studies focused on a joint custody subgroup that was entrenched in high-conflict disputes. The data from this research suggest that these children, assessed 2 to 3 years after the divorce, have both overcontrolled and undercontrolled profiles of disturbance characterized by such symptoms as depression, withdrawal, and diminished interest in communicating. Additionally, this group of children reported somatic complaints. Role reversal, the caretaking of a parent, was also observed in these children and found to be an important indicator of child disturbance. This was especially true when fathers reversed roles rather than mothers. Frequent access to the less-seen parent was identified as a central contributor to withdrawal in these children, as well as to inferior social competence compared to children living in sole mother custody arrangements. The sample sizes were relatively large for joint custody studies, and the ethnic diversity contributes to generalizability of the samples. A study drawing upon the Johnston et al. (1989) data confirm that frequent access actually predicts increased conflict and child symptomatology over time (Tschann et al., 1989). These studies do not unequivocally demonstrate that joint custody promotes conflict, only that among highly conflictual parents, the frequent access to each other serves to sustain hostilities and predict ongoing aggression.

Insofar as joint custody fosters more contact between divorced parents (e.g., Nelson, 1989), it appears to exacerbate interparental conflict among high-conflict families and concomitant negative effects on child adjustment. However, it is not at all clear that joint custody engenders conflict among the majority of the divorcing population. Two longitudinal studies indicate that conflict diminishes for the majority of parents and their children in the first several years after separation (Kelly, 1990; Maccoby et al., 1990). Ex-spouses simply have less to do with each other over time, with diminished sharing of information about child rearing. The clearest predictors in these studies were the extent of child-specific conflict during the marriage (Kelly, 1990), the degree of conflict at the beginning of the divorce process, and the amount of legal conflict, whether over support or custody (Albiston et al., 1990).

Another feature mediating conflict, adversely affecting the success of joint custody arrangements, is the manner in which the conflict is expressed or contained (Maccoby et al., 1993). The presence of interparental hostility and conflict is less harmful if parents can separate marital from parental dimensions of their relationship. Conflicts about child rearing, in particular, are associated with poorer child outcome. Clarke-Stewart (1977) reviewed numerous studies and concluded that inconsistencies between parents are commonly associated with social developmental lags, such as immaturity and dependency. Differences in child rearing and disciplinary practices may be most salient for preschool and preadolescent children (Clingempeel & Reppucci, 1982). If parents are different in ways that are internally consistent, that are supportive or at least clearly separate from the other, the detrimental impact on children may be lessened. For example, school-age preadolescents adjusted well to dissimilar home environments when their schedule was predictable and parents cooperated with one another (Greif, 1979). This finding must be considered only as preliminary given the very small sample size of eight families, and the selection bias inherent in the study.

The way in which parents protect or expose their children significantly affects how the conflict impacts children. Becoming the object of the battle, or the parentified child, has been linked to poorer adjustment (Buchanan et al., 1991; Johnston et al., 1989). Among adolescents, higher parental conflict makes it more likely that children will feel caught in the ongoing dissension (Buchanan et al., 1991). Yet even some parents who maintain a relatively high level of hostility refrain from implicating their child; likewise, some cooperative parents have children who report feeling caught between their parents. The authors found that dual-residence children are more vulnerable to feeling loyalty pulls or caught in the middle than sole-residence children. Thus, just as the benefits from cooperative parenting were stronger for joint than sole custody adolescents, so too are the negative effects of conflict stronger for this subgroup.

POTENTIAL FOR REDUCING LEGAL CONFLICT

Within high-conflict families, joint custody children are exposed to greater risk of being caught in the middle in pernicious ways that pose a serious detriment to their development. This raises concerns for the children from high-conflict families who live in states where joint custody is presumed to be in the best interests of the child if the parents are willing to accept it. There has not been sufficient time passed nor empirical study undertaken to determine how legal presumptions influence parental conflict. Data comparing outcomes in mandated joint custody versus mandated sole custody awards are scarce due to the complexity of obtaining this data and controlling for many of the relevant variables.

When parents freely enter into joint custody, studies have consistently found decreased relitigation for joint custody over sole custody parents (Dudley, 1991; Emery, Matthews, & Wyer, 1991; Emery & Wyer, 1987; Ilfeld, Ilfeld, & Alexander, 1982; Luepnitz, 1986). Luepnitz (1982) found that 50% of her sole custody families relitigated, while none of her joint custody families did. Ilfeld and colleagues (1982) found, that among 414 cases over a 2-year period, relitigation rates for joint custody were half those of sole custody families, except among cases where joint custody was imposed without the consent of one parent. In the involuntary joint custody cases, the relitigation rates for sole custody and joint custody families were comparable (32% vs. 33%, respectively). The authors conclude that unconsented joint custody is no more disruptive to family relations than sole custody. Although this result has been interpreted to mean that mandating joint custody does not increase preexisting parental conflict (e.g., Schepard, 1985), a more conservative interpretation is warranted. It does indicate that the joint custody designation may remove the stimulus for returning to court for some couples, preventing a crucial type of conflict. It does not automatically signal that conflict is not high, however, or that the children are not exposed to higher levels of conflict than they would be otherwise. Whether the ability to keep the conflict out of the legal system identifies a family strength likely to lead to attenuation of the hostilities and their fallout is an important area for further study.

Other studies concur that court-imposed custody awards do not reduce litigation. In states that have experimented with court-imposed joint legal custody orders, relitigation is higher among court-ordered cases than in sole custody cases. In Massachusetts, a 20% relitigation rate for joint custody cases was found compared with a 12% rate among sole custody cases (Phear et al., 1984), with a similar conclusion found in Michigan (see Kuehl, 1989). The benefits of joint custody may be lost, and the process of custody decision making may become even more costly, when it is imposed on parents who are not ready to undertake it. The experience of working out the conflict without legal interference may lead to one or both parents' increased ability to negotiate and compromise. Decision theory suggests that people who are forced to deal directly with each other are more likely to cooperate eventually than those whose relationships are mediated and less intertwined (Schepard, 1985). However, the argument against mandating joint custody is voiced consistently by clinicians who feel that children of high-conflict families pay too high a price in shared parenting arrangements (e.g., Johnston & Campbell, 1986; Johnston et al., 1987, 1989; Steinman et al., 1986). The presence of higher conflict increases the chance that children will become caught and used in the wars their parents wage (Johnston et al., 1989).

Parents may come to joint custody through several channels. Irving et al. (1984) described three kinds of joint custody groups, differentiated by the degree to which they selected joint custody voluntarily. One group is characterized by both ex-spouses wanting it and agreeing to it. The second group is reluctant but accepts it as a compromise. The third and final group is mandated to accept it. Most of the positive payoffs for parents and children of joint custody reside in the first group, those who selected joint custody because they felt their children needed and deserved an equal relationship with both parents. The horror stories of joint custody are most commonly drawn from the high-conflict, mandated group. The middle group presents the greatest challenge, since they fall into a gray area about which little is known. This is potentially a high-conflict group, but one that is situationally determined, and not yet entrenched in destructive conflictual interactions. This group could benefit from joint custody, with early intervention and support. For the present, what the best decisions are for this group is only conjecture, and requires research that clarifies interactions between the mediators across areas of divorce research—those variables relevant to the interparental relationship, parent-child connections, and parental and child characteristics and functioning.

When Conflict Escalates into Violence

The presence of postseparation spousal conflict is pervasive in the literature, but it does not usually reach truly destructive heights. More than a decade of research with various populations from across the state of California has shown fairly consistent findings: 60%–76% of mediated disputes result in agreements; of these, 40%–57% reach full resolutions (see full description in Johnston & Roseby, 1997). The highly conflicting group of families who cannot settle in brief mediation comprises 9%–15% of all divorcing families, and 24%–40% of those seeking a court-imposed decision (Johnston & Roseby 1997). A disproportionately large share of judicial resources are devoted to this select group.

There is concern from joint custody opponents that the assumption of shared parenting may escalate the level of violence already present in the family. Empirical knowledge does not support this fear. In one sample of joint physical custody families, extreme levels of verbal and physical aggression 2 to 3 years postseparation was not attributable to or predicted by custody arrangements (Nelson, 1989). The violence is likely to be a carryover from marital dynamics established before the separation. Mothers' reports of abuse in marriage are strong, consistent predictors of postdivorce physical abuse (Emery, 1982).

Another concern commonly voiced is for the protection of women. Women who are being abused may place themselves and their children in grave danger when they try to end the marriage and thereby break the cycle of abuse. Out of fear and intimidation, women tend to trade financial entitlements for custody in hopes that the intimidation from ex-spouses will stop (Pagelow, 1993). Children may then be at higher risk since research shows that children in abusive marriages are often victims of abuse themselves, and that the loss of one victim may lead to substitution of another (Geffner & Pagelow, 1990). These issues focus concern on mandated joint custody and mandated mediation. Some states consider spousal abuse as a reason not to mandate mediation, but in other states such as California, the presence of domestic violence is considered irrelevant for mediation (Geffner & Pagelow, 1990).

As a result of the higher proportion of mediations resulting in shared parenting agreements, mandated mediation is targeted by opponents of joint custody in violent families. Opponents argue that joint custody in the presence of domestic violence perpetuates cycles of unequal power and intimidation, undermining a central tenet of mediation: to equalize power among men and women by putting the negotiations in their own hands rather than the courts (Geffner & Pagelow, 1990; Pagelow, 1993). On the other hand, women of color and low socioeconomic status have not always been treated adequately in the adversarial system. They should not therefore be excluded from mediation due solely to a fairness question if they want to participate. Careful attention paid to whether a woman is freely consenting to mediation or joint custody, and inclusion of a mediator trained in domestic violence issues, contribute to correcting for power imbalances that skew the process (Geffner & Pagelow, 1990).

Although mandating mediation may compromise needed protections for battered women, high-conflict divorcing families are not unidimensional. Johnston and Campbell (1993) have developed an exploratory typology of violent couples from a sample of 140 families studied and provided mental health treatment. They distinguished four major categories: episodic/ongoing violence perpetuated by men against their wives throughout the marriage; female initiated; interactive violence that arises out of troubled communications instigated by either party but ultimately controlled by the men; and situational violence connected to the separation/divorce trauma and controlled by whichever partner is abandoned or left by the other. The first group resembles the classic "wife battering" syndrome (Walker, 1984). For a small group of perpetrators that span the first two categories, violence was fueled by disordered thinking and paranoia of clinical proportions. Johnston's typologies need to be revalidated with larger samples. If they hold under wider conditions, clinicians can begin to describe for decision makers judicious custody and access plans for these couples. Furthermore, interventions that mitigate the situational divorce-determined violence may strengthen some couples' capacity to cooperate for the benefit of their child. The well-founded concerns about high conflict result in typecasting all high-conflict families in a manner that does not tell the whole story about whether joint custody could be beneficial, or workable, over time.

JOINT CUSTODY IN THE LEGAL SYSTEM

The shadow of the law also encompasses the shadow of the adversarial process under which families negotiate joint custody. Several elements of the current legal context in which joint custody is decided are elucidated to guide decision makers in understanding how their values and biases impact joint custody.

The meaning of joint and sole custody to the people who are divorcing is one important issue. Legal commentators call for a move away from the terms "custody" and "visitation," implying ownership and nonparental relationships, toward terms of shared responsibility (e.g., Schepard, 1985). Patrician (1984) studied the connotations of joint versus sole legal custody and of custodial versus noncustodial parent for 90 men. Joint legal custody was most strongly associated with being fair, good, and equal. Sole legal custody, on the other hand, was associated with being unfair, selfish, unequal, bad, and useless. Similarly, custodial parents were viewed as powerful, strong, winners, and dominant compared with noncustodial parents. These results suggest that for men the vocabulary and meaning assigned to custody labels in the divorce process may exacerbate wounded pride, confidence, and sense of fairness and inflame anger. These emotions may undermine the spirit of cooperation needed for shared parenting and healthy child adjustment.

Another contextual consideration affecting how joint custody will be viewed by families is the influence of legal professionals on the joint custody process. Unless judges and attorneys are open to the possibilities of joint custody for different kinds of families, its potential benefits may be lost. Felner, Terre, Farber, Primavera, and Bishop (1985) sought opinions from 350 attorneys (75 of whom participated) and 43 judges about their legal preferences. This response rate is an extremely low one, indicating that a bias may be present in the data. Nevertheless, this group did not advocate for joint custody. Less than one-third of the participants felt that joint custody is the best option for minor children. They emphasized its viability for all children only under certain conditions: a good interparental relationship, financial resources, mutual motivation, and the ability to place a child's interests before their own. These conditions constitute the *ideal* environment for joint custody to take place. Judges and attorneys may be reluctant to recommend joint custody without substantial data indicating its potential for a wider range of families. Although it is most obvious in the ideal how joint custody can benefit family adjustment, the joint custody literature reviewed also indicates that a broader range of families could successfully share parenting responsibilities.

Increasing societal alarm about the possible perpetration of sexual abuse and domestic violence within families is also complicating divorce disputes. Judges denied custody significantly more often to the parent who had allegations levied against him or her, regardless of whether the information was substantiated (Sorensen et al., 1995). In fact, it was not substantiated in the majority of those cases. The potential for misuse of allegations by parents and decision makers plays a crucial role in determinations of joint legal custody and shared residential arrangements.

A number of states are attempting to reduce the adversarial nature of divorce by encouraging or mandating mediation for all families disagreeing about issues of custody and visitation (Emery, 1994). Mediation has been touted and condemned for its potential role in promoting joint custody. There is strong evidence that mediated agreements are more likely to yield joint custody than are lawyer-negotiated agreements (Bautz & Hill, 1991; Bohmer & Ray, 1994; Emery & Wyer, 1987; Pearson & Thoennes, 1986), although mediated child custody agreements also tend to break down at a higher rate than other custody agreements (Bohmer & Ray, 1994). It is possible that the parties are persuaded by the mediators to agree to joint custody, which helps to explain the frequency of joint custody arrangements found in the mediated samples (Grillo, 1991).

Although these data are used to recommend mediation as a means of promoting joint custody, the couples who mediate are more often a select group. They tend to have higher levels of interaction during and after the divorce, to cooperate more, and to have higher regard for their ex-spouse as a parent than are couples who litigate (Kelly, 1991; Pearson & Thoennes, 1984). The use of mediation to encourage joint custody also raises the specter of mandatory mediation. Grillo (1991) fears that under these conditions women will be disadvantaged, yet data show that women are not forced to give away custody entitlements (Emery & Jackson, 1989) nor are they disadvantaged financially (Maccoby & Mnookin, 1992).

CLOSING THE GAP BETWEEN EMPIRICAL KNOWLEDGE AND DECISION MAKING

Despite the gap left when empirical knowledge and joint custody became estranged years ago, joint custody research has established some fundamentals. To review the fundamentals to date:

- Legal custody status in and of itself is not significantly related to the parental relationship or the child's adjustment.
- JLC and JPC fathers feel more satisfied after divorce, which has a positive effect on their involvement with their child over time.

- JPC provides benefits in satisfaction and adjustment among more educated, child-centered families that are most likely to choose it. For these
  families, the structure may reinforce a natural tendency to work together
  as parents for their children after divorce.
- Custody arrangement does not affect parental cooperation or conflict.
- Research robustly indicates that when families are in high conflict, joint
  custody of any sort does not heal the relationship, and when parents cannot contain their conflict to the marital dyad, it can be destructive for children. School-age children may be most vulnerable to role reversals and
  other destructive dynamics in which parents involve their children. This
  use of the child can produce loyalty conflicts or unsavory alliances against
  the other parent. Conflict is harmful, and conflict plus frequent access to
  both warring parents is most destructive.

Instead of directing additional inquiries into relatively well-substantiated
areas, future research should address domains in which there is less complete
knowledge. Logistical and psychological mechanisms through which contact
with the less-seen parent leads to a better parent-child relationship constitute
one such domain. Joint custody is associated with increased contact, but how
that contact is developed and nurtured through living arrangements of various
types is less understood. A theme running through the literature is the importance of shared parenting agreements that encourage active involvement in
child care rather than just "time spent together." These arrangements foster a
sense of influence over a child's upbringing.

There are also a number of areas where research is needed to further inform
legal decision makers. These inquiries should be guided by theoretical models
that draw on empirical knowledge of divorce, understanding of the legal system,
and psychological knowledge of child development and family process. The
models should then be tested and refined. Figure 18.1 depicts an example of a research and intervention model presently being conducted by this chapter's senior author for divorcing families with children under the age of 6. The figure
illustrates the theoretical model that integrates clinical and legal interventions;
details of the clinical intervention are discussed elsewhere (Kline & Pruett, in
press). A central premise underlying the model assumes that divorce turns
parental gatekeeping from the married family on its head, such that father's
support of mother's child rearing becomes a means for retaliation or growth
through mother's support of father's child rearing after divorce. The role of legal
intervention is embodied in a cooperative model that challenges traditional roles
of attorneys, judges, mental health professionals, and mediators. This model elu-
cidates the processes of litigation or collaboration among families with young
children. The discussion that follows highlights areas needing further research.

Additional interventions that comprise psychoeducational, clinical, and
legal interventions must be formulated and tested; for example, interventions
for parents who believe in shared parenting, but who are too angry with each

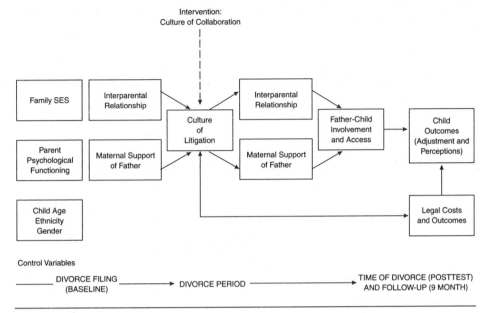

Figure 18.1   The Collaborative Divorce Project (CDP).

other to feel secure in their execution of it must be tested. Such interventions can be tested with families choosing different types of living arrangements. These families could benefit from short-term interventions within the legal context, such as family education, as well as brief therapeutic interventions aimed at helping couples separate marital from parental issues.

Other families require mental health intervention on a longer term basis, with evidence suggesting that it should begin as early in the separation process as possible and continue through the changes that evolve in the first year. Supporting a familial alliance during the divorce process may facilitate reasoned decisions that do not become as engulfed in the culture of the legal system with its accompanying adversarial probabilities.

We need much more information about effective interventions with high-risk families. Studies of children under the age of 6 and of high-conflict families are two such examples. Special techniques for families at an impasse (Johnston & Roseby, 1997) are needed to assess the foundation of the conflict and the best way to intervene under the varying conditions of different family dynamics.

Basic information from large samples of longitudinal studies that focus on the children's adjustment at several developmental stages will clarify the roles of age and gender as they relate to adjustment in various arrangements. The processes between transitions, overnights, and parents' emotional health and interparental relationship need to be elucidated. Under what conditions can children adjust well to different environments, at what developmental stages, and for what periods of time? How can families build in mechanisms for scheduling changes so that parents negotiate with each other and the children in a manner that enhances everyone's sense of fairness and commitment to healthy development, rather than become manipulations or narcissistic insults? How much time with a mother or a father is needed at what stages over the long course of development?

In addition to more clinically oriented studies, research must focus on the legal system itself. Researchers have not investigated the degree to which lawyers for parents feel compelled, or even try, to temper parents' positions when those positions threaten the child's relationship with the other parent (Schepard, 1985). Aggressive representation is considered a sine qua non of legal advocacy, and it is a difficult balancing act for lawyers to fulfill their legal obligation while keeping the child's interests present when the child is not the client.

Research is needed that examines legal options: the single judge calendar management system, custody decisions made with neutral evaluators, the presence or absence of child attorneys, and joint legal and joint physical custody determined under different kinds of legal processes. The use of mediation will require further research to clarify its strengths and weaknesses.

Postdecree remedies for parental violations of agreements must be researched to find the most effective deterrents from embroiling children as pawns in a game of chess, when coparenting and shared residential arrangements are the stakes of the game.

It is through research questions such as these that we can explore dimensions of shared parenting in detail, and examine the legal and psychological processes that impact it in tandem. Only then can we reach a sustained reconciliation between the realities of shared parenting, known also as joint custody, and its estranged empirical partner. Together, they can support the healthy adjustment and development of children and their families after divorce.

REFERENCES

Ahrons, C. (1979). The binuclear family: Two households, one family. *Alternative Lifestyles, 2,* 499–515.

Ahrons, C. (1981). The continuing coparental relationship between divorced spouses. *American Journal of Orthopsychiatry, 51,* 415–428.

Ahrons, C. (1983). Predictors of paternal involvement postdivorce: Mothers' and fathers' perceptions. *Journal of Divorce, 6,* 55–67.

Ahrons, C., & Miller, R. B. (1993). The effect of the postdivorce relationship on paternal involvement: A longitudinal relationship. *American Journal of Orthopsychiatry, 63,* 441–450.

Albiston, C. R., Maccoby, E. E., & Mnookin, R. H. (1990). Does joint legal custody matter? *Stanford Law and Policy Review, 2,* 167–179.

Amato, P. R., & Keith, B. (1991). Parental divorce and the well-being of children: A meta-analysis. *Psychological Bulletin, 110,* 26–46.

Arditti, J. A. (1992). Differences between fathers with joint custody and noncustodial fathers. *American Journal of Orthopsychiatry, 62,* 186–195.

Bahr, S. J., Howe, J. D., Mann, M. M., & Bahr, M. S. (1994). Trends in child custody awards: Has the removal of maternal preference made a difference? *Family Law Quarterly, 28*, 247–267.

Bautz, B. J., & Hill, R. M. (1991). Mediating the breakup: Do children win? *Mediation Quarterly, 8*, 199–210.

Benjamin, M., & Irving, H. H. (1990). Comparison of the experience of satisfied and dissatisfied shared parents. *Journal of Divorce and Remarriage, 14*, 43–61.

Bohmer, C., & Ray, M. L. (1994). Effects of different dispute resolution methods on women and children after divorce. *Family Law Quarterly, 28*, 223–245.

Bowman, M. E., & Ahrons, C. R. (1985). Impact of legal custody status on fathers' parenting postdivorce. *Journal of Marriage and Family, 47*, 481–488.

Braver, S. L., Wolchik, S. A., Sandler, I. N., Sheets, V. L., Fogas, B., & Bay, R. C. (1993). A longitudinal study of noncustodial parents: Parents without children. *Journal of Family Psychology, 7*, 9–23.

Brotsky, M., Steinman, S., & Zemmelman, S. (1988). Joint custody through mediation—reviewed: Parents assess their adjustment eighteen months later. *Conciliation Courts Review, 26*, 53–58.

Buchanan, C. M., Maccoby, E. E., & Dornbusch, S. M. (1991). Caught between parents: Adolescents' experience in divorced homes. *Child Development, 62*, 1008–1029.

Buchanan, C. M., Maccoby, E. E., & Dornbusch, S. M. (1996). *Adolescents after divorce.* Cambridge, MA: Harvard University Press.

Camara, K. A., & Resnick, G. (1988). Interparental conflict and cooperation: Factors moderating children's post-divorce adjustment. In E. M. Hetherington & J. D. Arasteh (Eds.), *Impact of divorce, single parenting, and stepparenting on children* (pp. 169–196). Hillsdale, NJ: Erlbaum.

Chambers, D. (1979). *Making fathers pay: The enforcement of child support.* Chicago: University of Chicago Press.

Chase-Lansdale, P. L., Cherlin, A. J., & Kiernan, P. K. (1995). The long-term effects of parental divorce on the mental health of young adults: A developmental perspective. *Child Development, 66*, 1614–1634.

Clarke-Stewart, A. (1977). *Child care in the family.* New York: Academic Press.

Clingempeel, W. G., & Reppucci, N. D. (1982). Joint custody after divorce: Major issues and goals for research. *Psychological Bulletin, 91*, 102–127.

Coysh, W., Johnston, J. R., Tschann, J., Wallerstein, J., & Kline, M. (1989). Parental postdivorce adjustment in joint and sole physical custody families. *Journal of Family Issues, 10*, 52–71.

Davies, P. T., & Cummings, E. M. (1994). Marital conflict and child adjustment: An emotional security hypothesis. *Psychological Bulletin, 116*, 387–411.

Derdeyn, A. P. (1976). Child custody contests in historical perspective. *American Journal of Psychiatry, 133*, 1369–1376.

Donnelly, D., & Finkelhor, D. (1993). Who has joint custody? Class differences in the determination of custody arrangements. *Family Relations, 42*, 57–60.

Dudley, J. R. (1991). The consequences of divorce proceedings for divorced fathers. *Journal of Divorce and Remarriage, 16*, 171–193.

Ehrenberg, M. F., Hunter, M. A., & Elterman, M. F. (1996). Shared parenting agreements after marital separation: The roles of empathy and narcissism. *Journal of Consulting and Clinical Psychology, 64*, 808–818.

Ellis, J. W. (1990). Plans, protections, and professional intervention: Innovations in divorce custody reform and the role of legal professionals. *University of Michigan Journal of Law Reform, 24,* 65–188.

Emery, R. E. (1982). Interparental conflict and the children of discord and divorce. *Psychological Bulletin, 92,* 310–330.

Emery, R. E. (1988). *Marriage, divorce, and children's adjustment.* Newbury Park, CA: Sage.

Emery, R. E. (1994). *Renegotiating family relationships: Divorce, child custody, and mediation.* New York: Guilford Press.

Emery, R. E., & Jackson, J. A. (1989). The Charlottesville mediation project: Mediated and litigated child custody disputes. *Mediation Quarterly, 24,* 3–18.

Emery, R. E., Matthews, S. G., & Kitzmann, K. M. (1994). Child custody mediation and litigation: Parents' satisfaction and functioning one year after settlement. *Journal of Consulting and Clinical Psychology, 62,* 124–129.

Emery, R. E., Matthews, S. G., & Wyer, N. M. (1991). Child custody mediation and litigation: Further evidence on the differing views of mothers and fathers. *Journal of Consulting and Clinical Psychology, 59,* 410–418.

Emery, R. E., & Wyer, N. M. (1987). Child custody mediation and litigation: An experimental evaluation of the experience of parents. *Journal of Consulting and Clinical Psychology, 55,* 179–186.

Felner, R. T., Terre, L., Farber, S. S., Primavera, J., & Bishop, T. A. (1985). Child custody: Practices and perspectives of legal professionals. *Journal of Clinical Child Psychology, 14,* 27–34.

Folberg, J. (1991). *Joint custody and shared parenting.* New York: Guilford Press.

Garfinkel, I., Melli, M. S., & Robertson, J. G. (1994). Child support orders: A perspective on reform. *The Future of Children: Children and Divorce, 4,* 84–100.

Geffner, R., & Pagelow, M. (1990). Mediation and child custody: Issues in abusive relationships. *Behavioral Sciences and the Law, 8,* 151–159.

Goldstein, J., Solnit, A. J., Goldstein, S., & Freud, A. (1996). *The best interests of the child.* New York: Free Press.

Greif, J. B. (1979). Fathers, children, and joint custody. *American Journal of Orthopsychiatry, 49,* 311–319.

Grillo, T. (1991). The mediation alternative: Process dangers for women. *Yale Law Journal, 100,* 1545–1610.

Grossberg, M. (1985). *Governing the hearth.* Chapel Hill: University of North Carolina Press.

Guidubaldi, J., & Perry, J. (1985). Divorce and mental health sequlae for children: A two year follow-up of a nationwide sample. *Journal of the American Academy of Child Psychiatry, 24,* 531–537.

Guidubaldi, J., Perry, J., & Cleminshaw, H. (1984). The legacy of parental divorce: A nationwide study of family status and selected mediating variables on children's academic and social competencies. In B. D. Lahey & A. E. Kazdin (Eds.), *Advances in clinical child psychology* (Vol. 7, pp. 109–151). New York: Plenum Press.

Healy, J. M., Malley, J. E., & Stewart, A. J. (1990). Children and their fathers after parental separation. *American Journal of Orthopsychiatry, 60,* 531–543.

Hess, R. D., & Camara, K. A. (1979). Post-divorce family relationships as mediating factors in the consequences of divorce for children. *Journal of Social Issues, 35,* 79–96.

Hetherington, E. E. (1989). Coping with family transitions: Winners, losers, and survivors. *Child Development, 60,* 1–14.

Hetherington, E. M. (1972). Effects of father absence on personality development in adolescent daughters. *Developmental Psychology, 7,* 313–326.

Hetherington, E. M., Cox, M., & Cox, R. (1979). Family interaction and the social, emotional, and cognitive development of children following divorce. In V. Vaughn & T. Brazelton (Eds.), *The family: Setting priorities* (pp. 71–87). New York: Science and Medicine.

Hetherington, E. M., Cox, M., & Cox, R. (1982). Effects of divorce on parents and children. In M. Lamb (Ed.), *Nontraditional families* (pp. 233–288). Hillsdale, NJ: Erlbaum.

Hetherington, E. M., Cox, M., & Cox, R. (1985). Long-term effects of divorce and remarriage on the adjustment of children. *Journal of the American Academy of Child Psychiatry, 24,* 518–530.

Hodges, W. F. (1991). *Interventions for children of divorce* (3rd ed.). New York: Wiley.

Ilfeld, F. W., Jr., Ilfeld, H. Z., & Alexander, J. R. (1982). Does joint custody work? A first look at outcome data of relitigation. *American Journal of Psychiatry, 1,* 62–66.

Irving, H. H., Benjamin, M., & Trocme, N. (1984). Shared parenting: An empirical analysis utilizing a large data base. *Family Process, 23,* 561–569.

Jacobson, D. (1978). The impact of marital separation and divorce on children: II. Interparental hostility and child adjustment. *Journal of Divorce, 2,* 3–20.

Johnston, J. R., & Campbell, L. E. G. (1986). *Preschool children in post-separation and divorce disputes.* Paper presented at the 63rd Annual Meetings of the American Orthopsychiatric Association, Chicago.

Johnston, J. R., & Campbell, L. E. G. (1988). *Impasses of divorce.* New York: Free Press.

Johnston, J. R., & Campbell, L. E. G. (1993). A clinical typology of interpersonal violence in disputed-custody divorce cases. *American Journal of Orthopsychiatry, 63,* 190–199.

Johnston, J. R., Gonzales, R., & Campbell, L. E. G. (1987). Ongoing post-divorce conflict and child disturbance. *Journal of Abnormal Child Psychology, 15,* 493–509.

Johnston, J. R., Kline, M., & Tschann, J. M. (1988). Ongoing post-divorce conflict in families contesting custody: Effects on children of joint custody and frequent access. *American Journal of Orthopsychiatry, 59,* 576–592.

Johnston, J. R., & Roseby, V. (1997). *In the name of the child: A developmental approach to understanding and helping children of conflicted and violent divorce.* New York: Free Press.

Kalter, N., Kloner, A., Schreier, S., & Okla, K. (1989). Predictors of children's postdivorce adjustment. *American Journal of Orthopsychiatry, 59,* 605–618.

Kelly, J. B. (1988). Longer-term adjustment in children of divorce: Converging findings and invocations for practice. *Journal of Family Psychology, 2,* 119–140.

Kelly, J. B. (1990). *Mediated and adversarial divorce resolution process: An analysis of postdivorce outcomes.* Final report prepared for the Fund for Research in Dispute Resolution.

Kelly, J. B. (1991). Parent interaction after divorce: Comparison of mediated and adversarial divorce processes. *Behavioral Sciences and the Law, 9,* 387–398.

Kelly, J. B. (1993). Current research on children's postdivorce adjustment: No simple answers. *Family and Conciliation Courts Review, 31,* 29–49.

King, V. (1994). Nonresident father involvement and child well-being. *Journal of Family Issues, 15,* 78–96.

Kline, M., Johnston, J. R., & Tschann, J. M. (1991). The long shadow of marital conflict: A model of children's postdivorce adjustment. *Journal of Marriage and the Family, 53,* 297–309.

Kline, M., Tschann, J. M., Johnston, J. R., & Wallerstein, J. S. (1989). Children's adjustment in joint and sole custody families. *Developmental Psychology, 25,* 430–438.

Kuehl, S. J. (1989). Against joint custody: A dissent to the general bullnose theory. *Family and Conciliation Courts Review, 27,* 37–45.

Luepnitz, D. A. (1982). *Child custody: A study of families after divorce.* Toronto, Ontario, Canada: Lexington Books.

Luepnitz, D. A. (1986). A comparison of maternal, paternal, and joint custody: Understanding the varieties of post-divorce family life. *Journal of Divorce, 9,* 1–12.

Maccoby, E. E. (1995). Divorce and custody: The rights, needs, and obligations of mothers, fathers, and children. *Nebraska Symposium on Motivation, 42,* 135–172.

Maccoby, E. E., Buchanan, C. M., Mnookin, R. H., & Dornbusch, S. M. (1993). Postdivorce roles of mothers and fathers in the lives of their children. *Journal of Family Psychology, 7,* 24–38.

Maccoby, E. E., Depner, C. E., & Mnookin, R. H. (1990). Coparenting in the second year after divorce. *Journal of Marriage and the Family, 52,* 141–155.

Maccoby, E. E., & Mnookin, R. H. (1992). *Dividing the child: Social and legal dilemmas of custody.* Cambridge, MA: Harvard University Press.

McKinnon, R., & Wallerstein, J. (1986). Joint custody and the preschool child. *Behavioral Science and the Law, 4,* 169–183.

Mnookin, R. H. (1975). Child-custody adjudication: Judicial functions in the face of indeterminacy. *Law and Contemporary Problems, 39,* 226–292.

Nehls, N., & Morgenbesser, M. (1980). Joint custody: An exploration of the issues. *Family Process, 19,* 117–125.

Nelson, R. (1989). Parental hostility, conflict, and communication in joint and sole custody families. *Journal of Divorce, 13,* 145–157.

Pagelow, M. D. (1993). Justice for victims of spouse abuse in divorce and child custody cases. *Violence and Victims, 8,* 69–83.

Patrician, M. (1984). Child custody terms: Potential contributors to custody dissatisfaction and conflict. *Mediation Quarterly, 3,* 41–57.

Pearson, J., & Thoennes, N. (1984). *Final report of the divorce mediation research project* (Report to the U.S. Children's Bureau). Denver: Research Unit, Association of Family and Conciliation Courts.

Pearson, J., & Thoennes, N. (1986). Mediation in custody disputes. *Behavioral Sciences and the Law, 4,* 203–216.

Pearson, J., & Thoennes, N. (1990). Custody after divorce: Demographic and attitudinal patterns. *American Journal of Orthopsychiatry, 60,* 233–249.

Phear, W. P. C., Beck, J. C., Hauser, B. B., Clark, S. C., & Whitney, R. A. (1984). An empirical study of custody agreements: Joint versus legal sole custody. In J. Folberg (Ed.), *Joint custody and shared parenting* (pp. 142–156). Washington, DC: The Bureau of National Affairs and The Association of Conciliation Courts.

Pruett, M. K. (in press). *Divorce in legal context: Outcomes for children.* Executive summary of the final report to the Smith-Richardson Foundation, reprinted in the *Connecticut Family Lawyer,* Winter, 1999.

Racusin, R. J., Albertini, R., Wishik, H. R., Schnurr, P., & Mayberry, J. (1989). Factors associated with joint custody awards. *Journal of the American Academy of Child and Adolescent Psychiatry, 28,* 164–170.

Radovanic, H., Bartha, C., Magnatta, M., Hood, E., Sagar, A., & McDonough, H. (1994). A follow-up of families disputing child custody/access: Assessment, settlement, family relationship outcomes. *Behavioral Sciences and the Law, 12,* 427–435.

Roman, M., & Haddad, W. (1978). *The disposable parent: The case for joint custody.* New York: Holt, Rinehart and Winston.

Rothberg, B. (1983). Joint custody: Parental problems and satisfactions. *Family Process, 22,* 43–52.

Santrock, J. W., & Warshak, R. A. (1979). Father custody and social development in boys and girls. *Journal of Social Issues, 35,* 112–125.

Schepard, A. (1985). Taking children seriously: Promoting cooperative custody after divorce. *Texas Law Review, 64,* 687–788.

Shiller, V. M. (1986). Joint versus maternal custody for families with latency age boys: Parent characteristics and child adjustment. *American Journal of Orthopsychiatry, 56,* 486–489.

Shrier, D. K., Simring, S. K., Shapiro, E. T., Greif, J. B., & Lindenthal, J. J. (1991). Level of satisfaction of fathers and mothers with joint or sole custody arrangements: Results of a questionnaire. *Journal of Divorce and Remarriage, 16,* 163–170.

Solomon, J., & George, C. (1996, April). *The effects on attachment of overnight visitation in divorced and separated families.* Paper presented at the biennial meetings of the International Conference on Infant Studies, Providence, RI.

Sorensen, E., Goldman, J., Ward, M., Albanese, H., Graves, L., & Chamberlain, C. (1995). Judicial decision-making in contested custody cases: The influence of reported child abuse, spouse abuse, and parental substance abuse. *Child Abuse and Neglect, 19,* 251–260.

Stack, C. B. (1976). Who owns the child? Divorce and custody decisions in middle class families. *Social Problems, 23,* 505–515.

Steinman, S. B. (1981). The experience of children in a joint-custody arrangement: A report of a study. *American Journal of Orthopsychiatry, 51,* 403–414.

Steinman, S. B., Zemmelman, S. E., & Knoblauch, T. M. (1986). *Children in joint custody: A report of a study of children in voluntary and court determined joint custody.* Paper presented at the 63rd Annual Meeting of the American Orthopsychiatric Association, Chicago.

Thomas, A. M., & Forehand, R. (1993). The role of paternal variables in divorced and married families: Predictability of adolescent adjustment. *American Journal of Orthopsychiatry, 63,* 127–135.

Tschann, J. M., Johnston, J. R., Kline, M., & Wallerstein, J. S. (1989). Family process and children's functioning during divorce. *Journal of Marriage and the Family, 51,* 431–444.

Tschann, J. M., Johnston, J. R., Kline, M., & Wallerstein, J. S. (1990). Conflict, loss, change and parent-child relationships: Predicting children's adjustment during divorce. *Journal of Divorce, 13,* 1–22.

Walker, L. E. (1984). *The battered woman syndrome.* New York: Springer.

Wallerstein, J. S., & Blakeslee, S. (1989). *Second chances: Men, women, and children a decade after divorce.* New York: Ticknor & Fields.

Wallerstein, J. S., & Kelly, J. B. (1980). *Surviving the breakup: How children actually cope with divorce.* New York: Basic Books.

Warshak, R. A., & Santrock, J. W. (1983). The impact of divorce in father-custody and mother-custody homes: The child's perspective. In L. A. Kurdek (Ed.), *New directions for child development: Children and divorce* (Vol. 19, pp. 19–46). San Francisco: Jossey-Bass.

Weiss, R. S. (1979). Growing up a little faster: The experience of growing up in a single parent household. *Journal of Social Issues, 35,* 97–111.

Weitzman, L. J. (1985). *The divorce revolution.* New York: Free Press.

Whiteside, M. F. (1995, April). *An integrative review of the literature pertinent to custody of children five years of age and younger.* Executive Summary to the Statewide Office of Family Court Services, San Francisco, CA. Ann Arbor, MI: Center for the Family.

Wolchik, S. A., Braver, S. L., & Sandler, I. N. (1985). Maternal versus joint custody: Children's post-separation experiences and adjustment. *Journal of Child Clinical Psychology, 14,* 5–10.

Zill, N. (1983). *Happy, healthy, and insecure.* New York: Doubleday.

CHAPTER 19

Children and High-Conflict Divorce: Theory, Research, and Intervention

DAVID B. DOOLITTLE and ROBIN DEUTSCH

IVORCE IS DISRUPTIVE for children at all ages. But the small percentage of divorces that are high conflict, where the separating parents continue to litigate and fail to come to a resolution of their postdivorce situation in the first 2 years, are qualitatively and quantitatively more disruptive of the child's continued psychological development. Further, the conflict itself interferes with the utility of the usual help available to children of divorce.

Children whose parents separate or divorce are consistently reported to have more feelings of depression, sadness, anxiety, anger, and lowered self-esteem. They experience more social disruption, academic decline, and behavioral difficulties at home and at school than their peers (Emery, 1982; Felner, Farber, & Primavera, 1980; Guidubaldi & Perry, 1985; Hess & Camara, 1979; Hetherington, 1979; Hetherington, Cox, & Cox, 1985; Hodges & Bloom, 1984; Jacobson, 1978; Kurdek & Berg, 1983; Peterson & Zill, 1986; Wallerstein & Kelly, 1980). Data from the National Center for Health Statistics indicate that compared with children from intact families, children from single-parent and re-married families were more than twice as likely to have emotional and behavioral problems (Zill & Schoenborn, 1990). Not only the existence but the magnitude of this difference is important (Emery, 1994). Researchers find that the differences are generally small. Children from divorced families who suffer the most often come from overlapping groups involving chronic interparental conflict (Amato & Keith, 1991; Emery, 1982, 1988; Grych & Fincham,

1990) and poor parent-child relationships (Maccoby & Mnookin, 1992). Interparental hostility and aggression, disruptions in attachment, and diminished parenting may continue well beyond the early stages of the divorce process and sometimes continue throughout the time the child is at home and beyond. In Maccoby and Mnookin's study of 1,124 families in California, one quarter of the couples studied were in high conflict and continued dispute 3½ years after the separation.

Children of divorced parents are at risk in adulthood of their own divorce (Glenn & Kramer, 1987). Wallerstein and Blakeslee (1989) found that children from divorced families are often ill prepared for the challenges of adult relationships. Additionally, divorce becomes a normalized solution to an unhappy or difficult marriage.

FACTORS CONTRIBUTING TO THE NEGATIVE IMPACT OF DIVORCE

The factors with a negative impact on children of divorced parents are complex. Wallerstein (1991) proposes that divorced parents often suffer from compromised parenting capacities, thus disturbing the parent-child relationship and consequently the child's psychological well-being. The absence of parental emotional, physical, and spiritual availability is an enduring fear of children of divorced parents (Wallerstein, 1991).

In high-conflict divorces, children are often involved in their parents' legal disputes over the custody or coparenting arrangements. These families present a particularly challenging group for clinicians and the family court system. Children of high-conflict divorce are at risk for more behavioral, cognitive, emotional, and social dysfunction than other children of separated and divorced parents (Amato & Keith, 1991; Grych & Fincham, 1990; Johnston & Campbell, 1993; Johnston, Gonzalez, & Campbell, 1987; Johnston, Kline, & Tschann, 1989; Long, Forehand, Fauber, & Brody, 1987; Radovanovic, 1993). These children continue to witness family hostility and violence, even after their parents divorce (Emery, 1982; Maccoby & Mnookin, 1992).

High-conflict divorces often involve the most severe impairments of parenting. Parental judgment is compromised as the conflict becomes the primary focus of the moment. Our clinical work, as well as that of others (Johnston & Campbell, 1988), suggests that often parents who are in high conflict have not been able to resolve the feelings of loss or betrayal associated with the marital separation. Clinical experience suggests that parents in high conflict will merge their needs with those of their child. The absence of appropriate caretaking or empathic response to the children may result in a "hypervigilant monitoring" (Wallerstein, 1991) by children, or a kind of learned helpless response. Children may stop expecting the parent to respond empathically to them. They may come to feel that parents respond only when the child's needs mirror the parents' or the child is undemanding. These children are often not seen by their parents as independent beings, but as extensions of the inter-parental conflict.

This chapter will review the literature examining the short- and long-term consequences of high-conflict divorce on children, and the specific family process factors and characteristics that affect the separation and divorce experience and what is known or not known about the interaction of these variables. To the extent that research can describe a child's expectable developmental course, the professional can provide the court with valuable information for custody, visitation, and coparenting decision making in the resolution of high-conflict divorce.

In divorces not involving high conflict, aspects of reintegration and stabilization following divorce involve improved communication between the ex-spouses, stable and predictable patterns of access and visitation between children and the noncustodial parent, resolution of property and financial disputes, and the subjective sense of the ex-spouses and children of divorce moving on with their lives in what Ahrons (1994) has termed the "binuclear family." In the binuclear family, both parents have created lives either singly or with new partners that are stable and permit them to cooperate together to support the developmental needs of the children. Thus the previous task of the nuclear family in supporting the needs of child development has become organized and met through a new configuration—a family comprising two separate but inter-related units.

Research on restabilization and reintegration following divorce shows a marked difference between highly conflictual and relatively nonconflictual divorcing families. Ahrons and Miller (1993) and Wallerstein and Kelly (1980) present findings consistent with an 18- to 24-month reintegration following divorce in families where severe interparental conflict does not continue following separation.

In highly conflictual divorcing families, however, there are often obstacles to the progression of family members and the family unit toward a new family configuration. Such obstacles are most often ways that either or both parents are psychologically or socially unable to relinquish and grieve the marital and family contract and result in what has been termed the "impasses of divorce" (Johnston & Campbell, 1988). In other conflictual divorces, significant impairments in familial functioning such as parent-child relationships or destructive and even violent interparental interactions prevent the development of new patterns of adaptation and stable family reorganization.

In the divorce follow-up study of families in Dane County, Wisconsin, Ahrons and Miller (1993) find specific patterns of reintegration after relatively nonconflictual divorce. This study considered the data from the initial evaluation in 1979 a year postdivorce as well as two follow-up periods, 2 and 4 years later. The final evaluation was 5 years postdivorce. They found that the quality of the postdivorce relationship and proximity of the divorcing marital partners had a significant correlation to postdivorce adjustment and the quality of paternal involvement with the children. This sample, however, may have been biased toward relatively stable divorcing families as couples had to live in the same county and the fathers had ongoing contact with the children for the family to be admitted to the study. The period of 18 to 24 months for reintegration following divorce found in this study may be considered a benchmark for more stable and less intensively conflictual divorcing families. Kaffman (1993) also presents data consistent with an adjustment to divorce within a 2-year period in his sample drawn from the kibbutz. He found, however, that where there was a longer period of marriage as well as more intense and overt conflict in the divorcing couple the initial adjustment to divorce did not reliably occur within 2 years. The 12% of couples characterized by more intense and overt conflict continued to show difficulties in postdivorce adjustment for 5 years after separation.

Thus, whereas many divorcing families will show an initial adjustment within 2 years—what Wallerstein and Blakeslee (1989) refer to as the acute period of adjustment after divorce—a minority of families will continue to have significant difficulty and disturbance for a more extended period. These families are characterized by intensive and enduring conflict between the divorcing couple and often compromised parent-child relationships. The parents' absorption in unremitting conflict with their ex-spouse renders them less available to address the intensified needs of children. Further, greater conflict between the ex-spouses often leads to intensified loyalty conflicts for the children and a correspondingly greater tendency to ally with one parent over the other.

Much has been learned from the study of families who litigate divorce and who utilize the court system chronically, typically the most highly conflictual divorce situations. Johnston and Campbell have conducted an ongoing study of such families in California and summarized their work in a series of papers (1985, 1987, 1988, 1993) as well as their book, *Impasses of Divorce* (1988). Intensive levels of enduring conflict and even physical violence in some families characterize the interactions of the divorcing couple. Children are often aligned with one parent against the other and at risk of sacrificing a relationship with one parent to stabilize and secure the relationship with the other parent. Johnston and Campbell's (1988) typology of divorce impasse situations focuses principally on the psychodynamic aspects of the marital partners and ways that they are unable to let each other go. This structural view of the impasse is augmented by a recommendation to formulate and understand the impasse at interactional and external/social levels. Their typology outlines divorces where reactivated trauma are one form of impasse and separation-individuation conflicts are the other general form of impasse.

Reactivated trauma impasses are considered to have a relatively good prognosis for resolution. The impasse here reflects a difficulty progressing through the stages of divorce transition because of an earlier unresolved loss. The parents have fewer psychological deficits than those impasses due to separation-individuation conflicts. In this latter form of impasse, the unresolved psychological development of the parents with respect to individuation and autonomy complicates the divorce transition process. Johnston and Campbell (1988) identify three subtypes of difficulty in divorce impasses due to conflicts concerning separation-individuation: dependent attachment, counterdependency, and oscillating dependency. Though subtypes show different behavioral manifestations, parents in each subtype are not able to relinquish the relationship with the ex-spouse as it has become entangled and enmeshed with their own identity. High conflict and especially litigating divorcing couples typically represent the separation-individuation form of divorce impasse.

Individuals in high-conflict divorces are alternately enraged and deeply emotionally injured by the actions of their ex-spouse. The intensive and unremitting emotional engagement with their ex-spouse reflects the degree to which the ex-spouse is psychologically entangled with their identity and sense of self.

Empirical research on child and adolescent adjustment following divorce can help in understanding variables in family members' reorientation following high-conflict versus relatively nonconflictual divorces. Fine, Moreland, and Schwebel (1983) studied long-term adjustment following divorce during childhood in a college sample and found that positive experiences in family life before divorce and better quality of relationships between ex-spouses following divorce predicted better adjustment. Thus, the extent to which parental and familial conflict is acted out within the family both before and after the divorce bears importantly on the extent to which postdivorce adjustment, at least in children, occurs. Other studies of postdivorce adjustment in children and adolescents following divorce (e.g., Black & Pedro-Carroll, 1993; Brody & Forehand, 1990) derive similar findings on the importance of intensity of interparental conflict and strength of parent-child relationships in mediating the adjustment of children and adolescents after divorce. These findings consistently show that the pattern of adjustment and reorientation following divorce correlates with the systemic relationship among family members.

The addition of overt violence to a high-conflict divorce situation only intensifies the difficulties in postdivorce adjustment and reorientation following divorce. Johnston and Campbell (1993) studied litigating high-conflict divorce families and identified a number of subtypes. Although subtypes varied in chronicity and mutuality of violent behaviors, all these families where the intensity of interparental conflict had erupted into physical violence faced intensive obstacles to postdivorce adjustment. The families' capacity to progress toward stability of visitation arrangements and viable communication between the ex-spouses was held hostage to the intensity and enduring nature of interparental conflict.

High-conflict divorces are especially likely to become obstructed in the postdivorce adjustment process. Interference with the progression to postdivorce adjustment may be so substantial that progression stops, resulting in a divorce impasse. Relinquishing the emotional bonds of an unsuccessful marriage to allow for new and more adaptive relationships for the spouses is blocked and children as well as parents are locked in a struggle around a marriage that has technically, though clearly not emotionally, ended. Children's heightened needs for consistent and supportive relationships with the noncustodial as well as the custodial parent are often neglected when parents are preoccupied with divorce conflict. Thus the quality of parent-child relationships, indicated by research as critical for mediating children's adjustment following divorce, tends to be compromised in high-conflict divorce and divorce impasse situations.

IMPACT OF HIGH-CONFLICT DIVORCE ON CHILDREN

Parental conflict, defined as verbal or physical aggression between parents, has emerged as the most robust predictor of children's functioning after their parents have separated (Amato & Keith, 1991; Radovanovic, 1993; Tschann, Johnston, Kline, & Wallerstein, 1989; Wallerstein, 1991). Interparental conflict before, during, and after a divorce is strongly associated with childhood behavior problems (Block, Block, & Gjerde, 1986; Emery, 1982; Grych & Fincham, 1990; Hess & Camara, 1979; Hetherington, 1979).

The preceding discussion of family process variables suggests that children's adjustment is moderated by the parent-child relationship, parenting style, and the parents' emotional adjustment. Yet there are significant variables in children that are associated with increased vulnerability to interparental conflict. Some studies suggest that individual differences among children account for much of the variability in the nature and intensity of their responses to parental divorce (Hetherington, 1979). Within child variables that have been shown to mediate the effects of interparental conflict on children include the age and developmental level of the child (Cummings, Zahn-Waxler, & Radke-Yarrow, 1984; Hetherington, 1989; Porter & O'Leary, 1980); temperament of the child (Block et al., 1986; Guidubaldi & Perry, 1985; Kurdek, 1988); and coping strategies (Radovanovic, 1993). Studies that assess children's reactions to conflict have not to date differentiated responses by the properties of the episodes of conflict. Grych and Fincham (1990) articulate a framework for assessing the impact of marital conflict on children by looking at the properties of a conflict episode. The properties of intensity, content, duration, and resolution, as well as the context of the conflict, likely affect children's processing of the conflict, and emotional and behavioral responses.

In the same way that children cope with divorce differently at different ages, children cope with interparental conflict differently at different ages. The age differences represent children's cognitive developmental level, that is, the way that children interpret the conflict between their parents. The child's understanding of the conflict is also shaped by the context in which the conflict occurs. The context of the conflict, which includes previous exposures, provides the framework in which the child can place the events or process. The child's understanding and responses to conflict are mediated in part by that framework (Grych & Fincham, 1990).

LONG-TERM EFFECTS OF HIGH-CONFLICT DIVORCE ON CHILDREN

There are few studies that examine the long-term effects of a high-conflict divorce on children's development (Chess, Thomas, Korn, Mittelman, & Cohen, 1983; Hetherington, 1989; Johnston, Kline, & Tschann, 1989). These studies as well as cross-sectional studies do indicate that interparental or family conflict is a potential stressor. Behavior, affect, and cognition are influenced as a result of the child's meaning making or interpretation of the conflict to which they are exposed. As children advance developmentally their resources for coping with this stressor are enhanced. They are better able to understand and cope with conflict. At the same time the longer or more chronic the conflict, the more feelings of social competence decrease (Radovanovic, 1993).

The ways in which internal and external factors combine are predictive of outcomes for children. Internal factors, including gender, age, temperament, the imprint of past experiences with conflict, stress, and trauma mediate children's responses to conflict. External factors that influence how children cope include economic factors, the parent-child relationships, and available support people including peers, family, and other adults.

Often children of high-conflict divorces do not grow up with a parental model for working intimate relationships. Even if they learned conflict resolution strategies in other venues, the most intimate and protective relationship failed to provide the model for effective problem-solving strategies. The parental function of facilitating mood regulation is compromised. The child does not learn a model of impulse control, mood regulation, and emotional management from parents in high conflict. Functioning is compromised when these critical capacities are undeveloped or wanting.

The parental failure to protect children results in anxiety, distress, and fear which then intrudes into the time and space necessary to accomplish normal developmental functions. The child's capacity to focus on identity development and formation is compromised. It is this potential weakness that likely leads to the failure in adulthood to maintain intimate relationships.

When exposure to interparental conflict is long, gender differences in children's responses may emerge over time. Aggression and conduct problems may be seen more in boys during school-age years and early adolescence (Block et al., 1986; Hetherington, 1989; Werner, 1989), whereas in adolescence girls may manifest more adjustment problems than boys (Werner, 1989).

DEVELOPMENTAL LEVEL AND SHORT-TERM EFFECTS OF DIVORCE CONFLICT

Infants and toddlers up to approximately 2½ or 3 years respond to the emotion of the conflict with distress. They do not understand the content, but are struck by the emotional arousal expressed by their parents. This generates fear and confusion in these children. Their primary need is to develop trust from being consistently well cared for and nurtured, and then with that foundation to develop autonomy and increased independence. Interparental conflict can interfere with both of those developmental processes, affecting the child's sense of security. It is not uncommon to see regression in infants and toddlers who have been exposed to conflict between their primary caregivers. They will frequently become fearful and resistant to separation. It is also not uncommon to notice that their developmental progress is arrested. Their attention is diverted from developing new skills and having new experiences.

> The case of Peter, age 2.9 years, is an example of the anxiety seen in response to exposure to unresolved anger between parents. Symptoms included fear of monsters, sleep disruption, toileting regression, and regressive clinginess. He also took on some self-blame stating "I bad." Over the next year, he became electively mute, language development halted as a response to the terror of the fighting between his parents. The energy typically used for developmental tasks, such as language development, was rechanneled in Peter's case to his attempts to withdraw from the conflict, and keep himself safe and protected.

Four- and five-year-old children experience things very concretely. They begin to understand the content of the arguments they hear and focus on the words that they can understand. For example, they might ask if it is true that daddy does not care about us; or ask if mommy is stupid. Children of 4 and 5 may ask if these things are true, or they may dwell on them internally.

Increased aggression with acting-out behaviors may be seen in children age 4 up to age 8. Children this age will often take on responsibility for the conflict. They are terribly worried about basic routines and concrete observable tasks. They may experience anxiety and may try to fix it or take care of the problems. Children this age are egocentric and feel quite powerful. They may take on the attributes of their favorite superheroes and attempt to care for the parent they see as suffering, or address the problem they have identified as the source of the conflict. When they discover that their powers do not work or that they are not effective in intervening, their sense of competence is devastated and they withdraw into a more helpless stance, often regressing and unable to continue development. Children this age believe that what they do or think has an effect on their environment. When they find it does not, and in fact it is their primary safety and protection figures whom they cannot affect, they are prone to confusion and disorganization that may be seen in aggressive acting-out behaviors, or in withdrawn, helpless behaviors.

In cases of great interparental conflict, where the other parent is represented as horrible, toxic, and frightening, the child experiences confusion as well as increased fear of both abandonment and punishment or rejection. Preschool children often regress, experience separation anxiety, and increased aggression.

Coping may include high use of fantasy, with imaginary friends. For example Lisa, aged 4½, experienced transitions between her parents as dangerous. She began to tell her mother "don't worry mommy, Lisa's not going to see daddy, Jessica is." In this case the child's sense of self was compromised in the transition process. Lisa used strategies of fantasy and compartmentalization to manage the task of maintaining relationships with both parents.

Early school-age children (ages 6 to 8) are often more involved with one or both parents' struggle. They may play messenger for one parent. This process of becoming involved in their parents' disputes intensifies and solidifies into adolescence.

Behavioral and emotional difficulties are more likely found in school-age children exposed to high conflict (Johnston et al., 1987; Radovanovic, 1993). As in other studies of school-age children of divorced parents, both internalizing and externalizing symptoms of general maladjustment were noted (Long, Slater, Forehand, & Fauber, 1988; Roseby & Deutsch, 1985).

These children in high-conflict families often have an underlying fragmentation of sense of self and others. If the response of either parent is unempathic or punitive during transitions, the child uses splitting as a defense, splitting off feelings of anger, shame, and helplessness. The child is doing the best he or she can to stay aligned with both parents. By feeding to each parent what they want to hear or believe, the child is working very hard to please them both, losing his or her sense of self in the process.

Later school-age children are less egocentric. They experience anger and often take sides with one parent against the other. They are quick to assess the causes of their parents' conflict and to make judgments about who is right.

School-age children tend to use repression as a defense. They can look frozen and constricted. Roseby, Johnston, Erdberg, and Bardenstein (1994) studied children (ages 6 to 12) of conflicted divorces. On the Rorschach, these children looked severely traumatized. They were guarded, hypervigilant, and had coping deficits. Almost half cope by relying on themselves for problem solving. They see themselves as their best and only resource, even though these children do not have the skills and resources to take care of themselves. These children look helpless and hopeless. There is an absence of normal fantasy or reaching out for human contact and relations. Basically the profile is of a helpless, constricted, empty child. This is the child who teachers and neighbors describe as well behaved. These children feel like nobody cares, and in fact they themselves will often say "I don't care." Often their sense of self is so submerged they cannot care.

Interparental conflict is associated for adolescents with increases in depression, anxiety, and somatic symptoms and social maladjustment. In addition, high interparental conflict is associated with parent-adolescent difficulties and difficulties at school (Forehand et al., 1991; Neighbors, Forehand, & McVicar, 1993; Wierson, Forehand, & McCombs, 1988). A study by Neighbors et al. (1993) found that adolescents' self-esteem in particular, but also their relationship with their mothers, predicted resiliency in coping with the experience of severe interparental conflict. Resiliency was defined as cognitive competence. Better school functioning is associated with a positive parent-child relationship for adolescents whose parents are in high conflict (Forehand et al., 1991; Neighbors et al., 1993). Those adolescents who did not score high on self-esteem measures or had poor relationships with their mothers had more depression and anxiety.

The parent-adolescent relationship does seem to mediate the effects of interparental conflict on school functioning. There is some evidence that adolescents who remain disengaged from their parent's struggle and do not feel caught in the middle, have fewer symptoms of depression, anxiety, and deviant behaviors than those adolescents who feel caught up in the conflict.

INTERVENTIONS FOR HIGH-CONFLICT DIVORCE

The phenomenon of high-conflict divorce has been recognized relatively recently and suitable interventions are only now in developmental stages. Only a few of a potential continuum of interventions to address the pernicious effects of high-conflict divorce are widely available. Interventions to address divorce generally have become available since the groundbreaking work of Wallerstein and Kelly on divorce in 1980. Wallerstein (1991) refers to the "tormented families who are locked into protracted high conflict" as requiring specialized intervention skills for mental health and legal professionals alike. Her view is that such families are not at one end of a continuum representing divorce conflict but rather constitute a separate subtype of divorcing families with unique characteristics and features. Certainly the defining feature of these families is the intensity and unremitting nature of virulent conflict between the ex-spouses. Often such conflict existed prior to the separation and has affected the children's lives. Children in the high-conflict situation align with or fear a parent figure as their relationships and internalized representations of parents are distorted. Children's intensified needs for support and consistency from parents following separation and divorce often are neglected.

The elements of intense interparental conflict and adequacy of parent-child relationships are a central focus of interventions. Research data cited earlier underscores that the intensity of interparental conflict and quality of parent-child relationships are the most critical factors in the outcome for the child of divorce, especially in situations of high conflict. Parent monitoring, mediation, mental health treatments and psychoeducational programs all attempt to ameliorate these destructive influences on all family members, with a special focus on the needs of the children.

Mediation is by definition quite difficult in high-conflict divorce situations. The qualities most useful in approaching a mediation of disputes tend to be those most lacking in high-conflict divorce situations: separation of the child's needs from those of the couple and that modicum of trust and goodwill in the partners that enables successful dispute resolution. Wallerstein (1991) and Grych and Fincham (1990) both relate concerns about the limitations of mediation in high-conflict divorce situations. Although mediation has demonstrated effectiveness in low and moderate conflicts, its effectiveness is more limited in high-conflict situations. In the latter, if a resolution can even be reached it often breaks down in the postmediation period. Because of the unresolved impasse that inhibits the divorcing couple's movement toward postdivorce adjustment the agreement falls prey to the tendency of the couple to reengage in conflict. Thus mediation should be seen as only one part of a broad strategy of intervention in high-conflict divorce situations.

Traditional mental health interventions of adult or child individual therapy can be problematic in situations of divorce impasse and high-conflict divorce. Although individual treatment can be helpful to family members moving toward postdivorce adjustment, in situations of divorce impasse therapists can become involved in the polarizing tensions of the divorce conflict. Adult individual therapists may, in a well-meaning way, reinforce and entrench the views of their patient, complicating the need for mediation and conflict resolution. Thus therapists may end up functioning as extended family members often do in high-conflict divorces, participating in and even intensifying what Johnston and Campbell (1988) refer to as "tribal warfare." Individual child therapists more often see the child's need for a region of relatedness free of interparental conflict but may support their child patient's alignment with or fear of one or the other parent. When individual therapy is underway or represents the only available alternative, communication among therapists is essential. Without such communication the likelihood of the therapists recapitulating and further polarizing the divorce conflict is very high.

More promising are mental health interventions specifically tailored to divorcing couples in a high-conflict divorce situation. Roseby and Johnston (1995) provide a review of group interventions for children in high-conflict divorce situations that at times involve domestic violence. Because of the high risk that these children will lose support of one parent entirely while another parent is compromised in parental functioning by the high-conflict divorce, there is a need for specialized groups for these children. Roseby and Johnston (1995, 1997) base their work theoretically on social-cognitive script formation and developmental object relations theories. The objectives of the group interventions are to enable children to formulate and review their experiences within their families, increase tolerance of negative and painful affective experiences, and encourage the development of new perspectives on divorcing family relations. Their time-limited group format for children is viewed as sufficient for low-intensity divorce conflict and as preparatory for long-term individual treatment in situations of high-conflict divorce.

Parent-focused interventions reviewed by Grych and Fincham (1990) have been found to have utility in general divorcing situations but their utility in high-conflict divorce situations has yet to be demonstrated. Interventions such as psychoeducational and supportive time-limited groups can be useful in facilitating postdivorce adjustment in many cases. Many states are now mandating such sessions as part of the legal requirements for divorce. For the approximately 10% of cases that represent high-conflict divorce, such general divorce adjustment groups are unlikely to influence adjustment significantly. More hopeful is the counseling and mediation intervention process presented by Campbell and Johnston (1987) specifically developed for litigating, high-conflict divorcing families. Their model program, conducted on a group or individual basis, has demonstrated effectiveness in facilitating dispute resolution and lessening post-agreement conflict with divorcing couples, also improving their ability to resolve conflicts on their own. The program prepares couples for mediation and dispute resolution through a series of prenegotiation counseling sessions. These sessions include extended family and therapists or attorneys when these individuals seem to be a part of the divorce impasse. Divorcing couples do not meet together until the negotiation or dispute resolution phase. Intervention is directed toward the divorce impasse. A follow-up period after agreement is reached in the negotiation phase is included to facilitate implementation and follow-through of the agreement. In this study, Campbell and Johnston studied 80 divorcing couples referred by courts due to unsuccessful attempts to mediate disputes. Individual work yielded as much success as their group approach, but staff stress and "burnout" was higher in individual approaches; and couples involved in the group approach showed a tendency to independently resolve new conflicts in the postagreement follow-up phase. This approach shows great promise as it combines the best of mediation and divorce impasse counseling in a process directed toward dispute resolution. The group method, while logistically more complicated, is important to consider as the strain of working individually with high-conflict divorcing couples is not to be underestimated.

Visitation is fraught with difficulties in high-conflict divorcing couples both before and after visitation orders are established. Visitation is a prime area for disputes and conflicts where fears, anxieties and resentments place important obstacles to reaching a visitation agreement and implementing it. Conflict over visitation, of course, involves the child more directly than conflicts over money and property. The quality of parent-child interaction is tremendously affected by divorce conflict about visitation. In the subgroup of high-conflict divorcing couples where domestic violence has occurred, visitation plans can be difficult to arrange in view of the child's need for safety and the intensity of conflict the child may experience during visitation transfers. Transfers between parents at the beginning and end of visitations are quite problematic as here the child and parents are directly exposed to the interactional process that was highly conflicted or overtly violent. Procedures are developing in many jurisdictions and communities to supervise transfers of the child between parents or, in some cases, supervise the visitations. Hess, Mintun, Moelhman, and Pitts (1992) present one such visitation center program where professional or para-professional staff are available for supervising visitation transfers, supervising on- or off-site visitations, and parent education. Utilization of such centers or locating supervisors for visitations, at least for a transitional period when agreements are being negotiated and conflict is being eased, can make visitation possible when children have been traumatized by witnessing or experiencing domestic violence. Divorcing couples who have been embroiled in such conflict or violence may require third parties to be present, at least for a transitional period, to ensure that violence or intensive conflict do not emerge when the child is being transferred between parents.

A new and useful professional role of parent monitor or special master in situations of high-conflict divorce has emerged. Parent monitors are assigned by family court judges to monitor and mediate visitation difficulties over the extended time that is required for resolution of high-conflict divorce. Such monitors are often involved in court-sanctioned evaluations that lead to visitation agreements but may be assigned when visitation plans are already in effect to implement and mediate difficulties with implementation of visitation plans. The parent monitor or special master appointment is made in order to monitor seriously conflictual visitation situations, reduce frequent nonproductive court appearances and provide ongoing court-sanctioned decision making to implement and/or mediate difficulties with visitation and decision making. These professionals require specialized training and skills in divorce conflict and mediation. Parent monitors can continue to be more or less involved as the divorcing couple and family needs over an extended time and often can significantly reduce the likelihood that disputes will require court involvement to settle. Modeling of dispute management and resolution as well as containment of conflict are important aspects of the parent monitor role. The child and the child's quality of relationship with each parent is a major beneficiary of the parent monitor role. The monitor's facilitation of visitation agreements and movement toward postdivorce adjustment ease the extent of conflict that the child must live with in the divorce process. This function is essential in the situation of high-conflict divorce.

Theoretical understanding of high-conflict divorces and practical understanding of the costs to children and parents embroiled in intense divorce conflict and impasse have led to interventions tailored to the specialized needs of these families. Further development of intervention models is especially needed to reduce the length of time required for postdivorce adjustment in these families. The length of postdivorce adjustment is critical for these children and families as the child's developmental process does not and cannot wait for resolution of divorce conflict. Children's developmental needs are increasingly compromised as divorce conflict becomes increasingly protracted.

REFERENCES

Ahrons, C. (1994). *The good divorce Keeping your family together when your marriage is coming apart.* New York: Harper Perennial.

Ahrons, C., & Miller, R. (1993). The effect of the postdivorce relationship on paternal involvement: A longitudinal analysis. *American Journal of Orthopsychiatry, 63*(3), 441–449.

Amato, P. R., & Keith, B. (1991). Parental divorce and the well-being of children: A meta-analysis. *Psychological Bulletin, 110*(1), 26–46.

Black, A., & Pedro-Carroll, J. (1993). Role of parent-child relationships in mediating the effects of marital disruption. *Journal of the American Academy of Child and Adolescent Psychiatry, 32*(5), 1019–1027.

Block, J. H., Block, J., & Gjerde, P. F. (1986). The personality of children prior to divorce: A prospective study. *Child Development, 57*(4), 827–840.

Brody, G., & Forehand, R. (1990). Interparental conflict, relationship with the noncustodial father, and adolescent post-divorce adjustment. *Journal of Applied Developmental Psychology, 11*, 139–147.

Campbell, L., & Johnston, J. (1987). Multifamily mediation The use of groups to resolve child custody disputes. *Mediation Quarterly, * (14/15), 137–162.

Chess, S., Thomas, A., Korn, Mittelman, & Cohen, J. (1983). Early parental attitudes, divorce, and separation, and young adult outcome: Findings of a longitudinal study. *Journal of the American Academy of Child Psychiatry, 22*, 47–51.

Cummings, E. M., Zahn-Waxler, C., & Radke-Yarrow, M. (1984). Developmental changes in children's reactions to anger in the home. *Journal of Child Psychology and Psychiatry, 25*, 63–74.

Emery, R. E. (1982). Interparental conflict and the children of discord and divorce. *Psychological Bulletin, 92*(2), 310–330.

Emery, R. E. (1988). *Marriage, divorce and children's adjustment.* Newbury Park, CA: Sage.

Emery, R. E. (1994). *Renegotiating family relationships: Divorce, child custody and mediation.* New York: Guilford Press.

Felner, R. D., Farber, S. S., & Primavera, J. (1980). Children of divorce, stressful life events and transitions: A framework for preventive efforts. In R. H. Price, R. F. Ketterer, B. C. Bader, & J. Monahan (Eds.), *Prevention in mental health: Research, policy, and practices* (Vol. 1, pp. 81–108). Beverly Hills, CA: Sage.

Fine, M., Moreland, J., & Schwebel, A. (1983). Long-term effects of divorce on parent-child relationships. *Developmental Psychology, 19*(5), 703–713.

Forehand, R., Wierson, M., Thomas, A. M., Fauber, R., Armistead, L., Kemptom, T., & Long, N. (1991). A short-term longitudinal examination of adolescent functioning following divorce: The role of family factors. *Journal of Abnormal Child Psychology, 19*(1), 97–111.

Glenn, N. D., & Kramer, K. B. (1987). The marriages and divorces of the children of divorce. *Journal of Marriage and the Family, 45*, 405–410.

Grych, J. H., & Fincham, F. D. (1990). Marital conflict and children's adjustment: A cognitive-contextual framework. *Psychological Bulletin, 108*(2), 267–290.

Grych, J., & Fincham, F. (1992). Interventions for children of divorce: Toward greater integration of research and action. *Psychological Bulletin, 111*(3), 434–454.

Guidubaldi, J., & Perry, J. D. (1985). Divorce and mental health sequelae for children: A two-year follow-up of a nationwide sample. *Journal of the American Academy of Child Psychiatry, 24*, 531–537.

Hess, P., Mintun, G., Moelhman, A., & Pitts, G. (1992). The family connection program: An innovative visiting program. *Child Welfare, 71*(1), 77–88.

Hess, R. D., & Camara, K. A. (1979). Post-divorce family relationships as mediating factors in the consequences of divorce for children. *Journal of Social Issues, 35*(4), 79–96.

Hetherington, E. M. (1979). Family interaction and the social, emotional, and cognitive development of children after divorce. In V. Vaughn & T. Brazeton (Eds.), *The family setting priorities* (pp. 71–87). New York: Science and Medicine.

Hetherington, E. M. (1984). Coping with family transitions: Winners, losers, and survivors. *Child Development, 60*, 1–14.

Hetherington, E. M. (1989). Coping with family transitions: Winners, losers, and survivors. *Child Development, 60*, 1–14.

Hetherington, E. M., Cox, M., & Cox, R. (1985). Long-term effects of divorce and remarriage on the adjustment of children. *Journal of the American Academy of Child and Adolescent Psychiatry, 24*(5), 518–530.

Hodges, W. F., & Bloom, B. L. (1984). Parent's report of children's adjustment to marital separation: A longitudinal study. *Journal of Divorce, 8*(1), 33–50.

Jacobson, D. S. (1978). The impact of marital separation/divorce on children: III. Parent-child communication and child adjustment, and regression analysis of findings from overall study. *Journal of Divorce, 2*(2), 175–194.

Johnston, J., & Campbell, L. (1988). *Impasses of divorce: The dynamics and resolution of family conflict.* New York: Free Press.

Johnston, J., & Campbell, L. (1993). Parent-child relationships in domestic violence families disputing custody. *Family and Conciliation Courts Review, 31*(3), 282–298.

Johnston, J. R., Gonzalez, R., & Campbell, L. E. G. (1987). Ongoing postdivorce conflict and child disturbance. *Journal of Abnormal Child Psychology, 15*(4), 493–509.

Johnston, J. R., Kline, M., & Tschann, J. M. (1989). Ongoing postdivorce conflict: Effects on children of joint custody and frequent access. *American Journal of Orthopsychiatry, 59*(4), 576–592.

Kaffman, M. (1993). Divorce in the Kibbutz: Lessons to be drawn. *Family Process, 32*, 117–133.

Kurdek, L. (1988). A 1-year follow-up of children's divorce adjustment, and post divorce parenting. *Journal of Applied Developmental Psychology, 9*, 315–328.

Kurdek, L. A., & Berg, B. (1983). Correlates of children's adjustment to their parents' divorce. In L. A. Kurdek (Ed.), *Children and divorce: New directions for child development.* San Francisco: Jossey-Bass.

Long, N. (1991). A short-term longitudinal examination of young adolescent functioning following divorce: The role of family factors. *Journal of Abnormal Child Psychology, 19*(1), 97–110.

Long, N., Forehand, R., Fauber, R., & Brody, G. H. (1987). Self-perceived and independently observed competence of young adolescents as a function of parental marital conflict and recent divorce. *Journal of Abnormal Child Psychology, 15*, 15–27.

Long, N., Slater, E., Forehand, R., & Fauber, R. (1988). Continued high or reduced interparental conflict following divorce: Relation to young adolescent adjustment. *Journal of Consulting and Clinical Psychology, 56*(3), 467–469.

Maccoby, E. E., & Mnookin, R. H. (1992). *Dividing the child.* Cambridge, MA: Harvard University Press.

Neighbors, B., Forehand, R., & McVicar, D. (1993). Resilient adolescents and interparental conflict. *American Journal of Orthopsychiatry, 63*(3), 462–471.

Peterson, J. L., & Zill, N. (1986). Marital disruption, parent-child relationships, and behavior problems in children. *Journal of Marriage and the Family, 48,* 295–307.

Porter, B., & O'Leary, K. D. (1980). Marital discord and child behavior problems. *Journal of Abnormal Child Psychology, 80,* 287–295.

Radovanovic, H. (1993). Parental conflict and children's coping styles in litigating separated families: Relationships with children's adjustment. *Journal of Abnormal Child Psychology, 29,* 697–713.

Roseby, V., & Deutsch, R. (1985). Children of separation and divorce: Effects of a social role-taking group intervention on fourth and fifth graders. *Journal of Abnormal Child Psychology, 14,* 55–60.

Roseby, V., & Johnston, J. (1997). *High conflict, violent, and separating families: A group treatment manual for school-age children.* New York: Free Press.

Roseby, V., & Johnston, J. (1995). Clinical interventions with latency-age children of high conflict and violence. *American Journal of Orthopsychiatry, 65*(1), 48–59.

Roseby, V., Johnston, J. R., Erdberg, P., & Bardenstein, K. (1994, July). *The development of personality disorders in children of highly conflictual and violent families.* Paper presented at the international congress of the International Association of Child and Adolescent Psychology and Allied Professionals, San Francisco.

Shaw, D. S., Vondra, J. I., Hommerding, K. D., Keenan, K., & Dunn, M. (1994). Chronic family adversity and early child behavior problems: Longitudinal study of low income families. *Journal of Child Psychology and Psychiatry, 35*(6), 1109–1122.

Tschann, J. M., Johnston, J. R., Kline, M., & Wallerstein, J. S. (1989). Family process and children's functioning during divorce. *Journal of Marriage & the Family, 51,* 431–444.

Wallerstein, J. S. (1994). The early psychological tasks of marriage. *American Journal of Orthopsychiatry, 64*(4), 640–650.

Wallerstein, J., & Blakeslee, S. (1989). *Second chances: Men, women and children a decade after divorce.* New York: Ticknor & Fields.

Wallerstein, J., & Kelly, J. (1980). *Surviving the breakup: How children and parents cope with divorce.* New York: Basic Books.

Wallerstein, J. S. (1991). Tailoring the intervention to the child in the separating and divorced family. *Family and Conciliation Courts Review, 29*(4), 448–459.

Werner, E. E. (1989). High-risk children in young adulthood: A logitudinal study from birth to 32 years. *American Journal of Orthopsychiatry, 59,* 72–81.

Wierson, M. Forehand, R., & McCombs, A. (1988). The relationship of early adolescent functioning to parent-reported and adolescent-perceived interparental conflict. *Journal of Abnormal Child Psychology, 16*(6), 707–718.

Zill, N., & Schoenborn, C. A. (1990). *Developmental learning and emotional problems: Health of our nation's children—United States 1988* (Advance data from Vital and Health statistics No. 190). Hyattsville, MD: National Center for Health Statistics.

CHAPTER 20

Conclusion

ROBERT M. GALATZER-LEVY

W E SET OUT to learn what is known of the impact of custody arrangements on children in the hope of giving courts, lawyers, and mental health professionals a solid base on which to make these life-shaping decisions. We knew that the issues were extensive and complex. As this book developed, it became ever clearer that although the mental health disciplines have much to offer toward decisions about custody, this information is seldom simple, sometimes sparse, and frequently not as thoroughly supported as one would hope. Some important matters are not adequately addressed in the literature. We found surprisingly little research on such important issues as the impact of visitation schedules on children, whereas certain other areas, such as the effect of parental sexual orientation, were surprisingly well investigated. Much remains to be known about the impact of custody and divorce arrangements. Given the very large number of children involved, our society should be investing more extensively in research to address outstanding issues in this field.

Families, and those who must aid them in making decisions about custody and visitation, cannot wait the outcome of research that in many instances has not even begun. In this book, we have attempted to present the best current information about a range of issues pertinent to custody decisions, along with an estimate of the credibility of that information, to help in making informed decisions. We believe that neither is the available information so good that mental health professionals can always confidently prescribe the best management of custody issues, nor is it so poor (as some critics claim) that their input is not valuable in reaching custody decisions.

The most useful body of knowledge about the well-being of children comes from the mental health and behavioral science disciplines, especially developmental psychology. The findings of these disciplines go far beyond common sense and are useful antidotes to personal prejudices that easily cloud decisions in this area. The wise use of scientific information in this and other areas requires that it be understood not as reflecting absolute certainty—scientific theories and findings are always subject to ongoing revision—but rather that they are likely to reflect the best information available combined with either direct estimates of their credibility or sufficient information about how they were gathered so that the user can make such estimates. This information has the strengths and weaknesses common to the discipline from which it derives.

There is a recurring theme in this book—the more we explore the internal subjective world of the individual, the more difficult it is to obtain reliable data. Very good data are available, for example, about the economic impact of divorce on children (i.e., we have quantitative data that reflect children of diverse background over extended periods). In contrast, the rich data we have about the internal experience of children of divorce largely comes from a small sample of unusually affluent families, primarily from California. In addition, information about effects distant in time from the divorce is more difficult to obtain than more proximate consequences. Because promoting the child's best interests entails attempts to ensure that the youngster will grow to as psychologically healthy maturity as possible, the paucity of satisfactory studies addressing long-term outcomes, especially from the point of view of the psychological well-being of the child, is a problem.

These problems are partly solved by generalizing from findings not specifically involving divorce. What is known about children in general and children in adverse situations can be applied to children of divorce provided appropriate care is taken to address the limits of applicability. The authors of this volume have felt confident that many such generalizations are reasonable. After all, it is unlikely that research will have been done that precisely addresses the situation of the child in question and reasonable generalization will always be necessary. At the same time, it is important to be constantly vigilant for the impact of the particular child's situation to avoid inappropriately applying research findings. Thus, for example, some vulnerable children may be greatly affected by features of a parent's personality that have little impact on most children, whereas particularly resilient children may be little harmed by parental influences that would damage most children. In applying research findings to particular situations, we need to remain constantly alert to the question of how well these findings apply to the situation at hand.

Certain important generalizations are possible from available research. One is that, within wide limits, children are less sensitive to variations in parental personality than was once thought. For variations in parental personality to rise to significance in custody decisions, it is necessary to demonstrate that those variations are likely to directly affect the child. Too often, because the primary training of mental health professionals is in the diagnosis and treatment of psychopathology, custody evaluations are heavy in information about parental psychiatric diagnoses and deviant test findings. Unless these results are closely linked to the care of the child, they are of little value to custody decisions. Another robust result is that the process of divorce itself, including the process of making custody decisions, is likely to have a great impact on youngsters. Therefore those interested in children's well-being will be attentive to means for facilitating the best possible divorce process and particularly ways to avoid high-conflict divorces. In addition, because everyone involved in divorce is in the midst of change, care is needed to differentiate stable from transient configurations in divorcing families. Finally, the range of children's specific needs is staggering, so that no single solution to custody issues is appropriate. Custody arrangements need to be tailor-made if they are to really fit children.

The impact of divorce on children challenges our society. Efforts to address this challenge range from endeavors to reshape society so that fewer children will be affected by divorce to attempts to refine the details of the legal process so that courts can apply existing laws more adequately. Wise decisions about these issues, whether for individual children or society as a whole, should be based on an understanding of the scientific information we have about the impact of divorce and family arrangements on children. This book is a contribution to that understanding.

Author Index

Subject Index